Brief Contents

The St. Martin's
Guide to Writing

TWELFTH EDITION

The St. Martin's Guide to Writing

Rise B. Axelrod
University of California, Riverside

Charles R. Cooper
University of California, San Diego

bedford/st.martin's
Macmillan Learning
Boston | New York

For Bedford/St. Martin's

Vice President, Editorial, Macmillan Learning Humanities: Edwin Hill
Executive Program Director for English: Leasa Burton
Senior Program Manager: Laura Arcari
Marketing Manager: Vivian Garcia
Director of Content Development, Humanities: Jane Knetzger
Executive Developmental Editor: Jane Carter
Senior Content Project Manager: Peter Jacoby
Senior Workflow Project Supervisor: Susan Wein
Production Supervisor: Lawrence Guerra
Senior Media Project Manager: Allison Hart
Associate Media Editor: Julia Domenicucci
Editorial Services: Lumina Datamatics, Inc.
Composition: Lumina Datamatics, Inc.
Text Permissions Manager: Kalina Ingham
Text Permissions Researcher: Arthur Johnson, Lumina Datamatics, Inc.
Permissions Editor: Angela Boehler
Photo Researcher: Brittani Morgan Grimes, Lumina Datamatics, Inc.
Director of Design, Content Management: Diana Blume
Text Design: Jerilyn Bockorick, Cenveo Publisher Services
Cover Design: William Boardman, Marine Miller
Printing and Binding: LSC Communications

Manufactured in the United States of America.

1 2 3 4 5 6   23 22 21 20 19 18

For information, write: Bedford/St. Martin's, 75 Arlington Street, Boston, MA 02116

ISBN 978-1-319-10437-5   (with Handbook)
ISBN 978-1-319-10438-2   (without Handbook)

Acknowledgments

Contents

3 | Writing Profiles 54

4 Explaining a Concept 106

5 | Analyzing and Synthesizing Opposing Arguments 154

6 | Arguing a Position 191

7 | Proposing a Solution 240

8 | Justifying an Evaluation 286

9 | Arguing for Causes or Effects 330

10 | Analyzing Stories 376

PART 2 Critical Thinking Strategies

11 | A Catalog of Invention and Inquiry Strategies 420

12 | A Catalog of Reading Strategies 432

PART 3 Writing Strategies

13 | Cueing the Reader 456

14 | Narrating and Describing 470

15 | Defining, Classifying, and Comparing 490

16 | Arguing 505

PART 4 Research Strategies

17 | Planning and Conducting Research 520

18 | Selecting and Evaluating Sources 535

19 | Using Sources to Support Your Ideas 542

20 | Citing and Documenting Sources in MLA Style 554

24 | Creating a Portfolio 626

25 | Writing in Business and Scientific Genres 630

26 | Writing for and about Your Community 642

27 | Writing Collaboratively 647

Handbook

Student Essays

*Available in *LaunchPad for The St. Martin's Guide to Writing* and *Sticks and Stones and Other Student Essays*.

*Available in *LaunchPad for The St. Martin's Guide to Writing* and *Sticks and Stones and Other Student Essays*.

Preface

Our goal for *The St. Martin's Guide to Writing* has always been to provide the clear guidance and practical strategies students need to harness their potential as writers, both in college and in the wider world. We also strive to provide both experienced and novice instructors with the time-tested tools they need to coach their students as they develop skills for writing successfully in college and beyond. In the twelfth edition, we continue in our mission to serve a diverse audience of schools and students with new support for metacognition, which encourages the transfer of writing skills; an accessible design; and a new *Student's Companion* for students taking co-requisite or ALP courses. Envisioned as a complete first-year composition course in a single book—with a full rhetoric, engaging readings, and a research manual—the new edition prepares students to read analytically and write successfully, and transfer these skills from first-year composition to courses across campus.

Core Features of the *Guide*

The St. Martin's Guide retains its emphasis on active learning, integrating reading and writing through hands-on activities for critical thinking, reading, analysis, and synthesis and by providing practical guides to reading and writing.

Sustained Attention to Critical Reading and Reflective Writing

The Guides to Reading in each Part 1 chapter help students hone their ability to read like a writer, with activities following each of the professional reading selections that ask students to reflect, analyze, and respond to a range of contemporary selections. These activities draw attention both to the writer's ideas and to the strategies the writer uses to present those ideas to readers. Each Guide to Reading provides

- an annotated student essay that prompts readers to answer questions about how it is composed;
- a range of compelling professional selections to demonstrate the basic features of the writing assignment;
- activities following each professional selection that prompt students to read actively by asking them to reflect on the essay and relate it to their own experience and also to read like writers by focusing their attention on the writer's strategies. (Chapter 12 also provides an array of strategies students can use to read critically.)

Part 2 includes "A Catalog of Reading Strategies," which provides the tools students need to understand, synthesize, analyze, contextualize, and evaluate texts, with models to support their own development as readers and writers. Part 4 further supports readers by providing strategies that help students find and evaluate reliable sources and synthesize those sources to create new ideas.

Practical, Classroom-Tested Guides to Writing

Based on classroom-tested, research-informed pedagogy, each of the Guides to Writing in Part 1 emphasizes the basic features of a piece of writing so that students can internalize a systematic yet flexible approach to the composing process that can be transferred to any writing situation.

Commonsensical and easy to follow, the Guides to Writing teach students how to

- assess the rhetorical situation, focusing on purpose and audience, with special attention given to the basic features of each assignment type;
- ask probing analytical questions about what they're reading, which can help make them more reflective writers;
- practice finding answers through various kinds of research, including memory search, field research, and traditional source-based research.

Each Guide to Writing begins with a **Starting Points** chart, offering students multiple ways of finding the help they need, when they need it. Each also includes a **Peer Review Guide**, to help students assess their own writing and the writing of their classmates, as well as a **Troubleshooting Guide**, to help students find ways to improve their drafts. All of the guides emphasize the assignment's basic features. In short, the Guides to Writing help students make their writing thoughtful, clear, organized, compelling, and effective for the rhetorical situation.

Purpose-Driven Assignment Chapters

Each chapter in Part 1 introduces a commonly assigned reason for writing. By working through several assignment types, students learn to identify and use relevant and effective strategies to achieve their purpose with their readers. For example, "Remembering an Event"—a memoir assignment—challenges students to reflect on the autobiographical and cultural significance of their experience. "Explaining a Concept"—an analysis assignment—asks students to explain a new subject while also making that subject interesting and informative for their readers. A cluster of argument chapters (Chapters 6–10) requires students to develop an argument that not only is well reasoned and well supported but also responds constructively to readers' likely questions and concerns. These five argument chapters ask students to argue for

- a position,
- a solution,
- an evaluation,
- a cause, and
- an interpretation.

The streamlined Chapter 5 lays the groundwork for students to build a convincing academic argument by analyzing competing viewpoints and synthesizing ideas across selections. It offers excellent preparation for students to understand an issue before adopting and arguing a position of their own.

Hands-On Strategies for Writing and Research

Part 2 offers practical strategies for invention and critical reading, and Part 3 includes writing strategies—from "Cueing the Reader" to using the modes—so students and instructors can dip in for more help as needed. Part 4 offers in-depth coverage of research, including how to cite sources in MLA and APA styles. Part 5 offers strategies for academic writing today, with a new chapter on analyzing and composing multimodal texts, and chapters on taking essay exams, creating a portfolio, writing in business and scientific genres, writing for and about the community, and writing collaboratively.

What's New

Although the twelfth edition of *The St. Martin's Guide to Writing* builds on the success of previous editions, many of the strategies the *Guide* employs have changed in order to support students who are challenged to compose multimodally but are stretched thin, with increasing demands on their time, attention, and energy.

New Support for Metacognition

The twelfth edition of the *Guide* includes new marginal annotations that encourage students to write *mindfully* by reflecting on their writing processes, rhetorical situations, and the reading-writing connection, among other topics. Together with activities like Practicing the Genre at the start of each Part 1 chapter; Test Your Choice, Peer Review, and Revision activities throughout the Guides to Writing; and Reflection activities at the end of each Part 1 chapter, these ultra-brief "meta-moments" help students consolidate their learning, bring distance and self-awareness to their writing, and develop an understanding of their own preferences and experiences as writers. Taken together, this new support for metacognition encourages transfer across assignments and courses.

A New Chapter on Analyzing and Composing Multimodal Texts

A new Chapter 22, "Analyzing and Composing Multimodal Texts," explains multimodality and walks students through the process of analyzing, composing, and designing a multimodal text; remixing text-based compositions in new modalities and genres; and creating presentations that take advantage of various modalities of communication, from the linguistic and spatial to the visual, aural, and gestural.

New Annotated Student Essays and Compelling Professional Readings

Demonstrating the basic features of the genres, the Part 1 chapters provide nine engaging new selections by well-known authors and fresh voices, from Ta-Nehisi Coates to Jean M. Twenge, as well as new selections by students, including a fresh literacy narrative to supplement Chapter 1, "Composing Literacy"; a new essay analyzing the concept of trigger-warning memes in Chapter 4, "Explaining a Concept"; and an essay in Chapter 5, "Analyzing and Synthesizing Opposing Arguments," analyzing free speech on college campuses.

A Student's Companion for The St. Martin's Guide to Writing

A new supplement to support students taking a co-requisite (or ALP) course alongside first-year composition, this text (available in print and in LaunchPad) is designed for students who need a little extra help to write successfully on the college level. The text includes

- material for student success, including coverage of time management, academic planning, and beating test anxiety;
- additional activities to help students read critically and mindfully, and transfer what they've learned to their own writing;
- assessment rubrics for every writing assignment in the text;
- sentence strategies for academic writing; and
- editing activities for students who need extra practice identifying and correcting some of the most common writing errors.

New Accessible Design

To ensure that the *Guide* continues to serve the needs of all students, the design of *The St. Martin's Guide* has been improved to meet accessibility standards, including in its use of color, annotations, and highlighting. The result is a book that has been thoughtfully and carefully imagined to meet the needs of its diverse student audience.

Council of Writing Program Administrators' Outcomes Statement

The St. Martin's Guide to Writing, Twelfth Edition, helps students build proficiency in the four categories of learning that writing programs across the country use to assess their students' work: rhetorical knowledge; critical thinking, reading, and composing; processes; and knowledge of conventions. The following chart shows in detail how *The St. Martin's Guide* helps students develop these proficiencies. (Note: This chart aligns with the latest WPA Outcomes Statement, ratified in July 2014.)

DESIRED OUTCOMES	RELEVANT FEATURES OF *THE ST. MARTIN'S GUIDE TO WRITING*, TWELFTH EDITION
Rhetorical Knowledge	
Learn and use key rhetorical concepts through analyzing and composing a variety of texts.	• Chapter 1, **"Composing Literacy,"** provides students with a clear, workable definition of the rhetorical situation and asks students to apply that knowledge as they read literacy narratives and compose one of their own.

DESIRED OUTCOMES	RELEVANT FEATURES OF *THE ST. MARTIN'S GUIDE TO WRITING*, TWELFTH EDITION
Rhetorical Knowledge (continued)	
	• In each of the chapters in Part 1, **"Writing Activities"** (Chapters 2–10), students **read**, **analyze**, and **compose a variety of texts**. A Guide to Reading asks students to analyze texts (including student writing and professional selections) in terms of **purpose**, **audience**, and **genre**. Each Guide to Writing supports students with detailed help for composing in a variety of genres, including memoir, profile, concept analysis, position argument, evaluation, causal argument, and literary analysis.
	• Chapter 12, **"A Catalog of Reading Strategies,"** provides tools for analyzing texts.
	• Part 5, **"Composing Strategies for College and Beyond"** (Chapters 22–27), encourages students to consider how genre expectations and discipline requirements affect compositions; chapters include **"Analyzing and Composing Multimodal Texts"** (Chapter 22), **"Taking Essay Examinations"** (Chapter 23), **"Creating a Portfolio"** (Chapter 24), **"Writing in Business and Scientific Genres"** (Chapter 25), **"Writing for and about Your Community"** (Chapter 26), and **"Writing Collaboratively"** (Chapter 27).
Gain experience reading and composing in several genres to understand how genre conventions shape and are shaped by readers' and writers' practices and purposes.	• Chapter 1 and the Part 1 chapters emphasize the connection between **reading and composing**: Each introduces students to the basic features of writing with a specific purpose; provides a group of engaging reading selections, with apparatus that ask students to think about how the readings demonstrate the basic features; then a Guide to Writing leads them through the process of composing their own text. The **readings** in Part 1 represent a range of topics and genres. Each is framed with comments and questions that focus students on **key features of the genre** and help spark ideas for their own compositions.
	• A streamlined Chapter 5, **"Analyzing and Synthesizing Opposing Arguments,"** invites students to build an understanding of a controversial topic from the ground up by first analyzing arguments on conflicting positions (in order to probe the ideas, beliefs, and values underlying each position) and then synthesizing what they've learned to create a thoughtful analysis.
	• The new Chapter 22, **"Analyzing and Composing Multimodal Texts,"** challenges students to analyze and compose selections in a variety of modalities and to reimagine writing originally composed primarily in the linguistic mode to take advantage of other modalities and genres.
	• Chapter 25 covers writing in **business and scientific genres**.
Develop facility in responding to a variety of situations and contexts, calling for purposeful shifts in voice, tone, level of formality, design, medium, and/or structure.	• In Part 1, students practice **responding to a variety of rhetorical situations and contexts**. These chapters also point out what makes a text structurally sound, while the Guides to Writing help students systematically develop their own processes and structures. Sentence strategies in these chapters help composers deal with issues of **voice**, **tone**, and **formality**.
	• Chapter 22, **"Analyzing and Composing Multimodal Texts,"** invites students to consider how changes to the rhetorical situation, especially genre and medium, shape decisions about tone, level of formality, design, medium, and structure. It also walks students through the rhetorical choices involved in the design of any text.

(continued)

DESIRED OUTCOMES	RELEVANT FEATURES OF *THE ST. MARTIN'S GUIDE TO WRITING*, TWELFTH EDITION
Rhetorical Knowledge (continued)	
Understand and use a variety of technologies to address a range of audiences.	• One of the book's assumptions is that most **students compose in digital spaces** for varied audiences and use different media for doing so. This idea is woven throughout the text. • Chapter 22, **"Analyzing and Composing Multimodal Texts,"** helps students understand the needs and requirements involved in design, both in print and online. It also offers instruction on how to prepare and deliver multimodal presentations. • Online tutorials in the **LaunchPad for *The St. Martin's Guide*** include **how-tos for using technology**; topics include digital writing for specific audiences and purposes, creating presentations, integrating photos, and appealing to a prospective employer.
Match the capacities of different environments (e.g., print and electronic) to varying rhetorical situations.	• Chapter 22, **"Analyzing and Composing Multimodal Texts,"** invites students to remix a textual composition into one that makes use of a variety of modalities. It also provides guidance on how to make effective design choices for electronic documents, from decisions about formatting and font sizes to those involving visuals and screenshots. • Advice on composing in a timed writing environment can be found in Chapter 23, **"Taking Essay Examinations."** • The **LaunchPad** version of *The St. Martin's Guide to Writing* offers **integrated digital tutorials** on topics such as photo-editing basics, audio recording and editing, creating presentations with PowerPoint and Prezi, cross-platform word processing, and building your professional brand with LinkedIn and Twitter, as well as a variety of tutorials on reading visuals that consider issues of framing, sequence, alignment, proximity, and color.
Critical Thinking, Reading, and Composing	
Use composing and reading for inquiry, learning, thinking, and communicating in various rhetorical contexts.	• Chapter 1, **"Composing Literacy,"** asks students to reflect on their own literacy experiences and to extrapolate from the literacy narratives they are reading. • **Analyze & Write** activities in Part 1 (Chapters 2–10) ask students to **read like a writer**, identifying ideas, techniques, and strategies that they can apply in their own compositions. • **Make Connections** activities encourage students to put what they've read in the context of the world they live in. These preliminary reflections come into play in the Guides to Writing, in which students are asked to draw on their thoughts and experiences to write meaningfully. **Reflection** sections, which conclude Chapters 2–10, ask students to consider what they have learned about the genre in which they have composed. • Chapter 5, **"Analyzing and Synthesizing Opposing Arguments,"** challenges students to think critically about texts representing opposing positions, to analyze and synthesize information, and to compare and contrast positions on a controversial issue. • Chapter 11, **"A Catalog of Invention and Inquiry Strategies,"** and Chapter 12, **"A Catalog of Reading Strategies,"** provide strategies students can use to read critically and apply what they've learned.

DESIRED OUTCOMES	RELEVANT FEATURES OF *THE ST. MARTIN'S GUIDE TO WRITING*, TWELFTH EDITION
Critical Thinking, Reading, and Composing (continued)	
	• Chapter 18, **"Selecting and Evaluating Sources,"** asks students to evaluate their sources critically to determine the message and underlying values; and Chapter 19, **"Using Sources to Support Your Ideas,"** challenges students to synthesize information from sources with their own ideas to develop knowledge.
Read a diverse range of texts, attending especially to relationships between assertion and evidence, patterns of organization, the interplay between verbal and nonverbal elements, and how these features function for different audiences and situations.	• Chapters 1–10 include a **range of professional selections** and **student essays**. The Guides to Reading and Writing in Chapters 2–10 include advice on **effective strategies for supporting claims**; the Guides to Writing include **assignment-specific suggestions for organization**, some tailored to specific types of audiences. • The Guides to Writing in the argument chapters (Chapters 6–10) offer advice on **framing** topics to appeal to the audience and recommend techniques and strategies for **responding to alternative views** readers may hold. • The section **"Reimagine your writing in a new genre or medium"** (Chapter 22) invites students to consider how a change of audience will affect aspects of the composition. • Part 4, **"Research Strategies"** (Chapters 17–21), especially Chapter 19, **"Using Sources to Support Your Ideas,"** emphasizes the importance of **using evidence** effectively to support one's views.
Locate and evaluate primary and secondary research materials, including journal articles, essays, books, databases, and informal Internet sources.	• The **Guides to Writing** throughout Part 1 (Chapters 2–10) offer **genre-specific research guidance**, from finding sources and analyzing and researching a position to citing a variety of sources and supporting a causal analysis. • Part 4, **"Research Strategies"** (Chapters 17–21), offers extensive coverage of **finding, evaluating**, and **using** print and electronic resources, with guidance on responsibly using online sources and communities for research. • Chapter 17, **"Planning and Conducting Research,"** addresses finding sources using **catalogs** and **databases** and developing sources through **field research**; it also explains differences between **primary** and **secondary** research. • Chapter 18, **"Selecting and Evaluating Sources,"** emphasizes strategies for **evaluating print** and **digital sources** and distinguishing between **scholarly** and **popular** sources.
Use strategies—such as interpretation, synthesis, response, critique, and design/ redesign—to compose texts that integrate the writer's ideas with those from appropriate sources.	• A new Chapter 5, **"Analyzing and Synthesizing Opposing Arguments,"** challenges students to synthesize, analyze, and compare sources on a controversial topic. It provides a bridge to help move students from personal and expository genres to argumentative ones by modeling how to review and critique persuasive texts in preparation for adopting and defending a position of their own. • Chapters 6–10 ask students to **argue** for a position, a solution, an evaluation, a preferred cause or effect, and a literary interpretation, and to **anticipate** and **respond to opposing positions** and **readers' objections**. • Chapter 16, **"Arguing,"** provides strategies for **making assertions, offering support**, and **avoiding logical fallacies**. • Chapter 19, **"Using Sources to Support Your Ideas,"** offers detailed **strategies** for **integrating research** into an academic research project. Specifically, this chapter provides advice on how to integrate and introduce quotations, how to cite paraphrases and summaries so as to distinguish them from the writer's own ideas, and how to avoid plagiarism. Sentence strategies and research coverage in several Part 1 chapters offer additional support.

(continued)

DESIRED OUTCOMES	RELEVANT FEATURES OF *THE ST. MARTIN'S GUIDE TO WRITING*, TWELFTH EDITION
Processes	
Develop a writing project through multiple drafts.	• In Chapters 2–10, Guides to Writing prompt students to **compose** and **revise**. These chapters include activities for **inventing**, **researching**, **planning**, **composing**, **evaluating**, and **revising** writing over the course of **multiple drafts**. • **A Writer at Work** sections toward the end of each Part 1 chapter (Chapters 2–10) demonstrate students' writing processes.
Develop flexible strategies for reading, drafting, reviewing, collaborating, revising, rewriting, rereading, and editing.	• The Guides to Writing in Chapters 2–10 offer extensive, assignment-specific advice on **reading**, **drafting**, **rethinking**, and **revising** at multiple stages. The **Ways In** and **Test Your Choice** activities as well as the **Starting Points** and **Troubleshooting** charts encourage students to discover, review, and revise. The activities urge students to start from their strengths, and the charts offer specific targeted advice for students facing different challenges. • Chapter 11, **"A Catalog of Invention and Inquiry Strategies,"** offers numerous helpful suggestions for idea generation. • Chapter 12, **"A Catalog of Reading Strategies,"** provides a variety of strategies for reading analytically and critically. • See also the section below, "Experience the **collaborative** and social aspects of writing processes."
Use composing processes and tools as a means to discover and reconsider ideas.	• Central to Chapters 2–10 is the idea of using **composing to discover ideas**, especially through the **Ways In** activities in each Guide to Writing. Strategies for **evaluating**, **revising**, and **editing** help students reconsider their ideas over the course of multiple drafts. • **A Writer at Work** sections toward the end of each Part 1 chapter demonstrate how student writers use writing as a means of discovery and reconsideration. • See also Chapter 11, **"A Catalog of Invention and Inquiry Strategies,"** and Chapter 17, **"Planning and Conducting Research."**
Experience the collaborative and social aspects of writing processes.	• This goal is implicit in several **collaborative activities** in Part 1: **Practicing the Genre** activities at the beginning of each chapter; **Make Connections** activities after the readings; and **Test Your Choice** activities and **Peer Review Guides** in the Guides to Writing all provide opportunities to work collaboratively. • Chapter 26, **"Writing for and about Your Community,"** emphasizes the social nature of writing and real-world applicability in its focus on service learning. • **"Writing Collaboratively"** is the focus of **Chapter 27**, which offers strategies for writing effectively in and managing groups.
Learn to give and act on productive feedback to works in progress.	• The **Evaluating the Draft**, **Peer Review Guide**, **Improving the Draft**, and **Troubleshooting Guide** sections in the Guides to Writing in each Part 1 chapter offer students specific advice on constructively criticizing—and praising—their own work and the work of their classmates, then reflecting and acting on the comments they've received. • Guidelines in Chapter 27, **"Writing Collaboratively,"** offer advice for evaluating another writer's work, from seeking information about the writer's purpose, audience, and genre to offering support and being sufficiently prepared to participate fully.

DESIRED OUTCOMES	RELEVANT FEATURES OF *THE ST. MARTIN'S GUIDE TO WRITING*, TWELFTH EDITION
Processes (continued)	
Adapt composing processes for a variety of technologies and modalities.	• As noted in the **rhetorical knowledge section** on (pp. xxvi–xxviii), one of the book's assumptions is that most students compose in digital spaces for varied audiences and use different media for doing so. This assumption is woven throughout, especially in Chapters 2–10.
	• Chapter 22, **"Analyzing and Composing Multimodal Texts,"** challenges students to analyze and compose in multiple modalities: linguistic, visual, aural, spatial, and gestural. It invites students to reimagine a primarily linguistic text in another medium or genre, addresses design differences related to the medium of delivery (print versus digital), and invites students to pull together what they've learned throughout the chapter to create a multimodal presentation.
	• The **LaunchPad** version of *The St. Martin's Guide to Writing* offers a digital course space and an interactive e-book. It also offers integrated digital tutorials, such as online **how-to's for using technology**; topics include digital writing, creating presentations, integrating photos, and appealing to a prospective employer.
Reflect on the development of composing practices and how those practices influence their work.	• Central to Chapters 2–10 is the idea of **reflecting on composing practices**, especially through the **Practicing the Genre** activities at the start of each chapter, the **Reflection** activities at the end of each chapter, and the new **"meta-moments"** tags that appear in the margins throughout these chapters. Each of these activities encourages self-awareness and invites students to develop an understanding of their own preferences and experiences as writers and to consolidate their learning through reflection.
	• **A Writer at Work** sections toward the end of each Part 1 chapter demonstrate how student writers use writing as a means of discovery and reconsideration.
	• See also Chapter 11, **"A Catalog of Invention and Inquiry Strategies,"** and Chapter 17, **"Planning and Conducting Research."**
Knowledge of Conventions	
Develop knowledge of linguistic structures—including grammar, punctuation, and spelling—through practice in composing and revising.	• **Editing** and **proofreading** advice for the most common issues students face appears at the end of the textbook.
	• The full version of the *Guide* also includes a concise yet remarkably comprehensive **handbook** that covers syntax, grammar, punctuation, and spelling.
Understand why genre conventions for structure, paragraphing, tone, and mechanics vary.	• Chapters 2–10 emphasize the importance of **audience** and how expectations differ. For example, several readings emphasize differences in expectations for documenting sources, depending on whether the audience is academic or popular.
	• Chapter 22, **"Analyzing and Composing Multimodal Texts,"** invites students to consider how changes to the rhetorical situation, especially genre and medium, shape decisions about tone, level of formality, design, medium, and structure.
Gain experience negotiating variations in genre conventions.	• Students **read**, **analyze**, and **compose a variety of texts** in Part 1, **"Writing Activities"** (Chapters 2–10). In each of these chapters, a Guide to Reading asks students to analyze texts in terms of **purpose**, **audience**, and the basic features of the **genre**.
	• Part 4, **"Research Strategies,"** allows students to gain experience as they compose an **academic research project**.
	• The chapters in Part 5, **"Composing Strategies for College and Beyond,"** provide students with opportunities to gain experience negotiating genre conventions.

(continued)

DESIRED OUTCOMES	RELEVANT FEATURES OF *THE ST. MARTIN'S GUIDE TO WRITING*, TWELFTH EDITION
Knowledge of Conventions (continued)	
Learn common formats and/ or design features for different kinds of texts.	• Chapter 22 covers elements of design in sections titled **"Design a Multimodal Text"** and **"Criteria for Analyzing Document Design."** • **Examples of MLA, APA, and presentation formats** appear at the ends of Chapters 20 ("Citing and Documenting Sources in MLA Style"), 21 ("Citing and Documenting Sources in APA Style"), and 22 ("Analyzing and Composing Multimodal Texts").
Explore the concepts of intellectual property (such as fair use and copyright) that motivate documentation conventions.	• The book's research coverage (mainly in Chapters 17–21) teaches strategies for **integrating** and **citing** sources. • Chapter 19, **"Using Sources to Support Your Ideas,"** offers detailed coverage of how to use sources fairly, and features sections dedicated to acknowledging sources and avoiding plagiarism.
Practice applying citation conventions systematically in their own work.	• Several of the activities following reading selections in Chapters 2–9 challenge students to **recognize differences in citation conventions** in popular and academic writing. • A number of reading selections in Part 1 include **citations** or **lists of links** to sources. • **Research sections** in each Guide to Writing section help students with the details of using and documenting sources by providing genre-specific examples of what (and what not) to do. • **Student essays** in Chapters 3–9 offer models for documenting sources in a list of works cited or references. • Chapter 19, **"Using Sources to Support Your Ideas,"** offers detailed advice for integrating and introducing quotations, citing paraphrases and summaries so as to distinguish them from the writer's own ideas, and avoiding plagiarism. • Chapters 20, **"Citing and Documenting Sources in MLA Style,"** and 21, **"Citing and Documenting Sources in APA Style,"** offer an overview of each style's requirements and a variety of common documentation models.

Acknowledgments

We owe an enormous debt to all the rhetoricians and composition specialists whose theory, research, and pedagogy have informed *The St. Martin's Guide to Writing*. We would be adding many pages to an already long book if we were to name everyone to whom we are indebted; suffice it to say that we have been eclectic in our borrowing. We must also acknowledge immeasurable lessons learned from all the writers—professional and student alike—whose work we analyzed and whose writing we used in this and earlier editions.

Many instructors and students have contributed ideas and criticism over the years. For responding to detailed questionnaires about the twelfth edition, we thank Mary Brantley, Holmes Community College; Joan Brickner, Minnesota State Community and Technical College; Jessica Brown, Holmes Community College; Wallace Cleaves, University of California at Riverside; Mark Collins, College of DuPage; Daniel Compton, Midlands Technical College Beltline; Jason DePolo, North Carolina A&T State University; Pamela Hardman, Cuyahoga Community College; Faye Spencer Maor, North Carolina A&T State University; James Mense, St. Louis Community College at Florissant Valley; Elizabeth Monske, Northern Michigan University; Karen O'Donnell, Finger Lakes Community College; Lonetta Oliver, St. Louis Community College at Florissant Valley; Elizabeth Onufer, Idaho State University; Arnetra Pleas, Holmes Community College; Suzanne Roszak, University of California at Riverside; Lisa Sharfstein, Carlow University; Minnette Smith, Hodges University; Wes Spratlin, Motlow State Community College; Jennifer Tronti, California Baptist University; Cassandra Van Zandt, University of California at Riverside; and Jeana West, Murray State College.

For helping us select new readings, we thank A. Beshears, Murray State College; Teresa Caruso, University of the Virgin Islands; Wallace Cleaves, University of California at Riverside; Jennifer Doke-Kerns, Des Moines Area Community College; Adam Hoffman, Arizona State University; Jennifer Levi, Cecil College; Lucinda Ligget, Ivy Tech Community College of Indiana; Coretta Pittman, Baylor University; Bryan Santin, Concordia University Irvine; Emily Standridge, University of Texas at Tyler; Marianne Trale, Community College of Allegheny County; Kathleen Weiss, Cecil College; and Shellie Welch, Georgia State University—Perimeter College.

For commenting on a revised sample chapter, we thank A. Beshears, Murray State College; Mary Brantley, Holmes Community College; Joan Bruckwicki, Tyler Junior College; Wallace Cleaves, University of California at Riverside; Kathryn Crowther, Georgia State University— Perimeter College; Roberta Foizey, Carlow University; Jennifer P. Gray, College of Coastal Georgia; Candace Grissom, Motlow State Community College; Nile Hartline, Des Moines Area Community College; Adam D. Hoffman, Arizona State University; Jody Jones, Alabama A&M University; Jennifer Levi, Cecil College; Lucinda Ligget, Ivy Tech Community College of Indiana; Dr. Jim Richey, Tyler Junior College; Jeana West, Murray State College; S. Russell Wood, Southwest Virginia Community College; and Renee Wright, Triton College.

For this new edition of the *Guide,* we are particularly grateful to Wallace Cleaves, who made recommendations of reading selections, helped draft some of the reading apparatus, and was generally available as a sounding board and a font of good advice, especially in rethinking Chapter 5. We also thank Wallace for his astute revisions and updates to the instructor's manual and for writing an entirely new supplement, *A Student's Companion for The St. Martin's Guide to Writing.* Finally, we are especially grateful to the student authors for allowing us to use their work in *Sticks and Stones* and the *Guide.*

We want to thank many people at Bedford/St. Martin's, especially Jane Carter, Executive Development Editor and our editor, whose invaluable expertise and indomitable good humor made this book possible; Senior Project Editor Peter Jacoby, who worked miracles keeping all the details straight and keeping the book on schedule; Editorial Assistant William Hwang, who single-handedly managed multiple reviews while also preparing the manuscript for production and supporting the permissions process; Sherry Mooney, Advanced Development Editor, who stepped in to take over the editing of *Sticks and Stones;* and Associate Media Editor Julia Domenicucci, who oversaw the editorial work on LaunchPad, our customizable course space and interactive e-book for *The St. Martin's Guide to Writing.*

Jamie Thaman made many valuable contributions to this revision with her careful copyediting, as did Umadevi Soundararajan and Lori Lewis with their meticulous proofreading and Julie Grady with her indexing of the text. Susan Wein and Lawrence Guerra kept the whole process running smoothly. Thanks also to the immensely talented design team—book designer Jerilyn Bockorick and Bedford/St. Martin's art director Diana Blume—who worked with strategies from Tech for All to make the text beautiful and accessible. Our gratitude also goes to Hilary Newman, Kalina Ingham, Angie Boehler, Brittani Morgan, Tom Wilcox, and Arthur Johnson for their thoughtful and conscientious work on the permissions program for visuals and text.

We also thank Leasa Burton, Senior Program Director—English, and Laura Arcari, Senior Program Manager for Rhetorics and Business and Technical Writing, both of whom offered valued advice at many critical stages in the process. Thanks as well to Edwin Hill, Vice President—Editorial (Humanities), for his adroit leadership of Bedford/St. Martin's, and to Marketing Manager Vivian Garcia, for her tireless efforts on behalf of the *Guide.*

Rise dedicates this book to her husband, Steven, and their son, Jeremiah, who are both distinguished teachers and scholars, and to Sophie and Amalia, two young women whose writing she very much looks forward to reading.

We're All In. As Always.

Bedford/St. Martin's is as passionately committed to the discipline of English as ever, working hard to provide support and services that make it easier for you to teach your course your way.

Find **community support** at the Bedford/St. Martin's English Community (community.macmillan.com), where you can follow our *Bits* blog for new teaching ideas, download titles from our professional resource series, and review projects in the pipeline.

Choose **curriculum solutions** that offer flexible custom options, combining our carefully developed print and digital resources, acclaimed works from Macmillan's trade imprints, and your own course or program materials to provide the exact resources your students need. Our approach to customization makes it possible to create a customized project uniquely suited for your students, and based on your enrollment size, return money to your department and raise your institutional profile with a high-impact author visit through the Macmillan Author Program ("MAP").

Rely on **outstanding service** from your Bedford/St. Martin's sales representative and editorial team. Contact us or visit **macmillanlearning.com** to learn more about any of the options below.

LaunchPad for *The St. Martin's Guide to Writing:* Where Students Learn

LaunchPad provides engaging content and new ways to get the most out of your book. Get an interactive e-book combined with assessment tools in a fully customizable course space; then assign and mix our resources with yours.

- **Autoscored reading quizzes and summary practice activities** are available for every professional selection in the text. Use these to test understanding and motivate preparation.

- **Diagnostics** provide opportunities to assess areas for improvement and assign additional exercises based on students' needs. Visual reports show performance by topic, class, and student as well as improvement over time.

- **Pre-built units**—including readings, videos, quizzes, and more—are easy to adapt and assign by adding your own materials and mixing them with our high-quality multimedia content and ready-made assessment options, such as **LearningCurve** adaptive quizzing, Exercise Central, and more than 100 Grammar Girl Podcasts.

- **More than 40 additional student essays** from *Sticks and Stones and Other Student Essays.*

- **Additional support for students in ALP/corequisite courses** from *A Student's Companion for The St. Martin's Guide to Writing.*

- Use LaunchPad on its own or **integrate it** with your school's learning management system so that your class is always on the same page.

LaunchPad for *The St. Martin's Guide to Writing* can be purchased on its own or packaged with the print book at a significant discount. An activation code is required. To order LaunchPad for *The St. Martin's Guide to Writing* with the print book, use one of the following ISBNs:

- *The St. Martin's Guide to Writing,* Twelfth Edition (with handbook): ISBN 978-1-319-23255-9

- *The St. Martin's Guide to Writing,* Short Twelfth Edition (without handbook): ISBN 978-1-319-24781-2

For more information, go to **launchpadworks.com**.

Choose from Alternative Formats of *The St. Martin's Guide to Writing*

Bedford/St. Martin's offers a range of formats. Choose what works best for you and your students:

- *Print text* To order *The St. Martin's Guide to Writing,* 12e (full edition—with handbook), use ISBN 978-1-319-10437-5; to order *The St. Martin's Guide to Writing* Short 12e (without handbook), use ISBN 978-1-319-10438-2.

- *Popular e-book formats* For details of our e-book partners, visit **macmillanlearning .com/ebooks**.

- *A Student's Companion for The St. Martin's Guide to Writing* To order *A Student's Companion* packaged with *The St. Martin's Guide to Writing* (with handbook), use 978-1-319-24836-9; to order *A Student's Companion* packaged with the short edition of the *Guide* (without the handbook), use ISBN 978-1-319-25873-3.

- LaunchPad for *The St. Martin's Guide to Writing* To order LaunchPad packaged with *The St. Martin's Guide to Writing* (with handbook), use ISBN 978-1-319-23255-9; to order LaunchPad packaged with the short edition of the *Guide* (without the handbook), use ISBN 978-1-319-24781-2.

For additional packages, such as *The St. Martin's Guide to Writing* (with or without handbook) packaged with *Sticks and Stones and Other Student Essays*—our companion student essay reader—contact your sales representative.

Instructor Resources

You have a lot to do in your course. We want to make it easy for you to find the support you need—and to get it quickly.

Instructor's Resource Manual for *The St. Martin's Guide to Writing* is available as a PDF that can be downloaded from **macmillanlearning.com**. Visit the instructor resources tab for *The St. Martin's Guide to Writing.* In addition to chapter overviews and teaching tips, the instructor's manual includes detailed chapter plans for every chapter in the text, sample syllabi, tips for evaluation and teaching, and a bibliography in composition studies.

1

Composing Literacy

People are writing more today than ever before, and many are switching comfortably from one genre or medium to another — from tweeting to blogging to creating multimedia Web pages. Learning to be effective as a writer is a continuous process as you find yourself in new writing situations using new technologies and trying to anticipate the concerns of different audiences. "The illiterate of the twenty-first century will not be those who cannot read and write," futurist Alvin Toffler predicted, "but those who cannot learn, unlearn, and relearn."

Understanding the Rhetorical Situation

Central to success in writing across the spectrum of possibilities today is understanding your **rhetorical situation**, any situation in which you produce or receive a text. Ask yourself these questions whenever you encounter a new rhetorical situation:

1. *Who* is the **audience**? How does the audience's prior knowledge, values, and beliefs influence the production and reception of the text?

2. *What* **genre** or type of text is it? How do genre conventions (what we call the text's *basic features*) influence the production and reception of the text?

3. *When*—at what time or for what **occasion**—is the text produced? Is it timely?

4. *Where*—in what social or cultural **context**—will the communication take place? How does the situation influence the production and reception of the text?

5. *How*—in what **medium**—is the text experienced? How does the medium influence the production and reception of the text?

6. *Why* communicate? What is the main **purpose** or goal driving the author's choices and affecting the audience's perceptions of the text?

Composing with an awareness of the rhetorical situation means writing not only to express yourself but also to engage your readers and respond to their concerns. You write to influence how your readers think and feel about a subject and, depending on the genre, perhaps also to inspire them to act.

To be an effective writer, you have to understand the central role of genre in the rhetorical situation. Genres are ways of categorizing texts—for example, a way to subdivide fiction into romance, mystery, and science fiction or break down mystery even further into hard-boiled detective, police procedural, true crime, and classic whodunit. But genre categories are not rigid, unchanging forms. They are dynamic patterns of communication that are variable and versatile.

Readers expect texts in a given genre to use a set of conventions, or **basic features**. Although individual texts within the same genre vary a great deal—no two *proposals*, even those arguing for the same solution, will be identical—they nonetheless include many of the same basic features. For example, everyone expects a proposal to identify the problem and to offer a solution. Writers must decide whether their particular rhetorical situation requires that they spend time trying to convince readers that the problem really exists or demonstrating that the proposed solution is preferable to alternative solutions because it is more effective, less expensive, or easier to implement.

In other words, the basic features are not recipes but frameworks within which writers make choices and are free to be creative. Most writers, in fact, find that frameworks make creativity possible. Depending on the formality of the rhetorical situation, the purpose of the composer, and the audience's openness to innovation, writers may also construct remixes by reimagining a text in a different genre or medium, for a different purpose, or for a new audience. For example, the student whose proposal appears in Chapter 7 (pp. 246–52) could reenvision his text as a Prezi presentation (as shown in Chapter 22, p. 610).

Reflecting on Your Own Literacy

Learning—especially learning to communicate with new audiences and in new genres—benefits from **reflection** (or metacognition)—thinking critically about *how* as well as *what* you are learning. Extensive research confirms that reflection makes learning easier and faster. In fact, recent studies show that writing even a few sentences about your thoughts and feelings before a high-stress paper or exam can help you reduce stress and boost performance.

Spend a few minutes thinking about your own literacy experiences: *What memories stand out as formative?* You may define *literacy* narrowly as the ability to read and write, as it has been traditionally defined, or you may think of it more broadly as the ability to make meaning in the multiplicity of languages and genres, media and communication practices, we are increasingly called on to use. Here are several questions and examples that may help you remember and reflect on your own literacy experiences:

> **Take a moment . . .**
>
> How do you think reflecting aids learning? Notice that marginal questions like this invite quick reflection.

- *What do you think are the personal and cultural effects of acquiring new literacies (such as learning another language, using social media, playing sports or video games)?*

  The first thing I remember watching on [television] was *Robot Monster*, a film in which a guy dressed in an ape-suit with a goldfish bowl on his head—Ro-Man, he was called—ran around trying to kill the last survivors of a nuclear war. I felt this was art of quite a high nature.

  I also watched *Highway Patrol* with Broderick Crawford as the fearless Dan Matthews, and *One Step Beyond*, hosted by John Newland, the man with the spookiest eyes. . . . There was a whole world of vicarious adventure which came packaged in black-and-white, fourteen inches across and sponsored by brand names which still sound like poetry to me.

  —Best-selling writer Stephen King, from *On Writing:*
  A Memoir of the Craft

- *What did you do to learn to write in a new genre?*

  I went back to good nature books that I had read. And I analyzed them. I wrote outlines . . . so that I could see their structure. And I copied down their transitional sentences or their main sentences or their closing sentences or their lead sentences.

  —Writer Annie Dillard, whose book about nature,
  Pilgrim at Tinker Creek, won the Pulitzer Prize

- *How did you learn to write effectively in school?*

  I was both devastated and determined when my first paper got 36 out of a possible 100—"for your imagination," written alongside the grade. My not belonging was verified but I was not ready to be shut down, not so quickly. So to the library to look up what the Professor himself had published. Proceedings of the Spenser Society. I had no idea what the Professor was going on about in his paper, but I could see the patterns: an introduction that said something about what others had said, what he was going to be writing about, in what order, and what all this would prove; details about what he said he was going to be writing about, complete with quotes, mainly from the poetry, not much from other writers on Spenser, and a "therefore." It wasn't the five-paragraph paper Mr. Lukens has insisted on, not just three points, not just repetition of the opening in the close, but the pattern was essentially the same. The next paper: 62 out of 100 and a "Much better."

—Writer and professor Victor Villanueva Jr., from
Bootstraps: From an American Academic of Color

- *How did your home or early school environment encourage or discourage your literacy development?*

    There were no books in our house. Not really any books at all. No kids' books. No adult books. Not even a dictionary. I mostly got books from the library or read magazines my mom brought home from the hospital where she was a housekeeper—a lot of *Reader's Digest* or the *Playboy*s my dad hid but not very well. . . .

    I think the truth is she hated that I liked to read. To her it was like I was just sitting in one place for two hours staring at a pineapple. It really drove her insane and I learned never to let her catch me reading, because if she saw me she'd make me do housework. I could, however, watch all the TV I wanted. I could also play endless games of solitaire. Just no books. No paper. No pencils or pens. . . .

    It's hard for me to believe how much drawing and reading and writing were discouraged in my house while I was growing up. My mother was actually upset by me reading, and she hated for me to use up paper. I got screamed at a lot for using up paper. . . .

—Cartoonist and author Lynda Barry, from Elissa Schappell's *Tin House* interview

Composing Your Own Literacy Narrative

This chapter invites you to compose a **literacy narrative**. Your instructor may add specific requirements to this assignment, but in general you are to write about a memorable literacy experience—learning, unlearning, or relearning, as Toffler would say, to communicate with others. Some ideas are offered below to help you choose a subject. But first let's consider the assignment's rhetorical situation.

Apply the rhetorical framework: who? what? when? where? how? and why?

To see a portion of Jean Brandt's memoir remixed as a graphic memoir, see p. 13; to see Patrick O'Mally's proposal essay remixed as a Prezi presentation, see Chapter 22.

Since this is the beginning of a new course, you could view this assignment as an opportunity to introduce yourself to your instructor and classmates by choosing a literacy experience, genre, or medium (assuming your instructor gives you leeway to choose) that would enable you to make a particular impression on your readers. For example, if you want to emphasize the importance of reading graphic novels or playing video games in your literacy development, you might consider composing your literacy narrative as a graphic memoir (p. 13) or video game.

Like the remembered event narrative discussed in Chapter 2, a literacy narrative tells a story about a person or an event from your own life. To be effective, it must

- tell a compelling story;
- vividly describe the people and places;
- convey the event's or person's significance in your life and how the event or person affected your literacy practices or your understanding of the power and complexity of the ways we try—and sometimes fail—to communicate with one another.

These are the basic features of the genre.

The first part of the Guide to Reading in Chapter 2 (pp. 14–34) provides a more detailed introduction to the basic features of remembered event narratives, and the Guide to Writing in that chapter (pp. 35–49) supports the drafting and revising of such narratives. Use those sections to help you invent as you draft and revise your literacy narrative.

Devise a topic.

You may already have an idea about what you'd like to write about. But if not, the following ideas may give you a jumping-off point:

- an influential person who played a role—for good or ill—in your literacy education
- a challenging project that required using a literacy you had not yet mastered
- an occasion when you had to display literacy in a particular academic discipline
- a new literacy you had to learn at a workplace
- an experience learning how to communicate better with classmates, team members, siblings, or people in your community

Your instructor may ask you to post your thoughts to a class discussion board or compose a fully developed literacy narrative like the examples by Katherine Kachnowski (pp. 5–8) and David Sedaris on pp. 8–10. If your instructor approves, you might also consider using multimedia—for example, creating a Web page with visuals, audio, and video.

Readings

| Katherine Kachnowski | *Beyond the Microwave, or How I Learned to Cook with a French Accent* |

Katherine Kachnowski, a student at the Ohio State University, originally wrote this literacy narrative in response to an assignment to think about an experience of learning something new. That something could be learning to read or write; learning the language of a new discourse community, like that of an academic discipline; or learning something beyond traditional print literacy, such as how to use unfamiliar technology or how to play a musical instrument. Kachnowski chose to write about her experience learning to cook at the side of her cousin Sophie.

As you read,

- skim the opening paragraph to see how Kachnowski engages her readers' interest; what impression do you get from the way Kachnowski describes the microwaved food and Sophie's reaction to it?

- notice how Kachnowski talks about becoming motivated to learn cooking "techniques, tools, and terminology" (in pars. 4–6, for example); how important in learning to cook does the terminology, or jargon, seem to be?

- answer the questions in the margins; your instructor may ask you to post your answers to a class blog or discuss them in class.

1   Not many people can say that they learned to cook thanks to a microwaveable meal. My culinary education began when my cousin Sophie caught me heating a frozen dinner. "What are you making?" she asked incredulously. A look of alarm spread across her face as she examined the limp vegetables, dry chicken, and sticky pasta on my tray. "That is not food!"

2   After growing up in France, Sophie was spending the summer with my family in the United States. She and I had very different definitions of cooking. Raised by parents who were both chefs, Sophie was skilled in the kitchen. Meanwhile, I barely knew the difference between the bake and broil settings on an oven; my cooking knowledge was limited to operating a microwave and a toaster. And when operating those small appliances seemed like too much of a chore, I resorted to ordering pizza.

How does Sophie serve as a mentor in Kachnowski's literacy education?

3   Immediately after eyeing that sad microwaveable meal, Sophie made it her summer project to instruct me in what she considered all-important basic culinary skills. Although she was my age, Sophie had an air of sophistication and competency that made her a natural mentor. She exuded a confidence in the kitchen that I never felt. During our first few lessons, I could barely comprehend her, and it wasn't solely because of her thick French accent. When Sophie cooked, she spoke in a jargon totally unfamiliar to me. She used culinary terminology, tossing around words like *sear the meat, prove the dough,* and *baste the chicken.* Despite being totally fluent in English, Sophie also had a tendency to mutter in French when she cooked with me. In the kitchen, I struggled to understand her instructions.

4   "An easy first task will be to julienne the potatoes," she advised me during our first lesson. When she saw my confusion, Sophie truly realized my inabilities. *"Mon dieu, this will be a challenge."*

5   I made plenty of mistakes due to my lack of knowledge and experience. *"Plus, plus.* I said *braise* not *glaze,"* she chided as I poured sauce over a piece of beef. Although I was discouraged, I kept my eyes and ears open and tried to keep up. Sophie had a certain dexterity with tools that made a whisk seem more like a wand. As I observed her and tried to mimic this grace, I slowly began to feel less awkward in the kitchen. The techniques, tools, and terminology became more straightforward as I practiced kneading dough, dicing onions, and roasting cuts of meat. The sounds of meat sizzling in a pan, the aromas of a *bouquet garni* flavoring a simmering soup, and the satisfaction of seeing an even, golden crust on a loaf of bread all seemed to cast a spell on me. I was no longer a reluctant cook and was motivated to become more fluent in culinary language.

6   One afternoon late in the summer, we were preparing ratatouille for dinner. "Pass me the mandoline, *rapidement s'il-te-plait,"* Sophie asked. I immediately handed it to her, then paused with an air of realization.

7   "I understood you!" I exclaimed. I had finally cracked the code. The feeling of accomplishment continued throughout the afternoon. As I sliced the zucchini, eggplant, and bell peppers, I noticed how easily I handled the paring knife that was once foreign and terrifying. Although I might never become as accomplished in the kitchen as Sophie, I now possessed the basic knowledge. By improving my cooking vocabulary, Sophie provided me with the skills I needed to fend for myself. While I once avoided anything more than three-step simple instructions, I was now capable of following and executing complex recipes.

8   My culinary education culminated with one final dinner for the family on the eve of Sophie's departure. She and I prepared coq au vin with fresh bread and roasted vegetables. There was even mousse for dessert. As we braised the chicken with a broth and red wine mixture, I thought back to the unappetizing microwave dinner I had prepared for myself on that fateful evening. My cooking knowledge had expanded from "Heat on low for 30 seconds" to lovingly preparing a healthy meal with fresh and flavorful ingredients. Cookbooks and online recipes no longer seemed to be written in a foreign gibberish.

Why do you think Kachnowski acknowledges making mistakes?

How do Kachnowski's reflections on literacy help readers understand her experience?

What does comparing literacy to cracking a code include — and leave out?

How does this ending reinforce the purpose of Kachnowski's literacy narrative?

9   Today, whenever I enjoy something delicious, I am transported back to the summer spent cooking with my cousin. I hear Sophie's French chatter, see the once-foreign, now familiar tools on the counter, and taste the flavors I have come to understand. Learning the language of chefs from Sophie not only helped to bond us, but it also shaped the way I view cooking and nourishing myself.

David Sedaris | *Me Talk Pretty One Day*

Bruce Glikas/Getty Images

David Sedaris, a writer of humorous essays like the one below, was born in upstate New York and grew up in suburban Raleigh, North Carolina. He was catapulted to fame in 1992, when he first read his "SantaLand Diaries" on National Public Radio. Since then, he has performed his pieces both in person and on television and radio, published numerous books and essays, and collaborated with his sister—actress Amy Sedaris—on plays produced under the name the Talent Family. The literacy narrative below was published in 2000 in a book of the same name, *Me Talk Pretty One Day*.

As you read,

- notice Sedaris's explanation, in the opening paragraphs, of when and why he took this class; how does his experience learning a foreign language compare to yours (assuming you have learned or tried to learn another language)?

- compare Sedaris's story about learning French to Katherine Kachnowski's essay about learning to cook; what similarities and differences do you notice?

- think about how Sedaris takes a fairly run-of-the-mill experience of learning something new in a class and makes it hilarious; what makes his story compelling and vivid?

1   At the age of forty-one, I am returning to school and have to think of myself as what my French textbook calls "a true debutant." After paying my tuition, I was issued a student ID, which allows me a discounted entry fee at movie theaters, puppet shows, and Festyland, a far-flung amusement park that advertises with billboards picturing a cartoon stegosaurus sitting in a canoe and eating what appears to be a ham sandwich.

2   I've moved to Paris with hopes of learning the language. My school is an easy ten-minute walk from my apartment, and on the first day of class I arrived early, watching as the returning students greeted one another in the school lobby. Vacations were recounted, and questions were raised concerning mutual friends with names like Kang and Vlatnya. Regardless of their nationalities, everyone spoke in what sounded to me like excellent

French. Some accents were better than others, but the students exhibited an ease and confidence I found intimidating. As an added discomfort, they were all young, attractive, and well dressed, causing me to feel not unlike Pa Kettle trapped backstage after a fashion show.

3   The first day of class was nerve-racking because I knew I'd be expected to perform. That's the way they do it here—it's everybody into the language pool, sink or swim. The teacher marched in, deeply tanned from a recent vacation, and proceeded to rattle off a series of administrative announcements. I've spent quite a few summers in Normandy, and I took a monthlong French class before leaving New York. I'm not completely in the dark, yet I understood only half of what this woman was saying.

4   "If you have not *meimslsxp* or *lgpdmurct* by this time, then you should not be in this room. Has everyone *apzkiubjxow*? Everyone? Good, we shall begin." She spread out her lesson plan and sighed, saying, "All right, then, who knows the alphabet?"

5   It was startling because (a) I hadn't been asked that question in a while and (b) I realized, while laughing, that I myself did *not* know the alphabet. They're the same letters, but in France they're pronounced differently. I know the shape of the alphabet but had no idea what it actually sounded like.

6   "Ahh." The teacher went to the board and sketched the letter *a*. "Do we have anyone in the room whose first name commences with an *ahh*?" Two Polish Annas raised their hands, and the teacher instructed them to present themselves by stating their names, nationalities, occupations, and a brief list of things they liked and disliked in this world. The first Anna hailed from an industrial town outside of Warsaw and had front teeth the size of tombstones. She worked as a seamstress, enjoyed quiet times with friends, and hated the mosquito.

7   "Oh, really," the teacher said. "How very interesting. I thought that everyone loved the mosquito, but here, in front of all the world, you claim to detest him. How is it that we've been blessed with someone as unique and original as you? Tell us, please."

8   The seamstress did not understand what was being said but knew that this was an occasion for shame. Her rabbity mouth huffed for breath, and she stared down at her lap as though the appropriate comeback were stitched somewhere alongside the zipper of her slacks.

9   The second Anna learned from the first and claimed to love sunshine and detest lies. It sounded like a translation of one of those Playmate of the Month data sheets, the answers always written in the same loopy handwriting. "Turn-ons: Mom's famous five-alarm chili! Turnoffs: insecurity and guys who come on too strong!!!!"

10   The two Polish Annas surely had clear notions of what they loved and hated, but like the rest of us, they were limited in terms of vocabulary, and this made them appear less than sophisticated. The teacher forged on, and we learned that Carlos, the Argentine bandoneon player, loved wine, music, and, in his words, "making sex with the womens of the world." Next came a beautiful young Yugoslav who identified herself as an optimist, saying that she loved everything that life had to offer.

11   The teacher licked her lips, revealing a hint of the saucebox we would later come to know. She crouched low for her attack, placed her hands on the young woman's desk, and leaned close, saying, "Oh yeah? And do you love your little war?"

12   While the optimist struggled to defend herself, I scrambled to think of an answer to what had obviously become a trick question. How often is one asked what he loves in this world? More to the point, how often is one asked and then publicly ridiculed for his answer? I recalled my mother, flushed with wine, pounding the tabletop late one night, saying, "Love? I love a good steak cooked rare. I love my cat, and I love . . ." My sisters and I leaned forward, waiting to hear our names. "Tums," our mother said. "I love Tums."

13   The teacher killed some time accusing the Yugoslavian girl of masterminding a program of genocide, and I jotted frantic notes in the margins of my pad. While I can honestly say that I love leafing through medical textbooks devoted to severe dermatological conditions, the hobby is beyond the reach of my French vocabulary, and acting it out would only have invited controversy.

14   When called upon, I delivered an effortless list of things that I detest: blood sausage, intestinal pâtés, brain pudding. I'd learned these words the hard way. Having given it some thought, I then declared my love for IBM typewriters, the French word for *bruise,* and my electric floor waxer. It was a short list, but still I managed to mispronounce *IBM* and assign the wrong gender to both the floor waxer and the typewriter. The teacher's reaction led me to believe that these mistakes were capital crimes in the country of France.

15   "Were you always this *palicmkrexis*?" she asked. "Even a *fiuscrzsa ticiwelmun* knows that a typewriter is feminine."

16   I absorbed as much of her abuse as I could understand, thinking—but not saying—that I find it ridiculous to assign a gender to an inanimate object incapable of disrobing and making an occasional fool of itself. Why refer to Lady Crack Pipe or Good Sir Dishrag when these things could never live up to all that their sex implied?

17   The teacher proceeded to belittle everyone from German Eva, who hated laziness, to Japanese Yukari, who loved paintbrushes and soap. Italian, Thai, Dutch, Korean, and Chinese—we all left class foolishly believing that the worst was over. She'd shaken us up a little, but surely that was just an act designed to weed out the deadweight. We didn't know it then, but the coming months would teach us what it was like to spend time in the presence of a wild animal, something completely unpredictable. Her temperament was not based on a series of good and bad days but, rather, good and bad moments. We soon learned to dodge chalk and protect our heads and stomachs whenever she approached us with a question. She hadn't yet punched anyone, but it seemed wise to protect ourselves against the inevitable. Though we were forbidden to speak anything but French, the teacher would occasionally use us to practice any of her five fluent languages.

18   "I hate you," she said to me one afternoon. Her English was flawless. "I really, really hate you." Call me sensitive, but I couldn't help but take it personally. After being singled out as a lazy *kfdtinvfm*, I took to spending four hours a night on my homework, putting in even more time whenever we were assigned an essay. I suppose I could have gotten by with less, but I was determined to create some sort of identity for myself: David the hard worker, David the cut-up. We'd have one of those "complete this sentence" exercises, and I'd fool with the thing for hours, invariably settling on something like "A quick run around the lake? I'd love to! Just give me a moment while I strap on my wooden leg." The teacher, through word and action, conveyed the message that if this was my idea of an identity, she wanted nothing to do with it.

19   My fear and discomfort crept beyond the borders of the classroom and accompanied me out onto the wide boulevards. Stopping for a coffee, asking directions, depositing money in my bank account: these things were out of the question, as they involved having to speak. Before beginning school, there'd been no shutting me up, but now I was convinced that everything I said was wrong. When the phone rang, I ignored it. If someone asked me a question, I pretended to be deaf. I knew my fear was getting the best of me when I started wondering why they don't sell cuts of meat in vending machines.

20   My only comfort was the knowledge that I was not alone. Huddled in the hallways and making the most of our pathetic French, my fellow students and I engaged in the sort of conversation commonly overheard in refugee camps.

21   "Sometime me cry alone at night."

22   "That be common for I, also, but be more strong, you. Much work and someday you talk pretty. People start love you soon. Maybe tomorrow, okay." Unlike the French class I had taken in New York, here there was no sense of competition. When the teacher poked a shy Korean in the eyelid with a freshly sharpened pencil, we took no comfort in the fact that, unlike Hyeyoon Cho, we all knew the irregular past tense of the verb *to defeat*. In all fairness, the teacher hadn't meant to stab the girl, but neither did she spend much time apologizing, saying only, "Well, you should have been *vkkdyo* more *kdeynfulh*."

23   Over time it became impossible to believe that any of us would ever improve. Fall arrived and it rained every day, meaning we would now be scolded for the water dripping from our coats and umbrellas. It was mid-October when the teacher singled me out, saying, "Every day spent with you is like having a cesarean section."

24   And it struck me that, for the first time since arriving in France, I could understand every word that someone was saying.

25   Understanding doesn't mean that you can suddenly speak the language. Far from it. It's a small step, nothing more, yet its rewards are intoxicating and deceptive. The teacher continued her diatribe and I settled back, bathing in the subtle beauty of each new curse and insult.

26   "You exhaust me with your foolishness and reward my efforts with nothing but pain, do you understand me?"

27   The world opened up, and it was with great joy that I responded, "I know the thing that you speak exact now. Talk me more, you, plus, please, plus."

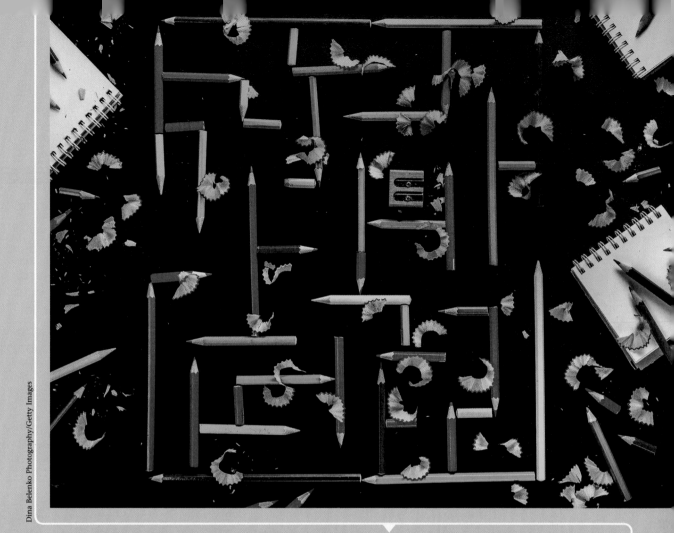

Dina Belenko Photography/Getty Images

PART 1

Writing
Activities

2

Remembering an Event

Were you arrested — when you were thirteen? Why would a child remember being chased by an adult stranger as glorious? Have you ever had a moment when you came face-to-face with your own mortality? These are just a few of the exhilarating, disquieting, even terrifying experiences remembered in this chapter. The kind of memoir you will be reading and writing in this chapter is public, intended to be read by others. Writing for others not only enables us to revisit our past but also gives us an opportunity to represent ourselves to others. Our own and other people's life stories can help us see ourselves differently. They can give us insight into the cultural influences that helped shape who we are and what we value. They can show us what we have in common with others as well as what makes each of us unique.

People write memoirs for various purposes and audiences and publish them as narratives or graphics in a variety of media (print, digital, audiovisual). In college courses, students can use their experiences to analyze or evaluate ideas they are studying. A sociology student, for example, might analyze an actual conversation to test the theory that women tend to view problems as opportunities to share their feelings whereas men typically treat problems as occasions for practical solutions. In professional and business settings, personal stories can play a role. At a conference, for example, a manager might use the story of his encounter with a disgruntled employee to open a discussion of ways to defuse confrontations in the workplace. In a personal context, a writer might convey a powerful experience in a graphic memoir. (The graphic here is based on the memoir by Jean Brandt.)

In this chapter, we ask you to write about a memorable event that you feel comfortable sharing. From reading and analyzing the selections in the Guide to Reading (pp. 14–34) that follows, you can see how others make their stories interesting, even exciting, to read. The Guide to Writing (pp. 35–49) will show you ways to use the basic features of the genre to tell a vivid and dramatic story in a way that not only entertains readers but also gives them insight into the event's significance—its personal and cultural meaning and importance.

To learn more about remixing an essay in a new genre or medium, see Chapter 22.

PRACTICING THE GENRE

Telling a Story

The success of remembered-event writing depends on how well you tell your story. The challenge is to make the story compelling and meaningful for readers — that is, to make readers care about the storyteller and curious to know what happened. To practice creating an intriguing story, follow these guidelines:

Part 1.   Get together with two or three other students.

1 Choose an event that you feel comfortable describing.

2 Think about what makes the event memorable (a conflict with someone else or within yourself, the strong or mixed feelings it evokes, the cultural attitudes it reflects); what will be the turning point, or *climax,* and how will you build up to it?

3 Take turns telling your stories.

Part 2.   After telling your stories, discuss what you learned:

- **What did you learn about the genre from listening to others' stories?** Describe what struck you most upon hearing one another's stories. For example, identify something in each story that was engaging (by being suspenseful, edgy, or funny, perhaps) or that helped you understand the event's significance.

- **What did you learn from the group's reaction to your story?** Knowing how people react to your story, what could you add or change to make your story more engaging or dramatic? What could you show or tell that might help others understand the event's personal or cultural significance?

Did you know?

Audience awareness is developed through practice and feedback, as in this activity.

Analyzing Remembered Event Essays

As you read the selections in this chapter, you will see how different authors craft stories about an important event in their lives.

- Jean Brandt looks back on getting caught shoplifting. (pp. 18–22)
- Annie Dillard recalls the consequences of a childhood prank. (pp. 22–24)
- Ta-Nehisi Coates remembers an earthshaking encounter he had when he was eleven. (pp. 26–28)
- Jenée Desmond-Harris reflects on the death of her idol, rapper Tupac Shakur. (pp. 30–32)

Analyzing how these writers tell a dramatic, well-focused story; using vivid, specific description to enliven their writing; and choosing details and words that help readers understand why the event was so memorable will help you see how you can employ these same techniques when writing your own autobiographical story.

Determine the writer's purpose and audience.

Many people write about important events in their lives to archive their memories and to learn something about themselves. Choosing events that are important to them personally, writers strive to imbue their stories with meaning and feeling that will resonate with readers. That is, they seek to help readers appreciate what we call the event's autobiographical **significance**—why the event is so memorable for the writer and what it might mean for readers. Often writers use autobiographical stories to reflect on a conflict that remains unresolved or that is not yet fully understood. Autobiographical stories may not only prompt readers to reflect on the writer's complicated and ambivalent emotions, puzzling motivations, and strained relationships, but also help readers see larger cultural themes in these stories or understand implications the writer may not have even considered.

When reading the stories that follow, ask yourself what the writers' main purpose is and how they want readers to react:

<table>
<tr><td>The writer's main purpose may be to</td><td>The writer wants readers to react by</td></tr>
<tr><td>

- relive an intense experience that might resonate with readers and lead them to reflect on similar experiences
- understand what happened and why, perhaps to confront hidden, possibly humiliating feelings
- win over readers, perhaps to justify or rationalize choices made, actions taken, or words used
- reflect on cultural attitudes at the time the event occurred, perhaps in contrast to current ways of thinking

</td><td>

- thinking anew about similar experiences—their own or ones they have heard or read about
- understanding what happened and why, perhaps identifying with or empathizing with the writer
- overlooking or excusing what the writer did, said, thought, or felt
- thinking about the writer's experience as symptomatic of social issues and concerns—now or in the past

</td></tr>
</table>

Reflect on . . .

Consider how the concept of *significance* answers readers' predictable "So what?" question.

Assess the genre's basic features.

As you read about the remembered events in this chapter, analyze and evaluate how different authors use the basic features of the genre. The examples that follow are taken from the reading selections that appear later in this Guide to Reading.

> ▮▮ **Basic Features**
> A Well-Told Story
> Vivid Description
> Significance

A WELL-TOLD STORY

Read first to see how the story attempts to engage readers:

- by letting readers into the storyteller's (or narrator's) point of view ("My private musings on identity and belonging—not original in the least, but novel to me—were interrupted when . . . " [Desmond-Harris, par. 2]);

- by arousing curiosity and suspense ("He ran after us, and we ran away from him. . . . All of a sudden, we were running for our lives." [Dillard, par. 10]);

- by clarifying or resolving the underlying conflict through a change or discovery of some kind ("I took the subway home that day, processing the episode all alone. I did not tell my parents. I did not tell my teachers, and if I told my friends I would have done so with all the excitement needed to obscure the fear that came over me in that moment" [Coates, par. 3]).

Many of these basic narrative elements can be visualized in the form of a **dramatic arc** (see Figure 2.1), which you can analyze to see how a story creates and resolves dramatic tension.

For more about narrating, see Chapter 14.

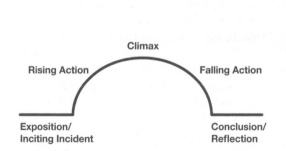

Exposition/Inciting Incident: Background information and scene setting, introducing the characters and the initial conflict or problem that sets off the action, arousing curiosity and suspense

Rising Action: The developing crisis, possibly leading to other conflicts and complications

Climax: The emotional high point, often a turning point marking a change for good or ill

Falling Action: Resolution of tension and unraveling of conflicts; may include a final surprise

Conclusion/Reflection: End, but perhaps not the resolution, of conflicts, and reflection on the event's meaning and importance — its significance

FIGURE 2.1   Dramatic arc
The shape of the arc varies from story to story: Not all stories devote the same amount of space to each element, and some may omit an element or include more than one.

*Notice the narrating strategies used to create **action sequences**.* Narrating action sequences relies on such strategies as using action verbs (such as *walked*) in different tenses or in conjunction with prepositional phrases or other cues of time or location to depict movement and show the relation among actions in time. In the following example, notice that *I walked* occurred in the past—after *I had found* and before *I was about to drop it*:

Action verbs

> I walked back to the basket where I had found the button and was about to drop it when suddenly, instead, I took a quick glance around, assured myself no one could see, and slipped the button into the pocket of my sweatshirt. (Brandt, par. 3)

In addition to moving the narrative along, action sequences may also contribute to the overall feeling—or *dominant impression*—and help readers understand the event's significance. In this example, Brandt's actions show her ambivalence or inner conflict. While her actions seem impulsive ("suddenly"), they are also self-conscious, evidenced by her stopping midway to see if anyone is watching.

VIVID DESCRIPTION OF PEOPLE AND PLACES

For more on describing strategies, see Chapter 14.

*Look for the describing strategies of **naming**, **detailing**, and **comparing**.* In this example, Annie Dillard uses all three strategies to create a vivid description of a Pittsburgh street on one memorable winter morning:

Naming
Detailing
Comparing

> The cars' tires laid behind them on the snowy street a complex trail of beige chunks like crenellated castle walls. I had stepped on some earlier; they squeaked. (Dillard, par. 5)

Notice the senses the description evokes. In the preceding example, Dillard relies mainly on visual details to identify the color, texture, and shape of the snowy tire tracks. But she also tells us what the chunks of snow sounded like when they were stepped on.

Think about the impression made by the descriptions, particularly by the comparisons (similes and metaphors). For example, Dillard's comparison of tire tracks to crenellated castle walls suggests a kind of starry-eyed romanticism, an impression that is echoed by her reflections at the end of the story. As you will see, descriptions like this contribute to the dominant impression, which helps readers grasp the event's significance.

*Notice how **dialogue** is used to portray people and their relationships.* Autobiographers use dialogue to characterize the people involved in the event, showing what they're like by depicting how they talk and interact. Speaker tags identify who is speaking and indicate the speaker's tone or attitude. Here's a brief example that comes at the climax of Dillard's story, when the man finally catches the kids he's been chasing:

Speaker tag

> "You stupid kids," he began perfunctorily. (Dillard, par. 18)

Consider why the writer chose to quote, paraphrase, or summarize. **Quoting** can give dialogue immediacy, intensify a confrontation, and shine a spotlight on a relationship. For example, Brandt uses quoting to make an inherently dramatic interaction that much more intense.

> "I don't understand. What did you take? Why did you do it? You had plenty of money with you."
>
> "I know but I just did it. I can't explain why. Mom, I'm sorry."
>
> "I'm afraid sorry isn't enough. I'm horribly disappointed in you." (pars. 33–35)

Paraphrasing enables the writer to choose words for their impact or contribution to the dominant impression:

> Next thing I knew, he was talking about calling the police and having me arrested and thrown in jail, as if he had just nabbed a professional thief instead of a terrified kid. (Brandt, par. 7)

Paraphrase cue

The clichés (*thrown in jail* and *nabbed*) mock the security guard, aligning Brandt with her father's criticism of the police at the story's end.

Summarizing gives the gist. Sometimes writers use summary because what was said or how it was said isn't as important as the mere fact that something was said:

> The chewing out was redundant, a mere formality, and beside the point. (Dillard, par. 19)
>
> They yelled and gestured. (Coates, par. 1)

Summary cue

AUTOBIOGRAPHICAL SIGNIFICANCE

Look for remembered feelings and thoughts from the time the event occurred. Notice in the first example that Brandt announces her thoughts and feelings before describing them, but in the second example she simply shows her feelings by her actions:

> The *thought* of going to jail terrified me. . . . I *felt* alone and scared. (par. 17)
>
> Long after we got off the phone, . . . I could still distinctly hear the disappointment and hurt in my mother's voice. I cried. (36)

Emotional response

Similarly, Coates acknowledges how surprising and confusing the experience was:

> I remember being amazed. . . . I knew. . . . I *felt,* but did not yet understand. (Coates, par. 4)

Look also for present perspective reflections about the past. In this example, Desmond-Harris uses rhetorical questions (questions she poses and then answers) to set up her present-day adult perspective on her past.

> Did we take ourselves seriously? Did we feel a real stake in the life of this "hard-core" gangsta rapper, and a real loss in his death? We did, even though we were two mixed-race girls raised by our white moms in a privileged community. (par. 8)

Rhetorical questions

Notice that writers sometimes express both their past and their present feelings, either to contrast them or to show that they have not changed. Observe the time cues Desmond-Harris uses to distinguish between past and present feelings:

Time cues

> I mourned Tupac's death then, and continue to mourn him now, because his music represents the years when I was both forced and privileged to confront what it meant to be black. (Desmond-Harris, par. 9)

Mark word choices in descriptive and narrative passages that contribute to the dominant impression and help show why the event or person was significant. For example, Brandt depicts her feeling of shame vividly in this passage:

> As the officers led me through the mall, I sensed a hundred pairs of eyes staring at me. My face flushed and I broke out in a sweat. (par. 18)

Dominant impression

Take a moment . . .
Creating a storyboard
(a series of illustrations like
a comic strip) can help
make a story more visual.

*Consider whether the story's **significance** encompasses mixed or ambivalent feelings and still-unresolved conflicts.* For example, notice the seesawing of feelings Brandt reports:

- Right after shoplifting, Brandt tells us, "I thought about how sly I had been" and "I felt proud of my accomplishment" (par. 5).

- After she is arrested, she acknowledges mixed feelings: "Being searched, although embarrassing, somehow seemed to be exciting. . . . I was having fun" (19).

- It is only when she has to face her mother that Brandt lets her intense feelings show: "For the first time that night, I was close to tears" (26).

Readings

Jean Brandt | *Calling Home*

As a first-year college student, Jean Brandt wrote a courageous story about shoplifting, being arrested and put on public display, and finally having to face her parents' disappointment in her.

As you read,

- consider that some readers, like Brandt's father, will think she was treated too roughly by the store manager and the police, whereas others will think that being a white, middle-class, suburban teenager gave her a "get-out-of-jail-free" card; how do you feel about the way Brandt was treated?

- imagine what Brandt thought her instructor and classmates would think of her after reading her story; how did you respond?

- think about how effectively Brandt uses the basic features of the genre (listed below), and answer the questions in the margins; your instructor may ask you to post your thoughts and answers to a class blog or discussion board or to bring your responses to class.

To learn about Brandt's
process of writing this
essay, turn to A Writer
at Work on pp. 49–51.
How did Brandt discover
the central conflict and
significance of her story?

Basic Features
A Well-Told Story
Vivid Description
Significance

1   As we all piled into the car, I knew it was going to be a fabulous day. My grandmother was visiting for the holidays; and she and I, along with my older brother and sister, Louis and Susan, were setting off for a day of last-minute Christmas shopping. On the way to the mall, we sang Christmas carols, chattered, and laughed. With Christmas only two days away, we were caught up with holiday spirit. I felt light-headed and full of joy. I loved shopping — especially at Christmas.

2   The shopping center was swarming with frantic last-minute shoppers like ourselves. We went first to the General Store, my favorite. It carried mostly knickknacks and other useless items which nobody needs but buys anyway. I was thirteen years old at the time, and things like buttons and calendars and posters would catch my fancy. This day was no different. The object of my desire was a 75-cent Snoopy button. Snoopy was the latest. If you owned anything with the Peanuts on it, you were "in." But since I was supposed to be shopping for gifts for other people and not myself, I couldn't decide what to do. I went in search of my sister for her opinion. I pushed my way through throngs of people to the back of the store where I found Susan. I asked her if she thought I should buy the button. She said it was cute, and if I wanted it to go ahead and buy it.

3   When I got back to the Snoopy section, I took one look at the lines at the cashiers and knew I didn't want to wait thirty minutes to buy an item worth less than one dollar. I walked back to the basket where I had found the button and was about to drop it when suddenly, instead, I took a quick glance around, assured myself no one could see, and slipped the button into the pocket of my sweatshirt.

4   I hesitated for a moment, but once the item was in my pocket, there was no turning back. I had never before stolen anything, but what was done was done. A few seconds later, my sister appeared and asked, "So, did you decide to buy the button?"

5   "No, I guess not." I hoped my voice didn't quaver. As we headed for the entrance, my heart began to race. I just had to get out of that store. Only a few more yards to go and I'd be safe. As we crossed the threshold, I heaved a sigh of relief. I was home free. I thought about how sly I had been and I felt proud of my accomplishment.

6   An unexpected tap on my shoulder startled me. I whirled around to find a middle-aged man, dressed in street clothes, flashing some type of badge and politely asking me to empty my pockets. Where did this man come from? How did he know? I was so sure that no one had seen me! On the verge of panicking, I told myself that all I had to do was give this man his button back, say I was sorry, and go on my way. After all, it was only a 75-cent item.

7   Next thing I knew, he was talking about calling the police and having me arrested and thrown in jail, as if he had just nabbed a professional thief instead of a terrified kid. I couldn't believe what he was saying.

How well do these descriptive details (highlighted) help you visualize the scene?

What is your first impression of Brandt based on paragraphs 1 and 2?

How do the action verbs (highlighted) and dialogue contribute to the drama?

8   "Jean, what's going on?"

9   The sound of my sister's voice eased the pressure a bit. She always managed to get me out of trouble. She would come through this time, too.

10   "Excuse me. Are you a relative of this young girl?"

11   "Yes, I'm her sister. What's the problem?"

12   "Well, I just caught her shoplifting and I'm afraid I'll have to call the police."

13   "What did she take?"

14   "This button."

15   "A button? You are having a thirteen-year-old arrested for stealing a button?"

16   "I'm sorry, but she broke the law."

17   The man led us through the store and into an office, where we waited for the police officers to arrive. Susan had found my grandmother and brother, who, still shocked, didn't say a word. The thought of going to jail terrified me, not because of jail itself, but because of the encounter with my parents afterward. Not more than ten minutes later, two officers arrived and placed me under arrest. They said that I was to be taken to the station alone. Then, they handcuffed me and led me out of the store. I felt alone and scared. I had counted on my sister being with me, but now I had to muster up the courage to face this ordeal all by myself.

How does your understanding of Brandt deepen or change through what she reveals about her feelings and thoughts?

18   As the officers led me through the mall, I sensed a hundred pairs of eyes staring at me. My face flushed and I broke out in a sweat. Now everyone knew I was a criminal. In their eyes I was a juvenile delinquent, and thank God the cops were getting me off the streets. The worst part was thinking my grandmother might be having the same thoughts. The humiliation at that moment was overwhelming. I felt like Hester Prynne being put on public display for everyone to ridicule.

19   That short walk through the mall seemed to take hours. But once we reached the squad car, time raced by. I was read my rights and questioned. We were at the police station within minutes. Everything happened so fast I didn't have a chance to feel remorse for my crime. Instead, I viewed what was happening to me as if it were a movie. Being searched, although embarrassing, somehow seemed to be exciting. All the movies and television programs I had seen were actually coming to life. This is what it was really like. But why were criminals always portrayed as frightened and regretful? I was having fun. I thought I had nothing to fear—until I was allowed my one phone call.

I was trembling as I dialed home. I didn't know what I was going to say to my parents, especially my mother.

20   "Hi, Dad, this is Jean."

21   "We've been waiting for you to call."

22   "Did Susie tell you what happened?"

23   "Yeah, but we haven't told your mother. I think you should tell her what you did and where you are."

24   "You mean she doesn't even know where I am?"

25   "No, I want you to explain it to her."

26   There was a pause as he called my mother to the phone. For the first time that night, I was close to tears. I wished I had never stolen that stupid pin. I wanted to give the phone to one of the officers because I was too ashamed to tell my mother the truth, but I had no choice.

27   "Jean, where are you?"

28   "I'm, umm, in jail."

29   "Why? What for?"

30   "Shoplifting."

31   "Oh no, Jean. Why? Why did you do it?"

32   "I don't know. No reason. I just did it."

33   "I don't understand. What did you take? Why did you do it? You had plenty of money with you."

34   "I know, but I just did it. I can't explain why. Mom, I'm sorry."

35   "I'm afraid sorry isn't enough. I'm horribly disappointed in you."

36   Long after we got off the phone, while I sat in an empty jail cell, waiting for my parents to pick me up, I could still distinctly hear the disappointment and hurt in my mother's voice. I cried. The tears weren't for me but for her and the pain I had put her through. I felt like a terrible human being. I would rather have stayed in jail than confront my mom right then. I dreaded each passing minute that brought our encounter closer. When the officer came to release me, I hesitated, actually not wanting to leave. We went to the front desk, where I had to sign a form to retrieve my belongings. I saw my parents a few yards away and my heart raced. A large knot formed in my stomach. I fought back the tears.

> How does the dialogue here and below add to the drama?

> What is the effect of interweaving storytelling and describing with remembered thoughts and feelings in this paragraph?

What do you learn from Brandt's account of her father's reaction?

37 Not a word was spoken as we walked to the car. Slowly, I sank into the back seat anticipating the scolding. Expecting harsh tones, I was relieved to hear almost the opposite from my father.

38 "I'm not going to punish you and I'll tell you why. Although I think what you did was wrong, I think what the police did was more wrong. There's no excuse for locking a thirteen-year-old behind bars. That doesn't mean I condone what you did, but I think you've been punished enough already."

What, if anything, does this final paragraph contribute to the story?

39 As I looked from my father's eyes to my mother's, I knew this ordeal was over. Although it would never be forgotten, the incident was not mentioned again.

Annie Dillard | From *An American Childhood*

Courtesy of Michele Strub

ANNIE DILLARD, professor emeritus at Wesleyan University, won the Pulitzer Prize for nonfiction writing with her first book, *Pilgrim at Tinker Creek* (1974). Since then, she has written twelve books in a variety of genres. These include *Teaching a Stone to Talk* (1988), *The Writing Life* (1990), and *The Abundance* (2016). Dillard also wrote an autobiography of her early years, *An American Childhood* (1987), from which the following selection comes.

As you read,

- think about how the first two paragraphs prepare readers to understand the story's significance;
- notice how Dillard sets the scene; why do you think she describes the time and place with so much specificity?

1 Some boys taught me to play football. This was fine sport. You thought up a new strategy for every play and whispered it to the others. You went out for a pass, fooling everyone. Best, you got to throw yourself mightily at someone's running legs. Either you brought him down or you hit the ground flat out on your chin, with your arms empty before you. It was all or nothing. If you hesitated in fear, you would miss and get hurt: you would take a hard fall while the kid got away, or you would get kicked in the face while the kid got away. But if you flung yourself wholeheartedly at the back of his knees—if you gathered and joined body and soul and pointed them diving fearlessly—then you likely wouldn't get hurt, and you'd stop the ball. Your fate, and your team's score, depended on your concentration and courage. Nothing girls did could compare with it.

2   Boys welcomed me at baseball, too, for I had, through enthusiastic practice, what was weirdly known as a boy's arm. In winter, in the snow, there was neither baseball nor football, so the boys and I threw snowballs at passing cars. I got in trouble throwing snowballs, and have seldom been happier since.

3   On one weekday morning after Christmas, six inches of new snow had just fallen. We were standing up to our boot tops in snow on a front yard on trafficked Reynolds Street, waiting for cars. The cars traveled Reynolds Street slowly and evenly; they were targets all but wrapped in red ribbons, cream puffs. We couldn't miss.

4   I was seven; the boys were eight, nine, and ten. The oldest two Fahey boys were there—Mikey and Peter—polite blond boys who lived near me on Lloyd Street, and who already had four brothers and sisters. My parents approved Mikey and Peter Fahey. Chickie McBride was there, a tough kid, and Billy Paul and Mackie Kean too, from across Reynolds, where the boys grew up dark and furious, grew up skinny, knowing, and skilled. We had all drifted from our houses that morning looking for action, and had found it here on Reynolds Street.

5   It was cloudy but cold. The cars' tires laid behind them on the snowy street a complex trail of beige chunks like crenellated castle walls. I had stepped on some earlier; they squeaked. We could not have wished for more traffic. When a car came, we all popped it one. In the intervals between cars we reverted to the natural solitude of children.

6   I started making an iceball—a perfect iceball, from perfectly white snow, perfectly spherical, and squeezed perfectly translucent so no snow remained all the way through. (The Fahey boys and I considered it unfair actually to throw an iceball at somebody, but it had been known to happen.)

7   I had just embarked on the iceball project when we heard tire chains come clanking from afar. A black Buick was moving toward us down the street. We all spread out, banged together some regular snowballs, took aim, and, when the Buick drew nigh, fired.

8   A soft snowball hit the driver's windshield right before the driver's face. It made a smashed star with a hump in the middle.

. . . this time, the only time in all of life, the car pulled over and stopped. Its wide black door opened; a man got out of it, running. He didn't even close the car door.

9   Often, of course, we hit our target, but this time, the only time in all of life, the car pulled over and stopped. Its wide black door opened; a man got out of it, running. He didn't even close the car door.

10   He ran after us, and we ran away from him, up the snowy Reynolds sidewalk. At the corner, I looked back; incredibly, he was still after us. He was in city clothes: a suit and tie, street shoes. Any normal adult would have quit, having sprung us into flight and made his point. This man was gaining on us. He was a thin man, all action. All of a sudden, we were running for our lives.

11   Wordless, we split up. We were on our turf; we could lose ourselves in the neighborhood backyards, everyone for himself. I paused and considered. Everyone had vanished except Mikey Fahey, who was just rounding the corner of a yellow brick house. Poor Mikey, I trailed him. The driver of the Buick sensibly picked the two of us to follow. The man apparently had all day.

12   He chased Mikey and me around the yellow house and up a backyard path we knew by heart: under a low tree, up a bank, through a hedge, down some snowy steps, and across the grocery store's delivery driveway. We smashed through a gap in another hedge, entered a scruffy backyard and ran around its back porch and tight between houses to Edgerton Avenue; we ran across Edgerton to an alley and up our own sliding woodpile to the Halls' front yard; he kept coming. We ran up Lloyd Street and wound through mazy backyards toward the steep hilltop at Willard and Lang.

13   He chased us silently, block after block. He chased us silently over picket fences, through thorny hedges, between houses, around garbage cans, and across streets. Every time I glanced back, choking for breath, I expected he would have quit. He must have been as breathless as we were. His jacket strained over his body. It was an immense discovery, pounding into my hot head with every sliding, joyous step, that this ordinary adult evidently knew what I thought only children who trained at football knew: that you have to fling yourself at what you're doing, you have to point yourself, forget yourself, aim, dive.

14   Mikey and I had nowhere to go, in our own neighborhood or out of it, but away from this man who was chasing us. He impelled us forward; we compelled him to follow our route. The air was cold; every breath tore

my throat. We kept running, block after block; we kept improvising, backyard after backyard, running a frantic course and choosing it simultaneously, failing always to find small places or hard places to slow him down, and discovering always, exhilarated, dismayed, that only bare speed could save us—for he would never give up, this man—and we were losing speed.

15   He chased us through the backyard labyrinths of ten blocks before he caught us by our jackets. He caught us and we all stopped.

16   We three stood staggering, half blinded, coughing, in an obscure hilltop backyard: a man in his twenties, a boy, a girl. He had released our jackets, our pursuer, our captor, our hero: he knew we weren't going anywhere. We all played by the rules. Mikey and I unzipped our jackets. I pulled off my sopping mittens. Our tracks multiplied in the backyard's new snow. We had been breaking new snow all morning. We didn't look at each other. I was cherishing my excitement. The man's lower pants legs were wet; his cuffs were full of snow, and there was a prow of snow beneath them on his shoes and socks. Some trees bordered the little flat backyard, some messy winter trees. There was no one around: a clearing in a grove, and we the only players.

17   It was a long time before he could speak. I had some difficulty at first recalling why we were there. My lips felt swollen; I couldn't see out of the sides of my eyes; I kept coughing.

18   "You stupid kids," he began perfunctorily.

19   We listened perfunctorily indeed, if we listened at all, for the chewing out was redundant, a mere formality, and beside the point. The point was that he had chased us passionately without giving up, and so he had caught us. Now he came down to earth. I wanted the glory to last forever.

20   But how could the glory have lasted forever? We could have run through every backyard in North America until we got to Panama. But when he trapped us at the lip of the Panama Canal, what precisely could he have done to prolong the drama of the chase and cap its glory? I brooded about this for the next few years. He could only have fried Mikey Fahey and me in boiling oil, say, or dismembered us piecemeal, or staked us to anthills. None of which I really wanted, and none of which any adult was likely to do, even in the spirit of fun. He could only chew us out there in the Panamanian jungle, after months or years of exalting pursuit. He could only begin, "You stupid kids," and continue in his ordinary Pittsburgh accent with his normal righteous anger and the usual common sense.

21   If in that snowy backyard the driver of the black Buick had cut off our heads, Mikey's and mine, I would have died happy, for nothing has required so much of me since as being chased all over Pittsburgh in the middle of winter—running terrified, exhausted—by this sainted, skinny, furious redheaded man who wished to have a word with us. I don't know how he found his way back to his car.

[REFLECT]   ## Make connections: Acting fearlessly.

At the beginning of the essay, Dillard tells about being taught by the neighborhood boys the joy of playing football, particularly the "all or nothing" of "diving fearlessly" (par. 1). Recall an occasion when you had an opportunity to dive fearlessly into an activity that posed some challenge or risk or required special effort. For example, you may have been challenged, like Dillard, by your teammates at a football game or by a group of volunteers helping during a natural disaster. Or you may have felt pressured by friends to do something that went against your better judgment, was illegal, or was dangerous. Your instructor may ask you to post and discuss your thoughts about the experience. Use these questions to get started:

- What made you embrace the challenge or resist it? What do you think your choice reveals about who you were at the time of the event?

- Dillard uses the value term *courage* to describe the fearless behavior she learned playing football. What value term would you use to describe your experience? For example, were you being *selfless* or *self-serving; responsible* or *irresponsible; a follower, a leader,* or *a self-reliant individual*?

Use the basic features.

A WELL-TOLD STORY: CONSTRUCTING AN ACTION SEQUENCE

Throughout this story, Dillard creates compelling *action sequences* by using a variety of strategies. In this first example, she combines action verbs with prepositional phrases to help readers visualize what it was like to move rapidly from place to place:

> He chased Mikey and me around the yellow house and up a backward path we knew by heart: under a low tree, up a bank, through a hedge, down some snowy steps, and across the grocery store's delivery driveway. We smashed through a gap in another hedge. (par. 12)

Action verb
Prepositional phrases

Here's an example in which she uses short phrases, often with similar sounding words and parallel sentence structures, to convey a sense of repeated action:

> He impelled us forward; we compelled him to follow our route. . . . We kept running, block after block; we kept improvising, backyard after backyard. (par. 14)

Similar sounds
Parallel structures

ANALYZE & WRITE

Write a paragraph analyzing one of Dillard's action sequences:

1 Skim paragraphs 11–14, marking similar words and parallel sentence structures, action verbs, and prepositional phrases. (Don't feel you have to mark every instance, but get a sense of how often Dillard uses these strategies.)

2 How well do these narrative strategies work to represent action? How does using the same strategies over and over contribute to the effect?

For more about action sequences, see Chapter 14.

3 Try writing an action sequence for your story, using parallel sentence structure, prepositional phrases, and words that echo one another, as Dillard does.

AUTOBIOGRAPHICAL SIGNIFICANCE: SHOWING AND TELLING

Writers use both *showing* and *telling* to convey the autobiographical significance of an event: what it meant at the time and why it continues to be memorable. As you've seen, **showing**—in narrating the story and describing people and places—not only helps make the writing vivid but also creates a dominant impression. However, showing alone cannot help readers fully grasp an event's significance. Readers also need **telling**—the writer's explicit comments and reflections. In this example, Brandt uses showing and telling to give readers a clear understanding of how she felt at the time:

> As the officers led me through the mall, I sensed a hundred pairs of eyes staring at me. My face flushed and I broke out in a sweat. Now everyone knew I was a criminal. . . . The humiliation at that moment was overwhelming. I felt like Hester Prynne being put on public display for everyone to ridicule. (par. 18)

Telling
Showing

Narrators may use telling to articulate remembered feelings and thoughts from the time the event occurred and to convey the writer's present perspective on the event—what the writer feels and thinks now, looking back on it after time has passed.

To alert readers that they are telling, writers sometimes announce their reflections with words like *felt* and *thought*. But they may also choose words that name or imply a particular emotion or thought (for example, "The humiliation at that moment was overwhelming" [Brandt, 18]).

Similarly, to signal a shift from the past to the present perspective, writers sometimes announce the transition with words such as *then* and *now*. But a more subtle strategy is to make a cultural reference or allusion, as Brandt does when she compares herself to Hester Prynne, from Nathaniel Hawthorne's novel *The Scarlet Letter*, "being put on public display for everyone to ridicule" [par. 18].

ANALYZE & WRITE

Write a paragraph analyzing Dillard's use of telling to convey the event's significance:

1 Skim paragraphs 11–21, noting where Dillard *tells* readers her thoughts and feelings. (Don't feel you have to mark every instance, but try to get a sense of how much she tells as well as what she tells readers.)

2 Review what you have highlighted to determine which of the passages indicate Dillard's remembered feelings and thoughts from the time the incident occurred and which indicate what she feels and thinks now, looking back on the event from her present adult perspective. How can you tell the difference between her past and present perspectives?

RESPOND ## Consider possible topics: Remembering unexpected adult actions and reactions.

Like Dillard, you could write about a time when an adult did something entirely unexpected during your childhood—an action that seemed dangerous or threatening to you, or something humorous, kind, or generous. Consider unpredictable actions of adults in your immediate or extended family, adults you had come to know outside your family, and strangers. As you consider these possible topics, think about your purpose and audience: What would you want your instructor and classmates to learn from reading about this event?

Ta-Nehisi Coates | *Losing My Innocence*

Tasos Katopodis/Getty Images

TA-NEHISI COATES is a national correspondent for the *Atlantic,* writes articles for publications such as the *New York Times Magazine* and the *Village Voice,* and is the author of the *Black Panther* graphic novel series. His most recent book is a collection of essays written during the Obama administration, *We Were Eight Years in Power* (2017). In 2015, *Between the World and Me*—his collection of essays written as a letter to his adolescent son—won the National Book

Award for Nonfiction, and Coates was awarded a MacArthur Foundation "genius" grant. In this brief selection, excerpted from *Between the World and Me,* Coates recounts an experience that helped him learn a startling lesson.

As you read, think about the following:

- consider how the experience Coates writes about relates to your own experience when you were around eleven years old;
- reflect on the fact that Coates frames this story as a letter to his fifteen-year-old son affect the ways you understand its significance.

1   I was eleven years old, standing out in the parking lot in front of the 7-Eleven, watching a crew of older boys standing near the street. They yelled and gestured at . . . who? . . . another boy, young, like me, who stood there, almost smiling, gamely throwing up his hands. He had already learned the lesson he would teach me that day: that his body was in constant jeopardy. Who knows what brought him to that knowledge? The projects, a drunken stepfather, an older brother concussed by police, a cousin pinned in the city jail. That he was outnumbered did not matter because the whole world had outnumbered him long ago, and what do numbers matter? This was a war for the possession of his body and that would be the war of his whole life.

2   I stood there for some seconds, marveling at the older boys' beautiful sense of fashion. They all wore ski jackets, the kind which, in my day, mothers put on layaway in September, then piled up overtime hours so as to have the thing wrapped and ready for Christmas. I focused in on a light-skinned boy with a long head and small eyes. He was scowling at another boy, who was standing close to me. It was just before three in the afternoon. I was in sixth grade. School had just let out, and it was not yet the fighting weather of early spring. What was the exact problem here? Who could know?

3   The boy with the small eyes reached into his ski jacket and pulled out a gun. I recall it in the slowest motion, as though in a dream. There the boy stood, with the gun brandished, which he slowly untucked, tucked, then untucked once more, and in his eyes I saw a surging rage that could, in an instant, erase my body. That was 1986. That year I felt myself to be drowning in the news reports of murder. I was aware that these murders very often did not land upon the intended targets but fell upon great-aunts, PTA mothers, overtime uncles, and joyful children — fell upon them random and relentless, like great sheets of rain. I knew this in theory but could not understand it as fact until the boy with the small eyes stood across from me holding my entire body in his small hands. The boy did not shoot. His friends pulled him back. He did not need to shoot. He had affirmed my place in the order of things. He had let it be known how easily I could be selected. I took the subway home that day, processing the episode all alone. I did not tell my parents. I did not tell my teachers, and if I told my friends I would have done so with all the excitement needed to obscure the fear that came over me in that moment.

4   I remember being amazed that death could so easily rise up from the nothing of a boyish afternoon, billow up like fog. I knew that West Baltimore, where I lived; that the north side of Philadelphia, where my cousins lived; that the South Side of Chicago, where friends of my father lived, comprised a world apart. Somewhere out there beyond the firmament, past the asteroid belt, there were other worlds where children did not regularly fear for their bodies. I knew this because there was a large television resting in my living room. In the evenings I would sit before this television bearing witness to the dispatches from this other world. There were little white boys with complete collections of football cards, and their only want was a popular girlfriend and their only worry was poison oak. That other world was suburban and endless, organized around pot roasts, blueberry pies, fireworks, ice cream sundaes, immaculate bathrooms, and small toy trucks that were loosed in wooded backyards with streams and glens. Comparing these dispatches with the facts of my native world, I came to understand that my country was a galaxy, and this galaxy stretched from the pandemonium of West Baltimore to the happy hunting grounds of *Mr. Belvedere.* I obsessed over the distance between that other sector of space and my own. I knew that my portion of the American galaxy, where bodies

were enslaved by a tenacious gravity, was black and that the other, liberated portion was not. I knew that some inscrutable energy preserved the breach. I felt, but did not yet understand, the relation between that other world and me. And I felt in this a cosmic injustice, a profound cruelty, which infused an abiding, irrepressible desire to unshackle my body and achieve the velocity of escape.

[REFLECT]

Make connections: The media as a window onto another world.

Coates describes his neighborhood as "a world apart" from that "other world" he witnessed on television, in particular the world that belonged to the idealized white, middle-class, suburban family of *Mr. Belvedere,* a popular television sitcom at the time:

> There were little white boys with complete collections of football cards, and their only want was a popular girlfriend and their only worry was poison oak. That other world was suburban and endless, organized around pot roasts, blueberry pies, fireworks, ice cream sundaes, immaculate bathrooms, and small toy trucks that were loosed in wooded backyards with streams and glens. (par. 4)

Reflect on how television, film, books, YouTube, and other media have opened up worlds for you, as the sitcom *Mr. Belvedere* did for the young Coates. Your instructor may ask you to post and discuss your ideas about the role of the media in influencing how we imagine other worlds. Use these questions to get started:

- Think of one or two examples of other worlds you have witnessed through the media and the impressions you have of them. For example, do you think the other worlds represented in the media are real and attainable or just a fantasy?

- Coates explains, "I felt, but did not yet understand, the relation between that other world and me" (par. 4). What do you feel and understand about the relation between the world in which you live and the other worlds you see in the media?

[ANALYZE]

Use the basic features.

VIVID DESCRIPTION: CREATING A DOMINANT IMPRESSION

The describing strategies of naming, detailing, and comparing portray people and places vividly:

Naming
Detailing
Comparing

> The shopping center was swarming with frantic last-minute shoppers like ourselves. (Brandt, par. 2)

Brandt *names* a familiar location for readers. She selects *details* carefully to conjure a specific image of that shopping center before Christmas. Perhaps most evocatively, she uses a metaphor to *compare* the shopping mall to a "swarming" beehive, a comparison that reinforces the image of "frantic" shoppers in a place teeming with hurried, excited people.

Describing strategies like Brandt's not only help readers imagine the scene and people at a particular place and time but also contribute to the dominant impression. The description evokes Brandt's youthful excitement, suggests the crowds and chaos that motivated Brandt to pocket the button, and foreshadows the swarm of intense and conflicted feelings Brandt experiences as the story unfolds.

ANALYZE & WRITE

Write a paragraph analyzing Coates's use of naming, detailing, and comparing to help readers visualize the boys he encountered outside the 7-Eleven and to create a dominant impression of the boy with the gun:

1. Review paragraphs 1–3, noting how Coates uses naming and detailing to help readers visualize the scene and, most important, to identify who does what to whom.

2. Coates begins by describing the scene as a bystander. How does he describe his vantage point, specifically where he is positioned in relation to the other boys in the scene?

3. Reread paragraph 3. How does Coates use comparison to convey his feelings? Identify the metaphor(s) he uses, and explain how they reinforce his description of feeling overwhelmed by "news reports of murder" that fell "random and relentless." What is the overall impression you get from this use of comparing?

AUTOBIOGRAPHICAL SIGNIFICANCE: USING SYMBOLS

Autobiographers occasionally use *symbols* to enrich a story's significance by adding another level of meaning. The symbol could be an object (such as the Snoopy button for Brandt), a person (such as Tupac for Desmond-Harris in the next reading), or a place (such as the Panamanian jungle for Dillard). On a literal level, the object, person, or place is simply what it is, nothing more. But on a symbolic level, the object, person, or place takes on additional meaning, often standing for an abstract idea. For example, when Brandt identifies herself with Hester Prynne, she associates herself with a symbol of social injustice and personal heroism, encouraging readers to see her as being mistreated but rising above it. Through this symbol, Brandt reinforces her father's judgment that although she had done something wrong, the police were even "more wrong" (par. 38).

ANALYZE & WRITE

Write a paragraph analyzing how Coates uses symbolism:

1. Reread paragraph 4 to see how Coates uses symbolism to describe what he calls "a cosmic injustice."

2. He describes the places he and his family and friends live as "a world apart." What do you think he means?

Consider possible topics: Thinking about the cultural context.

Clearly, Ta-Nehisi Coates has thought and written in-depth about the cultural context he explores in "Losing My Innocence." In fact, he uses a well-known device: framing his story as a letter to his son. Imagine you were writing a letter (more likely an e-mail) to a child or a younger sibling using an event from your life to share your insights; what event could you write about? For example, try to recall an event that taught you something about being a bully or standing up to one, that tested your sense of fairness and equality, or that challenged gender stereotypes or racial biases.

Jenée Desmond-Harris | *Tupac and My Non-thug Life*

Courtesy of Jenée Desmond-Harris

JENÉE DESMOND-HARRIS is a *New York Times* Op-Ed Page editor as well as the race, law, and politics reporter at Vox.com. A graduate of Howard University and Harvard Law School, Desmond-Harris has also been a contributor to such news outlets as *Time* magazine, CNN, MSNBC, and the *Huffington Post*. The following selection was published in the *Root* in 2011. It chronicles Desmond-Harris's reaction to the murder of gangsta rap icon Tupac Shakur in a Las Vegas drive-by shooting in 1996. Desmond-Harris mentions Tupac's mother, Afeni, as well as the "East Coast–West Coast war"—the rivalry between Tupac and the Notorious B.I.G. (Biggie Smalls), who was suspected of being involved in Tupac's murder.

As you read, think about being a fan:

- consider why people become a fan of a musical artist, actor, athlete, or other celebrity;

- reflect on how your fascination with a celebrity helps you understand Desmond-Harris's feelings about Tupac's death.

1　I learned about Tupac's death when I got home from cheerleading practice that Friday afternoon in September 1996. I was a sophomore in high school in Mill Valley, Calif. I remember trotting up my apartment building's stairs, physically tired but buzzing with the frenetic energy and possibilities for change that accompany fall and a new school year. I'd been cautiously allowing myself to think during the walk home about a topic that felt frighteningly taboo (at least in my world, where discussion of race was avoided as delicately as obesity or mental illness): what it meant to be biracial and on the school's mostly white cheerleading team instead of the mostly black dance team. I remember acknowledging, to the sound of an 8-count that still pounded in my head as I walked through the door, that

I didn't really have a choice: I could memorize a series of stiff and precise motions but couldn't actually dance.

2　My private musings on identity and belonging—not original in the least, but novel to me—were interrupted when my mom heard me slam the front door and drop my bags: "*Your friend died!*" she called out from another room. Confused silence. "*You know, that rapper you and Thea love so much!*"

Mourning a Death in Vegas

3　The news was turned on, with coverage of the deadly Vegas shooting. Phone calls were made. Ultimately my best friend, Thea, and I were left to our own 15-year-old devices to mourn that weekend. Her mother and step-father were out of town. Their expansive, million-dollar home was perched on a hillside less than an hour from Tupac's former stomping grounds in Oakland and Marin City. Of course, her home was also worlds away from both places.

4   We couldn't "pour out" much alcohol undetected for a libation, so we limited ourselves to doing somber shots of liqueur from a well-stocked cabinet. One each. Tipsy, in a high-ceilinged kitchen surrounded by hardwood floors and Zen flower arrangements, we baked cookies for his mother. We packed them up to ship to Afeni with a handmade card. ("Did we really do that?" I asked Thea this week. I wanted to ensure that this story, which people who know me now find hilarious, hadn't morphed into some sort of personal urban legend over the past 15 years. "Yes," she said. "We put them in a lovely tin.")

5   On a sound system that echoed through speakers perched discreetly throughout the airy house, we played "Life Goes On" on a loop and sobbed. We analyzed lyrics for premonitions of the tragedy. We, of course, cursed Biggie. Who knew that the East Coast–West Coast war had two earnest soldiers in flannel pajamas, lying on a king-size bed decorated with pink toe shoes that dangled from one of its posts? There, we studied our pictures of Tupac and re-created his tattoos on each other's body with a Sharpie. I got "Thug Life" on my stomach. I gave Thea "Exodus 1811" inside a giant cross. Both are flanked by "West Side."

6   A snapshot taken that Monday on our high school's front lawn (seen here) shows the two of us lying side by side, shirts lifted to display the tributes in black marker. Despite our best efforts, it's the innocent, bubbly lettering of notes passed in class and of poster boards made for social studies presentations. My hair has recently been straightened with my first (and last) relaxer and a Gold 'N Hot flatiron on too high a setting. Hers is slicked back with the mixture of Herbal Essences and Blue Magic that we formulated in a bathroom laboratory.

7   My rainbow-striped tee and her white wifebeater capture a transition between our skater-inspired Salvation Army shopping phase and the next one, during which we'd wear the same jeans slung from our hip

Courtesy of Jenée Desmond-Harris

The author (left) with her friend Thea

bones, revealing peeks of flat stomach, but transforming ourselves from Alternative Nation to MTV Jams imitators. We would get bubble coats in primary colors that Christmas and start using silver eyeliner, trying—and failing—to look something like Aaliyah.[1]

Mixed Identities: Tupac and Me

8   Did we take ourselves seriously? Did we feel a real stake in the life of this "hard-core" gangsta rapper, and a real loss in his death? We did, even though we were two mixed-race girls raised by our white moms in a privileged community where we could easily rattle off the names of the small handful of other kids in town who also had one black parent: Sienna. Rashea. Brandon. Aaron. Sudan. Akio. Lauren. Alicia. Even though the most subversive thing we did was make prank calls. Even though we hadn't yet met our first boyfriends, and Shock G's proclamations about putting satin on people's panties sent us into absolute giggling fits. And even though we'd been so delicately cared for, nurtured and protected from any of life's hard edges—with special efforts made to shield us from those involving race—that we sometimes felt ready to explode with boredom. Or maybe because of all that.

9   I mourned Tupac's death then, and continue to mourn him now, because his music represents the years

---

[1] A hit rhythm-and-blues and hip-hop recording artist. Aaliyah Dana Haughton died in a plane crash at age twenty-two. [Editor's note]

when I was both forced and privileged to confront what it meant to be black. That time, like his music, was about exploring the contradictory textures of this identity: The ambience and indulgence of the fun side, as in "California Love" and "Picture Me Rollin'." But also the burdensome anxiety and outright anger—"Brenda's Got a Baby," "Changes" and "Hit 'Em Up."

10   For Thea and me, his songs were the musical score to our transition to high school, where there emerged a vague, lunchtime geography to race: White kids perched on a sloping green lawn and the benches above it. Below, black kids sat on a wall outside the gym. The bottom of the hill beckoned. Thea, more outgoing, with more admirers among the boys, stepped down boldly, and I followed timidly. Our formal invitations came in the form of unsolicited hall passes to go to Black Student Union meetings during free periods. We were assigned to recite Maya Angelou's "Phenomenal Woman" at the Black History Month assembly.

11   Tupac was the literal sound track when our school's basketball team would come charging onto the court, and our ragtag group of cheerleaders kicked furiously to "Toss It Up" in a humid gymnasium. Those were the games when we might breathlessly join the dance team after our cheer during time-outs if they did the single "African step" we'd mastered for BSU performances.

Everything Black—and Cool

12   . . . Blackness became something cool, something to which we had brand-new access. We flaunted it, buying Kwanzaa candles and insisting on celebrating privately (really, just lighting the candles and excluding our friends) at a sleepover. We memorized "I Get Around"[2] and took turns singing verses to each other as we drove through Marin County suburbs in Thea's green Toyota station wagon. Because he was with us through all of this, we were in love with Tupac and wanted to embody him. On Halloween, Thea donned a bald cap and a do-rag, penciled in her already-full eyebrows and was a dead ringer.

13   Tupac's music, while full of social commentary (and now even on the Vatican's playlist), probably wasn't made to be a treatise on racial identity. Surely it wasn't created to accompany two girls (*little* girls, really) as they embarked on a coming-of-age journey. But it was there for us when we desperately needed it.

[REFLECT]   # Make connections: Searching for identity.

Remembering high school, Desmond-Harris describes the emergence of "a vague, lunchtime geography to race: White kids perched on a sloping green lawn and the benches above it. Below, black kids sat on a wall outside the gym" (par. 10).

School, particularly high school, is notorious for students' forming peer groups or cliques of various kinds—by ethnicity, gender, popularity, and so on. Recall the cliques in your own school and think about the roles they played, both positive and negative, in your search for identity. Your instructor may ask you to post and discuss your thoughts about your search for identity. Use these questions to get started:

- Did you associate with any particular groups, and if so, why did you choose those groups?

- How did being in a particular group or not being in that group affect your sense of yourself?

---

[2] Tupac Shakur's first top-twenty single, released in 1993 on *Strictly 4 My N.I.G.G.A.Z.*, Shakur's second studio album. [Editor's note]

- Why do you think it is important for her "coming-of-age journey" that Desmond-Harris felt "beckoned" by the group at the "bottom of the hill" (par. 10)? The word *beckoned* here can be read in two ways: that she felt the need to be a part of the group or that members of the group invited her to join them. Consider how these possible interpretations affect your understanding of her remembered event.

Use the basic features.

[ANALYZE]

VIVID DESCRIPTION OF PEOPLE AND PLACES: USING VISUALS AND BRAND NAMES

Desmond-Harris provides lots of concrete details to enliven her narrative. She also uses a photo and refers to brand names to convey to readers an exact sense of what the girls were like. Notice that she recounts the Sharpie tattooing and then actually shows us a photo of her and her friend Thea displaying their tattoos. But Desmond-Harris does not let the photo speak for itself; instead, she describes the picture, pointing out features, such as their hairstyles and outfits, that mark the girls' identity. Consider the references to particular styles and brand names (such as "our skater-inspired Salvation Army shopping phase") that tag the various roles they were trying on at that time of their lives (par. 7).

ANALYZE & WRITE

Write a paragraph or two analyzing Desmond-Harris's use of a photograph and brand names to enhance her descriptions:

1. Skim paragraphs 5–7, highlighting the specific details in the photo that Desmond-Harris points out as well as the brand names (usually capitalized) and the modifiers (like *skater-inspired*) that make them more specific.

2. Look closely at the photograph itself, and consider its purpose.
   - Why do you think Desmond-Harris included it?
   - What does the photograph contribute or show us that the text alone does not convey?

3. Consider the effect that the photo and the brand names have on you as a reader (or might have on readers close to Desmond-Harris's age). How do they help readers envision the girls? What is the dominant impression you get of the young Desmond-Harris from these descriptive details?

For more about analyzing illustrated or multimodal texts, see Chapter 22.

AUTOBIOGRAPHICAL SIGNIFICANCE: HANDLING COMPLEX EMOTIONS

Remembered events that have lasting significance nearly always involve mixed or ambivalent feelings. Therefore, readers expect and appreciate some degree of complexity. Multiple layers of meaning make autobiographical stories more, not less, interesting. Significance that seems simplistic or predictable makes stories less successful. For example, if Brandt's story had ended with her arrest and left out the conversations with her parents, readers would have less insight into Brandt's still intense and unresolved feelings.

ANALYZE & WRITE

Write a paragraph or two analyzing Desmond-Harris's handling of the complex personal and cultural significance of her remembered event:

1 Skim the last two sections (pars. 8–13), noting passages where Desmond-Harris tells readers her remembered feelings and thoughts at the time, and passages where she gives readers her present perspective as an adult reflecting on the experience. How does Desmond-Harris use her dual perspective — that of the fifteen-year-old experiencing the event and the thirty-year-old writing about it — to help readers understand the event's significance?

2 Look closely at paragraph 8, and consider how Desmond-Harris helps her readers grasp the significance of the event by using sentence strategies like these:

- rhetorical questions (questions writers ask and answer themselves)
- repeated words and phrases
- intentional sentence fragments (incomplete sentences used for special effect)

Note that in academic writing, sentence fragments — even those that are used purposely for rhetorical effect — may be frowned on. One of the instructor's purposes in assigning a writing project is to teach students to use formal academic writing conventions, a process that includes distinguishing between complete sentences and sentence fragments, and knowing how to identify and correct sentence fragments.

[RESPOND]

Consider possible topics: Recognizing a public event as a turning point.

Like Desmond-Harris, you could write about how a public event—such as a celebrity death or marriage, an act of heroism or charity, or even the passage of a law—helped (or forced) you to confront an aspect of your identity. Consider the complexities of your reaction—the significance the event had for you at the time, and the significance the event has for you now. You might make a list of physical traits, as well as beliefs about or aspects of your sense of identity, that changed as a result of the event.

The Writing Assignment

Write about an event in your life that will engage readers and that will, at the same time, help them understand the significance of the event. Tell your story dramatically and vividly.

This Guide to Writing is designed to help you depict your own remembered event and apply what you have learned from reading other selections in the same genre. The Starting Points chart will help you find the guidance you need, when you need it.

Did you know?

When you are experimenting with a new or especially challenging genre, scaffolding like this Guide to Writing can be very helpful. But when you are writing in a genre you know well, you may not need the support of the activities here.

STARTING POINTS: REMEMBERING AN EVENT

A Well-Told Story

How can I come up with an event to write about?

- Consider possible topics. (pp. 26, 30, 34)
- Choose an event to write about. (pp. 37–38)
- Test Your Topic: Considering Your Purpose and Audience (p. 38)

How can I interest my audience and hold its attention?

- Give your story a dramatic arc. (pp. 38–40)
- Test Your Story: Facing an Audience (p. 40)
- Write the opening sentences. (p. 44)
- A Troubleshooting Guide: A Well-Told Story (pp. 46–47)

How can I make my story dramatic?

- Assess the genre's basic features: A well-told story. (pp. 15–16)
- A Well-Told Story: Constructing an Action Sequence (p. 25)
- A Troubleshooting Guide: A Well-Told Story (pp. 46–47)

How should I organize my story?

- Give your story a dramatic arc. (pp. 38–40)
- Assess the genre's basic features: A well-told story. (pp. 15–16)
- Use tenses to clarify the sequence of actions. (pp. 40–41)
- A Troubleshooting Guide: A Well-Told Story (pp. 46–47)

Vivid Description of People and Places

How can I describe the place where the event occurred vividly and specifically?

- Assess the genre's basic features: Vivid description of people and places. (pp. 16–17)
- Describe key people and places vividly, and show their significance. (pp. 41–42)
- A Troubleshooting Guide: Vivid Description of People and Places (p. 47)

How can I make the people in my story come alive?

- Assess the genre's basic features: Vivid description of people and places. (pp. 16–17)
- Describe key people and places vividly, and show their significance. (pp. 41–42)
- Vivid Description of People and Places: Creating a Dominant Impression (pp. 28–29)
- Vivid Description of People and Places: Using Visuals and Brand Names. (p. 33)
- Use dialogue to portray people and dramatize relationships (p. 42)
- A Troubleshooting Guide: Vivid Description of People and Places (p. 47)

Autobiographical Significance

How can I help readers grasp the significance of my remembered event?

- Assess the genre's basic features: Autobiographical significance. (pp. 17–18)
- Autobiographical Significance: Showing and Telling (pp. 25–26)
- Autobiographical Significance: Handling Complex Emotions (pp. 33–34)
- Autobiographical Significance: Using Symbols (p. 29)
- Clarify your story's significance. (pp. 42–43)
- A Troubleshooting Guide: Autobiographical Significance (pp. 47–48)

How can I create a dominant impression?

- Assess the genre's basic features: Autobiographical significance. (pp. 17–18)
- Autobiographical Significance: Showing and Telling (pp. 25–26)
- Autobiographical Significance: Using Symbols (p. 29)
- Clarify your story's significance. (pp. 42–43)

Writing a Draft: Invention, Research, Planning, and Composing

The activities in this section will help you choose an event to write about and develop it into a story that is well-told, vivid, and meaningful. Do the activities in any order that makes sense to you (and your instructor), and return to them as needed as you revise.

Choose an event to write about.

To make a compelling story, the event you choose to write about should

- take place over a short period of time (preferably just a few hours);
- center on a conflict (an internal struggle or an external confrontation);
- disclose something significant about your life;
- reveal strong and possibly complex or ambivalent feelings (rather than superficial or sentimental ones).

Make a list of possible events in your life that you would feel comfortable writing about. If you are having trouble coming up with promising events to write about, think about the readings. Like Brandt, you could revisit an event that changed your relationship with your parents. Like Dillard, you could recall an event that you found exalting. Like Coates, you could reflect on an event that changed the way you saw the world. Or like Desmond-Harris, you could examine an event that helped you find your identity. You may also consult the Consider Possible Topics sections on pp. 26, 30, and 34, and reread any notes you made in response to those suggestions. Alternatively, check out Web sites where people post stories about their lives, such as the *Moth*, *Story Preservation Initiative*, *the Sixties Project*, or *StoryCorps*. Try also typing *memory project*, *survivor stories*, or a similar word string into the search box of your browser. If you need more ideas, the following may give you a jumping-off point:

- a difficult situation (for example, when you had to make a tough choice and face the consequences, or when you let someone down or someone you admired let you down)
- an occasion when things did not turn out as expected (for example, when you expected to be criticized but were praised or ignored instead, or when you were convinced you would succeed but failed)
- an incident that changed you or that revealed an aspect of your personality (such as initiative, insecurity, ambition, jealousy, or heroism)
- an incident in which a conflict or a serious misunderstanding with someone made you feel unjustly treated or caused you to mistreat someone else
- an experience that made you reexamine a basic value or belief (such as a time when you were expected to do something that went against your values, or a time when you had to make a decision about which you were deeply conflicted)

- an encounter with another person that led you to seriously consider someone else's point of view, changed the way you viewed yourself, or altered your ideas about how you fit into a group or community

- an event that revealed to you other people's surprising assumptions about you (as a student, friend, colleague, or worker)

TEST YOUR TOPIC

Considering Your Purpose and Audience

After you have made a tentative topic choice, ask yourself the following questions:

- Will I be able to reconstruct the story, place, and people in enough detail to help my readers imagine what the event was like? (As you probe your memory, you may remember more details, but you may also need to fill in or re-create some details.)

- Do I feel comfortable sharing this experience with my instructor and classmates — revealing what I did, thought, and felt at the time? What concerns or anxieties do I have about the impression they will have of me?

- Will I be able to help my readers understand the personal and social dimensions of the underlying conflict? Will my own understanding of its significance deepen as I write about it?

If you lose confidence in your choice after answering these questions, return to your list and choose another event.

▦ Give your story a dramatic arc.

Once you have selected an event, begin by making a simple sketch of your story. Here is a sample outline you can modify to fit your needs. (Remember that each section need not be the same length; the exposition and conclusion/reflection may be very brief — a sentence or two — while the rising action and climax may run for several paragraphs.)

I. **Exposition/Inciting Incident:** Set the scene, and show how the conflict or problem started.

II. **Rising Action:** Build tension and suspense, showing how the crisis developed or worsened.

III. **Climax:** End the suspense by dramatizing the most critical moment or turning point.

IV. **Falling Action:** Show how the tension diminished as the conflict moved toward resolution.

V. **Conclusion/Reflection:** Bring closure to the story, and reflect on the event's overall significance.

Then you can use the following Ways In activities to anticipate your readers' likely questions and flesh out your chronology.

HOW DO I DEVELOP A DRAMATIC ARC?

Ask yourself the following questions:

What is the underlying conflict, the dilemma facing my narrator?

To answer, provide some EXPOSITION, *the background information that will help your readers understand the situation:*

▶ I wanted .... but didn't want to .... So I ....

EXAMPLE   The object of my desire was a 75-cent Snoopy button. . . . I took one look at the lines at the cashiers and knew I didn't want to wait thirty minutes. (Brandt, pars. 2, 3)

What started it?

To answer, dramatize the **INCITING INCIDENT**, *the crisis that sets off the conflict or triggered the event.*

Use an action sequence:

▶ I did .... But then ....

EXAMPLE   A black Buick was moving toward us down the street. We all spread out, banged together some regular snowballs, took aim, and, when the Buick drew nigh, fired. (Dillard, par. 7)

Use dialogue:

▶ " .... ," .... announced excitedly.

EXAMPLE   *"Your friend died!"* she called out from another room. (Desmond-Harris, par. 2)

What will happen?

To answer, intensify the story's **RISING ACTION** *to arouse curiosity and build suspense and excitement:*

▶ He .... us. We ....

EXAMPLE   He ran after us, and we ran away from him, up the snowy Reynolds sidewalk. At the corner, I looked back; incredibly, he was still after us. . . . This man was gaining on us. He was a thin man, all action. All of a sudden, we were running for our lives. (Dillard, par. 10)

What did it lead to?

To answer, dramatize the **CLIMAX** *by reflecting on what you were feeling at the time:*

▶ He did .... , and I remember [the event] as if ....

EXAMPLE   The boy with the small eyes reached into his ski jacket and pulled out a gun. I recall it in the slowest motion, as though in a dream. There the boy stood, with the gun brandished, which he slowly untucked, tucked, then untucked once more. (Coates, par. 3)

(continued)

How did it turn out?

To answer, summarize the **FALLING ACTION**, *showing how the conflict subsides and complications unravel:*

▶ Finally, he ⸺⸺⸺⸺ , and I ⸺⸺⸺⸺ .

EXAMPLE   When the officer came to release me, I hesitated, actually not wanting to leave. We went to the front desk, where I had to sign a form to retrieve my belongings. (Brandt, par. 36)

Why does my story matter?

To answer, conclude with **REFLECTIONS** *on the event's significance:*

▶ I realized then that ⸺⸺⸺⸺ .

EXAMPLE   As I looked from my father's eyes to my mother's, I knew this ordeal was over. Although it would never be forgotten, the incident was not mentioned again. (Brandt, par. 39)

TEST YOUR STORY

Facing an Audience

Get together with two or three other students to try out your story. Your classmates' reactions will help you determine whether you are telling it in an interesting or exciting way.

Storytellers: Take turns telling your stories briefly. Try to pique your listeners' curiosity and build suspense, and watch your audience to see if your story is having the desired reaction.

Listeners: Briefly tell each storyteller what you found most intriguing about the story. For example, consider these questions:

- Were you eager to know how the story would turn out?
- What was the inciting incident? Did it seem sufficient to motivate the climax?
- Was there a clear conflict that seemed important enough to write about?

▦ Use tenses to clarify the sequence of actions.

Excerpts from the reading selections in this chapter demonstrate how writers clarify when different actions occur in relation to each other. Try using some of these strategies to help your readers keep track of what happened when.

Manage **tenses** *to show the sequence of actions occurring over time.* You can use the simple past tense (*yelled*) to depict an action that occurred at one point in the past, and the past perfect tense (*had already learned*) to indicate something that happened in the more distant past. You can also use the present progressive tense (*smiling*) to show an ongoing action, as well as the future conditional (*would teach*) to describe something that was going to happen later:

> They yelled and gestured at . . . who? . . . another boy, young, like me, who stood there, almost <u>smiling</u>, gamely <u>throwing up</u> his hands. He had already learned the lesson he **would teach** me that day. (Coates, par. 1)

Use **time cues** *(such as* when, now, then, *and* as*) to help readers understand how one action relates to another in the time sequence:*

> As we all piled into the car, I knew. . . . (Brandt, par. 1)

> <u>When</u> I got back to the Snoopy section, I took one look at the lines . . . and knew I didn't want to wait. (Brandt, par. 3)

Refer to **calendar** *or* **clock time** *to establish when the event took place:*

> On one weekday morning after Christmas. . . . (Dillard, par. 3)

Past

Present

Future

Both actions occur at the same time

One action follows another

For more on transitions of time, see Chapters 13 and 14.

▦ Describe key people and places vividly, and show their significance.

The following excerpts show how the writers whose stories appear in this chapter use strategies like naming, detailing, comparing, selecting sensory details, and providing an overview of the setting to bring key people and places to life. Try using some of these strategies in your own writing to make people and places come alive.

- *Use* **naming** *and* **detailing** *to help readers visualize people and understand the roles they play in your story.* For example, identify people by name, occupation, or relationship to you; specify how they act, talk, look, and gesture:

> A light-skinned boy with a long head and small eyes (Coates, par. 2)

> My rainbow-striped tee and her white wifebeater capture a transition between our skater-inspired Salvation Army shopping phase and the next one. . . . (Desmond-Harris, par. 7)

- *Add* **comparisons** *to convey what's distinctive about the person and to help create a dominant impression:*

> This sainted, skinny, furious redheaded man (Dillard, par. 21)

- *Specify* **sensory details**—*size, shape, color, sounds, textures, smells, tastes*—*of key features of the scene that contribute to the dominant impression you want to create:*

> Tupac was the literal sound track when our school's basketball team would come charging onto the court, and our ragtag group of cheerleaders kicked furiously to "Toss It Up" in a humid gymnasium. (Desmond-Harris, par. 11)

- *Give readers an* **overview** *of the place, or take them on a* **tour** *of it:*

> We ran across Edgerton to an alley and up our own sliding woodpile to the Halls' front yard; he kept coming. We ran up Lloyd Street and wound through mazy backyards toward the steep hilltop at Willard and Lang. (Dillard, par. 12)

- *Weave **active, specific verbs** and **vivid descriptive details** into your action sequences:*

  > I whirled around to find a middle-aged man, dressed in street clothes, flashing some type of badge. . . . (Brandt, par. 6)

  > I had just embarked on the iceball project when we heard tire chains come clanking from afar. (Dillard, par. 7)

- *Consider including a **photograph** (or **video**) to help readers picture people and places.* Make sure you introduce it or use a caption to demonstrate its relevance:

  > A snapshot taken that Monday on our high school's front lawn (seen here) shows the two of us lying side by side. . . . (Desmond-Harris, par. 6)

Use dialogue to portray people and dramatize relationships.

Dialogue—in the form of quotation, paraphrase, or summary—can give readers a vivid impression of the people and their relationships while also enhancing the drama. The following excerpts may give you ideas about how you might use dialogue in your own story.

- *Insert a **quotation** to dramatize a key moment or to characterize a relationship:*

  > I was too ashamed to tell my mother the truth, but I had no choice.

  > "Jean, where are you?"

  > "I'm, umm, in jail." (Brandt, pars. 26–28)

- *Use **summary** to emphasize thoughts, feelings, or actions or simply to move the story along:*

  > They yelled and gestured at . . . who? (Coates, par. 1)

- *Use **speaker tags** to identify each speaker and intersperse remembered thoughts:*

  > "Did we really do that?" I asked Thea this week. I wanted to ensure that this story, which people who know me now find hilarious, hadn't morphed into some sort of personal urban legend over the past 15 years. "Yes," she said. "We put them in a lovely tin." (Desmond-Harris, par. 4)

To learn more about quoting, paraphrasing, and summarizing, see Chapter 19.

Clarify your story's significance.

Try using some of these strategies to refine your understanding and presentation of the event's significance. Some of these sentences may make their way into your story; others may simply help you understand your reactions so that you can depict the event's significance more clearly.

WAYS IN

> **HOW CAN I HELP MY READERS UNDERSTAND THE SIGNIFICANCE OF MY STORY?**
>
> *Reexamine the* **UNDERLYING CONFLICT** *to determine what your story is really about:*
>
> ▶ I was confused, torn between _____ and _____ .
>
> **EXAMPLE**   Did we feel a real stake in the life of this "hard-core" gangsta rapper, and a real loss in his death? We did, even though we were . . . in a

privileged community. Even though . . . we'd been so delicately cared for, nurtured and protected from any of life's hard edges — with special efforts made to shield us from those involving race — that we sometimes felt ready to explode with boredom. Or maybe because of all that. (Desmond-Harris, par. 8)

Consider whether you now have **INSIGHT** *into your motivation that you did not have at the time or whether you feel just as bewildered today as you did then:*

▶ I still don't understand why I _____ .

EXAMPLE   ". . . I just did it. I can't explain why." (Brandt, par. 34)

▶ I knew _____ , I felt _____ , but _____ .

EXAMPLE   I knew that my portion of the American galaxy . . . I knew that. . . . I felt, but did not yet understand. (Coates, par. 4)

Recall your **REMEMBERED FEELINGS** *and* **THOUGHTS** *from when the event occurred:*

▶ Before / during / after the event, I felt _____ . I showed my feelings by _____ .

EXAMPLE   I could still distinctly hear the disappointment and hurt in my mother's voice. I cried. . . . I felt like a terrible human being. (Brandt, par. 36)

Explore your **PRESENT PERSPECTIVE***, what you think and feel now as you look back:*

▶ I realize now that my feelings have not changed. I still _____ .

▶ Looking back at the event, I realize I was probably trying to _____ , though I didn't appreciate that fact at the time.

EXAMPLE   ("Did we really do that?" I asked Thea last week. I want to ensure that this story . . . hadn't morphed into some sort of personal urban legend. . . .) (Desmond-Harris, par. 4)

Recall what you did and did not do:

▶ I remember doing _____ but not _____ because _____ .

EXAMPLE   I did not tell my parents. I did not tell my teachers, and if I told my friends I would have done so with all the excitement needed to obscure the fear that came over me in that moment. (Coates, par. 3)

Reconsider your **PURPOSE** *and* **AUDIENCE** *in light of your developing understanding of the event's significance.* Determine what you want your readers to think and feel after reading your story:

▶ When my readers finish the story, I want them to better appreciate _____ .

▶ The point was that _____ .

EXAMPLE   The point was that he had chased us passionately without giving up, and so he had caught us. Now he came down to earth. I wanted the glory to last forever. (Dillard, par. 19)

Take a moment . . .

How well do sentence templates and examples from actual memoirs help you construct your own sentences?

Write the opening sentences.

Review what you have already written to see if you have something that would work to launch your story, or try out some of these opening strategies:

Set the **scene**—*a specific time and place:*

> Some boys taught me to play football. (Dillard, par. 1)

> I was eleven years old, standing out in the parking lot in front of the 7-Eleven, watching a crew of older boys standing near the street. (Coates, par. 1)

Establish the **mood**:

> I knew it was going to be a fabulous day. . . . [We] were setting off for a day of last-minute Christmas shopping. (Brandt, par. 1)

Reflect on something from your past that provides **context** *for the event:*

> I'd been cautiously allowing myself to think during the walk home about a topic that felt frighteningly taboo (at least in my world . . .). (Desmond-Harris, par. 1)

But don't agonize over the first sentences, because you are likely to discover the best way to begin only after you have written a rough draft.

Draft your story.

By this point, you have done a lot of writing to

- develop a plan for a well-told story;
- come up with vivid details to help your readers imagine what happened;
- think of strategies for showing or telling the autobiographical significance of your event;
- try out a way to launch your story.

Now stitch that material together to create a draft. The next two parts of this Guide to Writing will help you evaluate and improve your draft.

Evaluating the Draft: Using Peer Review

Take a moment . . .
Consider what has (and has not) helped you during past peer reviews. What can you ask this time to make the process more helpful?

Your instructor may arrange a peer review session in class or online, where you can exchange drafts with your classmates and give one another a thoughtful critical reading, pointing out what works well and suggesting ways to improve the draft. A good critical reading does three things:

1. It lets the writer know how clear, vivid, and meaningful the story seems to readers.

2. It praises what works best.

3. It indicates where the draft could be improved and makes suggestions on how to improve it.

One strategy for evaluating a draft is to use the basic features of remembered event essays as a guide. Also be sure to respond to any concerns the writer has shared with you.

A PEER REVIEW GUIDE

A Well-Told Story

How effectively does the writer tell the story?

Summarize: Highlight the inciting incident and the climax of the story.

Praise: Cite a passage where the storytelling is especially effective — for example, a place where the story seems to flow smoothly and maintain the reader's interest, or where narrative action is compelling or exciting.

Critique: Tell the writer where the storytelling could be improved — for example, where the suspense slackens, the story lacks tension or conflict, or the chronology is confusing.

Vivid Description of People and Places

Do the descriptions help you imagine what happened?

Summarize: Choose a passage of description, and analyze how — and how well — it uses the describing strategies of naming, detailing, and comparing.

Praise: Identify a description that is particularly vivid — for example, a graphic sensory description or an apt comparison that makes a person or place come alive.

Critique: Tell the writer where the description could be improved — for example, where objects in the scene are not named or described with enough specific detail (colors, sounds, smells, textures), or where the description is sparse. Note any description that contradicts the dominant impression; this may suggest how the autobiographical or cultural significance can be made more complex and interesting.

Autobiographical Significance

Is it clear why the event was important to the writer?

Summarize: Briefly describe the story's dominant impression, and tell the writer why you think the event was significant.

Praise: Give an example of where the significance comes across effectively — for example, where remembered feelings are expressed poignantly, where the present perspective seems insightful, or where the description creates a strong dominant impression that clarifies the significance.

Critique: Tell the writer where the significance could be strengthened — for example, if the conflict is too easily resolved, if a moral seems tacked on at the end, or if more interesting meanings could be drawn out of the experience.

Did you know?
Research shows that writers sometimes don't figure out exactly what they want to say until they finish drafting. Do you ever use drafting to figure out your main point?

Improving the Draft: Revising, Editing, and Proofreading

Start improving your draft by reflecting on what you have written thus far:

- Review critical reading comments from your classmates, instructor, or writing center tutor. What are your readers getting at?
- Take another look at your notes and ideas. What else should you consider?
- Review your draft. What else can you do to make your story compelling?

Revise your draft.

If your readers are having difficulty with your draft, try some of the strategies listed in the Troubleshooting Guide that follows. They can help you fine-tune your presentation of the genre's basic features.

A TROUBLESHOOTING GUIDE

A Well-Told Story

My readers tell me that the story starts too slowly.

- Shorten the exposition, spread it out more within the story, or move it to a later part of the story.
- Move a bit of dialogue or narrative action to the beginning.
- Start with something surprising but critical to the story.

My readers find the chronology confusing.

- Add or change time transitions.
- Look for inadvertent tense shifts, and fix them.

My readers feel that the suspense slackens or that the story lacks drama.

- Add remembered feelings and thoughts to heighten anticipation.
- Add an action sequence to build to a climax or high point.
- Cut or shorten background exposition and unnecessary description.
- Build rising action in stages, with multiple high points.

A Well-Told Story

My readers find the conflict vague or unconnected to the autobiographical significance.

- Think about the conflict's multiple and possibly contradictory meanings.
- Add remembered feelings or thoughts to suggest multiple meanings, and cut those that don't clarify the significance.
- Add your present perspective to make the significance clearer and to bring out the implications.
- Add dialogue or narrative action to clarify the conflict.

Vivid Description of People and Places

My readers feel that the people in the story don't come alive.

- Add details about distinctive physical features or mannerisms.
- Add speaker tags to the dialogue to characterize people and relationships.
- Read your dialogue aloud, and revise to make the language more natural and appropriate to the person.

My readers have trouble visualizing the places I describe.

- Name objects in the scene.
- Add sensory details (colors, sounds, smells, textures).
- Use a comparison — metaphor or simile — to evoke a particular mood or attitude.
- Add a visual — a photograph or other memorabilia.

My readers feel that some descriptions weaken the dominant impression.

- Omit unnecessary details.
- Add adjectives, similes, or metaphors to strengthen the dominant impression.
- Rethink the impression you want your writing to convey and the significance it suggests.

Autobiographical Significance

My readers do not identify or empathize with me.

- Add background details, or explain the context.
- Reveal the cultural influences acting on you, or emphasize the historical period in which the event occurred.
- Show readers how you have changed or were affected by the experience.

Autobiographical Significance

My readers don't understand the significance of the story.

- Use irony or humor to contrast your present perspective with your past behavior, feelings, or attitudes.
- Show that the event ended but that the conflict was not resolved.
- Use dialogue to show how your relationship with someone in your story changed.
- Indicate how the event continues to influence your thoughts or actions.

My readers think the significance seems too pat or simplistic.

- Develop contradictions or show ambivalence to enrich the implications.
- Use humor to comment ironically on your past behavior or current contradictory feelings.
- Stress the social or cultural dimensions of the event.
- Revise Hollywood-movie clichés, simple resolutions, or tagged-on morals.

A Note on Grammar and Spelling Checkers

Spelling checkers cannot catch misspellings that are themselves words, such as *to* for *too,* and grammar checkers miss problems, give faulty advice, and even flag correct items as wrong. Use these tools as a second line of defense after your own (and, ideally, another reader's proofreading efforts).

Edit and proofread your final draft.

Editing means making changes to the text to ensure that it follows the conventions of style, grammar, spelling, and mechanics appropriate to the rhetorical situation. **Proofreading** involves checking to make sure the text follows these conventions and that no words are repeated or omitted. You have probably done some editing and proofreading while composing and improving your draft, but it is always good practice to edit and proofread a draft after you have revised it and before you submit it.

Most writers get the best results by leaving time — even just an hour or two — between the stages of revising, editing, and proofreading, so they can return to their writing project with fresh eyes. When possible, enlist a friend or classmate to proofread the final draft of your writing projects. When that is not possible, proofread from the last line to the first to avoid seeing what you expect to find rather than what is actually on the page (or screen).

As rhetorical situations change, so too do the conventions or expectations readers bring to the text. For example, whereas text messages to friends are usually quite informal, filled with abbreviations, emojis, and sentence fragments, final drafts of writing projects for college classes or the workplace are expected to follow a more formal set of conventions concerning clarity, style, grammar, and punctuation.

We recommend that you make a list of the problems your instructors frequently point out in your writing, then use that list to guide your editing and proofreading. A Guide to Editing and Proofreading (at the end of this text) provides a checklist of the most common problems writers face. For issues that go beyond those on this list, consult a handbook* or search for advice online at sites like the Purdue Online Writing Lab (owl.english.purdue.edu) or Grammarly (grammarly.com). For practice identifying and correcting errors, try the activities in LearningCurve, a gamelike adaptive quizzing program available on LaunchPad for *The St. Martin's Guide to Writing*. The less well you do on activities in one topic area, the more LearningCurve focuses on it; and the better you do, the more challenging the questions become.

A WRITER AT WORK

Developing Significance in Jean Brandt's Remembered Event Essay

This section compares Jean Brandt's first draft of "Calling Home" to her final revised draft. (See the complete revision on pp. 18–22).

1   It was two days before Christmas and my older sister and brother, my grandmother, and I were rushing around doing last-minute shopping. After going to a few stores we decided to go to Lakewood Center shopping mall. It was packed with other frantic shoppers like ourselves from one end to the other. The first store we went to (the first and last for me) was the General Store. The General Store is your typical gift shop. They mainly have the cutesy knick-knacks, posters, frames and that sort. The store is decorated to resemble an old-time western general store but the appearance doesn't quite come off.

2   We were all browsing around and I saw a basket of buttons so I went to see what the different ones were. One of the first ones I noticed was a Snoopy button. I'm not sure what it said on it, something funny I'm sure and besides I was in love with anything Snoopy when I was 13. I took it out of the basket and showed it to my sister and she said "Why don't you buy it?" I thought about it but the lines at the cashiers were outrageous and I didn't think it was worth it for a 75 cent item. Instead I figured just take it and I did. I thought I was so sly about it. I casually slipped it into my pocket and assumed I was home free since no one pounced on me.

---

* The full version of *The St. Martin's Guide to Writing* includes a handbook on yellow tinted pages at the end of the book.

3   Everyone was ready to leave this shop so we made our way through the crowds to the entrance. My grandmother and sister were ahead of my brother and I. They were almost to the entrance of May Co. and we were about 5 to 10 yards behind when I felt this tap on my shoulder. I turned around already terror struck, and this man was flashing some kind of badge in my face. It happened so fast I didn't know what was going on. Louie finally noticed I wasn't with him and came back for me. Jack explained I was being arrested for shoplifting and if my parents were here then Louie should go find them. Louie ran to get Susie and told her about it but kept it from Grandma.

4   By the time Sue got back to the General Store I was in the back office and Jack was calling the police. I was a little scared but not really. It was sort of exciting. My sister was telling me to try and cry but I couldn't. About 20 minutes later two cops came and handcuffed me, led me through the mall outside to the police car. I was kind of embarrassed when they took me through the mall in front of all those people. When they got me in the car they began questioning me, while driving me to the police station. Questions just to fill out the report—age, sex, address, color of eyes, etc.

5   Then when they were finished they began talking about Jack and what a nuisance he was. I gathered that Jack had every single person who shoplifted, no matter what their age, arrested. The police were getting really fed up with it because it was a nuisance for them to have to come way out to the mall for something as petty as that. To hear the police talk about my "crime" that way felt good because it was like what I did wasn't really so bad. It made me feel a bit relieved. When we walked into the station I remember the desk sergeant joking with the arresting officers about "well we got another one of Jack's hardened criminals." Again, I felt my crime lacked any seriousness at all.

6   Next they handcuffed me to a table and questioned me further and then I had to phone my mom. That was the worst. I never was so humiliated in my life. Hearing the disappointment in her voice was worse punishment than the cops could ever give me.

Brandt was confident in her choice of a topic. She was sure she could recall enough details to make the story dramatic and was confident it would resonate with readers: "I think many of my readers will be able to identify with my story, even though they won't admit it." Most important, Brandt had no doubt that the event was significant:

Being arrested for shoplifting was significant because it changed some of my basic attitudes. Since that night I've never again considered stealing anything. This event would reveal how my attitude toward the law has changed from disrespectful to very respectful.

However, as you compare the following excerpts from her first and last drafts, you will see that Brandt's understanding of the underlying conflict and the event's significance evolved. Initially, she thought the conflict would be about respecting the law. But her first draft doesn't even hint at this conflict, and the final draft barely mentions it.

First Draft

I took it out of the basket and showed it to my sister and she said "Why don't you buy it?" I thought about it but the lines at the cashiers were outrageous and I didn't think it was worth it for a 75 cent item. Instead I figured just take it and I did. I thought I was so sly about it. I casually slipped it into my pocket and assumed I was home free since no one pounced on me. (par. 2)

Final Draft

She said it was cute and if I wanted it to go ahead and buy it. . . . I took one look at the lines at the cashiers and knew I didn't want to wait thirty minutes to buy an item worth less than one dollar. . . . I took a quick glance around, assured myself no one could see, and slipped the button into the pocket of my sweatshirt.

I hesitated for a moment, but once the item was in my pocket, there was no turning back. I had never before stolen anything; but what was done was done. . . .

As we headed for the entrance, my heart began to race. I just had to get out of that store. Only a few more yards to go and I'd be safe. As we crossed the threshold, I heaved a sigh of relief. I was home free. I thought about how sly I had been and I felt proud of my accomplishment. (pars. 2–5)

The first draft does not show that Brandt had been conflicted about breaking the law before she stole the button or that she felt guilty afterward. In fact, her only remembered thought or feeling is pride at having pulled it off so neatly: "I thought I was so sly about it." The final draft is not very different, although it does add both a momentary hesitation before and some reflection afterward. But notice her choice of words: she uses clichés ("there was no turning back" and "what was done was done") that neither express guilt nor repentance.

It took some effort and a little help from her instructor for Brandt to realize that she was not really passionate about the conflict she had thought was at the heart of her story and that her strongest, most heartfelt emotions had to do with her mother's disappointment, not with the abstract idea of respecting the law. Pointing out that the first draft ended with a brief but powerful description of Brandt's phone conversation with her mother ("Hearing the disappointment in her voice was worse punishment than the cops could ever give me"), her instructor urged Brandt to try to dramatize the scene by adding dialogue, specific description, and an action sequence.

The benefit of reflection is proven and important: It helps reinforce what you have learned, so that you can remember and apply it well beyond this class. That is why we have included questions and comments in the margins and at the end of each chapter: to stimulate your thinking about reviews, your rhetorical situation, and the choices you make as a writer.

Reflecting on Reading and Writing about Remembered Events

To reflect on your experience reading and writing about a remembered event, try writing a blog post, a letter to your instructor, or an e-mail message to a student who will take this course next term that draws on what you have learned. Use any of these writing prompts that seem productive:

- Explain how the rhetorical situation you were in—being asked to write about something personal for an instructor and classmates you hardly know—affected your choice of an event. Describe your biggest concern—for example, that your readers would be disapproving or uninterested in your story.

- Consider how a different rhetorical situation might lead you to tell your story differently. If you were recounting the story in a different context—such as telling it to a friend or relative, posting it online, or remixing it as a comic strip or short film—what is one thing you might change?

- Reflect on how autobiographical stories that you have read, heard, or seen (including those in this chapter) helped you write about your own experience. Focus on one thing you learned. For example, what did you learn from Dillard's action sequences about how to make a story exciting? What did you learn from Coates or Desmond-Harris about how to probe the deeper cultural or personal significance of an event?

Reflecting on Your Composing Process

Thinking about your process for writing about a remembered event can be useful in helping you decide what works best for you as a writer. Using one or more of the following questions as a starting point, write a paragraph or two about your composing process:

- Did you do what you ordinarily do when you write, no matter what the genre or rhetorical situation, or did you go about this writing project differently? Identify one aspect of your composing process that worked well and one aspect that needs improvement.

- After deciding what to write about, how did you begin—for example, by planning or drafting one of the genre's basic features, such as constructing a dramatic story, reconstructing a bit of dialogue, or describing the scene?

- Did you do any invention writing (perhaps doing some of the activities in the Guide to Writing) before or while drafting, or did you write a rough draft in one sitting pretty much from beginning to end?

- If you reread and revised your draft, what kinds of things did you work on? Did you wait until the draft was complete, or did you reread and revise at various points in the drafting process? When, if at all, did you proofread your draft and edit for grammar and style?

- If someone read and commented on your draft, identify one observation or bit of advice that helped you revise it.

- How satisfied are you with the process you used? If you could go back in time, what would you have done differently? If you could continue working on your story, what would you like to do?

3

Writing Profiles

What goes on behind the scenes at a mortuary? What happens when kids visit their moms in prison? Can you really find edible food in a market dumpster? These are a few of the questions explored in the entertaining and thought-provoking profiles in this chapter. Profiles are mini-documentaries, like the podcasts and shows created by the producers of *Radiolab* and *This American Life*. They take us behind the scenes through slice-of-life portraits. As cultural ethnography, profiles range from a day in the life to a longer immersion study of people at work or at play. Intensively researched, they rely primarily on *field research* techniques of observation and interview to provide what is sometimes called *thick description,* because the information is interwoven with the profiler's analysis and interpretation — what we call **perspective** — to capture and convey a full experience.

People compose profiles for various purposes and audiences and publish them in a variety of media (print, digital, audiovisual). For example, a college student studying management might observe and interview a work group's collaborators, then post her profile on the class Web site. A participant in the restoration of a Depression-era mural might construct a multimedia profile of the community effort for the city's Web site to celebrate the project.

In this chapter, we ask you to compose a profile based primarily on your firsthand field research—observational visits and interviews. Whether you choose something you know well or something you want to learn about, you will need to focus on it as if for the first time and choose details that will not only make it come alive for your readers but also show them why your subject is intriguing and important. From reading and analyzing the selections in the Guide to Reading (pp. 56–80), you will learn how to weave information and insight to construct a rich tapestry that entertains as it informs. The Guide to Writing (pp. 81–100) will show you ways to use the basic features of the genre to depict your subject in a way that conveys your subject's cultural significance.

| PRACTICING THE GENRE |

Conducting an Interview

Part 1. Get together in a small group to practice interviewing, a crucial skill for composing profiles.

1 Choose someone from the group to act as the interviewee. It should be someone knowledgeable about a subject that is relatively unfamiliar to the other group members, such as a sport, hobby, type of music, video game, or profession.

2 Have the rest of the group compose a list of questions about the subject.

3 Choose one person to serve as the interviewer (or take turns asking questions). Group members should listen to the interview and take notes not only on what is said (quoting or summarizing) but also on the way it is said.

Part 2. Discuss what you learned about profiles and about conducting an interview:

- **What did you learn about how profiles can make information interesting?** For a profile to be effective, it must depict the subject vividly and be thought-provoking. Take turns identifying one thing the interviewee said — for example, an illuminating fact, an amusing anecdote, or a surprising judgment — that would be likely to engage the interest of an audience.

- **What did you learn about conducting an interview?** Compare your thoughts with those of the others in your group on what was easiest and hardest — for example, preparing questions, listening and following up, taking notes, or considering what might be interesting to an audience.

Did you know?

Research shows that learning by doing, as in this activity, can be very productive, especially when done with peers who can pool their knowledge and experience.

Analyzing Profiles

As you read the selections in this chapter, you will see how different authors create a compelling profile.

- Brian Cable anxiously visits a mortuary and ends up in the embalming room (pp. 59–65).
- Victoria C. Moré investigates freeganism by finding dinner in a dumpster (pp. 66–68).
- Amanda Coyne captures Mother's Day in a women's prison (pp. 71–74).
- Gabriel Thompson goes undercover to learn about harvesting lettuce firsthand (pp. 76–79).

Analyzing how these writers organize and present the information they gathered from firsthand observations, interviews, and background research; adopt a role as spectator or participant-observer; and convey a thought-provoking perspective on the subject will help you see how you can employ these same techniques when composing your own observational profile.

Determine the writer's purpose and audience.

Researching a profile gives writers a great deal of information about their subject, enabling them to impart their special perspective or insight into its cultural significance. Profilers seek to enlighten and entertain their audience, creating a fascinating—and occasionally disconcerting—portrait of other people at work or at play. When reading the profiles that follow, ask yourself what the writer's main purpose is and what he or she assumes about the reader:

The writer's main purpose may be to	The writer assumes readers will
- inform readers about an unfamiliar subject	- enjoy learning about unfamiliar subjects
- surprise readers with a new take on a familiar subject	- be surprised or intrigued about what they learn
- give readers a behind-the-scenes view	- be curious about how and why people do what they do
- challenge popular preconceptions about the subject	- have narrow or false preconceptions about the subject

Assess the genre's basic features.

As you read the profiles in this chapter, analyze and evaluate how profile writers employ the genre's basic features. The examples that follow are drawn from the reading selections that appear later in this Guide to Reading.

Basic Features

Specific Information

A Clear, Logical Organization

Writer's Role

A Perspective on the Subject

SPECIFIC INFORMATION ABOUT THE SUBJECT

Read first to learn about the subject. Much of the pleasure of reading a profile comes from the way the profile interweaves bits of information and insight into a rich tapestry of lively narrative, arresting quotations, and vivid descriptions.

*Notice the describing strategies of **naming**, **detailing**, and **comparing**.* These strategies help readers visualize places and people and create a dominant impression:

> We passed into a <u>bright, fluorescent-lit</u> "display room." Inside were <u>thirty</u> coffins. . . . **Like new cars on the showroom floor**, they gleamed (Cable, par. 18)

Naming

Detailing

Comparing

Using the detail *fluorescent-lit* clarifies what Cable means by *bright* and also reinforces the simile comparing the coffins to cars in a showroom.

Think about the different kinds *of information, or **topics**, the writer touches on.* In profiling a mortuary, for example, Cable identifies different jobs (funeral director and mortician), explaining the training people undergo and the tasks they perform, and also presents facts about the cost of funerals and ideas about cultural attitudes toward death.

Consider the sources of the information and how the information is presented. Some of the information comes from the writer's firsthand observation, but much of it comes from interviews and background research. To present this information, profile writers rely on three basic strategies—quotation, paraphrase, and summary:

For more on describing strategies, see Chapter 14.

QUOTATION	"We're in *Ripley's Believe It or Not,* along with another funeral home whose owners' names are Baggit and Sackit," Howard told me, without cracking a smile. (Cable, par. 14)
PARAPHRASE	Some, like Conrad's mother for example, insist that dumpsters are dirty and diseased, and express concern for the welfare of the dumpster divers. (Moré, par. 9)
SUMMARY	I came across several articles describing the causes of a farmworker shortage. The stories cited an aging workforce, immigration crackdowns, and long delays at the border that discourage workers with green cards. (Thompson, par. 5)

Did you know?

Readers expect profiles to include the genre's basic features, but they also expect the features to change to fit the situation, medium, purpose, and audience.

Profiles in academic contexts—for class and scholarly publication—are expected to cite their sources formally (see, for example, Moré's use of parenthetical citation and a works-cited list), but general-interest publications seldom include documentation beyond links to other Web pages. Ask your instructor whether you should cite your sources and, if so, what academic style you should follow.

See Chapters 20 and 21 to learn about the conventions for citing and documenting sources in two popular academic styles.

A CLEAR, LOGICAL ORGANIZATION

*Determine whether the profile's basic organizational plan is **narrative**, as a story occurring over time; **spatial**, as a guided tour of a place; or **topical**, as bits of information organized into categories.* Look for cues like these that help orient readers.

Narrative Cues

CALENDAR AND CLOCK TIME	On my first day (Thompson, par. 6)
ACTION VERBS	I bend over, noticing that most of the crew has turned to watch. (Thompson, par. 8)
TRANSITIONS OF TIME	First, I'm handed . . . Next comes the *gancho*. (Thompson, par. 6)
	During the cleaning process . . . After each veggie had a good scrub (Moré, par. 10)

Spatial Cues

PREPOSITIONAL PHRASES	the main lobby, adjacent to the reception room (Cable, par. 5)
	We are standing in front of the double glass doors that lead to the outside world. (Coyne, par. 20)
DIRECTIONS	To my left, . . . To my right (Thompson, par. 1)
LOCATIONS	visiting his mother in prisons in Kentucky, Texas, Connecticut (the Pit of Fire) (Coyne, par. 12)

Topical Cues or Logical Transitions

SEQUENCE	In addition, . . . (Cable, par. 24)
EMPHASIS	Even, or especially, if that world is a female federal prison camp. (Coyne, par. 4)
CONTRAST	Although this mind-set seems obsolete within the younger generation, it is a philosophy which our parents and grandparents grew up with. (Moré, par. 15)
CAUSE	Because of their difference (Coyne, par. 11)
CONCLUSION	So I am to be very careful and precise. (Thompson, par. 12)
SPECULATION	Perhaps such an air of comfort makes it easier for the family to give up their loved one. (Cable, par. 24)

To learn more about cueing the reader, see Chapter 13.

Also notice whether the writer uses a different organizational pattern in particular passages. For example, Cable's profile of a mortuary follows a spatial plan overall, beginning with him outside the building and moving first into the reception room and lobby, then into a chapel, then into the display room, and finally into the embalming room. But much of the information within this general structure is presented topically; for example, he uses his position in the display room to relate information about caskets—what they are made of, their price range, the cost of funerals and how it has increased over time, and so on.

THE WRITER'S ROLE

Think about the role the writer assumes in relation to the subject:

- As a **spectator**, the writer takes a position, like that of the reader, looking in on the people and their activities. Although profile writers sometimes refer to themselves using the first-person pronoun "I" to place themselves in the scene and tell us what they are thinking, they often maintain the role of a detached observer:

    I found the funeral director in the main lobby, adjacent to the reception room. Like most people, I had preconceptions about what an undertaker looked like. Mr. Deaver fulfilled my expectations entirely. Tall and thin, he even had beady eyes and a bony face. . . . Indeed, he looked like death on two legs. (Cable, par. 5)

- As a **participant-observer**, the writer participates in the activity being profiled in order to acquire insider knowledge. Participant-observers rely on the first-person pronoun "I" to place themselves in the scene and tell us what they are doing there, as this example from Thompson's profile of his work as a lettuce picker illustrates:

    I stand up gingerly. It's only my third day in the fields, but already my 30-year-old body is failing me. (par. 2)

A PERSPECTIVE ON THE SUBJECT

*Think about the writer's **perspective** on the subject.* What is the main idea or cultural significance of the profile? To understand the writer's perspective, it might help to also consider the writer's main purpose; the audience to whom the profile was originally addressed; as well as where, when, and how (in what medium) it was published. *Identify any passages where the perspective is communicated to readers*

- by **telling**—saying explicitly what the writer thinks about the subject:

    Death may be the great leveler, but one's coffin quickly reestablishes one's status. (Cable, par. 17)

- by **showing**—creating a dominant impression through description and narration:

    The mothers take deep whiffs from the backs of their children's necks. . . . They hold them tight and take in their own second scent—the scent assuring them that these are still their children and that they still belong to them. (Coyne, par. 2)

Readings

Brian Cable | *The Last Stop*

This profile of a neighborhood mortuary was originally written when Brian Cable was a first-year college student. "Death," as he explains in the opening sentence, "is a subject largely ignored by the living," so it is not surprising that he notices people averting their

Consider . . .

How would Cable's profile work as a documentary? How could you convey the writer's role and perspective on screen?

To learn how Cable conducted his interview with the funeral director and wrote up his notes, turn to A Writer at Work on pp. 100–104.

eyes as they walk past the mortuary on a busy commercial street. Cable, however, walks in and takes readers on a guided tour of the premises. As he presents information he learned from observing how the mortuary works—from the reception room up front to the embalming room in back—and from interviewing the people who work there, Cable invites us to reflect on our own feelings and cultural attitudes toward death.

As you read,

- notice how Cable uses humor to defuse the inherent seriousness of his subject;
- consider the significance of the quotation from Mark Twain with which Cable opens his profile;
- think about how effectively Cable uses the basic features of the genre (listed below), and answer the questions in the margins; your instructor may ask you to post your thoughts and answers to a class blog or discussion board or to bring your responses to class.

:: Basic Features

Specific Information

A Clear, Logical Organization

Writer's Role

A Perspective on the Subject

Cable tells us what he expected. How does this opening influence what you expect from his profile?

What organizational plan for the profile emerges in pars. 4 and 5?

Let us endeavor so to live that when we come to die even the undertaker will be sorry.

— Mark Twain, *Pudd'nhead Wilson*

1   Death is a subject largely ignored by the living. We don't discuss it much, not as children (when Grandpa dies, he is said to be "going away"), not as adults, not even as senior citizens. Throughout our lives, death remains intensely private. The death of a loved one can be very painful, partly because of the sense of loss, but also because someone else's mortality reminds us all too vividly of our own.

2   More than a few people avert their eyes as they walk past the dusty-tan building that houses the Goodbody Mortuary. It looks a bit like a church—tall, with gothic arches and stained glass. In the back, it looked somewhat like an apartment complex—low, with many windows stamped out of red brick. (See fig. 1.)

3   It wasn't at all what I had expected. I thought it would be more like Forest Lawn, serene with lush green lawns and meticulously groomed gardens, a place set apart from the hustle of day-to-day life. Here instead was an odd tan structure set in the middle of a business district.

4   I was apprehensive as I climbed the stone steps to the entrance. I feared rejection or, worse, an invitation to come and stay. The door was massive, yet it swung open easily on well-oiled hinges. "Come in," said the sign. "We're always open." Inside was a cool and quiet reception room. Curtains were drawn against the outside glare, cutting the light down to a soft glow.

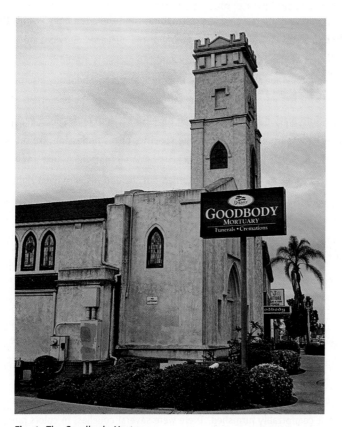

Fig. 1. The Goodbody Mortuary.

5   I found the funeral director in the main lobby, adjacent to the reception room. Like most people, I had preconceptions about what an undertaker looked like. Mr. Deaver fulfilled my expectations entirely. Tall and thin, he even had beady eyes and a bony face. A low, slanted forehead gave way to a beaked nose. His skin, scrubbed of all color, contrasted sharply with his jet black hair. He was wearing a starched white shirt, gray pants, and black shoes. Indeed, he looked like death on two legs.

6   He proved an amiable sort, however, and was easy to talk to. As funeral director, Mr. Deaver ("Call me Howard") was responsible for a wide range of services. Goodbody Mortuary, upon notification of someone's death, will remove the remains from the hospital or home. They then prepare the body for viewing, whereupon features distorted

> What does the detailed description of Deaver contribute to Cable's profile of the mortuary?

> What role has Cable adopted in writing the profile? When does it become clear?

by illness or accident are restored to their natural condition. The body is embalmed and then placed in a casket selected by the family of the deceased. Services are held in one of three chapels at the mortuary, and afterward the casket is placed in a "visitation room," where family and friends can pay their last respects. Goodbody also makes arrangements for the purchase of a burial site and transports the body there for burial.

7   All this information Howard related in a well-practiced, professional manner. It was obvious he was used to explaining the specifics of his profession. We sat alone in the lobby. His desk was bone clean, no pencils or paper, nothing — just a telephone. He did all his paperwork at home; as it turned out, he and his wife lived right upstairs. The phone rang. As he listened, he bit his lips and squeezed his Adam's apple somewhat nervously.

8   "I think we'll be able to get him in by Friday. No, no, the family wants him cremated."

9   His tone was that of a broker conferring on the Dow Jones. Directly behind him was a sign announcing "Visa and MasterCard Welcome Here." It was tacked to the wall, right next to a crucifix.

10   "Some people have the idea that we are bereavement specialists, that we can handle emotional problems which follow a death: Only a trained therapist can do that. We provide services for the dead, not counseling for the living."

11   Physical comfort was the one thing they did provide for the living. The lobby was modestly but comfortably furnished. There were several couches, in colors ranging from earth brown to pastel blue, and a coffee table in front of each one. On one table lay some magazines and a vase of flowers. Another supported an aquarium. Paintings of pastoral scenes hung on every wall. The lobby looked more or less like that of an old hotel. Nothing seemed to match, but it had a homey, lived-in look.

12   "The last time the Goodbodys decorated was in 2009, I believe. It still makes people feel welcome."

13   And so "Goodbody" was not a name made up to attract customers but the owner's family name. The Goodbody family started the business way back in 1915. Today, they do over five hundred services a year.

14   "We're in *Ripley's Believe It or Not*, along with another funeral home whose owners' names are Baggit and Sackit," Howard told me, without cracking a smile.

Margin questions:

Why do you think Cable summarizes the information in par. 6 instead of quoting Deaver?

What does this observation reveal about Cable's perspective?

Why do you think Cable quotes Howard in par. 10 instead of paraphrasing or summarizing?

What does this observation contribute to the dominant impression?

15   I followed him through an arched doorway into a chapel that smelled musty and old. The only illumination came from sunlight filtered through a stained glass ceiling. Ahead of us lay a casket. I could see that it contained a man dressed in a black suit. Wooden benches ran on either side of an aisle that led to the body. I got no closer. From the red roses across the dead man's chest, it was apparent that services had already been held.

16   "It was a large service," remarked Howard. "Look at that casket — a beautiful work of craftsmanship."

17   I guess it was. Death may be the great leveler, but one's coffin quickly reestablishes one's status.

18   We passed into a bright, fluorescent-lit "display room." Inside were thirty coffins, lids open, patiently awaiting inspection. Like new cars on the showroom floor, they gleamed with high-gloss finishes.

19   "We have models for every price range."

20   Indeed, there was a wide variety. They came in all colors and various materials. Some were little more than cloth-covered cardboard boxes, others were made of wood, and a few were made of steel, copper, or bronze. Howard told me prices started at $500 and averaged about $2,400. He motioned toward the center of the room: "The top of the line."

21   This was a solid bronze casket, its seams electronically welded to resist corrosion. Moisture-proof and air-tight, it could be hermetically sealed off from all outside elements. Its handles were plated with 14-karat gold. The Promethean casket made by the Batesville Casket Company is the choice of celebrities and the very wealthy. (See fig. 2.) The price: a cool $25,000–$30,000 (Russell).

22   A proper funeral remains a measure of respect for the deceased. But it is expensive. In the United States, the amount spent annually on funerals is around $12 billion (Grassley), with the average price about $7,000 ("NFDA Releases") — not counting the burial plot. Among ceremonial expenditures, funerals are second only to weddings. As a result, practices are changing. Howard has been in this business for forty years. He remembers a time when everyone was buried. Nowadays, with burials costing more than $7,000 a shot (Grassley), people often opt instead for cremation — as Howard put it, "a cheap, quick, and easy means of disposal." In some areas of the country, according

> How does Cable make the transition from topic to topic in pars. 15–18?

> What does the comparison to a new car showroom reveal about Cable's perspective?

> Where does the information in pars. 22–23 come from? How can you tell?

Fig. 2. "The top of the line." The Promethean casket that Michael Jackson was buried in.

Photo credit: Pool/Getty Images

> **Why do you think Cable uses a rhetorical question here?**

to Howard, the cremation rate is now over 60 percent. Observing this trend, one might wonder whether burials are becoming obsolete. Do burials serve an important role in society?

23   For Tim, Goodbody's licensed mortician, the answer is very definitely yes. Burials will remain in common practice, according to the slender embalmer with the disarming smile, because they allow family and friends to view the deceased. Painful as it may be, such an experience brings home the finality of death. "Something deep within us demands a confrontation with death," Tim explained. "A last look assures us that the person we loved is, indeed, gone forever."

24   Apparently, we also need to be assured that the body will be laid to rest in comfort and peace. The average casket, with its innerspring mattress and pleated satin lining, is surprisingly roomy and luxurious. Perhaps such an air of comfort makes it easier for the family to give up their loved one. In addition, the burial site fixes the deceased in the survivors' memory, like a new address. Cremation provides none of these comforts.

> **Whose perspective does this statement reflect? How do you know?**

25   Tim started out as a clerk in a funeral home but then studied to become a mortician. "It was a profession I could live with," he told me with a sly grin. Mortuary science might be described as a cross between pre-med and cosmetology, with courses in anatomy and embalming as well as in restorative art.

> **Is Tim's definition of mortuary science helpful? Why or why not?**

26   Tim let me see the preparation, or embalming, room, a white-walled chamber about the size of an operating room. Against the wall was a large sink with elbow taps and a draining board. In the center of the room stood a table with equipment for preparing the arterial embalming fluid, which consists primarily of formaldehyde, a preservative, and phenol, a disinfectant. This mixture sanitizes and also gives better color to the skin. Facial features can then be "set" to achieve a restful expression. Missing eyes, ears, and even noses can be replaced.

27   I asked Tim if his job ever depressed him. He bridled at the question: "No, it doesn't depress me at all. I do what I can for people and take satisfaction in enabling relatives to see their loved ones as they were in life." He said that he felt people were becoming more aware of the public service his profession provides. Grade-school classes now visit funeral homes as often as they do police stations and museums. The mortician is no longer regarded as a minister of death.

28   Before leaving, I wanted to see a body up close. I thought I could be indifferent after all I had seen and heard, but I wasn't sure. Cautiously, I reached out and touched the skin. It felt cold and firm, not unlike clay. As I walked out, I felt glad to have satisfied my curiosity about dead bodies, but all too happy to let someone else handle them.

> Which information in par. 26 comes from observation and which comes from interviewing Tim? How do you know?

> How effective is this ending?

Works Cited

Grassley, Chuck. Opening remarks. *Joint Hearing on Pension Tension: Does the Pension Benefit Guaranty Corporation Deliver for Retirees.* United States, Senate, Special Committee on Aging and the Committee on Small Business, Government Printing Office, 21 Sept. 2000, www.aging.senate.gov/imo/media/doc/publications/9212000.pdf. 106th Congress, 2nd session, Senate Hearing 106-38.

"NFDA Releases Results of Member General Price List Survey." *National Funeral Directors Association,* 1 Aug. 2013, nfda.org/news-a-events/all-press-releases/3719-nfda-releases-results-of-member-general-price-list-survey.html.

Russell, John. "Batesville Casket Is Coy about Starring Role in Jackson Funeral." *ABC News,* 9 July 2009, abcnews.go.com/Business/story?id=8042342.

Twain, Mark. *Pudd'nhead Wilson.* Pocket Books, 2004, p. 45.

Victoria C. Moré | *Dumpster Dinners: An Ethnography of Freeganism*

Courtesy of Victoria Moré

VICTORIA C. MORÉ profiles a group of freegans: people who are concerned about the wastefulness of consumer society. As a student at Illinois State University (ISU), Moré researched and wrote a longer version of this profile, which was subsequently published in the *Journal of Undergraduate Ethnography*. An **ethnography** is an in-depth profile used in many academic subjects, such as sociology, anthropology, and linguistics, to analyze the culture—behaviors, beliefs, and values—of a particular community. Because she was writing for a college course and subsequent academic publication, Moré provided a context for her firsthand field research (participant observation and interview) by doing secondary source research to learn what others have published about the topic, something your instructor may also ask you to do.

As you read, consider the following questions:

- What do the sources Moré cites in paragraphs 2 and 4 contribute to her profile?

- Why do you think Moré includes photos (figures 1 and 2) in her profile? What purpose do they serve for her readers?

Consider . . .

How might you remix Moré's profile as a *Radiolab* or a *This American Life*–type podcast? What would be an advantage or disadvantage of such a remix? For more on remixing, see Chapter 22 on multimodal composing.

1   On a misty evening, Rex Sunnyside approaches a dumpster, turns on the flashlight, and takes a look inside. "Ooooh . . . it's really nasty!" As she moves the light around, familiar things appear. "Oh, wow, there's a mango . . . a pear . . . look, there's a pineapple . . . and a cantaloupe . . . but it looks pretty funky!"

2   Americans dispose of billions of pounds of food waste per year; much of it still fit for consumption. In a study by the USDA Economic Research Service, it is estimated that 11.4 percent of fresh fruit and 9.7 percent of fresh vegetables per grocery store were lost due to inedibility from 2005–2006 (Buzby 2). Unfortunately, supermarkets often toss out these so-called "inedible" fruits and vegetables for superficial reasons. Some people, outraged by the "waste" grocers send to the landfill, have begun to salvage and eat it. These people, sometimes called "freegans," are "people who employ alternative strategies for living based on limited participation in the conventional economy and minimal consumption of resources" ("What").

3   In this paper, I describe a small group of young adult freegans living in Bloomington-Normal, Illinois. I describe freegan activities such as dumpster diving, bartering, and repurposing to show the symbolic transformation of garbage into groceries.

4   Although freeganism has received attention from the press (multiple news stories, magazine and newspaper articles, radio shows, and a discussion on *Oprah*), few ethnographic studies of freegans exist. An exception, Joan Gross explores freegan foodways in rural Oregon and describes freegans as "modern-day foragers who live off the waste of others and what they can gather in the wild" (Gross 57). These freegans demonstrate an extreme version of freeganism, separate from mainstream culture, and live for free all the time.

5   The freegans in my study, in contrast, are employed, have professional goals and are active community members. They either currently attend or have graduated from Illinois State University, and currently they all dumpster dive together regularly. Wimpy Oak, 26, started reclaiming thrown away goods while living by herself in college. Conrad and Sunnyside, both 21, would go around campus keeping an eye out for free things—like free food at club meetings or gallery openings—during their freshman year. When it came time for move-out from dorms and apartments for the summer, Sunnyside and Conrad saw for the first time how many hardly used items were discarded as trash. Sunnyside explained that once she got to college, she realized, "Wow. People get rid of a lot of stuff, and it's all useful." It is hard not to curb shop in college towns when items appear in such huge quantities.

Inside Local Dumpsters

6   My first dumpster dive was a chilly Sunday evening in late January. I met the girls at their apartment and we prepared for the dive. To ensure safety while diving, the divers either wear rain boots (preferably) or old gym shoes. Clothing does not usually get too dirty, but this is no place for your favorite jeans. Gloves, preferably sturdy gardening gloves, are good protection from anything sharp or nasty. In colder months, warm gloves underneath the protective ones are a necessity, along with the usual winter layers.

7   At first glance, dumpsters look grim and smell unpleasant. (See figure 1.) Eventually, your eyes adjust and familiar items appear, such as zucchini buried under wilted lettuce, or an upside down box hiding carrots and oranges. Shuffling around some more could reveal a bag of apples or onions. It takes your breath away when you see the amount of food that is unblemished, amongst a few rotten apples. Usually, the amount of food is so abundant that the freegans can be picky about what to take home. . . . From observations, it is plain to see anything and everything in the produce department ends up in the dumpster at some point, even baskets used to display fruit. Apples, zucchini, pre-sliced fruit in containers, celery, bagged or boxed lettuce, carrots, and peppers are found quite frequently. Sometimes there are boxes of yogurt, bags of onions, oranges, grapefruit and potatoes, boxes of strawberries, asparagus, broccoli,

Photo Courtesy of Victoria Moré

FIGURE 1.   Photo by author.

tomatoes, jalapenos, poblanos, and specialty health juices. A solitary bruise is enough for a vegetable to get thrown away. One moldy orange, potato, apple, or onion in a bag of 12 is enough for the entire bag to be tossed. For some items there is no obvious reason for their disposal.

8   Half-way into my first dive I was hooked. Initially I was shocked that we were pulling all of this nearly-perfect food out of a dumpster. Once we got to the second store, I was excited. It was thrilling to do something rebellious. This feeling of excitement grew when we got home and unloaded the car. Going up their apartment building stairs, we each had our arms full of heavy bags.

How Garbage Becomes Groceries

9   Once in the apartment, we put music on and began cleaning. With a sink full of soapy water, we started dunking veggies to get them clean, and to get rid of the faint lingering dumpster odor. Some, like Conrad's mother for example, insist that dumpsters are dirty and diseased, and express concern for the welfare of the dumpster divers. The mere fact that the food has been pulled from a dumpster tarnishes the image of the food inside it, no matter how pristine. . . . The concerns from Conrad's mom and society in general do not discourage the freegans at all. None of them have ever gotten sick from dumpstered foods. Freegans challenge our hegemonic "throw away" culture by interchanging the meaning of waste and food, insisting that found items are in fact still pure.

10   During the cleaning process, the plastic that wraps many of the items is thrown away, spoiled food is put in a container to be composted, and plastic containers that are reusable are washed and put away. After each veggie had a good scrub, we set them up to dry on the counter where, for purposes of this ethnography, we arranged our findings for a picture. Once the work was done and I saw the giant pile of beautiful food (see figure 2), I was changed. Clearly, some of what we label "garbage" is far from it. One trip to the dumpster can bring in the equivalent of $100–200 worth of food. One dive, on February 23, 2010, yielded $138 worth of groceries. This included boxes of guacamole, 28 zucchini, 14 wrapped containers of mushrooms, 11 bundles of radishes, and 10 bell peppers, lemons, fruit, lettuce, bread, broccoli, etc.

Photo Courtesy of Victoria Moré

FIGURE 2.   My first dumpster dive, January 26, 2010. Photo by author.

How Groceries Become Garbage

11 Picking out produce at the grocery store engages one's sense of sight to avoid imperfections, touch to determine a good firmness, and smell to gauge ripeness. Most Americans begin their relationship with fruit and vegetables when it is finally ripe. Prior to arrival at the store, the fruit has had a long life and possibly traveled a long distance.

12 Our detachment has blurred what is important when getting food. Consumers are very concerned with cosmetic qualities when choosing produce. After that lengthy life food has had before it appears on our shelves, we foolishly expect the items to look perfect. No one is about to spend his or her hard-earned money on produce that has a blemish, or is in some way sub-par. For this reason, stores are pressured to supply produce that meets our unreasonably high standards. Edible food that is deemed unworthy of our dollars is sent to the dumpster.

13 The innate value of food is overlooked in the current system; monetary value seems to be all that matters. Sadly, it seems stores can't or don't try to eliminate food waste. Employees are not allowed to take food home, and expired food cannot be donated because of legal risk. Besides a separate dumpster for corrugated cardboard, there is no attempt made by stores to recycle. Some of the packaging we find even says "please recycle," "compostable," or "biodegradable," but the stores probably consider the sorting process too much of a hassle. One night, we ironically found re-useable grocery bags with the words "[name of store] Recycles!" in the dumpster.

Identity and Way of Life

14 Although Oak, Conrad, and Sunnyside do consider themselves freegans, none participate full-time. They pay rent, pay for cell phones, attend a university (Sunnyside and Conrad), have a full-time job and drive a car (Oak). That said, when asked if they would be freegans for life, all of them replied with a confident "yes." Oak added that she might practice on a different level, maybe not always dumpster diving, but will always reclaim things and buy second hand. Additionally, the ISU freegans do not consider themselves anti-consumerists, but rather conscious consumers. They do participate in purchasing things like the rest of us, but do so much less frequently and with much more awareness than many Americans.

15 Freegans are committed to lengthening the life cycle of everything that comes into their lives, not just food. They don't believe in buying new, and try not to buy anything at all. This means they repair clothing, their bicycles, and anything else instead of throwing it away. They always seem to find new uses for old items and demonstrate a "Use it up, wear it out, make it do or do without" attitude. Although this mind-set seems obsolete within the younger generation, it is a philosophy which our parents and grandparents grew up with. . . . One of the biggest differences between freegans and the rest of society is their perspective of value. They do not only see value in terms of how much money it is "worth," but also in terms of its basic qualities and potential to be repurposed.

Works Cited

Buzby, Jean C., et al. "Supermarket Loss Estimates for Fresh Fruit, Vegetables, Meat, Poultry, and Seafood and Their Use in the ERS Loss-Adjusted Food Availability Data." *Economic Research Service: Report Summary*, no. 44, Mar. 2009, pp. 1–20, www.ers.usda.gov/webdocs/publications/44306/10894_eib44_reportsummary.pdf?v=41055.

Gross, Joan. "Capitalism and Its Discontents: Back-to-the-Lander and Freegan Foodways in Rural Oregon." *Food and Foodways*, vol. 17, no. 2, 2009, pp. 57–79, doi:10.1080/07409710902925797.

"What Is a Freegan?" *Freegan.Info: Strategies for Sustainable Living beyond Capitalism*, Activism Center at Wetlands Preserve, 2010, freegan.info/. Accessed 1 Feb. 2010.

Make connections: Throw-away society.

According to Moré, the fundamental critique driving freeganism is that ours is a throw-away society. As she puts it, "Freegans challenge our hegemonic 'throw away' culture by interchanging the meaning of waste and food" (par. 9). By "hegemonic," she means the ideas, values, and behaviors that are predominant in a society at a given time. Hegemonic ideas are usually taken for granted and not examined with a critical eye because they are assumed to be "normal." Most Americans assume that food thrown in the trash by a supermarket is inedible or unhealthy. But what about other items, such as clothing, dishes, and furniture? Think about your own experience as well as that of your friends and family members recycling or buying "hardly-used items" (par. 5). Your instructor may ask you to post and discuss your thoughts about the experience. Use these questions to get started:

- What do you think leads people to donate used clothes and furniture to Goodwill, Buffalo Exchange, or other outlets?

- What might lead people who are comfortable donating not to buy "hardly-used items" themselves?

- How does recycling and dumpster diving "challenge our hegemonic 'throw away' culture"? In what other ways, if any, can you see yourself questioning or changing the status quo?

Use the basic features.

A CLEAR, LOGICAL ORGANIZATION: CUEING READERS

Profile writers, like Cable, often organize their profiles narratively so that readers can, in a sense, come along with them on an exploration of the place and learn about it as they go. Moré chooses a different way of presenting her information. Because she is writing for an academic audience, Moré chooses to present the narrative of her experience dumpster diving within the context of the information she learned about freeganism, waste, and consumer culture. To present this information, she uses conventional academic methods for cueing readers, such as including a forecasting statement ("I describe freegan activities such as dumpster diving, bartering, and repurposing," par. 3), headings, and topic sentences.

Take a moment . . .

Why do you think cueing readers is especially valued in academic writing?

ANALYZE & WRITE

Write a couple of paragraphs analyzing how Moré uses cues to present information topically and to orient readers:

1 Reread paragraph 3, and consider how well it forecasts the profile's plan. How do you think a forecasting statement like this might help readers, particularly in an academic paper?

2 Review the headings, and consider what role they play in the profile. What can you learn about this profile or about freeganism generally from reading the forecast in paragraph 3 and skimming the headings?

3 To see how Moré uses topic sentences, skim paragraphs 2, 4, and 5, and highlight the topic sentence in each paragraph. Choose one of these paragraphs, and think about how the subsequent sentences give details or examples to back up the generalization in the topic sentence.

All the profiles in this chapter use a combination of showing and telling to convey the writer's perspective on the subject. Cable shows his anxiety about death, for example, by describing his hesitation to get close to and touch a dead body (pars. 15, 28). He uses comparisons to give readers a dominant impression of the funeral home as all business:

> His tone was that of a broker conferring on the Dow Jones. (par. 9)

> Inside were thirty coffins, lids open, patiently awaiting inspection. Like new cars on the showroom floor. (par. 18)

In addition, Cable tells readers directly about what he observed—for instance, in the opening paragraphs and in his questioning of Tim about whether burials play "an important role in society" (par. 22).

ANALYZE & WRITE

Write a paragraph or two analyzing how Moré uses showing and telling to convey her perspective on freegans:

1 Skim paragraphs 1 and 6–10, and assess how Moré uses narrating and describing to show readers what dumpster diving is like. Ask yourself questions like these: How does she acknowledge readers' possible preconceptions? What did you expect her to reveal about the look, smell, and feel of a supermarket dumpster filled with food? What, if anything, surprised you or seemed to be missing? What do the two photos add?

2 Now review paragraphs 11–13, highlighting what Moré tells readers directly.

3 Finally, consider the relationship between showing and telling. How well does Moré create a dominant impression by using what she *shows* to reinforce what she *tells* readers? Does what she shows and tells reinforce each other? If there are contradictions, how are they discussed?

[RESPOND]   ## Consider possible topics: Using profile to learn.

Moré uses ethnography to look closely at an aspect of consumer culture. Although she had read about food waste, it was only by accompanying a group of local freegans on a dumpster dive that she saw firsthand how much edible food was actually wasted. What aspect of consumer culture could you imagine researching firsthand? Consider researching the kinds of household products thrown away or recycled by going to the local dump or charity shop. Or compare "secondhand" clothes sold in a charity shop to "vintage" clothes sold at an upscale consignment shop.

Amanda Coyne | *The Long Good-Bye: Mother's Day in Federal Prison*

Courtesy of Amanda Coyne

AMANDA COYNE earned a master of fine arts degree in creative writing at the University of Iowa, where she was the recipient of an Iowa Arts Fellowship. She was the cofounder of and a writer for the *Alaska Dispatch*, an award-winning online news site. Her work has appeared in such publications as the *New York Times Magazine, Newsweek,* and the *Guardian*. Coyne coauthored a book about oil and politics in Alaska titled *Crude Awakening: Money, Mavericks, and Mayhem in Alaska* (2011). She also started a blog about Alaska politics in 2013.

"The Long Good-Bye," her first piece of published writing, originally appeared in *Harper's*. Coyne uses direct observation and interview to study the behavior of a particular community. In this profile, Coyne examines women who have been incarcerated and separated from their children to see how the mothers and children negotiate their difficult relationships.

As you read, consider the following questions:

- What stresses seem to affect the family relationships described in this profile?

- What do you think is the author's attitude toward these stresses? How can you tell what she thinks and feels?

1   You can spot the convict-moms here in the visiting room by the way they hold and touch their children and by the single flower that is perched in front of them—a rose, a tulip, a daffodil. Many of these mothers have untied the bow that attaches the flower to its silver-and-red cellophane wrapper and are using one of the many empty soda cans at hand as a vase. They sit proudly before their flower-in-a-Coke-can, amid Hershey bar wrappers, half-eaten Ding Dongs, and empty paper coffee cups. Occasionally, a mother will pick up her present and bring it to her nose when one of the bearers of the single flower—her child—asks if she likes it. And the mother will respond the way that mothers always have and always will respond when presented with a gift on this day. "Oh, I just love it. It's perfect. I'll put it in the middle of my Bible." Or, "I'll put it on my desk, right next to your school picture." And always: "It's the best one here."

2   But most of what is being smelled today is the children themselves. While the other adults are plunking coins into the vending machines, the mothers take deep whiffs from the backs of their children's necks, or kiss and smell the backs of their knees, or take off their shoes and tickle their feet and then pull them close to their noses. They hold them tight and take in their own second scent—the scent assuring them that these are still their children and that they still belong to them.

3   The visitors are allowed to bring in pockets full of coins, and today that Mother's Day flower, and I know from previous visits to my older sister here at the Federal Prison Camp for women in Pekin, Illinois, that there is always an aberrant urge to gather immediately around the vending machines. The sandwiches are stale, the coffee weak, the candy bars the ones we always pass up in a convenience store. But after we hand the children over to their mothers, we gravitate toward those machines. Like milling in the kitchen at a party. We all do it, and nobody knows why. Polite conversation ensues around the microwave while the popcorn is popping and the processed-chicken sandwiches are being heated. We ask one another where we are from, how long a drive we had. An occasional whistle through the teeth, a shake of the head. "My, my, long way from home, huh?" "Staying at the Super 8 right up the road. Not a bad place." "Stayed at the Econo Lodge last time. Wasn't a good place at all." Never asking the questions we really want to ask: "What's she in for?" "How much time's she got left?" You never ask in the waiting room of a doctor's office either. Eventually, all of us—fathers,

mothers, sisters, brothers, a few boyfriends, and very few husbands—return to the queen of the day, sitting at a fold-out table loaded with snacks, prepared for five or so hours of attempted normal conversation.

4   Most of the inmates are elaborately dressed, many in prison-crafted dresses and sweaters in bright blues and pinks. They wear meticulously applied makeup in corresponding hues, and their hair is replete with loops and curls—hair that only women with the time have the time for. Some of the better seamstresses have crocheted vests and purses to match their outfits. Although the world outside would never accuse these women of making haute-couture fashion statements, the fathers and the sons and the boyfriends and the very few husbands think they look beautiful, and they tell them so repeatedly. And I can imagine the hours spent preparing for this visit—hours of needles and hooks clicking over brightly colored yards of yarn. The hours of discussing, dissecting, and bragging about these visitors—especially the men. Hours spent in the other world behind the door where we're not allowed, sharing lipsticks and mascaras, and unraveling the occasional hair-tangled hot roller, and the brushing out and lifting and teasing . . . and the giggles that abruptly change into tears without warning—things that define any female-only world. Even, or especially, if that world is a female federal prison camp.

5   While my sister Jennifer is with her son in the playroom, an inmate's mother comes over to introduce herself to my younger sister, Charity, my brother, John, and me. She tells us about visiting her daughter in a higher-security prison before she was transferred here. The woman looks old and tired, and her shoulders sag under the weight of her recently acquired bitterness.

6   "Pit of fire," she says, shaking her head. "Like a pit of fire straight from hell. Never seen anything like it. Like something out of an old movie about prisons." Her voice is getting louder and she looks at each of us with pleading eyes. "My *daughter* was there. Don't even get me started on that place. Women die there."

7   John and Charity and I silently exchange glances.

8   "My daughter would come to the visiting room with a black eye and I'd think, 'All she did was sit in the car while her boyfriend ran into the house.' She didn't even touch the stuff. Never even handled it."

9   She continues to stare at us, each in turn. "Ten years. That boyfriend talked and he got three years. She

didn't know anything. Had nothing to tell them. They gave her ten years. They called it conspiracy. Conspiracy? Aren't there real criminals out there?" She asks this with hands outstretched, waiting for an answer that none of us can give her.

10   The woman's daughter, the conspirator, is chasing her son through the maze of chairs and tables and through the other children. She's a twenty-four-year-old blonde, whom I'll call Stephanie, with Dorothy Hamill hair and matching dimples. She looks like any girl you might see in any shopping mall in middle America. She catches her chocolate-brown son and tickles him, and they laugh and trip and fall together onto the floor and laugh harder.

11   Had it not been for that wait in the car, this scene would be taking place at home, in a duplex Stephanie would rent while trying to finish her two-year degree in dental hygiene or respiratory therapy at the local community college. The duplex would be spotless, with a blown-up picture of her and her son over the couch and ceramic unicorns and horses occupying the shelves of the entertainment center. She would make sure that her son went to school every day with stylishly floppy pants, scrubbed teeth, and a good breakfast in his belly. Because of their difference in skin color, there would be occasional tension—caused by the strange looks from strangers, teachers, other mothers, and the bullies on the playground, who would chant after they knocked him down, "Your Momma's white, your Momma's white." But if she were home, their weekends and evenings would be spent together transcending those looks and healing those bruises. Now, however, their time is spent eating visiting-room junk food and his school days are spent fighting the boys in the playground who chant, "Your Momma's in prison, your Momma's in prison."

12   He will be ten when his mother is released, the same age my nephew will be when his mother is let out. But Jennifer, my sister, was able to spend the first five years of Toby's life with him. Stephanie had Ellie after she was incarcerated. They let her hold him for eighteen hours, then sent her back to prison. She has done the "tour," and her son is a well-traveled six-year-old. He has spent weekends visiting his mother in prisons in Kentucky, Texas, Connecticut (the Pit of Fire), and now at last here, the camp—minimum security, Pekin, Illinois.

13   Ellie looks older than his age. But his shoulders do not droop like his grandmother's. On the contrary, his

Coyne *The Long Good-Bye: Mother's Day in Federal Prison* ▶ **GUIDE TO READING**
Guide to Writing
A Writer at Work
Reflection

73

bitterness lifts them and his chin higher than a child's should be, and the childlike, wide-eyed curiosity has been replaced by defiance. You can see his emerging hostility as he and his mother play together. She tells him to pick up the toy that he threw, say, or to put the deck of cards away. His face turns sullen, but she persists. She takes him by the shoulders and looks him in the eye, and he uses one of his hands to swat at her. She grabs the hand and he swats with the other. Eventually, she pulls him toward her and smells the top of his head, and she picks up the cards or the toy herself. After all, it is Mother's Day and she sees him so rarely. But her acquiescence makes him angrier, and he stalks out of the playroom with his shoulders thrown back.

14   Toby, my brother and sister and I assure one another, will not have these resentments. He is better taken care of than most. He is living with relatives in Wisconsin. Good, solid, middle-class, churchgoing relatives. And when he visits us, his aunts and his uncle, we take him out for adventures where we walk down the alley of a city and pretend that we are being chased by the "bad guys." We buy him fast food, and his uncle, John, keeps him up well past his bedtime enthralling him with stories of the monkeys he met in India. A perfect mix, we try to convince one another. Until we take him to see his mother and on the drive back he asks the question that most confuses him, and no doubt all the other children who spend much of their lives in prison visiting rooms: "Is my Mommy a bad guy?" It is the question that most seriously disorders his five-year-old need to clearly separate right from wrong. And because our own need is perhaps just as great, it is the question that haunts us as well.

15   Now, however, the answer is relatively simple. In a few years, it won't be. In a few years we will have to explain mandatory minimums, and the war on drugs, and the murky conspiracy laws, and the enormous amount of money and time that federal agents pump into imprisoning low-level drug dealers and those who happen to be their friends and their lovers. In a few years he might have the reasoning skills to ask why so many armed robbers and rapists and child-molesters and, indeed, murderers are punished less severely than his mother. When he is older, we will somehow have to explain to him the difference between federal crimes,

"Is my Mommy a bad guy?" It is the question that most seriously disorders his five-year-old need to clearly separate right from wrong.

which don't allow for parole, and state crimes, which do. We will have to explain that his mother was taken from him for five years not because she was a drug-dealer but because she made four phone calls for someone she loved.

16   But we also know it is vitally important that we explain all this without betraying our bitterness. We understand the danger of abstract anger, of being disillusioned with your country, and, most of all, we do not want him to inherit that legacy. We would still like him to be raised as we were, with the idea that we live in the best country in the world with the best legal system in the world—a legal system carefully designed to be immune to political mood swings and public hysteria; a system that promises to fit the punishment to the crime. We want him to be a good citizen. We want him to have absolute faith that he lives in a fair country, a country that watches over and protects its most vulnerable citizens: its women and children.

17   So for now we simply say, "Toby, your mother isn't bad, she just did a bad thing. Like when you put rocks in the lawn mower's gas tank. You weren't bad then, you just did a bad thing."

18   Once, after being given this weak explanation, he said, "I wish I could have done something really bad, like my Mommy. So I could go to prison too and be with her."

19   It's now 3:00. Visiting ends at 3:30. The kids are getting cranky, and the adults are both exhausted and wired from too many hours of conversation, too much coffee and candy. The fathers, mothers, sisters, brothers, and the few boyfriends, and the very few husbands are beginning to show signs of gathering the trash. The mothers of the infants are giving their heads one last whiff before tucking them and their paraphernalia into their respective carrying cases. The visitors meander toward the door, leaving the older children with their mothers for one last word. But the mothers never say what they want to say to their children. They say things like, "Do well in school," "Be nice to your sister," "Be good for Aunt Berry, or Grandma." They don't say, "I'm sorry I'm sorry I'm sorry. I love you more than anything else in the world and I think about you every minute and I worry about you with a pain that shoots straight to my heart, a pain so great I think I will just burst when I think of you alone, without me. I'm sorry."

20   We are standing in front of the double glass doors that lead to the outside world. My older sister holds her son, rocking him gently. They are both crying. We give her a look and she puts him down. Charity and I grasp each of his small hands, and the four of us walk through the doors. As we're walking out, my brother sings one of his banana songs to Toby.

21   "Take me out to the—" and Toby yells out, "Banana store!"

22   "Buy me some—"

23   "Bananas!!"

24   "I don't care if I ever come back. For it's root, root, root for the—"

25   "Monkey team!"

26   I turn back and see a line of women standing behind the glass wall. Some of them are crying, but many simply stare with dazed eyes. Stephanie is holding both of her son's hands in hers and speaking urgently to him. He is struggling, and his head is twisting violently back and forth. He frees one of his hands from her grasp, balls up his fist, and punches her in the face. Then he walks with purpose through the glass doors and out the exit. I look back at her. She is still in a crouched position. She stares, unblinking, through those doors. Her hands have left her face and are hanging on either side of her. I look away, but before I do, I see drops of blood drip from her nose, down her chin, and onto the shiny marble floor.

[REFLECT]   ## Make connections: Unfair punishment.

Coyne reflects near the end of the essay that she wishes her nephew Toby would "have absolute faith that he lives in a fair country" (par. 16). Yet she expects that, like Stephanie's son, Ellie, Toby will become bitter and angry when he understands that "his mother was taken from him for five years not because she was a drug dealer but because she made four phone calls for someone she loved" (par. 15).

Think about an occasion when you were punished unfairly—for breaking a school rule, perhaps, or neglecting to fulfill an expectation of your parents. Although you willingly admit having done it, you may still feel that the punishment was unjustified. Consider what you did and why you think the punishment was unfair. Your instructor may ask you to post and discuss your thoughts. Use these questions to get started:

- Why do you think the punishment was unfair? For example, were the rules or expectations that you broke unclear or unreasonable? Were they applied to everyone or applied selectively or at the whim of those in power?

- Coyne uses the value term *unfair* to describe what's wrong with the punishment her sister and some of the other women received. Why do you think Coyne believes her sister's punishment is unfair? Why does Stephanie's mother think Stephanie's punishment was unfair? Do you agree or disagree?

[ANALYZE]   ## Use the basic features.

SPECIFIC INFORMATION ABOUT THE SUBJECT: DESCRIBING AND NARRATING

Profiles, like remembered events (Chapter 2), succeed in large part by creating a vivid portrait of a place and the people in it by weaving together narrative and descriptive detail. Cable's narrative takes the form of a tour of the mortuary, the climax of which occurs when he touches a dead body. Similarly, Moré's profile includes a brief description of her experience dumpster diving, which offers insight into what motivates her freegan comrades.

To learn more about describing and narrating strategies, see Chapter 14.

ANALYZE & WRITE

Write a paragraph analyzing Coyne's use of describing and narrating strategies to give readers a vivid impression of the plight of incarcerated moms:

1. Skim paragraphs 1 and 4, highlighting the naming and detailing that stands out most graphically for you. What is the dominant impression you get from Coyne's descriptive language?

2. Now reread paragraph 13 to see how Coyne uses narration to capture a dramatic interaction. Coyne's storytelling is simple. Nothing out of the ordinary happens, but the incident carries a lot of weight for Coyne. How does she convey to readers the drama of this interaction?

> **Reflect on . . .**
> What do you learn by comparing the way specific information is conveyed in different profiles?

A PERSPECTIVE ON THE SUBJECT: USING CONTRAST

Unlike arguments supporting positions or justifying evaluations, which tell readers directly what the writer thinks and why, profiles often lead readers to draw a particular conclusion on their own, using strategies like comparing and contrasting. For example, Cable quotes the funeral director drawing a distinction between his job and that of a psychologist to clarify what a mortuary does and does not offer clients:

> "We provide services for the dead, not counseling for the living." (par. 10)

Contrast cue

Notice that he juxtaposes, or places side by side, the different professions.

Contrasts can also be used to foreground particular aspects of the subject. In this example, Cable uses contrast to call attention to the appearance and location of the mortuary, highlighting the difference between his expectations and the reality he finds:

> I thought it would be more like Forest Lawn, serene with lush green lawns and meticulously groomed gardens, a place set apart from the hustle of day-to-day life. Here instead was an odd tan structure set in the middle of a business district. (par. 3)

Contrast cue

ANALYZE & WRITE

Write a couple of paragraphs analyzing how Coyne uses contrast to convey her perspective:

To learn more about transitions, including those indicating contrasting or opposing views, see Chapter 13.

1. Skim Coyne's profile, highlighting the cues or transitional words and phrases that indicate contrast. Analyze at least one of the contrasts you find. What is being contrasted? How does the contrast help you understand the writer's perspective?

2. Note in the margin which paragraphs focus on Coyne's sister Jennifer and her son, Toby, and which focus on Stephanie and her son, Ellie. Does Coyne juxtapose the two families or use cues to highlight the contrasts — or does she use both strategies? What differences between the two families does Coyne emphasize? Since contrasts tend to be worth pointing out when there are also important similarities, consider what similarities Coyne wants readers to think about.

3. Consider how Coyne uses contrast — between people, between the world of the prison and the world outside, and between what is and what could have been — to help convey her perspective on the plight of women like her sister and children like her nephew.

[RESPOND] **Consider possible topics: Profiling one instance of a recurring event.**

Like Coyne, you could choose to profile an activity occurring over a short period of time, in a relatively small space, involving just a few people. Consider, for example, profiling a team practicing, a musical group rehearsing, or researchers working together in a lab. Try to make more than one observational visit to see the group in action, and arrange to talk with people on every visit, perhaps capturing a few digital images to help you understand the group and possibly also to illustrate it.

Gabriel Thompson | *A Gringo in the Lettuce Fields*

Courtesy of Gabriel Thompson

GABRIEL THOMPSON has worked as a community organizer and written extensively about the lives of undocumented immigrants in the United States. His books include *Calling All Radicals: How Grassroots Organizers Can Help Save Our Democracy* (2007), *America's Social Arsonist: Fred Ross and Grassroots Organizing in the Twentieth Century* (2016), and *Working in the Shadows: A Year of Doing the Jobs (Most) Americans Won't Do* (2010), from which the following selection is taken. The photograph showing lettuce cutters at work (p. 77) is from Thompson's blog, *Working in the Shadows*.

"A Gringo in the Lettuce Fields" falls into the category of immersion journalism, a cultural ethnography that uses undercover participant observation over an extended period of time to get an insider's view of a particular community.

As you read, consider the ethical implications of this kind of profile:

- What does Thompson's outsider status enable him to understand—or prevent him from understanding—about the community?

- How does Thompson avoid—or fail to avoid—stereotyping or exploiting the group being profiled?

- Toward the end, Thompson tells us that one of the workers "guesses" that he "joined the crew . . . to write about it" (par. 17). Not all participant-observers go undercover; why do you think Thompson chose to do so? What concerns would you have if you were the writer or if you were a member of the group being profiled?

1   I wake up staring into the bluest blue I've ever seen. I must have fallen into a deep sleep because I need several seconds to realize that I'm looking at the Arizona sky, that the pillow beneath my head is a large clump of dirt, and that a near-stranger named Manuel is standing over me, smiling. I pull myself to a sitting position. To my left, in the distance, a Border Patrol helicopter is hovering. To my right is Mexico, separated by only a few fields of lettuce. *"Buenos días,"* Manuel says.

2   I stand up gingerly. It's only my third day in the fields, but already my 30-year-old body is failing me.

I feel like someone has dropped a log on my back. And then piled that log onto a truck with many other logs, and driven that truck over my thighs. "Let's go," I say, trying to sound energetic as I fall in line behind Manuel, stumbling across rows of lettuce and thinking about "the five-day rule." The five-day rule, according to Manuel, is simple: Survive the first five days and you'll be fine. He's been a farmworker for almost two decades, so he should know. I'm on day three of five—the goal is within sight. Of course, another way to look at my situation is that I'm on day three of what I promised myself would be a two-month immersion in the work life of the people who do a job that most Americans won't do. But thinking about the next seven weeks doesn't benefit anyone. *Day three of five.*

3   "Manuel! Gabriel! Let's go! ¡*Vámonos!*" yells Pedro, our foreman. Our short break is over. Two dozen crew members standing near the lettuce machine are already putting on gloves and sharpening knives. Manuel and I hustle toward the machine, grab our own knives from a box of chlorinated water, and set up in neighboring rows, just as the machine starts moving slowly down another endless field.

4   Since the early 1980s, Yuma, Ariz., has been the "winter lettuce capital" of America. Each winter, when the weather turns cold in Salinas, California—the heart of the nation's lettuce industry—temperatures in sunny Yuma are still in the 70s and 80s. At the height of Yuma's growing season, the fields surrounding the city produce virtually all of the iceberg lettuce and 90 percent of the leafy green vegetables consumed in the United States and Canada.

5   America's lettuce industry actually needs people like me. Before applying for fieldwork at the local Dole headquarters, I came across several articles describing the causes of a farmworker shortage. The stories cited an aging workforce, immigration crackdowns, and long delays at the border that discourage workers with green cards who would otherwise commute to the fields from their Mexican homes.[1] Wages have been rising somewhat in response to the demand for laborers (one prominent member of the local growers association tells me average pay is now between $10 and $12 an hour), but it's widely assumed that most U.S. citizens wouldn't do the work at any price. Arizona's own Senator John McCain created a stir in 2006 when he issued a challenge to a group of union members in Washington, D.C. "I'll offer anybody here $50 an hour if you'll go pick lettuce in Yuma this season, and pick for the whole season," he said. Amid jeers, he didn't back down, telling the audience, "You can't do it, my friends."

6   On my first day I discover that even putting on a lettuce cutter's uniform is challenging (no fieldworkers, I learn, "pick" lettuce). First, I'm handed a pair of black galoshes to go over my shoes. Next comes the *gancho*, an

Courtesy of Gabriel Thompson

S-shaped hook that slips over my belt to hold packets of plastic bags. A white glove goes on my right hand, a gray glove, supposedly designed to offer protection from cuts, goes on my left. Over the cloth gloves I pull on a pair of latex gloves. I put on a black hairnet, my baseball cap, and a pair of protective sunglasses. Adding to my belt a long leather sheath, I'm good to go. I feel ridiculous.

7   The crew is already working in the field when Pedro walks me out to them and introduces me to Manuel. Manuel is holding an 18-inch knife in his hand. "Manuel has been cutting for many years, so watch him to see how it's done," Pedro says. Then he walks away. Manuel resumes cutting, following a machine that rolls along just ahead of the crew. Every several seconds Manuel bends down, grabs a head of iceberg lettuce with his left hand, and makes a quick cut with the knife in his right hand, separating the lettuce from its roots. Next, he lifts the lettuce to his stomach and makes a second cut, trimming the trunk. He shakes the lettuce, letting the outer leaves fall to the ground. With the blade still in his hand, he then brings the lettuce toward the gancho at his waist, and with a flick of the wrist the head is bagged and dropped onto one of the machine's extensions. Manuel does this over and over again, explaining each movement. "It's not so hard," he says. Five minutes later, Pedro reappears and tells me to grab a knife. Manuel points to a head of lettuce. "Try this one," he says.

8   I bend over, noticing that most of the crew has turned to watch. I take my knife and make a tentative

_____

[1] A green card is an immigration document that allows noncitizens to work legally in the United States, whether they live here or commute across the border. Undocumented workers (or illegal immigrants, depending on your position) lack green cards. [Editor's note]

sawing motion where I assume the trunk to be, though I'm really just guessing. Grabbing the head with my left hand, I straighten up, doing my best to imitate Manuel. Only my lettuce head doesn't move; it's still securely connected to the soil. Pedro steps in. "When you make the first cut, it is like you are stabbing the lettuce." He makes a quick jabbing action. "You want to aim for the center of the lettuce, where the trunk is," he says.

9   Ten minutes later, after a couple of other discouraging moments, I've cut maybe 20 heads of lettuce and am already feeling pretty accomplished. I'm not perfect: If I don't stoop far enough, my stab—instead of landing an inch above the ground—goes right through the head of lettuce, ruining it entirely. The greatest difficulty, though, is in the trimming. I had no idea that a head of lettuce was so humongous. In order to get it into a shape that can be bagged, I trim and trim and trim, but it's taking me upward of a minute to do what Manuel does in several seconds.

10   Pedro offers me a suggestion. "Act like the lettuce is a bomb," he says. "Imagine you've only got five seconds to get rid of it."

11   Surprisingly, that thought seems to work, and I'm able to greatly increase my speed. For a minute or two I feel euphoric. "Look at me!" I want to shout at Pedro; I'm in the zone. But the woman who is packing the lettuce into boxes soon swivels around to face me. "Look, this lettuce is no good." She's right: I've cut the trunk too high, breaking off dozens of good leaves, which will quickly turn brown because they're attached to nothing. With her left hand she holds the bag up, and with her right she smashes it violently, making a loud pop. She turns the bag over and the massacred lettuce falls to the ground. She does the same for the three other bags I've placed on the extension. "It's okay," Manuel tells me. "You shouldn't try to go too fast when you're beginning." Pedro seconds him. "That's right. Make sure the cuts are precise and that you don't rush."

12   So I am to be very careful and precise, while also treating the lettuce like a bomb that must be tossed aside after five seconds.

13   That first week on the job was one thing. By midway into week two, it isn't clear to me what more I can do to keep up with the rest of the crew. I know the techniques by this time and am moving as fast as my body will permit. Yet I need to somehow *double* my current output to hold my own. I'm able to cut only one row at a time while Manuel is cutting two. Our fastest cutter, Julio, meanwhile can handle three. But how someone could cut two rows for an hour—much less an entire day—is beyond me. "Oh, you will get it," Pedro tells me one day. "You will most definitely get it." Maybe he's trying to be hopeful or inspiring, but it comes across as a threat.

14   That feeling aside, what strikes me about our 31-member crew is how quickly they have welcomed me as one of their own. I encountered some suspicion at first, but it didn't last. Simply showing up on the second day seemed to be proof enough that I was there to work. When I faltered in the field and fell behind, hands would come across from adjacent rows to grab a head or two of my lettuce so I could catch up. People whose names I didn't yet know would ask me how I was holding up, reminding me that it would get easier as time went by. If I took a seat alone during a break, someone would call me into their group and offer a homemade taco or two.

15   Two months in, I make the mistake of calling in sick one Thursday. The day before, I put my left hand too low on a head of lettuce. When I punched my blade through the stem, the knife struck my middle finger. Thanks to the gloves, my skin wasn't even broken, but the finger instantly turned purple. I took two painkillers to get through the afternoon, but when I wake the next morning it is still throbbing. With one call to an answering machine that morning, and another the next day, I create my own four-day weekend.

16   The surprise is that when I return on Monday, feeling recuperated, I wind up having the hardest day of my brief career in lettuce. Within hours, my hands feel weaker than ever. By quitting time—some 10 hours after our day started—I feel like I'm going to vomit from exhaustion. A theory forms in my mind. Early in the season—say, after the first week—a farmworker's body gets thoroughly broken down. Back, legs, and arms grow sore, hands and feet swell up. A tolerance for the pain is developed, though, and two-day weekends provide just enough time for the body to recover from the trauma. My four-day break had been too long; my body actually began to recuperate, and it wanted more time to continue. Instead, it was thrown right back into the mix and rebelled. Only on my second

> *Pedro offers me a suggestion. "Act like the lettuce is a bomb. . . . Imagine you've only got five seconds to get rid of it."*

day back did my body recover that middle ground. "I don't think the soreness goes away," I say to Manuel and two other co-workers one day. "You just forget what it's like not to be sore." Manuel, who's 37, considers this. "That's true, that's true," he says. "It always takes a few weeks at the end of the year to get back to normal, to recover."

17   An older co-worker, Mateo, is the one who eventually guesses that I have joined the crew because I want to write about it. "That is good," he says over coffee at his home one Sunday. "Americans should know the hard work that Mexicans do in this country."

18   Mateo is an unusual case. There aren't many other farmworkers who are still in the fields when they reach their 50s. It's simply not possible to do this work for decades and not suffer a permanently hunched back, or crooked fingers, or hands so swollen that they look as if someone has attached a valve to a finger and pumped vigorously. The punishing nature of the work helps explain why farmworkers don't live very long; the National Migrant Resources Program puts their life expectancy at 49 years.

19   "Are you cutting two rows yet?" Mateo asks me. "Yes, more or less," I say. "I thought I'd be better by now." Mateo shakes his head. "It takes a long time to learn how to really cut lettuce. It's not something that you learn after only one season. Three, maybe four seasons—then you start understanding how to really work with lettuce."

Make connections: Switching perspectives.

[**REFLECT**]

Thompson temporarily joined a community of lettuce cutters to get an insider's perspective on their work. Think about your own experience as a member of a group that was visited and observed, even for a short period of time. Perhaps an administrator visited one of your classes or a potential coach or recruit observed your team. Consider what it was like being studied by a stranger. Your instructor may ask you to post and discuss your thoughts about the experience. Use these questions to get started:

- As an insider, how did you and the other group members feel about being the subject of someone else's gaze?

- What were you told about why your group was being visited and what assumptions or concerns did you have about the visitor? Were you concerned about the visitor's motives—for example, wondering if the person was really there to evaluate the group or its members?

- Suppose Thompson wanted to write a piece of immersion journalism about a community (such as a religious group, sports team, fraternity, or sorority) of which you are a member. What elements of Thompson's profile, if any, would cause you to trust or distrust his reporting? What ethical challenges might immersion journalists like Thompson face by going undercover?

Use the basic features.

[**ANALYZE**]

SPECIFIC INFORMATION ABOUT THE SUBJECT: USING QUOTATION, PARAPHRASE, AND SUMMARY

Profile writers—like all writers—depend on the three basic strategies for presenting source material: quoting, paraphrasing, and summarizing. Each strategy has advantages and disadvantages. It's obvious why Cable chose this quotation: "We're in *Ripley's Believe It or Not*, along with another funeral home whose owners' names are Baggit and Sackit" (par. 14). But making decisions about what to quote and what to paraphrase or summarize is not always that easy.

To learn more about quoting, paraphrasing, and summarizing, see Chapter 19.

| ANALYZE & WRITE |

Write a few paragraphs analyzing Thompson's decisions about how to present information from different sources:

1 Skim the essay to find at least one example of a quotation and one paraphrase or summary of information gleaned from an interview or from background research.

2 Why do you think Thompson chooses to quote certain things and paraphrase or summarize other things? What could be a good rule of thumb for you to apply when deciding whether to quote, paraphrase, or summarize? (Note that when writing for an academic audience, in a paper for a class or in a scholarly publication, all source material — whether it is quoted, paraphrased, or summarized — should be cited.)

THE WRITER'S ROLE: GOING UNDERCOVER

Like Moré, Thompson acts as a participant-observer. But unlike Moré, his role is covert. He does not watch lettuce cutters from the sidelines or announce himself as a journalist but instead works among them for two months. His informal interviews take place during work and on breaks (even at the homes of his coworkers over the weekend). Nevertheless, there is a significant difference between a two-month experiment and a personal account written by a lettuce cutter like Mateo after a lifetime on the job. A profile writer may participate but is always an outsider looking in.

| ANALYZE & WRITE |

Write a paragraph or two analyzing Thompson's use of the participant-observer role:

1 Skim the text, noting at least one place where Thompson

- reminds readers of his status as an outsider (for example, when he refers to a coworker as a "near-stranger" [par. 1]);
- tells readers about something he thinks will be unfamiliar to them (for example, when he explains that people do not "'pick' lettuce" [par. 6]);
- calls attention to his own incompetence or failings (for example, when he describes his first attempt to cut lettuce [par. 8]).

2 Why do you think Thompson tells us about his errors and reminds us that he is an outsider? What effect are these moves likely to have on his audience?

3 How do the writers whose profiles appear in this chapter use their outsider status to connect with readers?

[RESPOND] ## Consider possible topics: Immersing yourself.

Thompson's experience suggests two possible avenues for research: You could embed yourself in a group, participating alongside group members, and then write about that experience—for example, you might join a club on campus or try an unusual sport. Alternatively, you could observe life in an unfamiliar group, watching how a meeting or an event unfolds, interviewing members to learn about their practices, and conducting additional research to learn about the group.

The Writing Assignment

Profile an intriguing person, group, place, or activity in your community. Observe your subject closely, and then present what you have learned in a way that both informs and engages readers.

This Guide to Writing is designed to help you compose your own profile and apply what you have learned from reading other profiles. This Starting Points chart will help you find the guidance you need, when you need it.

> **Take a moment . . .**
> Why might a guide to writing like this be helpful to writers new to profiles? As you write, think about what you do (and do not) find helpful.

STARTING POINTS: WRITING A PROFILE

Specific Information about the Subject

How do I come up with an appropriate subject to profile?

- Choose a subject to profile. (p. 83)
- Test Your Choice: Considering Your Purpose and Audience (pp. 83–84)

How can I gather information on my subject?

- Conduct your field research. (pp. 84–88)
- Chapter 17, Planning and Conducting Research

How can I make my subject come to life?

- Assess the genre's basic features: Specific information about the subject. (p. 57)
- Specific Information about the Subject: Describing and Narrating (pp. 74–75)
- Specific Information about the Subject: Using Quotation, Paraphrase, and Summary (pp. 79–80)
- Use quotations that provide information and reveal character. (pp. 88–89)
- Consider adding visual or audio elements. (p. 89)
- A Troubleshooting Guide: Specific Information about the Subject (p. 97)

(continued)

A Clear, Logical Organization

How should I organize my profile?

- Assess the genre's basic features: A clear, logical organization. (pp. 57–58)
- A Clear, Logical Organization: Cueing Readers (p. 69)
- Create an outline that will organize your profile effectively for your readers. (pp. 89–90)
- A Troubleshooting Guide: A Clear, Logical Organization (p. 95)

The Writer's Role

What role should I adopt in researching and presenting my subject?

- Assess the genre's basic features: The writer's role. (p. 59)
- The Writer's Role: Going Undercover (p. 80)
- Determine your role in the profile. (pp. 90–91)
- A Troubleshooting Guide: The Writer's Role (p. 99)

A Perspective on the Subject

How do I develop and express a clear perspective on the subject?

- Determine the writer's purpose and audience. (p. 56)
- Assess the genre's basic features: A perspective on the subject. (p. 59)
- A Perspective on the Subject: Showing and Telling (p. 70)
- A Perspective on the Subject: Using Contrast (p. 75)
- Develop your perspective on the subject. (pp. 91–93)
- Clarify the dominant impression. (pp. 93–94)
- A Troubleshooting Guide: A Perspective on the Subject (p. 99)

Writing a Draft: Invention, Research, Planning, and Composing

The activities in this section will help you choose a subject to profile and develop your perspective on the subject. Do the activities in any order that makes sense to you (and your instructor), and return to them as needed as you revise.

Although some of the activities will take only a few minutes to complete, the essential field research — making detailed observations and conducting interviews — will take a good deal of time to plan and carry out. Your writing in response to many of these activities can be used as part of your rough draft, which you will be able to improve after receiving feedback from your classmates and instructor.

⊞ Choose a subject to profile.

To create an informative and engaging profile, your subject—whether it's a person, a group of people, a place, or an activity—should be one

- that sparks your interest or curiosity;
- that your readers will find interesting and informative;
- that you can gain access to and observe in detail in the time allowed;
- about which (or with whom) you can conduct in-depth interviews.

Note: Whenever you write a profile, consider carefully the ethics involved in such research: You will want to be careful to treat participants fairly and with respect in the way you both approach and depict them. Discuss the ethical implications of your research with your instructor, and think carefully about the goals of your research and the effect it will have on others. You may also need to obtain permission from your school's ethics review board.

> **Take a moment . . .**
> Why is it important to treat the people you profile ethically? Put yourself in the position of your subject.

Make a list of appropriate subjects. To come up with ideas, think about the readings: Like Moré, you could use the tools of ethnography to investigate an aspect of consumer culture firsthand, such as profiling a local dump or charity shop. Like Coyne, you could investigate an activity, such as a team practice or a rehearsal that occurs over a short period of time and involves only a few people. Or like Thompson, you could embed yourself in a club or an unusual sports team, and then write about how meetings or events unfold. Consult your school's Web site to find intriguing places, activities, or people on campus.

The following ideas may suggest additional possibilities to consider:

- a place where people come together because they are of the same age, gender, sexual orientation, or ethnic group (for example, a foreign language–speaking dorm or fraternity or sorority), or a place where people of different ages, genders, sexual orientations, or ethnic groups have formed a community (for example, a Sunday morning pickup basketball game in the park, LGBT club, or barbershop)
- a place where people are trained for a certain kind of work (for example, a police academy, cosmetology program, truck driving school, or boxing ring)
- a group of people working together for a particular purpose (for example, students and their teacher preparing for the academic decathlon, employees working together to produce something, law students and their professor working to help prisoners on death row, or scientists collaborating on a research project)

TEST YOUR CHOICE

Considering Your Purpose and Audience

After you have made a tentative choice, ask yourself the following questions:

- Do I feel curious about the subject?
- Am I confident that I will be able to make the subject interesting for my readers?
- Do I believe that I can research this subject sufficiently in the time I have?

Then get together with two or three other students:

Presenters.   Take turns identifying your subjects. Explain your interest in the subject, and speculate about why you think it will interest readers.

Listeners.   Briefly tell each presenter what you already know about his or her subject, if anything, and what might make it interesting to readers.

⠿ Conduct your field research.

To learn more about conducting observations and interviews, see Chapter 17.

To write an effective profile, conduct **field research** *— interviews and observations — to collect detailed, firsthand information about your subject.* Many writers begin with observations to get the lay of the land and identify people to interview, but you can start with interviews. You may even be able to make observations and conduct interviews during the same visit. If you are thinking of adopting the role of participant-observer, turn first to Determine Your Role in the Profile (pp. 90–91), and consider whether you need to request permission before conducting your research. Before your interview or observation, draft preliminary questions; when you appear for your interview or observation, dress appropriately and bring equipment for taking notes, recording, or filming. (Be sure to ask permission before recording or filming.) The following activities will help you plan and carry out your field research.

WAYS IN

HOW CAN I MANAGE MY TIME?

Try this BACKWARD PLANNING *strategy:*

1. Construct a calendar marking the date the project is due and any other intermediate due dates (such as the date the first draft, thesis, or topic is due). The calendar on the next page provides an example.

2. Work backward, adding dates by which key stages or milestones should be reached to make your due dates. For example, mark the following:

   - the date by which final revisions to text and images are needed
   - the date on which peer review is scheduled
   - the date by which the first draft should be completed
   - the date by which initial interviews and observations should be conducted (leave at least a week for this process)
   - the date by which interviews and observations must be scheduled (leave at least several days for this process)

Mon 10	Tue 11	Wed 12	Thu 13	Fri 14
Arrange interviews & observations				Research interview subjects
17	**18**	**19**	**20**	**21**
Conduct interviews/observations				
24	**25**	**26**	**27**	**28**
	Complete write-ups			First draft due
1	**2**	**3**	**4**	**5**
	Follow-up questions?	Revise draft		Final draft due

Did you know?

Research shows that suggestions like those in the Ways In activities help writers new to field research. How helpful do you find them?

WAYS IN

HOW DO I SET UP AND PREPARE FOR INTERVIEWS AND OBSERVATIONS?

1. *List the people you would like to interview or places you would like to observe.* Include a number of possibilities in case your first choice doesn't work out.

2. *Write out your intentions and goals so that you can explain them clearly to others.*

3. *Call or e-mail for an appointment with your interview subject, or make arrangements to visit the site.* Explain who you are and what you are doing. Student research projects are often embraced, but be prepared for your request to be rejected.

   Note: Be sure to arrange your interview or site visit as soon as possible. The most common error students report making on this assignment is waiting too long to make that first call. Be aware, too, that the people and places you contact may not respond immediately (or at all); be sure to follow up if you have not gotten an answer to your request within a few days.

4. *Make notes about what you expect to learn before you write interview questions, interview your subject, or visit your site.* Ask yourself questions like these:

Interview

- How would I define or describe the subject?
- What is the subject's purpose or function?
- Who or what is associated with it?
- What about the subject will interest me and my readers?
- What do I hope to learn about it?

Observation

- How would I define or describe my subject?
- What typically takes place at this location? Who or what will I likely observe?
- What will interest me and my readers?
- What do I expect to learn about my subject?
- How will my presence affect those I am observing?

(continued)

5. *Write some interview questions in advance, or ask yourself some observation questions to help you determine how best to conduct your site visit.*

Interview

Ask for stories:

▸ Tell me how you got into ....

▸ Tell me about something that surprised/pleased/frustrated you.

Let subjects correct misconceptions:

▸ What myths about .... would you most like to bust?

Ask about the subject's past and future:

▸ How has .... changed over the years, and where do you think it's going?

Observation

Consider your **PERSPECTIVE:**

▪ Should I observe from different vantage points or from the same location?

▪ Should I visit the location at different times of day or days of the week, or would it be better to visit at the same time every day?

▪ Should I focus on specific people, or should I identify roles and focus on people as they adopt those roles?

6. *Conduct some preliminary research on your subject or related subjects if possible, and revise your questions or plans accordingly.*

WAYS IN

HOW DO I CONDUCT INTERVIEWS?

Take notes:

▪ Clearly distinguish **QUOTATIONS** from **PARAPHRASES** or **SUMMARIES** by inserting quotation marks where needed.

▪ Record the interview, if allowed, but also take notes. Politely ask interviewees to speak slowly, repeat themselves, or confirm your quotations if necessary. (Interviewees often fear being misquoted and will usually appreciate your being careful.)

▪ In addition to writing down what your subject says, use **NAMING**, **DETAILING**, and **COMPARING** to capture the interviewee's tone, gestures, and mannerisms.

▪ To generate **ANECDOTES**, ask how the interviewee first got involved with the place or activity; if there was a key event worth noting; what most concerns the interviewee; and what has been the biggest influence on his or her experience, for good or ill.

HOW DO I CONDUCT OBSERVATIONS?

Take notes:

▪ Note your surroundings, using all of your senses: sight, hearing, smell, taste, touch.

▪ Describe the place from multiple vantage points, noting furnishings, decor, and so on, and sketch the layout.

▪ Describe people's appearance, dress, gestures, and actions.

▪ Make a record of interesting overheard conversation.

▪ Note your reactions and ideas, especially in relation to your preconceptions. What surprises you?

▪ If you can get permission, observe how people interact with one another.

Consider your **ROLE:**

▪ If you are new to the subject and would like to have a **PARTICIPANT-OBSERVER** role, ask permission to take part in a small way for a limited time.

- To elicit **PROCESS NARRATIVES**, ask how something works, what happens if it breaks, whether it has always been done the same way, how it has changed, and how it could be improved.

- To **CLASSIFY**, **COMPARE**, or **CONTRAST**, ask what kind of thing it is, how it's like and unlike others of its kind, and how it compares to what it was like in the past.

- To help you with your **PERSPECTIVE**, ask why the subject is important, how it contributes to the community, or how it could be improved. Ask who would disagree with these perspectives.

- Finally, ask for the interviewee's preferences (e-mail or phone) for handling your follow-up questions, if any.

Reflect on the interview. Review your notes right after the interview, adding any impressions and marking promising material, such as

- anything that calls into question your or your readers' likely preconceptions;

- details that could paint a vivid portrait of the person;

- quotable phrases that could help you capture the tone or mood of the subject;

- questions you still need answered.

Write up your interview. Write a few paragraphs reporting what you learned from the interview:

- Choose notable quotes, and summarize or paraphrase other bits of information.

- Try to add speaker tags to describe the person's tone of voice, gestures, and appearance while speaking.

- Consider whether something important was left unsaid or was misrepresented—and, if so, how that might extend or complicate your understanding of the subject.

- If you are an insider, adopt the position of a **SPECTATOR** to help you find a new angle and learn something new. (For example, if you're on the football team, focus on the cheerleaders or the people who maintain the field.)

Collect artifacts, or take videos or photos:

- Collect any brochures or other written material you might be able to use, either to prepare for interviews or to include in your essay.

- Consider taking photographs or videos, if allowed. Try a pan shot scanning the scene from side to side or a tracking shot indicating what you see as you enter or tour the place.

Reflect on your observations. Take five minutes right after your visit to think about what you observed, and write a few sentences about your impressions of the subject:

▶ The most interesting aspect of the subject is .... because ....

▶ Although my visit confirmed that ...., I was surprised to learn that ....

▶ My dominant impression of the subject is
....

Write up your observations:

- Write a few paragraphs reporting what you observed during your visit.

- Include as many sensory details as you can.

- Think of comparisons that might capture what's special or intriguing about the subject.

- Consider the dominant impression you want to make and what impression your word choices actually make. Explore contradictions between your intentions and your words to develop a more nuanced description.

(continued)

HOW DO I CONDUCT INTERVIEWS?

Do follow-up interviews, or interview another person:

- Follow up to check facts or get clarification, but be careful not to waste your interviewee's time.
- Arrange to talk to another person who has different kinds of information to share.

HOW DO I CONDUCT OBSERVATIONS?

Consider whether you need a follow-up observation:

- Consider a follow-up visit to observe from a new angle.
- Consider a follow-up observation to visit the site at another time.

WAYS IN

HOW SHOULD I PRESENT THE INFORMATION I'VE GLEANED FROM INTERVIEWS AND OBSERVATIONS?

Review the notes from your interviews and observations, selecting the information to include in your draft and how you might present it. Consider including the following:

- **DEFINITIONS** of key terms readers will find unfamiliar
- **COMPARISONS** or **CONTRASTS** that make information clearer or more memorable
- **LISTS** or **CATEGORIES** that organize information logically
- **PROCESSES** that readers will find interesting or surprising

⊞ Use quotations that provide information and reveal character.

Good profiles quote sources so that readers can hear what people have to say in their own voices. The most useful quotations are those that reveal the style and character of the people you interviewed. **Speaker tags** (like *she said*, *he asked*) help readers determine the source of a quotation. You may rely on an all-purpose verb or a more descriptive verb to help readers imagine speakers' attitudes and personal styles:

"Try this one," he says. (Thompson, par. 7)

"Take me out to the"—and Toby yells out, "Banana store!" (Coyne, par. 21)

Adding a word or phrase to a speaker tag can reveal something relevant about the speaker's manner or provide context:

"We're in *Ripley's Believe It or Not,* along with another funeral home whose owners' names are Baggit and Sackit," Howard told me, without cracking a smile. (Cable, par. 14)

Once, after being given this weak explanation, he said, "I wish I could have done something really bad, like my Mommy. So I could go to prison too and be with her." (Coyne, par. 18)

"Are you cutting two rows yet?" Mateo asks me. "Yes, more or less," I say. (Thompson, par. 19)

In addition to being carefully introduced, quotations must be precisely punctuated. Fortunately, there are only two general rules:

1. Enclose all quotations in a pair of quotation marks, one at the beginning and one at the end of the quotation.

2. Separate the quotation from its speaker tag with appropriate punctuation, usually a comma. (Commas and periods usually go inside the closing quotation mark, but question marks go inside or outside, depending on whether the question is the speaker's or the writer's.) If you are quoting more than one sentence, be careful to punctuate the separate sentences properly.

For more about integrating quotations, see Chapter 19.

▦ Consider adding visual or audio elements.

Think about whether visual or audio elements—photographs; postcards; menus; or snippets from films, television programs, or songs—would strengthen your profile. If you can recall profiles you've seen in magazines, on Web pages, or on television shows, what visual or audio elements were used to create a strong sense of the subject? Such elements aren't required to produce an effective profile, but they can be helpful.

Note: Be sure to cite the source of visual or audio elements you didn't create, and get permission from the source if your profile is going to be published on a Web site that is not password protected.

▦ Create an outline that will organize your profile effectively for your readers.

Here are two sample outlines you can modify to fit your needs, depending on whether you prefer a **narrative** plan (to give a tour of a place, for example) or a **topical** plan (to cluster related information). Even if you wish to blend features of both outlines, seeing how each basic plan works can help you combine them. Remember that each section need not be the same length; some sections may require greater detail than others.

For more on clustering and outlining, see Chapter 11.

Narrative Plan

I.   **Begin by describing the place from the outside.**

II.   **Present background information.**

III. **Describe what you see as you enter.**

IV.   **Introduce the people and their activities.** (This may require several paragraphs.)

V.   **Tour the place.** Describe what you see as you move from one space to the next. Integrate information wherever you can, and comment about the place or the people as you go. (This may require several paragraphs.)

VI.   **Conclude with reflections on what you have learned about the place.**

Topical Plan

I.   **Begin with a vivid image of the person in action.**

II.   **Present the first topic** (for example, a trait of the person or of his or her work). Use dialogue, description, narration, process description, evaluation, or interpretation to illustrate this topic. (Presentation of each topic may require several paragraphs.)

III. **Present the second topic** (and continue as above until you have presented all topics).

IV.   **Conclude with a bit of action or dialogue.**

The tentative plan you choose should reflect the possibilities in your material as well as your purpose and your understanding of your audience. When using a narrative plan, use verb tenses and transitions of space and time to make the succession of events clear; when using a topical plan, use logical transitions to help readers move from topic to topic. As you draft, you will almost certainly discover new ways of organizing parts of your material.

▦ Determine your role in the profile.

Consider the advantages and disadvantages of the spectator and participant-observer roles, noting the examples and sentence strategies illustrating them. Then choose the role that best allows you to achieve your purpose with your readers.

WAYS IN

WHICH ROLE WILL BEST HELP ME CONVEY THE EXPERIENCE OF MY PROFILE SUBJECT?

Choose the **SPECTATOR** *role to*

- provide readers with a detailed description or guided tour of the scene.

▶ X was dressed in _____ with _____ and _____ , doing _____ as she/he _____ -ed.

▶ Inside, you could see _____ . The room was _____ and _____ .

Writing a Draft   Guide to Reading
▶ **GUIDE TO WRITING**
A Writer at Work
Reflection   **93**

Define your **PURPOSE** *and* **AUDIENCE**. Write for five minutes exploring what you want your readers to learn about the subject and why. Use sentence strategies like these to help clarify your thinking:

- ▶ In addition to my teacher and classmates, I envision my ideal readers as ⸺ .

- ▶ They probably know ⸺ about my subject and believe ⸺ .

- ▶ They would be most surprised to learn ⸺ and most interested in ⸺ .

- ▶ I can help change their opinions of X by ⸺ and get them to think about X's social and cultural significance by ⸺ .

State your main point. Review what you have written, and summarize in a sentence or two the main idea you want readers to take away from your profile. Readers don't expect a profile to have an explicit thesis statement, but the descriptive details and other information need to work together to convey the main idea.

▦ Clarify the dominant impression.

The descriptive details, comparisons, and word choices you use and the information you supply should reinforce the dominant impression you are trying to create. For example, the dominant impression of Cable's profile is his—and our—anxiety about death, beginning with his apprehension upon entering the mortuary and ending with his daring to touch a dead body. But, as Cable shows, the dominant impression need not be simplistic. Readers appreciate profiles that reveal the richness and complexity of the subject, as Cable does by describing the Goodbody Mortuary looking "a bit like a church—tall, with gothic arches and stained glass"—and "somewhat like an apartment complex" (par. 2). Although he makes fun of the crass commercialism of Howard's side of the business, Cable lets Tim make the joke instead of being the joke: becoming a mortician "'was a profession I could live with,' he told me with a sly grin" (par. 25).

HOW DO I FINE-TUNE MY DOMINANT IMPRESSION?

Identify your intended **DOMINANT IMPRESSION**. Write for five minutes sketching out the overall impression you want readers to take away from your profile. What do you want readers to think and feel about your subject?

Reread your notes and write-ups, looking for words and phrases that help convey your overall impression. In Brian Cable's profile, phrases like "His desk was bone clean" (par. 7) help reinforce the sense of death Cable associated with the funeral director. A later sentence—"His tone was that of a broker conferring on the Dow Jones" (par. 9)—complicates his initial assessment and helps create the overall impression of the funeral home and its employees as being in the business of death.

WAYS IN

Did you know?
Research shows that experienced writers reconsider and fine-tune as they reread their writing. How do you fine-tune your drafts?

(continued)

If your initial dominant impression seems too simplistic, look for any contradictions or gaps in your notes and write-ups that you can use to develop the subject's complexity. You might start with one of the following sentence strategies and elaborate from there:

▶ Although X clearly seemed _____ , I couldn't shake the feeling that _____ .

▶ Although Y tries to/pretends to _____ , overall/primarily he/she/it _____ .

Write the opening sentences.

Review your invention writing to see if you have something that would work to launch your essay, or try out some of these opening strategies:

Begin with an **arresting scene:**

> You can spot the convict-moms here in the visiting room by the way they hold and touch their children and by the single flower that is perched in front of them—a rose, a tulip, a daffodil. (Coyne, par. 1)

Offer a **remarkable thought** *or* **occasion** *that triggered your observational visit:*

> Death is a subject largely ignored by the living. (Cable, par. 1)

Start with a **vivid description:**

> On a misty evening, Rex Sunnyside approaches a dumpster, turns on the flashlight, and takes a look inside. "Ooooh . . . it's really nasty!" As she moves the light around, familiar things appear. "Oh, wow, there's a mango . . . a pear . . . look, there's a pineapple . . . and a cantaloupe . . . but it looks pretty funky!" (Moré, par. 1)

But don't agonize over the first sentences because you are likely to discover the best way to begin only after you have written a first draft.

Draft your profile.

By this point, you have done a lot of research and writing to

- develop something interesting to say about a subject;
- devise a plan for presenting that information;
- identify a role for yourself in the essay;
- explore your perspective on the subject.

Now stitch that material together to create a draft. The next two parts of this Guide to Writing will help you evaluate and improve your draft.

Evaluating the Draft: Using Peer Review

Your instructor may arrange a peer review session in class or online, where you can exchange drafts with your classmates and give one another a thoughtful critical reading, pointing out what works well and suggesting ways to improve the draft. A good critical reading does three things:

1. It lets the writer know how well the reader understands the cultural significance of the subject.

2. It praises what works best.

3. It indicates where the draft could be improved and makes suggestions on how to improve it.

One strategy for evaluating a draft is to use the basic features of profiles as a guide. Also be sure to respond to any concerns the writer has shared with you.

A PEER REVIEW GUIDE

Specific Information about the Subject

> Does the writer portray the subject in enough well-chosen detail to show us why it's interesting?

Summarize: Tell the writer one thing you learned about the subject from reading the essay.

Praise: Point out one passage where the description seems especially vivid, a quotation stands out, or another writing strategy works particularly well to present information.

Critique: Point out one passage where description could be added or where the description could be made more vivid, where a quotation that falls flat should be paraphrased or summarized, or where another writing strategy could be used.

A Clear, Logical Organization

> Is the profile easy to follow?

Summarize: Identify the kind of organization — narrative, topical, or a blend of the two — that the writer uses.

Praise: Comment on the cues the writer gives that make the profile easy to follow. For example, point to a place where one topic leads logically to the next or where transitions help you follow the tour or narrative. Also, indicate what in the opening paragraphs grabs your attention or why you think the ending works well.

Critique: Point to information that seems out of place or instances where the chronology is confusing. If you think the opening or ending could be improved, suggest an alternative passage in the essay that could work as an opening or an ending.

(continued)

The Writer's Role

Is the author's role clear, whether it is spectator, participant-observer, or both?

Summarize: Identify the role the writer adopts.

Praise: Point to a passage where the spectator or participant-observer role enables you to identify with the writer, enhancing the essay's immediacy or interest.

Critique: Point out any problems with the role — for example, if the participant-observer role becomes distracting or if the spectator role seems too distant.

A Perspective on the Subject

Does the author have a clear point of view on the subject?

Summarize: State briefly what you believe to be the writer's perspective on the subject and the dominant impression you get from the essay.

Praise: Give an example of where you have a strong sense of the writer's perspective through a comment, description, quotation, or bit of information.

Critique: Tell the writer if the essay does not have a clear perspective or convey a dominant impression. To help him or her find one, explain what interests you about the subject and what you think is important. If you see contradictions in the draft that could be developed to make the profile more complex and illuminating, briefly explain.

Improving the Draft: Revising, Editing, and Proofreading

Start improving your draft by reflecting on what you have written thus far:

- Review critical reading comments from your classmates, instructor, or writing center tutor. What are your readers getting at?
- Take another look at the notes from your interviews, observations, and earlier writing activities. What else should you consider?
- Review your draft. What else can you do to make your profile fascinating?

Revise your draft.

If your readers are having difficulty with your draft, try some of the strategies listed in the Troubleshooting Guide that follows. They can help you fine-tune your presentation of the genre's basic features.

A TROUBLESHOOTING GUIDE

Specific Information about the Subject

My readers tell me that the people do not come alive.

- Describe a physical feature, a mannerism, or an emotional reaction that will help readers imagine or identify with each person.
- Include speaker tags that characterize how people talk.
- Paraphrase long, dry quotations that convey basic information.
- Use short quotations that reveal character or the way someone speaks.
- Make comparisons.
- Use anecdotes or action sequences to show the people in action.

My readers say the place is hard to visualize.

- Name objects in the scene.
- Add sensory detail — sight, sound, smell, taste, touch, temperature.
- Make comparisons.
- Consider adding a visual — a photograph or sketch, for example.

My readers say that there is too much information, and it is not clear what is important.

- Prioritize based on the perspective and dominant impression you want to convey, cutting information that does not reinforce the perspective.
- Break up long blocks of informational text with quotations, narration of events, or examples.
- Vary the writing strategies used to present the information: Switch from raw factual reporting to comparisons, examples, or process descriptions.
- Consider which parts of the profile would be more engaging if presented through dialogue or summarized more succinctly.

My readers say visuals could be added or improved.

- Use a photo, a map, a drawing, a cartoon, or any other visual that might make the place or people easier to imagine or the information more understandable.
- Consider adding textual references to any images in your essay or positioning images more effectively.

(continued)

A Clear, Logical Organization

My readers say the narrative plan drags or rambles.

- Try adding drama through dialogue or action sequences.
- Summarize or paraphrase any dialogue that seems dry or uninteresting.
- Give the narrative shape: Establish a conflict, build tension toward a climax, and resolve it.
- Make sure the narrative develops and has a clear direction.

My readers say my topically arranged essay seems disorganized or out of balance.

- Rearrange topics into new patterns, choosing the structure that makes the most sense for your subject. (Describe a place from outside to inside or from biggest to smallest; describe a process from start to finish or from cause to effect.)
- Add clearer, more explicit transitions or topic sentences.
- Move, remove, or condense information to restore balance.

My readers say the opening fails to engage their attention.

- Consider alternatives: Think of a question, an engaging image, or dialogue you could open with.
- Go back to your notes for other ideas.
- Recall how the writers in this chapter open their profiles: Cable stands outside, in front of the mortuary; Thompson awakens in the lettuce fields, his break over.

My readers say that transitions are missing or are confusing.

- Look for connections between ideas, and try to use those connections to help readers move from point to point.
- Add appropriate transitional words or phrases.

My readers say the ending seems weak.

- Consider ending earlier or moving a striking insight to the end. (Often first drafts hit a great ending point and then keep going. Deleting the last few sentences often improves essays.)
- Consider ending by reminding readers of something from the beginning.
- Recall how the writers in this chapter end their profiles: Cable touches the cold flesh of a cadaver; Coyne watches a mother bleed after being punched by her son.

My readers say the visual features are not effective.

- Consider adding textual references to any images in your essay or positioning images more effectively.
- Think of other design features — drawings, lists, tables, graphs, cartoons, headings — that might make the place and people easier to imagine or the information more understandable.

The Writer's Role

| My readers say the spectator role is too distant. |

- Consider placing yourself in the scene as you describe it.
- Add your thoughts and reactions to one of the interviews.

| My readers say my approach to participation is distracting. |

- Bring other people forward by adding material about them.
- Reduce the material about yourself.

A Perspective on the Subject

| My readers say the perspective or dominant impression is unclear. |

- Try stating your perspective by adding your thoughts or someone else's.
- Make sure the descriptive and narrative details reinforce the dominant impression you want to convey.
- If your perspective is complex, you may need to discuss more directly the contradictions or complications you see in the subject.

| My readers don't find my perspective interesting. |

- An "uninteresting" perspective is sometimes an unclear one. Check with your readers to see whether they understood it. If they didn't, follow the tips above.
- Readers sometimes say a perspective is "uninteresting" if it's too simple or obvious. Go back through your notes, looking for contradictions, other perspectives, surprises, or anything else that might help you complicate the perspective you are presenting.

Edit and proofread your final draft.

Editing means making changes to the text to ensure that it follows the conventions of style, grammar, spelling, and mechanics appropriate to the rhetorical situation. **Proofreading** involves checking to make sure the text follows these conventions and that no words are repeated or omitted. You have probably done some editing and proofreading while composing and improving your draft, but it is always good practice to edit and proofread a draft after you have revised it and before you submit it.

Most writers get the best results by leaving time—even just an hour or two—between the stages of revising, editing, and proofreading, so they can return to their writing project with fresh eyes. When possible, enlist a friend or classmate to proofread the final draft of your writing projects. When that is not possible, proofread from the last line to the first to avoid seeing what you expect to find rather than what is actually on the page (or screen).

As rhetorical situations change, so, too, do the conventions or expectations readers bring to the text. For example, whereas e-mail messages to friends are usually quite informal, filled with abbreviations, emojis, and sentence fragments, final drafts of writing projects for college classes or the workplace are expected to follow a more formal set of conventions concerning clarity, style, grammar, and punctuation.

We recommend that you make a list of the problems your instructors frequently point out in your writing, then use that list to guide your editing and proofreading. A Guide to Editing and Proofreading (at the end of this text) provides a checklist of the most common problems writers face. For issues that go beyond those on this list, consult a handbook* or search for advice online at sites like the Purdue Online Writing Lab (owl.english.purdue.edu) or Grammarly (grammarly.com). For practice identifying and correcting errors, try the activities in LearningCurve, a gamelike adaptive quizzing program available on LaunchPad for *The St. Martin's Guide to Writing*. The less well you do on activities in one topic area, the more LearningCurve focuses on it; the better you do, the more challenging the questions become.

> **A Note on Grammar and Spelling Checkers**
>
> Spelling checkers cannot catch misspellings that are themselves words, such as *to* for *too,* and grammar checkers miss problems, give faulty advice, and even flag correct items as wrong. Use these tools as a second line of defense after your own (and, ideally, another reader's proofreading efforts).

A WRITER AT WORK

Brian Cable's Interview Notes and Write-Up

Most profile writers take notes when interviewing people. Later, they may summarize their notes in a short write-up. In this section, you will see some of the interview notes and a write-up that Brian Cable prepared for his mortuary profile, "The Last Stop," on pp. 59–65.

Cable arranged to tour the mortuary and conduct interviews with the funeral director and mortician. Before each interview, he wrote out a few questions at the top of a sheet of paper and then divided it into two columns; he used the left-hand column for descriptive details and personal impressions, and the right-hand column for the information he got directly from the person he interviewed. Following are Cable's notes and write-up for his interview with the funeral director, Howard Deaver.

Cable used three questions to guide his interview with Deaver, then took brief notes during the interview. He did not concern himself too much with notetaking because he planned to spend a half hour directly afterward completing his notes. He focused his attention on Howard, trying to keep the interview comfortable and conversational and jotting down just enough to jog his memory and catch especially meaningful quotations. A typescript of Cable's interview notes follows.

---

*The full version of *The St. Martin's Guide to Writing* includes a handbook.

Brian Cable's Interview Notes and Write-Up

Guide to Reading
Guide to Writing
▶ A WRITER AT WORK
Reflection

101

The Interview Notes

Questions

1. How do families of the deceased view the mortuary business?
2. How is the concept of death approached?
3. How did you get into this business?

Descriptive Details & Personal Impressions	Information
weird-looking	Howard Deaver, funeral director,
tall	Goodbody Mortuary
long fingers	"Call me Howard"
big ears	How things work: Notification, pick up
low, sloping forehead	body at home or hospital, prepare for
like stereotype — skin colorless	viewing, restore distorted features —
	accident or illness, embalm, casket —
	family selects, chapel services (3 in bldg.),
	visitation room — pay respects, family & friends.
	Can't answer questions about death —
	"Not bereavement specialists. Don't
	handle emotional problems. Only a
	trained therapist can do that." "We
	provide services for the dead, not counseling
	for the living." (great quote) Concept of
	death has changed in last 40 yrs
	(how long he's been in the business)
plays with lips	Phone call (interruption)
blinks	"I think we'll be able to get him in
plays with Adam's apple	by Friday. No, no, the family wants
desk empty — phone, no	him cremated."
paper or pen	Ask about Neptune Society — cremation
	Cremation "Cheap, quick, easy means of disposal."
angry	
disdainful of the	Recent phenomenon. Neptune Society — erroneous
Neptune Society	claim to be only one.
	"We've offered them since the beginning. It's only
	now it's come into vogue."
	Trend now back toward burial.
	Cremation still popular in sophisticated areas
	60% in Marin Co. and Florida
	Ask about paperwork — does it upstairs,
	lives there with wife, Nancy.

musty, old stained glass	Tour around (happy to show me around)
sunlight filtered	Chapel — large service just done, Italian.
man in black suit	"Not a religious institution — a
roses	business."
wooden benches	casket — "beautiful craftsmanship" — admires, expensive
contrast brightness	Display room — caskets, about 30 of them
fluorescent lights	Loves to talk about caskets "models for every price
Plexiglas stands	range" glossy (like cars in a showroom) cardboard box, steel, copper, bronze starting at $500, averaging $2,400. Top of line: bronze, electronically welded, no corrosion

Cable's interview notes include many descriptive details of Deaver as well as of various rooms in the mortuary. Though most entries are short and sketchy, much of the language found its way into the final essay. In describing Deaver, for example, Cable noted that he fits the stereotype of the cadaverous undertaker, a fact that Cable emphasized in his essay.

He put quotation marks around Deaver's actual words, some of them written in complete sentences, others in fragments. We will see how Cable filled these quotes in when he wrote up the interview. In only a few instances did he take down more than he could use. Even though profile writers want good quotes, they should not use quotes to present information that can be more effectively expressed in their own words. In profiles, writers use direct quotation both to provide information and to capture the mood or character of the person speaking.

As you can see, Deaver was not able to answer Cable's questions about the families of the deceased and their attitudes toward death or mortuaries. The gap between these questions and Deaver's responses led Cable to recognize one of his own misperceptions about mortuaries — that they serve the living by helping people adjust to the death of loved ones. This misperception would become an important theme of his essay.

Immediately after the interview, Cable filled in his notes with details while they were still fresh in his mind. Next, he took some time to reflect on what he had learned from his interview with Howard. Here are some of his thoughts:

> I was surprised by how much Howard looked like the undertakers in scary movies. Even though he couldn't answer some of my questions, he was friendly enough. It's obviously a business for him (he loves to talk about caskets and to point out all their features, like a car dealer kicking a tire). Best quote: "We provide services for the dead, not counseling for the living." I have to bring up these issues in my interview with the mortician.

The Interview Write-Up

Writing up an account of the interview a short time afterward helped Cable fill in more details and reflect further on what he had learned. His write-up shows him

Brian Cable's Interview Notes and Write-Up

Guide to Reading
Guide to Writing
▶ **A WRITER AT WORK**
Reflection

103

already beginning to organize the information he had gained from his interview with the funeral director.

I. His physical appearance.

Tall, skinny, with beady blue eyes embedded in his bony face. I was shocked to see that he looks just like the undertakers in scary movies. His skin is white and colorless, from lack of sunshine. He has a long nose and a low, sloping forehead. He was wearing a clean white shirt. A most unusual man—have you ever seen those Ames Home Loan commercials? But he was friendly, and happy to talk with me. "Would I answer some questions? Sure."

II. What people want from a mortuary.

A. Well first of all, he couldn't answer my second question, about how families cope with the loss of a loved one. "You'd have to talk to a psychologist about that," he said. He did tell me how the concept of death has changed over the last ten or so years.

B. He has been in the business for forty years(!). One look at him and you'd be convinced he'd been there at least that long. He told me that in the old times, everyone was buried. Embalmed, put in a casket, and paid final homage before being shipped underground forever. Nowadays, many people choose to be cremated instead. Hence comes the success of the Neptune Society and others specializing in cremation. You can have your ashes dumped anywhere. "Not that we don't offer cremation services. We've offered them since the beginning," he added with a look of disdain. It's just that they've become so popular recently because they offer a "quick, easy, and efficient means of disposal." Cheap too—I think it is a reflection of a "no nonsense" society. The Neptune Society has become so successful because it claims to be the only one to offer cremations as an alternative to expensive burial. "We've offered it all along. It's just only now come into vogue."

Sophisticated areas (I felt "progressive" would be more accurate) like Marin County have a cremation rate of over 60 percent. The phone rang. "Excuse me," he said. As he talked on the phone, I noticed how he played with his lips, pursing and squeezing them. He was blinking a lot, too. I meant to ask him how he got into this business, but I forgot. I did find out his name and title: Mr. Howard Deaver, funeral director of Goodbody Mortuary (no kidding, that's the real name). He lives on the premises, upstairs with his wife. I doubt if he ever leaves the place.

III. It's a business!

Some people have the idea that mortuaries offer counseling and peace of mind— a place where everyone is sympathetic and ready to offer advice. "In some mortuaries, this is true. But by and large, this is a business. We provide services for the dead, not counseling for the living." I too had expected to feel an awestruck respect for the dead upon entering the building. I had also expected green lawns, ponds with ducks, fountains, flowers, peacefulness—you know, a "Forest Lawn" type deal. But it was only a tall, Catholic-looking building. "Mortuaries do not sell plots for burial," he was saying. "Cemeteries do that, after we embalm the body and select a casket. We're not a religious institution." He seemed hung up on caskets—though maybe he was just trying to impress upon me the differences between caskets. "Oh, they're very important.

A good casket is a sign of respect. Sometimes if the family doesn't have enough money, we rent them a nice one. People pay for what they get just like any other business."
I wondered when you had to return the casket you rented.

I wanted to take a look around. He was happy to give me a tour. We visited several chapels and visiting rooms — places where the deceased "lie in state" to be "visited" by family and friends. I saw an old lady in a "fairly decent casket," as Mr. Deaver called it. Again I was impressed by the simple businesslike nature of it all. Oh yes, the rooms were elaborately decorated, with lots of shrines and stained glass, but these things were for the customers' benefit. "Sometimes we have up to eight or nine corpses here at one time, sometimes none. We have to have enough rooms to accommodate." Simple enough, yet I never realized how much trouble people were after they died. So much money, time, and effort go into their funerals.

As I prepared to leave, he gave me his card. He'd be happy to see me again, or maybe I could talk to someone else. I said I was going to interview the mortician on another day. I shook his hand. His fingers were long and his skin was warm.

Writing up the interview helped Cable probe his subject more deeply. It also helped him express a humorous attitude toward his subject. Cable's interview notes and write-up were quite informal; later, he integrated this material more formally into his full profile of the mortuary.

REFLECTION

The benefit of reflection is proven and important: It helps consolidate what you have learned, so that you can remember and apply it well beyond this class. That is why we have included questions and comments in the margins and at the end of each chapter: to stimulate your thinking about reviews, your rhetorical situation, and the choices you make as a writer.

Reflecting on Reading and Writing a Profile

To reflect on your experience reading profiles and writing one of your own, try writing a blog post, a letter to your instructor, or an e-mail message to a student who will take this course next term that draws on what you have learned. Use any of these writing prompts that seem productive:

- Explain how your purpose and audience—what you wanted your readers to learn about your subject from reading your profile—influenced *one* of your decisions as a writer, such as what kinds of descriptive detail you included, what method of organization you used, or the ethics of the role you adopted in writing about your subject.

Reflecting on Your Composing Process

Guide to Reading
Guide to Writing
A Writer at Work
▶ REFLECTION

105

- Discuss what you learned about yourself as a writer in the process of writing this profile. Consider what part of the process you found most challenging—for example, making detailed observations or thinking of good questions to ask people you interviewed. Did you try anything new, like participating in a peer review of your draft or outlining your draft in order to revise it? If so, how successful was it?

- Describe one way a reading in this chapter influenced your essay. For example, perhaps something you read suggested a good subject, offered a way to organize your profile, or contributed a sentence pattern that helped you express yourself.

- Discuss what you learned about profiles as a genre. For example, were you surprised by how widely examples of the genre can differ—such as Cable's tour of the mortuary and Moré's ethnographic study of dumpster diving? Was it interesting to compare Moré's and Thompson's participant observations? If you looked at the remix of Cable's profile or if you're familiar with *Radiolab* podcasts or other multimedia profiles, consider how visual and audio elements can add to the effectiveness of a profile.

Reflecting on Your Composing Process

Thinking about your process for writing a profile can be useful in helping you decide what works best for you as a writer. Using one or more of the following questions as a starting point, write a paragraph or two about your composing process:

- How did you go about choosing a subject? Did you try out a few possibilities before making a final decision? How did having to conduct interviews and observations affect your choice?

- Explain how peer review helped you—perhaps by challenging your perspective in a way that enabled you to refocus your profile's dominant impression or by pointing out passages that needed more information or a clearer chronology to better orient readers.

- Did your perspective on your subject change or deepen as you revised? What helped you gain the most insight?

- How satisfied are you with the process you used? If you could go back in time, what would you have done differently? If you could continue working on your profile, what would you like to do?

4

Explaining a Concept

How have trigger warnings morphed from a courtesy to a put-down? Are the complex feelings of love rooted in simple biology? Can games really change their players? Could shyness really be a benefit? These are the questions that are answered in the intriguing concept explanations in this chapter. Much of your reading and writing as a college student involves learning the concepts that are the building blocks of academic subjects. These concepts may include principles (such as *equal justice*), theories (such as *evolution*), ideas (such as *commodification*), conditions (such as *state of flow*), phenomena (such as *inflation*), or processes (such as *socialization*). To communicate effectively and efficiently about a subject — whether you are writing to your instructor, your boss, or your friends or writing an essay exam, a blog post, or a presentation — you need to be able to use and explain concepts clearly and compellingly.

People analyze and explain concepts for various purposes and audiences and publish them in print and online. For example, a student in a cultural studies course might use the concept of cultural framing theory as a lens through which to analyze the politics of sexuality in advertising and publish her essay in a student journal. A business consultant might create a video to define and demonstrate 3-D imaging and to explain its role to potential buyers of driverless cars.

In this chapter, we ask you to analyze and explain a concept you know from school, work, sports, or some other area of interest. From reading and analyzing the selections in the Guide to Reading (pp. 108–33), you can see how others make their explanations clear, interesting, and informative. The Guide to Writing (pp. 134–51) will show you ways to use the basic features of the genre to make your explanation not only understandable but compelling for your readers.

PRACTICING THE GENRE

Explaining an Academic Concept

Did you know?

Research shows that explaining concepts you are learning helps you learn better.

Part 1.   Get together in small groups to practice explaining a concept.

1 Think of a concept that you recently learned in one of your courses.

2 Spend a few minutes jotting down notes about how to explain the concept to members of your group, who might not know anything about it. Choose an explanatory strategy that you think would work best with the people in your group — such as providing examples of the concept they can relate to or comparing the concept to something familiar.

3 Take two or three minutes to explain your concept.

Part 2.   Discuss what you learned by explaining a concept and listening to others' explanations:

- **What did you learn about explaining?** Compare your thoughts with those of others in your group about what was easiest and hardest about explaining a concept — for example, choosing a concept you understood well enough to explain to others; making it interesting, important, or useful to group members; or deciding what would best help your audience understand the concept in the time you had.

- **What could have been added to make a concept explanation more interesting and informative?** For instance, how could the concept's importance be demonstrated or its usefulness shown?

Analyzing Concept Explanations

As you read the selections in this chapter, you will see how different authors explain concepts:

- Rosa Alexander explains the evolution of the trigger-warning meme as a reflection of today's cultural division (pp. 111–17).
- Anastasia Toufexis analyzes the biochemical basis of love (pp. 118–20).
- Lindsay Grace explains the persuasive power of play (pp. 122–25).
- Susan Cain examines the evolutionary advantages of shyness and introversion (pp. 128–31).

Analyzing how these writers develop a surprising or interesting focus for their explanation, organize the explanation to draw readers in and keep them reading, use examples and other writing strategies to make the topic compelling, and integrate sources to make their claims convincing will help you see how you can employ these same techniques to make your own concept explanations successful.

Determine the writer's purpose and audience.

How well a writer analyzes and explains a concept can demonstrate how well he or she understands it. That is why this kind of writing is so frequently assigned in college courses. But it is also a popular genre outside the classroom, where effective writers manage to make the most esoteric topics interesting and important. These authors understand that a concept explanation risks being dry and uninteresting to those not already intrigued by the topic, so they make an effort to zero in on a focus that will excite the curiosity of their readers. When reading the concept explanations that follow, ask yourself what the writer's main purpose is and what he or she assumes about the reader:

The writer's main purpose may be to

- inform readers about an important idea or theory
- show how a concept has promoted original thinking and research in an area of study
- better understand the concept by explaining it to others
- demonstrate knowledge of the concept and the ability to apply it

The writer assumes readers will

- be unfamiliar with the concept and need an introduction that will capture their interest
- know something about the concept but want to learn more about it
- evaluate the writer's knowledge of the subject and his or her ability to explain it clearly

Assess the genre's basic features.

As you read the concept explanations in this chapter, analyze and evaluate how different authors employ the genre's basic features. The examples that follow are drawn from the reading selections that appear later in this Guide to Reading.

■■ Basic Features

A Focused Explanation

A Clear, Logical Organization

Appropriate Explanatory Strategies

Smooth Integration of Sources

A FOCUSED EXPLANATION

Read first to identify the concept. Ask yourself:

- What is the focus or main point? This point is the *thesis* of a concept explanation, comparable to what we call autobiographical significance in remembered-event essays and perspective in profiles. The point answers the "So what?" question: Why are you telling me about this concept? Why is it interesting or important? For example, Lindsay Grace focuses the concept of persuasive games this way:

  "We want to enhance people's understanding of complex topics, change their perspective and encourage them to think critically about the world around them." (par. 6)

- What should I include and what should I leave out? These decisions are often dictated by readers—how much they already know about the topic and how interested in the topic they are. For college writing and some other contexts, the focus may be dictated by a specific question or prompt. For example, Rosa Alexander's instructor advised her to avoid engaging in the debate surrounding the concept of trigger warnings on campus because she could do so later in the course, when they came to Chapter 6, "Arguing a Position."

A CLEAR, LOGICAL ORGANIZATION

Consider whether the concept explanation is clearly and logically organized. Notice how each writer develops a plan that does the following:

- states the thesis or main point early on

  Let's put love under a microscope.   Concept

  When rigorous people with Ph.D.s after their names do that, what they see is not
  some silly, senseless thing. No, their probe reveals that love rests firmly on the   Main point
  foundations of evolution, biology and chemistry. (Toufexis, pars. 1–2)

- divides the information into clearly distinguishable subtopics and forecasts them in the order in which they will be discussed

  As the concept of trigger warnings has evolved, it has not only been appropriated,   Concept
  but has also been weaponized in the culture wars over victimhood and political
  correctness. To understand this process, I will look briefly at the concept's origins in   Forecast of subtopics
  trauma theory, then at how it migrated from in-person to online support groups, and
  ultimately to how it became an Internet meme. (Alexander, par. 2)

- announces the subtopics with headings (as in Alexander's and Grace's essays) or topic sentences (as in Toufexis's essay):

Subtopics

Romance served the evolutionary purpose of pulling males and females into long-term partnership, which was essential to child rearing.

While Western culture holds fast to the idea that true love flames forever . . . , nature apparently meant passions to sputter out in something like four years.

What Fisher calls the "four-year itch" shows up unmistakably in today's divorce statistic. (Toufexis, pars. 5–7)

- guides readers by providing transitions and other cues or road signs

Cue

Before the concept of trigger warnings became popular on the Internet, the term *trigger* was used in the study of post-traumatic stress disorder (PTSD) among Vietnam War veterans. (Alexander, par. 3)

Games can relieve stress in other ways, too. (Grace, par. 7)

If, in nature's design, romantic love is not eternal, neither is it exclusive. (Toufexis, par. 8)

For more on writing strategies such as definition and classification, see the chapters in Part 3.

APPROPRIATE EXPLANATORY STRATEGIES

Look for explanatory strategies—such as definition, classification, comparison-contrast, example, illustration, and cause-effect—that help readers understand the topic:

Term being defined	**DEFINITION**	According to Wiktionary, *snowflake* is the pejorative term that refers to someone who is "hypersensitive to insult or offense, usually a young person with politically correct sensibilities." (Alexander, par. 10)
Class *Distinguishing characteristics*		
Items being contrasted *Cue*	**COMPARISON-CONTRAST**	Shyness and introversion are not the same thing. Shy people fear negative judgment; introverts simply prefer quiet, minimally stimulating environments. (Cain, par. 9)
Example	**EXAMPLE**	In 1904, Lizzie Magie patented "The Landlord's Game," a board game about property ownership, with the specific goal of teaching players about how a system of land grabbing impoverishes tenants and enriches property owners. The game, which went on to become the mass-market classic "Monopoly," was the first widely recognized example of what is today called "persuasive play." (Grace, par. 1)
Cue		
Example		We can see this agenda in figure 4, a meme that makes its ideology explicit. (Alexander, par. 8)
Cause *Cue* *Effect*	**CAUSE-EFFECT**	To play a game, players must accept its rules and then operate within the designed experience. As a result, games can change our perceptions, and ultimately our actions. (Grace, par. 2)
Concept *Categories*	**CLASSIFICATION**	When rigorous people with Ph.D.s after their names do that, what they see is not some silly, senseless thing. No, their probe reveals that love rests firmly on the foundations of evolution, biology and chemistry. (Toufexis, par. 2)

SMOOTH INTEGRATION OF SOURCES

Notice how writers draw on research, as well as their own experiences and observations, to explain the concept. How do writers use quotation, paraphrase, and summary to synthesize or integrate information from different sources smoothly into the explanation? How does each writer establish the source's expertise and credibility? The following examples demonstrate some strategies:

QUOTE   "If a woman was carrying the equivalent of a 20-lb. bowling ball in one arm and a pile of sticks in the other, it was ecologically critical to pair up with a mate to rear the young," explains anthropologist Helen Fisher, author of *Anatomy of Love.* (Toufexis, par. 5)   Signal phrase

PARAPHRASE   The U.S. Department of Defense After Deployment website uses the term "trauma triggers" for anything that makes the sufferer recall an earlier horrible experience. (Alexander, par. 3)   Signal phrase

SUMMARY   Another study, by the psychologists Eric Rolfhus and Philip Ackerman, tested 141 college students' knowledge of 20 different subjects, from art to astronomy to statistics, and found that the introverts knew more than the extroverts about 19 subjects. (Cain, par. 20)   Signal phrase

How writers treat sources depends on the writing situation. Certain formal situations, such as college assignments or scholarly publications, require writers to cite sources in the text and document them in a bibliography (called a list of **works cited** in many humanities disciplines and a list of **references** in the sciences and social sciences). Students and scholars are expected to cite their sources formally because readers will judge the work in part by what the writers have read and how they have used their reading. They may also be interested in locating the sources and reading more about the topic for themselves. (Rosa Alexander's essay, below, provides an example of academic citation.) For writing that appears in popular sources, such as magazine and newspaper articles, readers do not expect references or publication information to appear in the text, but they do expect sources to be identified and their expertise established in some way. (The articles by Toufexis, Grace, and Cain, on pp. 118–20, 122–25, and 128–31, provide examples of informal citation.)

> **Take a moment . . .**
>
> Why do you think college students are generally expected to use and cite their sources?

Readings

Rosa Alexander | *The Meme-ing of Trigger Warnings*

Rosa Alexander was still a high school student when the concept of trigger warnings became controversial on some college campuses, where classmates requested trigger warnings be included in the syllabus. The students wanted to alert vulnerable

> To learn about how Rosa Alexander reworked her focus to avoid taking a position on the issue of campus trigger warnings, turn to A Writer at Work on pp. 151–52. What steps did she take to refocus her topic? How did she change her language to avoid making an argument?

classmates about course material that might "trigger" memories of traumatic experience. But when Alexander wrote her concept essay on trigger warnings, she had to think about how to explain the concept without taking a position in the debate swirling around it.

As you read,

- consider the two figures in the opening paragraph. What do they suggest about how Alexander decided to explain the concept?

- think about the impression you get from the title and headings, as well as from the opening paragraph.

- think about how effectively Alexander uses the basic features of the genre (listed below), and answer the questions in the margins; your instructor may ask you to post your thoughts and answers to a class blog or discussion board or to bring your responses to class.

█ Basic Features

A Focused Explanation

A Clear, Logical Organization

Appropriate Explanatory Strategies

Smooth Integration of Sources

How effective is this opening?

Why does Alexander use telling and showing? Why isn't showing enough?

1   The evolution of the concept of trigger warnings offers a fascinating glimpse into our divided society. The following two examples show how the concept's meaning and significance has changed over the last two decades. Figure 1 is an alert introduced in the early 1990s on feminist bulletin boards as a courtesy to readers who have suffered trauma of some kind:

> **TRIGGER WARNING** This article or section, or pages it links to, contains information about sexual assault and/or violence which may be triggering to survivors.

Fig. 1. Source: geekfeminism.wikia.com/wiki/Trigger_warning.

In contrast, Figure 2 shows how the concept has been used for the opposite purpose. Instead of being a courtesy to sensitive readers, this remix from indie author and self-described "Gun Guy" Carlos Cunha's blog makes an outright threat to the "precious little snowflake" who dares to claim she needs and deserves a warning about potentially triggering material:

Fig. 2. Source: Carlos Cunha, "A Generation of Pussies," 23 Aug 2015, carloscunha .org/tag/trigger-warning/. Attributed to samizdata.net.

Alexander *The Meme-ing of Trigger Warnings*

GUIDE TO READING
Guide to Writing
A Writer at Work
Reflection

113

2   As the concept of trigger warnings has evolved, it has not only been appropriated but also been weaponized in the culture wars over victimhood and political correctness. To understand this process, I will look briefly at the concept's origins in trauma theory, then at how it migrated from in-person to online support groups, and ultimately to how it became an Internet meme.

The Origins of Trigger Warnings in PTSD

3   Before the concept of trigger warnings became popular on the Internet, the term *trigger* was used in the study of post-traumatic stress disorder (PTSD) among Vietnam War veterans. *Trigger* refers to the stimulus that sets off painful memories, flashbacks, or panic attacks. The U.S. Department of Defense After Deployment website uses the term "trauma triggers" for anything that makes the sufferer recall the earlier horrible experience. The effects of such triggers vary widely from emotions of distress (shame, anger, fear) to physical sensations (racing heart, flashbacks, suicide).

4   PTSD became an accepted diagnosis in 1987, when the American Psychiatric Association revised the Diagnostic and Statistical Manual of Mental Disorders (DSM-III) Although the DSM-III focuses on war-related traumas, it opened the door to refer to other traumas as well. "As silly as trigger warnings and safe spaces may seem," senior editor of the *New Republic* Jeet Heer notes in his article outlining the history of PTSD, "they are rooted in genuine, widely accepted science." By acknowledging the scientific basis of trauma triggers, the DSM has given legitimacy to the widespread use of the concept.

Trigger Warnings Go Online

5   When the concept of trigger warnings was first used on the Internet, its meaning was clear and uncontroversial. Trigger warnings made an easy transition from in-person group therapy to online consciousness-raising communities because the websites were for members only. An early example is the *Ms.* magazine bulletin board, where participants were expected to use trigger warnings to ensure that someone who has had a traumatic experience, such as child abuse or rape, would know in advance that the content of a blog post or link touched on sexual violence. "Before the 'trigger warning' became the accepted way to brace readers for explicit content," *Buzzfeed*

Why does a short essay like this need a forecasting statement?

How well does this paragraph introduce the topic? What explanatory strategies does Alexander use here?

Do the sources cited seem credible? Why or why not?

Why is broadening the use of trauma triggers relevant?

How would it help to refer to Figure 1 here?

author and video producer Alison Vingiano explains, "bloggers prefaced stories with 'This might be triggering,' or 'This deals with some eating disorder stuff,' or 'Warning: potential trigger.'"

6

Why does the original intention matter?

Whatever the phrasing, the concept was intended to give viewers time to prepare themselves to encounter distressing graphic content or to allow them to decide whether to avoid the potentially triggering content altogether. In fact, Vingiano cites a 2002 post asking users to "be courteous and use an lj-cut with a warning in the text before any possible triggers [for self-harm]." An lj-cut, she explains, "allows you to hide all or part of your entry behind a link."

What do these headings contribute?

Trigger Warnings Remixed as an Internet Meme

7

What's the function of the paragraphs following the headings?

Offering a trigger warning was an established courtesy in the early 2000s. But by the mid-2000s, with the rise of Twitter, Tumblr, and Facebook, the Internet changed from a group of closed, homogeneous communities to the open, heterogeneous wild west of the current social network. As the Internet exploded wide open, trigger warnings became memes. Image, gif, or video remixed and recirculated to trivialize, mock, and advance an agenda.

8

A popular early remix of the trigger warning was the meme #*I'm triggered*, often figured as an out-of-focus gif (fig. 3):

Fig. 3. Triggered (Source: Jamie Dillon, "'Triggered'—a Personal Response to a Popular Meme," 26 Apr. 2016, www.takethis.org/2016/04/triggered-a-personal-response-to-a -popular-meme.)

Why do you think Alexander quotes Dillon rather than using her own words?

"Triggered" became pervasive on the Internet, as blogger Jamie Dillon notes, "popping up in streams, chats, and comment threads." Dillon argues that from the very beginning, the *triggered* meme was "a snarky pushback at the concept of hyper-sensitivity." We can see this agenda in figure 4, a meme that makes its ideology explicit:

Fig. 4. Any Word. This image has appeared on a variety of websites and blogs, including this one: http://www.tikihumor.com/20076/any-word-can-be-a-trigger/any-word-can-be-a-trigger-jpg.

Take a look at the words in this image that trigger the woman's fear, words such as *denim, crisp, Oklahoma*. This meme makes her distress seem "silly," to borrow Heer's word. The meme clearly ridicules the very idea of political correctness embodied in the advice to "choose your words carefully." After all, those who enforce political correctness are often called the "language police" because they urge people to avoid using words that are thought of as sexist, racist, or simply insensitive. Trigger warnings are seen by Greg Lukianoff and Jonathan Haidt, in an often cited article, "The Coddling of the American Mind," as an effort to eliminate any "words, ideas, and subjects that might cause discomfort or give offense." The absurdity of the supposedly triggering words in this meme makes political correctness seem trivial and stupid.

> How does this close analysis of the meme help Alexander explain her concept?

> How well does Alexander keep her opinion to herself? Why should she do that?

9   Here's another viral triggered meme (fig. 5) that has been recirculated and remixed so often that it has a name: "the triggered feminist." Actually, she is a real person whose name is Melody Hensley. She was diagnosed with PTSD, which she claims was caused by cyberbullying. A "feminist and atheist" who is very active on Twitter, Hensley claimed her PTSD was "as bad as mental anguish suffered by those who do active duty" (Malm). Hensley became the online poster girl of what has been labeled "the culture of victimhood" (Friedersdorf). Anger toward Hensley and what she stands for inspired a meme storm (see figs. 6 and 7, for example).

Fig. 5. "The Triggered Feminist" (Source: TripleZed, "Triggered Comics," 28 Oct. 2016, knowyourmeme.com/memes/triggered-comics; updated by Brad Kim, 13 Dec. 2016.)

Fig. 6. You Just Triggered My PTSD Card (Source: adroitefficacy, 19 Sept. 2014, imgur.com/gallery/gVqNpqT)

PTSD: The Silent Killer

I KILLED.
MY FRIENDS WERE KILLED.
DEVELOPED PTSD.
DISCHARGED FROM THE MILITARY.
CAN'T SLEEP.
CAN'T KEEP A JOB.
SPOUSE LEFT ME.
DRUGS / BOOZE KILLED WHAT'S LEFT.
DON'T REALLY WANT TO TALK ABOUT IT.

SOMEBODY CALLED ME 'SMELLODY'.
DEVELOPED PTSD.
WON'T SHUT THE FUCK UP ABOUT IT.

Fig. 7. PTSD: The Silent Killer (Source: @Lightn1ngHand, "Smellody has PTSD," Twitter, 12 Oct. 2014, 10:49 AM, twitter.com/lightn1nghand/status/521356937829838848)

Alexander   *The Meme-ing of Trigger Warnings*

GUIDE TO READING
Guide to Writing
A Writer at Work
Reflection

117

10   The same anger that was expressed in the assault weapon trigger warning meme in figure 2 at the beginning of this essay is apparent here. In the blog post accompanying figure 2, Carlos Cunha claims that the "media, universities, and public schools" are to blame for "pushing a culture of victimization" that has given rise to people like Hensley and the "snowflakes" Cunha targets. According to Wiktionary, *snowflake* is the pejorative term that refers to someone who is "hypersensitive to insult or offense, usually a young person with politically correct sensibilities." It has been used to label college students who have taken the concept of the trigger warning from the Internet to the classroom.

11   The concept of trigger warnings, as originally defined, worked in homogeneous self-help communities. The call for courtesy and empathy was welcome in a group of like-minded people. But it appears not to be welcome in a society as divided and divisive as ours seems to be today, where mocking others and threatening them seems to have become the rule rather than the exception.

> Why do you think Alexander comes back to figure 2 here?

> What makes this conclusion work (or not)?

> How appropriate are these sources in number and kind for a college-level assignment?

Works Cited

Dillon, Jamie. "'Triggered'—a Personal Response to a Popular Meme." *Take This*, 29 Apr. 2016, www.takethis.org/author/jamie/.

Friedersdorf, Conor. "The Rise of Victimhood Culture." *The Atlantic*, 11 Sept. 2015, www .theatlantic.com/politics/archive/2015/09/the-rise-of-victimhood-culture/404794/.

Heer, Jeet. "The History of PTSD and the Evolution of Trigger Warnings." *The New Republic*, 20 May 2015, *newrepublic.com/article/121866/history-ptsd-and-evolution-trigger-warnings/*.

Lukianoff, Greg, and Jonathan Haidt. "The Coddling of the American Mind." *The Atlantic*, Sept. 2015, www.theatlantic.com/magazine/archive/2015/09/the-coddling-of-the -american-mind/399356/.

Malm, Sara. "'Twitter Gave Me PTSD': Woman Claims Mean Comments and 'Cyberstalking' Gave Her an Illness Usually Suffered by War Veterans." *The Daily Mail*, 17 Apr. 2014, www.dailymail.co.uk/news/article-2605888/Woman-claims-PTSD-Twitter -cyberstalking-says-bit-war-veterans.html.

"PTS Trauma Triggers and Memories—Overview." *After Deployment*, Defense Centers of Excellence and National Center for Telehealth & Technology, U.S. Department of Defense, afterdeployment.dcoe.mil/fact/post-traumatic-stress/pts-trauma-triggers -and-memories-overview.

Vingiano, Alison. "How the 'Trigger Warning' Took Over the Internet." *Buzzfeed*, 5 May 2014, www.buzzfeed.com/alisonvingiano/how-the-trigger-warning-took-over-the -internet?utm_term=.mm0YMdgKn#.dqLqEkDw0.

Anastasia Toufexis | *Love: The Right Chemistry*

ANASTASIA TOUFEXIS has been an associate editor of *Time*, senior editor of *Discover*, and editor in chief of *Psychology Today*. She has written on subjects as diverse as medicine, health and fitness, law, the environment, education, science, and national and world news. Toufexis has won a number of awards for her writing, including a Knight-Wallace Fellowship at the University of Michigan and an Ocean Science Journalism Fellowship at Woods Hole Oceanographic Institution. She has also lectured on science writing at Columbia University, the University of North Carolina, and the School of Visual Arts in New York.

As you read, consider the following questions:

- How would you describe the tone Toufexis adopts in this essay, at least in the beginning? How effective do you think this tone was for her original *Time* magazine readers? How appropriate would it be for a college paper?

- Given her purpose and audience, how effective is the visual in helping readers understand her rather technical explanation?

Love is a romantic designation for a most ordinary biological—or, shall we say, chemical?—process. A lot of nonsense is talked and written about it.

—Greta Garbo to Melvyn Douglas in *Ninotchka*

1 O.K., let's cut out all this nonsense about romantic love. Let's bring some scientific precision to the party. Let's put love under a microscope.

2 When rigorous people with Ph.D.s after their names do that, what they see is not some silly, senseless thing. No, their probe reveals that love rests firmly on the foundations of evolution, biology and chemistry. What seems on the surface to be irrational, intoxicated behavior is in fact part of nature's master strategy—a vital force that has helped humans survive, thrive and multiply through thousands of years. Says Michael Mills, a psychology professor at Loyola Marymount University in Los Angeles: "Love is our ancestors whispering in our ears."

3 It was on the plains of Africa about 4 million years ago, in the early days of the human species, that the notion of romantic love probably first began to blossom or at least that the first cascades of neurochemicals began flowing from the brain to the bloodstream to produce goofy grins and sweaty palms as men and women gazed deeply into each other's eyes. When mankind graduated from scuttling around on all fours to walking on two legs, this change made the whole person visible to fellow human beings for the first time. Sexual organs were in full display, as were other characteristics, from the color of eyes to the span of shoulders. As never before, each individual had a unique allure.

4 When the sparks flew, new ways of making love enabled sex to become a romantic encounter, not just a reproductive act. Although mounting mates from the rear was, and still is, the method favored among most animals, humans began to enjoy face-to-face couplings; both looks and personal attraction became a much greater part of the equation.

5 Romance served the evolutionary purpose of pulling males and females into long-term partnership, which was essential to child rearing. On open grasslands, one parent would have a hard—and dangerous—time handling a child while foraging for food. "If a woman was carrying the equivalent of a 20-lb. bowling ball in one arm and a pile of sticks in the other, it was ecologically critical to pair up with a mate to rear the young," explains anthropologist Helen Fisher, author of *Anatomy of Love*.

6 While Western culture holds fast to the idea that true love flames forever (the movie *Bram Stoker's Dracula* has the Count carrying the torch beyond the grave), nature apparently meant passions to sputter out in something like four years. Primitive pairs stayed together just "long enough to rear one child through infancy," says Fisher. Then each would find a new partner and start all over again.

7   What Fisher calls the "four-year itch" shows up unmistakably in today's divorce statistics. In most of the 62 cultures she has studied, divorce rates peak around the fourth year of marriage. Additional youngsters help keep pairs together longer. If, say, a couple have another child three years after the first, as often occurs, then their union can be expected to last about four more years. That makes them ripe for the more familiar phenomenon portrayed in the Marilyn Monroe classic *The Seven-Year Itch*.

8   If, in nature's design, romantic love is not eternal, neither is it exclusive. Less than 5% of mammals form rigorously faithful pairs. From the earliest days, contends Fisher, the human pattern has been "monogamy with clandestine adultery." Occasional flings upped the chances that new combinations of genes would be passed on to the next generation. Men who sought new partners had more children. Contrary to common assumptions, women were just as likely to stray. "As long as prehistoric females were secretive about their extramarital affairs," argues Fisher, "they could garner extra resources, life insurance, better genes and more varied DNA for their biological futures. . . ."

If, in nature's design, romantic love is not eternal, neither is it exclusive.

9   Lovers often claim that they feel as if they are being swept away. They're not mistaken; they are literally flooded by chemicals, research suggests. A meeting of eyes, a touch of hands or a whiff of scent sets off a flood that starts in the brain and races along the nerves and through the blood. The results are familiar: flushed skin, sweaty palms, heavy breathing. If love looks suspiciously like stress, the reason is simple: the chemical pathways are identical.

10   Above all, there is the sheer euphoria of falling in love—a not-so-surprising reaction, considering that many of the substances swamping the newly smitten are chemical cousins of amphetamines. They include dopamine, norepinephrine and especially phenylethylamine (PEA). Cole Porter knew what he was talking about when he wrote, "I get a kick out of you." "Love is a natural high," observes Anthony Walsh, author of *The Science of Love: Understanding Love and Its Effects on Mind and Body*. "PEA gives you that silly smile that you flash at strangers. When we meet someone who is attractive to us, the whistle blows at the PEA factory."

11   But phenylethylamine highs don't last forever, a fact that lends support to arguments that passionate romantic love is short-lived. As with any amphetamine, the body builds up a tolerance to PEA; thus it takes more and more of the substance to produce love's special kick. After two to three years, the body simply can't crank up the needed amount of PEA. And chewing on chocolate doesn't help, despite popular belief. The candy is high in PEA, but it fails to boost the body's supply.

12   Fizzling chemicals spell the end of delirious passion; for many people that marks the end of the liaison as well. It is particularly true for those whom Dr. Michael Liebowitz of the New York State Psychiatric Institute terms "attraction junkies." They crave the intoxication of falling in love so much that they move frantically from affair to affair just as soon as the first rush of infatuation fades.

13   Still, many romances clearly endure beyond the first years. What accounts for that? Another set of chemicals, of course. The continued presence of a partner gradually steps up production in the brain of endorphins. Unlike the fizzy amphetamines, these are soothing substances. Natural pain-killers, they give lovers a sense of security, peace and calm. "That is one reason why it feels so horrible when we're abandoned or a lover dies," notes Fisher. "We don't have our daily hit of narcotics."

14   Researchers see a contrast between the heated infatuation induced by PEA, along with other amphetamine-like chemicals, and the more intimate attachment fostered and prolonged by endorphins. "Early love is when you love the way the other person makes you feel," explains psychiatrist Mark Goulston of the University of California, Los Angeles. "Mature love is when you love the person as he or she is." It is the difference between passionate and compassionate love, observes Walsh, a psychobiologist at Boise State University in Idaho. "It's Bon Jovi vs. Beethoven."

15   Oxytocin is another chemical that has recently been implicated in love. Produced by the brain, it sensitizes nerves and stimulates muscle contraction. In women it helps uterine contractions during childbirth as well as production of breast milk, and seems to inspire mothers to nuzzle their infants. Scientists speculate that oxytocin might encourage similar cuddling between adult women and men. The versatile chemical may also enhance orgasms. In one study of men, oxytocin increased to three to five times its normal level during climax, and it may soar even higher in women.

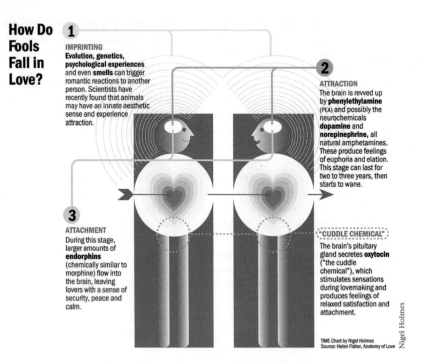

How Do Fools Fall in Love?

1
IMPRINTING
Evolution, genetics, psychological experiences and even **smells** can trigger romantic reactions to another person. Scientists have recently found that animals may have an innate aesthetic sense and experience attraction.

2
ATTRACTION
The brain is revved up by **phenylethylamine** (PEA) and possibly the neurochemicals **dopamine** and **norepinephrine,** all natural amphetamines. These produce feelings of euphoria and elation. This stage can last for two to three years, then starts to wane.

3
ATTACHMENT
During this stage, larger amounts of **endorphins** (chemically similar to morphine) flow into the brain, leaving lovers with a sense of security, peace and calm.

"CUDDLE CHEMICAL"
The brain's pituitary gland secretes **oxytocin** ("the cuddle chemical"), which stimulates sensations during lovemaking and produces feelings of relaxed satisfaction and attachment.

TIME Chart by Nigel Holmes
Source: Helen Fisher, Anatomy of Love

Nigel Holmes

16   Chemicals may help explain (at least to scientists) the feelings of passion and compassion, but why do people tend to fall in love with one partner rather than a myriad of others? Once again, it's partly a function of evolution and biology. "Men are looking for maximal fertility in a mate," says Loyola Marymount's Mills. "That is in large part why females in the prime child-bearing ages of 17 to 28 are so desirable." Men can size up youth and vitality in a glance, and studies indeed show that men fall in love quite rapidly. Women tumble more slowly, to a large degree because their requirements are more complex; they need more time to check the guy out. "Age is not vital," notes Mills, "but the ability to provide security, father children, share resources and hold a high status in society are all key factors."

17   Still, that does not explain why the way Mary walks and laughs makes Bill dizzy with desire while Marcia's gait and giggle leave him cold. "Nature has wired us for one special person," suggests Walsh, romantically. He rejects the idea that a woman or a man can be in love with two people at the same time. Each person carries in his or her mind a unique subliminal guide to the ideal partner, a "love map," to borrow a term coined by sexologist John Money of Johns Hopkins University.

18   Drawn from the people and experiences of childhood, the map is a record of whatever we found enticing and exciting—or disturbing and disgusting. Small feet, curly hair. The way our mothers patted our head or how our fathers told a joke. A fireman's uniform, a doctor's stethoscope. All the information gathered while growing up is imprinted in the brain's circuitry by adolescence. Partners never meet each and every requirement, but a sufficient number of matches can light up the wires and signal, "It's love." Not every partner will be like the last one, since lovers may have different combinations of the characteristics favored by the map.

19   O.K., that's the scientific point of view. Satisfied? Probably not. To most people—with or without Ph.D.s—love will always be more than the sum of its natural parts. It's a commingling of body and soul, reality and imagination, poetry and phenylethylamine. In our deepest hearts, most of us harbor the hope that love will never fully yield up its secrets, that it will always elude our grasp.

Make connections: How love works.

[REFLECT]

The chemistry of love is easily summarized: Amphetamines fuel romance; endorphins and oxytocin sustain lasting relationships. As Toufexis makes clear, however, these chemical reactions do not explain why people are attracted to each other in the first place. Rather, she claims that an attraction occurs because each of us carries a "unique subliminal guide," or "love map" (par. 17), that leads us unerringly to a partner. Make a short list of the qualities in a partner that would appear on your "love map," and then consider Toufexis's explanation. Your instructor may ask you to post your thoughts on a class discussion board or to discuss them with other students in class. Use these questions to get started:

- What role do factors such as family, friends, community, the media, and advertising play in constructing your love map?

- Why do you think Toufexis ignores the topic of sexual orientation?

- According to Toufexis, men typically look for "maximal fertility," whereas women look for security, resources, status, and a willingness to father children (par. 16). Does this explanation seem convincing to you? Why or why not?

Use the basic features.

[ANALYZE]

A FOCUSED EXPLANATION: EXCLUDING OTHER TOPICS

In writing about a concept as broad as love, Toufexis had to find a way to narrow her focus. Writers choose a focus in part by considering the **rhetorical situation**—the purpose, audience, genre, occasion, context, and medium—in which they are writing. Student Rosa Alexander was limited by the fact that she was writing in response to her instructor's assignment. As a science writer for *Time* magazine, Toufexis probably also had an assignment—to report on current scientific research. Her challenge, though, was to find a way to make the science interesting and understandable to her nonscientist readers.

ANALYZE & WRITE

Write a paragraph analyzing how Toufexis focuses her explanation:

1 What is the focus or main point of Toufexis's essay? How do you think she answers readers' potential "So what?" question?

2 How do the title, epigraph, and opening paragraphs help you identify this focus or main point?

3 How do you think Toufexis's purpose, audience, and genre (an article for a popular newsmagazine) affected her focus?

SMOOTH INTEGRATION OF SOURCES: ESTABLISHING CREDIBILITY

To establish their credibility on the subject, writers need to convince readers that the information they are using is authoritative. They can do this in a number of ways, but giving the professional credentials of their sources is a conventional strategy.

| ANALYZE & WRITE |

Write a paragraph or two analyzing how Toufexis establishes the credentials of her sources:

1 Skim the essay, underlining the name of each source she mentions. Then go back through the essay to highlight each source's credentials. When Toufexis provides credentials, what kinds of information does she include?

2 Consider the effectiveness of Toufexis's strategies for letting readers know the qualifications of her sources. Given her original audience (*Time* magazine readers), how well do you think she establishes her sources' credentials? If she were writing for an academic audience (for example, for your instructor), what would she have to add?

[RESPOND]

Consider possible topics: Examining other aspects of love.

Like Toufexis, you could write an essay about love or romance, but you could choose a different focus—for example, the history of romantic love (how did the concept of romantic love develop in the West, and when did it become the basis of marriage?), love's cultural characteristics (how is love regarded by different American ethnic groups or in world cultures?), its excesses or extremes (what is sex addiction?), or the phases of falling in and out of love (what is infatuation?). You could also consider writing about other concepts involving personal relationships, such as jealousy, codependency, stereotyping, or homophobia.

Lindsay Grace | *Persuasive Play: Designing Games That Change Players*

LINDSAY GRACE is an award-winning designer of games—his game Wait, 2013, entered the Games for Change Festival's Hall of Fame for its social impact over the last decade—and founding director of the Game Lab at American University, where he is also an associate professor. He has published widely on gaming and has given presentations at numerous prestigious conferences, including SXSW (South by Southwest) and the Games for Change Festival. The article that follows appeared in 2017 on the *Conversation US* website, a collaboration between professional editors and academic experts to bring ideas and information from the research community to a broader public.

As you read, consider the following questions:

- What does Grace's opening paragraph suggest about his rhetorical situation—specifically, what he assumes his readers already know about games in general and persuasive play in particular?

- Why do you think Grace begins with a historical example of persuasive play, especially in light of his focus on the new games developed by his Game Lab?

Grace *Persuasive Play: Designing Games That Change Players* ▶ **GUIDE TO READING**
Guide to Writing
A Writer at Work
Reflection

123

1 In 1904, Lizzie Magie patented "The Landlord's Game," a board game about property ownership, with the specific goal of teaching players about how a system of land grabbing impoverishes tenants and enriches property owners (Smith; Pilon, "Monopoly"). The game, which went on to become the mass-market classic "Monopoly," was the first widely recognized example of what is today called "persuasive play" (Pilon, "Lizzie Magie").

2 Games offer a unique opportunity to persuade their audiences, because players are not simply listening, reading or interpreting the game's message—they are subscribing to it. To play a game, players must accept its rules and then operate within the designed experience. As a result, games can change our perceptions, and ultimately our actions.

3 In American University's Game Lab and Studio (www.american.edu/gamelab), which I direct, we're creating a wide range of persuasive games to test various strategies of persuasion and to gauge players' responses. We have developed games to highlight the problems with using delivery drones (deliverydrone.augamelab.com), encourage cultural understanding (Jamieson et al.) and assess understanding of mathematics (Team Tangent).

4 And we're expanding the realm beyond education and health. With support from the Knight Foundation, we've been researching ways to connect

Games can change our perceptions, and ultimately our actions.

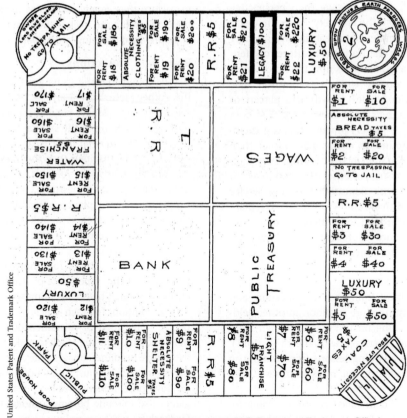

United States Patent and Trademark Office

"The Landlord's Game," the first persuasive game (U.S. Patent and Trademark Office)

games and journalism to engage people more deeply with issues in the news. (The Knight Foundation has also funded The Conversation US.) Our newest game, helping people and news organizations distinguish between real news and fake reports, is out now ("Game").

Game Play Involves Action

5 When talking about games as a persuasive tool, I often repeat the notion that readers read, viewers watch and players do. It's not a coincidence that when sitting down to learn a new game, a prospective player most often asks, "What do you do?" Persuasive play offers people the opportunity to do more than merely read or watch (Bogost)—they can engage with the game's subject matter (Grace et al.) in fundamentally valuable ways.

6   In our work, we want to enhance people's understanding of complex topics, change their perspective and encourage them to think critically about the world around them. For example, Game Lab faculty member Bob Hone worked with the National Institutes of Mental Health to create a game that is now in clinical trials as a treatment for anxiety without medication. The game "Seeing the Good Side" (Floyd) asks players to find numbers hidden in detailed drawings of classroom scenes. In the process, players practice calming themselves by looking around an entire space rather than focusing on one person's anxiety-provoking angry face.

7   Games can relieve stress in other ways, too. A recent study we conducted with Educational Testing Service (Lehman et al.) found that a game we created to replace multiple choice standardized tests offered a more positive test-taking experience for students. In addition, students were better able to demonstrate their abilities.

Turning to the News

8 Persuasive play is most common in education and health, but it's becoming more common in other fields too. We've been working on using game design techniques to get people to engage with the news (JoLT). We've also proposed adapting lessons from gaming to attract and retain audiences for news websites (Grace and Farley).

9   One project we did involved creating a game for WAMU, a National Public Radio affiliate in Washington, D.C. The station was covering public transportation failures in the city, specifically of the D.C. Metro subway and train service. We designed a game to increase audience engagement with the material.

10   WAMU sent an experienced reporter, Maggie Farley, into the field to interview a variety of Metro riders about their experience. We aggregated those stories into a single narrative and then made that story playable. In our "Commuter Challenge" (wamu.org/commuter-challenge), players have to make it through a week on the Metro system as a low-wage employee in the D.C. Metro service area. The problems facing players align with real-world trade-offs the reporter found people making: Should a worker choose a pricey ride-share service to get to the daycare in time for pickup or save money by taking the train but risk incurring fees for being late? Should a worker trust the announcement that the train will be only 15 minutes late or decline an extra shift because of rail service outages? Players have to balance their family, work and financial demands, in hopes of ending the week without running out of money or getting fired for being late to work.

Boosting Connections

11 WAMU found that the game got four times more visits than other Metro-related articles on its site. And people spent four times longer playing the game than they did reading or listening to the standard news coverage. People, it seemed, were far more eager to play a game about the plight of Metro riders than they were to hear about it.

12   Most recently, we released a game called "Factitious" (factitious.augamestudio.com/#/). It works like a simple quiz, giving players a headline and an article, at the bottom of which is a link to reveal the article's source. Players must decide whether a particular article is real news or fake. The game tells the player the correct answer and offers hints for improvement. This helps players learn the importance of reading skeptically and checking sources before deciding what to believe.

13   In addition, for each article we can see how many people understood or misunderstood it as real or fake news and how long they took to make the decision. When we change headlines, images or text, we can monitor how players' responses adjust, and report to news organizations on how those influence readers' understanding. We hope games like this one become a model for getting honest feedback from the general population.

14   While the original "Monopoly" aimed to explain the drawbacks of land grabbing, contemporary persuasive play has even grander hopes. This new generation of games aims to learn about its players, change their perceptions and revise their behavior in less time than it takes to build a hotel on Park Place.

Links

Bogost, Ian. "Persuasive Games: The Expressive Power of Videogames." MIT Press, 2007.

Floyd, Erika. "American University and NIMH Study Game Therapy as Treatment for Anxiety." *American University*, 9 Sept. 2015, http://www.american .edu/media/news/2015909_SOC_CAS_Game_Lab .cfm?_ga=2.211894611.658278306.1494972002 -1347323252.1494971299.

"Game Sets Sights on Fake News." *American University, School of Communication*, 22 May 2017, www .american.edu/soc/news/fake-news-game.cfm.

Grace, Lindsay, and Maggie Farley. "How Game Design Thinking Becomes Engagement Design." *Proceedings of the 20th International Academic Mindtrek Conference*. ACM, 2016, pp. 281–86, doi:10/1145/2994310.2994331.

Grace, Lindsay, et al. "Persuasive Content: Understanding In-Game Advertising Retention in Players and Onlookers." Foundations of Digital Games Society for the Advancement of the Science of Digital Games, Pacific Grove, California, 2015, www.lgrace.com/documents/Persuasive%20 Content%20Understanding%20In-Game%20 Advertising%20Retention%20in%20Players%20 and%20Onlookers.pdf.

Jamieson, Peter, et al. "A Simple Multi-Player Video Game Framework for Experimenting and Teaching Cultural Understanding." *Proceedings of the 20th International Academic Mindtrek Conference*. ACM, 2016, pp. 422–25, doi:10/1145/2994310.2994331.

JoLT: Innovation in Journalism through Game Design, edspace.american.edu/jolt/.

Lehman, Blair, et al. "Affect and Experience: Case Studies in Games and Test-Taking." *Proceedings of the 2017 CHI Conference Extended Abstracts on Human Factors in Computing Systems*. ACM, pp. 917–24.

Pilon, Mary. "Lizzie Magie Invented Monopoly, So Why Haven't We Heard of Her?" *The Guardian*, 10 Apr. 2015, www.theguardian.com/commentisfree/2015/ apr/10/lizzie-magie-invented-monopoly-landlords -game.

—. "Monopoly's Inventor: The Progressive Who Didn't Pass 'Go.'" Business Day. *The New York Times*, 13 Feb. 2015, www.nytimes.com/2015/02/15/ business/behind-monopoly-an-inventor-who -didnt-pass-go.html.

Smith, Monica M. "The Woman Inventor Behind Monopoly." Lemelson Center for the Study of Invention and Innovation, Smithsonian Institution, 26 Mar. 2015, http://invention.si.edu/ woman-inventor-behind-monopoly.

Team Tangent. *Function Force 4*. Office of Ed Tech, American University Game Lab and Operations Catalyst, White House Education Game Jam, White House Office of Science and Technology Policy, 6–8 Sept. 2014. *YouTube*, www.youtube.com/ watch?v=kDmpu0SwBe0.

Make connections: Your experience with persuasive play. [REFLECT]

Grace appears to assume that only certain games involve persuasive play. Think about the games you have played and whether any could be classified as persuasive. In your view, what makes a game persuasive? How does your view compare to Grace's? Your instructor may ask you to post or discuss your responses in class. Use these questions to get started:

- Grace claims that persuasive "games can change our perceptions, and ultimately our actions" (par. 2). Choose a game you've played that you consider persuasive. Which, if any, of your perceptions or actions have been affected by this game?

- Some of the games Grace refers to—such as the game that helps players learn to distinguish between real and fake news—seek to influence players' thinking about social issues. The Landlord's Game, Grace reports, had "the specific goal of teaching players about how a system of land grabbing impoverishes tenants and enriches property owners" (par. 1). How do the games you play seek to influence your thinking about social issues?

[ANALYZE] Use the basic features.

A CLEAR, LOGICAL ORGANIZATION: CUEING THE READER

Readers sometimes have trouble making their way through explanations of new concepts because the material is unfamiliar and may be complicated. To avoid having readers give up in frustration, writers strive to construct a reader-friendly organization by providing cues. Early in the essay, they usually provide an explanatory *thesis statement*, which identifies the subject, its focus, and the essay's main idea:

> The evolution of the concept of trigger warnings offers a fascinating glimpse into our divided society. (Alexander, par. 1)

Writers may also include a *forecasting statement*, which alerts readers to the subtopics in the order in which they will be introduced:

> To understand this process, I will look briefly at the concept's origins in trauma theory, then at how it migrated from in-person to online support groups, and ultimately to how it became an Internet meme. (Alexander, par. 2)

Occasionally, writers add subheadings to make it easy for readers to see at a glance how the essay is organized. Alexander includes three subheads that echo key terms in her forecasting statement:

> The Origins of Trigger Warnings in PTSD
>
> Trigger Warnings Go Online
>
> Trigger Warnings Remixed as an Internet Meme

Grace *Persuasive Play: Designing Games That Change Players*

GUIDE TO READING
Guide to Writing
A Writer at Work
Reflection

127

ANALYZE & WRITE

Write a paragraph or two analyzing the strategies Grace uses to organize his essay for readers:

1 Skim the essay, and note in the margin where he announces the concept and forecasts the subtopics he uses to organize the explanation.

2 Then highlight the passage where he discusses each subtopic. How well does the forecast work to make the essay readable?

3 Also note the subheadings Grace uses. How well do they line up with his forecast?

APPROPRIATE EXPLANATORY STRATEGIES: USING EXAMPLES

Examples are among the most common strategies writers use to explain concepts, because specific examples make it easier for readers to grasp abstract ideas. Anastasia Toufexis uses typical sentence patterns to introduce her examples:

> While Western culture holds fast to the idea that true love flames forever (the movie *Bram Stoker's Dracula* has the Count carrying the torch beyond the grave), nature apparently meant passions to sputter out in something like four years. (Toufexis, par. 6)

> Drawn from the people and experiences of childhood, the map is a record of whatever we found enticing and exciting—or disturbing and disgusting. Small feet, curly hair. The way our mothers patted our head or how our fathers told a joke. A fireman's uniform, a doctor's stethoscope. (Toufexis, par. 18)

Visuals are another kind of example. Rosa Alexander uses visuals to illustrate what trigger warnings look like online and how they have changed over time.

Main idea

Supporting example

Take a moment . . .
Toufexis uses sentence fragments intentionally here to emphasize each example. In your writing, avoid intentional fragments unless you're sure readers won't think they're a mistake.

ANALYZE & WRITE

Write a few sentences analyzing how Grace uses examples:

1 Begin with the visual illustrating "The Landlord's Game" (par. 1). What does this example illustrate? How do you know?

2 Skim the rest of the essay, looking for places where Grace includes examples of games. What do these examples show? How effectively do they illustrate the various types of persuasive play?

Consider possible topics: Explaining the differences between related concepts.

[RESPOND]

Grace's essay mentions the concepts of real and fake news, and the importance of learning to distinguish between them. You might consider explaining a set of paired concepts or opposites, like real vs. fake news, supply vs. demand, banking vs. problem-posing theories of education, or cooperative vs. competitive games.

Susan Cain | *Shyness: Evolutionary Tactic?*

Geoffrey Swaine/REX/Shutterstock

SUSAN CAIN is the author of the book *Quiet: The Power of Introverts in a World That Can't Stop Talking* (2012). She also writes a popular blog about introversion, and her TED talk has broken viewing records. Her writing has appeared in the *Atlantic*, the *Wall Street Journal, Psychology Today*, and many other publications. The selection that appears here was originally published in the *New York Times*. As you read, consider the following questions:

- Notice the title of this selection and the title of Cain's book. What do these titles lead you to expect?

- Given that this selection was first published in a newspaper, consider how effective the opening paragraph is as a hook to catch readers' attention.

1   A beautiful woman lowers her eyes demurely beneath a hat. In an earlier era, her gaze might have signaled a mysterious allure. But this is a 2003 advertisement for Zoloft, a selective serotonin reuptake inhibitor (SSRI) approved by the FDA to treat social anxiety disorder. "Is she just shy? Or is it Social Anxiety Disorder?" reads the caption, suggesting that the young woman is not alluring at all. She is sick.

2   But is she?

3   It is possible that the lovely young woman has a life-wrecking form of social anxiety. There are people too afraid of disapproval to venture out for a job interview, a date or even a meal in public. Despite the risk of serious side effects—nausea, loss of sex drive, seizures—drugs like Zoloft can be a godsend for this group.

4   But the ad's insinuation aside, it's also possible the young woman is "just shy," or introverted—traits our society disfavors. One way we manifest this bias is by encouraging perfectly healthy shy people to see themselves as ill.

5   This does us all a grave disservice, because shyness and introversion—or more precisely, the careful, sensitive temperament from which both often spring—are not just normal. They are valuable. And they may be essential to the survival of our species.

6   Theoretically, shyness and social anxiety disorder are easily distinguishable. But a blurry line divides the two. Imagine that the woman in the ad enjoys a steady paycheck, a strong marriage and a small circle of close friends—a good life by most measures—except that she avoids a needed promotion because she's nervous about leading meetings. She often criticizes herself for feeling too shy to speak up.

7   What do you think now? Is she ill, or does she simply need public-speaking training?

8   Before 1980, this would have seemed a strange question. Social anxiety disorder did not officially exist until it appeared in that year's Diagnostic and Statistical Manual, the DSM-III, the psychiatrist's bible of mental disorders, under the name "social phobia." It was not widely known until the 1990s, when pharmaceutical companies received FDA approval to treat social anxiety with SSRIs and poured tens of millions of dollars into advertising its existence. The current version of the Diagnostic and Statistical Manual, the DSM-IV, acknowledges that stage fright (and shyness in social situations) is common and not necessarily a sign of illness. But it also says that diagnosis is warranted when anxiety "interferes significantly" with work performance or if the sufferer shows "marked distress" about it. According to this definition, the answer to our question is clear: the young woman in the ad is indeed sick.

9   The DSM inevitably reflects cultural attitudes; it used to identify homosexuality as a disease, too. Though the DSM did not set out to pathologize shyness, it risks doing so, and has twice come close to identifying introversion as a disorder, too. (Shyness and introversion are

> *Shyness and introversion ... are not just normal. They are valuable. And they may be essential to the survival of our species.*

not the same thing. Shy people fear negative judgment; introverts simply prefer quiet, minimally stimulating environments.)

10   But shyness and introversion share an undervalued status in a world that prizes extroversion. Children's classroom desks are now often arranged in pods, because group participation supposedly leads to better learning; in one school I visited, a sign announcing "Rules for Group Work" included, "You can't ask a teacher for help unless everyone in your group has the same question." Many adults work for organizations that now assign work in teams, in offices without walls, for supervisors who value "people skills" above all. As a society, we prefer action to contemplation, risk-taking to heed-taking, certainty to doubt. Studies show that we rank fast and frequent talkers as more competent, likable and even smarter than slow ones. As the psychologists William Hart and Dolores Albarracin point out, phrases like "get active," "get moving," "do something" and similar calls to action surface repeatedly in recent books.

11   Yet shy and introverted people have been part of our species for a very long time, often in leadership positions. We find them in the Bible ("Who am I, that I should go unto Pharaoh?" asked Moses, whom the Book of Numbers describes as "very meek, above all the men which were upon the face of the earth"). We find them in recent history, in figures like Charles Darwin, Marcel Proust and Albert Einstein, and, in contemporary times: think of Google's Larry Page, or Harry Potter's creator, J. K. Rowling.

12   In the science journalist Winifred Gallagher's words: "The glory of the disposition that stops to consider stimuli rather than rushing to engage with them is its long association with intellectual and artistic achievement. Neither $E = mc^2$ nor *Paradise Lost* was dashed off by a party animal."

13   We even find "introverts" in the animal kingdom, where 15 percent to 20 percent of many species are watchful, slow-to-warm-up types who stick to the sidelines (sometimes called "sitters") while the other 80 percent are "rovers" who sally forth without paying much attention to their surroundings. Sitters and rovers favor different survival strategies, which could be summed up as the sitter's "Look before you leap" versus the rover's inclination to "Just do it!" Each strategy reaps different rewards.

14   In an illustrative experiment, David Sloan Wilson, a Binghamton evolutionary biologist, dropped metal traps into a pond of pumpkinseed sunfish. The "rover" fish couldn't help but investigate—and were immediately caught. But the "sitter" fish stayed back, making it impossible for Professor Wilson to capture them. Had Professor Wilson's traps posed a real threat, only the sitters would have survived. But had the sitters taken Zoloft and become more like bold rovers, the entire family of pumpkinseed sunfish would have been wiped out. "Anxiety" about the trap saved the fishes' lives.

15   Next, Professor Wilson used fishing nets to catch both types of fish; when he carried them back to his lab, he noted that the rovers quickly acclimated to their new environment and started eating a full five days earlier than their sitter brethren. In this situation, the rovers were the likely survivors. "There is no single best . . . [animal] personality," Professor Wilson concludes in his book *Evolution for Everyone* "but rather a diversity of personalities maintained by natural selection."

16   The same might be said of humans, 15 percent to 20 percent of whom are also born with sitter-like temperaments that predispose them to shyness and introversion. (The overall incidence of shyness and introversion is higher—40 percent of the population for shyness, according to the psychology professor Jonathan Cheek, and 50 percent for introversion. Conversely, some born sitters never become shy or introverted at all.)

17   Once you know about sitters and rovers, you see them everywhere, especially among young children. Drop in on your local Mommy and Me music class: there are the sitters, intently watching the action from their mothers' laps, while the rovers march around the room banging their drums and shaking their maracas.

18   Relaxed and exploratory, the rovers have fun, make friends and will take risks, both rewarding and dangerous ones, as they grow. According to Daniel Nettle, a Newcastle University evolutionary psychologist, extroverts are more likely than introverts to be hospitalized as a result of an injury, have affairs (men) and change relationships (women). One study of bus drivers even found that accidents are more likely to occur when extroverts are at the wheel.

19   In contrast, sitter children are careful and astute, and tend to learn by observing instead of by acting. They notice scary things more than other children do, but they also notice more things in general. Studies dating all the way back to the 1960s by the psychologists Jerome Kagan and Ellen Siegelman found that cautious, solitary children playing matching games spent more time considering all the alternatives than impulsive children did, actually using more eye movements to make decisions. Recent studies by a group of scientists at Stony Brook University and at Chinese universities using functional MRI technology echoed this research, finding that adults with sitter-like temperaments looked longer at pairs of photos with subtle differences and showed more activity in brain regions that make associations between the photos and other stored information in the brain.

20   Once they reach school age, many sitter children use such traits to great effect. Introverts, who tend to digest information thoroughly, stay on task, and work accurately, earn disproportionate numbers of National Merit Scholarship finalist positions and Phi Beta Kappa keys, according to the Center for Applications of Psychological Type, a research arm for the Myers-Briggs personality type indicator—even though their IQ scores are no higher than those of extroverts. Another study, by the psychologists Eric Rolfhus and Philip Ackerman, tested 141 college students' knowledge of 20 different subjects, from art to astronomy to statistics, and found that the introverts knew more than the extroverts about 19 subjects—presumably, the researchers concluded, because the more time people spend socializing, the less time they have for learning.

21   The psychologist Gregory Feist found that many of the most creative people in a range of fields are introverts who are comfortable working in solitary conditions in which they can focus attention inward. Steve Wozniak, the engineer who founded Apple with Steve Jobs, is a prime example: Mr. Wozniak describes his creative process as an exercise in solitude. "Most inventors and engineers I've met are like me," he writes in "iWoz," his autobiography. "They're shy and they live in their heads. They're almost like artists. In fact, the very best of them are artists. And artists work best alone. . . . Not on a committee. Not on a team."

22   Sitters' temperaments also confer more subtle advantages. Anxiety, it seems, can serve an important social purpose; for example, it plays a key role in the development of some children's consciences. When caregivers rebuke them for acting up, they become anxious, and since anxiety is unpleasant, they tend to develop pro-social behaviors. Shy children are often easier to socialize and more conscientious, according to the developmental psychologist Grazyna Kochanska. By six they're less likely than their peers to cheat or break rules, even when they think they can't be caught, according to one study. By seven they're more likely to be described by their parents as having high levels of moral traits such as empathy.

23   When I shared this information with the mother of a "sitter" daughter, her reaction was mixed. "That is all very nice," she said, "but how will it help her in the tough real world?" But sensitivity, if it is not excessive and is properly nurtured, can be a catalyst for empathy and even leadership. Eleanor Roosevelt, for example, was a courageous leader who was very likely a sitter. Painfully shy and serious as a child, she grew up to be a woman who could not look away from other people's suffering—and who urged her husband, the constitutionally buoyant F.D.R., to do the same; the man who had nothing to fear but fear itself relied, paradoxically, on a woman deeply acquainted with it.

24   Another advantage sitters bring to leadership is a willingness to listen to and implement other people's ideas. A groundbreaking study led by the Wharton management professor Adam Grant, to be published this month in *The Academy of Management Journal*, found that introverts outperform extroverts when leading teams of proactive workers—the kinds of employees who take initiative and are disposed to dream up better ways of doing things. Professor Grant notes that business self-help guides often suggest that introverted leaders practice their communication skills and smile more. But, he told me, it may be extrovert leaders who need to change, to listen more and say less.

25   What would the world look like if all our sitters chose to medicate themselves? The day may come when we have pills that "cure" shyness and turn introverts into social butterflies—without the side effects and other drawbacks of today's medications. (A recent study suggests that today's SSRIs not only relieve social anxiety but also induce extroverted behavior.) The day

may come—and might be here already—when people are as comfortable changing their psyches as the color of their hair. If we continue to confuse shyness with sickness, we may find ourselves in a world of all rovers and no sitters, of all yang and no yin.

26   As a sitter who enjoys an engaged, productive life, and a professional speaking career, but still experiences the occasional knock-kneed moment, I can understand why caring physicians prescribe available medicine and encourage effective non-pharmaceutical treatments such as cognitive-behavioral therapy.

27   But even non-medical treatments emphasize what is wrong with the people who use them. They don't focus on what is right. Perhaps we need to rethink our approach to social anxiety: to address the pain, but to respect the temperament that underlies it. The act of treating shyness as an illness obscures the value of that temperament. Ridding people of social unease need not involve pathologizing their fundamental nature, but rather urging them to use its gifts.

28   It's time for the young woman in the Zoloft ad to rediscover her allure.

Make connections: What's wrong with being quiet?

[REFLECT]

Cain asserts that "shyness and introversion share an undervalued status in a world that prizes extroversion. . . . As a society, we prefer action to contemplation, risk-taking to heed-taking, certainty to doubt" (par. 10). To explore these categories of introversion and extroversion and to test Cain's assertion about society's valuing one personality type over the other, think of someone you would describe as introverted and someone else who seems to be extroverted. (Include yourself, if you like.) What in particular leads you to classify these individuals as introverts or extroverts? Consider whether personality type has any effect on how other people react to them or whether they are more or less successful in school or in social or work contexts. Your instructor may ask you to post your thoughts on a class discussion board or to discuss them with other students in class. Use these questions to get started:

- What do you think are the defining characteristics of these two personality types?

- Which, if any, of these characteristics seem to be overvalued or devalued? By whom and in what contexts? Why?

- Cain raises a question about the way psychiatrists and the pharmaceutical industry may be pathologizing shyness or introversion—in other words, "encouraging perfectly healthy shy people to see themselves as ill" (par. 4). What do you think about this issue?

Use the basic features.

[ANALYZE]

APPROPRIATE EXPLANATORY STRATEGIES: USING COMPARISON-CONTRAST

Writers explaining concepts often use comparison and contrast. Research has shown that seeing how unfamiliar concepts are similar to or different from concepts we already know facilitates the learning of new concepts. Even when both concepts are unfamiliar, comparing foregrounds commonalities, while contrasting makes visible inconsistencies we might not otherwise notice.

Writers employ many strategies to signal comparisons and contrasts, including using transitions that emphasize similarity or difference, and repeating sentence patterns to highlight the differences:

Like emphasizes similarity

It works <u>like</u> a simple quiz. (Grace, par. 12)

Repeated sentence
pattern emphasizes
contrast

"Early love is <u>when</u> you love the way the other person makes you feel." . . . "Mature love is <u>when</u> you love the person as he or she is." It is the difference between passionate <u>and</u> compassionate love. . . . "It's Bon Jovi <u>vs.</u> Beethoven." (Toufexis, par. 14)

ANALYZE & WRITE

To learn more about
comparing and contrasting,
see Chapter 15

Write a paragraph or two analyzing Cain's strategies for showing contrast:

1 Find and highlight two or three of the sentence patterns Cain uses for cueing contrast in paragraphs 3–4, 9–10, 13, 18, and 19.

2 Analyze what is being contrasted and how each contrast works.

3 Why do you think Cain uses contrast so often in this essay?

SMOOTH INTEGRATION OF SOURCES: USING EVIDENCE FROM A SOURCE TO SUPPORT A CLAIM

Cain's article first appeared in the *New York Times*. So, like Toufexis whose article was originally published in a popular periodical, Cain names her sources and mentions their credentials but does not cite them, as you must do when writing a paper for a class. Although Cain does not cite her sources formally, she does integrate her sources effectively by

- making a claim of her own;

- providing appropriate, relevant supporting evidence;

- naming her source author(s) in a signal phrase (name plus an appropriate verb) and mentioning his, her, or their credentials;

- showing how the evidence supports her claim.

Look at how Cain achieves these goals:

Cain's idea

Supporting evidence

Signal phrase plus
credentials

Text linking Cain's idea with
research findings

As a society, we prefer action to contemplation, risk-taking to heed-taking, certainty to doubt. Studies show that we rank fast and frequent talkers as more competent, likable and even smarter than slow ones. **As the psychologists William Hart and Dolores Albarracin point out,** phrases like "get active," "get moving," "do something" and similar calls to action surface repeatedly in recent books. (par. 10)

| ANALYZE & WRITE |

Write a paragraph analyzing how Cain integrates source material elsewhere in her article:

1 Examine paragraphs 18–19 or 20–21 to see how Cain uses a pattern similar to the one described above.

2 Find and mark the elements: Cain's idea; the name(s) and credentials of the source or sources; what the source found; text linking the source's findings to the original idea or extending the idea in some way.

3 When writers use information from sources, why do you think they often begin by stating their own idea (even if they got the idea from a source)? What do you think would be the effect on readers if the opening sentence of paragraph 18 or 20 began with the source instead of with Cain's topic sentence?

Consider possible topics: Correcting a misunderstood concept.

[RESPOND]

Cain writes in this article about a concept she thinks has been misunderstood or misused. Consider other concepts that you think need clarification. For example, you might consider concepts such as *attention-deficit hyperactivity disorder (ADHD),* *autism spectrum,* or *transgender.* Alternatively, you might consider contested political concepts, such as *liberal, conservative, corporate personhood, American exceptionalism,* or *regime change.*

The Writing Assignment

Explain an important and interesting concept, one you already know well or are just learning about. Consider what your readers are likely to know and think about the concept, what they are likely to find interesting about the topic, what you might want them to learn about it, and whether you can research it sufficiently in the time you have.

This Guide to Writing is designed to help you compose your own concept explanation and apply what you have learned from analyzing other concept explanations. The Starting Points chart will help you find answers to questions you might have about explaining a concept. Use it to find the guidance you need, when you need it.

Did you know? . . .

When you are experimenting with a new or especially challenging genre, scaffolding like this Guide to Writing can be very helpful. But when you are writing in a genre you know well, you may not need the support of the activities here.

STARTING POINTS: EXPLAINING A CONCEPT

How do I come up with a concept to write about?

- Consider possible topics: Examining other aspects of love. (p. 122)
- Consider possible topics: Explaining the differences between related concepts. (p. 127)
- Consider possible topics: Correcting a misunderstood concept. (p. 133)
- Choose a concept to write about. (p. 136)
- Test Your Choice: Considering Your Purpose and Audience (p. 137)

A Focused Explanation

How can I decide on a focus for my concept?

- Assess the genre's basic features: A focused explanation. (p. 109)
- Conduct initial research on the concept. (pp. 137–38)
- Focus your explanation of the concept. (p. 138)
- Test Your Choice: Evaluating Your Focus (p. 139)
- Conduct further research on your focused concept. (p. 139)

How can I make my concept clear and interesting to my readers?

- A Focused Explanation: Excluding Other Topics (p. 121)
- Focus your explanation of the concept. (p. 138)
- Test Your Choice: Evaluating Your Focus (p. 139)
- A Troubleshooting Guide: A Focused Explanation (pp. 147–48)

A Clear, Logical Organization

> How should I organize my explanation so that it's logical and easy to read?

- Assess the genre's basic features: A clear, logical organization. (pp. 109–10)
- Draft your working thesis. (p. 139)
- Create an outline that will organize your concept explanation effectively for your readers. (p. 140)
- A Troubleshooting Guide: A Clear, Logical Organization (p. 148)

> What kinds of cues should I provide?

- Assess the genre's basic features: A clear, logical organization. (pp. 109–10)
- A Clear, Logical Organization: Cueing the Reader (p. 126)
- Draft your working thesis. (p. 139)
- Design your writing project. (p. 140)

Appropriate Explanatory Strategies

> What's the best way to explain my concept? What writing strategies should I use?

- Assess the genre's basic features: Appropriate explanatory strategies. (p. 110)
- Appropriate Explanatory Strategies: Using Examples (p. 127)
- Appropriate Explanatory Strategies: Using Comparison-Contrast (pp. 131–32)
- Consider the explanatory strategies you should use. (pp. 140–41)
- Use summaries, paraphrases, and quotations from sources to support your points. (p. 142)
- Use visuals or multimedia illustrations. (pp. 142–43)
- A Troubleshooting Guide: Appropriate Explanatory Strategies (p. 149)

Smooth Integration of Sources

> How should I integrate sources so that they support my argument?

- Assess the genre's basic features: Smooth integration of sources. (p. 111)
- Smooth Integration of Sources: Establishing Credibility (pp. 121–22)
- Smooth Integration of Sources: Using Evidence from a Source to Support a Claim (pp. 132–33)
- Use appositives to integrate sources. (p. 143)
- Use descriptive verbs in signal phrases to introduce information from sources. (p. 144)
- A Troubleshooting Guide: Smooth Integration of Sources (p. 150)

Writing a Draft: Invention, Research, Planning, and Composing

The activities in this section will help you choose a concept and develop an explanation that will appeal to your readers, using appropriate explanatory strategies as well as photographs, tables, charts, and other illustrations. Do the activities in any order that makes sense to you (and your instructor), and return to them as needed as you revise.

⊞ Choose a concept to write about.

List possible concepts you might write about. For the best results, your concept should be one that you

- understand well or are eager to learn more about;
- think is important and will interest your readers;
- can research sufficiently in the allotted time;
- can explain clearly in the length prescribed by your instructor.

To come up with ideas, think about the readings: Like Alexander or Cain, you could analyze a word (*spinster*, *awful*), a concept (democracy), or even a holiday (Thanksgiving) that has morphed over time. Like Toufexis, you could focus on some aspect of love or romance, such as love's cultural characteristics, its phases, or its excesses or extremes (What is sex addiction?). Or, like Grace, you could analyze an aspect of the digital world that most people think little about, such as the traits that make games addictive or that make clickbait enticing.

The following list suggests some additional concepts you could analyze:

- **Biology, nursing, and the physical sciences:** morphogenesis, electron transport, phagocytosis, homozygosity, diffusion, mass, energy, gravity, entropy, communicable diseases, epidemiology, toxicology, holistic medicine, pathogen

- **Business and economics:** opportunity cost, elasticity of demand, negative externalities, minimum wage, affirmative action, collective bargaining, robotics, flex time, family leave

- **Environment:** fracking, toxic waste, endangered species, sustainability, climate change

- **Identity and community:** multiculturalism, racism, sexism, social contract, community policing, social Darwinism, identity politics, public space

- **Literature and cultural studies:** irony, semiotics, dystopia, canon, postmodernism, realism, genre, connotation

- **Psychology and sociology:** assimilation/accommodation, social cognition, emotional intelligence, the Stroop effect, trauma, theory of mind, deviance, ethnocentrism, social stratification, acculturation, cultural relativism, patriarchy

- **Management and finance:** risk management, leveraged buyout, deregulation, branding, economy of scale, monopoly capitalism, socially conscious investing

Take a moment . . .
Why do you think you need to learn certain concepts to become literate in a particular field or area of expertise?

Evaluating the Draft

Guide to Reading
GUIDE TO WRITING
A Writer at Work
Reflection

145

Offer an **anecdote** *or* **example** *illustrating the concept:*

> In 1904, Lizzie Magie patented "The Landlord's Game," a board game about property ownership, with the specific goal of teaching players about how a system of land grabbing impoverishes tenants and enriches property owners (Smith; Pilon, "Monopoly"). The game, which went on to become the mass-market classic "Monopoly," was the first widely recognized example of what is today called "persuasive play." (Grace, par. 1)

Start with a **scenario:**

> A beautiful woman lowers her eyes demurely beneath a hat. In an earlier era, her gaze might have signaled a mysterious allure. But this is a 2003 advertisement for Zoloft, a selective serotonin reuptake inhibitor (SSRI) approved by the FDA to treat social anxiety disorder. "Is she just shy? Or is it Social Anxiety Disorder?" reads the caption, suggesting that the young woman is not alluring at all. She is sick.
> But is she? (Cain, pars. 1–2)

But don't agonize over the first sentences, because you are likely to discover the best way to begin only after you have written a rough draft.

Draft your explanation.

By this point, you have done a lot of research and writing to

- find an interesting focus and develop a working thesis statement;
- try out writing strategies that can help you explain your concept;
- create an outline for presenting that information;
- come up with ways to integrate your sources smoothly;
- try out a way to launch your explanation.

Now stitch that material together to create a draft. The next two parts of this Guide to Writing will help you evaluate and improve your draft.

Evaluating the Draft: Using Peer Review

Your instructor may arrange a peer review session in class or online, where you can exchange drafts with your classmates and give one another a thoughtful critical reading, pointing out what works well and suggesting ways to improve the draft. A good critical reading does three things:

1. It lets the writer know how well the reader understands the concept.
2. It praises what works best.
3. It indicates where the draft could be improved and makes suggestions on how to improve it.

One strategy for evaluating a draft is to use the basic features of concept essays as a guide. Also be sure to respond to any concerns the writer has shared with you.

A PEER REVIEW GUIDE

A Focused Explanation

Is the explanation focused?

Summarize: Tell the writer, in one sentence, what you understand the concept to mean and why it is important or useful.

Praise: Identify something in the draft that will especially interest readers.

Critique: Tell the writer about any confusion or uncertainty you have about the concept's meaning, importance, or usefulness. Indicate if the focus could be clearer or more appropriate, or if the explanation could have a more interesting focus.

A Clear, Logical Organization

Is the concept explanation clear and easy to follow?

Summarize: Look at the way the essay is organized by making a scratch outline.

Praise: Give an example of where the essay succeeds in being readable — for instance, in its overall organization, forecast of topics, or use of transitions to cue readers.

Critique: Identify places where readability could be improved — for example, the beginning made more appealing, a topic sentence made clearer, or transitions or headings added.

Appropriate Explanatory Strategies

Are writing strategies used effectively to analyze and explain the concept?

Summarize: Note which explanatory strategies the writer uses, such as definition, comparison, example, cause-effect, classification, or process analysis.

Praise: Point to an explanatory strategy that is especially effective, and highlight research that is particularly helpful in explaining the concept.

Critique: Point to any places where a definition is needed, where more (or better) examples might help, or where another explanatory strategy could be improved or added. Note where a visual (such as a flowchart or graph) would make the explanation clearer.

Smooth Integration of Sources

Are sources incorporated into the essay effectively?

Summarize: Note each source mentioned in the text, and check to make sure it appears in the list of works cited, if there is one. Highlight signal phrases and in-text citations, and identify appositives used to provide experts' credentials.

Praise: Give an example of the effective use of sources — a particularly well-integrated quotation, paraphrase, or summary that supports and illustrates the point. Note any especially descriptive verbs used to introduce information.

Critique: Point out where experts' credentials are needed. Indicate quotations, paraphrases, or summaries that could be more smoothly integrated or more fully interpreted or explained. Suggest verbs in signal phrases that may be more appropriate.

Improving the Draft

Guide to Reading
▶ **GUIDE TO WRITING**
A Writer at Work
Reflection

147

Improving the Draft: Revising, Editing, and Proofreading

Start improving your draft by reflecting on what you have written thus far:

- Review critical reading comments from your classmates, instructor, or writing center tutor: What problems do your readers identify?

- Take another look at the notes from your earlier research and writing activities: What else should you consider?

- Review your draft: What else can you do to make your explanation more effective?

Revise your draft.

If your readers are having difficulty with your draft, or if you think there is room for improvement, try some of the strategies listed in the Troubleshooting Guide that follows. They can help you fine-tune your presentation of the genre's basic features.

A TROUBLESHOOTING GUIDE

A Focused Explanation

My readers think that my topic seems thin, that I don't have enough to write about. (The focus is too narrow.)

- Broaden your concept by adding scientific, cultural, or historical comparisons and contrasts.
- Use reference sources to look up your concept in order to find more expansive subject terms.
- Conduct a Web search using the name of your concept and *overview* or *definition*. Use the Advanced Search feature to focus on sites with *.edu, .gov,* or *.org* domains.
- If your concept comes from another course you are taking, check your textbook or lecture notes for broader related topics.

(continued)

A Focused Explanation

> My readers don't find my focus interesting.

- Conduct additional research, focusing on finding information likely to be of value and interest to your readers.
- Consider how you can answer your readers' "So what?" question—perhaps by showing them how they can use the concept; building on their interests or what they already know; or clarifying their mistaken, faulty, or outdated assumptions or ideas.
- Consider using humor, anecdotes, or visuals to engage readers' interest.
- Ask yourself whether the focus is interesting to you. If it isn't, choose a different focus. If it is, ask yourself how you can communicate your enthusiasm to your readers — perhaps with anecdotes, examples, or illustrations.

A Clear, Logical Organization

> My readers don't find my organization clear and logical.

- Reread your thesis statement to be sure that it clearly announces the concept and perhaps forecasts the subtopics.
- Outline your material to be sure that it is divided into separate subtopics that are presented in a logical order.

> My readers say that the beginning doesn't capture their interest.

- Review your opening paragraphs to be sure that you clearly introduce your concept and your focus.
- Try starting with an anecdote, an interesting quotation, a surprising aspect of the concept, a concrete example, or a similar lead-in.
- Consider stating explicitly what makes the concept worth thinking about and how it relates to your readers' interests.

> My readers feel that the essay doesn't flow smoothly from one part to the next.

- Outline your essay, dividing it into major parts — introduction, main topics, and conclusion. Reread the end of each major part and the beginning of the next to make sure you have provided transitions or other cues (the strategic repetition of words or phrases, use of synonyms, rhetorical questions). If there are none, add some.
- Consider adding headings to make the topical sections easier to identify.

> My readers find that the ending falls flat.

- Consider ending by speculating on what the future will bring — how the concept might be redefined, for example.
- Consider relating the ending to the beginning — for example, by recalling an example or a comparison.

Appropriate Explanatory Strategies

My readers don't understand my explanation.

- Consider whether you have used the most appropriate writing strategies for your topic — defining, classifying, comparing and contrasting, narrating, illustrating, describing, or explaining cause and effect.
- Recheck your definitions for clarity. Be sure that you have explicitly defined any key terms your readers might not know.
- Add cues (transitional words and phrases, strategic repetition, rhetorical questions, and so on).
- Add headings and bulleted or numbered lists to help readers follow the discussion.

My readers want more information about certain aspects of the concept.

- Expand or clarify definitions by adding examples or using appositives.
- Add examples or comparisons and contrasts to relate the concept to something readers already know.
- Conduct additional research on your topic, and cite it in your essay.

My readers think visuals would help them better understand the concept.

- Check whether your sources use visuals (tables, graphs, drawings, photographs, and the like) that might be appropriate for your explanation. If you are publishing your concept explanation online, consider including video clips, audio files, and animated graphics as well.
- Consider drafting your own charts, tables, or graphs, or adding your own photographs or illustrations.

My readers think my summaries are vague, my paraphrases are too complicated, or my quotations are too long or uninteresting.

- Revise the summaries to emphasize a single key idea.
- Restate the paraphrases more succinctly, omitting irrelevant details. Consider quoting important words.
- Quote only a few memorable words or phrases from a source.

My readers aren't sure how source information supports my explanation of the concept.

- Check to be sure that you have appropriately commented on all cited material, making its relation to your own ideas absolutely clear.
- Expand or clarify accounts of research that your readers find unconvincing for reasons other than the credibility of the source.

(continued)

Smooth Integration of Sources

> My readers think that the quotations, summaries, and paraphrases don't flow smoothly with the rest of the essay.

- Reread all passages in which you quote sources. Ask yourself whether you provide enough context or clearly establish the author's credentials.
- Use signal phrases to place sources in context. Consider using descriptive verbs in signal phrases to give your readers more information about what your source is saying and why you are referring to it.
- Use appositives to integrate information about your sources smoothly and clearly.

> My readers are concerned that my list of sources is too limited.

- Do additional research to balance your list, taking particular care that you have an adequate number of credible sources.
- If you have difficulty finding sources, ask your instructor or a librarian for help.

> My readers wonder whether my sources are credible.

- Clearly identify all sources, and fully state the credentials of all cited authorities, using appositives where appropriate.
- Eliminate sources that are clearly identified and well integrated but that are not relevant, credible, or otherwise appropriate.

A Note on Grammar and Spelling Checkers

Spelling checkers cannot catch misspellings that are themselves words, such as *to* for *too*, and grammar checkers miss problems, give faulty advice, and even flag correct items as wrong. Use these tools as a second line of defense after your own (and, ideally, another reader's) proofreading efforts.

Edit and proofread your final draft.

Editing means making changes to the text to ensure that it follows the conventions of style, grammar, spelling, and mechanics appropriate to the rhetorical situation. **Proofreading** involves checking to make sure the text follows these conventions and that no words are repeated or omitted. You have probably done some editing and proofreading while composing and improving your draft, but it is always good practice to edit and proofread a draft after you have revised it and before you submit it.

Most writers get the best results by leaving time — even just an hour or two — between the stages of revising, editing, and proofreading, so that they can return to their writing project with fresh eyes. When possible, enlist a friend or classmate to proofread the final draft of your writing projects. When that is not possible, proofread from the last line to the first, to avoid seeing what you expect to find rather than what is actually on the page (or screen).

As rhetorical situations change, so, too, do the conventions or expectations readers bring to the text. For example, whereas e-mail messages to friends are usually quite informal, filled with abbreviations, emojis, and sentence fragments, final drafts of writing projects for college classes or workplaces are expected to follow a more formal set of conventions concerning clarity, style, grammar, and punctuation.

Rosa Alexander Focuses Her Concept Explanation

Guide to Reading
Guide to Writing
▶ **A WRITER AT WORK**
Reflection

151

We recommend that you make a list of the problems your instructors frequently point out in your writing, then use that list to guide your editing and proofreading. A Guide to Editing and Proofreading at the end of this text provides a check-list of the most common problems writers face. For issues that go beyond those on this list, consult a handbook* or search for advice online at sites like the Purdue Online Writing Lab (owl.english.purdue.edu) or Grammarly (grammarly.com). For practice identifying and correcting errors, try the activities in LearningCurve, a gamelike adaptive quizzing program available on LaunchPad for *The St. Martin's Guide to Writing*. The less well you do on activities in one topic area, the more LearningCurve focuses on it; the better you do, the more challenging the questions become.

A WRITER AT WORK

Rosa Alexander Focuses Her Concept Explanation

As the headnote to her essay explains, Rosa Alexander knew about trigger warnings before she wrote about them in her freshman composition course. In fact, she had a strong opinion about the controversy surrounding the proposal to give students trigger warnings. So when she began work on her concept essay, she found herself expressing her opinion rather than explaining a concept.

Alexander's instructor became aware of this problem during an in-class Test Your Choice activity. Students gathered in small groups, taking turns telling group members what aspect of the concept they intended to focus on and why they thought their readers would be interested. Alexander told her group that she thought her readers—whom she identified as her classmates—would be interested in the focus she planned to use: why trigger warnings should be required in college syllabi. Her instructor, overhearing the lively discussion that erupted in Alexander's group, joined the group and quickly realized he needed to say something—not just to Alexander or her group but to the class as a whole.

Using Alexander's focus statement as an example, he explained the difference between the genre of concept explanation and that of arguing an opinion on a controversial issue. After class, Alexander told the instructor she now understood why her focus was wrong, but she didn't see how she could focus an explanation of trigger warnings. Her instructor told her to make a list of possible ways of focusing the concept and to bring the list to the next day's office hour.

---

* The full version of *The St. Martin's Guide to Writing* includes a handbook.

To make a list, Alexander spent several hours on the Internet searching trigger warnings. Here is the list she brought to the meeting:

- The origin of trigger warnings in trauma study (PTSD)
- How a warning on the syllabus helps students who have experienced trauma
- Why trigger warnings are so controversial nowadays
- Social media and trigger warnings
- Politics and trigger warnings

Alexander discussed her list with her instructor, trying to figure out which topics would lead to a concept explanation rather than an argument. One of the topics that aroused her instructor's curiosity was the one about social media. Alexander showed him some of the outrageous images people were remixing and circulating. Both Alexander and her instructor believed this focus could work; plus, she could use some of the images she had found as examples.

Alexander left the office feeling energized. She thought she had a unique take on the concept of trigger warnings—something she had not thought of before that would be sure to interest her readers.

REFLECTION

The benefit of reflection is proven and important: It helps consolidate what you have learned so that you can remember and apply it well beyond this class. That is why we have included questions and comments in the margins and at the end of this chapter: to stimulate your thinking about explaining a concept, your rhetorical situation, and the choices you make as a writer.

Reflecting on Reading and Writing a Concept Analysis

To reflect on your experience reading concept analyses and writing one of your own, try writing a blog post, a letter to your instructor, or an e-mail message to a student who will take this course next term that draws on what you have learned. Use any of these writing prompts that seem productive:

- Explain how what you wanted your readers to learn by reading your concept analysis influenced *one* of your decisions as a writer, such as how you focused the concept analysis, organized your explanation, used writing strategies to convey information, or integrated sources into your essay.

Reflecting on Your Composing Process

Guide to Reading
Guide to Writing
A Writer at Work
▶ **REFLECTION**

153

- Discuss what you learned about yourself as a writer through the process of writing a concept analysis. Consider what part of the process you found most challenging—for example, choosing a focus or making the concept accessible and engaging to your reader. Did you try anything new, like imitating a strategy you noticed in a reading selection or reworking your introduction and conclusion so that they worked together effectively? If so, how successful was it?

- Describe one way a reading in this chapter influenced your essay. For example, perhaps something you read suggested a good concept to analyze, offered a way to engage your readers or explain why the concept matters, or contributed a sentence pattern that helped you express yourself.

- Consider what you learned about concept analyses as a genre. How are the concept explanations that you are familiar with from your classes similar to or different from the concept explanations that you read in this chapter? How might concept analyses change in relation to the rhetorical situation? For example, how would you present your concept as a podcast rather than an essay?

For more on multimodal composing, see Chapter 22.

Reflecting on Your Composing Process

Thinking about your process for writing a concept analysis can be useful in helping you decide what works best for you as a writer. Using one or more of the following questions as a starting point, write a paragraph or two about your composing process:

- How did you go about choosing a concept to analyze and explain? Did you choose a topic that you had learned about in class or one that relates to a personal interest? How did having to conduct research affect your choice? Did you have trouble finding appropriate sources?

- While conducting research on the concept, did you discover that some of the information had been challenged by experts, or did the body of knowledge seem settled and established? How did you decide what information might seem new or even surprising to readers? How did you integrate evidence from sources to support your own analysis?

- Explain how revising helped you shape your concept analysis, perhaps by giving you the opportunity to find a more engaging beginning, sharpen your focus, integrate information from sources more smoothly, or tweak your use of transitions.

- How satisfied are you with the process you used? If you could go back in time, what would you have done differently? If you could continue working on your concept analysis, what would you like to do?

5

Analyzing and Synthesizing Opposing Arguments

S hould conservative, even alt-right, speakers be allowed to address college students on campus? Should people be compensated for donating a kidney for transplant? Should citizens and noncitizens be required to carry proof that they are in the United States legally? Should college athletes be paid to play? Debates on issues like these are rampant online, at work, and in college classrooms. Whether you want to participate in the debate or simply educate yourself, a good place to start is by researching and analyzing the opposing arguments. This kind of intellectual work is done by individuals at their home computers; by community and business leaders in public forums; by professors in academic journals and at conferences; and by students in class reports, research projects, and oral presentations.

In this chapter, the main purpose of your analysis and synthesis is *explanatory*: to help your audience understand a controversial issue as well as how and why people argue different points of view. In Chapters 6–10, you will use these tools as you enter the debate to argue for your own

- point of view on a controversial issue (Chapter 6)
- solution to a problem (Chapter 7)
- evaluation and the criteria on which it is based (Chapter 8)
- preferred cause or effect (Chapter 9)
- analysis of a work of literature (Chapter 10)

The essays by students Max King (pp. 160–64) and Maya Gomez (pp. 165–67) in the Guide to Reading illustrate some of the strategies you might use in your own writing. The Guide to Writing (pp. 171–86) will show you ways to plan and compose your essay, possibly by constructing an annotated bibliography of background sources, analyzing the essays to identify their main arguments, and completing a comparative analysis to synthesize opposing arguments.

| PRACTICING THE GENRE |

Analyzing Opposing Arguments

Explore how people typically argue about a controversial issue.

Part 1.   With two or three other students, choose a controversial issue with which you are all familiar, such as paying college athletes, requiring community service for college graduation, and making college tuition-free for in-state students at public colleges and universities.

1 List several reasons for and against the position. For example:

- **Pro:** College should be paid for in the same way that public school is from kindergarten through twelfth grade. Well-educated voters are needed to keep our democracy healthy and our economy strong. Therefore, free public education benefits everyone.

- **Con:** Making public colleges and universities free would raise taxes for everyne, but only benefit students who attend public schools. Also, not paying for your own education undermines its value.

2 Speculate about whose interests, values, or beliefs are served by the different pro and con positions. Present your issue, the pro and con lists your group has come up with, and the reasons, interests, and values you think motivate each position.

Part 2.   Discuss what you learned by thinking about the reasons for and against a controversial issue:

- **What did you learn about the reasons and values motivating a position?** Was it easier to come up with pro or con arguments for values you shared? How did you come up with reasons for positions that differed from your own?

- **What did you learn about the genre from listening to others' analyses?** Were you more convinced by the pro or con arguments? Were you surprised by the values groups suggested underlay one position or the other?

Analyzing Opposing Arguments

This chapter differs from the ones that came before in that there are only two examples, essays by students Max King and Maya Gomez. Each essay focuses on two opposing arguments. King's essay addresses an issue that affects many college students: provocateurs speaking on college campuses. Gomez's essay examines a health crisis faced by people across America and around the world: the lack of organs available for transplant.

In these essays, you will see how both King and Gomez attempt to answer these basic questions:

- What is the crux of the disagreement?
- What values, ideas, or concerns drive the disagreement?
- Who benefits from or whose interests are served by the arguments on each side?

As you read, notice how King and Gomez try to remain fair and impartial in their essays, saving their opinions for the position essays they would write next.

Determine the writer's purpose and audience.

College courses throughout the curriculum require students to analyze and synthesize opposing points of view because these are fundamental critical-thinking skills, necessary for research, reading, and writing. They are also essential for thoughtful participation in our democracy as well as for many kinds of work. As you read Max King's essay and other analyses, ask yourself questions like these about the writer's purpose and audience:

The writer's main purpose may be to	The writer wants readers to react by
<ul><li>clarify the opposing arguments</li><li>pinpoint the crux of the disagreement</li><li>probe the underlying values, ideas, or beliefs on which people base their opinion of the issue</li><li>reveal who benefits from or whose interests are served by each side in the debate</li></ul>	<ul><li>understanding the opposing arguments</li><li>gaining insight into the disagreement</li><li>recognizing the values, ideas, or beliefs that underlie people's views on the issue</li><li>assessing the arguments in light of who benefits or whose interests are being served</li></ul>

Assess the genre's basic features.

Basic Features

An Informative Introduction

A Probing Analysis

A Fair and Impartial Presentation

A Clear, Logical Organization

As you read Max King's and Maya Gomez's comparative analyses, consider how they use the basic features to analyze and synthesize opposing arguments on a controversial issue.

AN INFORMATIVE INTRODUCTION

Read first to see how the issue is presented. Consider, for example, whether the writer assumes that readers are already well informed about the issue or need background information and whether they will be interested in the issue or will need to have their interest piqued. To inform and interest readers, writers in this genre often provide historical context, using a simple sentence strategy like this:

▪ On/in [date/year(s)], when _____ occurred [describe events or provide historical context], Author A voiced strong opinions about _____ [name controversy].

In the following example, Max King provides historical context for the controversy over the issue of what constitutes free speech on campus:

> From spring through fall of 2017, several universities across the nation were rocked by conflicts over who should and should not be allowed to speak on campus. Protests erupted on campuses from Auburn to UC Berkeley, igniting a war of words over the limits of free speech. (par. 1)

Consider how the authors of both arguments are described. Writers typically provide a brief description of the authors' background to help readers make judgments about the trustworthiness of each side in the debate, using a sentence strategy like this:

▪ "_____" [article title], published by Author A, a professor/researcher/business leader at institution/business B, appeared in Publication C, and the piece by Author X, a professor/researcher/business leader at institution/business Y, was published at Web site Z.

To learn more about contextualizing an issue, see Chapter 12.

EXAMPLE The first essay is a *New York Times* op-ed by NYU college administrator and professor Ulrich Baer, and the second was published . . . by a well-respected journalist, blogger, and editor at Reason.com, Robby Soave. (King, par. 3)

> Publication source
> Credentials
> Name

Most important, notice how the opposing positions are summarized and contrasted, as in this example from Gomez's comparative analysis, which makes clear the different perspectives:

EXAMPLE Whereas the NKF defends the status quo and urges retention of the valuable consideration clause, Satel deplores the "woeful inadequacy of our nation's transplant policy" and proposes "rewards" to "encourage more living and posthumous donation." (par. 3)

> Cues contrast
> Opposing positions

A PROBING ANALYSIS

Look for passages in which the opposing arguments are represented. To represent the arguments clearly and accurately, writers of essays that analyze and synthesize arguments usually rely heavily on **quotation**, although they may also use **summary** (giving the gist of the writer's argument) and **paraphrase** (putting the writer's argument into their own words), as we can see from the way King presents Baer's argument in paragraph 8:

> First, he is talking about hate speech. Although he doesn't use the term, his point is clear: Describing groups of people as "inferior to others, or illegal or unworthy of legal standing," is dehumanizing. Essentially, Baer suggests that the very speech campus provocateurs wish to protect is being used to diminish the rights of other, more marginalized groups to be respected as equal citizens.

> Summary
> Quotation
>
> Paraphrase

Examine the analysis and synthesis of the points of disagreement, and ask yourself how well the analysis helps you understand the disagreement as well as what may be motivating each side's arguments. For example, see if basic values are discussed, and look for words—such as *contention, concession,* or *rebuttal*—identifying the moves each writer is making:

Move Values and beliefs	This is the central point of disagreement between Soave and Baer. Baer contends that by demeaning and silencing people, hate speech makes debate impossible. Although Soave concedes that discriminatory speech "may be wrong and legitimately hurtful," he denies that such speech inherently threatens the rights of those who are denigrated by it. (King, par. 9)

A FAIR AND IMPARTIAL PRESENTATION

Determine whether the writer comes across as fair and impartial in presenting the opposing points of view. To win and hold readers' confidence, the writer's analysis needs to be thoughtful and unbiased. To achieve this, writers normally

- refrain from taking a position on the issue;
- avoid judging either side's arguments;
- use neutral or speculative language;
- give roughly equal attention to both views.

For example, writers will use neutral verbs to describe what was said:

- X claims ⸻.
- Y holds that ⸻.

EXAMPLE   Whereas Baer argues that these opposing values need to be balanced, Soave maintains that individual rights should be valued more highly than promoting the common good. (King, par. 5)

Writers of comparative analysis may also use conjecture, making clear that they are making an interpretation or inference that may not be accurate:

- X appears to assume that ⸻.
- Y may think that ⸻.

EXAMPLE   I suppose Baer could respond to this critique by characterizing Soave's slippery slope argument as a logical fallacy. (King, par. 10)

Another strategy writers sometimes use to make their analysis impartial is to quote one writer's criticism of the other or to bring in another expert to support a critique:

- X rebuts Y's argument by ⸻.
- Whereas X asserts ⸻, Y counters with ⸻.

Take a moment . . .
Why would writers analyzing opposing arguments try to come across as fair and impartial? If you have a strong opinion on an issue, how hard would it be for you to write impartially?

EXAMPLE   Even economics professors Gary S. Becker and Julio J. Elias, who have defended compensation, agree with the NKF that not only would a free market lead to a decline in kidney donation, but it would also exploit the poor. However, Becker and Elias see a remedy in what Satel calls "good policy." (Gomez, par. 13)

A CLEAR, LOGICAL ORGANIZATION

Examine the strategies the writer uses to make the points of agreement and disagreement clear and easy to follow, such as providing a clear *thesis* and *forecasting statement* announcing the areas of disagreement that the essay will focus on, and repeating the key terms (or synonyms for them) in headings or topic sentences:

> While Baer contends that white nationalist provocateurs should not be invited to campus or allowed to speak, Soave claims that preventing them from speaking denies their right to freedom of speech. At the heart of their disagreement is their radically different idea about whether freedom of speech is an absolute and unchanging individual right or a public good that has to be regularly adjusted to be fair to everyone. They also disagree over whether limiting freedom of speech or allowing it to be unlimited is the greater danger to democracy. (King, par. 3)

Cue signaling disagreement

Forecast of key topics

> **Consider . . .**
> How important are comparison and contrast cues in writing about opposing arguments?

Finally, *look for cues signaling comparison and contrast* of the two opposing points of view:

- Both X and Y agree that ⸏⸏⸏⸏⸏⸏ .
- Although X argues ⸏⸏⸏⸏⸏⸏ , Y contends ⸏⸏⸏⸏⸏⸏ .

EXAMPLE   Both appear to agree that exploitation of the poor would result. But whereas the NKF appears to think this problem is inescapable as well as inevitable, Satel seems to be confident that it could be handled administratively. (Gomez, par. 12)

Comparison cue
Contrast cue

Readings

The following essays by students Max King and Maya Gomez analyze opposing arguments on controversial issues. Whereas King is writing about free speech on college campuses, Gomez is addressing the law that prohibits paying kidney donors. Their topics differ, but they use similar strategies to analyze and synthesize the opposing arguments so that readers will better understand these debates and why they are important. By reading these essays, you will learn a good deal about how to write a comparative analysis of your own.

Max King | *Freedom of or from Speech*

To see how Max King developed his analysis of the opposing arguments, turn to the Writer at Work section on pp. 187–88.

In this essay, Max King writes about several incidents in which controversial speakers who were invited to give speeches at college campuses were met by student protests. The incidents led to a lively debate in print and online over freedom of speech on college campuses and whether hate speech should be protected as free speech. For his essay analyzing opposing arguments on this controversy, King used two position essays: Ulrich Baer's *New York Times* op-ed "What 'Snowflakes' Get Right about Free Speech" and Robby Soave's Reason.com blog post "Liberals Are Amazed That Campus Free Speech Outrage Gets So Much Attention; Here's Why It Matters."

As you read,

- think about the epigraph King uses to begin his essay. Why do you think he quotes the First Amendment?
- notice the two headings. What is their purpose?
- answer the questions in the margins. Your instructor may ask you to post your responses or bring them to class.

Basic Features

An Informative Introduction

A Probing Analysis

A Fair and Impartial Presentation

A Clear, Logical Organization

How well does this description arouse readers' interest?

Why do you think King cites sources here?

Why is it useful to know what others said?

Congress shall make no law . . . abridging the freedom of speech.

—First Amendment, Constitution of the United States

1   From spring through fall of 2017, several universities across the nation were rocked by conflicts over who should and should not be allowed to speak on campus. Protests erupted on campuses from Auburn to UC Berkeley, igniting a war of words over the limits of free speech. Some of the speakers who were banned from campus or whose visits were protested against were rabble-rousers—for example, the self-described white supremacist Richard Spencer (Reilly), Internet troll Milo Yiannopoulos (Steinmetz), and conservative firebrand Ann Coulter (McLaughlin)—who wanted to provoke the kinds of reactions they received.

2   What happened in 2017 appears to mark a turning point in the debate about freedom of speech, especially on college campuses. Some commentators accused student protesters of being "snowflakes" who can't handle a free and open exchange of different points of view (McLaughlin). Others countered that freedom of speech should not be a justification for hate speech—speech that dehumanizes and silences disempowered groups (Nielsen).

3   This essay examines the debate by analyzing two essays published during campus
protests at UC Berkeley. The first essay is a *New York Times* op-ed by NYU college
administrator and professor Ulrich Baer, and the second was published the following day
by a well-respected journalist, blogger, and editor at Reason.com, Robby Soave, who
specifically singled out Baer's arguments for response. While Baer contends that white
nationalist provocateurs should not be invited to campus or allowed to speak, Soave
claims that preventing them from speaking denies their right to freedom of speech.
At the heart of their disagreement is their radically different idea about whether
freedom of speech is an absolute and unchanging individual right or a public good that
has to be regularly adjusted to be fair to everyone. They also disagree over whether
limiting freedom of speech or allowing it to be unlimited is the greater danger to
democracy. As the country becomes increasingly polarized and campuses continue to be
an important front in the culture wars, it is important that we understand the debate
over whether and how freedom of speech should be limited on campus.

Is Freedom of Speech an Individual Right or a Public Good?

4   This question about the relative value of individual rights versus the public good
is not new. The tug of war between them is clear in America's Constitution and Bill
of Rights. While the Preamble to the Constitution stresses the need to "promote the
general welfare," the Bill of Rights echoes the Declaration of Independence's assertion
that individual rights are God-given and therefore cannot be taken away. The importance
of the right to free speech is evident in the fact that it is guaranteed by the very first
amendment to the Constitution.

5   Whereas Baer argues that these opposing values need to be balanced, Soave
maintains that individual rights should be valued more highly than promoting the
common good. We can see this disagreement in Soave's response to Baer's assertion
that "the parameters of public speech must be continually re-drawn." Soave claims "the
purpose of the First Amendment, and norms of free speech more generally, is to *prevent*
the authorities from re-drawing the parameters relating to speech, since they cannot be
trusted to do so fairly." This distrust of government reminds us of the conditions that
led to the Declaration of Independence in the first place.

6   Like Soave, Baer is concerned with fairness and the unequal distribution of power.
However, Baer's concern is not with King George's tyranny over the colonies but with

Why describe these authors?

What do you think these key terms mean?

Why end the introduction with this claim?

How well do the headings explain the disagreement?

How do the verbs King uses suggest impartiality?

Why include this historical reference?

How do these transitions help readers?

what he calls the "long history" of "discrimination" against disempowered groups such as African Americans. Unlike Soave, Baer seems less fearful of authoritarian government than of "an unholy alliance of so-called alt-right demagogues and campus liberals" who do not recognize what he sees as a real threat to our democracy. Soave labels Baer's views as "dangerous." But Baer says that, unlike those who agree with Soave, he is "not overly worried" that freedom of speech is endangered by protesters. What worries Baer is that select groups of Americans continue to be silenced and their humanity invalidated.

What Is the Danger of Restricting or Allowing Freedom of Speech?

7   Ulrich Baer and Robby Soave disagree over the harm that would result if free speech was limited or, indeed, if it was unlimited. For Baer, not restricting speech means that those in power are free to use speech that is offensive and demeaning, perhaps even hate speech against other less powerful people. In contrast, Robby Soave seems less concerned about the harm unfettered speech can do to people and more focused on what suppressing free speech would do to our democracy. He clearly fears that our essential First Amendment right to freedom of speech is at risk.

8   Instead of free speech protections being a tool to enhance the free exchange of views so highly valued in a democracy, Baer contends that they "should not mean that someone's humanity, or their right to participate in political speech as political agents, can be freely attacked, demeaned or questioned." Here, Baer is making two linked arguments. First, he is talking about hate speech. Although he doesn't use the term, his point is clear: Describing groups of people as "inferior to others, or illegal or unworthy of legal standing," is dehumanizing. Essentially, Baer suggests that the very speech campus provocateurs wish to protect is being used to diminish the rights of other, more marginalized groups to be respected as equal citizens. Second, Baer is arguing that speech that invalidates people's humanity does, indeed, restrict speech because people cannot be put into the position of defending their own basic humanity. To support this argument, Baer refers to Yale University's 1963 report: "Requiring of someone in public debate to defend their human worth conflicts with the community's obligation to assure all of its members equal access to public speech."

Why do you think King brings up this highly charged term?

9   This is the central point of disagreement between Soave and Baer. Baer contends that by demeaning and silencing people, hate speech makes debate impossible. Although Soave concedes that discriminatory speech "may be wrong and legitimately hurtful," he denies that such speech inherently threatens the rights of those who are denigrated by it. "Expressing views that invalidate the humanity of some people," according to Soave, "does precisely that: it invalidates the humanity of some people . . . but it does not restrict their speech." Soave clearly believes that First Amendment rights are so important that any attempt to weaken them could hurt us all far more than hate speech ever could.

10   Finally, Soave supports his contention that freedom of speech must be absolute by refuting Baer's argument about the need to adjust when and for whom the right to free speech should be applied. Soave maintains that treating free speech as an adjustable right, rather than as an unchanging absolute right, is a slippery slope because it inevitably leads to the silencing of critics or the less powerful. In fact, Soave argues that Baer does just that by defending the censoring of would-be campus speakers whose speech he doesn't like:

> Baer's own remarks demonstrate how the people who wish to re-draw speech parameters will always be tempted to do so in a manner that disadvantages their enemies. . . . In his article, he is attempting to craft a definition of free speech that obligates attacks on certain people's right to participate in political speech.

Soave's fear is that any restrictions on the freedom of speech will be used to silence those who have unpopular views and that those in power will always try to limit speech rather than foster open debate. I suppose Baer could respond to this critique by characterizing Soave's slippery slope argument as a logical fallacy. He could argue that denying free speech to one's enemies would not be inevitable. Moreover, he could repeat his basic argument that the powerless have already been silenced. In other words, the status quo that Soave defends as a free and open democracy is really already closed to a significant part of the population. Baer holds that free speech rights need to be adjusted because democracy will not be truly free and open until everyone's voice can be heard.

11   Both of these authors clearly see the college campus as the central battlefield testing our constitutional guarantee of free speech versus the wish to limit hate speech. Where they seem to most seriously part ways is in their idea of who the First Amendment

What does this term mean? Why do you think King uses it?

Why does King indent this quotation?

What does King do to appear fair and impartial despite his use of the first person (*I*) here?

What makes this conclusion effective or ineffective?

is intended to protect. Ulrich Baer clearly believes that its purpose is to protect the speech of those who have been marginalized and denied a voice in public discourse, while Robby Soave believes that freedom of speech is meant to protect our individual rights and that any infraction of that right is a danger to our core principles. This difference of opinion may well be the kind of disagreement that ends up at the Supreme Court.

What do you learn about citing sources from these examples?

Works Cited

Baer, Ulrich. "What 'Snowflakes' Get Right about Free Speech." *The New York Times,* 24 Apr. 2017, nyti.ms/2pVkD2z.

Jaschik, Scott. "Shouting Down a Lecture." *Inside Higher Ed,* 3 Mar. 2017, www .insidehighered.com/news/2017/03/03/middlebury-students-shout-down-lecture -charles-murray.

Lanney, Jillian, and Carolyn Cong. "Ray Kelly Lecture Canceled amidst Student, Community Protest." *The Brown Daily Herald,* 30 Oct. 2013, www.browndailyherald .com/2013/10/30/ray-kelly-lecture-canceled-amidst-student-community-protest/.

McLaughlin, Eliott C. "Ann Coulter Controversy Tests Berkeley's Free Speech Credentials." *CNN.com,* 27 Apr. 2017, www.cnn.com/2017/04/27/us/berkeley-ann-coulter-free -speech/index.html.

Nielsen, Laura Beth. "The Case for Restricting Hate Speech." *Los Angeles Times,* 21 June 2017, www.latimes.com/opinion/op-ed/la-oe-nielsen-free-speech-hate-20170621 -story.html.

Reilly, Katie. "Three Arrested in Clashes over White Nationalist Richard Spencer's Speech at Auburn University." *Time,* 19 Apr. 2017, time.com/4746276/richard-spencer -auburn-university-protests/.

Sguelglia, Kristina. "Condolezza Rice Declines to Speak at Rutgers after Student Protests." *CNN.com,* 5 May 2014, www.cnn.com/2014/05/04/us/condoleeza-rice -rutgers-protests/index.html.

Soave, Robby. "Liberals Are Amazed That Campus Free Speech Outrage Gets So Much Attention. Here's Why It Matters." *Reason,* 25 Apr. 2017, reason.com/ blog/2017/04/25/liberals-are-amazed-that-campus-free-spe.

Steinmetz, Katy. "Milo Yiannopoulos Finally Spoke at Berkeley. But the Protesters Were Louder." *Time,* 25 Sept. 2017, time.com/4955245/milo-yiannopoulos-berkeley-free -speech-week/.

Maya Gomez | *Should Kidney Donors Be Compensated?*

MAYA GOMEZ chose the option her instructor offered to analyze two opposing arguments about organ donation: the National Kidney Foundation's policy statement "Financial Incentives for Organ Donation" and Dr. Sally Satel's op-ed "When Altruism Isn't Moral." The debate centers on this issue: Should people be paid for donating a kidney, or must all kidney donations be altruistic? Before focusing on the opposing arguments, Gomez did some background research to learn about the issue. For example, she discovered that there is a diabetes epidemic in the United States that leads to chronic kidney disease for many people and ultimately to either kidney transplant or death. She also learned that people can donate one of their two kidneys and still live a long, healthy life.

As you read,

- think about the statistics in the opening paragraph. Why do you think Gomez decided to begin this way, given that her analysis of the debate is supposed to be impartial?

- notice that at the end of the opening paragraph Gomez brings up the "ultimate solution." Why do you think she mentions it only to put it aside?

1   The statistics tell a grim story. There is a wide gap between the supply of kidneys available for transplant and the nearly 100,000 Americans on the kidney transplant waiting list. According to the most recent data, 17,107 surgeries were performed in 2014, while 4,761 patients died awaiting a match and 3,668 people were removed from the list because they became too sick for a transplant ("Organ Donation"). The ultimate solution to the kidney shortage is likely to be the development of an implantable artificial kidney. The Kidney Project is making great strides, but clinical trials have not yet begun and it will take years before an artificial kidney is perfected for widespread use (Molteni).

2   For now, as kidney transplant recipient Dr. Sally Satel argues, a regulated market for live donor kidneys is the only alternative for end stage renal disease (ESRD) sufferers. In her opinion piece "When Altruism Isn't Moral," Satel holds the National Kidney Foundation (NKF), the nation's foremost nonprofit advocacy group for kidney disease patients, responsible for the ban on compensating donors. The NKF wouldn't be likely to object to Satel's characterization because it proudly claims responsibility for drafting the National Organ Transplant Act (NOTA) as well as for getting the law passed in Congress ("History"). The key passage of NOTA prohibiting compensation states that "it shall be unlawful for any person to knowingly acquire, receive, or otherwise transfer any human organ for valuable consideration for use in human transplantation" (Sec. 301a). Although the law has been modified to permit kidney exchanges and to remove several disincentives to donation, the "valuable consideration" clause outlawing compensation remains in force.

3   This essay compares the underlying values driving the arguments in the NKF position statement "Financial Incentives for Organ Donation" and Satel's article "When Altruism Isn't Moral." Their views are diametrically opposed. Whereas the NKF defends the status quo and urges retention of the valuable consideration clause, Satel deplores the "woeful inadequacy of our nation's transplant policy" and proposes "rewards" to "encourage more living and posthumous donation."

4   Satel's disagreement with the NKF is essentially about its framing the issue of compensation in terms of morality. Or rather, it is about what she sees as the NKF's moral absolutism in what she thinks should be viewed as "a morally pluralistic society." The basis of their disagreement is the proper role of altruism. The NKF emphatically endorses the current "altruistic system." Satel, in contrast, argues that current policy is failing precisely because it is an "altruism-only system."

5   Altruism, according to Satel, is "the guiding narrative of the transplant establishment," its underlying ideology or value system. The NKF would agree with Satel's

description of current policy requiring that "organs should be a 'gift of life'" and donating should be "an act of selfless generosity." In using the phrase "altruistic gift of life," the NKF statement makes explicit the connection between the act of giving and what is being given. If the act of giving is tainted, for example by self-interest rather than selflessness, then the gift itself becomes unacceptable. That is why, in the anecdote that Satel uses to begin her article, the transplant surgeons need to be convinced that Matt Thompson, the potential donor, "was donating his kidney for the right reasons"—namely, for purely altruistic reasons.

6   The NKF statement represents a worldview in which there are certain moral truths about which it is assumed everyone agrees. Examples of moral certainty in the NKF policy statement include the claims that "payment for organs is wrong" and "inconsistent with our values as a society."

7   We can see the NKF's and Satel's opposing views of morality played out in their arguments about the commodification of human organs. The NKF statement explains what is wrong with treating the human body as a commodity: "Any attempt to assign a monetary value to the human body, or body parts, either arbitrarily, or through market forces, diminishes human dignity." This argument is based on the belief that the human body is not something to be treated as "property" to be bought and sold. Rather, it is sacred, made in God's image.

8   Satel refutes the NKF's commodification argument in a number of ways. For example, she points out that commodifying body parts has a long legal tradition, from Hammurabi to current personal injury law. She also questions the cause-effect reasoning that commodifying body parts is necessarily dehumanizing: "There is little reason to believe—nor tangible evidence to suggest—that these practices depreciate human worth or undermine human dignity in any way." But her main argument is about how we evaluate "the goodness of an act"—in other words, our moral reasoning.

9   Satel critiques the NKF's way of assessing moral value by arguing that its moral logic relies on "false choice" reasoning. She summarizes the NKF's thinking this way: "Giving a kidney 'for free' is noble but accepting compensation is illegitimate." This distinction between altruistic gift giving and receiving a reward hinges on the idea that inserting a reward into the exchange commercializes it and damages the act's moral purity. Satel quotes Kieran

Healy, a professor at Duke University studying economic sociology, to describe the either/or dilemma that framing the debate around altruism creates: "the debate is cast as one in which existing relations of selfless, altruistic exchange are threatened with replacement by market-based, for-profit alternatives."

10   In other words, Satel thinks the NKF sets up a false choice between selflessness and self-interest. In contrast to the NKF, Satel believes that mixed motives probably drive most gift giving. For example, she suggests several self-interested motives that may be involved in giving the "gift of life"—such as offering "an organ as an act of redemption," "a way to elicit praise and social acceptance," or "a way to avoid the shame and guilt of allowing a relative to suffer needlessly and perhaps even die."

11   Purity of motivation plays a key role for the NKF in evaluating "the goodness of an act." But for Satel, what appears to matter most is that the act has the potential to save a human life. For her, it doesn't matter if the donor gains materially, earns enhanced social status, or just gets a "'warm glow'" of self-satisfaction "from performing acts of charity." Instead of "remuneration" crowding out "generosity," as critics of financial compensation like the National Kidney Foundation claim, Satel argues that the opposite is true: the combination of payment with the opportunity to do good could "increase the pool of transplantable organs."

12   The question of altruism is the center of Satel's disagreement with the NKF. But Satel and the NKF also disagree about what would happen if there was a legal market in kidneys. Both appear to agree that exploitation of the poor would result. But whereas the NKF appears to think this problem is inescapable as well as inevitable, Satel seems to be confident that it could be handled administratively. According to the NKF "Financial Incentives" statement, those in desperate need of money would feel they have no choice but to sell one of their kidneys. (People can live with only one kidney, but there may be lasting health consequences.) Moreover, because the poor would not be in a position to buy a kidney, they would not benefit, as richer people would, from the free market. The NKF calls this both coercion and exploitation.

13   Critics of the illegal global black market in kidneys support the NKF's judgment on this point. For example, transplant surgeons Anya Adair and Stephen J. Wigmore claim a free market would be "inherently exploitative,

with the poorest in society being the ones who come forward as sellers every time." Even economics professors Gary S. Becker and Julio J. Elias, who have defended compensation, agree with the NKF that not only would a free market lead to a decline in kidney donation, but it would also exploit the poor. However, Becker and Elias see a remedy in what Satel calls "good policy." They suggest that "Medicaid could help." But given the state of health care currently, one might respond with skepticism to this "good policy" argument.

14   So, while the National Kidney Foundation stakes out the moral high ground on the issue of compensating kidney donors, others—like Sally Satel—are struggling to find a practical solution to a literal life and death problem. Medical science and biotechnology seem to promise the best answer, but waiting is not a viable option for everyone.

Works Cited

Adair, Anya, and Stephen J. Wigmore. "Paid Organ Donation: The Case Against." *Annals of the Royal College of Surgeons of England,* vol. 93, no. 3, Apr. 2011, pp. 191–92, doi:10.1308/147870811X565061a.

Becker, Gary S., and Julio J. Elías. "Cash for Kidneys: The Case for a Market for Organs." *The Wall Street Journal,* 18 Jan. 2014, www.wsj.com/articles/cash-for-kidneys-the-case-for-a-market-for-organs-1389992925.

"Financial Incentives for Organ Donation." *National Kidney Foundation,* 1 Feb. 2003, www.kidney.org/news/newsroom/positionpaper03.

"History." *National Kidney Foundation,* www.kidney.org/about/history. Accessed 30 Apr. 2015.

Molteni, Megan. "Silicon Isn't Just for Computers. It Can Make a Pretty Good Kidney, Too." *Wired,* 6 Oct. 2017, www.wired.com/story/artificial-kidneys/.

"Organ Donation and Transplantation Statistics." *National Kidney Foundation,* 8 Sept. 2017, www.kidney.org/news/newsroom/factsheets/Organ-Donation-and-Transplantation-Stats.

Satel, Sally. "When Altruism Isn't Moral." *American Enterprise Institute,* 30 Jan. 2009, www.aei.org/publication/when-altruism-isnt-moral/.

United States, Congress, House. *National Organ Transplant Act.* Government Printing Office, 19 Oct. 1984. 98th Congress, House Report 98-1127.

Make connections: What do you think about this issue?   ⌈ REFLECT ⌉

Before examining this debate impartially to see how Gomez employs the basic features of the genre, think about what you would say if you entered the debate. Your instructor may ask you to post your thoughts or to discuss them in class. Use these questions to get started:

- Do you agree or disagree that
  - paying someone to donate a kidney is morally wrong?
  - "the goodness of an act" is undermined by selfish motives?
  - people usually act out of mixed motives?
  - if some people were paid for donating a kidney, no one would donate without being paid?
  - if there were a legal market in kidneys, desperately poor people would feel pressured to sell one of their kidneys?
  - "good policy" could protect poor people from being exploited?
- Now that you've considered your own opinion, what values and beliefs seem most important to you? Do you see the same values and beliefs reflected in the National Kidney Foundation statement or Sally Satel's op-ed? What seem to be their priorities?

$\Big[$ ANALYZE $\Big]$ # Use the basic features.

AN INFORMATIVE INTRODUCTION: ANSWERING THE JOURNALIST'S QUESTIONS

Writers analyzing opposing arguments usually begin by identifying the issue and the opposing positions. Max King chose to introduce the issue by answering a few of the journalist's questions: *who, what, where, when, why,* and *how.*

When
Where
What
Who

> From spring through fall of 2017, **several universities** across the nation were rocked by conflicts over who should and should not be allowed to speak on campus. . . . Some of the speakers who were banned from campus or whose visits were protested against were rabble-rousers—for example, the self-described white supremacist Richard Spencer (Reilly), Internet troll Milo Yiannopoulos (Steinmetz), and conservative firebrand Ann Coulter (McLaughlin). (par. 1)

The *what* question identifies the immediate controversy.

$\boxed{\text{ANALYZE \& WRITE}}$

Write a paragraph or two analyzing how Maya Gomez introduces the issue over which the opposing arguments she's analyzing are at odds:

1 Skim the first four paragraphs of the essay. Which of the *who, what, where, when, why* and *how* questions does Gomez answer?

2 How does she explain the different positions the National Kidney Foundation and Sally Satel take on the issue?

3 How well does Gomez help you understand why this issue matters?

A PROBING ANALYSIS: ANALYZING THE REBUTTALS

A strategy writers can use to probe opposing arguments is to examine how they rebut each other. When there is a rebuttal but no response, writers may speculate about the likely response. This strategy can be effective as long as it is clear that the response is the writer's best guess, based on the content of the source.

Notice how Max King begins by examining Soave's refutation of Baer's argument:

> Soave maintains that treating free speech as an adjustable right . . . is a slippery slope because it inevitably leads to the silencing of critics or the less powerful. (par. 10)

Then he speculates about how Baer probably would have responded to Soave's critique:

Speculation cues

> I suppose Baer could respond to this critique by characterizing Soave's slippery slope argument as a logical fallacy. (par. 10)

By highlighting how Soave attempts to refute Baer and how Baer might have responded, King helps readers better understand their disagreement.

| ANALYZE & WRITE |

Write a paragraph analyzing the strategies Gomez uses to probe the opposing positions:

1 Reread paragraphs 7–10 to see how Gomez analyzes the argument between the National Kidney Foundation and Sally Satel about the "commodification of human organs." What is Satel's critique of the NKF? How does Gomez speculate about how the NKF would respond?

2 In paragraphs 9 and 10, Gomez uses the terms "false choice" and "either/or dilemma" (quoted by Satel) to explain Satel's critique of the NKF's reasoning. What does Satel think is the problem with this kind of reasoning? How well do these terms help you understand the crux of the disagreement between Satel and the NKF?

A FAIR AND IMPARTIAL PRESENTATION: ESTABLISHING THE TONE

To earn their readers' confidence, writers of comparative analyses must come across as fair and accurate in their representation of opposing arguments, not biased in favor of one side and against the other. Readers expect writers analyzing a debate to keep their opinion to themselves and not let it influence the fairness and accuracy of their analysis. Therefore, writers usually strive for an academic tone that is evenhanded, judicious, and serious—in a word, impartial.

However, that does not mean that writers should come across as detached. In fact, if they appear uninterested, then they may not be able to interest readers in caring about the issue. So although writers reporting on a debate usually avoid emotional or inflammatory language, they often begin by establishing a tone of concern, even anxiety, about the controversy. We can see this in the way King dramatizes the campus incidents in his opening sentences:

> From spring through fall of 2017, several universities across the nation were rocked by conflicts over who should and should not be allowed to speak on campus. Protests erupted on campuses from Auburn to UC Berkeley, igniting a war of words over the limits of free speech.

| ANALYZE & WRITE |

Write a paragraph or two analyzing how Maya Gomez establishes her tone:

1 Reread the opening paragraph of Gomez's essay, highlighting any words that convey the writer's attitude toward the issue.

2 How would you describe the tone Gomez establishes with this opening? Where do you see this tone in her word choices?

3 What role, if any, do the statistics play in how Gomez establishes this tone?

A CLEAR, LOGICAL ORGANIZATION: USING KEY WORDS AS CUES

Comparative analysis essays can be hard to follow because the writer is juggling two different texts. To be fair in their treatment of each side, writers typically use either

For more about structuring a comparison-contrast essay, see Chapter 15.

an *alternating* or a *sequencing* pattern of organization. An alternating, or chunking, pattern focuses on one side for a paragraph and then switches to the other side for the next paragraph. A sequential pattern treats both sides within the same paragraph.

Whichever organizational pattern is used, cues signaling comparison and contrast (such as *like* and *similarly,* or *in contrast* and *on the one hand . . . on the other hand*) can be very helpful between and within sentences as well as between paragraphs and sections. Repetition of key words or their synonyms—in a forecasting statement, in topic sentences, and in headings—can also signal that a comparison of opinions is coming. Take a look at how King uses this cueing strategy:

THESIS WITH FORECAST Topic 1 Topic 2	At the heart of their disagreement is their radically different idea about whether freedom of speech is an absolute and unchanging individual right or a public good that has to be regularly adjusted to be fair to everyone. They also disagree over whether limiting freedom of speech or allowing it to be unlimited is the greater danger to democracy. (par. 3)
HEADING 1	**Is Freedom of Speech an Individual Right or a Public Good?**
TOPIC SENTENCE	This question about the relative value of individual rights versus the public good is not new. (par. 4)
HEADING 2	**What Is the Danger of Restricting or Allowing Freedom of Speech?**
TOPIC SENTENCE	Ulrich Baer and Robby Soave disagree over the harm that would result if free speech was limited or, indeed, if it was unlimited. (par. 7)

ANALYZE & WRITE

Write a paragraph assessing how effectively Maya Gomez uses cueing strategies to guide readers through her comparison:

1 Skim paragraph 3 to look for a forecast, and highlight any key words that announce the topics she plans to focus on.

2 Reread paragraphs 7 and 12, and underline the topic sentences. How effectively do you think Gomez's topic sentences work to orient readers? Why do you think she chose not to add headings?

3 Now reread paragraphs 8 and 10, and highlight the transitions Gomez uses to cue readers. How well do these cues work to help you track the logical progression from one sentence to another? Would you advise Gomez to keep all these transitions, cut or change particular ones, or add even more?

The Writing Assignment

Write an essay analyzing two opposing arguments on a controversial issue. Your purpose is to analyze their authors' main points of disagreement and to probe the ideas, beliefs, values, and concerns that underlie their disagreement.

This Guide to Writing is designed to help you compose your own essay analyzing and synthesizing opposing arguments. The Starting Points chart will help you find answers to questions you might have about the best way to analyze and synthesize opposing arguments. Use it to find the guidance you need, when you need it.

Did you know?

When you are experimenting with a new or especially challenging genre, scaffolding like this Guide to Writing can be very helpful. But when you are writing in a genre you know well, you may not need the support of the activities here.

STARTING POINTS: ANALYZING AND SYNTHESIZING OPPOSING ARGUMENTS

An Informative Introduction

How do I come up with an issue to write about?

- Choose a controversial issue to write about. (pp. 172–73)
- Choose opposing arguments to analyze. (p. 177)

How can I interest my readers in the issue?

- Assess the genre's basic features: An informative introduction. (pp. 156–57)
- An Informative Introduction: Answering the Journalist's Questions (p. 168)
- Test Your Choice: Selecting a Topic (p. 173)
- Conduct research. (p. 173)
- Analyze your audience. (p. 176)
- Draft the opening sentences. (p. 182)

How can I give readers an overview of the debate?

- Assess the genre's basic features: An informative introduction. (pp. 156–57)
- An Informative Introduction: Answering the Journalist's Questions (p. 168)
- Conduct research. (p. 173)

(continued)

A Probing Analysis	How do I identify the writers' values and areas of disagreement?	• Assess the genre's basic features: A probing analysis. (pp. 157–58) • A Probing Analysis: Analyzing the Rebuttals (p. 168) • Analyze and synthesize the opposing arguments. (pp. 177–78) • Draft a working thesis. (p. 179) • Develop your analysis. (pp. 180–81) • Test Your Choice: Evaluating Your Analysis (p. 178)
A Fair and Impartial Presentation	How do I avoid entering the debate myself?	• Assess the genre's basic features: A fair and impartial presentation. (pp. 158–59) • A Fair and Impartial Presentation: Establishing the Tone (p. 169) • Create an outline to plan or assess your organization. (p. 179)
A Clear, Logical Organization	How can I make my essay clear?	• Assess the genre's basic features: A clear, logical organization. (p. 159) • A Clear, Logical Organization: Using Key Words as Cues (pp. 169–70) • Create an outline to plan or assess your organization. (p. 179)

Writing a Draft: Invention, Research, Planning, and Composing

The activities in this section will help you

- choose a controversial issue
- find opposing arguments to analyze
- conduct background research
- compile an annotated working bibliography
- develop your analysis and synthesis of the arguments

Do the activities in any order that makes sense to you (and your instructor), and return to them as needed as you draft and revise your comparative analysis.

⊞ Choose a controversial issue to write about.

Whether your instructor assigned opposing arguments for you to analyze, recommended opposing arguments on one or more issues from which to choose, or gave you free rein to find opposing arguments on any controversial issue, you may want

Writing a Draft

Guide to Reading
GUIDE TO WRITING
A Writer at Work
Reflection

173

to do background research to learn more about how people debate the issue. The following Ways In activities will help you conduct research and construct a working bibliography.

TEST YOUR CHOICE

Selecting a Topic

Get together with two or three other students to take turns trying out your topics with potential readers. Ask group members questions like these:

- What, if anything, do you already know about the topic?
- What questions would you like answered?
- Do you have a strong opinion about the issue, or do I need to get you to see why it matters?

⊞ Conduct research.

If you need to find opposing arguments to analyze, use the tips in the Ways In activity to locate sources.

WAYS IN

HOW DO I RESEARCH OPPOSING ARGUMENTS?

Use the following suggestions to find a debate on a controversial issue:

- Search for op-eds (opinion pieces) in newspapers and blogs, using LexisNexis Academic or other databases accessible through your college library.
- Look for issues on Web sites such as debate.org, procon.org, or controversialissues .org, or on the Room for Debate page at nytimes.com.
- Google a controversial issue, such as voter ID laws or school uniforms, plus a term like *debate, opposing arguments,* or *controversy*.
- Conduct a search on a controversial issue, such as voter ID laws or school uniforms, in a database, such as Academic OneFile (InfoTrac) or Academic Search Complete (EBSCOhost), or another general database accessible through your college library.
- Revisit the topic you discussed in the Practicing the Genre activity earlier in this chapter (p. 155).
- Glance at the reading selections in Chapters 6–9 to see if any of the readings or topics pique your interest. For example, consider using as one of your sources Jessica Statsky's opinion essay on organized sports for kids (pp. 198–204), David Figlio's proposal to start high school an hour later (pp. 252–55), or Jean Twenge's essay on the destructive power of smartphones (pp. 344–47).

Once you have identified a debate you are interested in exploring, return to Google or a general database to learn more about the issue.

To learn more about conducting research, see Chapter 17.

⊞ Create an annotated working bibliography.

Creating an annotated bibliography can help you keep track of sources and begin to figure out how your sources might be related. Follow these steps when making entries for the most relevant potential sources you find:

For more about creating bibliographic citations in MLA and APA style, see Chapters 20 and 21.

1. Add a citation to your working bibliography that includes author, title, and publication information. For citation models and detailed instructions on creating a bibliographic citation for your annotated bibliography, see Chapter 20 (MLA style) or Chapter 21 (APA style).

Take a moment . . .

Think about how summarizing and commenting on each source could help you synthesize as well as analyze your sources.

2. Save a copy of the source—in PDF format or as a printout or photocopy—for further reference.

3. Annotate your working bibliography by briefly summarizing the source, adding a short commentary about how you plan to use it, and considering how it relates to other sources you may have read.

WAYS IN

For more about creating a scratch outline, see Chapters 11 and 12; for more about summarizing, see Chapters 12 and 19; for more about avoiding plagiarism, see Chapter 19.

HOW DO I WRITE A SUMMARY OR CONCISE "GIST" STATEMENT?

1. *Highlight the* **THESIS** *and* **MAIN SUPPORTING IDEAS (REASONS)** *as you read the source. (You may have to reread it several times to distinguish the main points from the details.)*

2. *Make a scratch* **OUTLINE** *of the main ideas, using your own words.*

3. *Put the source away, and draft the summary from your outline. (This can help you avoid inadvertent plagiarism and retain the order of your source's ideas.)*

   ■ Introduce the source in a **SIGNAL PHRASE** (author's name plus a verb that captures the move the author is making, such as *argues, supports,* or *describes*). Include the author's name and credentials, as well as the publication and date if relevant. Remember that all of this information will be included in the bibliographic citation:

   ▶ In this book/article/op-ed, X, professor of .... at School A, asserts/reports ....

   EXAMPLE   *Inside HigherEd* editor and co-founder Scott Jaschik reports on the events surrounding the disruption of Charles Murray's Middlebury College talk.

   ■ State the **THESIS** in your own words.

   ▶ X argues that the best way to solve the problem is to ....

   ▶ Professor X contradicts Dr. Y, explaining that ....

Writing a Draft

Guide to Reading
GUIDE TO WRITING
A Writer at Work
Reflection

175

EXAMPLE   Lawyer and sociology professor Laura Beth Nielsen argues in her *Los Angeles Times* op-ed that hate speech doesn't just hurt the feelings of "snowflakes"; it does real harm to those it targets.

- List the main supporting ideas (or reasons) in the same order in which they appear in the source.

  ▶ X responds to such criticisms as _____, _____, and _____.

  ▶ X claims that _____. He also argues that _____.

  EXAMPLE   Robby Soave rebuts Baer's claims that demeaning speech restricts others' freedom of speech and that speech protections should be adjusted with the changing times.

- Use **TRANSITIONS** of comparison or contrast (*like, while, but, therefore*) and other cues (such as strategic repetition of key words or synonyms for key words) to show readers how the ideas relate to one another.

  ▶ Although/Whereas/Unlike A's position, B's contention is that _____.

  EXAMPLE   Unlike Baer, Soave argues that as a right guaranteed under the Constitution, free speech is absolute and unchangeable. Whereas Baer thinks speech should be considered a "public good" that needs to be adjusted over time, Soave contends that making free speech protections adjustable would inevitably lead to those in power silencing the powerless.

4. *Check your draft summary against the source to make sure you have*
   - captured the author's ideas accurately and succinctly;
   - avoided inserting your own ideas or opinions;
   - used neutral verbs (*stated* or *responded* rather than *complained* or *whined*);
   - put terms borrowed from the source in quotation marks and avoided borrowing other words or sentence patterns.

An annotated working bibliography for a writing project includes not only a summary of each main source but also a commentary consisting of

- your thoughts on how you might use the source in your analysis;
- your ideas about the relationships among your sources (the beginning of your synthesis);
- a possible evaluation of each source's **credibility** (authority).

Use the following guidelines and sentence strategies as a jumping-off point for drafting the commentary for the sources you include in your working bibliography. You can make the sentences you generate on your own later, as you revise.

WAYS IN

HOW DO I DRAFT A COMMENTARY FOR AN ANNOTATED BIBLIOGRAPHY?

1. *Explore how you could use the source in your project(s).*

   ▶ I plan to use _____ [title of article/book] to show _____, _____, and _____.

   EXAMPLE   I can cite the news reports of the 2017 campus incidents in my opening paragraphs to give readers some background on the controversy.

2. *Make connections among your sources.*

   ▶ X is like/unlike Y in that _____.

   EXAMPLE   Soave rejects Baer's main argument that hate speech makes free speech impossible because it silences people; it hurts people's feelings but doesn't take away their rights.

3. *Assess the credibility of your sources.*

   ▶ X is likely to carry authority with most people because _____.

   EXAMPLE   Baer is likely to have some credibility as a professor and administrator, but his tone and reference to Lyotard may strike readers as too lecturing and superior.

⊞ Analyze your audience.

For more about brainstorming, freewriting, and other idea-generating strategies, see Chapter 11.

Once you have conducted research and added potential sources to your annotated bibliography, spend a few minutes thinking about your audience. Answering the questions that follow will help you decide how to engage your readers and how much background information to provide.

WAYS IN

WHAT WILL INTEREST MY READERS?

Analyze your **AUDIENCE** *by brainstorming or freewriting answers to the following questions:*

- Who are your readers, and what are they likely to know about the topic? What opinions are they likely to hold? (Reconsider what you learned from the Test Your Choice activity earlier in this Guide to Writing.)

- How would you answer your readers' "So what?" question? Think of at least one aspect of the topic that will clarify its importance for your readers.

- What is your relationship with your readers? What **TONE** is most appropriate for addressing this audience? How do you want your readers to perceive you? For an essay analyzing opposing viewpoints, a rational, impartial tone is most appropriate: *asserts* rather than *proclaims* or *rationalizes*; *argues* instead of *nitpicks* or *champions*. (In academic writing, a rational, impartial tone is generally appropriate.)

Writing a Draft

Guide to Reading
GUIDE TO WRITING
A Writer at Work
Reflection

177

▦ Choose opposing arguments to analyze.

If you have been asked to choose opposing arguments for a comparative analysis, you will need to select texts that

- take different positions on the same controversial issue;
- reflect different underlying basic values or worldviews.

It may also be helpful to choose opposing arguments that refer explicitly to each other, as in the Baer/Soave pairing Max King used. When compiling your annotated bibliography, you may have come across two (or three) essays that looked promising. If you have one promising text but need to find a good opposing one, consider doing additional research. You may also need to do research to provide the historical and cultural context surrounding the debate.

To learn more about contextualizing, see Chapter 12.

▦ Analyze and synthesize the opposing arguments.

The following activities will help you develop your analysis and synthesis of the opposing arguments.

WAYS IN

HOW CAN I ANALYZE AND SYNTHESIZE THE OPPOSING ARGUMENTS?

Reread each essay, noting in the margin where you find indications of the following:

Framing: How the writer defines what is important about the issue or what it is about

Position: The writer's main idea or THESIS STATEMENT—that is, the writer's opinion about the topic

Arguments: How the writer supports the position and responds to alternative points of view

Credibility and Tone: The writer's background and area of expertise and how the writer tries to win readers' trust

Motivating Factors:

- **Values:** Moral, ethical, or religious principles (justice, equality, "do unto others")
- **Worldviews and ideologies:** Political or religious belief systems (libertarianism, progressivism, conservatism, orthodoxy)
- **Ideas and ideals** (for example, democratic ideals, such as the right to vote and freedom of speech)
- **Concerns and fears** (personal safety, abuse of power, protecting the environment)
- **Goals and priorities** about what is most important or urgent (for example, whether obedience to authority is more important than independent thinking)
- **Interests served** (for example, whether an individual or group benefits financially or politically)

Reflect on . . .

Consider which factors seem most important to you? What, if any, motivations would you add to the list?

(continued)

Consider . . .

How does completing this chart help you synthesize as well as analyze the opposing arguments?

Fill in the Comparative Analysis Chart.

Enter your notes, useful quotations, and the page or paragraph numbers in which you found the borrowed information. Searching the text for evidence of underlying values and other motivating factors will deepen your analysis and help you go beyond summarizing what is said to explaining *why* each author holds her or his opinion. Creating this chart will also help you see points of comparison and contrast between the opposing arguments. (Remember that it is okay to leave some sections of the chart blank, as you may not find examples of all the features in each essay.)

Comparative Analysis Chart		
Author		
Framing of Issue		
Position		
Arguments		
Credibility and Tone		
Motivating Factors: Values, Beliefs, Concerns, Priorities, Interests Served, etc.		

To see Max King's completed comparative analysis chart, see the Writer at Work section (pp. 187–88).

TEST YOUR CHOICE

Evaluating Your Analysis

Get together with two or three other students to test the underlying value (or other motivating factor) you think plays an important role in the debate you are analyzing:

Presenters.   Briefly tell your listeners what the disagreement is about and what you think is the important motivating factor (such as a value, belief, or concern) driving the debate. Provide one or two examples to show where you see the factor you have identified in the opposing texts.

Listeners.   Tell the presenter what the examples suggest to you about the motivating factor underlying the disagreement. Share any questions, comments, or insights with the presenter.

▦ Draft a working thesis.

The thesis statement announces the purpose and the main idea in a comparative analysis and may also forecast the points of comparison or contrast:

> This essay **examines the debate** by analyzing two essays published during campus protests at UC Berkeley. . . . At the heart of their disagreement is their radically different idea about whether freedom of speech is an absolute and unchanging individual right or a public good that has to be regularly adjusted to be fair to everyone. They also disagree over whether limiting freedom of speech or allowing it to be unlimited is the greater danger to democracy. (Max King, par. 3)

Purpose

Thesis

Forecast

▦ Create an outline to plan or assess your organization.

You may want to create an outline before writing a draft (as a guide to organizing your essay) or after you have drafted your analysis (as a check to make sure your organization makes sense). An effective outline for a comparative analysis typically offers a sequenced (or alternating) comparison centered on points of disagreement because this pattern suggests that both sides of the debate are represented equally.

For help organizing a comparison or contrast, see Chapter 15.

I. **Introduction:** Provides background on issue and introduces debate (pars. 1–3)

II. **Conflict:** Is free speech an unchanging individual right or a public good? Which is more dangerous to democracy? (par. 4)

III. **Individual Right or Public Good:** Provides background over the conflict (par. 4), explains Baer's and Soave's position (pars. 5–6)

IV. **Restricting or Allowing Unrestricted Freedom of Speech:** Describes conflict (par. 7)

  A. **Baer's position** (par. 8)

  B. **Analysis of conflict—Baer vs. Soave** (par. 9)

  C. **Rebuttal** (par. 10)

V. **Conclusion:** Summarizes conflict, emphasizes importance of issue (par. 11)

I. **Introduction:** Shows seriousness of issue and provides background (pars. 1–2)

II. **Conflict:** Should organ donors be compensated to increase the availability of organs for transplantation? (par. 3)

III. **Satel's Objection:** NKF unfairly assumes *altruism* as a moral absolute (pars. 4–6)

  A. **Commodification of Body Parts:** NKF's position (par. 7), Satel's response (pars. 8–10)

  B. **Motivation for donating:** NKF's position, Satel's response (par. 11)

  C. **Market for organs:** Satel's position, NKF's response (par. 12); illegal black market, other views (par. 13)

IV. **Conclusion:** Summarizes conflict—morality vs. practicality (par. 14)

⊞ Develop your analysis.

Once you have a working thesis statement and outline, review your notes, including the writing you may have done to analyze your audience (p. 176) as well as the comparative analysis chart (p. 178) to determine how you can use the ideas and information you have to support your thesis.

The following Ways In activities provide some sentence strategies to help you analyze opposing arguments and develop supporting paragraphs using writing strategies like classification and comparison or contrast. Use the sentence strategies as a jumping-off point—you can always revise them later—or use language of your own from the start.

WAYS IN

HOW CAN I PRESENT MY ANALYSIS OF THE OPPOSING ARGUMENTS?

Analyze a quotation. Compose a few sentences explaining why you think a particular quotation (or group of quotations) suggests a **BASIC VALUE** or other **MOTIVATING FACTOR** that plays an important role in the arguments you are analyzing.

▶ Use of the words/phrase "_____" shows that factor A is central to X's way of thinking.

EXAMPLE   Soave claims "the purpose of the First Amendment, and norms of free speech more generally, is to *prevent* the authorities from re-drawing the parameters relating to speech, since they cannot be trusted to do so fairly." This distrust of government reminds us of the conditions that led to the Declaration of Independence in the first place. (par. 5)

SUMMARIZE *or* **PARAPHRASE** *the disagreement.*

▶ X disagrees with Y about _____ [describe approach]. The basis of their disagreement is _____. Y prefers _____, while X argues that _____ is flawed because _____.

EXAMPLE   Satel's disagreement with the NKF is essentially about its framing the issue of compensation in terms of morality. Or rather, it is about what she sees as the NKF's moral absolutism in what she thinks should be viewed as "a morally pluralistic society." The basis of their disagreement is the proper role of altruism. The NKF emphatically endorses the current "altruistic system." Satel, in contrast, argues that current policy is failing precisely because it is an "altruism-only system." (Gomez, par. 4)

Writing a Draft

Guide to Reading
GUIDE TO WRITING
A Writer at Work
Reflection

181

WHAT EXPLANATORY STRATEGIES COULD I USE?

Consider which explanatory strategies would be most useful in analyzing conflicting positions on the topic. Ask yourself questions like these:

How could I use **COMPARISON AND CONTRAST** *to sharpen similarities and differences between the different points of view?*

▶ While/Whereas X believes/argues/claims _____, Y claims _____.

▶ X is like Y in these ways: _____, _____, _____.

EXAMPLE Like Soave, Baer is concerned with fairness and the unequal distribution of power. However, Baer's concern is not with King George's tyranny over the colonies but with what he calls the "long history" of "discrimination" against disempowered groups such as African Americans. (King, par. 6)

How can I **CLASSIFY** *aspects of the topic or different points of view?*

▶ Topic X can be broken down into such categories as _____, _____, and

   _____.

▶ Some of the reasons Professor X supports _____ include _____, _____, and _____.

EXAMPLE Soave maintains that individual rights should be valued more highly than promoting the common good. (King, par. 5)

   It is about what she sees as the NKF's moral absolutism in what she thinks should be viewed as "a morally pluralistic society." (Gomez, par. 4)

How do I **DEFINE** *terms or concepts that may be unfamiliar to my readers?*

▶ X means _____.

▶ X, a type of _____, is characterized by _____, _____, and _____.

EXAMPLE First, he is talking about hate speech. Although he doesn't use the term, his point is clear: Describing groups of people as "inferior to others, or illegal or unworthy of legal standing," is dehumanizing. (King, par. 8)

What **CAUSES** *or* **EFFECTS** *are important to note?*

▶ The result of _____ is _____.

▶ Because of _____, we no longer do _____.

EXAMPLE If the act of giving is tainted, for example by self-interest rather than selflessness, then the gift itself becomes unacceptable. (Gomez, par. 5) Soave maintains that treating free speech as an adjustable right, rather than as an unchanging absolute right, is a slippery slope because it inevitably leads to the silencing of critics or the less powerful. In fact, Soave argues that Baer does just that by defending the censoring of would-be campus speakers whose speech he doesn't like. (par.11)

For more about definition, classification, and comparison and contrast, see Chapter 15; for more on cause and effect, see Chapter 9.

Draft the opening sentences.

Review what you have written to see if you have something that would help you start your analysis, or try out one or two of these opening strategies:

Cite **statistics** *to show readers the importance of the topic.*

> The statistics tell a grim story. There is a wide gap between the supply of kidneys available for transplant and the nearly 100,000 Americans on the kidney transplant waiting list. According to the most recent data, 17,107 surgeries were performed in 2014, while 4,761 patients died awaiting a match and 3,668 people were removed from the list because they became too sick for a transplant ("Organ Donation"). (Gomez, par. 1)

Begin with a **report of dramatic events** *to show the relevance or importance of the topic.*

> From spring through fall of 2017, several universities across the nation were rocked by conflicts over who should and should not be allowed to speak on campus. Protests erupted on campuses from Auburn to UC Berkeley. . . (King, par. 1)

Cite an interesting and relevant **quotation** *to intrigue your readers or show the topic's larger cultural relevance.*

> Congress shall make no law . . . abridging the freedom of speech.
>
> — First Amendment, Constitution of the United States (King epigraph)

At this point, you simply want an opening sentence to launch your draft. Later, you may discover a better way to capture your readers' attention.

Draft your comparative analysis.

By this point, you have done a lot of writing to

- summarize sources accurately and concisely;
- comment on how sources relate to one another;
- create bibliographic citations for sources;
- synthesize various background sources;
- analyze the opposing arguments;
- probe the factors motivating the opposing views;
- explore explanatory strategies you could use;
- draft a working thesis;
- organize your ideas to make them clear, logical, and effective for readers;
- consider possible opening sentences.

Now stitch that material together to create a draft. The next two parts of the Guide to Writing will help you evaluate and improve your draft.

Evaluating the Draft

Guide to Reading
GUIDE TO WRITING
A Writer at Work
Reflection

183

Evaluating the Draft: Using Peer Review

Your instructor may arrange a peer review session in class or online, where you can exchange drafts with your classmates and give one another a thoughtful critical reading, pointing out what works well and suggesting ways to improve the draft. A good critical reading does three things:

1. It lets the writer know how well the reader understands the point of the essay.

2. It praises what works best.

3. It indicates where the draft could be improved and makes suggestions on how to improve it.

One strategy for evaluating a draft is to use the basic features of the genre you are composing as a guide. Also, be sure to respond to any concerns the writer has shared with you.

Did you know?

Peer review helps writers become more confident as writers and as readers.

A PEER REVIEW GUIDE

An Informative Introduction

Has the writer explained the issue and opposing positions clearly and in a way that will engage readers' interest?

Summarize: Briefly tell the writer what you understand the issue to be and what the opposing positions are.

Praise: Indicate where the writer does a good job explaining the issue, introducing the authors, or engaging readers' interest.

Critique: Describe any confusion or uncertainty you have about the issue, about why it is important, or about the positions the essays being analyzed take on it.

A Probing Analysis

Is the writer's analysis of the points of disagreement interesting and insightful?

Summarize: Tell the writer what you understand to be the crux of the disagreement.

Praise: Identify one or two passages where the analysis seems especially effective — for example, where a motivating factor, such as a basic value or belief, is shown to be driving the debate.

Critique: Identify places where the choice of words in a quotation could be unpacked, an explanatory strategy could be used (such as defining key terms), or the analysis could be deepened. Let the writer know if you detect any other motivating factors that might be used to clarify the disagreement.

(continued)

A Fair and Impartial Presentation

Has the writer represented the opposing arguments in a balanced, unbiased way?

Summarize: Circle the words used to describe the proponents, and underline the words used to describe their views.

Praise: Note any passages where the writer comes across as being especially fair and impartial.

Critique: Tell the writer if the authors and their positions are presented unfairly or if one side seems to be favored over the other. Identify passages that seem critical of the proponents or their views, and suggest ways the writer could make his or her points less negative, such as by using quotations to state criticisms or replacing negative words with neutral ones.

A Clear, Logical Organization

Is the essay clear and readable?

Summarize: Underline the thesis, and circle key terms that forecast the topics the essay will focus on. Then circle those key terms when they appear elsewhere in the essay.

Praise: Pick one or two places where the essay is especially clear and easy to follow — for example, where the writer has repeated key terms or their synonyms effectively, or where the writer has used comparative transitions, such as *both* or *as well as* to signal similarity and *whereas* or *although* to signal differences.

Critique: Let the writer know where the readability could be improved — for example, where a topic sentence could be clearer or where a transition is needed. Suggest a better beginning or a more effective ending.

Improving the Draft: Revising, Editing, and Proofreading

Start improving your draft by reflecting on what you have written thus far:

- Review peer review comments from your classmates, as well as feedback from your instructor or a writing center tutor: What problems do your readers identify?
- Consider your invention writing: What else could you add? Is more research needed?
- Review your draft: What can you do to make your analysis more informative, interesting, perceptive, or clearly organized?

Revise your draft.

If your readers are having difficulty with your draft, or if you think there is room for improvement, try some of the strategies listed in the Troubleshooting Guide that follows. They can help you fine-tune your presentation of each genre's basic features.

Improving the Draft

Guide to Reading
▶ **GUIDE TO WRITING**
A Writer at Work
Reflection

185

A TROUBLESHOOTING GUIDE

An Informative Introduction

> My readers are not clear about the issue or the opposing positions.

- State the issue explicitly as a question.
- Explain the issue in more depth, perhaps providing an example or statistics to show why it is important.
- Put the issue in context by providing historical or cultural background.
- Use a transition (such as *whereas* or *although*), or repeat key words or synonyms to sharpen the contrast between the opposing positions.

> My readers are not interested or do not appreciate the issue's importance.

- Add information showing the impact of the issue or how it affects people's lives.
- Contextualize the issue in history, politics, or culture.
- Quote notable authorities to emphasize the issue's importance.
- Cite polls or research studies, or use graphics to convey statistical information demonstrating the widespread impact of the issue.

A Probing Analysis

> My readers do not understand my analysis.

- Determine whether you are trying to cover too many points.
- Explain in more detail the points that are harder for readers to grasp.
- Consider emphasizing the less obvious points of agreement.
- Add supporting summaries, paraphrases, or quotations from the texts you are analyzing.

> My analysis seems more like a summary of the arguments than a probing analysis.

- Ask yourself why the writer makes a particular kind of argument rather than another kind of argument.
- Consider how the writer's profession or biography could explain why a particular motivating factor (such as a value, belief, or fear) has so much persuasive power.
- Think about the social and political situation in which each essay was originally written and how the writer was trying to appeal to readers.
- Examine the concessions and refutations of opposing views.

(continued)

A Fair and Impartial Presentation

My presentation is not impartial or balanced.

- Give equal space to both arguments.
- Make sure that you are representing each writer accurately and fairly by relying more on quoting than on summarizing or paraphrasing.
- Consider your word choices, replacing judgmental words with neutral ones.

A Clear, Logical Organization

My readers are confused by my essay or find it difficult to read.

- Consider adding a forecasting statement to preview the topics you discuss.
- Add topic sentences or repeat key terms in topic sentences.
- Add transitions to signal comparisons or contrasts.

Edit and proofread your final draft.

Editing means making changes to the text to ensure that it follows the conventions of style, grammar, spelling, and mechanics appropriate to the rhetorical situation. **Proofreading** involves checking to make sure the text follows these conventions and that no words are repeated or omitted. You have probably done some editing and proofreading while composing and improving your draft, but it is always good practice to edit and proofread a draft after you have revised it and before you submit it.

Most writers get the best results by leaving time — even just an hour or two — between the stages of revising, editing, and proofreading, so that they can return to their writing project with fresh eyes. When possible, enlist a friend or classmate to proofread the final draft of your writing projects. When that is not possible, proofread from the last line to the first, to avoid seeing what you expect to find rather than what is actually on the page (or screen).

As rhetorical situations change, so, too, do the conventions or expectations readers bring to the text. For example, whereas e-mail messages to friends are usually quite informal, filled with abbreviations, emojis, and sentence fragments, final drafts of writing projects for college classes or the workplace are expected to follow a more formal set of conventions concerning clarity, style, grammar, and punctuation.

We recommend that you make a list of the problems your instructors frequently point out in your writing, then use that list to guide your editing and proofreading. A Guide to Editing and Proofreading (at the end of this text) provides a checklist of the most common problems writers face. For issues that go beyond those on this list, consult a handbook* or search for advice online at sites like the Purdue Online Writing Lab (owl.english.purdue.edu) or Grammarly (grammarly.com). For practice identifying and correcting errors, try the activities in LearningCurve, a game-like

A Note on Grammar and Spelling Checkers

Spelling checkers cannot catch misspellings that are themselves words, such as *to* for *too*, and grammar checkers miss problems, give faulty advice, and even flag correct items as wrong. Use these tools as a second line of defense after your own (and, ideally, another reader's) proofreading efforts.

---

* The full version of *The St. Martin's Guide to Writing* includes a handbook.

adaptive quizzing program available on LaunchPad for *The St. Martin's Guide to Writing*. The less well you do on activities in one topic area, the more LearningCurve focuses on it; the better you do, the more challenging the questions become.

A WRITER AT WORK

Max King's Analysis

Max King's instructor chose the issue "Should offensive speakers be allowed to speak on college campus?" He also posted several arguments from which students could choose. King chose those by Ulrich Baer and Robby Soave, which formed a clear debate in that Soave explicitly responds to Baer's arguments.

To decide how he could analyze and explain their debate, he began by carefully rereading and annotating each essay, highlighting key passages, making marginal comments that summarized the main points, and adding his own comments and questions.

To learn more about annotating sources, see Chapter 12.

Par.	Baer's text with King's highlighting	King's Comments
8	The great value and importance of freedom of expression, for higher education and for democracy, is hard to overestimate. But it has been regrettably easy for commentators to create a simple dichotomy between a younger generation's oversensitivity and free speech as an <u>absolute good</u> that leads to the truth. We would do better to focus on a more sophisticated understanding, such as the one provided by Lyotard, of the <u>necessary conditions</u> for speech to be a common, public good. This requires the realization that in politics, the parameters of public speech must be continually redrawn to accommodate those who previously had no standing.	Why "regrettable"? Too "simple"? Common view: free speech leads to truth NOT "absolute good"? To be a "common, public good": (1) must allow those denied a voice to speak
10	The idea of freedom of speech does <u>not</u> mean a blanket permission to say anything anybody thinks. It means balancing the inherent value of a given view with the obligation to ensure that other members of a given community can participate in discourse as fully recognized members of that community. Free-speech protections — not only but especially in universities, which aim to educate students in how to belong to various communities — should <u>not</u> mean that someone's humanity, or their right to participate in political speech as political agents, can be freely attacked, demeaned or questioned.	Redefines freedom of speech in terms of fairness & equality (2) must NOT demean or invalidate others' humanity

Then King filled in the comparative analysis chart from the Guide to Writing. Filling in the chart not only helped him deepen his analysis of each essay but also showed him how to synthesize—make connections—between the arguments. Notice that he did not try to be exhaustive, to cover every aspect of the essays. Instead, he tried to focus on the main debate over what freedom of speech actually means to Baer and Soave.

Comparative Analysis Chart		
Source	**Baer**	**Soave**
Framing of Issue	Should speakers who demean others be banned from college campuses?	Should all speakers be allowed to exercise their right to free speech on campus?
Position	Campuses should ban demeaning hate speech.	The right to free speech must be preserved, no matter who is offended by it.
Arguments	Because not all speech serves the "public good" (5)	Because freedom of speech is an "individual right," not a "public good" (3)
	Because free speech "is not an unchanging absolute" right. As a "public good," it "requires the vigilant and continuing examination of its parameters" to include those who have been excluded (15)	Because freedom of speech must remain absolute to prevent unfairness. No one's "right to participate in political speech" should be restricted, including Charles Murray's and Ann Coulter's (5)
	Because freedom of speech "should not mean that someone's humanity, or their right to participate in political speech as political agents, can be freely attacked, demeaned or questioned" (10)	Concedes speech that invalidates people's humanity "may be wrong and legitimately hurtful" (3), but argues it "does not restrict their speech" (3)
	Because "the internet, where all kinds of offensive expression flourish unfettered" replaces the university as the marketplace of ideas (7)	Because public universities must "defend speech and opportunity on an equal basis for all the members of its community" (6)
Credibility and Tone	Respected publication by distinguished professor. Tone: condescending, lecturing	Experienced journalist, important libertarian publication. Tone: self-righteous
Motivating Factors: Values, Beliefs, Concerns, Priorities, Interests Served, etc.	Balance values of free speech & human dignity	Preserves free speech rights
	Values fairness & inclusiveness — esp. for historically disempowered "minorities" (14)	Values fairness & inclusiveness — esp. "disfavored people — like Coulter" and Murray (5)
	Concerned about protecting people from hate speech	Concerned about protecting the First Amendment
	Fears silencing minority groups	Fears silencing unpopular voices
	Historically disempowered benefit	Society as a whole benefits, which benefits from exposure to unpopular views

Filling in the chart led King to a clear plan for his essay. He decided that the core of his analysis had to be the disagreement about whether freedom of speech should be seen as an individual right or as a public good. Analyzing this fundamental disagreement led King to examine what and who is endangered by restricting free speech (as Baer advocates) or by allowing complete freedom of speech, including offensive or hate speech (as Soave argues). He was planning to conclude by examining the role of the university in all of this but decided that there wasn't much said in either of the essays about this topic.

The benefit of reflection is proven and important: It helps consolidate what you have learned so that you can remember and apply it well beyond this class. That is why we have included questions and comments in the margins and at the end of this chapter: to stimulate your thinking about profiles, your rhetorical situation, and the choices you make as a writer.

Reflecting on Reading and Writing a Comparative Analysis Essay

To reflect on your experience analyzing opposing arguments, try writing a blog post, a letter to your instructor, or an e-mail message to a student who will take this course next term. Use any of these writing prompts that seem productive:

- Explain how your purpose and audience—what you wanted your readers to learn about the debate from reading your analysis—influenced *one* of your decisions as a writer, such as what you chose to quote and what you summarized, or how you organized your essay.

- Discuss what you learned about yourself as a writer in the process of writing this analysis. Consider what part of the process you found most challenging—for example, choosing opposing arguments you could write about with some authority, analyzing instead of just summarizing what each side said, keeping your own opinion out of the essay, or being evenhanded in your representation of the opposing views. Did you try anything new, like participating in a peer review of your draft or outlining your draft in order to revise it? If so, how successful was it?

- Describe one way a reading in this chapter influenced your essay. For example, perhaps something you read suggested how you could probe the disagreement or contributed a sentence pattern that helped you compare and contrast the different points of view.

Reflecting on Your Composing Process

Thinking about your process for analyzing opposing arguments can be useful in helping you decide what works best for you as a writer. Using one or more of the following questions as a starting point, write a paragraph or two about your composing process:

- How challenging was it to do background research on the debate? How well do you think you used what you learned to introduce your analysis of the opposing argument essays?

- How challenging was it to fill in the comparative analysis chart, and how well did the chart help you plan and compose your essay?

- Explain how peer review helped you—perhaps by suggesting a better way to engage readers' interest in the debate or by identifying an underlying value you had neglected.

- Did your own thinking about the issue being debated change or deepen as you analyzed and synthesized the opposing arguments? How well prepared are you now to write a position essay of your own?

- How satisfied are you with the process you used? If you could go back in time, what would you have done differently? If you could continue working on your analysis, what would you like to do?

6

Arguing a Position

Should parents think twice before signing up their kids for Little League? Might it *not* be a good idea for teens to get after-school jobs? Should hate speech be protected? Should you care about online privacy if you haven't done anything wrong? These are the compelling issues argued about in this chapter. Because of the in-your-face kind of arguing that is common in blogs and on talk shows, you may associate arguing with quarreling. Although this kind of "argument" lets people vent strong feelings, it seldom leads them to consider other points of view seriously or to think critically about their own reasons or underlying values. A more thoughtful, deliberative kind of argument, one that depends on critical analysis of an issue and involves logical reasoning rather than raised voices, is more likely to convince others of the validity of your position. Reasoned argument is also more likely to be expected in college courses and in the workplace.

You might compose this thoughtful kind of argument for a variety of purposes and audiences and publish your efforts in a variety of media. For example, in a college course on law and society, a student might write a blog post supporting the position that the race of a murder victim is the crucial factor determining whether the death penalty is sought. A group of parents might publish an open letter in the local newspaper arguing in favor of requiring teachers to give students trigger warnings when teaching potentially disturbing topics. In the workplace, a consultant may make a presentation, citing statistics and examples, to argue that sustainable environmental practices are good for business.

In this chapter, we ask you to compose a position argument on a controversial issue. Your argument should try to convince readers to adopt your point of view or at least to consider it seriously. From reading and analyzing the selections in the Guide to Reading (pp. 193–218) you will learn how writers frame and support a position so that readers will take it seriously. The Guide to Writing (pp. 219–35) will support your composing by showing you how to choose and frame an arguable position, marshal compelling evidence to support it, respond to naysayers, and organize it in a way that makes your argument as compelling as possible.

| PRACTICING THE GENRE |

Debating a Position

To get a sense of what's involved in arguing a position, get together with a small group of students to discuss an issue you have strong feelings about.

Part 1.   Choose an issue you all know something about, or pick one of the following:

- Should college be paid for by taxes the way K–12 is?
- Should general education requirements be continued (or discontinued) at your college?
- Should drinking alcohol be banned on campuses?
- Should online courses replace large face-to-face lecture courses?

First, decide on your audience and purpose: Is your audience other students, faculty, administrators, or the general public? Is your purpose to persuade audience members to change their minds, confirm their opinions, move them to action, or something else? Then take five minutes as a group to sketch out the arguments for and against your issue. Take turns presenting your arguments to the rest of the class.

Part 2.   After your presentations, discuss what you learned:

- **What did you learn about the genre from listening to others' arguments?** Were you convinced by the arguments? Would the intended audience have been convinced? That is, was the position presented with the audience's values in mind?

- **What did you learn about the genre from presenting your group's position?** Discuss with your group what was easiest and hardest about presenting your position — for example, finding enough evidence that your audience would find convincing, anticipating opposing views, or appealing to the values of your audience.

Take a moment . . .

In writing a position essay, why is it important to consider your readers' beliefs and values, not just your own?

Analyzing Position Arguments

As you read the selections in this chapter, you will see how different authors argue convincingly for their positions:

- Jessica Statsky argues that organized sports activities can be harmful for children aged six to twelve (pp. 198–204).
- Laura Beth Nielsen uses sociological research to support her argument that hate speech should not be protected under the First Amendment (pp. 205–6).
- Amitai Etzioni challenges the idea that after-school work, especially at fast food restaurants, is good for teenagers (pp. 209–11).
- Daniel J. Solove argues that protecting our privacy on the Internet is crucially important even if we feel we have "nothing to hide" (pp. 213–16).

Analyzing how these writers focus and frame their arguments to appeal to the hearts and minds of readers, anticipate and respond to opposing views, and select and present evidence that will convince readers and refute objections will help you see how you can employ these techniques to make your own position argument clear and compelling for your readers.

Determine the writer's purpose and audience.

Although arguing a position helps writers decide where they stand on the issue and why, writers typically compose arguments to influence their readers. As you read the position arguments that follow, ask yourself what the writer's main purpose is and what he or she assumes about the reader:

The writer's main purpose may be to

- change readers' minds by challenging their values and beliefs
- convince readers to look anew at the reasons and evidence
- confirm the writers' refutation of possible objections
- strengthen readers' opinions by providing them with convincing arguments
- move readers to take action by stressing the urgency or seriousness of the issue

The writer wants readers to react by

- thinking critically about the values and beliefs underlying their position
- reexamining the reasons and evidence
- seriously considering the writer's refutation
- reconsidering an issue they had been certain about
- inspiring readers to do something about the issue

Assess the genre's basic features.

As you read the position arguments in this chapter, consider how different authors incorporate the basic features of the genre. The examples that follow are drawn from the reading selections that appear later in this Guide to Reading.

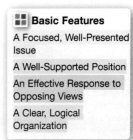

Basic Features

A Focused, Well-Presented Issue

A Well-Supported Position

An Effective Response to Opposing Views

A Clear, Logical Organization

A FOCUSED, WELL-PRESENTED ISSUE

Read first to identify the issue. An issue is a matter of opinion about which people may disagree. Look for key words in the title and opening paragraphs that indicate what people are arguing about.

Topic
Position

Why Privacy Matters Even if You Have "Nothing to Hide" (Solove)

To explain the rhetorical situation or context in which people are arguing about the issue, writers may use a simple sentence pattern like this:

To learn more about making an arguable claim, see Chapter 16.

▶ When X happens, most people think _____, but I think _____ because _____.

For example, Solove uses this strategy in his opening paragraph:

> When the government gathers or analyzes personal information, many people say . . . (par. 1)

For Solove, this "but I think . . . because . . ." response to the common view serves as his main argumentative strategy.

Reflect on . . .

Consider how writers' decisions about framing may affect their credibility with readers.

Notice how the writer frames the issue and establishes its significance. **Framing** an issue is like cropping and resizing a photograph to focus the viewer's eye on one part of the picture (see Figure 6.1). Writers frame an issue to set the stage for their argument and promote their point of view. They may suggest that particular values are at stake or raise in readers' minds certain concerns having to do with the issue. As you read, notice how each writer frames the issue, asking yourself questions like these:

FIGURE 6.1   Framing an issue

By cropping this photograph of a protest march to focus on the little boy, the photographer softens the message; the broader issue of climate change is framed in terms of saving the planet for these children.

- Who, or what groups of people, does the writer associate with each position, and how does the writer characterize their views? For example, does one side appear thoughtful, moderate, and knowledgeable, and the other side extreme, unreasonable, or self-interested?

- What does the writer suggest is really at stake, and for whom? If you were unfamiliar with the issue, what did the writer lead you to think and feel about it? If you were already familiar with it, which of your preconceptions were reinforced and which were challenged by the writer's way of framing the issue?

© Patrick Ward/Alamy Stock Photo

A WELL-SUPPORTED POSITION

Identify the writer's position, and determine whether the position is appropriately qualified. To argue effectively, writers need to assert an arguable position (an opinion, not a fact that can be proved or disproved or a belief that must be taken on faith). They may also need to *qualify* that position (for example, by using words like *may* and by specifying conditions) to avoid making a claim that is too strong to be defended given the available evidence.

Analyzing Position Arguments

GUIDE TO READING
Guide to Writing
A Writer at Work
Reflection

195

In a position argument, writers typically declare their positions in a thesis state-ment early on in the essay. Notice, for example, how Jessica Statsky states her thesis:

> When overzealous parents and coaches impose adult standards on children's sports, the result can be activities that are neither satisfying nor beneficial to children.
>
>   I am concerned about all organized sports activities for children between the ages of six and twelve. (pars. 1–2)

Qualifying terms

She makes a claim that reasonable people could dispute, and she qualifies her claim by limiting its scope (not all children, just those between six and twelve).

Examine the main reasons and the evidence the writer provides. Make sure that the reasons clearly support the writer's position and that the evidence (facts, statistics, examples, research studies, expert testimony) is credible.

Look for sentence strategies like these that introduce supporting reasons:

▶ What makes issue X problematic/praiseworthy is ....

▶ Because of ...., I support/oppose X.

EXAMPLE   Another reason I oppose competitive sports for children is that they are so highly selective that very few children get to participate. (Statsky, par. 10)

Credible evidence is both relevant and representative; that is, it must clearly support the reason (which must in turn support the topic sentence and thesis), and it must be typical. The following example demonstrates an approach to introducing supporting evidence:

> 24 percent . . . worked . . . five to seven days a week. . . . There is just no way such amounts of work will not interfere with school work, especially homework. In an informal survey . . . , 58 percent of seniors acknowledged that their jobs interfere with their school work. (Etzioni, par. 13)

Statistics
Reason

Also consider whether the evidence the writer provides appeals to readers' intellect, values, or emotions and avoids logical fallacies. Writers can draw on various types of evidence—from facts to anecdotes to photographs and flowcharts—to support their positions, but position arguments are most convincing when writers are able to appeal to readers on three levels:

- **Logos:** Appeal to readers' intellect, presenting readers with logical reasoning and reliable evidence
- **Ethos:** Appeal to readers' perception of the writer's credibility and fairness
- **Pathos:** Appeal to readers' values and feelings

Ask yourself how effectively the writer appeals to readers' intellect, sense of fairness, and emotions:

- Is the argument logical and reasonable (logos)?
- Does the writer appear credible and trustworthy (ethos)?
- Are the values and feelings sincere or manipulative (pathos)?

To learn more about making an arguable claim, supporting a claim with evidence, and arguing logically and effectively, see Chapter 16.

AN EFFECTIVE RESPONSE TO OPPOSING VIEWS

Notice whether the author anticipates readers' objections and opposing arguments, and whether he or she refutes or concedes those objections and arguments. Writers **refute** (rebut or argue against) opposing views when they can show that the opposing view is weak or flawed. A typical refutation (or rebuttal) states the problem with the opposing view and then explains why the view is problematic, using sentence strategies like these:

> ▶ One problem with position A is that _____ .

> ▶ Some claim _____ , but in reality _____ .

Writers often introduce the rebuttal with a **transition** or cue that indicates contrast, such as *but, although, nevertheless,* or *however*:

Transition
Refutation

The deeper problem with the nothing-to-hide argument is that it myopically views privacy as a form of secrecy. In contrast, understanding privacy as a plurality of related issues demonstrates that the disclosure of bad things is just one among many difficulties caused by government security measures. (Solove, par. 10)

Writers may also **concede** (accept) valid objections, concerns, or reasons. A typical way of conceding is to use sentence strategies like these:

> ▶ I agree that _____ .

> ▶ _____ is certainly an important factor.

Here is a concession from Jessica Statsky's essay:

> I acknowledge that some children may benefit from playing competitive sports. (par. 14)

Conceding a strong opposing view reassures readers that the writer shares their values and builds a bridge of shared concerns.

Frequently, though, writers reach out to readers by making a concession but then go on to point out where they differ. We call this the **concession-refutation move.** Like writers refuting a point, writers making the concession-refutation move often follow their concession with a transition indicating contrast to signal that an exception or refinement is coming. Here's an example:

Concession
Transition
Refutation

True, you still have to have the gumption to get yourself over to the hamburger stand, **but** once you don the prescribed uniform, your task is spelled out in minute detail. (Etzioni, par. 7)

While reading position arguments, assess the effectiveness of the responses by asking yourself questions like these:

- Do they appeal to shared values (pathos) or seem trite or maudlin?
- Do they offer compelling reasons and credible evidence (logos) or simply make unsubstantiated assertions or criticisms?

- Do they draw on authorities whose expertise is established (ethos) or merely refer vaguely to "some" or "many" people with whom they agree? Do the responses to opposing views seem significant and genuine or trivial and insincere?

- Do they misrepresent the opposition (committing a *straw man fallacy*) or attack people personally (committing an *ad hominem fallacy*)?

To learn more about logical fallacies, see Chapter 16.

A CLEAR, LOGICAL ORGANIZATION

Look for a thesis statement that asserts the writer's position and provides a forecast of the reasons the writer will offer. For instance, Amitai Etzioni grabs readers' attention with an alarming sentence — "McDonald's is bad for your kids" — and then goes on to explain just how McDonald's is bad for kids in the next sentence:

> I do not mean the flat patties and the white-flour buns; I refer to the jobs teen-agers undertake, mass-producing these choice items. (par. 1)

In addition to asserting the thesis, writers sometimes preview the reasons in the order they will bring them up later in the essay, as in this example of a *forecasting statement* by Jessica Statsky:

> Highly organized competitive sports . . . are too often played to adult standards, which are developmentally inappropriate for children and can be both physically and psychologically harmful. Furthermore, . . . they are actually counterproductive for developing either future players or fans. Finally, . . . they . . . provide occasions for some parents and coaches to place their own fantasies and needs ahead of children's welfare. (par. 2)

Reasons

Transitions

Notice also where the writer uses *logical transitions* to indicate

- supporting evidence (*because*),
- exceptions (*however*),
- concessions (*admittedly*),
- refutations (*on the other hand*),
- conclusions (*therefore*),
- reasons (*first, finally*).

Transitions may be useful in a forecasting statement, as in the preceding example, or in the *topic sentence* of a paragraph or group of paragraphs, as shown in these examples from Solove's position argument:

> One such harm, for example . . . Another potential problem with . . . is . . . A related problem involves . . . Yet another problem (pars. 11–14)

To learn more about using transitions to cue readers, see Chapter 13.

Readings

Jessica Statsky | *Children Need to Play, Not Compete*

To learn more about how
Jessica Statsky developed
her response to readers'
likely objections, see
A Writer at Work on
pp. 235–37. If you could
have given Statsky advice in
a peer review of her drafts,
what objections would you
have advised her to respond
to, and how do you think
she could have responded?

THIS ESSAY by Jessica Statsky about children's competitive sports was written for a college composition course. When you were a child, you may have had experience playing competitive sports, in or out of school, for example in Peewee Football, Little League Baseball, American Youth Soccer, or some other organization. Or you may have had relatives or friends who were deeply involved in sports.

As you read,

- reflect on your own experience and observation of youth sports. Was winning unduly emphasized or was more value placed on having a good time, learning to get along with others, developing athletic skills, or something else altogether?

- think about how effectively Statsky uses the basic features of the genre (listed below), and answer the questions in the margins; your instructor may ask you to post your thoughts and answers to a class blog or discussion board or to bring your responses to class.

▦ Basic Features

A Focused,
Well-Presented Issue

A Well-Supported Position

An Effective Response to
Opposing Views

A Clear, Logical
Organization

1   "Organized sports for young people have become an institution in North America," reports sports journalist Steve Silverman, attracting more than 44 million youngsters according to a survey by the National Council of Youth Sports. Though many adults regard Little League Baseball and Peewee Football as a basic part of childhood, the games are not always joyous ones. When overzealous parents and coaches impose adult standards on children's sports, the result can be activities that are neither satisfying nor beneficial to children.

How does Statsky qualify her position?

2   I am concerned about all organized sports activities for children between the ages of six and twelve. The damage I see results from noncontact as well as contact sports, from sports organized locally as well as those organized nationally. Highly organized competitive sports such as Peewee Football and Little League Baseball are too often played to adult standards, which are developmentally inappropriate for children and can be both physically and psychologically harmful. Furthermore, because they eliminate many children from organized sports before they are ready to compete, they are actually counterproductive for developing either future players or fans. Finally, because they emphasize competition and winning, they unfortunately provide occasions for some parents and coaches to place their own fantasies and needs ahead of children's welfare.

3   Yet many parents would disagree with my view that children should not be encouraged to participate in organized sports. Parents are correct to be frustrated by their children's lack of physical activity. We are living in a culture where too many children spend their time in front of the television, a computer screen playing video games, or on social media. A recent analysis of the National Health and Nutrition Examination Survey found that even young children are surprisingly inactive:

> Children should get at least an hour of moderate-to-vigorous exercise a day, according to the World Health Organization. But the study showed that among kids ages 6–11, 25% of boys and 50% of girls did not meet this recommendation. (Park)

There's no doubt that organized sports get children on their feet and out of the house. However, the risks of participating in competitive sports at a young age may well outweigh the health benefits.

4   One readily understandable danger of overly competitive sports is that they entice children into physical actions that are bad for growing bodies. "There is a growing epidemic of preventable youth sports injuries" according to the American Orthopaedic Society for Sports Medicine: "Among athletes ages 5 to 14, 28 percent of football players, 25 percent of baseball players, 22 percent of soccer players, 15 percent of basketball players, and 12 percent of softball players were injured while playing their respective sports" (*STOP Sports Injuries*). Although the official Little League Web site acknowledges that children do risk injury playing baseball, it insists that "severe injuries . . . are infrequent," the risk "far less than the risk of riding a skateboard, a bicycle, or even the school bus" ("What about My Child?"). Nevertheless, Leonard Koppett in *Sports Illusion, Sports Reality* claims that a twelve-year-old trying to throw a curve ball, for example, may put abnormal strain on developing arm and shoulder muscles, sometimes resulting in lifelong injuries (294). Contact sports like football can be even more hazardous. Thomas Tutko, a psychology professor at San Jose State University and coauthor of the book *Winning Is Everything and Other American Myths*, writes:

> I am strongly opposed to young kids playing tackle football. It is not the right stage of development for them to be taught to crash into other kids. Kids under the age of fourteen are not by nature physical. Their main concern is self-preservation. They don't want to meet head on and slam into each other. But tackle football absolutely requires that they try to hit each other as hard as they can. And it is too traumatic for young kids. (qtd. in Tosches A1)

Why do you think Statsky begins with the concession/refutation move?

How does Statsky try to establish the credibility (ethos) of her sources in pars. 4–7?

Why do you think Statsky uses block quotations instead of integrating these quotes into her own sentences?

5   As *New York Times* health columnist Jane Brody reports in "Concussions Can Occur in All Youth Sports," the discovery that professional football players suffer long-term brain damage from multiple concussions "has prompted a much closer look at how children and adolescents who participate in sports can be protected from similar consequences." Although the focus has been on high school athletes, Brody notes that "sports-related concussions account for more than half of all emergency room visits by children aged 8 through 13." Moreover, a new Boston University School of Medicine study found that any head injury — whether a concussion or something less (often called a subconcussive, or micro, injury that builds up over time) — can result in the degenerative brain disease called chronic traumatic enceph-alopathy (CTE) (Boren). For young people especially, the cumulative effect of small hits (what has been called "the bobblehead effect") appears to do the lasting dam-age. Few sports are free from the risk of head injury. For boys, the most risky sport is predictably tackle football, followed closely by lacrosse, ice hockey, and wrestling. For girls, soccer seems to be the most dangerous (apparently resulting more from collisions between players than from heading the ball), followed by basketball and gymnastics.

6   Even when children are not injured, Tutko points out, fear of being hurt detracts from their enjoyment of the sport. The Little League Web site ranks fear of injury as the seventh of seven reasons children quit ("What about My Child?"). One mother of an eight-year-old Peewee Football player explained, "The kids get so scared. They get hit once and they don't want anything to do with football anymore. They'll sit on the bench and pretend their leg hurts" (qtd. in Tosches A1). Some children are driven to even more desperate measures. For example, in one Peewee Football game, a reporter watched the following scene as a player took himself out of the game:

> "Coach, my tummy hurts. I can't play," he said. The coach told the player to get back onto the field. "There's nothing wrong with your stomach," he said. When the coach turned his head the seven-year-old stuck a finger down his throat and made himself vomit. When the coach turned back, the boy pointed to the ground and told him, "Yes there is, coach. See?" (Tosches A33)

7   Besides physical hazards and anxieties, competitive sports pose psychological dangers for children. Martin Rablovsky, a former sports editor for the *New York Times*, says that in all his years of watching young children play organized sports, he has noticed very few of them smiling. "I've seen children enjoying a spontaneous pre-practice scrimmage become somber and serious when the coach's whistle blows," Rablovsky says. "The spirit of play suddenly disappears, and sport becomes job-like" (qtd. in Coakley 94). The primary goal of a professional athlete — winning — is not appropriate for children. Their goals should be having fun, learning, and being with friends. Although winning does add to the fun, too many adults lose sight of what matters and make winning the most important goal. Several studies have shown that when children are asked whether they would rather be warming the bench on a winning team or playing regularly on a losing team, about 90 percent choose the latter (Smith, Smith, and Smoll 11).

8   Winning and losing may be an inevitable part of adult life, but they should not be part of childhood. Too much competition too early in life can affect a child's development. Children are easily influenced, and when they sense that their competence and worth are based on their ability to live up to their parents' and coaches' high expectations — and on their ability to win — they can become discouraged and depressed. Little League advises parents to "keep winning in perspective" ("Your Role"), noting that the most common reasons children give for quitting, aside from change in interest, are lack of playing time, failure and fear of failure, disapproval by significant others, and psychological stress ("What about My Child?"). "According to a poll from the National Alliance for Youth Sports," Julianna W. Miner writes in the *Washington Post*, "around 70 percent of kids in the United States stop playing organized sports by the age of 13 because 'it's just not fun anymore.'"

9   Some parents would no doubt argue that learning to compete is important. Children cannot start too soon preparing to live in a free-market economy. After all, secondary schools and colleges require students to compete for grades, and college admission is extremely competitive. In addition, it is perfectly obvious how important competitive skills are in finding a job. Yet most parents will admit that the ability to cooperate is also important for success in life. Before children are psychologically ready

> How does Statsky try to refute this objection? How effective is her rebuttal? Why?

for competition, maybe we should emphasize cooperation and individual performance in team sports rather than winning.

10   Another reason I oppose competitive sports for children is that they are so highly selective that very few children get to participate. Far too soon, a few children are singled out for their athletic promise, while many others, who may be on the verge of developing the necessary strength and ability, are screened out and discouraged from trying out again. Like adults, children fear failure, and so even those with good physical skills may stay away because they lack self-confidence. Consequently, teams lose many promising players who with some encouragement and experience might have become stars. The problem is that many parent-sponsored, out-of-school programs give more importance to having a winning team than to developing children's physical skills and self-esteem.

> In criticizing some parents' behavior in pars. 11–12, Statsky risks alienating her readers. How effective is this part of her argument?

11   Indeed, it is no secret that too often scorekeeping, league standings, and the drive to win bring out the worst in adults who are more absorbed in living out their own fantasies than in enhancing the quality of the experience for children (Smith, Smith, and Smoll 9). Newspaper articles on children's sports contain plenty of horror stories. *Los Angeles Times* reporter Rich Tosches, for example, tells the story of a brawl among seventy-five parents following a Peewee Football game (A33). As a result of the brawl, which began when a parent from one team confronted a player from the other team, the teams are now thinking of hiring security guards for future games. Another example is provided by a *Los Angeles Times* editorial about a Little League manager who intimidated the opposing team by setting fire to one of their team's jerseys on the pitcher's mound before the game began. As the editorial writer commented, the manager showed his young team that "intimidation could substitute for playing well" ("The Bad News").

12   Although not all parents or coaches behave inappropriately, the seriousness of the problem is illustrated by the fact that Adelphi University in Garden City, New York, offers a sports psychology workshop for Little League coaches, designed to balance their "animal instincts" with "educational theory" in hopes of reducing the "screaming and hollering," in the words of Harold Weisman, manager of sixteen Little Leagues in New York City (Schmitt). In a three-and-one-half-hour Sunday

morning workshop, coaches learn how to make practices more fun, treat injuries, deal with irate parents, and be "more sensitive to their young players' fears, emotional frailties, and need for recognition." Little League is to be credited with recognizing the need for such workshops.

13   There have been some efforts to make organized sports emphasize the fun in playing sports. For example, a New York Little League official who had attended the Adelphi workshop tried to ban scoring from six- to eight-year-olds' games — but parents wouldn't support him (Schmitt). An innovative children's sports program in New York City, City Sports for Kids, emphasizes fitness, self-esteem, and sportsmanship. In this program's basketball games, every member on a team plays at least two of six eight-minute periods. The basket is seven feet from the floor, rather than ten feet, and a player can score a point just by hitting the rim (Bloch). I believe this kind of local program should replace overly competitive programs like Peewee Football and Little League Baseball. As one coach explains, significant improvements can result from a few simple rule changes, such as including every player in the batting order and giving every player, regardless of age or ability, the opportunity to play at least four innings a game (Frank).

14   Some children *want* to play competitive sports; they are not being forced to play. These children are eager to learn skills, to enjoy the camaraderie of the team, and earn self-respect by trying hard to benefit their team. I acknowledge that some children may benefit from playing competitive sports. While some children do benefit from these programs, however, many more would benefit from programs that avoid the excesses and dangers of many competitive sports programs and instead emphasize fitness, cooperation, sportsmanship, and individual performance.

How effective is Statsky's way of concluding her argument?

Works Cited

"The Bad News Pyromaniacs?" *Los Angeles Times,* 16 June 1990, articles.latimes
     .com/1990-06-16/local/me-31_1_team-manager. Editorial.
Bloch, Gordon B. "Thrill of Victory Is Secondary to Fun." *The New York Times,* 2 Apr.
     1990, late ed., p. C12.

Boren, Cindy. "A New Study Shows That Hits to the Head, Not Concussions, Cause CTE." *The Washington Post,* 18 Jan. 2018, www.washingtonpost.com/news/early-lead/wp/2018/01/18/a-new-study-shows-that-hits-to-the-head-not-concussions-cause-cte/?utm_term=.b970.

Brody, Jane. "Concussions Can Occur in All Youth Sports." *The New York Times,* 24 Aug. 2015, nyti.ms/2jVB8In.

Coakley, Jay J. *Sport in Society: Issues and Controversies.* 12th ed., McGraw-Hill Education, 2015.

Frank, L. "Contributions from Parents and Coaches." *CYB Message Board,* 8 July 1997, members.aol.com/JohnHoelter/b-parent.html.

Koppett, Leonard. *Sports Illusion, Sports Reality: A Reporter's View of Sports, Journalism, and Society.* U of Illinois P, 1994.

Miner, Julianna W. "Why 70 percent of Kids Quit Sports by Age 13." *The Washington Post,* 1 June 2016, www.washingtonpost.com/news/parenting/wp/2016/06/01/why-70-percent-of-kids-quit-sports-by-age-13/?utm_term=.1e33111f5912.

Park, Alice. "Teens Are Just as Sedentary as 60 Year Olds." *Time,* 16 June 2017, time.com/4821963/teens-sedentary-lifestyle-exercise.

Schmitt, Eric. "Psychologists Take Seat on Little League Bench." *The New York Times,* 14 Mar. 1988, nyti.ms/2qFsRx0.

Smith, Nathan, et al. *Kidsports: A Survival Guide for Parents.* Addison-Wesley, 1983.

STOP Sports Injuries. American Orthopaedic Society for Sports Medicine. 2017, www.stopsportsinjuries.org/STOP/Resources/Statistics/STOP/Resources/Statistics.aspx?hkey=24daffdf-5313-4970-a47d-ed621dfc7b9b.

Tosches, Rich. "Game's Critics Are Not Amused: Pee Wee Football: Is It Time to Blow the Whistle?" *Los Angeles Times,* 3 Dec. 1988, articles.latimes.com/1988-12-03/news/mn-936_1_youth-football-games.

"What about My Child?" *Little League Online,* 1999, www.eteamz.com/whlittleleague/files/What_About_My_Child.doc.

"Your Role as a Little League Parent." *Little League Online,* 1999, www.littleleagues.org/parents.htm.

Nielsen *The Case for Restricting Hate Speech*

GUIDE TO READING
Guide to Writing
A Writer at Work
Reflection

205

Laura Beth Nielsen | *The Case for Restricting Hate Speech*

Northwestern University,
photo by John Zich

LAURA BETH NIELSEN is a professor of sociology and the director of legal studies at Northwestern University. Nielsen—who has received awards from the MacArthur Foundation, the Ford Foundation, and the National Science Foundation—serves as a research professor at the American Bar Foundation, focusing on law and social change. She has written several books, including *License to Harass: Law, Hierarchy, and Offensive Public Speech* (2004), as well as a number of articles for both scholarly journals and popular news outlets such as the *Huffington Post* and the *Los Angeles Times*, in which this op-ed originally appeared in 2017.

As you read,

- think about your understanding of the part of the First Amendment concerning freedom of speech—"Congress shall make no law . . . abridging the freedom of speech, or of the press"—in light of what Nielsen explains about curtailments of speech in the opening paragraph.

- consider how Nielsen uses a recent Supreme Court decision to frame the issue for her readers. How does this framing affect your attitude toward the issue?

1 As a sociologist and legal scholar, I struggle to explain the boundaries of free speech to undergraduates. Despite the 1st Amendment—I tell my students—local, state, and federal laws limit all kinds of speech. We regulate advertising, obscenity, slander, libel, and inciting lawless action to name just a few. My students nod along until we get to racist and sexist speech. Some can't grasp why, if we restrict so many forms of speech, we don't also restrict hate speech. Why, for example, did the Supreme Court on Monday rule that the trademark office cannot reject "disparaging" applications—like a request from an Oregon band to trademark "the Slants" as in Asian "slant eyes."

2 The typical answer is that judges must balance benefits and harms. If judges are asked to compare the harm of restricting speech—a cherished core constitutional value—to the harm of hurt feelings, judges will rightly choose to protect free expression. But perhaps it's nonsense to characterize the nature of the harm as nothing more than an emotional scratch; that's a reflection of the deep inequalities in our society, and one that demonstrates a profound misunderstanding of how hate speech affects its targets.

People can't falsely yell fire in a theater but can yell the N-word at a person of color.

3 Legally, we tell members of traditionally disadvantaged groups that they must live with hate speech except under very limited circumstances. The KKK can parade down Main Street. People can't falsely yell fire in a theater but can yell the N-word at a person of color. College women are told that a crowd of frat boys chanting "no means yes and yes means anal" is something they must tolerate in the name of (someone else's) freedom.

4 At the same time, our regime of free speech protects the powerful and popular. Many city governments, for instance, have banned panhandling at the behest of their business communities. The legal justification is that the targets of begging (commuters, tourists, and consumers) have important and legitimate purposes for being in public: to get to work or to go shopping. The law therefore protects them from aggressive requests for money.

5 Consider also the protections afforded to soldiers' families in the case of Westboro Baptist anti-gay demonstrations. When the Supreme Court in 2011 upheld that church's right to stage offensive protests at veterans' funerals, Congress passed the Honoring America's Veterans' Act, which prohibits any protests 300 to 500 feet

Members of the Westboro Baptist Church picket in front of the Supreme Court in Washington on October 6, 2010.

around such funerals. (The statute made no mention of protecting LGBTQ funeral attendees from hate speech, just soldiers' families.)

6   So soldiers' families, shoppers and workers are protected from troubling speech. People of color, women walking down public streets or just living in their dorm on a college campus are not. The only way to justify this disparity is to argue that commuters asked for money on the way to work experience a tangible harm, while women catcalled and worse on the way to work do not — as if being the target of a request for change is worse than being racially disparaged by a stranger.

7   In fact, empirical data suggest that frequent verbal harassment can lead to various negative consequences. Racist hate speech has been linked to cigarette smoking, high blood pressure, anxiety, depression and post-traumatic stress disorder, and requires complex coping strategies. Exposure to racial slurs also diminishes academic performance. Women subjected to sexualized speech may develop a phenomenon of "self-objectification," which is associated with eating disorders.

8   These negative physical and mental health outcomes — which embody the historical roots of race and gender oppression — mean that hate speech is not "just speech." Hate speech is doing something. It results in tangible harms that are serious in and of themselves and that collectively amount to the harm of subordination. The harm of perpetuating discrimination. The harm of creating inequality.

9   Instead of characterizing racist and sexist hate speech as "just speech," courts and legislatures need to account for this research and, perhaps, allow the restriction of hate speech as do all of the other economically advanced democracies in the world.

10   Many readers will find this line of thinking repellent. They will insist that protecting hate speech is consistent with and even central to our founding principles. They will argue that regulating hate speech would amount to a serious break from our tradition. They will trivialize the harms that social science research undeniably associates with being the target of hate speech, and call people seeking recognition of these affronts "snowflakes."

11   But these free-speech absolutists must at least acknowledge two facts. First, the right to speak already is far from absolute. Second, they are asking disadvantaged members of our society to shoulder a heavy burden with serious consequences. Because we are "free" to be hateful, members of traditionally marginalized groups suffer.

[REFLECT]   # Make connections: Handling hate speech.

As a legal scholar, Nielsen's focus is on the law and court decisions. But as a sociologist, she's also concerned about "the harms that social science research undeniably associates with being the target of hate speech" (par. 10). To reflect on her argument and the debate surrounding hate and harassing speech, think about your own experience and observation. Your instructor may ask you to post your thoughts on a class discussion board or to discuss them with other students in class. Use these questions to get started:

- Think of an example of hate or harassing speech you have experienced personally, seen, or read about. How widespread or serious a problem does hate speech seem to be in your community, workplace, or school?

- How convincing do you find Nielsen's argument that hate speech should be restricted because it does harm to its victims? If you have witnessed or experienced hate speech, what harm do you think it did?

Use the basic features.

[ANALYZE]

A WELL-SUPPORTED POSITION: USING EXAMPLES

Examples and anecdotes can be especially effective as evidence because they often appeal to readers' values and feelings. Jessica Statsky, for instance, relates an anecdote about a seven-year-old Peewee Football player who made himself vomit to avoid playing. This anecdote delivers the message powerfully, although it runs the risk of being perceived by readers as exaggerated or emotionally manipulative. Writers can also use examples to bring home their claims, making them more concrete, graphic, and convincing, as Statsky does when she tells of "a brawl among seventy-five parents following a Peewee Football game" (par. 11). Because examples are isolated instances, however, they do not necessarily prove the general rule. To get around this, Statsky introduces this example as one of many "horror stories" to suggest that it is not all that unusual, but a fairly typical incident that should be taken seriously as evidence to support her position.

| ANALYZE & WRITE |

Write a paragraph analyzing and evaluating Nielsen's use of examples:

1 Reread paragraphs 3–6, highlighting the examples of hate speech. Which examples are protected, and which are unprotected? What does the photo of the Westboro Baptist Church protest contribute to your understanding of the disparity between protected and unprotected speech?

2 Look closely at paragraphs 7–8. How do the examples in the preceding paragraphs support Nielsen's argument that "hate speech is not 'just speech'" (par. 8)?

3 Consider whether you are persuaded by Nielsen's examples. What additional evidence (if any) would you need to be persuaded to adopt her position?

AN EFFECTIVE RESPONSE: THE CONCESSION-REFUTATION MOVE

Writers of position essays try to anticipate other widely held positions on the issue. Representing opposing points of view fairly and accurately enhances the writer's credibility (or ethos) and also strengthens the argument. When readers holding an opposing position recognize that the writer takes their position seriously, they are more likely to listen to what the writer has to say. It can also reassure readers that they share certain important values and interests with the writer, potentially building a bridge to connect people separated by difference and antagonism. For example, when Statsky acknowledges that parents may be "frustrated by their children's lack of physical activity" (par. 3), she is suggesting that she recognizes her readers' values.

But many writers of position essays (like Statsky) not only acknowledge alternative viewpoints; they also go on to rebut opposing views. In other words, they make the *concession-refutation move*:

Transition

> There's no doubt that organized sports get children on their feet and out of the house. However, the risks of participating in competitive sports at a young age may well outweigh the health benefits. (par. 3)

In this example, Statsky signals that a rebuttal is coming by inserting a transition of contrast (*however*).

ANALYZE & WRITE ────────────────────────────────

Write a paragraph analyzing and evaluating how Nielsen presents and responds to an opposing point of view:

1 Reread paragraphs 10–11, noting how Nielsen represents her opponents' views.

2 Now reread paragraph 2. How does Nielsen use the concession-refutation move here? What does she concede, and how does she go on to argue against the opposing position?

3 Finally, analyze the effectiveness of Nielsen's response to opposing views. Given her rhetorical situation — her audience; her purpose; and the type, or *genre*, of text she is writing (an op-ed, on the newspaper's editorial page) — how smart do you think it is to call her opponents "free-speech absolutists" (par. 11)? How effective do you think her use of the concession-refutation move is likely to be for her readers?

[RESPOND] ## Consider possible topics: Issues regarding free speech.

Nielsen wants readers to think about what kinds of speech should be protected by the First Amendment, arguing that court decisions and commentators tend to "trivialize the harms that social science research undeniably associates with being the target of hate speech" (par. 10). The debate over free speech has been in the news following the Charlottesville White Nationalist demonstration in August 2017, college campus invitations to self-described provocateurs like Anne Coulter and Milo Yiannopoulos, and the request by some students to add trigger warnings to syllabi. You might consider writing about one of these aspects of the free speech debate or taking up a specific kind of speech or another type of protected expression.

Amitai Etzioni | *Working at McDonald's*

Pokłekowski/ullstein bild via Getty Images

AMITAI ETZIONI is a sociologist who has taught at Columbia, Harvard, and George Washington University. He has written numerous articles for scholarly and general publications and more than two dozen books, including *The Spirit of Community: The Reinvention of American Society* (1983); *The Limits of Privacy* (2004); and, most recently, *Happiness Is the Wrong Metric* (2018). The following reading was originally published on the opinion page of the *Miami Herald* newspaper.

As you read,

- consider what Etzioni's teenage son Dari, who helped his father write the essay, may have contributed.

- think about the kinds of summer and school-year jobs or volunteer opportunities that you or your friends have held while in high school or college. What, if anything, did you learn from them?

1   McDonald's is bad for your kids. I do not mean the flat patties and the white-flour buns; I refer to the jobs teen-agers undertake, mass-producing these choice items.

2   As many as two-thirds of America's high school juniors and seniors now hold down part-time paying jobs, according to studies. Many of these are in fast-food chains, of which McDonald's is the pioneer, trend-setter and symbol.

3   At first, such jobs may seem right out of the Founding Fathers' educational manual for how to bring up self-reliant, work-ethic-driven, productive youngsters. But in fact, these jobs undermine school attendance and involvement, impart few skills that will be useful in later life, and simultaneously skew the values of teen-agers—especially their ideas about the worth of a dollar.

4   It has been a longstanding American tradition that youngsters ought to get paying jobs. In folklore, few pursuits are more deeply revered than the newspaper route and the sidewalk lemonade stand. Here the youngsters are to learn how sweet are the fruits of labor and self-discipline (papers are delivered early in the morning, rain or shine), and the ways of trade (if you price your lemonade too high or too low . . .).

5   Roy Rogers, Baskin Robbins, Kentucky Fried Chicken, et al. may at first seem nothing but a vast extension of the lemonade stand. They provide very large numbers of teen jobs, provide regular employment, pay quite well compared to many other teen jobs and, in the modern equivalent of toiling over a hot stove, test one's stamina.

6   Closer examination, however, finds the McDonald's kind of job highly uneducational in several ways. Far from providing opportunities for entrepreneurship (the lemonade stand) or self-discipline, self-supervision and self-scheduling (the paper route), most teen jobs these days are highly structured— what social scientists call "highly routinized."

> *Far from providing opportunities for entrepreneurship . . . most teen jobs these days are highly structured.*

7   True, you still have to have the gumption to get yourself over to the hamburger stand, but once you don the prescribed uniform, your task is spelled out in minute detail. The franchise prescribes the shape of the coffee cups; the weight, size, shape and color of the patties; and the texture of the napkins (if any). Fresh coffee is to be made every eight minutes. And so on. There is no room for initiative, creativity, or even elementary rearrangements. These are breeding grounds for robots working for yesterday's assembly lines, not tomorrow's high-tech posts.

Drew Angerer/Getty Images

8   There are very few studies on the matter. One of the few is a 1984 study by Ivan Charper and Bryan Shore Fraser. The study relies mainly on what teen-agers write in response to questionnaires rather than actual observations of fast-food jobs. The authors argue that the employees develop many skills such as how to operate a food-preparation machine and a cash register. However, little attention is paid to how long it takes to acquire such a skill, or what its significance is.

9   What does it matter if you spend 20 minutes to learn to use a cash register, and then—"operate" it? What "skill" have you acquired? It is a long way from learning to work with a lathe or carpenter tools in the olden days or to program computers in the modern age.

10   A 1980 study by A. V. Harrell and P. W. Wirtz found that, among those students who worked at least 25 hours per week while in school, their unemployment rate four years later was half of that of seniors who did not work. This is an impressive statistic. It must be seen, though, together with the finding that many who begin as part-time employees in fast-food chains drop out of high school and are gobbled up in the world of low-skill jobs.

11   Some say that while these jobs are rather unsuited for college-bound, white, middle-class youngsters, they are "ideal" for lower-class, "non-academic," minority youngsters. Indeed, minorities are "over-represented" in these jobs (21 percent of fast-food employees). While it

is true that these places provide income, work and even some training to such youngsters, they also tend to perpetuate their disadvantaged status. They provide no career ladders, few marketable skills, and undermine school attendance and involvement.

12   The hours are often long. Among those 14 to 17, a third of fast-food employees (including some school dropouts) labor more than 30 hours per week, according to the Charper-Fraser study. Only 20 percent work 15 hours or less. The rest: between 15 and 30 hours.

13   Often the stores close late, and after closing one must clean up and tally up. In affluent Montgomery County, Md., where child labor would not seem to be a widespread economic necessity, 24 percent of the seniors at one high school in 1985 worked as much as five to seven days a week; 27 percent, three to five. There is just no way such amounts of work will not interfere with school work, especially homework. In an informal survey published in the most recent yearbook of the high school, 58 percent of seniors acknowledged that their jobs interfere with their school work.

14   The Charper-Fraser study sees merit in learning teamwork and working under supervision. The authors have a point here. However, it must be noted that such learning is not automatically educational or wholesome. For example, much of the supervision in fast-food places leans toward teaching one the wrong kinds of compliance: blind obedience, or shared alienation with the "boss."

15   Supervision is often both tight and woefully inappropriate. Today, fast-food chains and other such places of work (record shops, bowling alleys) keep costs down by having teens supervise teens with often no adult on the premises.

16   There is no father or mother figure with which to identify, to emulate, to provide a role model and guidance. The work-culture varies from one place to another: Sometimes it is a tightly run shop (must keep the cash registers ringing); sometimes a rather loose pot party interrupted by customers. However, only rarely is there a master to learn from, or much worth learning. Indeed, far from being places where solid adult work values are being transmitted, these are places where all too often delinquent teen values dominate. Typically, when my son Oren was dishing out ice cream for Baskin Robbins in upper Manhattan, his fellow teen-workers considered him a sucker for not helping himself to the till. Most youngsters felt they were entitled to $50 severance "pay" on their last day on the job.

17   The pay, oddly, is the part of the teen work-world that is most difficult to evaluate. The lemonade stand

or paper route money was for your allowance. In the old days, apprentices learning a trade from a master contributed most, if not all, of their income to their parents' household. Today, the teen pay may be low by adult standards, but it is often, especially in the middle class, spent largely or wholly by the teens. That is, the youngsters live free at home ("after all, they are high school kids") and are left with very substantial sums of money.

18   Where this money goes is not quite clear. Some use it to support themselves, especially among the poor. More middle-class kids set some money aside to help pay for college, or save it for a major purchase—often a car. But large amounts seem to flow to pay for an early introduction into the most trite aspects of American consumerism: flimsy punk clothes, trinkets and whatever else is the last fast-moving teen craze.

19   One may say that this is only fair and square; they are being good American consumers and spend their money on what turns them on. At least, a cynic might add, these funds do not go into illicit drugs and booze. On the other hand, an educator might bemoan that these young, yet unformed individuals, so early in life driven to buy objects of no intrinsic educational, cultural or social merit, learn so quickly the dubious merit of keeping up with the Joneses in ever-changing fads, promoted by mass merchandising.

20   Many teens find the instant reward of money, and the youth status symbols it buys, much more alluring than credits in calculus courses, European history or foreign languages. No wonder quite a few would rather skip school—and certainly homework—and instead work longer at a Burger King. Thus, most teen work these days is not providing early lessons in the work ethic; it fosters escape from school and responsibilities, quick gratification and a short cut to the consumeristic aspects of adult life.

21   Thus, parents should look at teen employment not as automatically educational. It is an activity—like sports—that can be turned into an educational opportunity. But it can also easily be abused. Youngsters must learn to balance the quest for income with the needs to keep growing and pursue other endeavors that do not pay off instantly—above all education.

22   Go back to school.

Make connections: Useful job skills.

[REFLECT]

Etzioni argues that fast-food jobs do not qualify as meaningful work experience because they do not teach young people the skills and habits they will need for fulfilling careers: "entrepreneurship . . . or self-discipline, self-supervision and self-scheduling" (par. 6).

To judge Etzioni's argument against your own experience and expectations, consider what you have learned from summer and after-school jobs, either paid or volunteer. Your instructor may ask you to post your thoughts on a class discussion board or to discuss them with other students in class. Use these questions to get started:

- Which, if any, of the skills and habits Etzioni lists as important do you think young people learn at summer or after-school jobs?

- Why do you think these skills and habits are worth learning? If you think other skills and habits are as important or even more important, explain what they are and why you think so.

Use the basic features.

[ANALYZE]

A FOCUSED, WELL-PRESENTED ISSUE: FRAMING AN ARGUMENT FOR A DIVERSE GROUP OF READERS

When Jessica Statsky wrote "Children Need to Play, Not Compete," she knew she would be addressing her classmates. But writers of position essays do not always have such a homogeneous audience. Often, they have to direct their argument to a diverse group of readers, many of whom do not share their concerns or values. From the first sentence, it is clear that Etzioni's primary audience is the parents of teenagers, but his concluding sentence is a direct address to the teenagers themselves: "Go back to school."

| ANALYZE & WRITE |

Write a paragraph analyzing and evaluating how Etzioni presents the issue to a diverse group of readers:

1 Reread paragraphs 1–7, highlighting the qualities — values and skills — associated with traditional jobs (the newspaper route and lemonade stand of yesteryear) and today's McDonald's-type jobs, at least according to Etzioni. How does Etzioni use this comparison to persuade parents to reconsider their assumption that McDonald's-type jobs are good for their kids?

2 Now skim the rest of the essay, looking for places where Etzioni appeals to teenagers themselves. (Notice, for example, how he represents teenagers' experience and values.) How effective do you think Etzioni's appeal would be to teenage readers? How effective is it for you and your classmates?

AN EFFECTIVE RESPONSE: PRESENTING AND REINTERPRETING EVIDENCE TO UNDERMINE OBJECTIONS

At key points throughout his essay, Etzioni acknowledges readers' likely objections and then responds to them. One strategy Etzioni uses is to cite research that appears to undermine his claim and then offer a new interpretation of that evidence. For example, he cites a study by Harrell and Wirtz (par. 10) that links work as a student with greater likelihood of employment later on. He then reinterprets the data from this study to show that the high likelihood of future employment could be an indication that workers in fast-food restaurants are more likely to drop out of school rather than an indication that workers are learning important employment skills. This strategy of presenting and reinterpreting evidence can be especially effective in academic writing, as Etzioni (a professor of sociology) well knows.

| ANALYZE & WRITE |

Write a paragraph or two analyzing and evaluating Etzioni's strategy of reinterpreting data elsewhere in his essay:

1 Reread paragraphs 8–9, in which Etzioni responds to the claim that employees in McDonald's-type jobs develop many useful skills.

2 Reread paragraphs 14–16, in which Etzioni discusses the benefits and shortcomings of various kinds of on-the-job supervision.

3 For each section, identify the claim that appears in the research Etzioni cites. How does Etzioni reinterpret it? Do you find his reinterpretation persuasive? Why or why not?

Consider . . .
How might this reinterpretation of evidence or other forms of the concession-refutation move affect the writer's credibility?

Solove *Why Privacy Matters*

GUIDE TO READING
Guide to Writing
A Writer at Work
Reflection

213

Consider possible topics: Issues facing students.

Etzioni focuses on a single kind of part-time work, takes a position on how worthwhile it is, and recommends against it. You could write a similar kind of essay. For example, you could take a position for or against students' participating in other kinds of part-time work or recreation during the high school or college academic year or over the summer—for example, playing on a sports team, volunteering, completing an internship, studying a musical instrument or a foreign language, or taking an elective class. If you work to support yourself and pay for college, you could focus on why the job either strengthens or weakens you as a person, given your life and career goals. Writing for other students, you would either recommend the job or activity to them or discourage them from pursuing it, giving reasons and support for your position.

Daniel J. Solove | *Why Privacy Matters Even if You Have "Nothing to Hide"*

© Drik Anschütz

DANIEL J. SOLOVE is the John Marshall Harlan Research Professor of Law at the George Washington University Law School. In addition to writing numerous books and articles on issues of privacy and the Internet, Solove is the founder of a company that provides privacy and data security training to corporations and universities. Among his books are *The Future of Reputation: Gossip, Rumor, and Privacy on the Internet* (2007) and *Nothing to Hide: The False Tradeoff between Privacy and Security* (2011).

An early version of this essay in a law review journal included citations, which had to be eliminated for publication in the *Chronicle of Higher Education* in 2011; we have restored them here so that you can see how Solove uses a variety of sources to support his position.

As you read, consider the following questions:

- How do the sources cited in the opening paragraphs contribute to your understanding of why so many people think privacy is not something they should be concerned about?

- Do you use Internet privacy settings? How concerned are you about protecting your privacy on social networking and other Web sites?

1   When the government gathers or analyzes personal information, many people say they're not worried. "I've got nothing to hide," they declare. "Only if you're doing something wrong should you worry, and then you don't deserve to keep it private." The nothing-to-hide argument pervades discussions about privacy. The data-security expert Bruce Schneier calls it the "most common retort against privacy advocates." The legal scholar Geoffrey Stone refers to it as an "all-too-common refrain." In its most compelling form, it is an argument that the privacy interest is generally minimal, thus making the contest with security concerns a foreordained victory for security.

2   The nothing-to-hide argument is everywhere. In Britain, for example, the government has installed millions of public-surveillance cameras in cities and towns,

which are watched by officials via closed-circuit television. In a campaign slogan for the program, the government declares: "If you've got nothing to hide, you've got nothing to fear" (Rosen 36). Variations of nothing-to-hide arguments frequently appear in blogs, letters to the editor, television news interviews, and other forums. One blogger in the United States, in reference to profiling people for national-security purposes, declares: "I don't mind people wanting to find out things about me, I've got nothing to hide! Which is why I support [the government's] efforts to find terrorists by monitoring our phone calls!"

3   On the surface, it seems easy to dismiss the nothing-to-hide argument. Everybody probably has something to hide from somebody. As Aleksandr Solzhenitsyn declared, "Everyone is guilty of something or has something to conceal. All one has to do is look hard enough to find what it is" (192). . . . One can usually think of something that even the most open person would want to hide. As a commenter to my blog post noted, "If you have nothing to hide, then that quite literally means you are willing to let me photograph you naked? And I get full rights to that photograph—so I can show it to your neighbors?". . .

4   But such responses attack the nothing-to-hide argument only in its most extreme form, which isn't particularly strong. In a less extreme form, the nothing-to-hide argument refers not to all personal information but only to the type of data the government is likely to collect. Retorts to the nothing-to-hide argument about exposing people's naked bodies or their deepest secrets are relevant only if the government is likely to gather this kind of information. In many instances, hardly anyone will see the information, and it won't be disclosed to the public. Thus, some might argue, the privacy interest is minimal, and the security interest in preventing terrorism is much more important. In this less extreme form, the nothing-to-hide argument is a formidable one. However, it stems from certain faulty assumptions about privacy and its value. . . .

5   Most attempts to understand privacy do so by attempting to locate its essence—its core characteristics or the common denominator that links together the various things we classify under the rubric of "privacy." Privacy, however, is too complex a concept to be reduced to a singular essence. It is a plurality of different things that do not share any one element but nevertheless bear a resemblance to one another. For example, privacy can be invaded by the disclosure of your deepest secrets. It might also be invaded if you're watched by a peeping Tom, even if no secrets are ever revealed. With the disclosure of secrets, the harm is that your concealed information is spread to others. With the peeping Tom, the harm is that you're being watched. You'd probably find that creepy regardless of whether the peeper finds out anything sensitive or discloses any information to others. There are many other forms of invasion of privacy, such as blackmail and the improper use of your personal data. Your privacy can also be invaded if the government compiles an extensive dossier about you. Privacy, in other words, involves so many things that it is impossible to reduce them all to one simple idea. And we need not do so. . . .

6   To describe the problems created by the collection and use of personal data, many commentators use a metaphor based on George Orwell's *Nineteen Eighty-Four*. Orwell depicted a harrowing totalitarian society ruled by a government called Big Brother that watches its citizens obsessively and demands strict discipline. The Orwell metaphor, which focuses on the harms of surveillance (such as inhibition and social control), might be apt to describe government monitoring of citizens. But much of the data gathered in computer databases, such as one's race, birth date, gender, address, or marital status, isn't particularly sensitive. Many people don't care about concealing the hotels they stay at, the cars they own, or the kind of beverages they drink. Frequently, though not always, people wouldn't be inhibited or embarrassed if others knew this information.

7   Another metaphor better captures the problems: Franz Kafka's *The Trial*. Kafka's novel centers around a man who is arrested but not informed why. He desperately tries to find out what triggered his arrest and what's in store for him. He finds out that a mysterious court system has a dossier on him and is investigating him, but he's unable to learn much more. *The Trial* depicts a bureaucracy with inscrutable purposes that uses people's information to make important decisions about them, yet denies the people the ability to participate in how their information is used.

8   The problems portrayed by the Kafkaesque metaphor are of a different sort than the problems caused by surveillance. They often do not result in inhibition. Instead they are problems of information processing—the

storage, use, or analysis of data—rather than of information collection. They affect the power relationships between people and the institutions of the modern state. They not only frustrate the individual by creating a sense of helplessness and powerlessness, but also affect social structure by altering the kind of relationships people have with the institutions that make important decisions about their lives.

9   Legal and policy solutions focus too much on the problems under the Orwellian metaphor—those of surveillance—and aren't adequately addressing the Kafkaesque problems—those of information processing. The difficulty is that commentators are trying to conceive of the problems caused by databases in terms of surveillance when, in fact, those problems are different. Commentators often attempt to refute the nothing-to-hide argument by pointing to things people want to hide. But the problem with the nothing-to-hide argument is the underlying assumption that privacy is about hiding bad things. By accepting this assumption, we concede far too much ground and invite an unproductive discussion about information that people would very likely want to hide. As the computer-security specialist

> *The problem with the nothing-to-hide argument is the underlying assumption that privacy is about hiding bad things.*

Schneier aptly notes, the nothing-to-hide argument stems from a faulty "premise that privacy is about hiding a wrong." Surveillance, for example, can inhibit such lawful activities as free speech, free association, and other First Amendment rights essential for democracy.

10   The deeper problem with the nothing-to-hide argument is that it myopically views privacy as a form of secrecy. In contrast, understanding privacy as a plurality of related issues demonstrates that the disclosure of bad things is just one among many difficulties caused by government security measures. To return to my discussion of literary metaphors, the problems are not just Orwellian but Kafkaesque. Government information-gathering programs are problematic even if no information that people want to hide is uncovered. In *The Trial*, the problem is not inhibited behavior but rather a suffocating powerlessness and vulnerability created by the court system's use of personal data and its denial to the protagonist of any knowledge of or participation in the process. The harms are bureaucratic

ones—indifference, error, abuse, frustration, and lack of transparency and accountability.

11   One such harm, for example, which I call aggregation, emerges from the fusion of small bits of seemingly innocuous data. When combined, the information becomes much more telling. By joining pieces of information we might not take pains to guard, the government can glean information about us that we might indeed wish to conceal. For example, suppose you bought a book about cancer. This purchase isn't very revealing on its own, for it indicates just an interest in the disease. Suppose you bought a wig. The purchase of a wig, by itself, could be for a number of reasons. But combine those two pieces of information, and now the inference can be made that you have cancer and are undergoing chemotherapy. That might be a fact you wouldn't mind sharing, but you'd certainly want to have the choice.

12   Another potential problem with the government's harvest of personal data is one I call exclusion. Exclusion occurs when people are prevented from having knowledge about how information about them is being used, and when they are barred from accessing and correcting errors in that data. Many government national-security measures involve maintaining a huge database of information that individuals cannot access. Indeed, because they involve national security, the very existence of these programs is often kept secret. This kind of information processing, which blocks subjects' knowledge and involvement, is a kind of due-process problem. It is a structural problem, involving the way people are treated by government institutions and creating a power imbalance between people and the government. To what extent should government officials have such a significant power over citizens? This issue isn't about what information people want to hide but about the power and the structure of government.

13   A related problem involves secondary use. Secondary use is the exploitation of data obtained for one purpose for an unrelated purpose without the subject's consent. How long will personal data be stored? How will the information be used? What could it be used for in the future? The potential uses of any piece of personal information are vast. Without limits on or accountability

for how that information is used, it is hard for people to assess the dangers of the data's being in the government's control.

14   Yet another problem with government gathering and use of personal data is distortion. Although personal information can reveal quite a lot about people's personalities and activities, it often fails to reflect the whole person. It can paint a distorted picture, especially since records are reductive—they often capture information in a standardized format with many details omitted. For example, suppose government officials learn that a person has bought a number of books on how to manufacture methamphetamine. That information makes them suspect that he's building a meth lab. What is missing from the records is the full story: The person is writing a novel about a character who makes meth. When he bought the books, he didn't consider how suspicious the purchase might appear to government officials, and his records didn't reveal the reason for the purchases. Should he have to worry about government scrutiny of all his purchases and actions? Should he have to be concerned that he'll wind up on a suspicious-persons list? Even if he isn't doing anything wrong, he may want to keep his records away from government officials who might make faulty inferences from them. He might not want to have to worry about how everything he does will be perceived by officials nervously monitoring for criminal activity. He might not want to have a computer flag him as suspicious because he has an unusual pattern of behavior. . . .

15   Privacy is rarely lost in one fell swoop. It is usually eroded over time, little bits dissolving almost imperceptibly until we finally begin to notice how much is gone. When the government starts monitoring the phone numbers people call, many may shrug their shoulders and say, "Ah, it's just numbers, that's all." Then the government might start monitoring some phone calls. "It's just a few phone calls, nothing more." The government might install more video cameras in public places. "So what? Some more cameras watching in a few more places. No big deal." The increase in cameras might lead to a more elaborate network of video surveillance. Satellite surveillance might be added to help track people's movements. The government might start analyzing people's bank records. "It's just my deposits and some of the bills I pay—no problem." The government may then start combing through credit-card records, then expand to Internet-service providers' records, health records, employment records, and more. Each step may seem incremental, but after a while, the government will be watching and knowing everything about us.

16   "My life's an open book," people might say. "I've got nothing to hide." But now the government has large dossiers of everyone's activities, interests, reading habits, finances, and health. What if the government leaks the information to the public? What if the government mistakenly determines that based on your pattern of activities, you're likely to engage in a criminal act? What if it denies you the right to fly? What if the government thinks your financial transactions look odd—even if you've done nothing wrong—and freezes your accounts? What if the government doesn't protect your information with adequate security, and an identity thief obtains it and uses it to defraud you? Even if you have nothing to hide, the government can cause you a lot of harm.

> *Privacy is rarely lost in one fell swoop. It is usually eroded over time, little bits dissolving almost imperceptibly until we finally begin to notice how much is gone.*

Works Cited

Rosen, Jeffrey. *The Naked Crowd: Reclaiming Security and Freedom in an Anxious Age.* Random House, 2004.

Schneier, Bruce. "The Eternal Value of Privacy." *Wired,* 18 May 2006, www.wired.com/2006/05/the -eternal-value-of-privacy.

Solzhenitsyn, Aleksandr. *Cancer Ward.* Translated by Nicholas Bethell and David Burg, Farrar, Straus and Giroux, 1969.

Stone, Geoffrey R. "Freedom and Public Responsibility." *Chicago Tribune,* 21 May 2006, p. 11, articles.chi -cagotribune.com/2006-05-21/news/0605210386_1 _phone-records-nsa-freedoms.

Solove   *Why Privacy Matters*

GUIDE TO READING
Guide to Writing
A Writer at Work
Reflection

217

Make connections: Privacy concerns on the Internet.

Whereas Solove's argument focuses on concerns about government collection and use of personal information, many people today are concerned as well about the collection and use of personal information to influence people's purchasing or voting decisions. For example, potential employers review blogs and social media Web sites to gather information about job candidates and to check their résumés. Corporations and political candidates use data mining to personalize advertising on Facebook, as was done during the 2016 presidential election.

Think about the implications of corporate or political data mining, and reflect on how it could affect your own sense of online privacy. Your instructor may ask you to post your thoughts on a class discussion board or to discuss them with other students in class. Use these questions to get started:

- How, if at all, do you manage the privacy preferences or settings on sites you use? Do you ever defriend people or click the "do not track" tool when you have the opportunity to do so? Would you untag photos or delete comments on social networking sites like Facebook that you didn't want potential employers to see?

- What are the advantages and disadvantages of data mining? Have targeted advertisements been a boon to you, or are you distressed that a candidate for office or a corporation knows so much about you?

Use the basic features.

A WELL-SUPPORTED POSITION: USING SOURCES

Writers of position arguments often quote, paraphrase, and summarize sources. Usually they use sources to support their positions, as Jessica Statsky does in her argument about children's sports. Sometimes, however, they use sources to highlight opposing positions to which they will respond, as Solove does on occasion in this essay.

In the following example, Solove signals his opinion through the words he chooses to characterize the source:

> As the computer-security specialist Schneier aptly notes, the nothing-to-hide argument stems from a faulty "premise that privacy is about hiding a wrong." (par. 9)

Elsewhere, readers have to work a little harder to determine how Solove is using the source.

Solove also uses what we might call **hypothetical quotations**—sentences that quote not what someone actually said but what they *might* have said:

> Many people say they're not worried. "I've got nothing to hide," they declare. "Only if you're doing something wrong should you worry, and then you don't deserve to keep it private." (par. 1)

Signal phrase
Hypothetical quotation

> "My life's an open book," people might say. "I've got nothing to hide." (par. 16)

You can tell from a signal phrase like "people might say" or "many people say" that no actual person made the statement, but Solove does not always supply such cues.

| ANALYZE & WRITE |

Write a paragraph analyzing and evaluating Solove's use of quotations:

1 Find and mark the quotations, noting which actually quote someone and which are hypothetical.

2 Identify the quotations — real or hypothetical — that Solove agrees with and those that represent an opposing view.

3 How effective did you find Solove's quoting strategy, given his purpose and audience? (Remember that this article appeared in the *Chronicle of Higher Education*, a weekly newspaper for college faculty and administrators.)

A CLEAR, LOGICAL ORGANIZATION: USING CUEING DEVICES

Solove uses a number of cueing devices to help readers keep track of his argument. Perhaps the most obvious and helpful cues are the topic sentences that begin each paragraph and the logical transitions ("One such harm," "Another potential problem," "A related problem," "Yet another problem" [pars. 11–14]) that signal connections between and within paragraphs. In addition, Solove uses rhetorical questions, such as the series of "What if" questions in the final paragraph.

| ANALYZE & WRITE |

Write a paragraph or two analyzing and evaluating the effectiveness of Solove's use of cueing devices to help readers follow his argument:

1 Choose a couple of paragraphs that use topic sentences and logical transitions effectively. Look closely at the way Solove uses these cueing devices, and determine what makes them so effective.

2 Highlight the rhetorical questions posed in paragraphs 12–14 and 16. Why do you imagine Solove uses so many of them, especially in the final paragraph? Given his purpose and audience, how effective do you think these rhetorical questions were likely to have been? How effective do you find them?

[RESPOND]   ## Consider possible topics: Issues concerning privacy.

Solove focuses on one concern about the erosion of privacy. You could write a similar type of essay, taking a position on issues such as state laws requiring women to have ultrasounds before terminating a pregnancy; airport security requiring passengers either to go through a full-body scanner or to submit to a "pat-down" before boarding a flight; cell phones making it possible for individuals to be located and tracked without their consent or knowledge; or houses, offices, and even people on the street being depicted on Google Maps without permission.

The Writing Assignment

Compose a position argument on a controversial issue. This Guide to Writing is designed to help you write a well-supported, clearly organized argument that will confirm, challenge, or change your readers' views.

The Starting Points chart will help you find answers to questions you might have about composing a position argument. Use it to find the guidance you need, when you need it.

> **Did you know?**
> You may not need the support of this Guide to Writing when composing in a genre you know well, but it can be very helpful when experimenting with a new or challenging genre.

STARTING POINTS: ARGUING A POSITION

A Focused, Well-Presented Issue

How do I come up with an issue to write about?

- Consider possible topics: Issues regarding free speech. (p. 208)
- Consider possible topics: Issues facing students. (p. 213)
- Consider possible topics: Issues concerning privacy. (p. 218)
- Choose a controversial issue on which to take a position. (pp. 221–22)
- Test Your Choice: Choosing an Issue (pp. 222–23)

How can I effectively frame the issue for my readers?

- Assess the genre's basic features: A focused, well-presented issue. (p. 194)
- A Focused, Well-Presented Issue: Framing an Argument for a Diverse Group of Readers (pp. 211–12)
- Frame the issue for your readers. (pp. 223–24)
- Test Your Choice: Frame Your Issue (p. 224)
- A Troubleshooting Guide: A Focused, Well-Presented Issue (p. 233)

(continued)

A Well-Supported Position

How do I come up with a plausible position?

- Assess the genre's basic features: A well-supported position. (pp. 194–95)
- Formulate a working thesis stating your position. (pp. 224–25)
- Develop the reasons supporting your position. (p. 225)
- Research your position. (p. 226)
- Use sources to reinforce your credibility. (pp. 226–27)

How do I come up with reasons and evidence supporting my position?

- A Well-Supported Position: Using Examples (p. 207)
- A Well-Supported Position: Using Sources (pp. 217–18)
- Formulate a working thesis stating your position. (pp. 224–25)
- Develop the reasons supporting your position. (p. 225)
- Research your position. (p. 226)
- A Troubleshooting Guide: A Well-Supported Position (p. 234)

An Effective Response to Opposing Views

How do I respond to possible objections to my views?

- Assess the genre's basic features: An effective response to opposing views. (pp. 196–97)
- An Effective Response: The Concession-Refutation Move (pp. 207–8)
- Identify and respond to your readers' likely reasons and objections. (pp. 227–29)

How do I respond to possible alternative positions?

- Assess the genre's basic feature: An effective response to opposing views. (pp. 196–97)
- An Effective Response: The Concession-Refutation Move (pp. 207–8)
- An Effective Response: Presenting and Reinterpreting Evidence to Undermine Objections (p. 212)
- Identify and respond to your readers' likely reasons and objections. (pp. 227–29)
- A Troubleshooting Guide: An Effective Response to Opposing Views (p. 234)

Writing a Draft

Guide to Reading
GUIDE TO WRITING
A Writer at Work
Reflection

221

A Clear, Logical Organization

> How can I help my readers follow my argument?

- Assess the genre's basic features: A clear, logical organization. (p. 197)
- A Clear, Logical Organization: Using Cueing Devices (p. 218)
- Create an outline that will organize your argument effectively for your readers. (pp. 229–30)
- Consider document design. (p. 230)
- A Troubleshooting Guide: A Clear, Logical Organization (p. 234)

Writing a Draft: Invention, Research, Planning, and Composing

The activities in this section will help you choose and research an issue as well as develop and organize an argument for your position. Your writing in response to many of these activities can be used as part of your rough draft, which you will be able to improve after receiving feedback from your classmates and instructor. Do the activities in any order that makes sense to you (and your instructor), and return to them as needed as you revise.

Choose a controversial issue on which to take a position.

When choosing an issue, keep in mind that it must be

- controversial—an issue that people disagree about;
- arguable—a matter of opinion on which there is no absolute proof or authority;
- one that you can research, as necessary, in the time you have;
- one that you care about.

To come up with ideas, think about the readings: Like Etzioni, you could choose a controversial topic related to students working full- or part-time or in work-study programs. Like Nielsen, you could take a stand on another of the freedoms protected in the Bill of Rights, such as freedom of assembly (should rules against groups of young people hanging out on street corners be protected?) or freedom of the press (should college administrators be allowed to censor your college newspaper?) Or like Solove, you could take a position on a privacy-related issue, such as the proliferation of security cameras on campus or the business of selling personal data gleaned from a listener's streaming habits.

Choosing an issue about which you have special interest or knowledge usually works best. Also, if you are thinking about addressing an issue of national concern, focus on a local or a very specific aspect of it. For example, instead of addressing censorship in general, write about a local lawmaker's recent effort to enact a law censoring the Internet, a city council's attempt to block access to Internet sites at the public library, or your school board's ban on certain books.

You may already have an issue in mind. If you do, skip to Test Your Choice: Choosing an Issue (pp. 222–23). If you do not, the topics that follow, in addition to those following the readings (pp. 208, 213, 218), may suggest an issue you can make your own:

- Should particular courses, community service, or an internship be a graduation requirement at your high school or college?
- Should students attending public colleges be required to pay higher tuition fees if they have been full-time students but have not graduated within four years?
- Should your large lecture or online courses have frequent (weekly or biweekly) exams instead of only a midterm and final?
- Should children raised in this country whose parents entered illegally be given an opportunity to become citizens upon finishing college or serving in the military?
- Should the football conference your school (or another school in the area) participates in be allowed to expand?
- Should you look primarily for a job that is well paid or for a job that is personally fulfilling or socially responsible?
- Should the racial, ethnic, or gender makeup of a police force resemble the makeup of the community it serves?
- Should public employees be allowed to unionize and to bargain collectively for improved working conditions, pay, or pensions?
- Should the state or federal government provide job training to those who are unemployed but able to work?

| TEST YOUR CHOICE |

Choosing an Issue

First, ask yourself the following questions:

- Does the issue matter to me and my readers? If not, could I argue convincingly that it ought to be of concern?
- Do I know enough about the issue to take a position that I can support effectively, or can I learn what I need to know in the time I have?
- Can I frame or reframe the issue in a way that might open readers to my point of view or help them reconsider what's at stake?

Then get together with two or three other students to take turns trying out your issues with potential readers. Ask group members questions like the following:

- What, if anything, do you already know about the issue?
- What about the issue (if anything) seems particularly important to you?
- Do you already hold a position on this issue? If so, how strongly do you hold it? Would you be open to considering other points of view? If you don't care about the issue, what might convince you that it matters?

Consider these questions and their responses as you plan and draft your argument.

⊞ Frame the issue for your readers.

Once you have made a preliminary choice of an issue, consider how you can frame (or reframe) the issue so that readers who support opposing positions will listen to your argument. Consider how the issue has been debated in the past and what your readers are likely to think. Use the following questions and sentence strategies to help you put your ideas in writing.

WAYS IN

HOW CAN I EXPLORE THE ISSUE?

To explore the ISSUE, ask yourself questions like these and answer them using the sentence strategies as a jumping-off point.

What groups or notable individuals have shaped the debate on this issue? What positions have they taken?

- ▶ Although many people take Issue X for granted, groups A, B, and C oppose it on the grounds that _____ .

- ▶ Whereas supporters of Issue X have argued that _____ , opponents such as A, B, and C contend that _____ .

How has the issue, or people's opinions about the issue, changed? What makes the issue important now?

- ▶ Recent research/news reports have changed some people's minds on this issue. Instead of assuming _____ , many people now think _____ .

- ▶ The debate over Issue X was initially focused on _____ , but now the main concern seems to be _____ .

WHAT DO MY READERS THINK?

To determine what your READERS are likely to think, ask yourself questions like these and answer them using the sentence strategies as a jumping-off point.

What values and concerns do my readers and I share regarding the issue?

- ▶ Concern about Issue X leads many of us to oppose _____ . We worry about the consequences if _____ is implemented.

- ▶ X is a basic human right that needs to be protected. But what does it mean in everyday practice when _____ ?

What fundamental differences in worldview or experience might keep my readers from agreeing with me?

- ▶ Those who disagree about Issue X often see it as a choice between _____ and _____ . But we don't have to choose between them.

- ▶ While others may view it as a matter of _____ , for me what's at stake is _____ .

(continued)

HOW CAN I FRAME THE ISSUE EFFECTIVELY?

Once you have a good idea of how the issue has been debated and what your readers think, use these sentence strategies to **FRAME** *the issue for your readers.*

What is the issue, and why should my readers be concerned about it?

▶ Issue X is of concern to all members of group A because _____.

EXAMPLE   I'm concerned about the high cost of tuition at state colleges like ours because students have to borrow more money to pay for their education than they will be able to earn once they graduate.

Why are popular approaches or attitudes inappropriate or inadequate?

▶ Although many in the community claim X, I think Y because _____.

EXAMPLE   Some argue that college football players should be paid because of the money the school is earning off players' labor. I disagree. I think the current system should be maintained because without the money earned from football, less lucrative sports programs, like fencing and wrestling, would have to be cut.

TEST YOUR CHOICE

Frame Your Issue

Ask two or three other students to consider the way you have framed your issue.

Presenters. Briefly explain the values and concerns you think are at stake. (The sentence strategies in the Ways In section can help you articulate your position and approach.)

Did you know?
Research shows that words used to frame an issue evoke connotations — feeling, beliefs, or values — in readers' minds. What connotations will your key words have for readers?

Listeners. Tell the presenter how you respond to this way of framing the issue, and why. You may use the language that follows as a model for structuring your response, or use language of your own.

▶ I'm also/not concerned about Issue X because _____.

▶ I agree/disagree with you about Issue X because _____.

▦ Formulate a working thesis stating your position.

Try drafting a working thesis statement now. (If you prefer to conduct research or develop your argument before trying to formulate a thesis, skip this activity and return to it when you are ready.) As you develop your argument, rework your assertion into a compelling thesis statement by making the language clear and straightforward. You may also need to qualify it with words like *often, sometimes,* or *in part.* Be sure to forecast your reasons.

Writing a Draft

Guid
GUII
A Wr
Refle

CHA

226

HOW CAN I DEVISE AN ARGUABLE THESIS?

Begin by describing the ISSUE, possibly indicating where others stand on it or what's at stake, and then stating your POSITION. These sentence strategies may help you get started:

▶ At a recent meeting, many people argued .... Although I sympathize with their point of view, this is ultimately a question of ...., not .... Therefore, we must do ....

▶ This issue is dividing our community. Some people argue X, others contend Y, and still others believe Z. However, it is in all of our interests to do .... because

....

▶ Conventional wisdom claims that .... But I take a different view: I believe .... because ....

▦ Develop the reasons supporting your position.

The following activities will help you find plausible reasons and evidence for your position. You can do some focused research later to fill in the details, or skip ahead to conduct research now.

For more idea-generating strategies, see Chapter 11.

HOW CAN I COME UP WITH REASONS THAT SUPPORT MY POSITION?

Write nonstop for at least five minutes exploring your reasons. Ask yourself questions like these:

- How can I show readers that my reasons lead logically to my position (**LOGOS**)?
- How can I convince my readers that I am trustworthy (**ETHOS**)?
- How can I appeal to my readers' feelings (**PATHOS**)?

At this point, don't worry about the exact language you will use in your final draft. Just write the reasons you hold your position and the evidence (anecdotes, examples, statistics, expert testimony) that supports it. Keep your readers and their values in mind—what would they find most convincing, and why?

To brainstorm a list of reasons, try this:

- Start by writing your position at the top of the page.
- On the left half of the page, list as many potential reasons as you can think of to support your position. (Don't judge at this point.)
- On the right half of the page, make notes about the kinds of evidence you would need to provide in order to convince readers of each reason and to show how each supports your position.

▉ Research your position.

Do some research to find out how others have argued in support of your position:

- Try entering keywords or phrases related to the issue or your position in the search box of an all-purpose database, such as Academic OneFile (InfoTrac) or Academic Search Complete (EBSCOhost), to find relevant articles in magazines and journals, or use the database Lexis/Nexis to find articles in newspapers. For example, Jessica Statsky could have tried a combination of keywords, such as *children's sports*, or variations of those terms (*youth sports*) to find relevant articles. A similar search of your library's catalog could also be conducted to locate books and other resources on your topic.

- If you think your issue has been dealt with by a government agency, explore the state, local, or tribal sections of USA.gov—the U.S. government's official Web portal—or visit the Library of Congress page on state government information (www.loc.gov/rr/news/stategov/stategov.html) and follow the links.

Remember to bookmark promising sites and to record the URL and other information you will need to cite and document any sources or visuals you use.

▉ Use sources to reinforce your credibility.

How you represent your sources can quickly establish your credibility (ethos)—or the reverse. For example, by briefly describing the author's credentials the first time you *summarize, paraphrase,* or *quote* from a source, you establish the source's authority and demonstrate that you have selected sources appropriately:

> Martin Rablovsky, a former sports editor for the *New York Times,* says that in all his years of watching young children play organized sports, he has noticed very few of them smiling. "I've seen children enjoying a spontaneous pre-practice scrimmage become somber and serious when the coach's whistle blows," Rablovsky says . . . (qtd. in Coakley 94). (Statsky, par. 7)

Quotations can also reinforce the accuracy of your summary or paraphrase and establish your fairness to opposing points of view. In the following sentence, Jessica Statsky demonstrates her fairness by quoting from the Web site of the Little League, a well-known organization, and establishes her credibility by demonstrating that even those who disagree with her recognize that injuries occur:

> Although the official Little League Web site acknowledges that children do risk injury playing baseball, it insists that "severe injuries . . . are infrequent," the risk "far less than the risk of riding a skateboard, a bicycle, or even the school bus" ("What about My Child?"). (Statsky, par. 4)

In both of these examples from "Children Need to Play, Not Compete," Statsky introduces the source to her readers, explaining the relevance of the source material—including the author's credentials—to readers rather than leaving them to figure out its relevance for themselves.

Consider . . .
When using multiple sources, an annotated working bibliography can help you keep track of your sources.

To learn more about searching a database or catalog, or finding government documents, consult Chapter 17; to learn more about documenting sources, consult Chapters 20 and 21.

Signal phrase and author's credentials

Source summary

Statsky's introduction: Summarizes source

In-text citation follows quotation

Writing a Draft

Guide to Reading
GUIDE TO WRITING
A Writer at Work
Reflection

227

Whenever you borrow information from sources, be sure to double-check that you are summarizing, paraphrasing, and quoting accurately and fairly. Compare Statsky's sentence from paragraph 4 with its source passage, which follows. (The portions she uses are highlighted.) Notice that she has inserted ellipsis marks (. . .) to indicate that she has left out words from her source's second sentence.

Source

Injuries seem to be inevitable in any rigorous activity, especially if players are new to the sport and unfamiliar with its demands. But because of the safety precautions taken in Little League, severe injuries such as bone fractures are infrequent. Most injuries are sprains and strains, abrasions and cuts and bruises. The risk of serious injury in Little League Baseball is far less than the risk of riding a skateboard, a bicycle, or even the school bus.

In both of the preceding examples, Statsky uses quotation marks to indicate that she is borrowing the words of a source and provides an in-text citation so that readers can locate the sources in her list of works cited. Doing both is essential to avoiding plagiarism; one or the other is not enough.

> For more on integrating language from sources into your own sentences and avoiding plagiarism, see Chapter 19.

▦ Identify and respond to your readers' likely reasons and objections.

The following activity will help you anticipate reasons your readers may use to support their argument or objections they may have. You may want to return to this activity as you do additional research and learn more about the issue and the arguments people make. Return to the section "Research your position" on p. 226, or consult Chapter 17, "Planning and Conducting Research."

HOW CAN I FIGURE OUT WHAT MY READERS WILL BE CONCERNED ABOUT?

1. **List** the **reasons** you expect your readers to have for their position and the **objections** (including those based on logical fallacies) you expect them to raise to your argument. How do your **values, beliefs,** and **priorities** differ from those of your readers?

2. *Analyze your list of likely* **reasons** *and* **objections**. Which can you refute, and how? Which may you need to concede?

HOW CAN I RESPOND TO READERS' REASONS AND OBJECTIONS?

Now, choose a **reason** *or an* **objection**, *and try out a response:*

1. Summarize it accurately and fairly. (Do not commit the straw man fallacy of knocking down something that no one really takes seriously.)

2. Decide whether you can refute it, need to concede it, or can refute part and concede part.

> For more logical fallacies, see Chapter 16.

(continued)

Try sentence strategies like these to **refute, concede,** *or* **concede** *then* **refute** *reasons supporting readers' arguments or their objections to your argument:*

To Refute

Reason or Objection Lacks Credible Support

▶ My opponents cite research to support their reason/objection, but the credibility of that research is questionable because _____. In contrast, reliable research by Professor X shows _____.

▶ This reason/objection seems plausible on the surface, but evidence shows _____.

Readers' Values and Concerns Are Better Served by Your Position

▶ Some insist _____ without realizing that it would take away a basic right/make things even worse.

▶ X and Y think this issue is about _____. But what is really at stake here is _____.

Reasoning Is Flawed

▶ Proponents object to my argument on the grounds that _____. However, they are confusing results with causes. What I am arguing is _____.

▶ Polls show that most people favor _____, but an opinion's popularity does not make it true or right.

▶ While most would agree that _____, it does not necessarily follow that _____.

Times Have Changed

▶ One common complaint is _____. In recent years, however, _____.

To Concede

Accept an Objection Well Taken

▶ To be sure, _____ is true.

▶ Granted, _____ must be taken into consideration.

Qualify on Common Ground

▶ Some people argue that _____. I understand this reservation, and therefore, I think we should _____.

Refocus Your Argument

▶ A common concern about this issue is _____. That's why my argument focuses on [a different aspect of the issue].

To Concede, Then Refute

Yes, But

▶ I agree that _____ is important, but my opponents also need to consider _____ .

On the One Hand . . . On the Other Hand

▶ On the one hand, I accept X's argument that _____ , but on the other hand, I still think _____ is ultimately more important because _____ .

Note: If a reason or an objection seems so damaging that you cannot refute it convincingly or concede it without undermining your own argument, discuss with your instructor how you could modify your position or whether you should choose a new issue to write about. If you do not know enough about readers' views to anticipate their reasons or likely objections to your argument, do more research.

⊞ Create an outline that will organize your argument effectively for your readers.

Whether you have rough notes or a complete draft, making an outline of what you have written can help you organize your essay effectively for your audience. Compare the possible outlines that follow to see how you might organize the essay depending on whether your readers primarily agree or disagree with you.

For more on outlining, see Chapters 11 and 12.

Readers Primarily Agree with You

Strengthen their convictions by organizing your argument around a series of reasons backed by supporting evidence or by refuting opposing arguments point by point:

I. **Present the issue.**

II. **Provide a thesis statement**—a direct statement of your position.

III. **Present your most plausible reasons and evidence.**

IV. **Concede or refute opposing reasons or objections to your argument.**

V. **Conclude:** Reaffirm your position.

Readers Primarily Disagree with You

Begin by emphasizing common ground, and make a concession to show that you have considered the opposing position carefully and with an open mind:

I. **Present the issue:** Reframe the issue in terms of common values.

II. **Concede:** Acknowledge the wisdom of an aspect of the opposing position.

III. **Provide a thesis statement**—a direct statement of your position, qualified as necessary.

VI. **Present your most plausible reasons and evidence.**

V. **Conclude:** Reiterate shared values.

Whatever organizational strategy you adopt, do not hesitate to change your outline as necessary while drafting and revising. For instance, you might find it more effective to hold back on presenting your own position until you have discussed unacceptable alternatives. Or you might find a more powerful way to order the reasons for supporting your position. The purpose of an outline is to identify the basic components of your argument and to help you organize them effectively, not to lock you into a particular structure.

Consider document design.

To learn more about multimodal composing, see Chapter 22.

Think about whether visual or audio elements—photographs, graphics, snippets of interviews with experts—would strengthen your position argument. If you can recall position arguments you've read in newspapers (op-eds and editorials generally argue for positions), on Web pages, and on blogs, what visual or audio elements were used to establish the writer's credibility and to appeal to the reader logically, ethically, or emotionally? Position arguments do not require visual or audio elements, yet they can be an effective tool.

Note: Be sure to cite the source of visual or audio elements you didn't create, and get permission from the source if your essay is going to be published on a Web site that will be accessible outside your class or college.

Take a moment . . .
How does the design of a document affect the reader's experience? How does design signal genre?

Consider also whether your readers might benefit from design features such as headings, bulleted or numbered lists, or other typographic elements that can make your argument easier to follow.

Write the opening sentences.

Review what you have written to see if you have something that would help you frame or reframe the issue for your readers while also grabbing their attention or try out some of these opening strategies:

Begin with **statistics** *that would help readers grasp the importance of your topic:*

> "Organized sports for young people have become an institution in North America," reports sports journalist Steve Silverman, attracting more than 44 million youngsters according to a recent survey by the National Council of Youth Sports. (Statsky, par. 1)

Use a **personal anecdote** *to make the issue tangible or to appeal to readers' emotions:*

> My students nod along until we get to racist and sexist speech. Some can't grasp why, if we restrict so many forms of speech, we don't also restrict hate speech. (Nielsen, par. 1)

Start with a **surprising statement** *to capture readers' attention:*

> McDonald's is bad for your kids. (Etzioni, par. 1)

Use a hypothetical quotation to indicate how people typically think about the issue:

> When the government gathers or analyzes personal information, many people say they're not worried. "I've got nothing to hide," they declare. (Solove, par. 1)

Draft your position argument.

By this point, you have done a lot of writing to

- devise a focused, well-presented issue and take a position on it;
- frame your issue so that readers will be open to your argument;
- support your position with reasons and evidence your readers will find persuasive;
- refute or concede alternative viewpoints on the issue;
- organize your ideas to make them clear, logical, and effective for readers.

Now stitch that material together to create a draft. The next two parts of this Guide to Writing will help you evaluate and improve your draft.

Evaluating the Draft: Using Peer Review

Your instructor may arrange a peer review session in class or online, where you can exchange drafts with your classmates and give one another a thoughtful critical reading, pointing out what works well and suggesting ways to improve the draft. A good critical reading does three things:

1. It lets the writer know how well the reader understands the point of the argument.
2. It praises what works best.
3. It indicates where the draft could be improved and makes suggestions on how to improve it.

One strategy for evaluating a draft is to use the basic features of a position argument as a guide. Also be sure to respond to any concerns the writer has shared with you.

A PEER REVIEW GUIDE

A Focused, Well-Presented Issue

How well does the writer present the issue?

Summarize: Tell the writer what you understand the issue to be. If you were already familiar with it and understand it differently, briefly explain.

Praise: Give an example from the essay where the issue and its significance come across effectively.

Critique: Tell the writer where more information about the issue is needed, where more might be done to establish its seriousness, or how the issue could be framed or reframed in a way that would better prepare readers for the argument.

(continued)

A Well-Supported Position

How well does the writer argue in support of the position?

Summarize: Underline the thesis statement and the main reasons.

Praise: Give an example in the essay where the argument is especially effective; for example, indicate which reason is especially convincing or which supporting evidence is particularly compelling.

Critique: Tell the writer where the argument could be strengthened; for example, indicate how the thesis statement could be made clearer or more appropriately qualified, how the argument could be developed, or where additional support is needed.

An Effective Response to Opposing Views

How effectively has the writer responded to others' reasons and likely objections?

Summarize: Identify where the writer responds to a reason others use to support their argument or an objection they have to the writer's argument.

Praise: Give an example in the essay where a concession seems particularly well done or a refutation is convincing.

Critique: Tell the writer how a concession or a refutation could be made more effective, identify a reason or an objection the writer should respond to, or note where common ground could be found.

A Clear, Logical Organization

How clearly and logically has the writer organized the argument?

Summarize: Find the sentence(s) in which the writer states the thesis and forecasts supporting reasons, as well as transitions or repeated key words and phrases.

Praise: Give an example of how or where the essay succeeds in being especially easy to read, perhaps in its overall organization, clear presentation of the thesis, clear transitions, or effective opening or closing.

Critique: Tell the writer where the readability could be improved. Can you, for example, suggest better forecasting or clearer transitions? If the overall organization of the essay needs work, make suggestions for rearranging parts or strengthening connections.

Improving the Draft

Guide to Reading
GUIDE TO WRITING
A Writer at Work
Reflection

233

Improving the Draft: Revising, Editing, and Proofreading

Start improving your draft by reflecting on what you have written thus far:

- Review critical reading comments from your classmates, instructor, or writing center tutor: What problems do your readers identify?
- Consider your invention writing: What else should you consider?
- Review your draft: What else can you do to support your position more effectively?

Revise your draft.

If your readers are having difficulty with your draft, or if you think there is room for improvement, try some of the strategies listed in the Troubleshooting Guide that follows. They can help you fine-tune your presentation of the genre's basic features.

A TROUBLESHOOTING GUIDE

A Focused, Well-Presented Issue

My readers don't get the point.

- Quote experts or add information — statistics, examples, anecdotes, and so on — to help readers understand what's at stake.
- Consider adding visuals, such as photos, graphs, tables, or charts, to present the issue more clearly.

My readers have a different perspective on the issue than I do.

- Show the limitations of how the issue has traditionally been understood.
- Reframe the issue by showing how it relates to the values, concerns, needs, and priorities you share with readers.
- Give concrete examples or anecdotes, facts, and details that could help readers see the issue as you see it.

(continued)

A Well-Supported Position

My readers do not find my argument clear and/or persuasive.

- Revisit your thesis statement to make sure your position is stated clearly and directly.
- Reconsider your reasons, or explain how they support your position.
- Add supporting evidence — statistics, examples, authorities, and so on.
- Consider adding visuals, graphs, tables, or charts to support your argument.
- Strengthen the logical, ethical, and emotional appeals of your argument.
- Try outlining your argument; if your organization is weak or illogical, or if your transitional strategies are not working, try reorganizing the material, adding transitional words and phrases, or repeating key words strategically.

An Effective Response to Opposing Views

My readers question my response to opposing arguments or objections to my argument.

- If your refutation is weak, strengthen it with additional or more compelling reasons and evidence.
- If your concession weakens your argument, qualify your position with words like *sometimes* or *often*.
- Consider adding a refutation to your concession.

A Clear, Logical Organization

My readers are confused by my essay or find it difficult to follow.

- Outline your essay. If necessary, move, add, or delete sections to strengthen coherence.
- Consider adding a forecasting statement with key terms that are repeated in topic sentences throughout the essay.
- Check for appropriate transitions between sentences, paragraphs, and major sections of your essay.
- Review your opening and closing paragraphs. Be sure that your thesis is clearly expressed and that you reaffirm your position in your closing.

Edit and proofread your final draft.

Editing means making changes to the text to ensure that it follows the conventions of style, grammar, spelling, and mechanics appropriate to the rhetorical situation. **Proofreading** involves checking to make sure the text follows these conventions and that no words are repeated or omitted. You have probably done some editing and proofreading while composing and improving your draft, but it is always good practice to edit and proofread a draft after you have revised it and before you submit it.

Jessica Statsky's Response to Opposing Positions

Guide to Reading
Guide to Writing
▶ A WRITER AT WORK
Reflection

235

Most writers get the best results by leaving time — even just an hour or two — between the stages of revising, editing, and proofreading, so that they can return to their writing project with fresh eyes. When possible, enlist a friend or classmate to proofread the final draft of your writing projects. When that is not possible, proofread from the last line to the first, to avoid seeing what you expect to find rather than what is actually on the page (or screen).

As rhetorical situations change, so, too, do the conventions or expectations readers bring to the text. For example, whereas e-mail messages to friends are usually quite informal, filled with abbreviations, emojis, and sentence fragments, final drafts of writing projects for college classes or the workplace are expected to follow a more formal set of conventions concerning clarity, style, grammar, and punctuation.

We recommend that you make a list of the problems your instructors frequently point out in your writing, then use that list to guide your editing and proofreading. A Guide to Editing and Proofreading (at the end of this text) provides a checklist of the most common problems writers face. For issues that go beyond those on this list, consult a handbook* or search for advice online at sites like the Purdue Online Writing Lab (owl.english.purdue.edu) or Grammarly (grammarly.com). For practice identifying and correcting errors, try the activities in LearningCurve, a gamelike adaptive quizzing program available on LaunchPad for *The St. Martin's Guide to Writing*. The less well you do on activities in one topic area, the more LearningCurve focuses on it; the better you do, the more challenging the questions become.

> **A Note on Grammar and Spelling Checkers**
>
> Spelling checkers cannot catch misspellings that are themselves words, such as *to* for *too*, and grammar checkers miss problems, give faulty advice, and even flag correct items as wrong. Use these tools as a second line of defense after your own (and, ideally, another reader's) proofreading efforts.

A WRITER AT WORK

Jessica Statsky's Response to Opposing Positions

In this section, we look at how Jessica Statsky tried to anticipate opposing positions and respond to them. To understand Statsky's thinking about possible opposing positions, look first at the invention writing she did while analyzing her potential readers.

I think I will write mainly to parents who are considering letting their children get involved in competitive sports and to those whose children are already on teams and who don't know about the possible dangers. Parents who are really into competition

Three potential groups of readers

Two groups of parents

---

* The full version of *The St. Martin's Guide to Writing* includes a handbook.

and winning probably couldn't be swayed by my arguments anyway. I don't know how to reach coaches (but aren't they also parents?) or league organizers. I'll tell parents some horror stories and present solid evidence from psychologists that competitive sports can really harm children under the age of twelve. I think they'll be impressed with this scientific evidence.

I share with parents one important value: the best interests of children. Competition really works against children's best interests. Maybe parents' magazines (don't know of any specific ones) publish essays like mine.

Notice that Statsky lists three potential groups of readers here, but she is already leaning toward making parents her primary audience. Moreover, she divides these parents into two camps: those who are new to organized sports and unaware of the adverse effects of competition, and those who are really into winning. Statsky decides early on against trying to change the minds of parents who place great value on winning. But as you will see in the next excerpt from her invention writing, Statsky gave a lot of thought to the position these parents would likely favor.

Listing Reasons for the Opposing Position

In continuing her invention writing, Statsky listed the following reasons she thought others might have for their position that organized competitive sports teach young children valuable skills:

> --because playing sports is healthy
> --because competition teaches children how to succeed in life
> --because playing sports--especially winning--is fun
> --because winning boosts children's self-esteem

This list appears to pose serious challenges to Statsky's argument, but she benefited by considering the reasons her readers might give for opposing her position before she drafted her essay. By preparing this list, she gained insight into how she had to develop her own argument in light of these predictable arguments, and she could begin thinking about which reasons she might concede and which she had to refute. Her essay ultimately gained authority because she could demonstrate a good understanding of the opposing arguments that might be offered by her primary readers — parents who have not considered the dangers of competition for young children.

Conceding a Plausible Reason

Looking over her list of reasons, Statsky decided that she could accommodate readers by conceding that competitive sports can sometimes be fun for children — at least for those who win. Here are her invention notes:

Jessica Statsky's Response to Opposing Positions

Guide to Reading
Guide to Writing
▶ **A WRITER AT WORK**
Reflection

237

It is true that children do sometimes enjoy getting prizes and being recognized as winners in competitions adults set up for them. I remember feeling very excited when our sixth-grade relay team won a race at our school's sports day. And I felt really good when I would occasionally win the candy bar for being the last one standing in classroom spelling contests. But when I think about these events, it's the activity itself I remember as the main fun, not the winning. I think I can concede that winning is exciting to six- to twelve-year-olds, while arguing that it's not as important as adults might think. I hope this will win me some friends among readers who are undecided about my position.

We can see this concession in paragraph 7 of Statsky's revised essay (p. 201), in which she concedes that winning "does add to the fun" but reports on studies that say that children would rather play regularly on a losing team than sit on the bench on a winning team.

Refuting an Implausible Reason

Statsky recognized that she had to attempt to refute the other objections in her list. She chose the second reason in her list and tried out the following refutation:

It irritates me that adults are so eager to make first and second graders go into training for getting and keeping jobs as adults. I don't see why the pressures on adults need to be put on children. Anyway, both my parents tell me that in their jobs, cooperation and teamwork are keys to success. You can't get ahead unless you're effective in working with others. Maybe we should be training children and even high school and college students in the skills necessary for cooperation, rather than competition. Sports and physical activity are important for children, but elementary schools should emphasize achievement rather than competition--race against the clock rather than against each other. Rewards could be given for gains in speed or strength instead of for defeating somebody in a competition.

This brief invention activity led to the argument in paragraph 9 of the revised essay (pp. 201–2), in which Statsky acknowledges the importance of competition for success in school and work, but goes on to argue that cooperation is also important. To support this part of her argument, she gives examples in paragraph 13 (p. 203) of sports programs that emphasize cooperation over competition.

You can see from Statsky's revised essay that her refutation of this opposing argument runs through her entire essay. The invention activities Statsky did advanced her thinking about her readers and purpose; they also brought an early, productive focus to her research on competition in children's sports.

The benefit of reflection is proven and important: It helps consolidate what you have learned so that you can remember and apply it well beyond this class. That is why we have included questions and comments in the margins and at the end of this chapter: to stimulate your thinking about profiles, your rhetorical situation, and the choices you make as a writer.

Reflecting on Reading and Writing a Position Argument

To reflect on your experience reading position arguments and writing one of your own, try writing a blog post, a letter to your instructor, or an e-mail message to a student who will take this course next term that draws on what you have learned. Use any of these writing prompts that seem productive:

- Explain how your purpose and audience—what you wanted your readers to learn about your subject from reading your position essay—influenced *one* of your decisions as a writer, such as what kinds of supporting evidence you included or how you responded to objections.

- Discuss what you learned about yourself as a writer in the process of writing this position essay. Consider what part of the process you found most challenging—for example, framing the issue to appeal to and inform your readers, qualifying your thesis statement, or refuting opposing arguments. Did you try anything new, like participating in a peer review of your draft or outlining your draft in order to revise it? If so, how successful was it?

- Describe one way a reading in this chapter influenced your essay. For example, perhaps something you read suggested a good subject, offered a way to organize your essay, or contributed a sentence pattern that helped you express yourself.

- Discuss what you learned about position essays as a genre. For example, were you surprised by how widely examples of the genre can differ—such as Nielsen's op-ed on hate speech versus Statsky's thoroughly researched academic argument about kids' sports?

Reflecting on Your Composing Process

Thinking about your process for writing a position essay can be useful in helping you decide what works best for you as a writer. Using one or more of the following questions as a starting point, write a paragraph or two about your composing process:

- How did you go about choosing a subject? Did you try out a few possibilities before making a final decision? Did doing research help you choose a subject? If so, how?

People make proposals for various purposes and audiences and publish them in a variety of media. For example, a group of students in an environmental health sciences course might collaborate on a project to build a Web page that informs the community about a water quality problem, evaluates the feasibility of alternative solutions that have been discussed, and argues for their preferred solution. A blogger might post a proposal to solve the problem of the rising college loan default rate, arguing that truth in advertising laws should be used to crack down on for-profit colleges that use aggressive recruiting tactics to target low-income students. A retired chef might offer to set up a program at a local day-care center to instill healthy eating habits by having kids plant a garden and then cook and eat the food they grow.

In this chapter, we ask you to identify a problem you care about and write a proposal to solve it. By analyzing the selections in the Guide to Reading (pp. 242–67), you will learn how to make a convincing case for the solution you propose. The Guide to Writing (pp. 268–82) will show you ways to use the basic features of the genre to make your proposal inventive as well as practical.

PRACTICING THE GENRE

Arguing That a Solution Is Feasible

Proposals often succeed or fail on the strength of the argument that the proposed solution is feasible.

Part 1.   Practice making a feasibility argument:

1 Get together in small groups of two or three students.

2 Identify a problem that you face as students in one of your college courses (this course or a different one).

3 Come up with a solution to your problem.

4 Take a few minutes discussing the feasibility of your solution. Ask yourselves:

- **Is it doable?** List specific steps that you, the instructor, or the administration would need to take.

- **Is it worth doing?** Identify what implementing the solution would cost in terms of time or money, and compare that investment with how much it would benefit students (in terms of learning, for example).

- **Would it work?** To prove that it would actually help solve the problem, you could show how it would eliminate a cause of the problem or how it has worked elsewhere, for example.

Part 2.   Discuss what you learned about making a feasibility argument:

- **What did you learn about arguing for your proposed solution?** Typically, a proposal tries to convince the audience that the solution is doable, is worth the time and money, and would actually help solve the problem. Are all three elements of feasibility necessary? If not, which is most important? Why?

- **Think about how the rhetorical situation of your proposal — the purpose, audience, and medium — affects how you should argue for your solution's feasibility.** For example, how would you change your argument about the negative effects of relying on high-stakes exams if you were trying to convince a group of professors at a conference about undergraduate teaching versus an administrator who controls the budget or schedule? Would feasibility be equally important to both groups?

> **Take a moment . . .**
> Think about how a proposed solution can be a form of social action, a way of acting that brings people together around shared values and concerns.

Analyzing Proposals

As you read the selections in this chapter, you will see how different writers argue for a solution:

- Patrick O'Malley argues for more low-stakes exams (pp. 246–52).
- David Figlio contends that having high schools start later in the day would improve student performance (pp. 252–55).
- David J. Smith proposes a national student exchange to help Americans get to know one another better (pp. 257–59).
- Kelly D. Brownell and Thomas R. Frieden propose raising taxes on sugary soft drinks as a way to stem the "obesity epidemic" (pp. 262–65).

Analyzing how these writers define their problems, argue for their solutions, respond to opposing views, and organize their writing will help you see how you can use these techniques to make your own proposals clear and compelling for your readers.

Determine the writer's purpose and audience.

Consider . . .

How does the rhetorical situation — especially the purpose and audience — affect the way the writer uses these basic features?

When reading the proposals that follow, ask yourself what the writer's main purpose is and what he or she assumes about the reader:

The writer's main purpose may be to

- convince readers the problem exists

- inspire readers to take action by stressing the problem's urgency or seriousness

- persuade readers that the writer's proposed solution is feasible and can be implemented

- confirm the writers' refutation of objections and alternative solutions

The writer wants readers to react by

- recognizing that the problem exists and is serious

- deciding to take action to solve the problem

- committing to implementing the writer's proposed solution

- preferring the writer's solution over alternative solutions

Assess the genre's basic features.

 **Basic Features**

A Focused, Well-Defined Problem

A Well-Argued Solution

An Effective Response to Objections and Alternative Solutions

A Clear, Logical Organization

As you read the proposals in this chapter, consider how different authors incorporate the basic features of the genre. The examples that follow are drawn from the reading selections that appear later in this Guide to Reading.

A FOCUSED, WELL-DEFINED PROBLEM

Read first to see how the writer defines or frames the problem. Framing a problem is a way of preparing readers for the proposed solution by focusing on the aspect of the problem the proposal tries to solve. In "More Testing, More Learning," for example, student Patrick O'Malley frames the problem in terms of the detrimental effects of

Analyzing Proposals

GUIDE TO READING
Guide to Writing
A Writer at Work
Reflection

243

high-stakes exams on students' learning. If O'Malley were writing to students instead of their teachers, he might have framed the problem in terms of students' poor study habits or procrastination. By framing the problem as he does, he indicates that teachers, rather than students, have the ability to solve the problem and tries to convince readers that it is real and serious.

Determine, how (and how well) the writer frames the problem—for example,

- by recounting *anecdotes* or constructing *scenarios* to show how the problem affects people:

EXAMPLE   It's late at night. The final's tomorrow. (O'Malley, par. 1)

- by giving *examples* to make the problem less abstract

EXAMPLE   For example, research by Karpicke and Blunt (2011) published in *Science* found that testing was more effective than other, more traditional methods of studying both for comprehension and for analysis. (O'Malley, par. 4)

- by listing the negative *effects* of the problem

EXAMPLE   Sugar-sweetened beverages (soda sweetened with sugar, corn syrup, or other caloric sweeteners and other carbonated and uncarbonated drinks, such as sports and energy drinks) may be the single largest driver of the obesity epidemic. A recent meta-analysis found that the intake of sugared beverages is   Cause
associated with increased body weight, poor nutrition, and displacement of   Effect
more healthful beverages; increasing consumption increases risk for obesity and diabetes. (Brownell and Frieden, par. 2)

Consider also how the writer uses research studies and statistics to demonstrate the severity of the problem. Look for source material, and notice how the writer establishes the credibility of the research by including the expert's name and credentials or by identifying the publication in which the study appeared:

- ▶ Dr. X at University of Y has found that _____ .

- ▶ A study published in *Journal X* shows that _____ .

EXAMPLE   A 2006 study reported in the journal *Psychological Science* concluded that "taking repeated tests . . . leads to better . . . retention . . . ," according to the study's coauthors, Henry L. Roediger and Jeffrey Karpicke (ScienceWatch .com, 2008). (O'Malley, par. 4)

EXAMPLE   A recent CNN poll revealed that 85 percent of Americans feel we are more divided than ever. (Smith, par. 2)

In contexts where sources are not normally cited (such as newspapers and certain Web sites) or where the information is widely available, the writer may cite statistics without indicating a specific source; in academic writing, the sources of such statistics must be cited.

Reflect on . . .

Why do you think writers in acdemic contexts are expected to cite their sources formally, in a list of references or works cited?

A WELL-ARGUED SOLUTION

To argue convincingly for a solution to a problem, writers need to *make clear exactly what is being proposed and offer supporting reasons and evidence* showing that the proposed solution

- will help solve the problem;
- can be implemented;
- is worth the expense, time, and effort to do so.

Read first to find the proposed solution, usually declared in a *thesis statement* early in the essay. Typically, the thesis describes the proposed solution briefly and indicates how it would solve the problem, as in this example, which contrasts the problem's disadvantages with the solution's benefits:

<table>
<tr>
<td>Problem and its disadvantages

Thesis proposing solution and its benefits</td>
<td>So, not only do high-stakes exams discourage frequent study and undermine students' performance, they also do long-term damage to students' cognitive development. If professors gave brief exams at frequent intervals, students would be spurred to learn more and worry less. They would study more regularly, perform better on tests, and enhance their cognitive functioning. (O'Malley, par. 2)</td>
</tr>
</table>

Then check to see how the writer presents the supporting reasons *and* evidence, *and consider how compelling the argument is likely to be, given the writer's purpose and audience.* The following sentence strategies and accompanying examples suggest the kinds of reasons and evidence proposal writers often employ to present their argument, as well as the writing strategies they represent:

- The proposed solution would reduce or eliminate a major cause of the problem and would (or could) have beneficial effects:

Cause/effect ▶ As research shows, solution X would stop ...., change ...., reverse ...., and would lead to/encourage ....

> EXAMPLE   What happens when children get an extra hour of sunlight before starting school? . . . math scores improve by eight percent and reading score improvements remain at six percent. (Figlio, par. 6)

- A similar solution has worked elsewhere:

Comparison ▶ Solution X has worked for problem Y, so it could work for .... as well.

> EXAMPLE   Taxes on tobacco products have been highly effective in reducing consumption, and data indicate that higher prices also reduce soda consumption. (Brownell and Frieden, par. 3)

- The necessary steps to put the solution into practice can be taken without excessive cost or inconvenience:

Process analysis ▶ This solution is easy to implement: first do .... and then do ....

> EXAMPLE   Ideally, a professor would give an in-class test or quiz after each unit. . . . These exams should be given weekly or at least twice monthly. . . . Exams should take no more than 15 or 20 minutes. (O'Malley, par. 3)

AN EFFECTIVE RESPONSE TO OBJECTIONS AND ALTERNATIVE SOLUTIONS

Read to see how the writer responds to readers' likely objections and to the alternative solutions readers may prefer—for example, by

- **conceding** (accepting) a valid objection.

  ▶ X and Y are right when they say that _____, _____, and _____ are likely to be problems.

EXAMPLE   There are, of course, potential costs associated with this type of schedule change. . . . For instance, later school start times might mean that more students participating in after-school activities will arrive home after dark, which might also cause concern. And given a school start time, at least one study shows that students learn more in the morning than they do in the afternoon. (Figlio, par. 12)

- **refuting** (arguing against) criticism—for example, by demonstrating that an objection is without merit or arguing that an alternative solution would be more costly or less likely to solve the problem than the proposed solution.

  ▶ Some object that my proposal would cost too much/cause too much disruption. But inaction would cost even more/cause more disruption by increasing _____ or inhibiting _____.

EXAMPLE   Some argue that government should not interfere in the market and that products and prices will change as consumers demand more healthful food, but several considerations support government action. . . . The contribution of unhealthful diets to health care costs is already high and is increasing. . . . Diet-related diseases also cost society in terms of decreased work productivity, increased absenteeism, poorer school performance, and reduced fitness on the part of military recruits, among other negative effects. (Brownell and Frieden, par. 5)

- **conceding** and then **refuting** (or making the concession-refutation move).

  ▶ Yes, this solution might result in Problem X, but X can be overcome/avoided by _____, _____, and _____.

EXAMPLES   Some believe that . . . From the student's perspective, however, this time is well spent. (O'Malley, par. 9)

Some argue that . . . , but several considerations support . . . action. The first is . . . The second consideration is . . . A third consideration is . . . (Brownell and Frieden, par. 5)

Contrasts alternative and proposed solutions

If weekly exams still seem too time-consuming to some professors, their frequency could be reduced to every other week or their length to 5 or 10 minutes. In courses where multiple-choice exams are appropriate, several questions could be designed to take only a few minutes to answer. (O'Malley, par. 9)

When reading a proposal, consider whether the writer presents other views fairly and accurately and whether the writer's rebuttal is likely to be convincing to readers.

To learn more about constructing arguments, see Chapter 16.

Pay special attention to the writer's tone in responding to other views, noting any place the tone seems sarcastic or dismissive and considering whether such a tone would be effective given the writer's purpose and audience.

A CLEAR, LOGICAL ORGANIZATION

For more about writing a thesis statement and topic sentences, see Chapter 13.

Look for cues or signposts that help readers identify the parts of the proposal. Identify the topic and find the thesis, which in a proposal asserts the solution. Look also for topic sentences, particularly those that announce the parts of the proposal argument. Notice also any transitions and how they function. For example, all of the transitions in the following topic sentences (*another, moreover, still,* and *furthermore*) indicate items in a list. Other transitions you can expect in proposals signal causes or effects (*because, as a result*), exceptions (*but*), concessions (*although*), refutations (*however*), emphasis (*more important*), conclusions (*then, therefore*), and enumerations (*first, second*). Here are the beginnings of several topic sentences from O'Malley's essay:

Transitions

The main reason professors should give frequent exams is that (par. 4)

Another, closely related argument in favor of multiple exams is that (par. 6)

Moreover, professors object to frequent exams because (par. 10)

Still another solution might be to (par. 12)

Furthermore, professors could (par. 13)

Finally, if headings or visuals (such as flowcharts, graphs, tables, photographs, or cartoons) are included, determine how they contribute. Notice whether visuals are referred to in the text and whether they have titles or captions.

Readings

To learn about how O'Malley responds to professors' likely objections to his proposed solution and argues against their preferred solutions to the problem, look at A Writer at Work on pp. 283–84.

Patrick O'Malley | *More Testing, More Learning*

FRUSTRATED BY what he calls "high-stakes exams," Patrick O'Malley wrote the following proposal while he was a first-year college student. To conduct research into opposing viewpoints, O'Malley interviewed two professors, talked with several students, and read published research on testing. He cited his sources using APA style, as his instructor requested.

As you read,

- consider how you feel about high-stakes exams. How well does the opening scenario resonate for you?

- consider O'Malley's audience: Who is the intended audience for his essay, and how convincing do you think his reader(s) will find the sources he uses?

- think about how effectively O'Malley uses the basic features of the genre (listed below), and answer the questions in the margins; your instructor may ask you to post your thoughts and answers to a class blog or discussion board or to bring your responses to class.

■■ **Basic Features**
A Focused, Well-Defined Problem
A Well-Argued Solution
An Effective Response to Objections and Alternative Solutions
A Clear, Logical Organization

1   It's late at night. The final's tomorrow. You got a C on the midterm, so this one will make or break you. Will it be like the midterm? Did you study enough? Did you study the right things? It's too late to drop the course. So what happens if you fail? No time to worry about that now—you've got a ton of notes to go over.

2   Although this last-minute anxiety about midterm and final exams is only too familiar to most college students, many professors may not realize how such major, infrequent, high-stakes exams work against the best interests of students both psychologically and cognitively. They cause unnecessary amounts of stress, placing too much importance on one or two days in the students' entire term, judging ability on a single or dual performance. Reporting on recent research at Cornell University Medical School, Sian Beilock, a psychology professor at the University of Chicago, points out that "stressing about doing well on an important exam can backfire, leading students to 'choke under pressure' or to score less well than they might otherwise score if the stakes weren't so high." Moreover, Cornell's research using fMRI brain scans shows that "the pressures of a big test can reach beyond the exam itself—stunting the cognitive systems that support the attention and memory skills every day" (Beilock, 2010). So, not only do high-stakes exams discourage frequent study and undermine students' performance, they also do long-term damage to students' cognitive development. If professors gave brief exams at frequent intervals, students would be spurred to learn more and worry less. They would study more regularly, perform better on tests, and enhance their cognitive functioning.

3   Ideally, a professor would give an in-class test or quiz after each unit, chapter, or focus of study, depending on the type of class and course material. A physics class might require a test on concepts after every chapter covered, while a history class could necessitate quizzes covering certain time periods or major events. These exams should be given weekly or at least twice monthly. Whenever possible, they should consist of two or three essay questions rather than many multiple-choice or short-answer questions. To preserve class time for lecture and discussion, exams should take no more than 15 or 20 minutes.

4   The main reason professors should give frequent exams is that when they do and when they provide feedback to students on how well they are doing, students learn more in the course and perform better on major exams, projects, and papers. It makes sense that in a challenging course containing a great deal of material, students will learn

What is the function of the opening paragraph?

How does framing the problem this way set up the solution?

How does O'Malley use the key terms introduced here throughout the essay?

What does par. 3 contribute to the argument?

How effectively does O'Malley introduce this reason? What kinds of support does he offer?

more of it and put it to better use if they have to apply or "practice" it frequently on exams, which also helps them find out how much they are learning and what they need to go over again. A 2006 study reported in the journal *Psychological Science* concluded that "taking repeated tests on material leads to better long-term retention than repeated studying," according to the study's coauthors, Henry L. Roediger and Jeffrey Karpicke (ScienceWatch.com, 2008). When asked what the impact of this breakthrough research would be, they responded: "We hope that this research may be picked up in educational circles as a way to improve educational practices, both for students in the classroom and as a study strategy outside of class." The new field of mind, brain, and education research advocates the use of "retrieval testing." For example, research by Karpicke and Blunt (2011) published in *Science* found that testing was more effective than other, more traditional methods of studying both for comprehension and for analysis. Why retrieval testing works is not known. UCLA psychologist Robert Bjork speculates that it may be effective because "when we use our memories by retrieving things, we change our access" to that information. "What we recall," therefore, "becomes more recallable in the future" (qtd. in Belluck, 2011).

How does O'Malley integrate and cite sources in pars. 4 and 5?

5   Many students already recognize the value of frequent testing, but their reason is that they need the professor's feedback. A Harvard study notes students' "strong preference for frequent evaluation in a course." Harvard students feel they learn least in courses that have "only a midterm and a final exam, with no other personal evaluation." Students believe they learn most in courses with "many opportunities to see how they are doing" (Light, 1990, p. 32). In a review of a number of studies of student learning, Frederiksen (1984) reports that students who take weekly quizzes achieve higher scores on final exams than students who take only a midterm exam and that testing increases retention of material tested.

How does O'Malley support this reason? Why does he include it?

6   Another, closely related argument in favor of multiple exams is that they encourage students to improve their study habits. Greater frequency in test taking means greater frequency in studying for tests. Students prone to cramming will be required — or at least strongly motivated — to open their textbooks and notebooks more often, making them less likely to resort to long, kamikaze nights of studying for major exams. Since there is so much to be learned in the typical course, it makes sense that frequent, careful study and review are highly beneficial. But students need motivation to study regularly, and nothing works like an exam. If students had frequent exams in all their courses,

they would have to schedule study time each week and would gradually develop a habit of frequent study. It might be argued that students are adults who have to learn how to manage their own lives, but learning history or physics is more complicated than learning to drive a car or balance a checkbook. Students need coaching and practice in learning. The right way to learn new material needs to become a habit, and I believe that frequent exams are key to developing good habits of study and learning. The Harvard study concludes that "tying regular evaluation to good course organization enables students to plan their work more than a few days in advance. If quizzes and homework are scheduled on specific days, students plan their work to capitalize on them" (Light, 1990, p. 33).

> How does O'Malley introduce and respond to this possible objection?

7   By encouraging regular study habits, frequent exams would also decrease anxiety by reducing the procrastination that produces anxiety. Students would benefit psychologically if they were not subjected to the emotional ups and downs caused by major exams, when after being virtually worry-free for weeks they are suddenly ready to check into the psychiatric ward. Researchers at the University of Vermont found a strong relationship among procrastination, anxiety, and achievement. Students who regularly put off studying for exams had continuing high anxiety and lower grades than students who procrastinated less. The researchers found that even "low" procrastinators did not study regularly and recommended that professors give frequent assignments and exams to reduce procrastination and increase achievement (Rothblum, Solomon, & Murakami, 1986, pp. 393–394).

> How effectively does O'Malley use this source?

8   Research supports my proposed solution to the problem I have described. Common sense as well as my experience and that of many of my friends support it. Why, then, do so few professors give frequent brief exams?

> What is the purpose of this question?

9   Some believe that such exams take up too much of the limited class time available to cover the material in the course. Most courses meet 150 minutes a week — three times a week for 50 minutes each time. A 20-minute weekly exam might take 30 minutes to administer, and that is one-fifth of each week's class time. From the student's perspective, however, this time is well spent. Better learning and greater confidence about the course seem a good trade-off for another 30 minutes of lecture. Moreover, time lost to lecturing or discussion could easily be made up in students' learning on their own through careful regular study for the weekly exams. If weekly exams still seem too time-consuming to some professors, their frequency could be reduced to every other week or their length to 5 or 10 minutes. In courses where multiple-choice exams are appropriate, several questions could be designed to take only a few minutes to answer.

How does O'Malley argue against possible objections in pars. 9 and 10?

10   Moreover, professors object to frequent exams because they take too much time to read and grade. In a 20-minute essay exam, a well-prepared student can easily write two pages. A relatively small class of 30 students might then produce 60 pages, no small amount of material to read each week. A large class of 100 or more students would produce an insurmountable pile of material. There are a number of responses to this objection. Again, professors could give exams every other week or make them very short. Instead of reading them closely, they could skim them quickly to see whether students understand an idea or can apply it to an unfamiliar problem; and instead of numerical or letter grades, they could give a plus, check, or minus. Exams could be collected and responded to only every third or fourth week. Professors who have readers or teaching assistants could rely on them to grade or check exams. And the Scantron machine is always available for instant grading of multiple-choice exams. Finally, frequent exams could be given *in place of* a midterm exam or out-of-class essay assignment.

How effectively does O'Malley present alternative solutions in pars. 11 and 12?

11   Since frequent exams seem to some professors to create too many problems, however, it is reasonable to consider alternative ways to achieve the same goals. One alternative solution is to implement a program that would improve study skills. While such a program might teach students how to study for exams, it cannot prevent procrastination or reduce "large test anxiety" by a substantial amount. One research team studying anxiety and test performance found that study skills training was not effective in reducing anxiety or improving performance (Dendato & Diener, 1986, p. 134). This team, which also reviewed other research that reached the same conclusion, did find that a combination of "cognitive/relaxation therapy" and study skills training was effective. This possible solution seems complicated, however, not to mention time-consuming and expensive. It seems much easier and more effective to change the cause of the bad habit rather than treat the habit itself. That is, it would make more sense to solve the problem at its root: the method of learning and evaluation.

How do the highlighted words and phrases make the argument easy to follow?

12   Still another solution might be to provide frequent study questions for students to answer. These would no doubt be helpful in focusing students' time studying, but students would probably not actually write out the answers unless they were required to. To get students to complete the questions in a timely way, professors would have to collect and check the answers. In that case, however, they might as well devote the time to grading an exam. Even if it asks the same questions, a scheduled exam is preferable to

a set of study questions because it takes far less time to write in class, compared to the time students would devote to responding to questions at home. In-class exams also ensure that each student produces his or her own work.

13   Furthermore, professors could help students prepare for midterm and final exams by providing sets of questions from which the exam questions will be selected or announcing possible exam topics at the beginning of the course. This solution would have the advantage of reducing students' anxiety about learning every fact in the textbook, and it would clarify the course goals, but it would not motivate students to study carefully each new unit, concept, or text chapter in the course. I see this as a way of complementing frequent exams, not as substituting for them.

14   From the evidence and from my talks with professors and students, I see frequent, brief in-class exams as the only way to improve students' study habits and learning, reduce their anxiety and procrastination, and increase their satisfaction with college. These exams are not a panacea, but only more parking spaces and a winning football team would do as much to improve college life. Professors can't do much about parking or football, but they can give more frequent exams. Campus administrators should get behind this effort, and professors should get together to consider giving exams more frequently. It would make a difference.

How effective is this conclusion?

References

Beilock, S. (2010, September 3). Stressing about a high-stakes exam carries consequences beyond the test [Web log post]. Retrieved from http://www.psychologytoday.com/blog/choke/201009/stressing-about-high-stakes-exam-carries-consequences-beyond-the-test

Belluck, P. (2011, January 20). To really learn, quit studying and take a test. *The New York Times.* Retrieved from http://www.nytimes.com/2011/01/21/science/21memory.html

Dendato, K. M., & Diener, D. (1986). Effectiveness of cognitive/relaxation therapy and study skills training in reducing self-reported anxiety and improving the academic performance of test-anxious students. *Journal of Counseling Psychology, 33,* 131–135.

Frederiksen, N. (1984). The real test bias: Influences of testing on teaching and learning. *American Psychologist, 39,* 193–202.

Karpicke, J. D., & Blunt, J. R. (2011, February 11). Retrieval practice produces more learning than elaborative studying with concept mapping. *Science, 331*(6018), 772–775. doi: 10.1126/science.1199327

Light, R. J. (1990). *Explorations with students and faculty about teaching, learning, and student life.* Cambridge, MA: Harvard University Graduate School of Education and Kennedy School of Government.

Rothblum, E. D., Solomon, L., & Murakami, J. (1986). Affective, cognitive, and behavioral differences between high and low procrastinators. *Journal of Counseling Psychology, 33*, 387–394.

ScienceWatch.com (2008, February). Henry L. Roediger and Jeff Karpicke talk with ScienceWatch.com and answer a few questions about this month's fast breaking paper in the field of psychiatry/psychology [Interview]. Retrieved from http://sciencewatch.com/dr/fbp/2008/08febfbp/08febfbpRoedigerETAL

David Figlio | *Starting High School Later*

Leslie E. Kossoff/LK Photos/ Northwestern University

DAVID FIGLIO is the dean and Orrington Lunt Professor of Education and Social Policy at Northwestern University. Figlio has published in major scholarly journals, including the *Journal of Human Resources,* where he serves as editor in chief. In addition to serving on various task forces and panels, Figlio is a member of the executive board of the National Center for Analysis of Longitudinal Data in Education Research. His research deals with a range of health and education policy issues, including the effects of online instruction, persistent gender gaps in education, and the effects on adolescents of early high school start times, which is the subject of this proposal, published originally on the Brookings Institution Web site in 2017.

As you read,

- recall your own experience with the starting time of your high school and how it affected your health and performance as a student.
- skim the works-cited list at the end of the proposal and consider how you think the number and type of sources he cites would have been received by Figlio's original audience.

1   Many proposals for improving student performance involve very costly interventions. And while quite a few of these costly interventions surely pass benefit-cost tests, they can be extremely challenging, politically or financially, to implement. One possible source of "low-hanging fruit" involves . . . starting school later in the day for middle and high school students (Jacob and Rockoff). . . . This would permit adolescents to sleep later and therefore arrive at school more ready to learn.

2   Why start school later for adolescents? The answer rests in our biology. Circadian rhythms influence our sleep patterns, and the degree of light on the outside of our eyelids affects our melatonin secretion and feelings of alertness or fatigue (Arendt). As children enter puberty, their nocturnal melatonin production shifts several hours later than what occurred when they were younger—or when they become adults (Carskadon et al.). As a consequence, the American Academy of Pediatrics suggests that adolescents sleep until at least 8:00 A.M. But thanks to a wide range of factors, half of all U.S. high schools start by that time ("Average Start Time"). Given this discordance between natural sleep rhythms and school start times for adolescents, it's no surprise that students lose as much as two hours of sleep per night when they start school in the fall relative to the summer (Hansen et al.).

3   It's difficult to know exactly how this disconnect between teenagers' optimal sleep times and school schedules affects their classroom performance because school districts that start high schools later might be better-resourced or otherwise support students better than do those that start high schools earlier in the day. One innovative study looks at U.S. Air Force Academy freshmen cadets who were randomly assigned to earlier or later start times (thanks to having a class in the first period or not) and shows that having a first period class substantially reduces achievement—both for the first period class and for the rest of the day (Carrell et al.). There also exists some case study evidence from Wake County, NC, which changed middle school busing schedules, suggesting that later start times for adolescents improves test scores (Edwards). Other case study evidence from Minneapolis, which shifted start times later by an hour and a half, is more mixed, with increased teacher-assigned grades and other aspects of student well-being but no improvements in ACT scores.

4   A major just-published study by Heissel and Norris provides the first evidence using large-scale population-level data on this topic. One way in which this paper represents a large step forward is that it is the first study, to my knowledge, to investigate this question using data from more than one institution or one school district—thereby substantially enhancing external validity. This new paper also has strong internal validity as well: The authors focus their attention on the relationship between sunlight and sleep, and take advantage of the fact that the state of Florida, where they conduct their research, is divided into two time zones. The sun comes up an hour later, on the clock, in the Eastern Time Zone than a few miles west in the Central Time Zone, but schools only partially account for this difference when setting their start times, so, on average, students in the Central Time Zone in Florida have more than half an hour more sunlight before school starts than do their counterparts in the Eastern Time Zone, and some have an hour or more additional sunlight, depending on when school starts.

5   One might be concerned that people living in different parts of Florida are somehow different in other ways as well, and Heissel and Norris are able to deal with this concern by concentrating on students who *moved between time zones,* while remaining in the northern part of Florida (typically called the Panhandle). Some students moved between the Eastern Time Zone and the Central Time Zone, thereby gaining extra sunlight in the morning before school, while others moved from the Central Time Zone to the Eastern Time Zone, thereby losing some sunlight before school starts. Their strategy, therefore, is to compare the same students' test performance before versus after their cross-time zone moves. The authors found that people making these eastward and westward moves in the Florida Panhandle were similar across a large range of characteristics, and tended to follow similar over-time test score trends prior to their moves.

6   What happens when children get an extra hour of sunlight before starting school? If they are young, math scores are barely affected, although reading scores increase by six percent. But once they reach puberty (approximately at age 11 for girls and age 13 for boys) math scores improve by eight percent and reading score improvements remain at six percent. The increased amounts of sunlight prior to school start only modestly

reduces absence rates—and more for young children than for teenagers—indicating that these improved student outcomes are probably due to increased alertness, rather than to more time in school.

7   The post-adolescent math performance bumps associated with more daylight prior to school are about the same for boys and girls alike. They are present for both white and non-white students (with slightly higher estimated effects for non-white students). They are present for both relatively affluent and relatively disadvantaged students (with somewhat higher estimated effects for students not eligible for free or reduced-price lunches). In sum, it appears that more daylight before school starts helps a wide range of adolescents better learn math. Moreover, the authors show that the benefits occur immediately and persist for years.

8   Do these results reflect the cumulative effect of more sunlight over the course of the entire school year, or do they just reflect alertness on the day of the exam? The answer to this question has important implications for whether it makes sense to shift the school day back in general for adolescents, or whether this is really just a test-day phenomenon. To address this question, Heissel and Norris take advantage of the fact that Florida changed the timing of its high-stakes testing from year to year and the dates of the start of daylight savings time changed from year to year. As a consequence, in some years the high-stakes testing took place just before the start of daylight savings time, when pre-school daylight was highest; in other years, the high-stakes testing took place just after the start of daylight savings time, when pre-school daylight was nearly an hour less; and in still other years, the high-stakes testing took place a month after the start of daylight savings time, when pre-school daylight was somewhere in the middle.

9   When the authors make this comparison, they find that the amount of sunlight on the day of the test can explain a portion of the reading results—recall that they find that more sunlight in general helps pre-pubescent and adolescent children approximately equally in reading as well—but it doesn't explain much of the math results. Most of the boost in adolescent test performance that we observe when students have more daylight in the morning is due not to the amount of daylight before school on days when children take tests, but rather to the amount of daylight before school experienced across the school year. Daylight before school apparently boosts cumulative learning for adolescents—and not just test-day alertness.

10   What do these findings imply for optimal school schedules—at least, from the point of view of maximizing student math and reading achievement? Heissel and Norris carried out a thought exercise in which, for every Florida panhandle school district, they assigned the school district's earliest start times to elementary students, the middle start times to middle school students, and the latest start times to high school students. This calculation would move elementary school start times 22 minutes earlier, middle school start times 13 minutes earlier, and high school start times 44 minutes later, on average.

11   Heissel and Norris estimate that making these scheduling switches would raise average math performance by six percent of a standard deviation and average reading performance by four percent of a standard deviation. While not earth-shattering performance changes, they are extremely impressive for a policy change that would cost school districts little to implement—and are approximately one-fourth the difference between an excellent-performing school and an average-performing school. (Recall, also, that most parts of the United States have less daylight between September and March than Florida does!)

12   There are, of course, potential costs associated with this type of schedule change. Parents might be more comfortable with high schoolers traveling to school in the dark than they are with elementary school-aged children doing the same. Starting elementary school relatively early could have implications for parents' after-school child care arrangements as well. High schoolers have more after-school activities, sports, and the like, and later school start times might put the squeeze on these types of activities. For instance, later school start times might mean that more students participating in after-school activities will arrive home after dark, which might also cause concern. And given a school start time, at least one study shows that students learn more in the morning than they do in the afternoon (Pope). Nevertheless, there are also a few "quick wins" in education when it comes to boosting learning at a very low cost, and paying attention to—and scheduling school start times in line with—human biology seems to be one of them.

Works Cited

American Academy of Pediatrics Adolescent Sleep Working Group, Committee on Adolescence, and Council on School Heath. "School Start Times for Adolescents." *Pediatrics*, vol. 134, no. 3, Sept. 2014, pp. 642–49, pediatrics.aappublications.org /content/pediatrics/early/2014/08/19/peds .2014-1697.full.pdf.

Arendt, Josephine. "Melatonin, Circadian Rhythms, and Sleep." *New England Journal of Medicine*, vol. 242, 12 Oct. 2000, pp. 1114–16, doi:10.1056 /NEJM200010123431510.

"Average Start Time for Public High Schools and Percentage Distribution of Start Times in Public High Schools, by Selected School Characteristics." National Center for Education Statistics, Institute of Education Sciences, 2012, nces.ed.gov/surveys /sass/tables/sass1112_201381_s1n.asp.

Carrell, Scott, et al. "A's from Zzzz's? The Causal Effect of School Start Time on the Academic Achievement of Adolescents." *American Economic Journal: Economic Policy*, vol. 3, no. 3, Aug. 2011, pp. 62–81, doi:10.1257/pol.3.3.62.

Carskadon, Mary, et al. "Regulation of Adolescent Sleep: Implications for Behavior." *Annals of the New York Academy of Science*, vol. 1021, June 2004, pp. 276–91, doi:10.1196/annals.1308.032.

Edwards, Finley. "Early to Rise? The Effect of Daily Start Times on Academic Performance." *Economics of Education Review*, vol. 31, no. 6, Dec. 2012, pp. 970–83, doi:10.1016/j.econedurev .2012.07.006.

Hansen, Martha, et al. "The Impact of School Daily Schedule on Adolescent Sleep." *Pediatrics*, vol. 115, no. 6, 2005, pp. 1555–61, doi:10.1542/peds .2004-1649.

Heissel, Jennifer, and Samuel Norris. "Rise and Shine: The Effect of School Start Times on Academic Performance from Childhood through Puberty." *Journal of Human Resources*, 19 Apr. 2017, doi:10.3368/jhr.53.4.0815 -7346R1.

Jacob, Brian, and Jonah Rockoff. "Organizing Schools to Improve Student Achievement: Start Times, Grade Configurations, and Teacher Assignments." *The Hamilton Project*, Discussion Paper 2011–08, September 2011, www.brookings .edu/wp-content/uploads/2016/06/092011 _organize_jacob_rockoff_paper.pdf.

Pope, Nolan. "How the Time of Day Affects Productivity: Evidence from School Schedules." *Review of Economics and Statistics*, vol. 98, no. 1, Mar. 2016, pp. 1–11, doi:10.1162/ REST_a_00525.

Make connections: Consider your own experience.

[REFLECT]

Readers often use their own experience and observation to assess the proposed solution. To judge Figlio's argument against your own experience, recall your high school years. Your instructor may ask you to post your thoughts on a class discussion board or to discuss them with other students in class. Use these questions to get started:

- Did your sleep pattern change when you became an adolescent? Would you have benefited from a later start time for school? Why or why not?

- Figlio concludes by mentioning objections readers might have with his proposal, particularly the fact that later school start times might cause a problem for after-school activities. How troubling do you think this objection is likely to be for most readers? What other objections do you think could be raised?

Did you know?

Research shows that we learn better when what we are learning connects to our real-world experience. Is that true for you?

$\left[\,\text{ANALYZE}\,\right]$ # Use the Basic Features.

A WELL-ARGUED SOLUTION: USING RESEARCH

Proposal writers often need to do research to demonstrate either that the problem exists or that the proposed solution will help solve the problem. Sometimes, they do both. O'Malley, for example, cites research to support his analysis of the problem—

> Cornell's research using fMRI brain scans shows that "the pressures of a big test can reach beyond the exam itself—stunting the cognitive systems that support the attention and memory skills every day" (Beilock, 2010). (par. 2).

and his argument for the solution—

> A 2006 study reported in the journal *Psychological Science* concluded that "taking repeated tests on material leads to better long-term retention than repeated studying," according to the study's coauthors, Henry L. Roediger and Jeffrey Karpicke (ScienceWatch.com, 2008). (par. 4)

ANALYZE & WRITE

Write a paragraph analyzing and evaluating how Figlio uses research to support his argument:

1   Reread paragraph 2 to see how Figlio uses biological research. What conclusion does he draw from this research, and why is it important for his proposal?

2   Making the cause-effect connection between this biological change and improved school performance is, as Figlio acknowledges, "difficult" (par. 3). How convincing is Figlio's use of the Heissel and Norris study? How well do you think this research supports his proposal to start high school later in the morning?

Take a moment . . .

Think about the difficulty of proving a cause-effect connection and the central role causal analysis plays in many proposals to solve a problem.

A CLEAR, LOGICAL ORGANIZATION: CUEING THE READER

It's important, especially in complicated proposals, to provide cues to help the audience move from paragraph to paragraph without losing sight of the main point. O'Malley, for example, provides a forecast of what his essay will cover and repeats key terms from his thesis statement—or their synonyms—in each of his topic sentences:

THESIS STATEMENT Key terms Forecast	If professors gave brief exams at frequent intervals, students would be spurred to learn more and worry less. They would study more regularly, perform better on tests, and enhance their cognitive functioning. (par. 2)
TOPIC SENTENCE Key terms	The main reason professors should give frequent exams is that when they do and when they provide feedback to students on how well they are doing, students learn more in the course and perform better. (par. 4)

O'Malley also uses rhetorical questions (a question to which no answer is expected) to make a transition from one topic to the next. For example, he uses a rhetorical question at the end of paragraph 8—"Why, then, do so few professors give frequent brief exams?"—as a transition to the section dealing with likely objections. The two paragraphs following the rhetorical question begin with an answer:

"Some believe that such exams . . ." (par. 9)

"Moreover, professors object to frequent exams because" (par. 10)

ANALYZE & WRITE

Write a paragraph analyzing and evaluating the strategies Figlio uses to cue readers:

1 Where does Figlio state his thesis, the solution he's proposing? What do you think Figlio's key terms are? Where do you see them repeated in the essay?

2 Notice that Figlio includes several rhetorical questions. How effective are they in helping readers follow his argument?

Consider possible topics: Problems involving schools.

[RESPOND]

Figlio focuses his proposal on what he calls "low-hanging fruit," solutions that are easy and inexpensive to implement but are likely to improve student performance. You might also have ideas about other changes that would both solve a problem for students and cost little to implement. For example, consider problems with bullying, lack of study time, or elimination of after-school activities at the middle school or high school you attended. How might problems like those be lessened or eliminated altogether? Consider low-cost options, such as involving older students for community service credit or joining forces with local retirees.

David J. Smith | *Getting to "E Pluribus Unum"*

Courtesy of George Mason University

DAVID J. SMITH is an attorney as well as a consultant specializing in conflict resolution. He has taught at various colleges, including Georgetown and the School for Conflict Analysis and Resolution at George Mason University. He is currently president of the Forage Center for Peacebuilding and Humanitarian Education, a nonprofit, nonpartisan consulting firm. Previously, he was the program officer at the U.S. Institute of Peace and a member of the Global Education Committee of the World Affairs Council. He has written several books, including *Peace Jobs: A Student's Guide to Starting a Career Working for Peace* (2016) and a number of articles for such publications as the *Journal of Peace Education*, the *Chronicle of Higher Education*, the *New York Times*, and *Inside Higher Education*, in which this proposal originally appeared in January 2017.

As you read,

- think about the phrase *e pluribus unum* (Latin for "one out of many"). What does it tell readers about the goal of this proposal?

- consider the rhetorical situation in which Smith is writing. Who is his audience? How does he reach out to all readers—in "blue America and red America" (par. 5)?

1   President Obama, as part of his swan song, recently traveled overseas, touting the benefits of international engagement and study abroad. In mid-November we also celebrated International Education Week, sponsored by the U.S. Department of State to advance global understanding. As a college educator for over thirty years, as well as someone who was a U.S. Fulbright Scholar (and now has a son in the Peace Corps), I believe the benefits of international education are incontrovertible.

2   But we learned something about our nation as a result of the presidential election that has caused me to reflect on whether the emphasis on international exchange has come at the expense of achieving important domestic understanding. Like a couple who spend little time with each other and instead seek individual pursuits, then wake up one morning realizing they no longer have much in common, Americans woke up the day after the election realizing that they no longer knew one another. We have become, in a broad context, a nation of strangers. We are now at a place where our failure to engage with one another has resulted in the most significant divide since the civil rights era or maybe even the Civil War. A recent CNN poll (Agiesta) revealed that 85 percent of Americans feel we are more divided than ever.

3   That is not surprising to me. I spend much of my time visiting college campuses in rural red and urban blue America promoting international education. In particular, I focus on community colleges: institutions that frequently are windows into local communities. I often start my talks with, "I'm from Washington and am here to help you." The laughter that follows has increasingly moved from being lighthearted to snickering. (I've decided to stop making the remark.) For years, I have warned my inside-the-Beltway colleagues that we live and work in a bubble. And this distortion has given us a perspective that is alien—like being from Mars—to folks in many parts of the country.

4   Pundits are replete with answers addressing the reasons for the election results. Was it educational differences, with Clinton supporters having more education than Trump supporters? Was it economic differences: the Trump supporters having never recovered from the Great Recession? Or was it anxiety from middle-aged white voters rejecting the social liberalism of the West Coast, New England and especially Washington, D.C.? We will debate this for a long time, and I'm not sure that there is one answer: it is probably a convergence of conditions.

5   But I do have one idea of where we might go from here, or a way of helping our couple—blue America and red America—to get to know each other again. We should establish a national exchange program for American college students that takes them from their often comfortable environments and provides them with the opportunity to get to know people in other parts of the country and in different settings.

6   In international exchange, the emphasis is cultural. The objective of going abroad is not to learn from other exchange students (although this happens), but rather to learn about how people in local and culturally rich environments live: what their struggles, hopes and values are. Every international educator hopes their returning students have had transformational experiences in which they learn about the conditions other people live under—and, in the process, develop empathy for others. As a result, they are better-informed global citizens, not afraid to travel, and most important, can engage in a meaningful way with those who are different than they are.

7   ProPublica reporter Alec MacGillis recently suggested in *The New York Times* that if hipsters wanted to promote their progressive agendas, they should move to Iowa. But I'm not thinking here about political change as much as improving political understanding. Too often engagement and dialogue are viewed as an occasion to change another's mind: it's a chance to make arguments (at times logical, but more often emotional) to convert someone to your camp. Although some people would contend that is needed, we must promote shared understanding and not conversion right now for our nation to move forward.

8   By providing students with a chance to live in a different type of community-based setting in an unfamiliar part of the country, we can foster a better understanding of the aspirations and needs of others. The overall objective would be to provide students with the opportunity to experience life in a part of the America that is unfamiliar to them and might have been characterized disparagingly. Remember Ted Cruz's

comment about "New York values" during one of the presidential debates, or Hillary Clinton's remark that half of Trump's supporters consist of a "basket of deplorables"?

9 I could imagine a student from the rural South spending a semester with an ethnic family in New York learning about cultural diversity and the challenges of immigrants. And I can imagine an urban West Coast student spending a semester living with a farm family in the Midwest learning about the importance of manual labor to support our economy and the values of small-town America.

10 The program could be set up similarly to how international exchange is run. For example, for more developed international programs, they often have a satellite campus abroad where students go to study, thereby replicating some of what the students have at home. The second model—more relevant in this case—is where students from a number of institutions go to a foreign university to study. Here, the home colleges and universities have entered into arrangements with the foreign host to accept students for the term, and often students stay with host families or other people in the country. For example, when my son did study abroad in Turkey, he didn't live on campus with other exchange students; rather, he got a flat with other local Turkish students. That provided him with an experience that was more genuine.

11 For a domestic exchange program, I could imagine institutions in red rural and blue urban parts of America hosting and housing students. But a model that probably would provide the best cultural immersion would be having students live with host families.

12 Fortunately, this concept is not a new one. The idea of students participating in programs in other parts of America has been done. American University has long hosted students in its Washington Semester Program. But the objective is not cultural—rather it is to learn about public affairs. A closer model ("Brown") could be the program between Brown University (an Ivy League, predominately white institution in Rhode Island) and Tougaloo College (a historically black institution in Mississippi) that has operated since 1964 and was established to promote better understanding of race relations.

13 Could such a program be replicated nationally with the help of federal funding and grants from educational foundations? The various higher education associations—for instance, the American Association of State Colleges and Universities or the American Association of Community Colleges—already have members from all parts of the country and could facilitate exchanges and help with coordination.

14 A national collegiate exchange program would allow students to see another person who differs from them not as a foe or someone to fear, but as an individual whom they could build relationships with. By offering opportunities to connect Americans in a domestic residential setting, they can explore values, dreams and aspirations. That would promote commonality and identify shared experiences and make real our national motto: e pluribus unum, or from many one.

filo/Getty Images

Links

Agiesta, Jennifer. "CNN/ORC Poll: A Nation Divided, and Is It Ever." CNN, 27 Nov. 2016, www.cnn .com/2016/11/27/politics/cnn-poll-division -donald-trump.

"Brown and Tougaloo: Transforming Lives since 1964." Brown University, 2016, www.brown.edu /academics/college/special-programs/tougaloo /get-involved/students.

MacGillis, Alec. "Go Midwest, Young Hipster." *The New York Times,* 22 Oct. 2016, nyti.ms/2jIsaBa.

[REFLECT] # Make connections: Broadening perspectives.

Smith argues that if students lived for a time in another part of the country, their cultural and political perspectives might be expanded. Not only would they forge new relationships but, Smith thinks, they would "develop empathy for others" (par. 6) as well.

Write a few paragraphs discussing the possibility that Smith's proposal could help blue America and red America come to a better understanding. Your instructor may ask you to post your thoughts on a class discussion board or to discuss them with other students in class. Use these questions to get started:

- What kinds of new experiences do you think you would have if you were a student living in another family's home in a different part of the country? What might you learn about their daily "struggles, hopes and values" (par. 6) that might foster understanding?

- Smith does not seem to be suggesting that students debate or try to educate people they encounter while participating in a national exchange program. How do you think the students and the people with whom they come into contact might broaden their perspectives?

[ANALYZE] # Use the basic features.

A FOCUSED, WELL-DEFINED PROBLEM: MAKING THE AUDIENCE CARE

Every proposal begins with a problem. What writers say about the problem and how much space they devote to it depends on what they assume their audience already knows and thinks about it. A savvy proposal writer tries to present even a familiar problem in a way that reminds readers of the problem's seriousness and prepares them for the writer's preferred solution. If many readers are unlikely to care about the problem, or if people aren't convinced it exists, any solution may seem too expensive or hard to implement. For this reason, a proposal writer must frame the problem so that the audience will want a solution.

In his proposal, Patrick O'Malley begins by addressing his fellow students: "You got a C on the midterm" (par. 1). But he knows that students are not his primary audience, so he shifts to the intended audience in paragraph 2: "many professors may not realize." To convince professors that the problem is important, O'Malley uses a couple of strategies:

- He enlists readers' attention and sympathy, using the opening scenario and rhetorical questions to remind professors what it was like to be a student:

  "It's late at night. . . . Did you study enough? Did you study the right things?" (par. 1)

- He cites credible sources to show that he is not just whining about a personal problem:

  "Reporting on recent research at Cornell University Medical School, Sian Beilock, a psychology professor at the University of Chicago" (par. 2)

| ANALYZE & WRITE |

Write a paragraph analyzing and evaluating how Smith makes his readers (mainly faculty, administrators, and staff) care about the issue:

1 Reread paragraph 1. Why do you think Smith mentions his many years in academia as well as his personal and professional experience with international education? How do you think Smith's readers would respond?

2 Now skim paragraphs 2–4. What evidence does Smith provide to establish the seriousness of the problem? Do you think more evidence would be necessary to convince readers that the nation is seriously divided? How does his anecdote about opening college talks with "I'm from Washington and am here to help you" serve to establish the problem?

A WELL-ARGUED SOLUTION: DEMONSTRATING FEASIBILITY

For proposals to be convincing, they have to seem feasible. That means readers need to be persuaded that the solution (highlighted in green) can be implemented without too much expense or inconvenience.

To persuade readers that more testing would help students, O'Malley makes clear in his thesis statement exactly what he wants faculty to do and why:

> If professors gave brief exams at frequent intervals, students would be spurred to learn more and worry less. They would study more regularly, perform better on tests, and enhance their cognitive functioning. (par. 2)

He then cites scientific studies and news reports about scientific studies to persuade readers that the results he promises are realistic.

| ANALYZE & WRITE |

Write a paragraph analyzing and evaluating how Smith demonstrates that his proposed solution is feasible:

1 Reread paragraphs 10–11. How does Smith's comparison help demonstrate that his proposed solution is feasible? Given his audience, what additional evidence might make his proposed solution more persuasive?

2 Now skim paragraphs 12 and 13. What do these paragraphs add to this argument for feasibility? Does the rhetorical question — "Could such a program be replicated nationally with the help of federal funding and grants from educational foundations?" — make the proposal sound more or less feasible and why?

Consider possible topics: Bringing Americans together.

[RESPOND]

Many people today are concerned about what appear to be deep divisions within America. Smith cites a CNN poll showing "that 85 percent of Americans feel we are more divided than ever" (par. 2). Smith's proposal is based on what he sees as

a lack of understanding and communication among Americans who live in different parts of the country. Think about the community you live and work in as well
as where you attend school. What opportunities are there in these communities
to increase communication among people? For example, are there sports, theater,
or music venues where people with diverse points of view might get to know one
another? What could be done on a local level to build a bridge of shared concerns?
For example, could people mobilize around the need for a stop sign or traffic signal
where there have been accidents, or could they volunteer to clean up neighborhood parks or plant trees? How might neighborhood actions like these help bring
people together?

| Kelly D. Brownell and Thomas R. Frieden | *Ounces of Prevention: The Public Policy Case for Taxes on Sugared Beverages* |

Courtesy of Kelly Brownell

KELLY D. BROWNELL is a professor of psychology and
neuroscience at Duke. An international expert who has published
numerous books and articles, including *Food Fight: The Inside Story
of the Food Industry, America's Obesity Crisis, and What We Can Do
about It* (2003), Brownell received the 2012 American Psychological
Association Award for Outstanding Lifetime Contributions to
Psychology. He was also featured in the Academy Award–nominated
film *Super Size Me.*

Centers for Disease Control and Prevention

THOMAS R. FRIEDEN, a physician specializing in public health,
served as the director of the U.S. Centers for Disease Control
and Prevention (CDC) under President Obama and served
for several years as the health commissioner for the City of
New York.

Brownell and Frieden's proposal "Ounces of Prevention: The
Public Policy Case for Taxes on Sugared Beverages" was originally
published in 2009 in the highly respected *New England Journal of
Medicine,* which calls itself "the most widely read, cited, and influential general medical periodical in the world." In fact, research published there is
often referred to widely throughout the media.

As you read, consider the effect that Brownell and Frieden's use of graphs and
formal citation of sources has on their credibility:

- How do the graphs help establish the seriousness of the problem? How do they
  also help demonstrate the feasibility of the solution the authors propose?

- How do the citations help persuade you to accept the authors' solution? What
  effect might they have had on their original readers? (Note that the authors use
  neither of the two citation styles covered in Part 4 of this text. Instead, they use
  one common to medical journals and publications of the U.S. National Library of
  Medicine.)

Sugar, rum, and tobacco are commodities which are nowhere necessaries of life, which are become objects of almost universal consumption, and which are therefore extremely proper subjects of taxation.

—Adam Smith, *The Wealth of Nations*, 1776

1   The obesity epidemic has inspired calls for public health measures to prevent diet-related diseases. One controversial idea is now the subject of public debate: food taxes. Forty states already have small taxes on sugared beverages and snack foods, but in the past year, Maine and New York have proposed large taxes on sugared beverages, and similar discussions have begun in other states. The size of the taxes, their potential for generating revenue and reducing consumption, and vigorous opposition by the beverage industry have resulted in substantial controversy. Because excess consumption of unhealthful foods underlies many leading causes of death, food taxes at local, state, and national levels are likely to remain part of political and public health discourse.

2   Sugar-sweetened beverages (soda sweetened with sugar, corn syrup, or other caloric sweeteners and other carbonated and uncarbonated drinks, such as sports and energy drinks) may be the single largest driver of the obesity epidemic. A recent meta-analysis found that the intake of sugared beverages is associated with increased body weight, poor nutrition, and displacement of more healthful beverages; increasing consumption increases risk for obesity and diabetes; the strongest effects are seen in studies with the best methods (e.g., longitudinal and interventional vs. correlational studies);* and interventional studies show that reduced intake of soft drinks improves health.[1] Studies that do not support a relationship between consumption of sugared beverages and health outcomes tend to be conducted by authors supported by the beverage industry.[2] Sugared beverages are marketed extensively to children and adolescents, and in the mid-1990s, children's intake of sugared beverages surpassed that of milk. In the past decade, per capita intake of calories from sugar-sweetened beverages has increased by nearly 30 percent (see bar graph Daily Caloric Intake from Sugar-Sweetened Drinks in the United States);[3] beverages now account for 10 to 15 percent of the calories consumed by children and adolescents. For each extra can or glass of sugared beverage

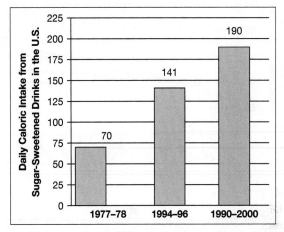

Daily Caloric Intake from Sugar-Sweetened Drinks in the United States.
Data are from Nielsen and Popkin.[3]

consumed per day, the likelihood of a child's becoming obese increases by 60 percent.[4]

3   Taxes on tobacco products have been highly effective in reducing consumption, and data indicate that higher prices also reduce soda consumption. A review conducted by Yale University's Rudd Center for Food Policy and Obesity suggested that for every 10 percent increase in price, consumption decreases by 7.8 percent. An industry trade publication reported even larger reductions: as prices of carbonated soft drinks increased by 6.8 percent, sales dropped by 7.8 percent, and as Coca-Cola prices increased by 12 percent, sales dropped by 14.6 percent.[5] Such studies—and the economic principles that support their findings—suggest that a tax on sugared beverages would encourage consumers to switch to more healthful beverages, which would lead to reduced caloric intake and less weight gain.

4   The increasing affordability of soda—and the decreasing affordability of fresh fruits and vegetables

---

* In a *longitudinal* study, researchers observe changes taking place over a long period of time; in an *interventional* study, investigators give research subjects a measured amount of whatever is being studied and note its effects; and in a *correlational* study, researchers examine statistics to see if two or more variables have a mathematically significant similarity. [Editor's note]

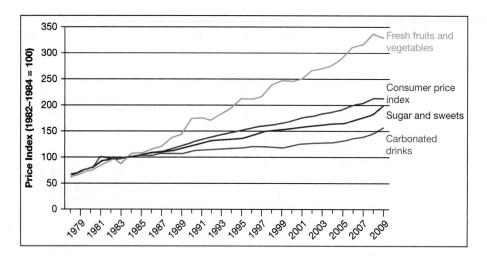

Relative Price Changes for Fresh Fruits and Vegetables, Sugar and Sweets, and Carbonated Drinks, 1978–2009.
Data are from the Bureau of Labor Statistics and represent the U.S. city averages for all urban consumers in January of each year.

(see line graph)—probably contributes to the rise in obesity in the United States. In 2008, a group of child and health care advocates in New York proposed a one-penny-per-ounce excise tax on sugared beverages, which would be expected to reduce consumption by 13 percent—about two servings per week per person. Even if one quarter of the calories consumed from sugared beverages are replaced by other food, the decrease in consumption would lead to an estimated reduction of 8,000 calories per person per year—slightly more than 2 pounds each year for the average person. Such a reduction in calorie consumption would be expected to substantially reduce the risk of obesity and diabetes and may also reduce the risk of heart disease and other conditions.

5   Some argue that government should not interfere in the market and that products and prices will change as consumers demand more healthful food, but several considerations support government action. The first is externality—costs to parties not directly involved in a transaction. The contribution of unhealthful diets to health care costs is already high and is increasing—an estimated $79 billion is spent annually for overweight and obesity alone—and approximately half of these costs are paid by Medicare and Medicaid, at taxpayers' expense. Diet-related diseases also cost society in terms of decreased work productivity, increased absenteeism, poorer school performance, and reduced fitness on the part of military recruits, among other negative effects. The second consideration is information asymmetry

between the parties to a transaction. In the case of sugared beverages, marketers commonly make health claims (e.g., that such beverages provide energy or vitamins) and use techniques that exploit the cognitive vulnerabilities of young children, who often cannot distinguish a television program from an advertisement. A third consideration is revenue generation, which can further increase the societal benefits of a tax on soft drinks. A penny-per-ounce excise tax would raise an estimated $1.2 billion in New York State alone. In times of economic hardship, taxes that both generate this much revenue and promote health are better options than revenue initiatives that may have adverse effects.

6   Objections have certainly been raised: that such a tax would be regressive, that food taxes are not comparable to tobacco or alcohol taxes because people must eat to survive, that it is unfair to single out one type of food for taxation, and that the tax will not solve the obesity problem. But the poor are disproportionately affected by diet-related diseases and would derive the greatest benefit from reduced consumption; sugared beverages are not necessary for survival; Americans consume about 250 to 300 more calories daily today than they did several decades ago, and nearly half this increase is accounted for by consumption of sugared beverages; and though no single intervention will solve the obesity problem, that is hardly a reason to take no action.

7   The full impact of public policies becomes apparent only after they take effect. We can estimate changes in sugared-drink consumption that would be prompted by a tax, but accompanying changes in the consumption of other foods or beverages are more difficult to predict. One question is whether the proportions of calories consumed in liquid and solid foods would change. And shifts among beverages would have different effects depending on whether consumers substituted water, milk, diet drinks, or equivalent generic brands of sugared drinks.

8   Effects will also vary depending on whether the tax is designed to reduce consumption, generate revenue, or both; the size of the tax; whether the revenue is earmarked for programs related to nutrition and health; and where in the production and distribution chain the tax is applied. Given the heavy consumption of sugared beverages, even small taxes will generate substantial revenue, but only heftier taxes will significantly reduce consumption. Sales taxes are the most common form of food tax, but because they are levied as a percentage of the retail price, they encourage the purchase of less-expensive brands or larger containers. Excise taxes structured as a fixed cost per ounce provide an incentive to buy less and hence would be much more effective in reducing consumption and improving health. In addition, manufacturers generally pass the cost of an excise tax along to their customers, including it in the price consumers see when they are making their selection, whereas sales taxes are seen only at the cash register.

9   Although a tax on sugared beverages would have health benefits regardless of how the revenue was used, the popularity of such a proposal increases greatly if revenues are used for programs to prevent childhood obesity, such as media campaigns, facilities and programs for physical activity, and healthier food in schools. Poll results show that support of a tax on sugared beverages ranges from 37 to 72 percent; a poll of New York residents found that 52 percent supported a "soda tax," but the number rose to 72 percent when respondents were told that the revenue would be used for obesity prevention. Perhaps the most defensible approach is to use revenue to subsidize the purchase of healthful foods. The public would then see a relationship between tax and benefit, and any regressive effects would be counteracted by the reduced costs of healthful food.

10   A penny-per-ounce excise tax could reduce consumption of sugared beverages by more than 10 percent. It is difficult to imagine producing behavior change of this magnitude through education alone, even if government devoted massive resources to the task. In contrast, a sales tax on sugared drinks would generate considerable revenue, and as with the tax on tobacco, it could become a key tool in efforts to improve health.

References

1. Vartanian LR, Schwartz MB, Brownell KD. Effects of soft drink consumption on nutrition and health: a systematic review and meta-analysis. Am J Public Health 2007;97:667–675.

2. Forshee RA, Anderson PA, Storey ML. Sugar-sweetened beverages and body mass index in children and adolescents: a meta-analysis. Am J Clin Nutr 2008;87:1662–1671.

3. Nielsen SJ, Popkin BM. Changes in beverage intake between 1977 and 2001. Am J Prev Med 2004;27:205–210.

4. Ludwig DS, Peterson KE, Gortmaker SL. Relation between consumption of sugar-sweetened drinks and childhood obesity: a prospective, observational analysis. Lancet 2001;357:505–508.

5. Elasticity: big price increases cause Coke volume to plummet. Beverage Digest. November 21, 2008:3–4.

Make connections: Government problem-solving.   [REFLECT]

Brownell and Frieden explicitly argue in favor of federal or state government taking action to address public health problems, such as those related to obesity and smoking. Imposing taxes is one thing government can do. Another action is to require that foods be labeled with accurate nutritional information.

Write a few paragraphs considering the right and responsibility of government to solve public health problems. Your instructor may ask you to post your thoughts on a class discussion board or to discuss them with other students in class. Use these questions to get started:

- Consider what actions government *could* take to address public health problems and whether government *should* take such actions.
- Think about how you would respond to Brownell and Frieden's argument that "though no single intervention will solve the obesity problem, that is hardly a reason to take no action" (par. 6).

[ANALYZE]   # Use the basic features.

A FOCUSED, WELL-DEFINED PROBLEM: CITING RESEARCH STUDIES

Brownell and Frieden identify the problem for which they are proposing a solution in broad terms as the "obesity epidemic" (par. 1). However, they frame the issue by focusing on "sugar-sweetened beverages" (par. 2). To support a causal connection between consuming sugar-sweetened beverages and obesity, they cite research studies.

ANALYZE & WRITE ──────────────────────────────

Write a paragraph or two analyzing and evaluating Brownell and Frieden's use of research to establish a causal connection between sweetened drinks and obesity:

1 Reread paragraphs 2–4, and assess how well the findings reported there support Brownell and Frieden's cause-effect argument.

2 Consider the two graphs: How do they help convince readers that the problem exists and is serious?

3 Think about Brownell and Frieden's rhetorical situation. Why might *New England Journal of Medicine* readers want to know the kinds of studies used and which ones employ "the best methods" and get "the strongest effects" (par. 2)?

AN EFFECTIVE RESPONSE: HANDLING OBJECTIONS

Proposal writers usually try to anticipate readers' objections or questions and concede or refute them. How writers handle objections and questions affects their credibility with readers, who usually expect writers to be respectful of other points of view and to take criticism seriously while still arguing assertively for their solution. Brownell and Frieden anticipate and respond to five objections they would expect their readers to raise.

ANALYZE & WRITE ──────────────────────────────

Write a couple of paragraphs analyzing and evaluating how Brownell and Frieden respond to objections:

1 Reread paragraph 5. First, summarize the objection and their argument refuting it. Then, evaluate their refutation: How effective is it likely to be with readers?

2 Reread paragraph 6, in which the authors respond to a number of other objections. What cues do they provide to help you follow their argument?

Brownell and Frieden *Ounces of Prevention*

GUIDE TO READING
Guide to Writing
A Writer at Work
Reflection

267

3 Given their purpose and audience, why do you think Brownell and Frieden focus so much attention on the first objection and group the other objections together in a single paragraph?

4 How would you describe the tone of Brownell and Frieden's refutation? How is their credibility with readers likely to be affected by the way they respond to objections?

Consider possible topics: Improving a group to which you belong.

[RESPOND]

Consider making a proposal to improve the operation of an organization, a business, or a club to which you belong. For example, you might propose that your college keep administrative offices open in the evenings or on weekends to accommodate working students, or that a child-care center be opened for students who are parents of young children. For a business, you might propose a system to handle customer complaints or a fairer way for employees to arrange their schedules. If you belong to a club that has a problem with the collection of dues, you might propose a new collection system or suggest alternative ways of raising money.

The Writing Assignment

Write an essay proposing a solution to a problem. Choose a problem faced by a community or group to which you belong, and address your proposal to one or more members of the group or to outsiders who might help solve the problem.

This Guide to Writing is designed to help you compose your own proposal and apply what you have learned from reading other essays in the same genre. The Starting Points chart will help you find answers to questions you might have about composing a proposal. Use it to find the guidance you need, when you need it.

Did you know?

You may not need the support of this Guide to Writing when composing in a genre you know well, but it can be very helpful when experimenting with a new or challenging genre.

STARTING POINTS: PROPOSING A SOLUTION

A Focused, Well-Defined Problem

How do I come up with a problem to write about?

- Assess the genre's basic features: A focused, well-defined problem. (pp. 242–49)
- Consider possible topics: Problems involving schools. (p. 257)
- Consider possible topics: Bringing Americans together. (pp. 261–62)
- Consider possible topics: Improving a group to which you belong. (p. 267)
- Choose a problem for which you can propose a solution. (p. 270)

How can I best define the problem for my readers?

- A Focused, Well-Defined Problem: Making the Audience Care (p. 260)
- A Focused, Well-Defined Problem: Citing Research Studies (p. 266)
- Frame the problem for your readers. (pp. 271–72)
- Test Your Choice: Defining the Problem (p. 273)
- Assess how the problem has been framed, and reframe it for your readers. (pp. 273–74)
- A Troubleshooting Guide: A Focused, Well-Defined Problem (p. 281)

The Writing Assignment

Guide to Reading
GUIDE TO WRITING
A Writer at Work
Reflection

269

A Well-Argued Solution

How do I come up with a plausible solution?

- Assess the genre's basic features: A well-argued solution. (p. 244)
- A Well-Argued Solution: Using Research (p. 256)
- A Well-Argued Solution: Demonstrating Feasibility (p. 261)
- Develop a possible solution. (pp. 274–75)
- Research your proposal. (p. 276)

How do I construct an argument supporting my solution?

- Assess the genre's basic features: A well-argued solution. (p. 244)
- A Well-Argued Solution: Demonstrating Feasibility (p. 261)
- Explain your solution. (p. 275)
- Research your proposal. (p. 276)
- A Troubleshooting Guide: A Well-Argued Solution (p. 281)

An Effective Response to Objections and Alternative Solutions

How do I respond to possible objections and alternative solutions?

- Assess the genre's basic features: An effective response to objections and alternative solutions. (pp. 245–46)
- An Effective Response: Handling Objections (p. 266)
- Develop a response to objections or alternative solutions. (pp. 276–77)
- A Troubleshooting Guide: An Effective Response to Objections and Alternative Solutions (p. 281)

A Clear, Logical Organization

How can I help my readers follow my argument?

- Assess the genre's basic features: A clear, logical organization. (p. 246)
- A Clear, Logical Organization: Cueing the Reader (pp. 256–57)
- Create an outline that will organize your proposal effectively for your readers. (pp. 277–78)
- A Troubleshooting Guide: A Clear, Logical Organization (p. 282)

Writing a Draft: Invention, Research, Planning, and Composing

The activities in this section will help you choose and research a problem as well as develop and organize an argument for your proposed solution. Your writing in response to many of these activities can be used as part of your rough draft, which you will be able to improve after receiving feedback from your classmates and instructor. Do the activities in any order that makes sense to you (and your instructor), and return to them as needed as you revise.

Choose a problem for which you can propose a solution.

When choosing a problem, keep in mind that it must be

- important to you and of concern to your readers;
- solvable, at least in part;
- one that you can research sufficiently in the time you have.

To come up with ideas, think about the readings: Like Figlio, you could offer a solution to a problem with student performance, such as retaining recess to improve student attentiveness or helping struggling students by starting a mentoring program. Like Smith, you could propose a way to unify students with differing perspectives, such as by challenging students from another campus organization to a bowling match or a debate. Or like Brownell and Frieden, you could offer a solution to a campus health issue, such as having the campus serve organic food to tackle the problem of unhealthy student eating habits, or starting a food pantry on campus to solve the problem of hunger or inadequate nutrition among students.

Choosing a problem affecting a group to which you belong (for example, as a classmate, teammate, participant in an online game site, or garage band member) or a place at which you have worked (a coffee shop, community pool, or radio station) gives you an advantage: You can write as an expert. You know the history of the problem as well as who to interview, and perhaps you have already thought about possible solutions. Moreover, you know who to address and how to persuade that audience to take action on your proposed solution.

If you already have a problem and possible solution(s) in mind, skip to "Frame the problem for your readers" (pp. 271–72). If you need to find a problem, consider the possible topics following the readings and the suggestions here:

	Problems	**Possible Solutions**
School	Can't get into required courses	Make them large lecture courses. Make them online or hybrid courses. Give priority to majors.
Community	No safe place for children to play	Use school yards for after-school sports. Get high school students or senior citizens to tutor kids. Make pocket parks for neighborhood play. Offer programs for kids at branch libraries.

Writing a Draft

Guide to Reading
▶ **GUIDE TO WRITING**
A Writer at Work
Reflection

271

| Work | Inadequate training for new staff | Make a training video or Web site. Assign experienced workers to mentor trainees (for bonus pay). |

⊞ Frame the problem for your readers.

Once you have made a preliminary choice of a problem, consider what you know about it, what research will help you explore what others think about it, and how you can interest your readers in solving it. Then determine how you can frame or reframe it in a way that appeals to readers' values and concerns. Use the questions and sentence strategies that follow as a jumping-off point; you can make them your own as you revise later.

For advice on listing, cubing, and freewriting, see Chapter 11; to learn more about conducting surveys and interviews, consult Chapter 17.

WAYS IN

WHAT IS THE PROBLEM?

What do I already know about the problem?

BRAINSTORM *a list:* Spend 10 minutes listing everything you know about the problem. Write quickly, leaving judgment aside for the moment. After the 10 minutes are up, you can review your list and highlight or star the most promising information.

Use **CUBING**: Probe the problem from a variety of perspectives:

- Describe the problem.
- Compare the problem to other, similar problems, or contrast it with other, related problems.
- Connect the problem to other problems you have experienced.
- Analyze the problem to identify its parts, its causes, or its effects.
- Apply the problem to a real-life situation.

FREEWRITE (write without stopping) for 5 or 10 minutes about the problem. Don't stop to reflect or consider; if you hit a roadblock, just keep coming back to the problem. At the end of the specified time, review your writing and highlight or underline promising ideas.

WHY SHOULD READERS CARE?

How can I convince readers the problem is real and deserves attention?

Give an **EXAMPLE** *to make the problem specific:*

▶ Consider the case of ...., in which a similar approach was implemented.

EXAMPLE　For example, when my son did study abroad in Turkey, he didn't live on campus with other exchange students; rather, he got a flat with other local Turkish students. That provided him with an experience that was more genuine. (Smith, par. 10)

Use a **SCENARIO** *or an* **ANECDOTE** *to dramatize the problem:*

▶ Imagine that you're in situation X when .... happens.

EXAMPLE　It's late at night. The final's tomorrow. You got a C on the midterm, so this one will make or break you. (O'Malley, par. 1)

Cite **STATISTIC** *to show the severity of the problem:*

▶ It has recently been reported that .... percent of group A are [specify problem].

(continued)

What do others think about the problem?

Conduct SURVEYS:

- Talk to a variety of students at your school (your friends and others).
- Discuss the problem with neighbors or survey shoppers at a local mall.
- Discuss the problem with coworkers or people who work at similar jobs.

Conduct INTERVIEWS:

- Interview faculty experts.
- Discuss the issue with businesspeople in the community.
- Interview local officials (members of the city council, the fire chief, the local labor union representative).

What do most of my potential readers already think about the problem?

▶ Many complain about _____ but do nothing because solving it seems too hard/too costly.

▶ Some think _____ is someone else's responsibility/not that big of a problem.

▶ Others see _____ as a matter of fairness/human decency.

Who suffers from the problem?

▶ Studies have shown that _____ mostly affects groups A, B, and C.

EXAMPLE   For each extra can or glass of sugared beverage consumed per day, the likelihood of a child's becoming obese increases by 60 percent. (Brownell and Frieden, par. 2)

EXAMPLE   A recent CNN poll (Agiesta) revealed that 85 percent of Americans feel we are more divided than ever. (Smith, par. 2)

Describe the problem's NEGATIVE CONSEQUENCES:

▶ According to Professor X, group A is suffering as a result of _____ [insert quote from expert].

EXAMPLE   Sian Beilock, a psychology professor at the University of Chicago, points out that "stressing about doing well on an important exam can backfire, leading students to 'choke under pressure' or to score less well than they might otherwise score if the stakes weren't so high." (O'Malley, par. 2)

Why should readers care about solving the problem?

▶ We're all in this together. _____ is not a win-lose proposition. If group A loses, we all lose.

▶ If we don't try to solve _____, no one else will.

▶ Doing nothing will only make _____ worse.

▶ We have a moral responsibility to do something about _____ .

Writing a Draft

Guide to Reading
GUIDE TO WRITING
A Writer at Work
Reflection

273

TEST YOUR CHOICE

Defining the Problem

Ask two or three other students to help you develop your plan to frame the problem.

Presenters.   Briefly explain how you are thinking of framing or reframing the problem for your audience. Use the following language as a model for presenting your problem, or use language of your own.

▶ I plan to define the problem not as _____ but as _____ /in terms of _____ because I think my readers will share my concerns/values/priorities.

Listeners.   Tell the presenter what response this way of framing the problem elicits from you and why. You may also explain how you think other readers might respond. Use the following language as a model for structuring your response, or use your own words.

▶ I'm also/not concerned about X because of _____, _____, and _____.

▶ I agree/disagree that _____ because _____.

⊞ Assess how the problem has been framed, and reframe it for your readers.

Once you have a good idea of what you and your readers think about the problem, consider how others have framed the problem and how you might be able to reframe it for your readers.

> **Did you know . . .**
>
> Research suggests the best way to reframe a problem is by appealing to your readers' values and concerns.

◀ WAYS IN

HOW HAS THE PROBLEM BEEN FRAMED?	HOW CAN I REFRAME THE PROBLEM?
Sink or Swim Argument	**Teaching Should Not Be Punitive Argument**
EXAMPLE Providing tutoring for students who are failing a course is wrong because students should do what they need to do to pass the course or face the consequences. That's the way the system is supposed to work.	**EXAMPLE** Providing tutoring for students who are failing a course assumes that the purpose of education is learning, not testing for its own sake or punishing those who have not done well.
Don't Reward Failure Argument	**Encourage Success Argument**
EXAMPLE Providing tutoring for students who are failing a course is like a welfare system that makes underprepared students dependent and second class citizens.	**EXAMPLE** Providing tutoring for students who are failing a course encourages students to work hard and value doing well in school.

(continued)

Reverse Discrimination Argument

EXAMPLE   Providing tutoring for students who are failing a course is unfair to the other students who don't need assistance.

Win-Lose Argument

EXAMPLE   Providing tutoring for students who are failing a course ignores the fact that grades should fall on a bell curve — that is, an equal proportion of students should get an *F* as get an *A*.

Level Playing Field Argument

EXAMPLE   Providing tutoring for students who are failing a course is a way to make up for inadequacies in previous schooling.

Win-Win Argument

EXAMPLE   Providing tutoring for students who are failing a course assumes that it would be a good thing if every student earned an *A*. Providing tutoring enhances learning.

▦ Develop a possible solution.

The following activities will help you devise a solution and develop an argument to support it. If you have already found a solution, you may want to skip this activity and go directly to the Explain Your Solution section (p. 275).

WAYS IN

HOW CAN I SOLVE THIS PROBLEM?

One way to generate ideas is to write steadily for at least five minutes, exploring some of the possible ways of solving the problem. Consider using the following approaches as a jumping-off point:

- Adapt a solution that has been tried or proposed for a similar problem.

    EXAMPLE   Smith's proposal for a national student exchange program is based on the successful international program.

- Focus on eliminating a cause or minimizing an effect of the problem.

    EXAMPLE   O'Malley's solution to stressful high-stakes exams is to eliminate the cause of the stress by inducing instructors to give more frequent low-stakes exams.

- See the problem as part of a larger system, and explore solutions to the system.

    EXAMPLE   Figlio argues that changing high school start times will help improve student performance.

- Focus on solving a small part of the problem.

Writing a Draft

Guide to Reading
GUIDE TO WRITING
A Writer at Work
Reflection

275

> **EXAMPLE**   Brownell and Frieden's solution to obesity is to reduce the consumption of sugared beverages through taxation.

- Look at the problem from different points of view.

> **EXAMPLE**   Consider what students, teachers, parents, or administrators might think could be done to help solve the problem.

- Think of a specific example of the problem, and consider how you could solve it.

For more idea-generating strategies, see Chapter 11.

> **EXAMPLE**   O'Malley could have focused on solving the problem of high-stakes exams in his biology course.

Explain your solution.

You may not yet know for certain whether you will be able to construct a convincing argument to support your solution, but you should choose a solution that you feel motivated to pursue. Use the questions and sentence strategies that follow to help you put your ideas in writing. You will likely want to revise what you come up with later, but the questions and sentence strategies may provide a convenient jumping-off point.

WAYS IN

HOW CAN I EXPLAIN HOW MY SOLUTION WOULD HELP SOLVE THE PROBLEM?

It would eliminate a cause of the problem.

▶ Research shows it would reduce _____ .

It has worked elsewhere.

▶ It works in _____ , _____ , and _____ , as studies evaluating it show.

It would change people's behavior.

▶ _____ would discourage/encourage people to _____ .

HOW CAN I EXPLAIN THAT MY SOLUTION IS FEASIBLE?

It could be implemented.

Describe the major stages or steps necessary to carry out your solution.

We can afford it.

Explain what it would cost to put the solution into practice.

It would not take too much time.

Create a rough schedule or timeline to show how long it would take to make the necessary arrangements.

⊞ Research your proposal.

You may have already begun researching the problem and familiarizing yourself with alternative solutions that have been offered, or you may have ideas about what you need to research. If you are proposing a solution to a problem about which others have written, use the following research strategies to help you find out what solutions others have proposed or tried. You may also use these strategies to find out how others have defined the problem and demonstrated its seriousness.

For more about searching for information, consult Chapter 17; for more about avoiding plagiarism and creating an annotated bibliography, see Chapter 19; for more about documenting sources, consult Chapter 20 (MLA style) or Chapter 21 (APA style).

- Enter keywords or phrases related to your solution (or problem) into the search box of an all-purpose database, such as Academic OneFile (InfoTrac) or Academic Search Complete (EBSCOhost), to find relevant articles in magazines and journals; in the database Lexis/Nexis to find articles in newspapers; or in library catalogs to find books and other resources. (Database names may change, and what is available will differ from school to school. Some libraries may even combine all three into one search link on the library's home page. Ask a librarian if you need help.) Patrick O'Malley could have tried a combination of keywords, such as *learning* and *test anxiety,* or variations on his terms (*frequent testing, improve retention*) to find relevant articles.

Consider . . .
An annotated working bibliography can help you keep track of multiple sources.

- Bookmark or keep a record of the URLs of promising sites, and download or copy information you could use in your essay. When available, download PDF files rather than HTML files because these are likely to include visuals, such as graphs and charts. If you copy and paste relevant information into your notes, be careful to distinguish all material from sources from your own ideas.

- Remember to record source information and to cite and document any sources you use, including visuals and interviews.

⊞ Develop a response to objections or alternative solutions.

The topics you considered when developing an argument for your solution may be the same topics you need to consider when developing a response to likely criticisms of your proposal—answering possible objections to your solution or alternative solutions readers may prefer. The following sentence strategies may help you start drafting an effective response.

WAYS IN

> **HOW CAN I DRAFT A REFUTATION OR CONCESSION?**
>
> *To draft a* **REFUTATION**, *try beginning with sentence strategies like these:*
>
> ▶ Some people think we can't afford to do X, but it would cost only $ .... to put my solution in place compared to $ .... , the cost of doing nothing/ implementing an alternative solution.
>
> ▶ Although it might take X months/years to implement this solution, it would actually take longer to implement solution A.

▶ There are critics who think that only a few people would benefit from solving this problem, but _____ would benefit because _____ .

▶ Some may suggest that I favor this solution because I would benefit personally; however, the fact is we would all benefit because _____ .

▶ Some may claim that this solution has been tried and hasn't worked. But research shows that [explain how proposed solution has worked] *or* my solution differs from past experiments in these important ways: _____ , _____ , and _____ .

To draft a CONCESSION, *try beginning with sentence strategies like these:*

▶ I agree with those who claim X/object on X grounds; therefore, instead of _____ , I think we should pursue _____ .

▶ If _____ seems too time-consuming/expensive, let's try _____ .

▶ Where _____ is a concern, I think _____ [name alternative] should be followed.

▶ Although _____ is the best way to deal with a problem like this, under _____ [describe special circumstances], I agree that _____ should be done.

Create an outline that will organize your proposal effectively for your readers.

For more on outlining, see Chapters 11 and 12.

Whether you have rough notes or a complete draft, making an outline of what you have written can help you organize your essay effectively for your audience. Compare the possible outlines that follow to see how you might organize the essay depending on whether your readers agree that a serious problem exists and are open to your solution—or not.

If you are writing primarily for readers who *acknowledge that the problem exists and are open to your solution:*

I. **Introduce the problem,** concluding with a thesis statement asserting your solution.

II. **Demonstrate the problem's seriousness:** Frame the problem in a way that prepares readers for the solution.

III. **Describe the proposed solution:** Show what could be done to implement it.

IV. **Refute objections.**

V. **Conclude:** Urge action on your solution.

If you are writing primarily for readers who *do not recognize the problem or are likely to prefer alternative solutions:*

I. **Reframe the problem:** Identify common ground, and acknowledge alternative ways readers might see the problem.

II. **Concede strengths, but emphasize the weaknesses of alternative solution(s) that readers might prefer.**

III. **Describe the proposed solution:** Give reasons and provide evidence to demonstrate that it is preferable to the alternative(s).

IV. **Refute objections.**

V. **Conclude:** Reiterate shared values.

Whatever organizational strategy you adopt, do not hesitate to change your outline as necessary while drafting and revising. For instance, you might find it more effective to hold back on presenting your solution until you have discussed unacceptable alternatives. The purpose of an outline is to identify the basic components of your proposal and to help you organize it effectively, not to lock you into a particular structure.

Write the opening sentences.

Review what you have written to see if you have something that would work to launch your proposal, or try out one or two of these opening strategies:

Begin with an **engaging scenario:**

> It's late at night. The final's tomorrow. You got a C on the midterm, so this one will make or break you. Will it be like the midterm? Did you study enough? Did you study the right things? It's too late to drop the course. So what happens if you fail? No time to worry about that now—you've got a ton of notes to go over. (O'Malley, par. 1)

Refer to the shortcomings of **alternative solutions:**

> Many proposals for improving student performance involve very costly interventions. And while quite a few of these costly interventions surely pass benefit-cost tests, they can be extremely challenging, politically or financially, to implement. (Figlio, par. 1)

Cite a **recent event** *establishing the problem or suggesting how to solve it:*

> President Obama, as part of his swan song, recently traveled overseas, touting the benefits of international engagement and study abroad. In mid-November we also celebrated International Education Week, sponsored by the U.S. Department of State to advance global understanding. (Smith, par. 1)

Offer a **quotation** *that highlights support for your solution:*

> Sugar, rum, and tobacco are commodities which are nowhere necessaries of life, which are become objects of almost universal consumption, and which are therefore extremely proper subjects of taxation.
>
> —Adam Smith, *The Wealth of Nations*, 1776 (Brownell and Frieden, par. 1)

Draft your proposal.

By this point, you have done a lot of research and writing to

- focus and define a problem, and develop a solution to it;
- support your solution with reasons and evidence your readers will find persuasive;
- refute or concede objections and alternative solutions;
- organize your ideas to make them clear, logical, and effective for readers.

Now stitch that material together to create a draft. The next two parts of this Guide to Writing will help you evaluate and improve your draft.

Evaluating the Draft
Guide to Reading
GUIDE TO WRITING
A Writer at Work
Reflection
279

Evaluating the Draft: Using Peer Review

Your instructor may arrange a peer review session in class or online, where you can exchange drafts with your classmates and give one another a thoughtful critical reading, pointing out what works well and suggesting ways to improve the draft. A good critical reading does three things:

1. It lets the writer know how well the reader understands the problem and the proposed solution.

2. It praises what works best.

3. It indicates where the draft could be improved and makes suggestions on how to improve it.

One strategy for evaluating a draft is to use the basic features of a proposal as a guide. Also be sure to respond to any concerns the writer has shared with you.

PEER REVIEW GUIDE

A Focused, Well-Defined Problem

> How well does the writer establish that the problem exists and is serious?

Summarize: Tell the writer what you understand the problem to be.

Praise: Give an example from the essay where the problem and its significance come across effectively, such as where an example dramatizes the problem or where statistics establish its significance.

Critique: Tell the writer where readers might need more information about the problem's causes and consequences, or where more might be done to establish its seriousness.

A Well-Argued Solution

> Has the writer argued effectively for the solution?

Summarize: Tell the writer what you understand the proposed solution to be.

Praise: Give an example from the essay where support for the solution is presented especially effectively — for example, note particularly strong reasons, writing strategies that engage readers, or design or visual elements that make the solution clear and accessible.

Critique: Tell the writer where the argument for the solution could be strengthened — for example, where steps for implementation could be laid out more clearly, where the practicality of the solution could be established more convincingly, or where additional support for reasons should be added.

(continued)

An Effective Response to Objections and Alternative Solutions

> Has the writer responded effectively to objections or alternative solutions?

Summarize: Tell the writer what you understand to be the objections or alternative solutions that he or she is responding to.

Praise: Give an example from the essay where the writer concedes or refutes a likely objection to the argument effectively, and where reasons showing the limitations of alternative solutions are most effectively presented.

Critique: Tell the writer where concessions and refutations could be more convincing, where possible objections or reservations should be taken into account or where alternative solutions should be discussed, where reasons for not accepting other solutions need to be strengthened, or where common ground should be sought with advocates of other positions.

A Clear, Logical Organization

> Is the proposal clearly and logically organized?

Summarize: Underline the sentence(s) in which the writer establishes the problem and proposes a solution. Also identify the places where the writer forecasts the argument, supplies topic sentences, and uses transitions or repeats key words and phrases.

Praise: Give an example of how the essay succeeds in being readable — for example, in its overall organization, its use of forecasting statements or key terms introduced in the thesis and strategically repeated elsewhere, its use of topic sentences or transitions, or its inclusion of an especially effective opening or closing.

Critique: Tell the writer where the readability could be improved. For example, point to places where adding key terms would help, where a topic sentence could be made clearer, or where transitions could be improved or added; also indicate whether the beginning or ending could be more effective.

Improving the Draft: Revising, Editing, and Proofreading

Start improving your draft by reflecting on what you have written thus far:

- Review the Test Your Choice responses and critical reading comments from your classmates, instructor, or writing center tutor: What problems do your readers identify?

- Take another look at the notes from your earlier research and writing activities: What else should you consider?

- Review your draft: What else can you do to make your proposal more effective?

Improving the Draft   ▶ Guide to Reading
GUIDE TO WRITING
A Writer at Work
Reflection   **281**

Revise your draft.

If your readers are having difficulty with your draft, or if you think there is room for improvement, try some of the strategies listed in the Troubleshooting Guide that follows. They can help you fine-tune your presentation of the genre's basic features.

A TROUBLESHOOTING GUIDE

A Focused, Well-Defined Problem

My readers aren't convinced that my problem is serious or even exists.

- Change the way you present the problem to address readers' concerns more directly.
- Add information — statistics, examples, description, and so on — that members of your audience are likely to find persuasive or that they can relate to.
- Consider adding visuals, such as graphs, tables, or charts, if these would help clarify the problem for your audience.

A Well-Argued Solution

My readers aren't convinced that my solution is a good one.

- Try to make your solution more convincing by discussing similar solutions used successfully elsewhere or by demonstrating more clearly how it will solve the problem.
- Add evidence (such as facts, statistics, and examples) to support your reasons.
- Review the steps needed to enact your solution; if necessary, lay them out more clearly.

An Effective Response to Objections and Alternative Solutions

My readers have raised objections to my solution.

- Cite research studies, statistics, or examples to refute readers' objections.
- Concede valid points or modify your solution to accommodate the criticism.
- If you can neither refute nor accommodate objections, rethink your solution.

My readers have proposed alternative solutions that I don't discuss.

- If possible, establish shared values with those who propose alternative solutions, but show why their solutions will not work as well as yours.
- If you cannot demonstrate that your solution is preferable, consider arguing that both solutions deserve serious consideration.

(continued)

A Clear, Logical Organization

My readers are confused by my proposal or find it hard to follow.

- Try outlining your proposal to be sure that the overall organization is strong; if it is not, try moving, adding, or deleting sections to strengthen coherence.
- Consider adding a forecasting statement and using key terms in your thesis and repeating them when you discuss your main points.
- Check to see that you use topic sentences to introduce your main points and that you provide appropriate transitions.

Edit and proofread your final draft.

Editing means making changes to the text to ensure that it follows the conventions of style, grammar, spelling, and mechanics appropriate to the rhetorical situation. **Proofreading** involves checking to make sure the text follows these conventions and that no words are repeated or omitted. You have probably done some editing and proofreading while composing and improving your draft, but it is always good practice to edit and proofread a draft after you have revised it and before you submit it.

Most writers get the best results by leaving time — even just an hour or two — between the stages of revising, editing, and proofreading, so that they can return to their writing project with fresh eyes. When possible, enlist a friend or classmate to proofread the final draft of your writing projects. When that is not possible, proofread from the last line to the first, to avoid seeing what you expect to find rather than what is actually on the page (or screen).

As rhetorical situations change, so, too, do the conventions or expectations readers bring to the text. For example, whereas e-mail messages to friends are usually quite informal, filled with abbreviations, emojis, and sentence fragments, final drafts of writing projects for college classes or the workplace are expected to follow a more formal set of conventions concerning clarity, style, grammar, and punctuation.

We recommend that you make a list of the problems your instructors frequently point out in your writing, then use that list to guide your editing and proofreading. A Guide to Editing and Proofreading (at the end of this text) provides a checklist of the most common problems writers face. For issues that go beyond those on this list, consult a handbook* or search for advice online at sites like the Purdue Online Writing Lab (owl.english.purdue.edu) or Grammarly (grammarly.com). For practice identifying and correcting errors, try the activities in LearningCurve, a gamelike adaptive quizzing program available on LaunchPad for *The St. Martin's Guide to Writing*. The less well you do on activities in one topic area, the more LearningCurve focuses on it; the better you do, the more challenging the questions become.

A Note on Grammar and Spelling Checkers

Spelling checkers cannot catch misspellings that are themselves words, such as *to* for *too*, and grammar checkers miss problems, give faulty advice, and even flag correct items as wrong. Use these tools as a second line of defense after your own (and, ideally, another reader's) proofreading efforts.

---

* The full version of *The St. Martin's Guide to Writing* includes a handbook.

Patrick O'Malley's Revision Process

This section focuses on student writer Patrick O'Malley's successful efforts to strengthen his argument for the solution he proposes in his essay, "More Testing, More Learning." Compare the following three paragraphs from his draft with paragraphs 4–7 of his final essay on pp. 247–52. As you read, take notes on the differences you observe.

The predominant reason students perform better with multiple exams is that they improve their study habits. Greater regularity in test taking means greater regularity in studying for tests. Students prone to cramming will be forced to open their textbooks more often, keeping them away from long, "kamikaze" nights of studying. Regularity prepares them for the "real world" where you rarely take on large tasks at long intervals. Several tests also improve study habits by reducing procrastination. An article about procrastination from the *Journal of Counseling Psychology* reports that "students view exams as difficult, important, and anxiety provoking." These symptoms of anxiety leading to procrastination could be solved if individual test importance was lessened, reducing the stress associated with the perceived burden.

With multiple exams, this anxiety decrease will free students to perform better. Several, less important tests may appear as less of an obstacle, allowing the students to worry less, leaving them free to concentrate on their work without any emotional hindrances. It is proven that "the performance of test-anxious subjects varies inversely with evaluation stress." It would also be to the psychological benefit of students if they were not subjected to the emotional ups and downs of large exams where they are virtually worry-free one moment and ready to check into the psychiatric ward the next.

Lastly, with multiple exams, students can learn how to perform better on future tests in the class. Regular testing allows them to "practice" the information they learned, thereby improving future test scores. In just two exams, they are not able to learn the instructor's personal examination style, and are not given the chance to adapt their study habits to it. The *American Psychologist* concludes: "It is possible to influence teaching and learning by changing the type of tests."

One difference you may have noted between O'Malley's draft and revised paragraphs is the sequence of reasons he offers.

Draft	Revision
1. Improve study habits	1. Learn more
2. Decrease anxiety and improve performance	2. Perform better on tests
3. Perform better on future tests	3. Improve study habits
	4. Decrease anxiety

O'Malley made learning more his first reason after a classmate commented that professors (the target audience) would probably be more convinced by increased student' learning than by improved study habits or decreased anxiety. Here are some other improvements you may have noticed:

- **O'Malley's revised paragraphs are better focused.** For example, in the first draft paragraph, O'Malley switches from study habits to procrastination to anxiety. The revised paragraph (par. 6), by contrast, focuses on study habits. Also, reduced anxiety as a result of less procrastination is discussed in a single paragraph in the revision (par. 7), whereas in the draft it is mixed in with intellectual benefits in the first two paragraphs.

- **O'Malley's language is more precise.** For example, he changes "predominant reason" to "main reason" and "future tests" to "major exams, projects, and papers."

- **O'Malley's supporting evidence is more relevant.** For example, in the first draft paragraph, O'Malley includes a quotation that adds nothing, whereas in the revised paragraph (par. 6) the quotation he uses from the Harvard report provides convincing support for his claims and offers an effective conclusion to the paragraph.

Can you find other examples of better focus, more precise language, or relevant support? Did you notice any other improvements?

REFLECTION

The benefit of reflection is proven and important: It helps consolidate what you have learned so that you can remember and apply it well beyond this class. That is why we have included questions and comments in the margins and at the end of each chapter: to stimulate your thinking about proposals, your rhetorical situation, and the choices you make as a writer.

Reflecting on Reading and Writing Proposals

To reflect on your experience reading proposals and writing one of your own, try writing a blog post, a letter to your instructor, or an e-mail message to a student who will take this course next term that draws on what you have learned. Use any of these writing prompts that seem productive:

- Explain how your purpose and audience influenced *one* of your decisions as a writer, such as how you defined the problem, the strategies you used in presenting your solution, or the ways in which you attempted to refute possible objections.

Reflecting on Your Composing Process

Guide to Reading
Guide to Writing
A Writer at Work
▶ REFLECTION

285

- Discuss what you learned about yourself as a writer in the process of writing this particular essay. For example, what part of the process did you find most challenging? Did you try anything new, like getting a critical reading of your draft or outlining your draft in order to revise it?

- If you were to give advice to a friend who was about to write an essay proposing a solution to a problem, what would you say?

- Which of the readings in this chapter influenced your essay? Explain the influence, citing specific examples from your essay and the reading.

- If you got good advice from a critical reader, explain exactly how the person helped you—perhaps by questioning the way you addressed your audience or the kinds of evidence you offered in support of your proposed solution.

Reflecting on Your Composing Process

Thinking about your process for writing a proposal can be useful in helping you decide what works best for you as a writer. Using one or more of the following questions as a starting point, write a paragraph or two about your composing process:

- How did you go about choosing a problem to solve? Did you try out a few possibilities before making a final decision? How did having to make a strong case for the seriousness of your problem or the feasibility of your solution affect your choice?

- Explain how peer review helped you—perhaps by helping you think about ways of implementing your solution or responding to objections readers might raise.

- What was the hardest part of the process for you—developing a solution or coming up with an argument to convince readers your solution is feasible?

- How satisfied are you with the process you used? If you could go back in time, what would you have done differently? If you could continue working on your proposal, what would you like to do?

8

Justifying an Evaluation

Does *Scott Pilgrim vs. the World* deserve its status as a cult film? If you like Disney films, should you go out of your way to see *Moana*? What made the original *Pokémon Go* such a successful game? Does the popular *U.S. News* "Best Colleges" guide use a reliable system for ranking schools? These are the questions the evaluations in this chapter answer.

People make evaluations for various purposes and audiences and publish them in a variety of media. For example, students in a history course might be asked to write and post to the class blog a review of a scholarly book that includes a summary of the book's main assertions and an assessment of how well the author supports those claims with factual evidence and authoritative sources. A business executive might use Prezi slides to present her evaluation of how the company could benefit from investing in 3-D printer technology. A motorcycle enthusiast might review his tour of the Harley-Davidson factory in York, Pennsylvania, and publish it in a newsletter for motorcyle hobbyists.

In this chapter, we ask you to choose a subject for evaluation that you can examine closely. By analyzing the selections in the Guide to Reading (pp. 288–311), you will learn how to use appropriate *criteria* to support your judgment. The Guide to Writing (pp. 312–27) will show you ways to use the basic features of the genre to make your evaluation interesting and persuasive.

PRACTICING THE GENRE
_____

Choosing Appropriate Criteria

The success of evaluation depends on whether readers agree that the criteria being applied are sound and based on widely accepted standards of judgment.

Part 1. To practice developing an evaluative argument based on appropriate criteria, get together with two or three other students. Choose a film everyone in the group has seen, and then take turns devising and applying evaluative criteria:

1 Identify the type of film you think it was (romantic comedy, science fiction, action, and so on).

2 Say one thing you expect from films of this type. For example, do you usually expect a film like this to have a surprising or predictable story; to present believable characters in realistic situations; to be all about special effects or exciting action sequences; to be funny, scary, or thought-provoking?

3 Say whether this particular film surpassed, met, or fell short of your expectations for this type of film and, why.

Now tell the class which film your group discussed and which criteria you used to evaluate it.

Part 2. Discuss what you learned by devising criteria and listening to the criteria others presented:

- **What did you learn about criteria, or standards for evaluating a film?** What is your *must have* (your main criterion) for judging a comedy, an action film, or a thriller? Were you surprised by how groups categorized a film or by any of their criteria?

- **Think about how the purpose, audience, and medium (the rhetorical situation) would affect the criteria you use.** If you were going to post your evaluation on Facebook, be graded on your review, or submit it to an audience review Web site such as Flixster, would you use the same criteria you used in your group? How could you justify the criteria you think are most important?

Analyzing Evaluations

As you read the selections in this chapter, you will see how different writers argue for an evaluation:

- William Akana argues that the cult classic film *Scott Pilgrim vs. the World* is "a hell of a ride" (pp. 292–97).
- Tasha Robinson praises *Moana* for building on and improving the Disney movie tradition (pp. 297–300).
- Katherine Isbister analyzes the reasons for the phenomenal success of the game *Pokémon Go* (pp. 302–5).
- Malcolm Gladwell argues that the *U.S. News* college guide uses a flawed ranking system (pp. 307–10).

Analyzing how these writers present their subject, assert and justify their judgment, respond to alternative viewpoints, and organize their writing will help you see how you can use these techniques to make your own evaluations clear and compelling for your readers.

Determine the writer's purpose and audience.

Although writing a review usually helps writers think through their own preferences, most writers hope to influence other people as well. As you read the evaluations that follow, ask yourself what the writer's main purpose is and what he or she assumes about the reader:

The writer's main purpose may be to

- influence readers' judgment

- question the criteria on which readers base their judgment of the subject
- convince readers the writer's analysis is well founded and based on solid support
- encourage readers to reject alternative judgments and objections to the writer's argument

The writer wants readers to react by

- accepting or at least taking seriously the writer's judgment
- reexamining the appropriateness of their criteria for evaluation
- reconsidering the validity of the writer's supporting evidence
- accepting the writer's refutation of an alternative judgment or objections to the writer's argument

Basic Features

A Well-Presented Subject

A Well-Supported Judgment

An Effective Response to Objections and Alternative Judgments

A Clear, Logical Organization

Assess the genre's basic features.

As you read the evaluations in this chapter, consider how different authors make their evaluations helpful and convincing. The examples that follow are taken from the reading selections that appear later in this Guide to Reading.

Analyzing Evaluations

GUIDE TO READING
Guide to Writing
A Writer at Work
Reflection

289

A WELL-PRESENTED SUBJECT

Read first to identify the subject of the review, which is often named in the title (for example, *"Scott Pilgrim vs. the World:* A Hell of a Ride") and described briefly in the opening paragraphs. Look also to see how the writer classifies the subject in terms of its genre. Here's an example from the first reading selection in the chapter, by student William Akana:

> From start to finish, *Scott Pilgrim vs. the World* delivers intense <u>action</u> in a hilarious <u>slacker</u> movie that also somehow reimagines <u>romantic comedy</u>. (par. 1)

Subgenres

Genre

Even if readers don't recognize the title, Akana makes clear that the film he is reviewing combines elements of three different kinds of movies (or subgenres), so readers can determine whether he is using appropriate criteria, as you will see in the next section.

Knowing the genre is also important because readers need different kinds of information for different genres. For example, most readers of film reviews want to know what the story is about but do not want to know how it turns out. Film reviewers, therefore, try not to give too much plot detail, as you can see in this concise plot summary from Akana's essay:

> Pilgrim's life takes a dramatic turn when he falls in love with Ramona Flowers (Mary Elizabeth Winstead), who is, quite literally, the girl of his dreams. However, he soon discovers that Ramona's former lovers have formed a league of evil exes to destroy him, and he is forced to fight to the death to prove his love. (par. 2)

A WELL-SUPPORTED JUDGMENT

Identify the judgment the writer asserts, and determine whether the writer thinks the subject is good or bad, better or worse, than other things in the same genre. Typically, writers announce their judgment in a *thesis statement* early in the evaluation. Sentence strategies typically used for thesis statements in evaluations follow, along with examples from reviews in this chapter:

▶ What makes X a success/a failure is _____ and _____ .

▶ X can be appreciated/criticized for _____, _____, and _____, but ultimately it is a success/failure because of _____ .

EXAMPLES   Although the film is especially targeted for old-school gamers, anime fans, and comic book fanatics, *Scott Pilgrim vs. the World* <u>can be appreciated and enjoyed by all audiences</u> because of its <u>inventive special effects</u>, <u>clever dialogue</u>, and <u>artistic cinematography and editing</u>. (Akana, par. 2)

Judgment

Reasons

Moana makes *Tangled* feel like one of many experiments at tinkering with the formula, getting it exactly right. All the beats proceed exactly as expected, but they hit with <u>admirably precise timing</u>, amid <u>a strikingly beautiful landscape where every leaf is rendered with loving clarity</u>. The <u>humor</u>, the <u>wonder</u>, and the <u>awwww moments</u> all hit home comfortably. This is such a perfect execution of the Disney formula, it feels like the movie the studio has been trying to make since *Snow White*. (Robinson, par. 3)

For advice on when to indent quotations rather than use quotation marks, see Chapter 19.

Examine the thesis to see whether the writer asserts an overall judgment, *noting the features of the subject that are being praised or criticized and the reasons supporting the judgment. Finally, consider whether the reasons are based on criteria you would expect to be used for evaluating something of this kind.* For example, one of William Akana's reasons is that the film uses "special effects" that are "inventive." To support this reason, he devotes two paragraphs to detailing some of the film's special effects. He also gives examples of "video-game-like gimmicks" such as "gamertags," describing them and also providing a screen shot to show what they look like (par. 3).

Consider the types of evidence provided, such as examples and visuals, and whether the writer cites sources by quoting, paraphrasing, *or summarizing source material.*

Signal phrase
Summary
Quotation

Some reviewers have criticized the film because they think that in the end it fails as a romantic comedy. For example, *Miami Herald* film reviewer Rene Rodriguez argues that the film ultimately fails because of the lack of **"chemistry"** or **"emotional involvement"** in the romance between Pilgrim and Ramona. (Akana, par. 9)

How writers treat sources depends on the rhetorical situation. Certain formal situations, such as college assignments or scholarly publications, require writers to cite sources in the text and document them, as we see in Akana's essay. In writing for a general audience, readers do not expect references to appear in the text, but they do expect links to be provided or sources to be named and their credentials to be identified in a signal phrase.

Notice also whether the reviewer uses comparison and contrast. Malcolm Gladwell, for example, sets up his evaluation of the ranking system used by *U.S. News & World Report*'s annual "Best Colleges" guide by comparing it to the system used by *Car and Driver* magazine. Similarly, Tasha Robinson and Katherine Isbister use comparison or contrast or both to support their judgments:

Comparison cue

Like Rapunzel in *Tangled*, Moana . . . is brave and ambitious, but also naïve and sheltered. . . . Like Rapunzel, Moana defies family to pursue her own quest. And like Rapunzel, Moana seeks the help of a more worldly and experienced man, who holds her in dismissive contempt until she's proved herself enough times to earn his admiration. . . . (Robinson, par. 2)

Contrast cue

In contrast to many "hard core" games such as League of Legends that can require hours or even years of skills training and background, Pokémon Go's design draws upon the principles of folk games such as scavenger hunts. (Isbister, par. 5)

AN EFFECTIVE RESPONSE TO OBJECTIONS AND ALTERNATIVE JUDGMENTS

Notice how the writer responds to objections to the argument or to alternative judgments that readers might prefer. Writers may **concede** (accept), **refute** (argue against) alternatives, or a combination of the two, providing a transition or other cues to alert readers.

The basic structure of a concession is:

- ▶ Of course, ... is an important factor.

- ▶ Granted, ... must be taken into consideration.

Transition indicating concession

The basic structure of a refutation is:

- ▶ Although ...., I think ....

- ▶ X says ...., but I disagree because ....

Transition indicating refutation

> There have been missteps along the way—a controversy over a Maui costume that looked suspiciously like a brownface suit; early complaints that Maui's thick build was a Samoan stereotype—and telling lapses, like the animators making Maui bald, which required an intervention from a Tahitian cultural consultant. But mostly, *Moana* is refreshingly free from groan-inducing stereotypes, or ridiculous twists. . . . (Robinson, par. 5)

Concession cue

Refutation cue

> Some reviewers have criticized the film because they think that in the end it fails as a romantic comedy. . . . But I agree with *New York Times* reviewer A. O. Scott, who argues that "the movie comes home to the well-known territory of the coming-of-age story, with an account of lessons learned and conflicts resolved." (Akana, par. 9)

> **Consider . . .**
> In position and proposal arguments, responding to opposing views is central. Why might an evaluation also respond to opposing views by, say, conceding a minor weakness but rebutting an alternative judgment?

A CLEAR, LOGICAL ORGANIZATION

Read to see if the reviewer provides cues *to help readers follow the logic of the argument.* Notice, for example, if the reasons are *forecast* in the thesis or elsewhere in the opening and, if so, where they are brought up again later in the essay. Here are examples from William Akana's film review:

> *Scott Pilgrim vs. the World* can be appreciated and enjoyed by all audiences because of its inventive special effects, clever dialogue, and artistic cinematography and editing. (par. 2)

Thesis with topics forecast

> *Scott Pilgrim vs. the World* shines bright with superb special effects that serve to reinforce the ideas, themes, and style of the film. (par. 3)

> Another strong point of *Scott Pilgrim vs. the World* is its clever and humorous dialogue. (par. 6)

> The best attribute by far is the film's creative cinematography and editing. . . . (par. 7)

Topic sentences with reasons forecast

Also notice how the writer uses logical transitions—such as *because* to introduce reasons and *another* to indicate the next reason in a list.

Finally, where visuals—*such as film stills, cartoons, screen shots, and diagrams*—*are included, determine how they are integrated into the text.* Akana, for example, uses the conventional phrase "see fig. 1" in parentheses following his written description and includes a descriptive caption with the visual. In contrast, writers publishing in newspapers and magazines may simply intersperse screen shots to illustrate their points.

Look at how student writer William Akana integrated visuals into his essay on pp. 292–97.

Readings

William Akana | Scott Pilgrim vs. the World: *A Hell of a Ride*

To learn how Akana developed his thesis and responses to objections, turn to A Writer at Work on pp. 327–28.

THIS EVALUATION ESSAY was written by student William Akana for his composition course. The assignment prompt asked students to choose a film and write a review that includes a close analysis of the cinematic techniques used in at least one important scene. Akana's instructor illustrated various cinematic techniques, such as camera angles and movements, and demonstrated how to take screen shots, explaining that students can use visuals for a class project without asking permission, but to publish them they would have to get permission, as we did. As you read, consider:

- How would you answer the questions in the margin? Your instructor may ask you to post your answers or discuss them in class.

▨ Basic Features

A Well-Presented Subject

A Well-Supported Judgment

An Effective Response to Objections and Alternative Judgments

A Clear, Logical Organization

How appropriate is this informal narrative style for a film review? For a college paper?

Why do you think Akana gives readers a plot summary and information about the film, its director, and its cast?

1   As I leaned back in the movie theater seat, accompanied by my friends on a typical Saturday night, I knew I was in for something special. I was reassured; not only had my friends and I reached a unanimous vote to watch *Scott Pilgrim vs. the World,* but two of my friends had already seen the film and were eager to see it again. As soon as the film began, with its presentation of the classic Universal Studios introduction in old-timer eight-bit music and pixilated format, I knew I was in for one hell of a ride. From start to finish, *Scott Pilgrim vs. the World* delivers intense action in a hilarious slacker movie that also somehow reimagines romantic comedy.

2   *Scott Pilgrim vs. the World,* released in 2010 by Universal Studios, came into production as a comic book adaptation film under the direction of Edgar Wright (best known for the zombie movie masterpiece *Shaun of the Dead*). Scott Pilgrim (Michael Cera) is a twenty-two-year-old Canadian who plays bass for his indie band, Sex Bob-omb, located in Toronto, Canada. Pilgrim's life takes a dramatic turn when he falls in love with Ramona Flowers (Mary Elizabeth Winstead), who is, quite literally, the girl of his dreams. However, he soon discovers that Ramona's former lovers have formed a league of evil exes to destroy him, and he is forced to fight to the death to prove his love. Although the film is especially targeted for old-school gamers, anime fans, and

Akana Scott Pilgrim vs. the World: *A Hell of a Ride*

GUIDE TO READING
Guide to Writing
A Writer at Work
Reflection

293

comic book fanatics, *Scott Pilgrim vs. the World* can be appreciated and enjoyed by all audiences because of its inventive special effects, clever dialogue, and artistic cinematography and editing.

3   *Scott Pilgrim vs. the World* shines bright with superb special effects that serve to reinforce the ideas, themes, and style of the film. Special effects are plentiful throughout the entire film, ranging from superimposed annotations echoing classic gaming features to artful backgrounds and action sequences modeled on colorful comic book pages. For example, each of the main characters is described for the first time with "gamertags," short-timed boxes of information that include name, age, and rating (see fig. 1).

4   *Scott Pilgrim vs. the World* contains numerous amounts of other fun video-game-like gimmicks that were made possible through special effects. One humorous scene presents a pee bar that depletes as Pilgrim relieves himself. Another scene presents a bass battle between Pilgrim and one of the evil exes in the format of PlayStation's popular Guitar Hero (see fig. 2). It goes without saying that anyone who has ever dabbled in video games will greatly appreciate the gaming-culture inside jokes. As the reviewer for the Web site *Cinema Sight* wrote, this film is intended for "the video game generation" ("Review").

Fig. 1. Screen shot showing gamertags.

How well does this thesis statement forecast Akana's argument? Skim the essay, noting where he discusses the reasons he gives here.

How well do these details and the illustration he chose support Akana's claim that the special effects are "inventive" and "superb"?

Fig. 2. Guitar face-off.

5   Comic book references are also installed using special effects. In almost every battle between Pilgrim and his enemies, comic-book-like backgrounds, added through CGI, enhance the eye-popping fight sequences as characters fly into the air to deliver devastating punches accompanied with traditional onomatopoeic "POWs" and "KAPOWs" (see fig. 3). However, comic book annotations are not reserved merely for fight scenes. Annotations range from even the simplest "RIIIINGs" of a telephone to trails of shout-ing "AAAAHs" of Pilgrim as he is thrown into the air in battle. To make the film even more visually appealing, *Scott Pilgrim vs. the World* portrays flashbacks using white and black comic strips similar to the original Scott Pilgrim comic books. Special effects play a truly vital part in enlivening the style of the film.

6   Another strong point of *Scott Pilgrim vs. the World* is its clever and humorous dialogue. One memorable scene in the film involves Knives Chau (Ellen Wong) and Scott Pilgrim in an awkward situation where Knives states sheepishly: "I've never even kissed a guy." In a supposedly intimate gesture of affection, Pilgrim moves closer only to pause shortly before saying "Hey . . . me neither." Additionally, *Scott Pilgrim vs. the World* is rich in cultural satire that pokes fun at adolescent and young adult behaviors. One scene contains Pilgrim telling Ramona Flowers: "I feel like I'm on drugs when I'm with you, not that I do drugs, unless you do — in which case, I do drugs all the time."

Akana   Scott Pilgrim vs. the World: *A Hell of a Ride*

▶ **GUIDE TO READING**
Guide to Writing
A Writer at Work
Reflection

295

Fig. 3. Comic-book-style annotations.

Dialogue like this gives the film a raw yet rich sense of humor that is one of the many inventive risks of the film that pay off.

7   The best attribute by far is the film's creative cinematography and editing, which can be illustrated in the ultimate fight scene of the movie. Pilgrim finally confronts his former band members, who are playing in an underground lair for Ramona's seventh evil ex, Gideon (Jason Schwartzman). As Pilgrim admits his faults and proceeds to apologize to the band for former wrongs, the shot assumes a point of view from Pilgrim's perspective looking up to the band on stage. Shortly before Pilgrim is finished, Gideon, sitting on his throne atop a miniature pyramid, interrupts him. The shot quickly cuts to a close-up of Gideon's eyes, emphasizing his anger at Pilgrim. From this point, soft focusing is utilized to blur the background as a tracking shot follows Pilgrim in a medium close-up as he marches to the base of the pyramid. Then, reverse shots are used between high- and low-angled frames to illustrate Pilgrim's challenge to Gideon for a final duel.

8   Gideon, in response to the challenge, asks Pilgrim if he is fighting for Ramona, which leads to a climactic epiphany for Pilgrim as he realizes his true motive, admitting in a tight close-up: "No. I want to fight you for me." As Pilgrim finishes this confession, a deep narrating voice announces that "Scott Pilgrim has earned the power

> How do the highlighted transitions help readers follow Akana's analysis?

Fig. 4. Threshold of a new beginning?

of self-respect," and in turn, he is awarded a magical sword with which he can defeat Gideon. Subsequently, the camera pans from left to right in a subjective shot to illustrate Gideon's goons closing in on Pilgrim. Pilgrim, in a series of fast-paced jump cuts, quickly dispatches the bad guys before charging up the pyramid. After an extended battle, deep focusing is used with a long shot to establish that the hierarchy has changed between hero and villain: Pilgrim is seen standing atop the pyramid, looking down at the kneeling Gideon before Pilgrim kicks him to smithereens.

9   This brilliantly executed scene illustrates the artful cinematography of *Scott Pilgrim vs. the World*. More importantly, it delivers the film's thematic message, which undercuts the cliché "love conquers all" and instead focuses on the fresh concept that, in the grand scheme of things, the only person you are fighting for is yourself. Some reviewers have criticized the film because they think that in the end it fails as a romantic comedy. For example, *Miami Herald* film reviewer Rene Rodriguez argues that the film ultimately fails because of the lack of "chemistry" or "emotional involvement" in the romance between Pilgrim and Ramona. But I agree with *New York Times* reviewer A. O. Scott, who argues that "the movie comes home to the well-known territory of the coming-of-age story, with an account of lessons learned and conflicts resolved." Fighting Ramona's exes forces Pilgrim to wake up out of his slacker stupor. Before he can begin a grown-up

For what purposes does Akana use these sources? How effective is his response to an opposing view?

Robinson   Moana: *The Perfect Disney Movie*

GUIDE TO READING
Guide to Writing
A Writer at Work
Reflection

297

relationship with Ramona, he has to come to terms with his own failures, especially in relation to his own exes. The film ends, as director Edgar Wright explained in an interview, on the threshold of a new beginning: "Scott and Ramona might not make it past the end credits, or it might be the start of a beautiful relationship" (Cozzalio).

Works Cited

Cozzalio, Dennis. "Scott Pilgrim's Dreamscape and the Glories of the Wright Stuff II: An interview with director Edgar Wright." *Sergio Leone and the Infield Fly Rule,* 15 Jan. 2011, sergioleoneifr.blogspot.com/2011/01/scott -pilgrims-dreamscape-and-glories.html.

Review of *Scott Pilgrim vs. The World. Cinema Sight,* 13 Sept. 2010, www.cinemasight .com/review-scott-pilgrim-vs-the-world-2010/.

Rodriguez, Rene. Review of *Scott Pilgrim vs. the World. Miami Herald,* 11 Aug. 2010, www.miami.com/things-to-do-in-miami/scott-pilgrim-vs-the-world-pg-13-4511/.

Scott, A. O. "This Girl Has a Lot of Baggage, and He Must Shoulder the Load." *The New York Times,* 12 Aug. 2010, www.nytimes.com/2010/08/13/movies/13scott.html.

Tasha Robinson | Moana: *The Perfect Disney Movie*

TASHA ROBINSON is the film and television editor at the *Verge*, a technology and media network operated by *Vox*. Robinson has written reviews and commentary for newspapers, such as the *Chicago Tribune* and the *Los Angeles Times*; the radio (NPR); and podcasts (*Filmspotting* and the *Next Picture Show*). Robinson's review of *Moana* first appeared in the *Verge* shortly after the film debuted in theaters.

As you read,

- reflect on your own evaluation of *Moana*, if you have seen it, or your view of any other Disney film Robinson mentions.

- notice that Robinson includes a few images ("stills") from the film. What impression do these stills have on you as a reader?

Timothy Hiatt/Getty Images

1   Virtually everything about Disney's latest fairy tale, *Moana*, is familiar from past Disney films. The studio is still following the broad parameters it started laying down in 1937, with *Snow White and the Seven Dwarfs*, by reshaping a culturally specific fairy tale to fit a family-friendly, accessible template. Once again, there's a young woman leaving a safe, comfortable home, venturing into a dangerous world, and finding her destiny, all while singing catchy songs about what she wants and how she'll get it.

2   All the narrow parameters are familiar, too, this time from Disney's *Tangled*. Like Rapunzel in *Tangled*, Moana (Hawaiian newcomer Auli'i Cravalho) is brave and ambitious, but also naïve and sheltered, because she's been held back by overprotective parents with their own agenda for her life. Like Rapunzel, Moana defies family to pursue her own quest. And like Rapunzel, Moana seeks the help of a more worldly and experienced man, who holds her in dismissive contempt until she's proved herself enough times to earn his admiration. The fact that he's a boastful demigod instead of a smug thief seems almost beside the point: Both Maui (Dwayne Johnson) in *Moana* and Flynn Rider in *Tangled* are flashy, arrogant, and headed for breakdowns when they realize the limits of their talents. And they're both overshadowed by their plucky young protégés, who start out less cocksure and brash, so they suffer smaller falls whenever they hit a crisis of confidence. Naturally, in both films, there's an animal companion, a lot of bantery comedy, a solemn moment where the heroine has to decide to press on alone, and some big explosive action when she does.

3   But the familiarity of the formula doesn't matter nearly as much as the execution. *Moana* makes *Tangled* feel like one of many experiments at tinkering with the formula, getting it exactly right. All the beats proceed exactly as expected, but they hit with admirably precise timing, amid a strikingly beautiful landscape where every leaf is rendered with loving clarity. The humor, the wonder, and the awwww moments all hit home comfortably. This is such a perfect execution of the Disney formula, it feels like the movie the studio has been trying to make since *Snow White*.

4   It's no wonder Disney keeps coming back to different forms of this fairy-tale-derived story, which encourages viewers to relate to a character with boundless drive and goodwill, then lets her triumph in a world that seems determined to make her fail. The Disney-heroine formula isn't just a standard feel-good underdog story, it's specifically a story about how determination and good intentions count for more than experience and age. That narrative is particularly friendly to younger viewers, who get to see their fantasies of heroism play out on-screen. But it's a satisfyingly idealistic stance for older watchers, too.

5   *Moana* also draws on a wrinkle familiar from films like *Mulan* and *Pocahontas*: The heroine isn't just buoyed by her own inner strength, she's drawing on the teachings and traditions of her culture as well. Moana is the daughter of a Polynesian chief, being groomed to succeed her father and advise her people, but she's as much the recipient of received wisdom as she is its arbiter. *Moana* directors John Musker and Ron Clements (*The Little Mermaid*, *Aladdin*, *Hercules*, *The Princess and the Frog*) built an extensive brain trust around designing and vetting the movie to respect the South Pacific myths it incorporates, and to accurately reflect the culture it portrays. There have been missteps along the way—a controversy over a Maui costume that looked suspiciously like a brownface suit; early complaints that Maui's thick build was a Samoan stereotype—and telling lapses, like the animators making Maui bald, which required an intervention from a Tahitian cultural consultant. But mostly, *Moana* is refreshingly free from groan-inducing stereotypes, or ridiculous twists like the European invaders leaving the American natives in peace and returning to England at the end of *Pocahontas*. *Moana* is respectful to the world it's evoking—sometimes to a fault, given how carefully calculated and celebratory it is when addressing those cultures.

6   If the worst that can be said about a Disney film is that it's too conscious and crafted about its messaging, though, it's mostly doing diversity right. And within all these familiar parameters and cultural caution, Musker and Clements still find ways to make *Moana* stand out, and to make it feel spontaneous, joyous, and beautiful. Character movements are based in Polynesian traditional dances and Samoan war dances. Apart from a weak, instantly dated joke about Twitter, the comedy is lively and rambunctious, and it works well to establish the characters. The songs, crafted by Samoan musician Opetaia Foa'i, composer Mark Mancina, and *Hamilton* composer/star Lin-Manuel Miranda, draw on Polynesian drumming and choral vocals for a rich, hypnotic sound. And the best of them—Maui's smarmy "look how great I am" anthem "You're Welcome" and the twisty, Bowie-esque phantasmagoria "Shiny," sung by Flight of the Conchords' Jemaine Clement—are just upbeat, earwormy show tunes, the kind that send audiences out of the theater humming.

7   Above all, though, *Moana* feels like the endpoint of the slow-burn modernization process that Walt Disney Animation started shortly after the Disney Renaissance kicked off. *The Little Mermaid* revived the studio's reputation for memorable animation, songs, and stories, but *Beauty and the Beast* started bringing its old stories into a modern era, by giving its heroines personality beyond the traditional "I Want" song, and agency that wasn't usurped as soon as the bland love interest entered the picture. It's been a slow road to self-realization for Disney heroines, but the old tropes have steadily been strengthened through films like *Mulan, Lilo & Stitch, The Princess and the Frog, Tangled, Zootopia*, and *Frozen*.

8   And now here's Moana, a fully rounded character with an idealized yet believable body, flaws that she acknowledges and fights, and a resourcefulness that makes her admirable even when she's failing. She doesn't even need a love interest to define her story. Maui, a tattooed trickster with all Johnson's gleaming-toothed charm, is compelling, but he's also ageless and inhuman,

so it's a relief when he doesn't start giving his traveling companion the hey-baby eye. *Moana* is all about familiar patterns, refined to their ultimate forms, and presented with a satisfying energy and power. But Musker and Clements also have the sense to pick and choose which tropes make sense for their story. As perfectly as these old beats work in this new context, *Moana* functions as well as it does because the story team ultimately focused on finding everything about Disney stories that worked in 2016, and improving everything that didn't.

[REFLECT]   # Make connections: The Disney princess culture.

There has been a lot of commentary and criticism about what has been called the Disney Princess culture—for example, Peggy Orenstein's best-seller *Cinderella Ate My Daughter* (2011) and Brigham Young University professor Sarah Coyne's research report, "Pretty as a Princess" (2016). Both describe the negative effects of princess culture on girls, such as encouraging stereotypical gender concepts and idealized body image. Against this backdrop, Tasha Robinson summarizes what she thinks makes Moana an improved Disney princess:

> And now here's Moana, a fully rounded character with an idealized yet believable body, flaws that she acknowledges and fights, and a resourcefulness that makes her admirable even when she's failing. She doesn't even need a love interest to define her story. (par. 8)

To think about Disney princess culture or, more broadly, the effects of media on children's beliefs about appropriate gendered behavior and body image, reflect on your own experience as well as your observations of others. Your instructor may ask you to post your thoughts on a class discussion board or to discuss them with other students in class. Use these questions to get started:

- Was there an image from the media (television, film, music, advertising) when you were growing up that influenced your or your friends' beliefs about appropriate gendered behavior and body image?

- Robinson argues that the Disney princess tradition has changed over time, culminating in *Moana*. How, if at all, do you think images in the media that influenced you as a child have changed?

[ANALYZE]   # Use the basic features.

A WELL-PRESENTED SUBJECT: IDENTIFYING THE SUBJECT

Reviews usually begin by naming the subject and providing some basic information that readers would expect to find in a review, such as the name of the director (and his or her well-known films), the main actors and their roles, the setting, and a brief summary of the plot.

> *Scott Pilgrim vs. the World,* released in 2010 by Universal Studios, came into production as a comic book adaptation film under the direction of Edgar Wright

(best known for the zombie movie masterpiece *Shaun of the Dead*). Scott Pilgrim (Michael Cera) is a twenty-two-year-old . . . in Toronto, Canada. Pilgrim's life takes a dramatic turn when he falls in love with Ramona Flowers (Mary Elizabeth Winstead), . . . and he is forced to fight to the death to prove his love. (Akana, par. 2)

Although Robinson is also reviewing a film, her rhetorical situation differs from Akana's because her evaluation was published at the same time as the film's initial theatrical release. Therefore, she could assume that her readers may have heard about the film from advertising or other reviews and that most readers would be reading her review to find out whether they should go see the film.

ANALYZE & WRITE

Write a paragraph analyzing and evaluating how Robinson presents her subject:

1 Skim the essay, highlighting the kinds of information Robinson tells her readers about *Moana*. For example, what do you learn about the film's plot, its main characters and actors, its directors, and its writers?

2 Given that her original *Verge* readers were likely reading her review to decide whether to see the film, why do you think Robinson spends so much time placing *Moana* in the Disney tradition, comparing and contrasting it to other Disney films? How effective do you think her approach was given her rhetorical situation?

A WELL-SUPPORTED JUDGMENT: BASING A JUDGMENT ON CRITERIA

Reviewers assert an overall judgment of a subject in a thesis statement, which usually appears early in the review. Akana, for example, concludes his opening paragraph with this thesis statement:

> From start to finish, *Scott Pilgrim vs. the World* delivers <u>intense</u> action in a <u>hilarious</u> slacker movie that also somehow <u>reimagines</u> romantic comedy.

Evaluation
Genre

Notice that Akana praises the film here, making his overall judgment clear. (Of course, an evaluation doesn't have to be all positive or all negative; reviews are often mixed.) He also uses specific evaluative language: He doesn't claim simply that *Scott Pilgrim* is good. Instead, he points out what is good about the film based on the three genres it draws on (action, slacker, and romantic comedy) and the criteria typically used for evaluating those genres.

Akana goes on to support his judgment with analysis, using carefully chosen value terms to explain, for example, what is noteworthy about the film's climactic fight scene:

> This <u>brilliantly</u> <u>executed</u> scene illustrates the <u>artful</u> <u>cinematography</u> of *Scott Pilgrim vs. the World*. More importantly, it delivers the film's <u>thematic message</u>, which <u>undercuts the cliché</u> "love conquers all" and instead focuses on the <u>fresh</u> concept that, in the grand scheme of things, the only person you are fighting for is yourself. (par. 9)

Value terms
Criteria

ANALYZE & WRITE

Write a paragraph analyzing and evaluating how Robinson bases her judgment on clear criteria:

1 Skim the essay. Where do you first find Robinson's overall judgment of *Moana*, her thesis statement? Where, if anywhere, does she restate her thesis?

2 What criteria does Robinson base her judgment on? How appropriate does it seem to you to evaluate a film like *Moana* based on these criteria? What other criteria would you apply to the film?

3 What value terms does Robinson use? How clear and appropriate are the value terms she uses to assess the effectiveness of the film, given her criteria?

Take a moment . . .

Think about how a writer of evaluation can establish credibility with readers. Why is it important that readers consider the writer credible?

[RESPOND]

Consider possible topics: Reviewing media.

Like Robinson and Akana, you could consider reviewing a film, a television show, or a series. If you can put together a multimedia presentation or Web page, you might be able to include music and video snippets as well as stills to convey a plot outline, introduce the main characters, and support your evaluation. Be sure to consider your rhetorical situation—not only the medium you are using but also your purpose and your readers' expectations—before deciding to make a presentation or create a Web page. Will your instructor accept a presentation instead of a more traditional essay?

Katherine Isbister | *Why Pokémon Go Became an Instant Phenomenon*

Carolyn A Lagattuta

KATHERINE ISBISTER is a professor and game designer, whose research focuses on developing digital games that foster social connection. She is currently a professor in the Department of Computational Media at the University of California, Santa Cruz, and a member of the Center for Games and Playable Media. Formerly, she was founding research director of the Game Innovation Lab at New York University. Among her many scholarly articles and books are the award-winning *Better Game Characters by Design* (2006) and *How Games Move Us* (2016). Her review in *The Conversation* of *Pokémon Go* appeared shortly after the game's launch in July 2016.

As you read,

- think about your own experience either playing or watching other players involved in a collaborative game like *Pokémon Go*. (You might consider team scavenger hunts, charades, Pictionary, or similar.)

- notice the headings Isbister uses to identify the criteria on which she bases her evaluation. Which of these criteria, if any, would you use? What other criteria would you use to evaluate a game like *Pokémon Go*?

Isbister   *Why Pokémon Go Became an Instant Phenomenon*

GUIDE TO READING
Guide to Writing
A Writer at Work
Reflection

303

Pokémon Go puts virtual characters in the real world — which is just part of its appeal.

1   Pokémon Go, an augmented reality game for mobile phones, has taken off. Daily traffic for the game exceeded Twitter and Facebook use. What is driving this intense interest and involvement? One way to understand is to take a closer look at the game's design.

2   First, for those who haven't played or watched, a brief overview of how the game works. To play Pokémon Go, you download an app onto your phone, which allows you to search for and "see" virtual creatures called Pokémon that are scattered throughout the real world. You need to be physically close to a Pokémon's location to see it on your mobile screen. Pokémon Go uses augmented reality technology—the game overlays the creature image on top of video from your phone's camera, so it looks as if the creature is floating in the real world. When you find a Pokémon, you try to catch it by swiping an on-screen ball at it. The simplest aim of the game is to "catch 'em all." To do this, you'll have to wander outside your own real-world neighborhood, because different types of creatures are scattered throughout your town and all around the world. You

can easily share snapshots of creatures you've collected and where you found them on social media sites like Facebook, if you want.

3   As you get better at the game, you discover that you can train the creatures in "gyms," which are virtual spaces accessible by visiting real world public locations (for example, the White House is a gym). When you've reached level 5 in the game, you get a chance to join one of three teams: Team Mystic, Team Valor or Team Instinct. These teams compete to maintain control over the gyms where Pokémon go and train. You and your friends can choose the same team, and work together if you like. You'll also have teammates from around your community (and the world) who join in.

4   Several aspects of the game's design help to make the experience so compelling. A look at gaming research shows several of the game's elements can explain why playing Pokémon Go has been such a massive worldwide hit for players of all ages.

Simple gameplay

5   Playing Pokémon Go is simple and accessible. It's easy to grasp what to do—just "catch 'em all" by walking around. In contrast to many "hard core" games such as League of Legends that can require hours or even years of skills training and background, Pokémon Go's design draws upon the principles of folk games such as scavenger hunts. Folk games have simple rules and typically make

Pokémon can appear almost anywhere!

Krista Kennell/Shutterstock

Catch one by flicking the Poké Ball catcher up toward the Pokémon.

use of everyday equipment, so that the game can spread readily from person to person. They often involve physical interaction between players—think of duck-duck-goose or red rover. These sorts of games are designed to maximize fun for a wide age range, and are typically extremely quick to grasp. Pokémon Go's designers made it very simple for everyone to learn how to play and have fun quickly.

Getting moving

6   Pokémon Go also leverages the power of physical movement to create fun. Simply moving about in the world raises one's arousal level and energy, and can improve mood. Exercise is frequently recommended as part of a regimen to reduce depression.

7   Pokémon Go's design gives players powerful motivation to get out of the house and move around. Not only are the creatures distributed over a wide geographic area, but also, players can collect Pokémon eggs that can be hatched only after a certain amount of movement. Players have reported radically increasing the amount of exercise that they get as they start playing the game.

Connecting with others

8   The most powerful wellspring of fun in the game's design is how it cultivates social engagement. There are several astute design choices that make for increased collaborative fun and interaction. For one thing, everyone who shows up to collect a creature at a location can catch a copy of that creature if they want. So players have motivation to communicate with one another and share locations of creatures, engaging in deeply collaborative rather than competitive play. Not all

Pacific Press/Getty Images

The game requires players to be on the go.

Isbister *Why Pokémon Go Became an Instant Phenomenon*

▸ **GUIDE TO READING**
Guide to Writing
A Writer at Work
Reflection

305

Tinxi/Shutterstock

Friends can play it together, and strangers can meet each other too.

gamers like fierce competition, so the collaborative aspects of the game broaden its appeal.

9   For those who do love competition, the three-team structure allows for friendly rivalry and challenge. The ease of joining a team keeps it from being exclusionary, preserving the game's inclusive style. Because there are only three teams worldwide, there's a lot of friendly banter online about which team is the best, adding to the fun.

10   Also, collecting Pokémon is a distinctive-looking thing to do with a phone. Players can tell when a stranger is collecting Pokémon at a place they happen to be, and can join in and collect for themselves. This has sparked many conversations among strangers. Finally, making it easy to take snapshots of collected creatures and share them on social media has meant that players recruit other players into the game at astonishing rates. Building collaboration and connection into the game in these ways creates a broadly accessible flavor of play, so that many people are willing to engage and share.

11   Pokémon Go's rapid success demonstrates the potential for well-designed augmented reality games to connect people to one another and their physical environment. That forms a stark contrast to the typical stereotype of video games as socially isolating and encouraging inactivity. It bodes well for the future of augmented reality gaming.

Make connections: Evaluating a game.

[REFLECT]

As a game designer, Isbister has certain criteria she uses to evaluate games. Think about your own experience playing digital or other games, and consider the criteria you apply in evaluating them. Your instructor may ask you to post your thoughts on a class discussion board or to discuss them with other students in class. Use these questions to get started:

- Think of a particular game you would like to review. What do you see as the strengths and weaknesses of this game?

- Why do you think others should accept your criteria? What other criteria might they apply to the game?

- For Isbister, getting players moving and collaborating are important criteria for evaluating *Pokémon Go*. Do you think most players of *Pokémon Go* would share these values with Isbister? Why or why not?

Use the basic features.

[ANALYZE]

A WELL-PRESENTED SUBJECT: PROVIDING INFORMATION

Katherine Isbister's review of the game *Pokémon Go* and Tasha Robinson's review of the film *Moana* share the same rhetorical situation: They were published around the time that their subject was initially introduced. So it's a safe bet that many of their readers would have heard of the game and the film from advertising, word of mouth, or other reviews. As reviewers, Isbister's and Robinson's primary purpose is to inform their readers about the subject so that they can decide whether they want to play the game or see the film. The kind of information readers need to make this decision depends, of course, on the kind of subject. For a film, as we've seen in Robinson's and Akana's reviews, readers need to know what kind of film it is—the genre or combination of genres—because the criteria typically used to evaluate a film depends on its genre. The following activity invites you to think about the kinds of information most helpful for readers in understanding a game review.

ANALYZE & WRITE

Write a paragraph analyzing and evaluating how Isbister describes the game *Pokémon Go*:

1 Reread paragraphs 1–3, highlighting the specific information Isbister gives readers about the game. If you are familiar with *Pokémon Go,* think about Isbister's choice of details: Would you have included anything else? Left anything out? Why or why not? If you are unfamiliar with the game, think about how well the information she provides helps you understand the game. What more do you need to know?

2 Look back at the images included in the review. How well do you think they help present the subject to readers unfamiliar with it?

3 Consider the criteria Isbister uses to evaluate *Pokémon Go.* What else do you think is important to consider when evaluating a game like this?

A CLEAR, LOGICAL ORGANIZATION: CUEING THE READER

Evaluation essays often include an array of cueing devices—the same kinds of devices we have seen in other explanatory and argumentative essays. Chief among these is a clear thesis statement that asserts the writer's overall judgment. The thesis statement may also include key terms that identify and forecast the criteria that will be developed in the body of the essay. For example, take a look at William Akana's thesis statement, in which he forecasts the criteria he uses to evaluate the film *Scott Pilgrim vs. the World*:

> Criteria
>
> *Scott Pilgrim vs. the World* can be appreciated and enjoyed by all audiences because of its inventive special effects, clever dialogue, and artistic cinematography and editing. (par. 2)

Akana also uses visuals that illustrate key moments in the film and offers examples of how the film excels based on the criteria he has chosen. Katherine Isbister's game review adds another cueing device: headings.

ANALYZE & WRITE

Write a paragraph analyzing and evaluating how Isbister uses cueing devices:

1 Find Isbister's thesis statement, and highlight the key terms she uses in this statement and repeats elsewhere in the essay. Where does she tend to repeat these key terms? How effectively does this repetition keep readers on track and help connect the parts of her essay?

2 Akana specifically forecasts the main topics, or criteria, he goes on to develop in his essay. In contrast, Isbister's forecast is general or even vague: "several aspects of the game's design" (par. 4). How effective do you think this kind of forecast is? Why do you think she chose not to make a more specific forecast?

3 Look closely at the way Isbister uses headings, noting key terms in the headings as well as in the topic sentences that begin each new section. Given that her review is so brief, why do you think Isbister uses both headings and topic sentences? How effective would it have been had she used headings without topics sentences, or vice versa?

Consider possible topics: Analyzing a game — old or new.   [RESPOND]

Like Isbister, you might be knowledgeable about novel or unfamiliar games or sports. As a game designer, Isbister was especially interested in *Pokémon Go,* the new "augmented reality game for mobile phones" (par. 1). You might be interested in reviewing a new game or a new version of a game you have played. Or you might choose to revisit an old favorite (as William Akana does in reviewing a cult film) to see how the game compares to more recent games.

Malcolm Gladwell | *What College Rankings Really Tell Us*

Theo Wargo/Getty Images

MALCOLM GLADWELL is a staff writer for the *New Yorker* magazine and has written a number of best-selling books, including *David and Goliath: Underdogs, Misfits, and the Art of Battling Giants* (2013); *Outliers: The Story of Success* (2008); and *Blink: The Power of Thinking without Thinking* (2005). He received the American Sociological Association Award for Excellence in the Reporting of Social Issues and was named one of the hundred most influential people by *Time* magazine. As he explains on his Web site (gladwell.com), giving public readings, particularly to academic audiences, has helped him "re-shape and sharpen [his] arguments."

"What College Rankings Really Tell Us" (2011) evaluates the popular *U.S. News* annual "Best Colleges" guide. You may be familiar with this guide and may have even consulted it when selecting a college. Excerpted from a longer *New Yorker* article, Gladwell's evaluation focuses on the *U.S. News* ranking system.

As you read, consider these questions:

• *U.S. News* created a numbered list of "variables" it uses to rank colleges. For whom do you suppose *U.S. News*'s criteria are important? Why?

• If these criteria are important for you, why? If they are not important for you, why not? What criteria for choosing a college are important for you?

1   *Car and Driver* conducted a comparison test of three sports cars, the Lotus Evora, the Chevrolet Corvette Grand Sport, and the Porsche Cayman S. . . . Yet when you inspect the magazine's tabulations it is hard to figure out why *Car and Driver* was so sure that the Cayman is better than the Corvette and the Evora. The trouble starts with the fact that the ranking methodology *Car and Driver* used was essentially the same one it uses for all the vehicles it tests—from S.U.V.s to economy sedans. It's not set up for sports cars. Exterior styling, for example, counts for four per cent of the total score. Has anyone buying a sports car ever placed so little value on how it looks? Similarly, the categories of "fun to drive" and "chassis"—which cover the subjective experience of driving the car—count for only eighty-five points out of the total of two hundred and thirty-five. That may make sense for S.U.V. buyers. But, for people interested in Porsches and Corvettes and Lotuses, the subjective experience of driving is surely what matters most. In other words, in trying to come up with a ranking that is heterogeneous—a methodology that is broad enough to cover all vehicles—*Car and Driver* ended up with a system that is absurdly ill-suited to some vehicles. . . .

The first difficulty with rankings is that it can be surprisingly hard to measure the variable you want to rank.

2   A heterogeneous ranking system works if it focuses just on, say, how much fun a car is to drive, or how good-looking it is, or how beautifully it handles. The magazine's ambition to create a comprehensive ranking system—one that considered cars along twenty-one variables, each weighted according to a secret sauce cooked up by the editors—would also be fine, as long as the cars being compared were truly similar. It's only when one car is thirteen thousand dollars more than another that juggling twenty-one variables starts to break down, because you're faced with the impossible task of deciding how much a difference of that degree ought to matter. A ranking can be heterogeneous, in other words, as long as it doesn't try to be too comprehensive. And it can be comprehensive as long as it doesn't try to measure things that are heterogeneous. But it's an act of real audacity when a ranking system tries to be comprehensive and heterogeneous—which is the first thing to keep in mind in any consideration of *U.S. News & World Report*'s annual "Best Colleges" guide.

3   The *U.S. News* rankings . . . relies on seven weighted variables:

1. Undergraduate academic reputation, 22.5 per cent
2. Graduation and freshman retention rates, 20 per cent
3. Faculty resources, 20 per cent
4. Student selectivity, 15 per cent
5. Financial resources, 10 per cent
6. Graduation rate performance, 7.5 per cent
7. Alumni giving, 5 per cent

From these variables, *U.S. News* generates a score for each institution on a scale of 1 to 100. . . . This ranking system looks a great deal like the *Car and Driver* methodology. It is heterogeneous. It doesn't just compare U.C. Irvine, the University of Washington, the University of Texas–Austin, the University of Wisconsin–Madison, Penn State, and the University of Illinois, Urbana–Champaign—all public institutions of roughly the same size. It aims to compare Penn State—a very large, public, land-grant university with a low tuition and an economically diverse student body, set in a rural valley in central Pennsylvania and famous for its football team—with Yeshiva University, a small, expensive, private Jewish university whose undergraduate program is set on two campuses in Manhattan (one in midtown, for the women, and one far uptown, for the men) and is definitely not famous for its football team.

4   The system is also comprehensive. It doesn't simply compare schools along one dimension—the test scores of incoming freshmen, say, or academic reputation. An algorithm takes a slate of statistics on each college and transforms them into a single score: it tells us that Penn State is a better school than Yeshiva by one point. It is easy to see why the *U.S. News* rankings are so popular. A single score allows us to judge between entities (like Yeshiva and Penn State) that otherwise would be impossible to compare. . . .

5   A comprehensive, heterogeneous ranking system was a stretch for *Car and Driver*—and all it did was rank inanimate objects operated by a single person. The Penn State campus at University Park is a complex institution with dozens of schools and departments, four thousand faculty members, and forty-five thousand students. How on earth does anyone propose to assign a number to something like that?

6   The first difficulty with rankings is that it can be surprisingly hard to measure the variable you want to rank—even in cases where that variable seems perfectly objective. . . . There's no direct way to measure the quality of an institution—how well a college manages to inform, inspire, and challenge its students. So the *U.S. News* algorithm relies instead on proxies for quality—and the proxies for educational quality turn out to be flimsy at best.

7   Take the category of "faculty resources," which counts for twenty per cent of an institution's score (number 3 on the chart above). "Research shows that the more satisfied students are about their contact with professors," the College Guide's explanation of the category begins, "the more they will learn and the more likely it is they will graduate." That's true. According to educational researchers, arguably the most important variable in a successful college education is a vague but crucial concept called student "engagement"—that is, the extent to which students immerse themselves in the intellectual and social life of their college—and a major component of engagement is the quality of a student's contacts with faculty. . . . So what proxies does *U.S. News* use to measure this elusive dimension of engagement? The explanation goes on:

> We use six factors from the 2009–10 academic year to assess a school's commitment to instruction. Class size has two components, the proportion of classes with fewer than 20 students (30 percent of the faculty resources score) and the proportion with 50 or more students (10 percent of the score). Faculty salary (35 percent) is the average faculty pay, plus benefits, during the 2008–09 and 2009–10 academic years, adjusted for regional differences in the cost of living. . . . We also weigh the proportion of professors with the highest degree in their fields (15 percent), the student-faculty ratio (5 percent), and the proportion of faculty who are full time (5 percent).

8   This is a puzzling list. Do professors who get paid more money really take their teaching roles more seriously? And why does it matter whether a professor has the highest degree in his or her field? Salaries and degree attainment are known to be predictors of research productivity. But studies show that being oriented toward research has very little to do with being good at teaching. Almost none of the *U.S. News* variables, in fact, seem to be particularly effective proxies for engagement. As the educational researchers Patrick Terenzini and Ernest Pascarella concluded after analyzing twenty-six hundred reports on the effects of college on students:

> After taking into account the characteristics, abilities, and backgrounds students bring with them to college, we found that how much students grow or change has only inconsistent and, perhaps in a practical sense, trivial relationships with such traditional measures of institutional "quality" as educational expenditures per student, student/faculty ratios, faculty salaries, percentage of faculty with the highest

degree in their field, faculty research productivity, size of the library, [or] admissions selectivity. . . .

9   There's something missing from that list of variables, of course: it doesn't include price. That is one of the most distinctive features of the *U.S. News* methodology. Both its college rankings and its law-school rankings reward schools for devoting lots of financial resources to educating their students, but not for being affordable. Why? [Director of Data Research Robert] Morse admitted that there was no formal reason for that position. It was just a feeling. "We're not saying that we're measuring educational outcomes," he explained. "We're not saying we're social scientists, or we're subjecting our rankings to some peer-review process. We're just saying we've made this judgment. We're saying we've interviewed a lot of experts, we've developed these academic indicators, and we think these measures measure quality schools."

10   As answers go, that's up there with the parental "Because I said so." But Morse is simply being honest. If we don't understand what the right proxies for college quality are, let alone how to represent those proxies in a comprehensive, heterogeneous grading system, then our rankings are inherently arbitrary. . . . *U.S. News* thinks that schools that spend a lot of money on their students are nicer than those that don't, and that this niceness ought to be factored into the equation of desirability. Plenty of Americans agree: the campus of Vanderbilt University or Williams College is filled with students whose families are largely indifferent to the price their school charges but keenly interested in the flower beds and the spacious suites and the architecturally distinguished lecture halls those high prices make possible. Of course, given that the rising cost of college has become a significant social problem in the United States in recent years, you can make a strong case that a school ought to be rewarded for being affordable. . . .

11   The *U.S. News* rankings turn out to be full of these kinds of implicit ideological choices. One common statistic used to evaluate colleges, for example, is called "graduation rate performance," which compares a school's actual graduation rate with its predicted graduation rate given the socioeconomic status and the test scores of its incoming freshman class. It is a measure of the school's efficacy: it quantifies the impact of a school's culture and teachers and institutional support mechanisms. Tulane, given the qualifications of the students that it admits, ought to have a graduation rate of eighty-seven per cent; its actual 2009 graduation rate was seventy-three per cent. That shortfall suggests that something is amiss at Tulane. Another common statistic for measuring college quality is "student

selectivity." This reflects variables such as how many of a college's freshmen were in the top ten per cent of their high-school class, how high their S.A.T. scores were, and what percentage of applicants a college admits. Selectivity quantifies how accomplished students are when they first arrive on campus.

12   Each of these statistics matters, but for very different reasons. As a society, we probably care more about efficacy: America's future depends on colleges that make sure the students they admit leave with an education and a degree. If you are a bright high-school senior and you're thinking about your own future, though, you may well care more about selectivity, because that relates to the prestige of your degree. . . .

13   There is no right answer to how much weight a ranking system should give to these two competing values. It's a matter of which educational model you value more—and here, once again, *U.S. News* makes its position clear. It gives twice as much weight to selectivity as it does to efficacy. . . .

14   Rankings are not benign. They enshrine very particular ideologies, and, at a time when American higher education is facing a crisis of accessibility and affordability, we have adopted a de-facto standard of college quality that is uninterested in both of those factors. And why? Because a group of magazine analysts in an office building in Washington, D.C., decided twenty years ago to value selectivity over efficacy.

[REFLECT] **Make connections: Ideology underlying judgments.**

Gladwell asserts that "implicit ideological choices" underlie ranking systems (par. 11). The word *ideology* refers to the values and beliefs that influence people's thinking. An important sign of underlying ideology is the fact that the *U.S. News* rankings leave out how much it costs to go to each college. This omission is significant, especially at a time when there is "a crisis of accessibility and affordability" (par. 14).

To think about the role of ideology in your own choice of a college, reflect on your personal experience as well as your observations of others choosing a college. Your instructor may ask you to post your thoughts on a class discussion board or to discuss them with other students in class. Use these questions to get started:

- What colleges did you consider, and what criteria (cost, location, standing in the *U.S. News* college ranking, and so on) did you use?

- Choose one or two of your criteria, and consider what values and beliefs were behind your choice. For example, was it important to you to attend a college with a winning football team, with a particular religious orientation, with opportunities for undergraduates to do scientific research?

- How would comparing the criteria you used with the criteria your classmates used help you better understand the ideology—values and beliefs—behind your choices?

[ANALYZE] **Use the basic features.**

AN EFFECTIVE RESPONSE: SINGLING OUT A COMMENT FOR RESPONSE

Because it is a negative evaluation, one could say that Gladwell's entire essay is an implied refutation of those who think well of the *U.S. News* college rankings. However, Gladwell also responds specifically to comments made by Robert Morse, the director of data research for *U.S. News & World Report*.

ANALYZE & WRITE

Write a paragraph analyzing Morse's response to Gladwell and Gladwell's response to Morse:

1 Reread paragraph 9, then describe Morse's response to Gladwell's criticism: Which points does Morse concede or refute? Is Morse's response effective? Why or why not?

2 Now reread paragraphs 10–12. How does Gladwell respond to Morse? How would you describe the tone of Gladwell's response? Is he fair, mean, sarcastic?

3 Given Gladwell's purpose and audience, how would readers react to Morse's response to Gladwell and Gladwell's handling of Morse's response? How did you respond?

A CLEAR, LOGICAL ORGANIZATION: USING COMPARISON AND CONTRAST

Lengthy evaluations can be difficult to follow, but writers have a number of strategies at their disposal to help guide readers. They may use transitional words and phrases or numbered lists, as Gladwell does. But they may also use more subtle strategies to help create cohesion. Gladwell, for example, uses comparison and contrast and strategic repetition to help readers follow his analysis.

ANALYZE & WRITE

Write a paragraph analyzing how Gladwell uses these two strategies:

1 Skim paragraphs 1–3, 5, and 10, noting where Gladwell mentions *Car and Driver* or compares *Car and Driver*'s ranking system with the ranking system used by *U.S. News*, and highlight Gladwell's repeated use of the word *heterogeneous* to describe these ranking systems. Consider the comparison Gladwell is making between *Car and Driver*'s and *U.S. News*'s ranking systems. How does this comparison help him structure his article logically?

2 Skim paragraphs 3, 8, and 11–14, underlining the words *selectivity* and *efficacy*. How does Gladwell use the contrast between selectivity and efficacy? How does this contrast help him guide readers and make his point?

3 Finally, evaluate Gladwell's use of these strategies. How effective are they in helping you follow Gladwell's logic? What, if anything, would you suggest Gladwell do to make his analysis easier to follow?

Consider possible topics: Evaluating a text.

[RESPOND]

List several texts you would consider evaluating, such as an essay from one of the chapters in this book; a children's book that you read when you were young or that you now read to your own children; a magazine for people interested in a particular topic, like computers or cars; or a scholarly article you read for a research paper. If you choose an argument from Chapters 6–9, you could evaluate its logic, its use of emotional appeals, or its credibility. You need not limit yourself to texts written on paper. You might also evaluate a Web site or blog, a radio or television program or advertisement, or even a work of art (such as a story from Chapter 10). Choose one possibility from your list, and then come up with two or three criteria for evaluation.

The Writing Assignment

Write an essay evaluating a specific subject. Examine your subject closely, and make a judgment about it. Give reasons for your judgment that are based on widely recognized criteria or standards for evaluating a subject like yours. Support your reasons with examples and other details primarily from your subject.

This Guide to Writing is designed to help you compose your own evaluation and apply what you have learned from reading other essays in the same genre. The Starting Points chart will help you find answers to questions you might have about composing an essay evaluating a subject. Use it to find the guidance you need, when you need it.

> **Did you know?**
> When you are experimenting with a new or especially challenging genre, scaffolding like this Guide to Writing can be very helpful. When you know a genre well, such support may not be needed.

STARTING POINTS: JUSTIFYING AN EVALUATION

How do I come up with a subject to write about?

- Consider possible topics: Reviewing media. (p. 302)
- Consider possible topics: Analyzing a game — old or new. (p. 307)
- Consider possible topics: Evaluating a text. (p. 311)
- Choose a subject to evaluate. (p. 314)
- Test Your Choice: Choosing a Subject (pp. 314–15)
- Assess your subject and consider how to present it to your readers. (pp. 315–16)

A Well-Presented Subject

How can I present my subject clearly and convincingly?

- Assess the genre's basic features: A well-presented subject. (p. 289)
- A Well-Presented Subject: Identifying the Subject (pp. 300–301)
- A Well-Presented Subject: Providing Information (pp. 305–6)
- Assess your subject, and consider how to present it to your readers. (pp. 315–16)
- A Troubleshooting Guide: A Well-Presented Subject (p. 325)

A Well-Supported Judgment

How do I come up with a thesis statement?

- Assess the genre's basic features: A well-supported judgment. (pp. 289–90)
- Formulate a working thesis stating your overall judgment. (p. 316)

Writing a Draft

Guide to Reading
GUIDE TO WRITING
A Writer at Work
Reflection

313

<table>
<tr><td>

**A Well-Supported
Judgment**

</td><td>

How do I construct an
argument supporting
my judgment?

</td><td>

- Assess the genre's basic features: A well-supported
  judgment. (pp. 289–90)
- A Well-Supported Judgment: Basing a Judgment on Criteria
  (pp. 301–2)
- Develop the reasons and evidence supporting your
  judgment. (p. 317)
- Research your evaluation. (p. 318)
- A Troubleshooting Guide: A Well-Supported Judgment (p. 325)

</td></tr>
<tr><td>

**An Effective
Response to
Objections
and Alternative
Judgments**

</td><td>

How do I respond to
possible objections and
alternative judgments?

</td><td>

- Assess the genre's basic features: An effective response to
  objections and alternative judgments. (pp. 290–91)
- An Effective Response: Singling Out a Comment for
  Response (pp. 310–11)
- Respond to a likely objection or alternative judgment.
  (pp. 318–19)
- A Troubleshooting Guide: An Effective Response to
  Objections and Alternative Judgments (p. 326)

</td></tr>
<tr><td>

**A Clear, Logical
Organization**

</td><td>

How can I help my readers
follow my argument?

</td><td>

- Assess the genre's basic features: A clear, logical
  organization. (p. 291)
- A Clear, Logical Organization: Cueing the Reader (pp. 306–7)
- A Clear, Logical Organization: Using Comparison and
  Contrast (p. 311)
- Organize your evaluation to appeal to your readers. (p. 320)
- A Troubleshooting Guide: A Clear, Logical Organization
  (p. 326)

</td></tr>
</table>

Writing a Draft: Invention, Research, Planning, and Composing

The activities in this section will help you choose and research a subject as well as develop and organize an evaluative argument. Do the activities in any order that makes sense to you (and your instructor), and return to them as needed as you revise. Your writing in response to many of these activities can be used as part of your rough draft, which you will be able to improve after receiving feedback from your classmates and instructor.

▦ Choose a subject to evaluate.

When choosing a subject for evaluation, keep in mind that it must be one that

- has strengths or weaknesses you could write about;
- you can view and review (for example, a location you can visit, a printed text, or a Web site or digital recording from which you can capture stills or video clips to use as examples in a multimedia presentation);
- is typically evaluated according to criteria or standards of judgment that you understand and share with your readers.

You may already have a subject in mind. If you do, skip to Test Your Choice: Choosing a Subject. If you do not, think about the readings: Like Akana and Robinson, you could evaluate a cultural production, like a film, a television show or series, or even a style of dress or haircut. Like Isbister, you could assess some type of game, comparing it to another successful game or evaluating it on its own terms. Or like Gladwell, you could evaluate a text—a book or an article, an advertisement, a work of art, or even another review.

- Evaluate some aspect of your high school or college—for example, a particular program or major you are considering; a residence hall, library, or lab; its sports facilities or teams; a campus research institute or center; or campus work-study or student support services.
- Evaluate an article, an essay, a textbook, or another book assigned in a course; a campus newspaper blog, editorial, or opinion piece; or a campus performance, exhibit, or film series.
- Evaluate how well one of the following meets the needs of residents of your town or city: public library, health clinic, neighborhood watch or block parent program, meals-on-wheels program, theater, or symphony.
- Evaluate a job you have had or currently have, or evaluate the job of someone you have observed closely, such as a coworker or supervisor.

TEST YOUR CHOICE

Choosing a Subject

After you have made a provisional choice, ask yourself the following questions:

- Do I know enough about the subject, or can I learn enough in the time I have?
- Do I already have a judgment (either tentative or certain) about this subject?
- Do I know what criteria or standards my readers are likely to use for judging something of this kind? Would I use the same criteria?

To try out your choice of a subject and get ideas about criteria, get together with two or three other students.

Presenters. Take turns describing your subject.

Listeners. Briefly tell each presenter what criteria or standards of judgment you would use to evaluate a subject of this kind.

Writing a Draft

Guide to Reading
▶ **GUIDE TO WRITING**
A Writer at Work
Reflection

315

As you plan and draft your evaluation, you may need to reconsider your choice of subject (for example, if you discover your criteria for evaluating are different from those your readers would use). If you have serious doubts about your choice, discuss them with your instructor before starting over with a new subject.

⊞ Assess your subject, and consider how to present it to your readers.

Once you have made a preliminary choice of a subject, consider how you can frame or reframe it so that readers will be open to your evaluation. To do this, consider first how you regard the subject and what your readers are likely to think. Use the following questions and sentence strategies as a jumping-off point. You can make the sentences you generate your own later, as you revise.

WHAT DO I THINK?

List those qualities of your **SUBJECT** that you like and dislike, or list its strengths and weaknesses or advantages and disadvantages.

▶ What makes X good/bad is ...., ..., and ....

▶ Although X is stellar in .... [ways], it falls short in .... [other ways].

What **GENRE** or kind of subject is it?

▶ X is a .... [name genre or category of subject, such as romantic comedy or horror movie].

▶ X is an innovative example of .... [name category in which the subject belongs], which combines elements of .... and ....

▶ X is rather unconventional for a .... [name category in which the subject belongs].

WHAT DO MY READERS THINK?

Who are your **READERS**, and why will they be reading your review? Is the subject new or familiar to them?

▶ My readers are .... and are probably reading my review to learn about the subject/to decide whether to see it, play it, or buy it.

▶ My readers will probably be familiar with the subject. They may be curious to know what I think because ....

How might **DEMOGRAPHIC FACTORS** such as the readers' age, gender, cultural background, or work experience affect their judgment of the subject?

▶ Older/Younger readers are less/more likely to ....

▶ People who work in .... or who are familiar with .... may be more/less critical, or apply different standards to a subject like this one.

WAYS IN

(continued)

What **CRITERIA** or standards of judgment do you usually use to evaluate things of this kind?

▶ I expect X to be .... or ....

▶ I dislike it when .... are ....

How does your subject **COMPARE** to other examples of the genre?

▶ Compared to X, Y has the best/worst .... [name trait].

▶ X is like Y in that both are/do/make ...., but X is more/less ....

▶ Whereas Y can be faulted/praised for ...., X ....

What **CRITERIA** or standards of judgment do you expect your readers to use when evaluating subjects of this kind? What other **EXAMPLES** of the genre would they be familiar with?

▶ I expect readers to share my criteria.

▶ If they like/dislike Y, they are sure to like/dislike X.

▶ Judging X on the basis of .... is likely to surprise readers because they are probably more familiar with .... and ....

⊞ Formulate a working thesis stating your overall judgment.

Consider . . .
Why might it be helpful to concede shortcomings in a favorable review or admirable qualities in a negative review?

You may already have a good idea about how you want to assert your thesis: stating whether your subject is good or bad, or better or worse than something else in the same genre or category. Remember that evaluations can be mixed—you can concede shortcomings in a generally favorable review or concede admirable qualities in a mostly negative assessment. If you feel comfortable drafting a working thesis statement now, do so. You may use the following sentence strategies as a jumping-off point—you can always revise them later—or use language of your own. (Alternatively, if you prefer to develop your argument before trying to formulate a thesis, skip this activity now and return to it later.)

As you develop your argument, you may want to rework your thesis to make it more compelling by sharpening the language and perhaps forecasting your reasons. You may also need to qualify your judgment with words like *generally, may,* or *in part.*

WAYS IN

HOW CAN I ASSERT A TENTATIVE OVERALL JUDGMENT?

A good strategy is to begin by **NAMING** the subject and **IDENTIFYING** the kind of subject it is, then using **VALUE TERMS** to state your judgment of the subject's strengths and weaknesses:

▶ X is a brilliant embodiment of .... [genre/category], especially notable for its superb .... and thorough ....

▶ Because I admire .... [another artist's other work], I expected X to be .... But I was disappointed/surprised by ....

▶ X has many good qualities, including .... and .... ; however, its pluses do not outweigh its one major drawback, namely that ....

Writing a Draft

Guide to Reading
▶ **GUIDE TO WRITING**
A Writer at Work
Reflection

317

⊞ Develop the reasons and evidence supporting your judgment.

The following activities will help you find reasons and evidence to support your evaluation. Begin by writing down what you already know. You can do some focused research later to fill in the details.

For more idea-generating strategies, see Chapter 11.

HOW CAN I COME UP WITH REASONS AND EVIDENCE TO SUPPORT MY JUDGMENT?

List the good and bad qualities of the subject. Begin by reviewing the **CRITERIA** and the **VALUE TERMS** you have already used to describe the good and bad qualities of the subject. These are the potential **REASONS** for your judgment. Try restating them using this basic sentence strategy, which is also illustrated by an example from student William Akana's film review:

> ▶ X is _____ [your overall judgment] because _____, _____, and _____ .

EXAMPLE *Scott Pilgrim vs. the World* can be appreciated and enjoyed by all audiences because of its inventive special effects, clever dialogue, and artistic cinematography and editing. (par. 2)

Write steadily for at least five minutes, developing your reasons. Ask yourself questions like these:

> ▶ Why are the characteristics I'm pointing out for praise or criticism so important in judging my subject?

EXAMPLE Akana singles out special effects, dialogue, cinematography and editing because of the particular kind of film *Scott Pilgrim vs. the World* is — "a hilarious slacker movie that also somehow reimagines romantic comedy" (par. 1).

> ▶ How can I prove to readers that the value terms I'm using to evaluate these characteristics are fair and accurate?

EXAMPLE Akana analyzes the film's special effects and gives readers specific examples, including screen shots, to demonstrate that they are indeed "inventive."

Make notes of the **EVIDENCE** you will use to support your judgment. Evidence you might use to support each reason may include the following:

- examples
- quotations from authorities
- textual evidence (quotations, paraphrases, or summaries)
- images
- statistics
- comparisons or contrasts

You may already have some evidence you could use. If you lack evidence for any of your reasons, make a research-to-do note for later.

WAYS IN

Did you know?
Research shows that readers are more likely to agree with your judgment if you emphasize values they endorse.

⊞ Research your evaluation.

To learn more about
conducting research,
including searching a
database or catalog,
see Chapter 17.

Consult your research-to-do notes to determine what you need to find out. If you are evaluating a subject that others have written about, try searching for articles or books on your topic. Enter keywords or phrases related to the subject, genre, or category into the search box of

- an all-purpose database—such as Academic OneFile (InfoTrac) or Academic Search Complete (EBSCOhost)—to find relevant articles in magazines and journals;
- the database *Lexis/Nexis* to find newspaper reviews;
- a search engine like *Google or Yahoo!* (Akana used *Movie Review Query Engine* [mrqe.com] and *Rotten Tomatoes* to find film reviews of *Scott Pilgrim vs. the World*);
- your library's catalog to locate books on your topic.

Turn to databases and search engines for information on more recent items, like films and popular novels; use books, databases, and search engines to find information on classic topics. (Books are more likely to provide in-depth information, but articles in print or online are more likely to be current.)

⊞ Respond to a likely objection or alternative judgment.

For more on idea-
generating strategies,
see Chapter 11.

Start by identifying an objection or an alternative judgment you expect some readers to raise. To come up with likely objections or alternative judgments, you might try the following:

- *Brainstorm* a list on your own or with fellow students.
- *Freewrite* for ten minutes on this topic.
- Conduct research to learn what others have said about your subject.
- Conduct interviews with experts.
- Distribute a survey to a group of people similar to your intended readers.

Then figure out whether to concede or refute a likely objection or alternative judgment. You may be able to simply acknowledge an objection or alternative judgment. But if the criticism is serious, consider conceding the point and qualifying your judgment. You might also try to refute an objection or alternative judgment by arguing that the standards you are using are appropriate and important. Use the following strategies for generating ideas and sentences as a jumping-off point, then revise them later to make them your own.

Writing a Draft

Guide to Reading
▶ **GUIDE TO WRITING**
A Writer at Work
Reflection

319

HOW CAN I RESPOND EFFECTIVELY TO MY READERS?

Assess your subject, and consider how to present it to your readers.

1. Start by listing **OBJECTIONS** you expect readers to have as well as their preferred **ALTERNATIVE JUDGMENTS**. In the Ways In activity on p. 315, you considered your readers and the criteria they are likely to favor. If their criteria differ from yours, you may need to explain or defend your criteria.

2. Analyze your list of objections and alternative judgments to determine which are likely to be most powerful for your readers.

3. Draft **REFUTATIONS** and **CONCESSION** statements:

To Refute

▶ Reviewer A claims that .... But I agree with Reviewer B, who argues that ....

▶ Some people claim that subject X is .... because of ...., ..., and .... Although one can see why they might make this argument, the evidence does not back it up because ....

▶ In contrast to popular opinion, a recent study of .... showed that ....

To Concede

▶ Indeed, the more hard-core enthusiasts, like A, B, and C, may note that .... is not sufficiently ....

▶ The one justifiable criticism that could be made against X is ....

▶ As some critics have pointed out, X follows the tried-and-true formula of ....

To Concede and Refute

Frequently, writers concede a point only to come back with a refutation. To make the **CONCESSION-REFUTATION MOVE**, follow concessions like those above with sentences that begin with a **TRANSITION**—like *but, however, yet,* or *nevertheless*—and then explain why you believe that your interpretation or position is more powerful or compelling.

▶ As some critics have pointed out, X follows the tried-and-true formula of .... Still, the director/writer/artist is using the formula effectively to ....

Research Note: You may want to return to this activity after conducting further research. (For example, when he researched published reviews of *Scott Pilgrim,* student William Akana found objections to his argument as well as alternative judgments he could quote and refute.)

For more on the concession-refutation move, see Chapter 6.

⊞ Organize your evaluation to appeal to your readers.

Whether you have rough notes or a complete draft, making an *outline* of what you have written can help you organize your essay effectively for your audience. An evaluative essay contains as many as four basic parts:

1. presentation of the subject
2. judgment of the subject
3. presentation of reasons and support
4. consideration of readers' objections and alternative judgments

These parts can be organized in various ways; two options follow:

If you are writing primarily for readers who disagree with your judgment, you could start by showing them what you think they have overlooked or misjudged about the subject. Then you could anticipate and refute their likely objections before presenting your own reasons.

  I. **Present the subject:** Reframe the subject in terms that support your judgment.

 II. **Provide a thesis statement:** State your judgment directly.

III. **Refute alternative judgments.**

IV. **Present first reason and support with refutation of objection.**

 V. **Present second reason and support.**

VI. **Present third reason and support (and so on).**

VII. **Conclude:** Reiterate why your judgment is preferable to the alternatives.

If you expect some readers to disagree with your judgment even though they share your standards, you could begin by restating these standards, and then demonstrate how the subject fails to meet them. Then you could present your reasons and support before responding to alternative judgments.

  I. **Present the issue:** Reassert shared criteria.

 II. **Provide a thesis statement:** State judgment that subject fails to meet shared criteria.

III. **Present first reason and support showing how subject falls short.**

IV. **Present second reason and support.**

 V. **Present third reason and support (and so on).**

VI. **Refute alternative judgment.**

VII. **Conclude:** Reassert judgment based on shared criteria.

For more on outlining, see Chapters 11 and 12.

Never be a slave to an outline: As you draft, you may see ways to improve your original plan, and you should be ready to shift parts around or drop or add parts as needed. If you use the outlining function of your word processing program, changing your outline will be simple, and you may be able to write the essay simply by expanding the outline.

Writing a Draft

Guide to Reading
GUIDE TO WRITING
A Writer at Work
Reflection

321

Consider document design.

Because evaluations depend heavily on excerpts from the subject, they frequently include quotations, paraphrases, or summaries of the subject. When the subject of evaluation is in a visual medium (as with films, television shows, works of art, and Web sites), writers may use movie stills, photographs, or screen shots as evidence to support their claims. Consider how William Akana used film stills from *Scott Pilgrim vs. the World* as evidence to support his claim that this film "can be appreciated and enjoyed by all audiences because of its inventive special effects" (par. 2).

Take a moment . . .

Why might academic writing use explicit references to visuals (*Fig. 1*) whereas popular writing usually doesn't?

Scott Pilgrim vs the World shines bright with superb special effects that serve to reinforce the ideas, themes, and style of the film. Special effects are plentiful throughout the entire film, ranging from superimposed annotations echoing classic gaming features to artful backgrounds and action sequences modeled on colorful comic book pages. For example, each of the main characters is described for the first time with "gamertags," short-timed boxes of information that include name, age, and rating (see fig. 1).

Uses a film still to support his claim that the film offers inventive special effects (film still shows "gamertags")

Connects text discussion to the illustration with a figure callout

Fig. 1. Screen shot showing gamertags.

Uses a caption to highlight what the illustration shows

Universal/Everett Collection

Write the opening sentences.

Review what you have written to see if you have something that would work to launch your concept explanation, or try out some of these opening strategies:

- Offer an **anecdote**:

    As I leaned back in the movie theater seat, accompanied by my friends on a typical Saturday night, I knew I was in for something special. I was reassured; not only had my friends and I reached a unanimous vote to watch *Scott Pilgrim vs. the World*, but two of my friends had already seen the film and were eager to see it again. (Akana, par. 1)

- Begin with a **comparison** your readers are likely to be familiar with:

    Car and Driver conducted a comparison test of three sports cars, the Lotus Evora, the Chevrolet Corvette Grand Sport, and the Porsche Cayman S. (Gladwell, par. 1)

- Offer a **surprising or provocative statement**:

    Virtually everything about Disney's latest fairy tale, *Moana,* is familiar from past Disney films. (Robinson, par. 1)

But don't agonize over the first sentences because you are likely to discover the best way to begin only after you have written a rough draft.

Draft your evaluation.

By this point, you have done a lot of writing to

- devise a well-presented subject and make a judgment about it;
- support your judgment with reasons and evidence that your readers will find persuasive;
- refute or concede objections and alternative judgments;
- organize your ideas to make them clear, logical, and effective for readers.

Now stitch that material together to create a draft. The next two parts of this Guide to Writing will help you evaluate and improve your draft.

Evaluating the Draft: Using Peer Review

Your instructor may arrange a peer review session in class or online, where you can exchange drafts with your classmates to give one another a thoughtful critical reading, pointing out what works well and suggesting ways to improve the draft. A good critical reading does three things:

1. It lets the writer know how well the reader understands how the subject is being evaluated.
2. It praises what works best.
3. It indicates where the draft could be improved and makes suggestions on how to improve it.

One strategy for evaluating a draft is to use the basic features of evaluative essays as a guide. Also, be sure to respond to any concerns the writer has shared with you.

A PEER REVIEW GUIDE

A Well-Presented Subject

> Has the writer presented the subject effectively?

Summarize: Tell the writer what you understand the subject of the evaluation to be, and identify the kind of subject it is.

Praise: Point to a place where the subject is presented effectively — for example, where it is described vividly and accurately, where it is named, or where it is clearly placed in a recognizable genre or category.

Critique: Tell the writer where readers might need more information about the subject, and whether any information about it seems inaccurate or possibly only partly true. Suggest how the writer could clarify the kind of subject it is, either by naming the category or by giving examples of familiar subjects of the same type.

A Well-Supported Judgment

> Has the writer supported the judgment effectively?

Summarize: Tell the writer what you understand the overall judgment to be, and list the criteria on which it is based.

Praise: Identify a passage in the essay where support for the judgment is presented effectively — for example, note particularly strong supporting reasons, appeals to criteria readers are likely to share, or especially compelling evidence.

Critique: Let the writer know if you cannot find a thesis statement or think the thesis is vague or overstated. Tell the writer where the evaluation could be improved — for example, suggest another reason that could be added, propose a way to justify one of the criteria on which the evaluation is based, or recommend a source or an example that could be used to bolster support for the judgment.

An Effective Response to Objections and Alternative Judgments

> Has the writer responded effectively to objections and alternative judgments?

Summarize: Choose an objection or alternative judgment about the subject, and explain it in your own words.

Praise: Identify a passage in the essay where the writer responds effectively to an objection or alternative judgment. An effective response may include making a concession — for example, agreeing that a subject the writer is primarily criticizing has some good points, or agreeing that the subject has weaknesses as well as strengths.

Critique: Tell the writer where a response is needed or could be made more effective — for example, suggest a likely objection or alternative judgment that should be taken into account, help the writer understand the criteria behind an alternative judgment, or offer an example that could be used to refute an objection.

(continued)

A Clear, Logical Organization

> Is the evaluation clearly and logically organized?

Summarize: Briefly describe the strategies used to make the essay clear and easy to follow.

Praise: Give an example of where the essay succeeds in being readable — in its overall organization, in its clear presentation of the thesis, in its effective opening or closing, or by other means.

Critique: Tell the writer where the readability could be improved. Can you, for example, suggest a better beginning or a more effective ending? If the overall organization of the essay needs work, make suggestions for rearranging parts or strengthening connections.

Improving the Draft: Revising, Editing, and Proofreading

Take a moment . . .

Think about how you usually work on improving a draft. How helpful is it to get a peer review or to use a troubleshooting guide like this one?

Start improving your draft by reflecting on what you have written thus far:

- Review critical reading comments from your classmates, instructor, or writing center tutor: What problems do your readers identify?

- Consider whether you can add any of the notes from your earlier writings: What else should you consider?

- Review your draft: What else can you do to present your judgment more compellingly?

Revise your draft.

If your readers are having difficulty with your draft, or if you think there is room for improvement, try some of the strategies listed in the Troubleshooting Guide that follows. They can help you fine-tune your presentation of the genre's basic features.

Improving the Draft

Guide to Reading
GUIDE TO WRITING
A Writer at Work
Reflection

325

A TROUBLESHOOTING GUIDE

A Well-Presented Subject

> My readers find my subject vague or do not think it has been identified clearly.

- Identify the subject, name the author or director, and give the title.
- Describe the subject — summarize what it is about, cite statistics that establish its importance, or give examples to make it concrete.
- Consider adding visuals — photographs, tables, or charts — to help clarify the subject.

> My readers aren't sure what kind of subject it is.

- Classify the subject by naming the genre or category it fits into.
- Refer to reviews or reviewers of subjects of this kind.
- Compare your subject to other, better-known subjects of the same kind.

A Well-Supported Judgment

> My readers don't find my thesis or overall judgment clear.

- State your thesis early in the essay.
- Clarify the language in your thesis statement to indicate your overall judgment.
- Consider whether your judgment is arguable (not simply a matter of taste). If you cannot provide reasons and support for it, then your judgment probably isn't arguable; ask your instructor about modifying your judgment or writing about a different subject.

> My readers aren't convinced that my evaluation is reasonable or persuasive.

- Clarify the criteria on which you base your judgment, and justify them by citing authorities or reviews of similar subjects, making comparisons, or explaining why your criteria are appropriate and perhaps even preferable to criteria readers may be more familiar with.
- Add support for your reasons by, for example, quoting respected experts or research studies; providing facts or statistics; giving specific examples; or quoting, summarizing, or paraphrasing the subject of your evaluation.

> My readers don't understand my evaluation.

- Review the way you present your evaluation to make sure that you have explained it clearly and that you state your supporting reasons clearly.
- Outline your argument to be sure that it is clearly organized; if it is not, try rearranging parts or strengthening connections.
- Make sure that you have cut out any irrelevant content, and revise to strengthen the connections among your ideas.

(continued)

An Effective Response to Objections and Alternative Judgments

My readers raise objections I haven't considered or find fault with my response to alternative judgments.

- If readers raise only a minor concern, you may be able to ignore or dismiss it. (Not every objection requires a response.)
- If readers raise a serious objection, one that undermines your argument, try to refute it by showing that it's not based on widely held or appropriate criteria or that it's based on a misunderstanding of your argument or the subject.
- If readers raise a serious objection that you can't refute, acknowledge it but try to demonstrate that it doesn't invalidate your judgment.

My readers have proposed alternative judgments or have found fault with how I handle alternatives.

- Address the alternative judgments directly by conceding good or bad qualities of the subject that others focus on, but emphasize that you disagree about the overall value of the subject.
- Point out where you and your readers agree on criteria but disagree on how well the subject meets the criteria.
- Where you disagree with readers on criteria, try to justify the standards you are applying by citing authorities or establishing your own authority.

A Clear, Logical Organization

My readers find my essay confusing or hard to follow.

- Outline your essay to review its structure, and move, add, or delete sections as necessary to strengthen coherence.
- Consider adding a forecasting statement early in your essay.
- Repeat your key terms or use synonyms of key terms to keep readers oriented.
- Check to see that you introduce your reasons clearly in topic sentences.
- Check to be sure that you provide appropriate transitions between sentences, paragraphs, and sections of your essay, especially at points where your readers have trouble following your argument.
- Review your opening and closing paragraphs to be sure that your overall judgment is clear and appropriately qualified.

Edit and proofread your final draft.

Editing means making changes to the text to ensure that it follows the conventions of style, grammar, spelling, and mechanics appropriate to the rhetorical situation. **Proofreading** involves checking to make sure the text follows these conventions and that no words are repeated or omitted. You have probably done some editing and proofreading while composing and improving your draft, but it is always good practice to edit and proofread a draft after you have revised it and before you submit it.

Most writers get the best results by leaving time — even just an hour or two — between the stages of revising, editing, and proofreading, so that they can return to their writing project with fresh eyes. When possible, enlist a friend or

William Akana's Thesis and Response to Objections

Guide to Reading
Guide to Writing
▶ **A WRITER AT WORK**
Reflection

327

classmate to proofread the final draft of your writing projects. When that is not possible, proofread from the last line to the first, to avoid seeing what you expect to find rather than what is actually on the page (or screen).

As rhetorical situations change, so, too, do the conventions or expectations readers bring to the text. For example, whereas e-mail messages to friends are usually quite informal, filled with abbreviations, emojis, and sentence fragments, final drafts of writing projects for college classes or the workplace are expected to follow a more formal set of conventions concerning clarity, style, grammar, and punctuation.

We recommend that you make a list of the problems your instructors frequently point out in your writing, then use that list to guide your editing and proofreading. A Guide to Editing and Proofreading (at the end of this text) provides a checklist of the most common problems writers face. For issues that go beyond those on this list, consult a handbook* or search for advice online at sites like the Purdue Online Writing Lab (owl.english.purdue.edu) or Grammarly (grammarly.com). For practice identifying and correcting errors, try the activities in LearningCurve, a gamelike adaptive quizzing program available on LaunchPad for *The St. Martin's Guide to Writing*. The less well you do on activities in one topic area, the more LearningCurve focuses on it; the better you do, the more challenging the questions become.

> **A Note on Grammar and Spelling Checkers**
>
> Spelling checkers cannot catch misspellings that are themselves words, such as *to* for *too*, and grammar checkers miss problems, give faulty advice, and even flag correct items as wrong. Use these tools as a second line of defense after your own (and, ideally, another reader's) proofreading efforts.

A WRITER AT WORK

William Akana's Thesis and Response to Objections

In this section, we look at how William Akana anticipated his readers' objections. Using the Ways In activities on responding to a likely objection or alternative judgment (p. 319), Akana determined that readers would be interested in his review to decide whether the movie is worth seeing although he realized that his instructor would be reading the review to assess how effectively he used the basic features of evaluative essays and whether he included an insightful analysis of the cinematic techniques used in at least one important scene.

After writing for a few minutes on the first part of the Test Your Choice activity on pp. 314–15, Akana got together with three other students in the class to test out his idea for a subject and his criteria for evaluation. One of his group's members told him that she had gone to see the movie on a date and had found the film lacking as a romantic comedy. Akana realized that this was an objection that he could respond to.

A few days later, Akana received some helpful advice from a student who read his draft. Using the Peer Review Guide in this chapter (pp. 323–24), the student noted

---

* The full version of *The St. Martin's Guide to Writing* includes a handbook.

that she could not find a clear statement of his judgment in the draft. She told him that although the evidence he provided made it pretty clear that he liked the movie, she couldn't find where he stated his judgment directly. So he went back to the Ways In activity on drafting a tentative overall judgment (p. 316) and used one of the sentence strategies to help him draft a thesis:

> *Scott Pilgrim vs. the World* is a brilliant embodiment of the slacker film, especially notable for its superb special effects and clever dialogue.

When he finished his first draft, he revisited his thesis to polish it and to add another reason he had been discussing in his supporting paragraphs. He also realized that he needed to acknowledge the target audience but wanted to make sure readers who were *not* video game or anime enthusiasts knew they would also enjoy the movie. Here's the final version of his thesis:

> Although the film is especially targeted for old-school gamers, anime fans, and comic book fanatics, *Scott Pilgrim vs. the World* can be appreciated and enjoyed by all audiences because of its inventive special effects, clever dialogue, and artistic cinematography and editing.

Another student reader noted that Akana's draft provided lots of strong evidence, especially the analysis of film stills, but she found his response to an objection weak and unconvincing. This assessment hit home because Akana had inserted his classmate's criticism—that the movie failed as a romantic comedy—without really thinking about it. To strengthen his response to the criticism, Akana conducted research to find an expert reviewer who agreed with his classmate. He found a review by Rene Rodriguez in the *Miami Herald* that offered a reason why the romance was not convincing, and then he brainstormed his own response—that the romance is really secondary to Pilgrim's personal development. Akana then did more research and found a review that he could use to support this claim. His paragraph (par. 9), which originally focused solely on Rodriguez's criticism of the romance theme, developed into one in which Akana argued what he really believed—that the romance is pretty much beside the point.

REFLECTION

The benefit of reflection is proven and important: It helps consolidate what you have learned so that you can remember and apply it well beyond this class. That is why we have included questions and comments in the margins and at the end of this chapter: to stimulate your thinking about reviews, your rhetorical situation, and the choices you make as a writer.

Reflecting on Reading and Writing an Evaluation

To reflect on your experience reading reviews and writing one of your own, try writing a blog post, a letter to your instructor, or an e-mail message to a student who will

Reflecting on Your Composing Process

Guide to Reading
Guide to Writing
A Writer at Work
► **REFLECTION**

329

take this course next term that draws on what you have learned. Use any of these writing prompts that seem productive:

- Explain how your purpose and audience influenced *one* of your decisions as a writer, such as how you presented the subject, the strategies you used in justifying your evaluation, or the ways in which you attempted to refute possible objections.

- Discuss what you learned about yourself as a writer in the process of writing this particular essay. For example, what part of the process did you find most challenging? Did you try anything new, like getting a critical reading of your draft or outlining your draft in order to revise it?

- If you were to give advice to a friend who was about to write an essay justifying an evaluation, what would you say?

- Which of the readings in this chapter influenced your essay? Explain the influence, citing specific examples from your essay and from the reading.

- If you got good advice from a critical reader, explain exactly how the person helped you—perhaps by questioning the way you addressed your audience or the kinds of support you offered in support of your judgment.

Reflecting on Your Composing Process

Thinking about your process for writing an evaluation can be useful in helping you decide what works best for you as a writer. Using one or more of the following questions as a starting point, write a paragraph or two about your composing process:

- How did you go about choosing a subject? Did you try out a few possibilities before making a final decision? Did you choose something you loved, something you hated, or something in between?

- Explain how peer review helped you—perhaps by helping you clarify your criteria or helping you provide better transitions to cue readers.

- What was the hardest part of the process for you—defining the criteria, finding a way to convince readers that your examples or other evidence actually support your overall judgment, responding to readers who disagreed with your judgment, or something else?

- How satisfied are you with your writing process for this assignment? If you could go back in time, what would you have done differently? If you could continue working on your review, what would you like to change?

9

Arguing for Causes or Effects

Why is social media *really* so popular? Why do we watch horror movies, even though they make our skin crawl? Are smartphones causing loneliness and depression? Why are people moved more by the plight of an individual than by the plight of a crowd? The quest for answers to our questions inspires scientific inquiry, which can fully and satisfactorily explain the causes and effects of many things. But for questions like those addressed by the readings in this chapter, the causes and effects are uncertain and may never be known conclusively. For such subjects, it is helpful to think of analyzing causes or effects as a special kind of *argument* that considers evidence to determine whether a cause is likely to play an important — perhaps surprising — role in bringing about the effect or whether surprising effects might be the result of a particular cause.

People make cause-effect arguments for various purposes and audiences and publish them in a variety of media. For example, a college student in an ecology course might write a research paper analyzing why coral reefs are dying off, a serious problem that could alter coastal communities around the world. The captain of a Neighborhood Watch committee might write to the op-ed page of his community's online newspaper arguing that ignoring vandalism can lead to more serious deterioration of a neighborhood (the "broken-window effect"). A teacher might write an article on why boys are falling behind in educational achievement and the consequences to society of such a fact.

In this chapter, we ask you to choose a subject that does not have a single, definitive cause or effect that everyone accepts as fact, and then to *argue* that one (or more than one) cause or effect is the most plausible culprit, providing *reasons* and *evidence* to support your claim. From reading and analyzing the selections in the Guide to Reading (pp. 332–55), you will learn how to develop your own causal analysis. The Guide to Writing (pp. 356–72) will show you ways to use the basic features of the genre to compose an original, thought-provoking cause-effect argument of your own.

PRACTICING THE GENRE

Arguing That a Cause Is Plausible

For readers to accept your cause-effect argument, you have to offer convincing evidence.

Part 1. To practice developing a causal argument, get together with two or three other students to discuss why teens continue to take up smoking despite clear evidence that it is harmful and addictive.

1 Choose your audience and purpose:

- Are you addressing other college students, faculty, administrators, the general public, or teens themselves?
- Is your goal to change opinions or behavior, or to inspire the creation of useful school policies?

2 Brainstorm a list of causes that could explain why some high school students choose to smoke.

3 Pick your most plausible cause, and discuss these questions:

- What evidence would you need to support an argument for your preferred cause?
- Where could you find the supporting evidence you need?

Part 2. As a group, discuss what you learned from this activity:

- **How did your group initially come up with possible causes?** For example, did you recall your own experiences and observations? Did you consider different categories of causes, such as cultural, biological, psychological, or social?

- **What did you assume about your audience?** Did you think audience members would already be interested in your argument or, if your audience consisted of teens, that they would resent being the focus of this kind of inquiry? What kinds of supporting evidence did you think your audience would find persuasive?

> **Take a moment . . .**
> Think about why, to be effective, a cause needs to be seen by readers as plausible.

Analyzing Cause-Effect Arguments

As you read the selections in this chapter, you will see how different authors make a provocative cause-effect argument:

- Clayton Pangelinan argues that the popularity of social media is driven not only by our need to connect but also by our curiosity and desire for fame (pp. 336–40).

- Stephen King offers causes for why we crave horror movies—beyond the simple shiver effect (pp. 341–42).

- Jean M. Twenge analyzes the negative effects of social media and smartphones on teens (pp. 344–47).

- Shankar Vedantam tries to explain why people are often generous toward individuals or small groups but do not help large groups (pp. 350–53).

Analyzing how these writers present their subjects to their readers, persuade readers that their cause-effect reasoning is plausible, respond to alternative viewpoints, and organize their writing will help you see how you can employ similar strategies to make your own cause-effect argument clear and compelling for your readers.

Determine the writer's purpose and audience.

In analyzing possible causes or effects, writers exercise their imagination along with their logical thinking skills, but they also want to influence the way their readers think. As you read the cause-effect arguments that follow, ask yourself what the writer's main purpose is and what he or she assumes about the reader:

The writer's main purpose may be to	The writer wants readers to react by
■ introduce readers to an unfamiliar subject's causes or effects	■ becoming interested in understanding the subject's causes or effects
■ challenge readers to reexamine a well-known subject whose causes or effects they thought they understood	■ considering new causes or effects of a familiar subject
■ convince readers to take seriously causes or effects that have been rejected	■ reexamining with an open mind all potential causes or effects
■ persuade readers to look deeper for underlying causes or effects	■ looking deeper for underlying causes or effects

Basic Features

A Well-Presented Subject

A Well-Supported Cause-Effect Analysis

An Effective Response to Objections and Alternative Causes or Effects

A Clear, Logical Organization

Assess the genre's basic features.

As you analyze the cause-effect arguments in this chapter, consider how different authors incorporate the basic features of the genre. The examples that follow are drawn from the reading selections that appear later in this Guide to Reading.

A WELL-PRESENTED SUBJECT

Look first at the title and opening paragraphs to see what the subject is and whether it is clearly and vividly established. Frequently, the title of a cause-effect argument will identify the focus:

> #socialnetworking: Why It's *Really* So Popular (Pangelinan, title)
> Why We Crave Horror Movies (King, title)

To establish the subject, a writer may cite statistics or provide graphic illustrations:

> As Figure 1 below shows, the rise in popularity [of social media] cuts across all age groups. The most dramatic growth has been among young adults. . . . A 2015 survey reported that 71% of all teens use Facebook, along with sites like Instagram and Snapchat (Lenhart). Facebook has tended to outpace other networking outlets for adults as well, with 71% of online adults reporting they use Facebook ("Social Networking Fact Sheet"). (Pangelinan, par. 1)

A common approach to arousing the reader's curiosity is to begin with a compelling anecdote:

> The *Insiko 1907* was a tramp tanker that roamed the Pacific Ocean. . . . The ship was about eight hundred miles south of Hawaii's Big Island, and adrift. Its crew could not call on anyone for help, and no one who could help knew of the *Insiko*'s existence, let alone its problems. (Vedantam, par. 1)

Another common strategy for stimulating the audience to read on is to pose *why* questions:

> The fact *that* social networking is popular is well established. The question is *why* is it so popular? (Pangelinan, par. 2)

> Why did so many people come forward to save Hokget? . . . Why did they feel a single abandoned dog on a stateless ship was *their* problem? (Vedantam, par. 11)

A WELL-SUPPORTED CAUSE-EFFECT ANALYSIS

Find where the writer identifies and discusses each possible cause or effect, and note which one(s) the writer favors as being the most plausible (the most likely to have played a significant role) *as well as the one the writer finds most interesting* (possibly because the cause or effect has been overlooked or underappreciated).

EXAMPLE   When we [see] a horror movie, we are daring the nightmare. Why? Some of the reasons are simple and obvious. To show that we can, that we are not afraid. . . .
. . . to re-establish our feelings of essential normality. . . .
. . . to have fun.
Ah, but this is where the ground starts to slope away, isn't it?
(King, pars. 2–5)

Then assess the persuasiveness of the supporting evidence:

Research
studies

Quotation from
expert

Examples

Recent research suggests that screen time, in particular social-media use, does indeed cause unhappiness. One study asked college students with a Facebook page to complete short surveys on their phone over the course of two weeks. They'd get a text message with a link five times a day, and report on their mood and how much they'd used Facebook. The more they'd used Facebook, the unhappier they felt, but feeling unhappy did not subsequently lead to more Facebook use. (Twenge, par. 11)

Writing in the journal *Psychology of Popular Media Culture*, psychology professor Dara Greenwood (Vassar College) reviews research showing that "a craving for positive feedback and validation may be a common thread that links a desire for fame with social media use" (223). (Pangelinan, par. 7)

When, as children, we hug our rotten little puke of a sister and give her a kiss, all the aunts and uncles smile and twit and cry, "Isn't he the sweetest little thing?" . . . But if we deliberately slam the rotten little puke of a sister's fingers in the door, sanctions follow—angry remonstrance from parents, aunts, and uncles. (King, par. 9)

Also check that the cause-effect argument makes sense—in particular, that the cause (or causes) could actually bring about the effect (or effects). Note whether either of these logical fallacies or errors of causal reasoning have been made:

Consider . . .

What do you know about these typical problems in cause-effect thinking?

For more about logical fallacies, see Chapter 16.

- **Mistaking chronology for causation:** Assuming that because one thing preceded another, the former caused the latter. (This fallacy is often called by its Latin name, *post hoc, ergo propter hoc*, which means "after this, therefore because of this.")

- **Mistaking correlation for causation:** Assuming that because two things seem to be related or complementary, one thing caused the other. (This fallacy is sometimes called "with this, therefore because of this.")

AN EFFECTIVE RESPONSE TO OBJECTIONS AND ALTERNATIVE CAUSES OR EFFECTS

Notice where the author anticipates and responds to objections and alternative causes or effects. Often writers mention the well-known, predictable causes or effects first, quickly putting them aside to make room for a more detailed consideration of their preferred cause or effect. Here are a couple of sentence strategies that you might look for, followed by examples of these strategies in context:

▶ Most people assume X; however, _____.

▶ X and Y are the usual suspects, but let's look at a totally new possibility: _____.

Acknowledges positive
aspects of rescue

Prepares reader for
alternative perspective

Sets aside alternative
explanations

EXAMPLES   Saving the dog . . . was an act of pure altruism, and a marker of the remarkable capacity human beings have to empathize with the plight of others.
     There are a series of disturbing questions, however. (Vedantam, pars. 6–7)

Some of the reasons are simple and obvious. To show that we can, that we are not afraid, that we can ride this roller coaster. . . .
     We also go to re-establish our feelings of essential normality. . . .
     And we go to have fun.

Ah, but this is where the ground starts to slope away, isn't it? Because this is a very peculiar sort of fun, indeed. The fun comes from seeing others menaced—sometimes killed. (King, pars. 2–5)

Offers surprising, new explanation

There are many explanations for the discrepancy between our response to Hokget and our response to genocide. Some argue that Americans care little about foreign lives—but then what should we make about their willingness to spend thousands of dollars to rescue a dog, a foreign dog on a stateless ship in international waters? Well, perhaps Americans care more about pets than people? But that does not stand up to scrutiny, either. . . .

States alternative explanation

Refutes alternative

I believe our inability to wrap our minds around large numbers is responsible for our apathy toward mass suffering. (Vedantam, pars. 8–9)

In addition to responding to alternative causes or effects, writers may acknowledge and try to refute readers' likely objections. This is the same concession-refutation move we have seen in other kinds of argument essays:

Depression and suicide have many causes; too much technology is clearly not the only one. And the teen suicide rate was even higher in the 1990s, long before smartphones existed. Then again, about four times as many Americans now take antidepressants, which are often effective in treating severe depression, the type most strongly linked to suicide. (Twenge, par. 16)

Concession

Transition signaling refutation

A CLEAR, LOGICAL ORGANIZATION

Read to see if the writer provides cues to help readers follow the logic of the cause-effect argument. Essays arguing for causes or effects tend to be rather complicated because the writer has to establish that the subject exists, present a variety of causes or effects, and argue for those that are more likely to play an important role. Thus, cues to help readers follow the argument are needed. Notice whether the writer asserts the preferred cause or effect in a thesis statement:

I believe our inability to wrap our minds around large numbers is responsible for our apathy toward mass suffering. (Vedantam, par. 9)

Cause

Effect

Some thesis statements may also include a forecasting statement. Typically, a forecasting statement in a cause-effect argument identifies the main causes, effects, key supporting topics, or examples in the order they will be explored in the essay.

The fact *that* social networking is popular is well established. The question is *why* is it so popular? The most basic answer is that social networking is popular because it's available. . . . A better answer, though, is that social media offer people a way to satisfy their desire to connect with others and maybe also be "world-famous for fifteen minutes" (as Andy Warhol supposedly remarked). (Pangelinan, par. 2)

Forecast of key causes

Writers may cue readers by repeating key terms from the forecasting statement. They may also repeat sentence patterns from the forecasting statement in the essay's *topic sentences* to emphasize that another cause or effect, response to objections, or supporting example is coming.

Repeats sentence
structure

FORECASTING STATEMENT   Why? Some of the reasons are simple and obvious. To show that we can, that we are not afraid, that we can ride this roller coaster. (King, par. 2)

TOPIC SENTENCE   We also go to re-establish our feelings of essential normality. (3)

TOPIC SENTENCE   And we go to have fun. (4)

By repeating the same subject (*we*) and an active verb (*can, are, go*), King helps readers identify each new cause.

Writers may also use parallel grammatical structures to help readers recognize a series of supporting examples:

For example, consider the story of Emmalene Pruden, a YouTube sensation who began posting her video blogs on YouTube. . . .

Consider also the story of Lisa Sargese, who "started blogging as a way to tell the truth about her life. . . . " (Pangelinan, pars. 3–4)

Each of these examples provides support for the claim that "our wiring impels us not only to share but also to hear" (par. 2). Other cues writers may provide to guide readers include the following:

- a thesis statement and a forecast of the main cause or causes
- topic sentences announcing each new cause or example
- clear transitional words and phrases
- visuals (such as charts, graphs, and tables) that present information in an easy-to-read format
- headings that break selections up into sections by topic or cause

Readings

Clayton Pangelinan | *#socialnetworking: Why It's Really So Popular*

To learn how Pangelinan generated ideas for his essay, turn to A Writer at Work on pp. 372–74.

ORIGINALLY WRITTEN for Clayton Pangelinan's first-year college composition course, this essay analyzes what may be some surprising reasons for social networking's popularity.

As you read,

- reflect on your own attitudes toward social networking. Why do you think social networking is so popular? What are your own reasons for using (or avoiding) social media?

- consider whether the author addresses any of the causes that you speculated about or that have motivated you.

Reflect on . . .
How might genre expectations change in response to changes in the audience?

- think about how effectively Pangelinan uses the basic features of the genre (listed below), and answer the questions in the margins; your instructor may ask you to post your thoughts and answers to a class blog or discussion board or to bring your responses to class.

Pangelinan   *#socialnetworking: Why It's Really So Popular*

▶ **GUIDE TO READING**
Guide to Writing
A Writer at Work
Reflection

337

■■ **Basic Features**

A Well-Presented Subject

A Well-Supported
Cause-Effect Analysis

An Effective Response to
Objections and Alternative
Causes or Effects

A Clear, Logical
Organization

1   Complain about problems in a *tweet* over Twitter; add a *friend*, virtually *poke* each other, and *like* friends' postings and ramblings on Facebook; send images and videos to each other using Snapchat; capture a *selfie* with Instagram, edit it, add hashtags, and share it for your friends to see and comment on: Social networking is only a click away with apps like Vine and YouTube, Twitter, Facebook, Snapchat, Instagram, and Whatsapp on smartphones and tablets everywhere. Over the last decade or so, there has been a remarkable increase in the popularity of social networking. As Figure 1 below shows, the rise in popularity cuts across all age groups. The most dramatic growth has been among young adults. The percentage of 18 to 29-year-olds using social media rose from 7% to 41% in just 17 months, from February 2005 to August 2006. Like young adults, teenagers have flocked to social media. A 2015 survey reported that 71% of all teens use Facebook, along with sites like Instagram and Snapchat (Lenhart). Facebook has tended to outpace other networking outlets for adults as well, with 71% of online adults reporting they use Facebook ("Social Networking Fact Sheet"). Preferences among social networking sites have changed over the years, but the bottom line is that social networking continues to be enormously popular.

2   The fact *that* social networking is popular is well established. The question is *why* is it so popular? The most basic answer is that social networking is popular because it's available. Without the technological advances that transformed the static read-only Web into the dynamic, interactive virtual community known as

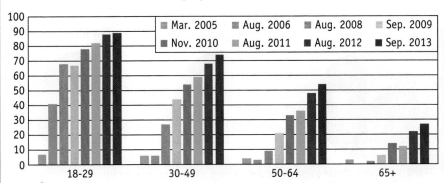

Social Media Use by Age in the United States, 2005-2013

Fig. 1. Social Media Use by Age in the United States, 2005–2013. Data from Wormald, Benjamin. "Social Media Use by Age Group over Time." *Pew Research Center,* 10 June 2015, http://www.pewinternet.org/chart/social-media-use-by-age-group-over-time/.

What is the effect on you of this opening paragraph?

How effective are the data Pangelinan provides to establish the fact that social networking has increased significantly?

How is the rhetorical question and its answer a response to objections?

How do these two answers help structure Pangelinan's essay?

How does this source support Pangelinan's argument?

Why does Pangelinan include this chart?

Web 2.0, none of the social networking we all engage in today would have been possible. A better answer, though, is that social media offer people a way to satisfy their desire to connect with others and maybe also be "world-famous for fifteen minutes" (as Andy Warhol supposedly remarked). When people were asked what their motivations were for using social networking sites like Facebook and Twitter, two-thirds of those surveyed reported that they go online primarily to connect with friends and family and meet new people (see fig. 2). As social animals, people have an inherent need for human connection. Professor Matthew Lieberman, in his recent book *Social: Why Our Brains Are Wired to Connect*, reports experiments using fMRIs to prove that the need to connect is hard-wired. According to Lieberman, our wiring impels us not only to share but also to hear. Communication naturally flows both ways: Not only

Staying in touch with ...

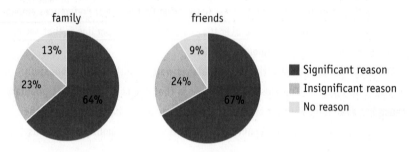

Connecting with ...

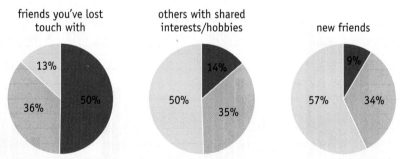

Fig. 2.   Motivations for using social networking sites. Data from Smith, Aaron. "Why Americans Use Social Media." *Pew Research Center*, 15 Nov. 2011, www.pewinternet .org/2011/11/15/why-americans-use-social-media/.

Pangelinan   *#socialnetworking: Why It's Really So Popular*

GUIDE TO READING
Guide to Writing
A Writer at Work
Reflection

339

are we "driven by deep motivations to stay connected with friends and family" but we are also "naturally curious about what is going on in the minds of other people" (ix).

3   Social media outlets offer a way to satisfy both impulses. For example, consider the story of Emmalene Pruden, reported by Hal Niedzviecki in *The Peep Diaries: How We're Learning to Love Watching Ourselves and Our Neighbors*. Emmalene is a YouTube sensation who began posting her video blogs after moving and feeling "cut off from her friends" (Niedzviecki 37). Emmalene shows how social media allow individuals to feel connected to a larger community: "If nothing else," as Niedzviecki claims, "peeping your problem, suspicion, or outrage is guaranteed to make you feel less alone" (142). But Emmalene's popularity also suggests that "it is these quotidian revelations that make her enticing to her viewers" (39). Viewers may feel less lonely knowing that their own everyday struggles and daily trivialities are no different than Emmalene's.

> How does Pangelinan make a connection between this paragraph and the one before?

4   Consider also the story of Lisa Sargese, who "started blogging as a way to tell the truth about her life as a morbidly obese, single woman determined to return to mobility and health via stomach-shrinking surgery" (Niedzviecki 51-52). She chronicled the effects of her surgery, growing her readership as she lost weight. Like Emmalene and her YouTube videos, Lisa was able to produce something that made her audience adore her: the sympathy effect. Readers also found hope by watching her overcome her problems. Niedzviecki makes a powerful statement that applies to both Emmalene and Lisa, as well as to their fans, when he concludes:

> How does repeating this phrase cue readers?

> We're alone all the time. We're alone on the bus, we're alone walking down the street, we're alone at the office and in the classroom, alone waiting in line at Disney World. We're tired of being alone, which is why increasingly we are barely hesitating to do whatever we feel we need to do to push out of solitude. (212–13)

5   This statement rings true throughout the social networking world but especially on Facebook, where users often post whatever is on their minds, however intimate. From the status of their relationships to pornographic home videos, social networkers can find it in a Facebook post. What motivates the extreme sharers?

> How effective is a rhetorical question here?

6   One answer might be a desire for celebrity. Consider the story of a woman who calls herself Padme. For her, social networking has turned into an obsession apparently motivated by her need for fame: "In our case you get to 1.6 million readers it's really hard to just walk away from that" (qtd. in Niedzviecki 26). Padme appears to be a typical suburban housewife and mother, except that she is also a fantastically popular writer of a sexually explicit Star Wars–themed blog, *Journey to the Darkside*. Padme's popularity appears to come not only from

> How effective is this transition to a new topic?

her sexual confessions (and visuals), but also from her story of living a double life, as both a mother and as a Star Wars sex slave. In addition to recording her rather ordinary day-to-day activities as a stay-at-home mom, she also writes "about her need to be dominated by the man she calls Master Anakin, the man she's been . . . 'married to for 4 years, living with for 12 years, and best friends with for 18 years'" (Niedzviecki 23).

How does this source support Pangelinan's argument?

7   Writing in the journal *Psychology of Popular Media Culture,* psychology professor Dara Greenwood (Vassar College) reviews research showing that "a craving for positive feedback and validation may be a common thread that links a desire for fame with social media use" (223). More specifically, she points to the correlation between the desire to be seen and valued and the need to feel connected, "to feel meaningfully embedded in social networks," as Greenwood puts it (223). While Padme carries her blogging to extremes that Emmalene and Lisa don't reach, what Greenwood writes applies to all three. The underlying cause of this need for visibility may be narcissism, fairly obvious in all three cases but especially so in Padme's as demonstrated by the "increased tendency to engage in exhibitionist postings on social media sites" (224).

How is Pangelinan's conclusion a response to objections? How effective is his conclusion?

8   Of course, most of us participate in social networks without getting as carried away as Emmalene, Lisa, or Padme. In fact, if you understood the first paragraph in this essay, then chances are you sign in, sign up, tune in, and engage in many of these forms of social media. So ask yourself: What are your reasons for joining in? To connect? To tune in to what others are up to? To show off? Whatever your reasons, you can be sure you are not alone.

Works Cited

Greenwood, Dara N. "Fame, Facebook, and Twitter: How Attitudes about Fame Predict the Frequency and Nature of Social Media Use." *Psychology of Popular Media Culture,* vol. 2, no. 4, 2013, pp. 222-36. *PsycINFO,* doi:10.1037/ppm0000013.

Lenhart, Amanda. "Teens, Social Media & Technology Overview 2015." *Pew Research Center,* 9 Apr. 2015, www.pewinternet.org/2015/04/09/teens-social-media-technology-2015/.

Lieberman, Matthew. *Social: Why Our Brains Are Wired to Connect.* Crown Publishing, 2013.

Niedzviecki, Hal. *The Peep Diaries: How We're Learning to Love Watching Ourselves and Our Neighbors.* City Lights Books, 2009.

Smith, Aaron. "Why Americans Use Social Media." *Pew Research Center,* 15 Nov. 2011, www.pewinternet.org/2011/11/15/why-americans-use-social-media/.

"Social Networking Fact Sheet." *Pew Research Center,* www.pewinternet.org/fact -sheets/social-networking-fact-sheet/. Accessed 15 Oct. 2015.

King *Why We Crave Horror Movies*

▶ **GUIDE TO READING**
Guide to Writing
A Writer at Work
Reflection

341

Stephen King | *Why We Crave Horror Movies*

AFP/Getty Images

STEPHEN KING is America's best-known writer of horror fiction. In 2015, he won the prestigious Edgar Award for best novel, for *Mr. Mercedes* (2014), in which a serial killer taunts the retired cop who never solved the crime. He has also won many other awards, including a Lifetime Achievement Award from the Horror Writers Association and the National Book Foundation Medal for Distinguished Contribution to American Letters, both in 2003. A prolific writer in many genres and media, King has recently published the novels *The Outsider* (2018), *Sleeping Beauties*, with his son Owen (2017), and *End of Watch* (2016); the graphic novel series Dark Tower and Road Rage; and a short story collection *The Bazaar of Bad Dreams* (2015). Many films and television movies have been based on King's work, including the classics *The Shawshank Redemption* (1994) and *Stand by Me* (1986). King offers this wise advice to beginning writers in *On Writing* (2000): "You have to read a lot and write a lot. There's no way around these two things . . . no shortcut."

In this classic essay, King analyzes why some of us love horror movies. As you read, consider the following:

- What's your feeling about horror films, roller coasters, or other scary rides? For you personally, what makes them attractive or something to avoid?

- What reasons can you think of for why we like horror movies?

1 I think that we're all mentally ill; those of us outside the asylums only hide it a little better — and maybe not all that much better, after all. We've all known people who talk to themselves, people who sometimes squinch their faces into horrible grimaces when they believe no one is watching, people who have some hysterical fear — of snakes, the dark, the tight place, the long drop . . . and, of course, those final worms and grubs that are waiting so patiently underground.

2 When we [see] a horror movie, we are daring the nightmare. Why? Some of the reasons are simple and obvious. To show that we can, that we are not afraid, that we can ride this roller coaster. Which is not to say that a really good horror movie may not surprise a scream out of us at some point, the way we may scream when the roller coaster twists through a complete 360 or plows through a lake at the bottom of the drop. And horror movies, like roller coasters, have always been the special province of the young; by the time one turns 40 or 50, one's appetite for double twists or 360-degree loops may be considerably depleted.

3 We also go to re-establish our feelings of essential normality; the horror movie is innately conservative, even reactionary. Freda Jackson as the horrible melting woman in *Die, Monster, Die!* confirms for us that no matter how far we may be removed from the beauty of a Robert Redford or a Diana Ross, we are still light-years from true ugliness.

4 And we go to have fun.

5 Ah, but this is where the ground starts to slope away, isn't it? Because this is a very peculiar sort of fun, indeed. The fun comes from seeing others menaced — sometimes killed. One critic has suggested that if pro football has become the voyeur's version of combat, then the horror film has become the modern version of the public lynching.

6 It is true that the mythic, "fairy tale" horror film intends to take away the shades of gray. . . . It urges us to put away our more civilized and adult penchant for analysis and to become children again, seeing things in pure blacks and whites. It may be that horror movies provide psychic relief on this level because this invitation to lapse into simplicity, irrationality, and even

and we recognize that it demands its own exercise to maintain proper muscle tone. Certain of these emotional muscles are accepted—even exalted—in civilized society; they are, of course, the emotions that tend to maintain the status quo of civilization itself. Love, friendship, loyalty, kindness—these are all the emotions that we applaud, emotions that have been immortalized in the couplets of Hallmark cards and in the verses (I don't dare call it poetry) of Leonard Nimoy.

9   When we exhibit these emotions, society showers us with positive reinforcement; we learn this even before we get out of diapers. When, as children, we hug our rotten little puke of a sister and give her a kiss, all the aunts and uncles smile and twit and cry, "Isn't he the sweetest little thing?" Such coveted treats as chocolate-covered graham crackers often follow. But if we deliberately slam the rotten little puke of a sister's fingers in the door, sanctions follow—angry remonstrance from parents, aunts, and uncles; instead of a chocolate-covered graham cracker, a spanking.

10   But anticivilization emotions don't go away, and they demand periodic exercise. We have such "sick" jokes as "What's the difference between a truckload of bowling balls and a truckload of dead babies?" ("You can't unload a truckload of bowling balls with a pitchfork" . . . a joke, by the way, that I heard originally from a ten-year-old.) Such a joke may surprise a laugh or a grin out of us even as we recoil, a possibility that confirms the thesis: If we share a brotherhood of man, then we also share an insanity of man. None of which is intended as a defense of either the sick joke or insanity but merely as an explanation of why the best horror films, like the best fairy tales, manage to be reactionary, anarchistic, and revolutionary all at the same time.

11   The mythic horror movie, like the sick joke, has a dirty job to do. It deliberately appeals to all that is worst in us. It is morbidity unchained, our most base instincts let free, our nastiest fantasies realized . . . and it all happens, fittingly enough, in the dark. For those reasons, good liberals often shy away from horror films. For myself, I like to see the most aggressive of them—*Dawn of the Dead,* for instance—as lifting a trap door in the civilized forebrain and throwing a basket of raw meat to the hungry alligators swimming around in that subterranean river beneath.

12   Why bother? Because it keeps them from getting out, man. It keeps them down there and me up here. It was Lennon and McCartney who said that all you need is love, and I would agree with that.

13   As long as you keep the gators fed.

outright madness is extended so rarely. We are told we may allow our emotions a free rein . . . or no rein at all.

7   If we are all insane, then sanity becomes a matter of degree. If your insanity leads you to carve up women like Jack the Ripper or the Cleveland Torso Murderer, we clap you away in the funny farm (but neither of those two amateur-night surgeons was ever caught, heh-heh-heh); if, on the other hand, your insanity leads you only to talk to yourself when you're under stress or to pick your nose on your morning bus, then you are left alone to go about your business . . . though it is doubtful that you will ever be invited to the best parties.

8   The potential lyncher is in almost all of us (excluding saints, past and present; but then, most saints have been crazy in their own ways), and every now and then, he has to be let loose to scream and roll around in the grass. Our emotions and our fears form their own body,

King *Why We Crave Horror Movies*

GUIDE TO READING
Guide to Writing
A Writer at Work
Reflection

343

Make connections: Media violence.

King seems to assume that horror films perform a social function by allowing us to exercise (or possibly exorcise) our least civilized emotions. In fact, King even argued against a proposed ban on the sale of violent video games for the same reason. To analyze King's ideas about violence in the media, reflect on your own observations and experiences with film, video games, or other media that may be considered violent. Your instructor may ask you to post your thoughts or to discuss them in class. Use these questions to get you started:

- King asserts that we all have what he calls "anticivilization emotions" (par. 10). What have you seen, heard, or felt that suggests that you or others harbor such emotions?

- The argument against violence in the media is basically that images of violence—or, in the case of video games, performing virtual acts of violence—arouse anti-civilization feelings and perhaps even inspire people (especially young people) to commit acts of real violence. King seems to agree that there is a cause-effect relationship, but what does he think is the cause and the effect? What do you think?

- If you think media violence inspires real violence, do you support censorship of movies, television programs, books, or Internet sites that portray violence? If so, should this material be censored just for children or for all viewers? If you oppose outright censorship, do you support movie rating systems or the television V-chip, which gives parents some control over what their children watch? Explain your responses.

Use the basic features.

A WELL-PRESENTED SUBJECT: REFRAMING THE SUBJECT FOR READERS

Writers try to present their subjects in a way that intrigues readers, making them want to know more. To do so, they typically frame or reframe their subjects, emphasizing new ways of looking at and understanding them. How does King make room for his less predictable causes and convince readers to go along for the ride?

| ANALYZE & WRITE |

Write a couple of paragraphs analyzing and evaluating how King reframes his subject:

1 The title suggests that the subject of this essay is horror movies, but the key term in the title is the word "crave." Look up the verb *crave* and the related noun *craving* to see what they mean. Also highlight some of the other words and phrases King associates with the appeal of horror movies, such as "mentally ill" and "hysterical fear" (par. 1). How do the words you highlighted relate to the word *crave*?

2 Given these key terms, how would you describe the way King reframes the subject for readers? How do these key terms enable him to plant the seed of his main idea at the very beginning of the essay?

AN EFFECTIVE RESPONSE: PUTTING ASIDE OBVIOUS CAUSES OR EFFECTS

People analyzing causes sometimes consider an array of possibilities before focusing on one or two serious probabilities. They may concede that these other causes or effects play some role, or they may simply dismiss them as trivial or irrelevant, as Clayton Pangelinan does when he says, *"The most basic answer* is that social networking is popular because it's available" (par. 2, italics added).

ANALYZE & WRITE

Write a couple of paragraphs analyzing and evaluating how well King uses concession and refutation:

1 Look closely at the causes King considers in the opening paragraphs to determine how he actually responds to them. For example, how does he support the assertion that some of them are "simple and obvious"? What other arguments, if any, does he use to refute them?

2 Given his purpose and audience, why do you think King chooses to begin by presenting causes he thinks are simple and obvious?

[RESPOND] **Consider possible topics: Popular culture.**

Following King, you could consider writing about some aspect of popular culture. Consider, for example, why particular social networking sites, apps or video games, or genres of fiction or film are so popular with college students or other demographic groups. Why do ads appealing to sex work so well to sell cars and other consumer products? Why are negative political ads so effective?

Jean M. Twenge | *Have Smartphones Destroyed a Generation?*

Jean M. Twenge is a prolific author and psychology professor at San Diego State University. In addition to writing for academic audiences in such publications as the *Journal of Cross-Culture Psychology* and the *Journal of Social Psychology,* Twenge writes for a more general readership in her *Psychology Today* blog *Our Changing Culture* and in magazines such as the *Atlantic,* in which a longer version of this article originally appeared (itself, an adaptation from her most recent book). Twenge has written a number of books, including two influential textbooks and several books for general readers, such as *Generation Me* (2nd ed., 2014) and *iGen: Why Today's Super-Connected Kids Are Growing Up Less Rebellious, More Tolerant, Less Happy—and Completely Unprepared for Adulthood—and What That Means for the Rest of Us* (2017).

As you read,

- think about Twenge's speculations about the effects of social media in light of your own experience and, if you read it, Clayton Pangelinan's essay on social media's popularity earlier in this chapter (pp. 336–40).

- notice that Twenge chose not to include formal academic citations or links to the surveys and research studies she refers to. Given her rhetorical situation—her expected readers, what she wanted to accomplish, the genre, and media conventions—how appropriate do you think it was for Twenge not to cite her sources? How do you think not citing sources may have affected her credibility with her original *Atlantic* readers?

1   I've been researching generational differences for 25 years, starting when I was a 22-year-old doctoral student in psychology. Typically, the characteristics that come to define a generation appear gradually, and along a continuum. Beliefs and behaviors that were already rising simply continue to do so. Around 2012, I noticed abrupt shifts in teen behaviors and emotional states. The gentle slopes of the line graphs became steep mountains and sheer cliffs, and many of the distinctive characteristics of the Millennial generation began to disappear. In all my analyses of generational data—some reaching back to the 1930s—I had never seen anything like it.

2   At first I presumed these might be blips, but the trends persisted, across several years and a series of national surveys. The changes weren't just in degree, but in kind. The biggest difference between the Millennials and their predecessors was in how they viewed the world; teens today differ from the Millennials not just in their views but in how they spend their time. The experiences they have every day are radically different from those of the generation that came of age just a few years before them.

3   What happened in 2012 to cause such dramatic shifts in behavior? It was after the Great Recession, which officially lasted from 2007 to 2009 and had a starker effect on Millennials trying to find a place in a sputtering economy. But it was exactly the moment when the proportion of Americans who owned a smartphone surpassed 50 percent.

4   The more I pored over yearly surveys of teen attitudes and behaviors, and the more I talked with young people, the clearer it became that theirs is a generation shaped by the smartphone and by the concomitant rise of social media. I call them iGen. Born between 1995 and 2012, members of this generation are growing up with smartphones, have an Instagram account before they start high school, and do not remember a time before the internet. The Millennials grew up with the web as well, but it wasn't ever-present in their lives, at hand at all times, day and night. iGen's oldest members were early adolescents when the iPhone was introduced, in 2007, and high-school students when the iPad entered the scene, in 2010. A 2017 survey of more than 5,000 American teens found that three out of four owned an iPhone.

5   The advent of the smartphone and its cousin the tablet was followed quickly by hand-wringing about the deleterious effects of "screen time." But the impact of these devices has not been fully appreciated, and goes far beyond the usual concerns about curtailed attention spans. The arrival of the smartphone has radically changed every aspect of teenagers' lives, from the nature of their social interactions to their mental health. These changes have affected young people in every corner of the nation and in every type of household. The trends appear among teens poor and rich; of every ethnic background; in cities, suburbs, and small towns. Where there are cell towers, there are teens living their lives on their smartphone.

6   Some generational changes are positive, some are negative, and many are both. More comfortable in their bedrooms than in a car or at a party, today's teens are physically safer than teens have ever been. They're markedly less likely to get into a car accident and, having less of a taste for alcohol than their predecessors, are less susceptible to drinking's attendant ills. Psychologically, however, they are more vulnerable than Millennials were: Rates of teen depression and suicide have skyrocketed since 2011. It's not an exaggeration to describe iGen as being on the brink of the worst mental-health crisis in decades. Much of this deterioration can be traced to their phones.

7   Even when a seismic event—a war, a technological leap, a free concert in the mud—plays an outsize role in shaping a group of young people, no single factor ever defines a generation. Parenting styles continue to change, as do school curricula and culture, and these things matter. But the twin rise of the smartphone and

social media has caused an earthquake of a magnitude we've not seen in a very long time, if ever. There is compelling evidence that the devices we've placed in young people's hands are having profound effects on their lives—and making them seriously unhappy. . . .

8   The number of teens who get together with their friends nearly every day dropped by more than 40 percent from 2000 to 2015; the decline has been especially steep recently. It's not only a matter of fewer kids partying; fewer kids are spending time simply hanging out. That's something most teens used to do: nerds and jocks, poor kids and rich kids, C students and A students. The roller rink, the basketball court, the town pool, the local necking spot—they've all been replaced by virtual spaces accessed through apps and the web.

9   You might expect that teens spend so much time in these new spaces because it makes them happy, but most data suggest that it does not. The Monitoring the Future survey, funded by the National Institute on Drug Abuse and designed to be nationally representative, has asked 12th-graders more than 1,000 questions every year since 1975 and queried eighth- and 10th-graders since 1991. The survey asks teens how happy they are and also how much of their leisure time they spend on various activities,

including nonscreen activities such as in-person social interaction and exercise, and, in recent years, screen activities such as using social media, texting, and browsing the web. The results could not be clearer: Teens who spend more time than average on screen activities are more likely to be unhappy, and those who spend more time than average on nonscreen activities are more likely to be happy.

10   There's not a single exception. All screen activities are linked to less happiness, and all nonscreen activities are linked to more happiness. Eighth-graders who spend 10 or more hours a week on social media are 56 percent more likely to say they're unhappy than those who devote less time to social media. Admittedly, 10 hours a week is a lot. But those who spend six to nine hours a week on social media are still 47 percent more likely to say they are unhappy than those who use social media even less. The opposite is true of in-person interactions. Those who spend an above-average amount of time with their friends in person are 20 percent less likely to say they're unhappy than those who hang out for a below-average amount of time.

11   Of course, these analyses don't unequivocally prove that screen time *causes* unhappiness; it's possible that unhappy teens spend more time online. But recent research suggests that screen time, in particular social-media use,

Donald Iain Smith/Getty Images

The amount of time teenagers hang out with their friends has plummeted since 2000.

does indeed cause unhappiness. One study asked college students with a Facebook page to complete short surveys on their phone over the course of two weeks. They'd get a text message with a link five times a day, and report on their mood and how much they'd used Facebook. The more they'd used Facebook, the unhappier they felt, but feeling unhappy did not subsequently lead to more Facebook use.

12   Social-networking sites like Facebook promise to connect us to friends. But the portrait of iGen teens emerging from the data is one of a lonely, dislocated generation. Teens who visit social-networking sites every day but see their friends in person less frequently are the most likely to agree with the statements "A lot of times I feel lonely," "I often feel left out of things," and "I often wish I had more good friends." Teens' feelings of loneliness spiked in 2013 and have remained high since.

13   This doesn't always mean that, on an individual level, kids who spend more time online are lonelier than kids who spend less time online. Teens who spend more time on social media also spend more time with their friends in person, on average—highly social teens are more social in both venues, and less social teens are less so. But at the generational level, when teens spend more time on smartphones and less time on in-person social interactions, loneliness is more common.

14   So is depression. Once again, the effect of screen activities is unmistakable: The more time teens spend looking at screens, the more likely they are to report symptoms of depression. Eighth-graders who are heavy users of social media increase their risk of depression by 27 percent, while those who play sports, go to religious services, or even do homework more than the average teen cut their risk significantly.

15   Teens who spend three hours a day or more on electronic devices are 35 percent more likely to have a risk factor for suicide, such as making a suicide plan. (That's much more than the risk related to, say, watching TV.)

For all their power to link kids day and night, social media also exacerbate the age-old teen concern about being left out.

One piece of data that indirectly but stunningly captures kids' growing isolation, for good and for bad: Since 2007, the homicide rate among teens has declined, but the suicide rate has increased. As teens have started spending less time together, they have become less likely to kill one another, and more likely to kill themselves. In 2011, for the first time in 24 years, the teen suicide rate was higher than the teen homicide rate.

16   Depression and suicide have many causes; too much technology is clearly not the only one. And the teen suicide rate was even higher in the 1990s, long before smartphones existed. Then again, about four times as many Americans now take antidepressants, which are often effective in treating severe depression, the type most strongly linked to suicide.

What's the connection between smartphones and the apparent psychological distress this generation is experiencing? For all their power to link kids day and night, social media also exacerbate the age-old teen concern about being left out. Today's teens may go to fewer parties and spend less time together in person, but when they do congregate, they document their hangouts relentlessly—on Snapchat, Instagram, Facebook. Those not invited to come along are keenly aware of it. Accordingly, the number of teens who feel left out has reached all-time highs across age groups. Like the increase in loneliness, the upswing in feeling left out has been swift and significant. . . .

18   What's at stake isn't just how kids experience adolescence. The constant presence of smartphones is likely to affect them well into adulthood. Among people who suffer an episode of depression, at least half become depressed again later in life. Adolescence is a key time for developing social skills; as teens spend less time with their friends face-to-face, they have fewer opportunities to practice them. In the next decade, we may see more adults who know just the right emoji for a situation, but not the right facial expression.

Make Connections: Effects of Social Media   [REFLECT]

In paragraph 8, Twenge writes: "The number of teens who get together with their friends nearly every day dropped by more than 40 percent from 2000 to 2015," a statistic she supports with a graph titled "Not Hanging Out with Friends." She suggests that the lack of face-to-face time hanging out with friends contributes to people's feelings of loneliness, being left out, and depression.

To analyze Twenge's ideas about the effects of not hanging out with friends, reflect on your own experience. Your instructor may ask you to post your thoughts on a class discussion board or to discuss them with other students in class. Use these questions to get you started:

- In your observation, do young people today appear to hang out a lot? When they are together, do they seem to spend a lot of time looking at their phones?
- Twenge cites various surveys, including the Monitoring the Future graphs, to suggest that there is a cause-effect relationship between the increase of social media and reduced face-to-face socializing, which in turn has led to increased feelings of loneliness and depression. What do you think about this chain of causes and effects? How convincing does it seem to you?

[ANALYZE]   Use the basic features.

A WELL-SUPPORTED CAUSE-EFFECT ANALYSIS: PROVIDING COMPELLING EVIDENCE

Essays speculating about causes and effects need to provide support to convince readers to take seriously the thesis—the preferred causes or effects—for which the author is arguing. Writers use various strategies to support their argument. Clayton Pangelinan, for instance, relies mainly on examples of people who have become famous for blogging their personal stories. To bolster this anecdotal evidence, Pangelinan also quotes authorities and includes a bar graph from a credible source (the Pew Research Center). Because he is examining the causes of people's fascination with horror films, Stephen King refers to a movie he finds especially horrifying: *Die, Monster, Die!* The fact that few, if any, of his readers are likely to be familiar with this particular film (or likely to find it horrifying) doesn't seem to matter to King, as he probably assumes that readers will be able to think of their own example of a truly horrifying film. He also offers causes he thinks readers can relate to and examples he thinks readers will find compelling (such as a "sick" joke and the hypothetical example of getting punished for maltreating his "little puke of a sister").

ANALYZE & WRITE

Write a paragraph analyzing and evaluating how Twenge supports her thesis about the "deleterious effects" (par. 5) of the iGen's use of the smartphone and social media:

1 Skim the essay to see how Twenge uses survey data, including the graphs from the Monitoring the Future survey, to support her argument about the effects of smartphone and social media use.

2 How convincing do you think this kind of supporting evidence is likely to be for Twenge's readers? How convincing do you find it?

3 What other kinds of evidence does Twenge use (or could she have used) to make her essay more convincing or compelling?

A CLEAR, LOGICAL ORGANIZATION: USING RHETORICAL QUESTIONS

Essays speculating about causes and effects need to make clear to readers the thesis—the causes or effects—for which the author is arguing. Sometimes writers assert the thesis at the outset (as Clayton Pangelinan does), and sometimes they wait until later in the essay, after putting aside other, less interesting causes or effects (as Stephen King does). Wherever the thesis statement is placed, it has to identify the subject and name the cause or effect (single or multiple) that the writer is asserting and supporting.

Pangelinan and King use rhetorical questions both to emphasize their preferred cause and to put aside alternative causes. For example, in paragraph 2, Pangelinan introduces his thesis with a rhetorical question:

> The fact *that* social networking is popular is well established. The question is *why* is it so popular? The most basic answer is that social networking is popular because it's available. . . . A better answer, though, is that social media offer people a way to satisfy their desire to connect with others and maybe also be "world-famous for fifteen minutes" (as Andy Warhol supposedly remarked). (par. 2)

Rhetorical question

Thesis/Preferred cause

In paragraph 2, King uses a rhetorical question to dismiss alternative causes:

> Why? Some of the reasons are simple and obvious. To show that we can, that we are not afraid, that we can ride this roller coaster. (par. 2)

Additionally, King uses a rhetorical question toward the end of his essay to highlight why the issue matters:

> Why bother? Because it keeps them from getting out, man. (par. 12)

ANALYZE & WRITE

Write a paragraph analyzing and evaluating Twenge's use of cueing devices:

1 Reread paragraphs 1–7 to find and highlight the thesis statement — the sentence (or sentences) that best present Twenge's main idea about the effect (or complex of effects) she is analyzing. How do you know this is the thesis of Twenge's essay?

2 Skim paragraphs 3 and 17. How does Twenge's use of rhetorical questions compare to Pangelinan's and King's?

Did you know?

Research indicates that rhetorical questions may soften criticism and strengthen assertions, as well as orient readers. How do Twenge, Pangelinan, or King use rhetorical questions?

Consider possible topics: Social media and new technologies.

RESPOND

New technologies offer an array of possible topics for cause-effect analysis. Twenge and Pangelinan analyze causes and effects of social media. Think of other topics related to social media that might interest you, such as its effects on dating, music production and consumption, and politics. You might also analyze how playing video games has affected the way we think, learn, and solve problems. Other possible topics ripe for cause-effect analysis include virtual and augmented reality, artificial intelligence, wearable computers, and self-driving cars—all of which may have substantial effects on our lives in the future.

Shankar Vedantam | *The Telescope Effect*

Julia Vitullo-Martin

SHANKAR VEDANTAM is a correspondent for National Public Radio, reporting on the psychology of human behavior. He also hosts the podcast *Hidden Brain* for NPR, and for ten years he wrote the Department of Human Behavior column for the *Washington Post*. He has been honored with fellowships and awards by Harvard University, the World Health Organization, the Society of Professional Journalists, and the American Public Health Association. In addition to his many articles, Vedantam writes plays and fiction, including his short story collection, *The Ghosts of Kashmir* (2005). "The Telescope Effect" is excerpted from his book *The Hidden Brain: How Our Unconscious Minds Elect Presidents, Control Markets, Wage Wars, and Save Our Lives* (2010). The photograph of the rescued dog, Hokget, that appears in the reading selection is from the *Honolulu Star-Bulletin*. As you read, consider the following questions:

- How does Vedantam engage readers' interest in the opening paragraphs?

- How do you think including a photograph of the dog affects readers' perspectives?

- What do you think is the most thought-provoking question Vedantam raises in this selection?

1   The *Insiko 1907* was a tramp tanker that roamed the Pacific Ocean. Its twelve-man Taiwanese crew hunted the seas for fishing fleets in need of fuel; the *Insiko* had a cargo of tens of thousands of gallons of diesel. It was supposed to be an Indonesian ship, except that it was not registered in Indonesia because its owner, who lived in China, did not bother with taxes. In terms of international law, the *Insiko 1907* was stateless, a two-hundred-sixty-foot microscopic speck on the largest ocean on earth. On March 13, 2002, a fire broke out in the *Insiko*'s engine room. . . . The ship was about eight hundred miles south of Hawaii's Big Island, and adrift. Its crew could not call on anyone for help, and no one who could help knew of the *Insiko*'s existence, let alone its problems.[1]

2   Drawn by wind and currents, the *Insiko* eventually got within two hundred twenty miles of Hawaii, where it was spotted by a cruise ship called the *Norwegian Star* on April 2. The cruise ship diverted course, rescued the Taiwanese crew, and radioed the United States Coast Guard. But as the *Norwegian Star* pulled away from the *Insiko* and steamed toward Hawaii, a few passengers on the cruise ship heard the sound of barking. The captain's puppy had been left behind on the tanker.

3   It is not entirely clear why the cruise ship did not rescue the Jack Russell mixed terrier, or why the Taiwanese crew did not insist on it. . . . Whatever the reason, the burned-out tanker and its lonely inhabitant were abandoned on the terrible immensity of the Pacific. The *Norwegian Star* made a stop at Maui. A passenger who heard the barking dog called the Hawaiian Humane Society in Honolulu. . . . The Humane Society alerted fishing boats about the lost tanker. Media reports began appearing about the terrier, whose name was Hokget.

4   Something about a lost puppy on an abandoned ship on the Pacific gripped people's imaginations. Money poured into the Humane Society to fund a rescue. One check was for five thousand dollars. . . . "It was just about a dog," [Hawaiian Humane Society president Pamela] Burns told me. . . . "This was an opportunity for people to feel good about rescuing a dog. People poured out their support. A handful of people were incensed. These people said, 'You should be giving money to the homeless.'" But Burns felt the great thing about America was that people were free to give money to whatever cause they cared about, and people cared about Hokget. . . .

5   On April 26, nearly one and a half months after the puppy's ordeal began, the *American Quest* found the *Insiko* and boarded the tanker. The forty-pound female pup was still alive, and hiding in a pile of tires. It was a hot day, so Brian Murray, the *American Quest*'s

salvage supervisor, went in and simply grabbed the terrier by the scruff of her neck. The puppy was terrified and shook for two hours. Her rescuers fed her, bathed her, and applied lotion to her nose, which was sunburned.

6   The story of Hokget's rescue is comical, but it is also touching. Human beings from around the world came together to save a dog. The vast majority of people who sent money to the Humane Society knew they would never personally see Hokget, never have their hands licked in gratitude. Saving the dog, as Pamela Burns suggested to me, was an act of pure altruism, and a marker of the remarkable capacity human beings have to empathize with the plight of others.

7   There are a series of disturbing questions, however. Eight years before Hokget was rescued, the same world that showed extraordinary compassion in the rescue of a dog sat on its hands as a million human beings were killed in Rwanda. . . . The twentieth century reveals a

Richard Walker/Honolulu Star-Advertiser

Hokget, the rescued dog, with Dr. Becky Rhoades, the veterinarian with the Kauai (Hawaii) Humane Society who examined her

shockingly long list of similar horrors that have been ignored by the world as they unfolded. . . . Why have successive generations of Americans—a people with extraordinary powers of compassion—done so little to halt suffering on such a large scale? . . .

8   There are many explanations for the discrepancy between our response to Hokget and our response to genocide. Some argue that Americans care little about foreign lives—but then what should we make about their willingness to spend thousands of dollars to rescue a dog, a foreign dog on a stateless ship in international waters? Well, perhaps Americans care more about pets than people? But that does not stand up to scrutiny, either. Hokget's rescue was remarkable, but there are countless stories about similar acts of compassion and generosity that people show toward their fellow human beings every day. No, there is something about genocide, about mass death in particular, that seems to trigger inaction.

9   I believe our inability to wrap our minds around large numbers is responsible for our apathy toward mass suffering. We are unconsciously biased in our moral judgment, in much the same way we are biased when we think about risk. Just as we are blasé about heart disease and lackadaisical about suicide, but terrified about psychopaths and terrorists, so also we make systematic errors in thinking about moral questions—especially those involving large numbers of people.

10   The philosopher Peter Singer once devised a dilemma that highlights a central contradiction in our moral reasoning. If you see a child drowning in a pond, and you know you can save the child without any risk to your own life—but you would ruin a fine pair of shoes worth two hundred dollars if you jumped into the water—would you save the child or save your shoes?[2] Most people react incredulously to the question; obviously, a child's life is worth more than a pair of shoes. If this is the case, Singer asked, why do large numbers of people hesitate to write a check for two hundred dollars to a reputable charity that could save the life of a child halfway around the world—when there are millions of such children who need our help? Even when people are absolutely certain their money will not be wasted and will be used to save a child's life, fewer people are willing to write the check than to leap into the pond.

11   Our moral responsibilities feel different in these situations even though Singer is absolutely right in arguing they are equivalent challenges; one feels immediate

and visceral, the other distant and abstract. We feel personally responsible for one child, whereas the other is one of millions who need help. Our responsibility feels diffused when it comes to children in distant places—there are many people who could write that check. But distance and diffusion of responsibility do not explain why we step forward in some cases—why did so many people come forward to save Hokget? Why did they write checks for a dog they would never meet? Why did they feel a single abandoned dog on a stateless ship was *their* problem?

12   I want to offer a disturbing idea. The reason human beings seem to care so little about mass suffering and death is precisely *because* the suffering is happening on a mass scale. The brain is simply not very good at grasping the implications of mass suffering. Americans would be far more likely to step forward if only a few people were suffering, or a single person were in pain. Hokget did not draw our sympathies because we care more about dogs than people; she drew our sympathies because she was a *single* dog lost on the biggest ocean in the world. If the hidden brain biases our perceptions about risk toward exotic threats, it shapes our compassion into a telescope. We are best able to respond when we are focused on a single victim. We don't feel twenty times sadder when we hear that twenty people have died in a disaster than when we hear that one person has died, even though the magnitude of the tragedy *is* twenty times larger. . . . We can certainly reach such a conclusion abstractly, in our conscious minds, but we cannot *feel it viscerally*, because that is the domain of the hidden brain, and the hidden brain is simply not calibrated to deal with the difference between a single death and a million deaths.

13   But the paradox does not end there. Even if ten deaths do not make us feel ten times as sad as a single death, shouldn't we feel five times as sad, or even at least twice as sad? There is disturbing evidence that shows that in many situations, not only do we not care twice as much about ten deaths as we do about one, but we may actually care *less*. I strongly suspect that if the *Insiko* had been carrying a hundred dogs, many people would have cared less about their fate than they did about Hokget. A hundred dogs do not have a single face,

We respond to mass suffering in much the same way we respond to most things in our lives. We fall back on rules of thumb, on feelings, on intuitions.

a single name, a single life story around which we can wrap our imaginations—and our compassion. . . .

14   The evidence for what I am going to call the telescope effect comes from a series of fascinating experiments.[3] At the University of Oregon, the psychologist Paul Slovic asked . . . groups of volunteers to imagine they were running a philanthropic foundation. Would they rather spend ten million dollars to save 10,000 lives from a disease that caused 15,000 deaths a year, or save 20,000 lives from a disease that killed 290,000 people a year? Overwhelmingly, volunteers preferred to spend money saving the ten thousand lives rather than the twenty thousand lives. Rather than tailor their investments to saving the largest number of lives, people sought to save the largest *proportion* of lives among the different groups of victims. An investment directed toward disease A could save two-thirds of the victims, whereas an investment directed at disease B could save "only" seven percent of the victims.

15   We respond to mass suffering in much the same way we respond to most things in our lives. We fall back on rules of thumb, on feelings, on intuitions. People who choose to spend money saving ten thousand lives rather than twenty thousand lives are not bad people. Rather, like those who spend thousands of dollars rescuing a single dog rather than directing the same amount of money to save a dozen dogs, they are merely allowing their hidden brain to guide them.

16   I have often wondered why the hidden brain displays a telescope effect when it comes to compassion. Evolutionary psychology tends to be an armchair sport, so please take my explanation for the paradox as one of several possible answers. The telescope effect may have arisen because evolution has built a powerful bias into us to preferentially love our kith and kin. It is absurd that we spend two hundred dollars on a birthday party for our son or our daughter when we could send the same money to a charity and save the life of a child halfway around the world. How can one child's birthday party mean more to us than another child's life? When we put it in those terms, we sound like terrible human beings. The paradox, as with the rescue of Hokget, is that our impulse springs from love, not callousness.

Evolution has built a fierce loyalty toward our children into the deepest strands of our psyche. Without the unthinking telescope effect in the unconscious mind, parents would not devote the immense time and effort it takes to raise children; generations of our ancestors would not have braved danger and cold, predators and hunger, to protect their young. The fact that you and I exist testifies to the utility of having a telescope in the brain that caused our ancestors to care intensely about the good of the few rather than the good of the many.

17   This telescope is activated when we hear a single cry for help—the child drowning in the pond, the puppy abandoned on an ocean. When we think of human suffering on a mass scale, our telescope does not work, because it has not been designed to work in such situations.

18   What makes evolutionary sense rarely makes moral sense. (One paradox of evolution is that ruthless natural selection has produced a species that recoils at the ruthlessness of natural selection.) Humans are the first and only species that is even aware of large-scale suffering taking place in distant lands; the moral telescope in our brain has not had a chance to evolve and catch up with our technological advances. When we are told about a faraway genocide, we can apply only our conscious mind to the challenge. We can reason, but we cannot feel the visceral compassion that is automatically triggered by the child who is drowning right before us. Our conscious minds can tell us that it is absurd to spend a boatload of money to save one life when the same money could be used to save ten—just as it can tell us it is absurd to be more worried about homicide than suicide. But in moral decision-making, as in many other domains of life where we are unaware of how unconscious biases influence us, it is the hidden brain that usually carries the day.

Editor's Notes

1. Lee, Chris, and George Butler. "Complex Response to Tankship *Insiko 1907.*" *Proceedings of the Marine Safety Council,* vol. 60, no. 1, Jan.-Mar. 2003, pp. 49–51.

2. Peter Singer has mentioned the story about the drowning child in a number of publications, including his book *The Life You Can Save,* Random House, 2009.

3. Slovic, Paul. "'If I Look at the Mass I Will Never Act': Psychic Numbing and Genocide." *Judgment and Decision Making,* vol. 2, no. 2, Apr. 2007, pp. 79–95.

Make connections: Thinking about — and feeling — others' suffering.

$\boxed{\text{REFLECT}}$

Moral dilemma experiments—scenarios that challenge our ability to decide what is the right thing to do—can be useful in helping us analyze our moral intuitions. Consider one of the moral dilemmas that follow, and then think about how scenarios like these help you think through a moral decision:

- Vedantam's scenario: Would you have sent money to support Hokget's rescue?

- Singer's dilemma: Would you be more likely to ruin expensive shoes to save a drowning child than to send the same amount of money to save an anonymous child halfway around the world?

- Slovic's dilemma: Would you rather spend $10 million to save 10,000 lives from a disease that caused 15,000 deaths a year or save 20,000 lives from a disease that killed 290,000 people a year?

- Sinking Lifeboat dilemma: Your cruise ship has sunk and you are in a dangerously overcrowded lifeboat. One person is gravely ill and not likely to survive the journey. Could you throw the sick person overboard in order to increase the chances of survival of the rest of the people in the lifeboat?

- Runaway Trolley dilemma: A runaway trolley is heading toward a group of people who can't be warned in time. Throwing a switch would shift the train from the track headed toward the group of people to another track on which one person is standing. Only you can divert the trolley by throwing the switch. What would you do?

Your instructor may ask you to post your thoughts on a class discussion board or to discuss them with other students in class. Use these questions to get started:

- What would you do if you were in the situation described in the dilemma? Briefly explain your choice. If you and your classmates are considering the same dilemma, discuss your various responses to it.

- How did you decide what was the right thing to do? For example, how did your feeling of closeness or identification with the potential victims or beneficiaries of your action influence you? How did the magnitude or the consequences of your action or inaction affect your choice?

- What is the value of participating in a thought experiment like this?

[ANALYZE]   ## Use the basic features.

A WELL-PRESENTED SUBJECT: USING AN ANECDOTE TO DRAMATIZE THE SUBJECT

In "The Telescope Effect," Vedantam begins his causal analysis with an *anecdote*, a story about an actual event. Vedantam could have summarized the anecdote about Hokget in a sentence or two:

> A dog was stranded on a ship adrift in the ocean, and after an outpouring of concern, the dog was ultimately rescued.

Instead, he gives readers a brief but dramatic *narrative* about how Hokget got stranded (in pars. 1–3) and rescued (par. 5).

ANALYZE & WRITE

Write a paragraph or two analyzing how Vedantam uses anecdote and examples to support his analysis:

1 Reread paragraphs 1–3 and 5, highlighting the details that help dramatize Hokget's story. What feelings do these narrative details evoke in you as a reader? Given his purpose, why do you think Vedantam would want to arouse readers' feelings at the beginning of his analysis?

2 Reread paragraph 7, contrasting the detail Vedantam provides in telling Hokget's story with the concise way in which he presents the example of the genocide in Rwanda. Why do you think Vedantam says so much about Hokget's story but so little about the Rwandan genocide?

AN EFFECTIVE RESPONSE: USING COUNTEREXAMPLES

A common strategy writers use to refute alternative causes or effects is to give counterexamples. A counterexample contradicts the causal explanation and shows that the analysis is flawed or at least incomplete. We can see this strategy at work in Vedantam's response to the cause proposed by Pamela Burns, the president of the Hawaiian Humane Society:

> Saving the dog, as Pamela Burns suggested to me, was an act of pure altruism, and a marker of the remarkable capacity human beings have to empathize with the plight of others.
>
> There are a series of disturbing questions, **however**. Eight years before Hokget was rescued, the same world that showed extraordinary compassion in the rescue of a dog sat on its hands as a million human beings were killed in Rwanda. (pars. 6–7)

Paraphrase of Burns's cause

Transition cueing refutation

Counterexample

ANALYZE & WRITE

Write a paragraph or two analyzing and assessing how Vedantam refutes philosopher Peter Singer's causal analysis:

1 Reread paragraphs 10 and 11. What example and counterexample does Singer use? How does Vedantam explain what Singer's thought experiment demonstrates?

2 Now examine paragraph 11, noting where Vedantam appears to accept Singer's causal analysis and also where he cues readers that he is about to question it. How does Vedantam use the counterexample of Hokget to refute Singer's explanation?

3 How effective is Vedantam's response? Does Singer's thought experiment raise interesting moral issues outside the context of Hokget?

Consider possible topics: Current events.

[RESPOND]

Following Vedantam, you could consider the causes of a current event. For example, think about why people voted a certain way in a recent election, or why a particular news story or YouTube video went viral. Or you could think about the causes of something ongoing, such as why the risk of auto accidents is higher among teenage drivers than among older motorists, or why the rate of teen pregnancy is the lowest it has been in twenty years.

The Writing Assignment

Write an essay about an important or intriguing subject, and speculate about why it might have occurred or what its effects might be. Make sure that it is an appropriate subject for a speculative cause-effect analysis and not simply a report of widely accepted causes or effects. Be sure to argue for the plausibility of certain causes or effects, while anticipating your readers' likely objections to your argument as well as their preferred alternative.

This Guide to Writing is designed to help you compose your own cause-effect analysis and apply what you have learned from reading other selections in the same genre. The Starting Points chart will help you find answers to questions you might have about composing an essay arguing for causes or effects. Use it to find the guidance you need, when you need it.

STARTING POINTS: ARGUING FOR CAUSES OR EFFECTS

How do I come up with a subject to write about?

- Consider possible topics: Popular culture. (p. 344)
- Consider possible topics: Social media and new technologies. (p. 349)
- Consider possible topics: Current events. (p. 355)
- Choose a subject to analyze. (pp. 358–59)
- Test Your Choice: Choosing a Topic (p. 359)

A Well-Presented Subject

How can I present my subject clearly and effectively?

- Assess the genre's basic features: A well-presented subject. (p. 333)
- A Well-Presented Subject: Reframing the Subject for Readers (p. 343)
- A Well-Presented Subject: Using an Anecdote to Dramatize the subject (p. 354)
- Present the subject to your readers. (p. 360)
- A Troubleshooting Guide: A Well-Presented Subject (p. 370)

A Well-Supported Cause-Effect Analysis

How do I come up with a list of possible causes to explore?

- Analyze possible causes or effects. (p. 361)
- Conduct research. (p. 362)

Writing a Draft

Guide to Reading
GUIDE TO WRITING
A Writer at Work
Reflection

357

A Well-Supported Cause-Effect Analysis

How can I convince my readers that the causes I identify are plausible?

- Assess the genre's basic features: A well-supported cause-effect analysis. (pp. 333–34)
- A Well-Supported Cause-Effect Analysis: Providing Compelling Evidence (p. 348)
- Analyze possible causes or effects. (p. 361)
- Conduct research. (p. 362)
- Cite a variety of sources to support your cause-effect analysis. (p. 363)
- Formulate a working thesis stating your preferred cause(s) or effect(s). (pp. 363–64)
- A Troubleshooting Guide: A Well-Supported Cause-Effect Analysis (p. 371)

An Effective Response to Objections and Alternative Causes or Effects

How do I deal with my readers' likely objections or alternative causes?

- Assess the genre's basic features: An effective response to objections and alternative causes or effects. (pp. 334–35)
- An Effective Response: Putting Aside Obvious Causes or Effects (p. 344)
- An Effective Response: Using Counterexamples (p. 355)
- Draft a response to objections readers are likely to raise. (pp. 364–65)
- Draft a response to the causes or effects your readers are likely to favor. (pp. 365–66)
- A Troubleshooting Guide: An Effective Response to Objections and Alternative Causes or Effects (p. 371)

A Clear, Logical Organization

How can I help my readers follow my argument?

- Assess the genre's basic features: A clear, logical organization. (pp. 335–36)
- Create an outline that will organize your cause-effect argument effectively for your readers. (pp. 366–67)
- A Troubleshooting Guide: A Clear, Logical Organization (p. 371)

Writing a Draft: Invention, Research, Planning, and Composing

The activities in this section will help you choose and research a subject as well as develop and organize your cause-effect analysis. Your writing in response to many of these activities can be used as part of your rough draft, which you will be able to improve after receiving feedback from your classmates and instructor. Do the activities in any order that makes sense to you (and your instructor), and return to them as needed as you revise.

⊞ Choose a subject to analyze.

When choosing a subject for a cause-effect analysis, keep in mind that it must be one that

- you can show exists (such as with examples or statistics);
- has no definitive, proven causes or effects;
- you can research, as necessary, in the time you have;
- will puzzle—or at least interest—you and your readers.

You may already have a subject in mind and a clear idea of the causes or effects you want to discuss. If so, go to Test Your Choice: Choosing a Topic (p. 359). If you do not, think about the readings: Like Pangelinan and Twenge, you could analyze the possible causes or effects of a relatively new social media outlet, digital game, or product, such as the effects on privacy of a digital assistant like Amazon's Alexa or a surprising reason that drones may overtake humans in package delivery. Like King, you could examine why a pop-culture phenomenon, such as K-pop, has taken off or what made the film *Get Out* such a hit. Or like Vedantam, you could examine the surprising causes or effects of a recent news story or a viral YouTube video. The subjects that follow may suggest a cause you can analyze effectively:

- What are the most or the least popular majors among undergraduates at your college? Why do you think these fields are so popular or unpopular?
- What were the underlying causes or effects of a recent surprising or controversial event at your college, such as a campus protest, the closing of an important student resource, or the firing of a coach or popular teacher?
- Why has hooking up replaced dating, or living together replaced getting married, for many young people? What are the results of such social changes?
- Why are people embracing or abandoning social media, getting or removing tattoos or body piercings, or becoming vegetarians or giving up vegetarianism?
- Why is collaborating with others or being able to communicate clearly in writing especially valuable in the workplace today?
- Why is the attitude that one should "work to live" more prevalent among young people than the attitude that one should "live to work"? How might such a change affect society for good or ill?

Writers often find it helpful to consider several possibilities before choosing a subject. Making a chart of subjects that interest you and their possible causes or effects can help you decide which subject is most promising.

Writing a Draft

Guide to Reading
GUIDE TO WRITING
A Writer at Work
Reflection

359

Subject	Possible Causes	Possible Effects
Bullying	Kids may bully because	Bullying may cause

Kids may bully because

- putting down others makes them feel powerful
- they are performing for their friends
- they are sociopaths without empathy for others

Bullying may cause

- other students to band together
- other students to withdraw socially

Procrastination

Students may procrastinate because

- they have better things to do
- they are lazy
- they are actually using time efficiently

Procrastination may cause

- students to do less well in school
- heightened feelings of anxiety
- learning to be undermined

TEST YOUR CHOICE

Choosing a Topic

After you have made a provisional choice, ask yourself the following questions:

- Do I know enough about the subject, or can I learn enough in the time I have?
- Do I know what causes or effects readers would be likely to think of, and do I have any ideas about what causes or effects might surprise and interest them?

To try out your choice of a subject and find out what other people think caused it, get together with two or three other students:

Presenters.   Take turns describing your subject.

Listeners.   Briefly tell each presenter what you think is a likely cause and why you think so.

Research Note

As you begin exploring the subject and its possible causes or effects, you may discover that you need to conduct research before you can go further. If so, skip ahead to the Conduct Research section (p. 362), and return to the activities here later on in the writing process. Alternatively, you may be able simply to make a research-to-do list for later.

▦ Present the subject to your readers.

Once you have made a preliminary choice of a subject and have some idea about its possible causes or effects, consider how you can present the subject in a way that will interest your readers. To do this, consider what you think about the subject and what your readers are likely to think. Use the questions and sentence strategies that follow to help you put your ideas in writing.

WAYS IN →

WHAT DO I THINK?	WHAT DO MY READERS THINK?
Why do I find this subject intriguing?	**What will readers know about the subject?**
▶ I think X is important because _____.	▶ My readers will probably be familiar with X because _____.
▶ X is changing the way we think/do _____.	▶ X is likely to be new to my readers, so I will need to show that it is widespread and serious by providing evidence such as _____.
▶ X has widespread effects, such as _____.	
▶ I know what the obvious causes/effects of X are, but I'm curious about the underlying cultural/psychological/ideological causes/effects because _____.	▶ My readers are likely to be curious about X because _____.
Which possible causes/effects will surprise readers or help them think about the subject in a constructive new way?	**How might readers' age, gender, work, or cultural background affect their thinking?**
▶ I think X will enable readers to understand that _____.	▶ Readers who are/have trait A may assume that X is caused by individuals who should have _____.
▶ Thinking about X will challenge readers to _____.	▶ Readers who are/have trait B are likely to think the causes/effects are part of a larger system that involves _____.
How do your subject and its causes/effects compare or contrast with other, more familiar subjects?	▶ Readers who have experienced C may think of X in terms of _____.
	What causes or effects are readers likely to know about?
▶ X is like Y in that they are both caused by _____.	▶ My readers will have heard of X from _____ [name source].
▶ Whereas Y is _____, X is _____.	▶ Readers' experience of D will lead them to assume that X was caused by _____.

Writing a Draft

Guide to Reading
GUIDE TO WRITING
A Writer at Work
Reflection

361

▦ Analyze possible causes or effects.

The following activity will help you analyze an array of possible causes or effects and decide which ones you could use in your essay. Remember that cause-effect analysis essays often speculate about several possible causes or effects but usually also argue for an especially interesting or plausible cause or effect.

WAYS IN

HOW CAN I ANALYZE POSSIBLE CAUSES OR EFFECTS?

1. List the possible causes or effects you've identified so far—ones that your readers are likely to think of, that your classmates suggested, that you found while doing research, and that you thought of on your own.

2. Write a few sentences about each cause or effect, answering questions like these:

   ▶ Why do my readers think _____ could have caused X?

   ▶ Why do I think _____ could have caused X?

   ▶ Is _____ necessary to bring about X; that is, could X not happen without _____? Is X sufficient — enough in itself — to cause _____?

   ▶ If X is one of several contributing factors, what role does it play? For example, is it a minor or a major cause, an obvious or a hidden cause, a triggering cause (the one that got the cause-effect process started), or a continuing cause (the one that keeps it going)?

   ▶ What kinds of evidence could I use to argue in favor of or against X? (If you don't already have supporting evidence, make a research-to-do note indicating what kind of evidence you need and where you might possibly find it.)

3. Classify the causes or effects you plan to discuss in your essay into three categories: plausible cause(s)/effect(s) you want to argue for, causes/effects your readers may favor that you can **CONCEDE** but put aside as obvious or minor, and causes/effects you should **REFUTE** because your readers are likely to think they are important.

Plausible cause(s)/ effect(s) to argue for	Readers' causes/effects to concede/put aside	Readers' causes/effects to refute

Turn to A Writer at Work on pp. 372–74 to see how Clayton Pangelinan used this activity to analyze his list of possible causes.

Remember that the only category you must include in your essay is the first: One or more causes or effects you will argue played a major, and perhaps surprising, role.

⊞ Conduct research.

If you are analyzing a cause that others have written about, try searching for articles or books on your topic. Enter keywords or phrases related to your cause/effect or subject into the search box of

To learn more about searching a database, finding government documents, or annotating a working bibliography, see Chapter 17.

- an all-purpose database, such as Academic OneFile (InfoTrac) or Academic Search Complete (EBSCOhost), to find relevant articles in magazines and journals;
- a database like Lexis/Nexis to find articles in newspapers;
- a search engine like Google to find relevant Web sites, blogs, podcasts, and discussion lists;
- your library's catalog, to find books and other resources on your topic.

To locate numerical or statistical evidence or to draw graphs or tables, try the following sites:

- USA.gov, the U.S. government's official Web portal, for information about the federal government
- Library of Congress page on State Government Information, loc.gov/rr/news/stategov/stategov.html; follow the links for information on state and local government
- U.S. Census Bureau, census.gov, especially the Quick Facts and Fact Finder pages and the Statistical Abstracts for various years, for demographic information
- The Centers for Disease Control and Prevention, cdc.gov, especially the FastStats pages, for statistics about diseases and illnesses
- National Center for Education Statistics, nces.ed.gov, for reports, such as *America's Youth: Transitions to Adulthood*
- Pew Research Center, pewresearch.org, for research data and public opinion polling data
- Gallup, gallup.com, or Rasmussen Reports, rasmussenreports.com, for public opinion polling data

Consider . . .
An annotated working bibliography can help you keep track of multiple sources.

Bookmark or keep a record of the URLs of promising sites. If you find useful information, you may want to download or copy it to use in your essay. When they are available, download PDF files rather than HTML files because the PDFs are more likely to include visuals, such as graphs and charts. If you copy and paste relevant information from sources into your notes, be careful to distinguish all source material from your own ideas and to record source information so you can cite and document any sources you use, including graphics.

Another option is to conduct field research and to use personal experience. Field research, such as interviews, surveys, and direct observation, can offer statistical data and information about public opinion. Your own experience may also provide anecdotal evidence that might interest readers.

Writing a Draft

Guide to Reading
▶ **GUIDE TO WRITING**
A Writer at Work
Reflection

363

⊞ Cite a variety of sources to support your cause-effect analysis.

Writers of cause-effect analyses often rely on evidence from experts to support some causes or effects and refute others. For college assignments, your instructor may require that certain kinds of sources be used and may even specify a minimum number of sources. But for most writing situations, you have to decide whether your sources are appropriate and sufficient. Using too few sources or sources that are too narrow in scope can undercut the effectiveness of your analysis. Consequently, it is important to offer information from a number of sources and from sources that reflect a variety of areas of expertise. The fact that student Clayton Pangelinan uses three stories of intimate social media sharing from a single book by Hal Niedzviecki in his essay "#socialnetworking: Why It's *Really* So Popular" (pp. 336–40) could make readers question Pangelinan's argument if they were not already familiar with similar examples from their own experience of social media.

Pangelinan does use a number of sources beyond Niedzviecki's book to support his causal analysis. Because he is writing for a class, Pangelinan includes both in-text citations and a list of works cited. Like Vedantam, he uses *signal phrases* (the author's name and an appropriate verb, plus the author's background where context is needed) and cites sources his readers are likely to find credible, such as the Pew Research Center and an academic article. The number of sources, their authority, and their variety lend credibility to Pangelinan's speculations.

As you determine how many and what kinds of sources to cite in your essay, ask yourself questions like these:

- Are my sources **appropriate**—will my audience accept them as authoritative?
- Are my sources **sufficient**—do I have enough sources, and do they reflect a variety of areas of expertise?
- Do I paraphrase or summarize my sources accurately, without borrowing too much of the source's language or sentence structures?
- Do I use signal phrases to provide the credentials of my sources?

⊞ Formulate a working thesis stating your preferred cause(s) or effect(s).

Once you have identified one or more interesting and plausible causes or effects that could be the focus of your analysis, try drafting a working thesis. (Some writers may want to skip this activity and return to it after they have developed their analysis and completed some research.)

WAYS IN

HOW CAN I ASSERT MY THESIS?

To get an idea about how you might formulate your thesis, take a look at the thesis statements from the reading selections you've studied in this chapter.

> The fact *that* social networking is popular is well established. The question is *why* is it so popular? . . . A better answer . . . is that social media offer people a way to satisfy their desire to connect with others and maybe also be "world-famous for fifteen minutes" (as Andy Warhol supposedly remarked). (Pangelinan, par. 2)

> The mythic horror movie, like the sick joke, has a dirty job to do. It deliberately appeals to all that is worst in us. It is morbidity unchained, our most base instincts let free, our nastiest fantasies realized . . . and it all happens, fittingly enough, in the dark. (King, par. 11)

> I want to offer a disturbing idea. The reason human beings seem to care so little about mass suffering and death is precisely *because* the suffering is happening on a mass scale. The brain is simply not very good at grasping the implications of mass suffering. (Vedantam, par. 12)

Now draft your own thesis statement, using the examples from the readings or the sentence strategies that follow as a jumping-off point. You can put your ideas into your own words now or when you revise:

▶ The reasons for X may surprise you, such as _____, _____, and _____ .

▶ The effects of X may be alarming, but they are clear: _____ .

▶ X plays a disturbing role in our lives/our families/our communities/our workplaces: It does/is/provides _____ .

▶ For many years, Group A has believed that _____ . Now there is research supporting this claim, but not for the reasons you may think. It's not _____ that has been causing this phenomenon but _____ .

▦ Draft a response to objections readers are likely to raise.

The following activity will help you respond to possible objections your readers might raise. Start by analyzing the reasons your readers object to your cause or effect, and then consider ways you might respond to their objections.

WAYS IN

HOW CAN I RESPOND EFFECTIVELY TO MY READERS' OBJECTIONS?

1. For each of your preferred causes or effects, consider the questions your readers might raise. Some possibilities include the following:

   ▶ Even if you can prove that X and Y increased/decreased at the same time, how do you know X actually caused Y?

Writing a Draft

Guide to Reading
▶ **GUIDE TO WRITING**
A Writer at Work
Reflection

365

> ▸ Even if you can prove that Y occurred after X, how do you know X actually caused Y?

> ▸ Could X and Y both have been caused by something else altogether?

> ▸ X seems to have been an effect of Y, but was it really a major effect or just one of many insignificant results?

2. Use the following sentence strategies or language of your own to respond to one of these objections:

> ▸ The objection that Y may result from things other than X may be true. But there is strong evidence showing that X played a central role by ....

> ▸ Researchers studying .... have shown a causal connection between X and Y. They claim that .... [quote/paraphrase/summarize information from source] (cite source).

> ▸ A large number of people have been polled on this question, and it appears that X was an important factor in their decision to ....

Research Note

You may need to conduct research to find evidence to support your refutation. If so, revisit the sections Conduct Research (p. 362) and Cite a Variety of Sources to Support Your Cause-Effect Analysis (p. 363).

▦ Draft a response to the causes or effects your readers are likely to favor.

In the preceding activity, you analyzed and drafted a response to the objections your readers are likely to raise. The next activity will help you respond to your readers' preferred causes or effects.

HOW CAN I RESPOND TO MY READERS' PREFERRED CAUSES OR EFFECTS?

WAYS IN

- **Choose an alternative cause or effect, and summarize it.** Be sure to summarize it accurately and fairly. Do not commit the straw man fallacy of knocking down something that no one really takes seriously.

- **Decide whether you can REFUTE the alternative cause or effect or whether you need to CONCEDE it.** Refute the alternative cause or effect if you can show that it lacks credible support or if the underlying reasoning is flawed. Concede it either by pointing out that the cause or effect is obvious and setting it aside or by showing that it plays a less important role than the cause or effect you are championing. Try the following sentence strategies, or use language of your own.

(continued)

To Refute

Lacks Credible Support

▶ Just because Y caused _____ does not mean that it caused _____ [a similar subject]. Here's why: _____.

▶ The scenario/anecdote others sometimes use to explain why X occurred certainly helps dramatize _____, but it doesn't really explain why X happened.

▶ If X is the result of Y, then one would expect _____ to happen, too, but it hasn't/the opposite has happened.

Reasoning Is Flawed

Mistakes correlation for causation.

▶ Some argue that Y caused X because X and Y occurred/began rising sharply at the same time. But, in fact, this is merely a coincidence/both were caused by something else altogether.

Mistakes chronology for causation.

▶ Just because Y occurred before/after X doesn't prove that X caused/resulted from Y.

▶ Proponents of _____ have not provided convincing evidence to show how Y could have caused X.

To Concede

Set Aside a Well-Known Cause

▶ An obvious explanation is _____. But if we dig deeper, we find that _____.

▶ Typical explanations include _____ and _____, but let's consider a totally different possibility: _____.

Show That an Alternative Cause Is Minor

▶ _____ is one of the answers, but it may not play as central a role as most people think it does.

▶ _____ may have kept the process going, but X was the trigger: Without it, Y would never have gotten started.

▶ _____ may have been a factor at the outset, getting the process started, but what keeps it going is X.

▦ Create an outline that will organize your cause-effect argument effectively for your readers.

Whether you have rough notes or a complete draft, making an outline of what you have written can help you organize your essay effectively for your audience. A cause-effect argument may contain as many as four basic parts:

1. a presentation of the subject
2. plausible causes/effects, logically sequenced

Writing a Draft

Guide to Reading
GUIDE TO WRITING
A Writer at Work
Reflection

367

3. convincing support for each cause or effect

4. a consideration of readers' questions, objections, and alternative causes or effects

Compare the possible outlines that follow to see how you might organize your essay depending on whether your readers primarily agree with you—or not.

If your readers are *not* likely to favor any alternatives, you may want to anticipate and respond to any possible objections to your causes or effects.	If you think that readers *are* likely to favor alternatives, you may want to concede or refute them before offering your own cause or effect.
I. **Present the subject:** Demonstrate that the subject exists and that its causes/effects are uncertain.	I. **Present the subject:** Demonstrate that the subject exists and that its causes/effects are uncertain.
II. **Provide a thesis and forecasting statement:** Announce the causes/effects you will offer.	II. **Provide a thesis statement:** Acknowledge alternative causes/effects readers are likely to know about.
III. **Present first cause/effect with supporting evidence and refutation of objection.**	III. **Concede first alternative cause/effect to set it aside.**
IV. **Present second cause/effect with supporting evidence and refutation of objection (and so on).**	IV. **Refutate second alternative cause/effect with supporting evidence.**
V. **Conclude:** Reassert judgment.	V. **Present writer's preferred cause/effect with supporting evidence.**
	VI. **Refute objection(s).**
	VII. **Conclude:** Reassert judgment based on shared criteria.

Whatever organizational strategy you adopt, do not hesitate to change your outline as necessary while drafting and revising. For instance, you might find it more effective to begin with your own preferred cause or effect and to hold back on presenting unacceptable alternatives until you've made the case you think is most plausible and interesting. The purpose of an outline is to identify the basic components of your analysis and to help you organize them effectively, not to lock you into a particular structure.

For more on outlining, see Chapters 11 and 12.

Write the opening sentences.

Review what you have written to see if you have something that would help you present the subject of your cause-effect argument effectively for your audience or try out one or two of these opening strategies:

*Demonstrate the **relevance** of your topic by putting it in context for your reader:*

> Complain about problems in a *tweet* over Twitter; add a *friend*, virtually *poke* each other, and *like* friends' postings and ramblings on Facebook; send images and videos to each other using Snapchat; capture a *selfie* with Instagram, edit it, add hashtags, and share it for your friends to see and comment on: Social networking is only a click away. . . . (Pangelinan, par. 1)

Begin with a **surprising assertion** *that would help grab your readers' attention:*

> I think that we're all mentally ill; those of us outside the asylums only hide it a little better—and maybe not all that much better, after all. (King, par. 1)

Begin with a **scenario** *or an* **anecdote**:

> The *Insiko 1907* was a tramp tanker that roamed the Pacific Ocean. Its twelve-man Taiwanese crew hunted the seas for fishing fleets in need of fuel; the *Insiko* had a cargo of tens of thousands of gallons of diesel. (Vedantam, par. 1)

Describe the writer's **authority** *to establish credibility*:

> I've been researching generational differences for 25 years, starting when I was a 22-year-old doctoral student in psychology. . . . In all my analyses of generational data—some reaching back to the 1930s—I had never seen anything like it. (Twenge, par. 1)

Draft your cause-effect argument.

By this point, you have done a lot of writing to

- devise a well-presented subject and analyze its causes or effects;
- support your preferred causes or effects with evidence your readers will find persuasive;
- refute or concede objections and alternative causes or effects;
- organize your ideas to make them clear, logical, and effective for readers.

Now stitch that material together to create a draft. The next two parts of this Guide to Writing will help you evaluate and improve your draft.

Evaluating the Draft: Using Peer Review

Did you know?

Peer review can be especially helpful when responses suggest how the writer can use a genre's basic features and strategies.

Your instructor may arrange a peer review session in class or online, where you can exchange drafts with your classmates and give one another a thoughtful critical reading, pointing out what works well and suggesting ways to improve the draft. A good critical reading does three things:

1. It lets the writer know how well the reader understands the cause-effect analysis.
2. It praises what works best.
3. It indicates where the draft could be improved and makes suggestions for how to improve it.

One strategy for evaluating a draft is to use the basic features of the cause-effect analysis as a guide. Also be sure to respond to any concerns the writer has shared with you.

Evaluating the Draft

Guide to Reading
GUIDE TO WRITING
A Writer at Work
Reflection

369

A PEER REVIEW GUIDE

A Well-Presented Subject

> How effectively does the writer present the subject?

Summarize: Tell the writer what you understand the subject to be and why he or she thinks it is important and worth analyzing.

Praise: Give an example of something in the draft that you think will especially interest the intended readers and help them understand the subject.

Critique: Tell the writer if you have any confusion or uncertainty about the subject. What further explanation, examples, or statistics do you need to understand it better? If you can think of a more interesting way to present the subject, share your ideas with the writer.

A Well-Supported Cause-Effect Analysis

> How plausible are the proposed causes or effects, and how well does the writer support the cause-effect analysis?

Summary: Identify the possible causes or effects that the writer argues are the most plausible and interesting.

Praise: Tell the writer which cause or effect seems most convincing. Point to any support (such as a particular example, a statistic, a research study, or a graph) that you think is especially strong.

Critique: Tell the writer if any of the causes or effects seem too obvious or minor, and if you think an important cause or effect has been left out. Where the support seems lacking or unconvincing, explain what is missing or seems wrong. If the reasoning seems flawed, what makes you think so?

An Effective Response to Objections and Alternative Causes or Effects

> How effectively does the writer respond to readers' objections and alternative causes or effects?

Summary: Identify the objections or alternative causes or effects to which the writer responds.

Praise: Point out any response you think is especially effective, and tell the writer what makes you think so. For example, indicate where the support is especially credible and convincing.

Critique: Point to any objections or alternative causes or effects that the writer could have responded to more effectively, and suggest how the response could be improved. Also indicate if the writer has overlooked any serious objections.

(continued)

A Clear, Logical Organization

> How clear and logical is the cause-effect analysis?

Summary: Underline the thesis statement and topic sentences.

Praise: Give an example of where the essay succeeds in being especially clear and easy to follow — for example, in its overall organization, its use of key terms and transitions, or its use of visuals.

Critique: Point to any passages where the writing could be clearer, where topic sentences or transitions could be added, or where key terms could be repeated to make the essay easier to follow. Try suggesting a better beginning or a more effective ending.

Improving the Draft: Revising, Editing, and Proofreading

Did you know?

Many great writers, from Vladimir Nabokov to Anne Lamott, believe that revision is the most important part of the writing process.

Start improving your draft by reflecting on what you have written thus far:

- Review critical reading comments from your classmates, instructor, or writing center tutor: What problems do readers identify?
- Consider your invention writing: What else should you consider?
- Review your draft: What else can you do to present your cause-effect analysis more compellingly?

Revise your draft.

If your readers are having difficulty with your draft, or if you think there is room for improvement, try some of the strategies listed in the Troubleshooting Guide that follows. They can help you fine-tune your presentation of the genre's basic features.

A TROUBLESHOOTING GUIDE

A Well-Presented Subject

> My readers don't understand the subject or see why it is important.

- Reconsider what your readers already know, and provide additional background if necessary.
- Try providing examples or an anecdote to interest readers in the subject.
- Quote authorities and explain research findings, including statistics, to demonstrate the subject's importance — that it is widespread and significant.
- Use visuals — graphs, tables, photographs, or screen shots — to make the subject more vivid.
- Review your research to see if you can add anything to help clarify the subject for your readers, or do some additional research.
- Pose the subject directly or indirectly as a *why* question, and then answer it.

A Well-Supported Cause-Effect Analysis

> My readers don't understand which of the causes or effects I am arguing are the most plausible.

- Be explicit about which causes or effects are the ones you think are most plausible, and why you think so.
- Use a thesis and forecasting statement followed by topic sentences with key terms to announce your main causes or effects.

> My readers do not find my cause-effect argument convincing.

- Whenever possible, explain how the cause-effect relationship works, backing up your explanation with appropriate support.
- Cite more credible experts, being sure to give their credentials.
- Cite research studies and statistics rather than limiting yourself to examples and anecdotes.
- Review your sources to make sure they are varied, or do additional focused research to fill in where your analysis is weak.
- Make sure your sources are cited properly.

An Effective Response to Objections and Alternative Causes or Effects

> My readers do not think my responses are effective.

- Respond directly to criticism of your reasoning by showing that you are not mistaking correlation or chronology for causation.
- Demonstrate that you understand the complexity of the cause-effect relationship you are analyzing — for example, by indicating how your cause relates to other contributing causes.
- If your readers think you have overlooked an objection, consider it seriously and do further research to respond to it if necessary.

A Clear, Logical Organization

> My readers think my analysis is not clear or logical.

- If readers have difficulty finding the thesis statement or topic sentences, consider revising them.
- Add a forecasting statement early in the essay to help guide readers.
- Review your use of transitions, and consider adding transitions to make the logical relationships among sentences and paragraphs clear to readers.
- Refer to visuals explicitly (for example, by adding the direction, "see fig. 1"), and include a caption tying each visual to the text discussion.
- Outline your essay to review its structure, and move, add, or delete sections as necessary to strengthen coherence.

Edit and proofread your final draft.

Editing means making changes to the text to ensure that it follows the conventions of style, grammar, spelling, and mechanics appropriate to the rhetorical situation. **Proofreading** involves checking to make sure the text follows these conventions and that no words are repeated or omitted. You have probably done some editing and proofreading while composing and improving your draft, but it is always good practice to edit and proofread a draft after you have revised it and before you submit it.

Most writers get the best results by leaving time—even just an hour or two— between the stages of revising, editing, and proofreading, so that they can return to their writing project with fresh eyes. When possible, enlist a friend or classmate to proofread the final draft of your writing projects. When that is not possible, proofread from the last line to the first, to avoid seeing what you expect to find rather than what is actually on the page (or screen).

As rhetorical situations change, so, too, do the conventions or expectations readers bring to the text. For example, whereas e-mail messages to friends are usually quite informal, filled with abbreviations, emojis, and sentence fragments, final drafts of writing projects for college classes or the workplace are expected to follow a more formal set of conventions concerning clarity, style, grammar, and punctuation.

We recommend that you make a list of the problems your instructors frequently point out in your writing, then use that list to guide your editing and proofreading. A Guide to Editing and Proofreading (at the end of this text) provides a checklist of the most common problems writers face. For issues that go beyond those on this list, consult a handbook* or search for advice online at sites like the Purdue Online Writing Lab (owl.english.purdue.edu) or Grammarly (grammarly.com). For practice identifying and correcting errors, try the activities in LearningCurve, a gamelike adaptive quizzing program available on LaunchPad for *The St. Martin's Guide to Writing*. The less well you do on activities in one topic area, the more LearningCurve focuses on it; the better you do, the more challenging the questions become.

> **A Note on Grammar and Spelling Checkers**
>
> Spelling checkers cannot catch misspellings that are themselves words, such as *to* for *too*, and grammar checkers miss problems, give faulty advice, and even flag correct items as wrong. Use these tools as a second line of defense after your own (and, ideally, another reader's) proofreading efforts.

A WRITER AT WORK

Clayton Pangelinan's Analysis of Possible Causes

Using the Ways In activity "How can I analyze possible causes or effects?" on p. 361, Clayton Pangelinan sorted through the notes he had made doing preliminary research for his essay "#socialnetworking: Why It's *Really* So Popular" (pp. 336–40).

---

* The full version of *The St. Martin's Guide to Writing* includes a handbook.

He began with the vague idea of examining the popularity of social networking, which he could establish easily with information he found from the Pew Research Center—a solid source. The Pew Research Center also offered reasons for the popularity of social media based on polling; its research suggested that staying in touch with friends and family and connecting with people with shared interests were the main reasons people use social media. But Pangelinan thought these reasons seemed too obvious and wanted to delve more deeply.

Following is the list of possible causes and a few sentences he wrote analyzing each cause. Notice that in a few cases he refers to research he has already found.

Possible Causes	Analysis of Causes
1. We have the technology for it now.	The Pew Research Center shows how social networking increased hugely in all age groups in 2005–6. We had to have Web 2.0 to create interactive use; without the technology, it simply couldn't have existed. So I will establish that the increase exists with a useful chart from Pew, and then I'll examine why social media is the form interactive behavior has taken.
2. People can connect with the lives and activities of friends and family.	The phone increased our connections, and e-mail did too, but not until people joined social media did they have a chance to be in touch daily—sometimes hourly—with everyone they cared about all at once. This is an obvious cause. You can share what you want with friends, acquaintances, and followers, and learn about their lives, too. It's interactive rather than read-only. (Research-to-do note: Find Matthew Lieberman's article recommended by my professor about why our brains are "wired to connect.")
3. People can shape how their lives look and how other people see them.	When people post to social media, they can revise what they write to create the impression they want. However, some people post really spontaneously, so I don't know whether this is a valid cause. Interview friends? This would be a more hidden cause.
4. People can reach more than one person at a time.	You have a larger audience when you post to social media. It's not like writing a letter or making a phone call—you can reach countless people all at once. This is a continuing cause. Appeals to people who want attention? Narcissists?
5. People can satisfy a desire for celebrity.	Could use Andy Warhol's 15 minutes of fame. Find examples of people who are clearly posting so they will get attention (Padme). Other examples?
6. It is a way to keep current in the world.	Can be a way to be "up" on current events without having to read newspapers, magazines, and books—too time-consuming? Twitter, for example, provides snippets of news that keep you up to date on what's happening right now. You can choose your own topics—politics, movies, animal rights, climate change, cartoons—it's all out there—and get different perspectives on the same sites. Some sites attract only one kind of perspective, though, and that might be a drawback—but keeping current is still a cause.

Pangelinan decided he couldn't use all these causes because of the time and space limits for his essay, so he decided to concentrate on humans' need for connection, their curiosity about other people's lives, and the desire to be the center of attention. He began with cause 1 because it was obvious that the technology had to have reached a certain point to allow social networking. He merged causes 2 and 3 because they were related and he knew these causes were valid from his own experience; he was sure he could find good examples to support them. He then developed cause 4 into a significant portion of his essay, folding in cause 5 because you can't get fame without an audience. *Narcissism* is a strong word that would generate strong opinions, and he thought some people might find it surprising. Finally, he dropped cause 6 altogether because he could write a whole essay just on that cause, and he found causes 2 through 5 more interesting.

REFLECTION

The benefit of reflection is proven and important: It helps consolidate what you have learned so that you can remember and apply it well beyond this class. That is why we have included questions and comments in the margins and at the end of this chapter: to stimulate your thinking about reviews, your rhetorical situation, and the choices you make as a writer.

Reflecting on Reading and Writing a Cause-Effect Analysis

To reflect on your experience reading cause-effect analysis essays and writing one of your own, try writing a blog post, a letter to your instructor, or an e-mail message to a student who will take this course next term that draws on what you have learned. Use any of these writing prompts that seem productive:

- Explain how your purpose and audience influenced *one* of your decisions as a writer, such as how you explained the subject, how you supported your preferred causes or effects, or how you responded to readers' likely objections.

- Discuss what you learned about yourself as a writer in the process of writing this argument. For example, what part of the process did you find most challenging? Did you try anything new, like getting a critical reading of your draft or re-envisioning your essay as a proposal or a presentation?

Reflecting on Your Composing Process

Guide to Reading
Guide to Writing
A Writer at Work
▶ **REFLECTION**

375

- If you were to give advice to a friend who was about to write a cause-effect argument, what would you say?

- Which of the readings in this chapter influenced your essay? Explain the influence, citing specific examples from your essay and the reading.

- If you got good advice from a critical reader, explain exactly how the person helped you—perhaps by questioning your use of support, your choice of medium, your use of visuals, the way you began or ended your essay, or the kinds of sources you used.

Reflecting on Your Composing Process

Thinking about your process for writing a cause-effect analysis can be useful in helping you decide what works best for you as a writer. Using one or more of the following questions as a starting point, write a paragraph or two about your composing process:

- How did you go about choosing a subject? Did you try out a few possibilities before making a final decision?

- Explain how peer review helped you—perhaps by helping you choose the most convincing causes or effects to develop or helping you strengthen your refutation of alternative causes or effects.

- What was the hardest part of the process for you—convincing readers that the subject is important, thinking of plausible causes or effects that are not obvious, finding evidence to make your claim plausible, responding to alternative causes or effects, or something else?

- How satisfied are you with the process you used? If you could go back in time, what would you have done differently? If you could continue working on your review, what would you like to do?

10

Analyzing Stories

Stories have a special place in most cultures. They can lead us to look at others with sensitivity and, for a brief time, to see the world through another person's eyes. They can also lead us to see ourselves differently, to gain insight into our innermost feelings and thoughts. Although writing about stories is an important academic kind of discourse, many people who are not in school enjoy discussing stories and writing about how a story resonates in their lives. That is why book clubs, reading groups, and online discussion forums are so popular. Good stories tend to be enigmatic in that they usually do not reveal themselves fully on first reading. So it can be enjoyable and enlightening to analyze stories and discuss them with other readers. Even very short stories can elicit fascinating analyses. For example, Ernest Hemingway wrote this six-word story, which he reportedly claimed was his best work:

For sale: baby shoes, never worn.

| PRACTICING THE GENRE |

Analyzing a Story Collaboratively

Sharing the experience of reading stories with others exposes us to different ways of interpreting and responding to them — expanding our openness to new perspectives, deepening our insight, and enhancing our pleasure. To benefit from this kind of discussion with others, work together with one or two other students to analyze Hemingway's ultrabrief story. Here are some guidelines to follow:

Part 1.   Discuss the story, using these questions to get started:

- It reads like an ad, but who would try to sell baby shoes, and why? What is the likely relationship between the person trying to sell the shoes and the baby for whom the shoes were originally bought?
- Who could be a potential buyer for the shoes?
- Where and when was the ad written? (In a country where there are land mines? In a time of severe economic depression?)
- Why is the story so short? What could its brevity say about the underlying emotion? What could the fact that the story is written in the form of an advertisement suggest about commercialism?

Part 2.   After you have discussed the story for half of the time allotted for this activity, reflect on the process of analyzing the story in your group:

- Before you began, what were your expectations of how the group would work together? For example, did you think your group should or would agree on one "right answer" to the questions, or did you expect significant disagreement? What actually happened once you began to discuss the story?
- How did the discussion affect your attitude about the story or about the process of analyzing stories? What, if anything, did you learn?

Your instructor may ask you to write about what you learned and to present your conclusions to the rest of the class.

Take a moment . . .

What are the benefits and drawbacks of working with others to analyze a story? Do you prefer to work alone or with others?

In this chapter, we ask you to write an analysis of a story. Analyzing the selections in the Guide to Reading that follows will help you learn the basic features and strategies writers typically use when writing about stories. The readings, as well as the questions and discussion surrounding them, will help you consider strategies you might want to try out when writing your own analysis.

Analyzing Essays That Analyze Stories

As you read the essays in this chapter, you will see how two students have analyzed the short story "The Use of Force" by William Carlos Williams (pp. 414–16).

- Iris Lee interprets the story through the lens of the doctor's Hippocratic Oath to "do no harm" (pp. 382–85).
- Isabella Wright interprets the story as a breaking away from convention (pp. 386–88).

Examining how these writers present an arguable thesis about the story, support this thesis, and guide readers through their argument will help you write an insightful literary analysis of your own. The example passages in the sections that follow are drawn from these two essays.

Determine the writer's purpose and audience.

When reading the short story analysis essays that appear in this chapter, ask yourself what the writer's main purpose is and what he or she assumes about the reader:

The writer's main purpose may be to	The writer wants readers to react by
■ illuminate the story	■ thinking about the story in greater depth
■ change or expand the way readers understand the story	■ accepting the writer's interpretation
■ impress readers with the writer's insight and close reading	■ learning something about the story that they hadn't known or expected

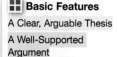
Basic Features
A Clear, Arguable Thesis
A Well-Supported Argument
A Clear, Logical Organization

Assess the genre's basic features.

As you read the essays that analyze stories in this chapter, you will see how different writers incorporate the basic features of the genre. The following discussions of these features include examples from the essays as well as sentence strategies you can experiment with later, as you write your own analysis of a story.

Analyzing Essays That Analyze Stories

GUIDE TO READING
Guide to Writing
A Writer at Work
Reflection

379

A CLEAR, ARGUABLE THESIS

Read first to find the thesis statement, *which is often one or two sentences long but can run to several paragraphs.* A good thesis statement in an essay analyzing a story

- asserts the main idea or claim;

- is arguable, not a simple statement of fact (for example, "'The Use of Force' tells the story of a doctor's visit to a sick little girl") or an obvious conclusion (for example, "The doctor grows frustrated by the little girl's behavior");

- is appropriately qualified, not overgeneralized or exaggerated (for example, "The behavior of the doctor at the center of 'The Use of Force' shows that no medical professional can be trusted");

- is clearly stated, not vague or ambiguous.

Often, the thesis is part of an introduction that is at least a paragraph in length. In most cases, this introduction identifies the story being analyzed by giving the title and author, and it may also provide some historical, biographical, or cultural context. In effective writing, the thesis and other sentences in the opening paragraph (or paragraphs) introduce *key terms* for ideas that are echoed and further developed later in the essay. In this way, the introductory sentences and thesis *forecast* how the argument will be developed.

Inexperienced writers are sometimes afraid to ruin the surprise by forecasting their argument at the beginning of their essays. But explicit forecasting is a convention of literary analysis, similar in purpose to the abstract that precedes many articles in academic journals.

Take a look at Iris Lee's lead-up to the thesis in her essay on "The Use of Force." In it, she introduces key terms that are *repeated* (exactly, closely, or through synonyms) and underscored in her thesis:

> The Hippocratic Oath binds doctors to practice ethically and, above all, to "do no harm." The doctor narrating William Carlos Williams's short story "The Use of Force" comes dangerously close to breaking that oath, yet ironically is able to justify his actions by invoking his professional image and the pretense of preserving his patient's well-being. As an account of a professional doing harm under the pretense of healing, the story uncovers how a doctor can take advantage of the intimate nature of his work and his professional status to overstep common forms of conduct, to the extent that his actions actually hurt rather than help a patient. In this way, the doctor-narrator actually performs a valuable service by warning readers, indirectly through his story, that blindly trusting members of his profession can have negative consequences. (par. 1)

Key terms

Thesis

Sometimes, the thesis of a literary analysis contradicts or complicates a surface reading of a work. Look for sentence strategies like this one:

▶ A common/superficial reading of X [title or author] is that .... [surface reading], but in fact .... [insert your own interpretation].

Consider . . .

Why do you think that surprising readers by withholding the thesis is frowned upon in literary analysis and other types of academic writing?

In Isabella Wright's essay on "The Use of Force," the surface reading actually appears in the sentences leading up to the thesis. A transition introduces the contradiction/complication that constitutes the thesis:

Surface reading

By any reasonable standards, the story of a doctor prying a little girl's mouth open as she screams in pain and fear should leave readers feeling nothing but horror and

Transition

disgust at the doctor's actions. William Carlos Williams's story "The Use of Force" is surprising in that it does not completely condemn the doctor for doing just that. Instead,

Contradiction/
complication

through his actions and words (uttered or thought), readers are able to see the freeing, transformative power of breaking with social conventions. (par. 1)

A WELL-SUPPORTED ARGUMENT

Consider how the writer provides support for the argument. Because essays analyzing stories usually present ideas that are not obvious and that readers may disagree with, writers need to make an argument that includes

- *reasons*—the supporting ideas or points that develop the essay's thesis or main claim;
- *evidence* or *examples* from the story;
- *explanations* or *analyses* showing how the examples support the argument.

In addition, writers may provide other kinds of support—for example, *quotations from experts* or historical, biographical, or cultural evidence. But *textual evidence* from the work of literature is the primary support readers expect in literary analysis essays.

Evidence from the text often takes the form of *quotation* of words, phrases, sentences, and, occasionally, even paragraphs. Quoting is the most important method of providing support for essays that analyze short stories, but effective writers do not expect a quotation to do the work by itself. Instead, they analyze the language of the story to show how particular words' **connotations** (cultural and emotional associations), *figurative* use in *images* and *metaphors,* or **symbolism** (ideas or qualities they suggest) enrich the story's meanings.

When reading a literary analysis, look for sentence strategies like this one:

▶ ....[type of evidence from the text], such as "..............................." and "..............................." [quotations], demonstrates/shows .... [analysis].

Now look at the extended example from paragraph 4 of Iris Lee's essay. In this excerpt, Lee supports an assertion about the author's use of "militaristic diction" by quoting from several parts of the story:

Evidence (quotations)

Examples of militaristic diction include calling his struggle with the girl a "battle" (p. 415), the tongue depressor a "wooden blade" (p. 415), his bodily effort an "assault" (p. 416). She too is a party in this war, moving from fighting "on the

Analysis

defensive" to surging forward in an attack (p. 416). Such metaphors of fighting and warfare, especially those associated with the doctor and his actions, figuratively convey that his character crosses a crucial boundary. They present the argument that,

Analyzing Essays That Analyze Stories

GUIDE TO READING
Guide to Writing
A Writer at Work
Reflection

381

despite his honorable pretentions, his actions—at least during the height of his conflict with the girl—align more with violence than with healing. The doctor's thoughts even turn more obviously (and more consciously) violent at times, such as when, in a bout of frustration, he wants "to kill" the girl's father (p. 415), or when he says, "I could have torn the child apart in my own fury and enjoyed it" (p. 416). Although these statements are arguably exaggerated or hyperbolic, they, like the metaphors of war, imply a tendency to do harm that goes directly against the narrator's duty as a doctor. While the story's opening introduces him as a person whose occupation is enough to overcome the parents' distrust, by the end of the story he leaves his readers thoroughly horrified by his forceful handling of the little girl. By investigating the calculated artifice and military metaphors, we might conclude that the narrator is conscious both of his deceptive rhetoric and of the harm it allows him to inflict upon his patient.

In addition to quoting, evidence can also take the form of *summary* or *paraphrase*. Writers can use this type of evidence to set up an extended close textual analysis like the example from Lee's essay. Or they might use summary or paraphrase in brief snippets of analysis, as in sentence strategies like the following:

▶ When X says/does .... [summary/paraphrase], readers can readily see .... [analysis].

For more on quotation, summary, and paraphrase, see Chapter 19.

For example, to support her thesis, Isabella Wright summarizes the doctor's conflict with the girl instead of describing it in detail. The summary is introduced by repeating key terms from the thesis statement:

The doctor also breaks with social conventions by willingly engaging in a physical struggle with the little girl. (par. 5)

Analysis

Summary

A CLEAR, LOGICAL ORGANIZATION

To make the argument in a literary analysis easy to follow, writers usually include some or all of the following:

- *topic sentences* introducing paragraphs or groups of paragraphs (often using key terms from the thesis statement)
- key terms—words or phrases—introduced in the thesis or other introductory text as a way of forecasting the development of the argument (see the previous section); these key terms are repeated strategically throughout the essay
- clear *transitional words* and *phrases* (such as "although," "in addition," and "at the story's beginning")

Writers tend to place topic sentences at or near the beginning of a paragraph because they help readers make sense of the details, examples, and explanations that follow. Often, topic sentences repeat key terms from the thesis or other introductory text. Look, for example, at the first topic sentence of Iris Lee's essay, which repeats key terms from the introduction in paragraph 1.

Key terms   In the way the story and its characters introduce us to the narrator, we see how people automatically grant a doctor status and privilege based on his profession alone, creating an odd sort of intimacy that is uncommon in ordinary social relations. (par. 2)

The paragraph then gives examples of the extreme politeness the young patient's parents show to the doctor, and in describing and analyzing the scene, Lee repeats the words "privilege" and "intimacy."

Topic sentences can also serve as transitions from one paragraph to the next. In reading literary analyses, look for sentence strategies like the following:

▶ In comparison with/in contrast to/in addition to/because of subject A [discussed in the previous paragraph], subject B [discussed in this paragraph] does _____.

In her analysis of "The Use of Force," Isabella Wright uses this strategy:

Subject A   **EXAMPLE**   In contrast to the little girl's parents, the doctor breaks social conventions
Subject B   in his interactions with the family and in doing so highlights the absurdity
                            of these rules. (par. 3)

Notice that Wright includes the phrase "social conventions," which she introduces in her thesis and repeats throughout the essay.

Readings

The following essays by students Iris Lee and Isabella Wright analyze the short story "The Use of Force," by William Carlos Williams (pp. 414–16). As you will see, both Lee and Wright attempt to answer questions that many readers have asked of this story: What is the purpose—aside from vividly describing his anger and frustration—of portraying a doctor's use of force on an uncooperative patient? What larger points are being made? Lee and Wright arrive at different answers to these questions. By reading their essays, you will learn a great deal about how writers argue for their own analysis of a story.

Iris Lee | *Performing a Doctor's Duty*

For guidelines on formatting a writing project and acknowledging sources in MLA style, see Chapter 20.

WRITTEN FOR A FIRST-YEAR COMPOSITION COURSE, this essay by Iris Lee emphasizes the "doctor's duty." As you read, consider the following:

• What, from Lee's perspective, is the doctor's duty, as indicated in the title?

• What evidence from the story does Lee use to support her main idea?

Also consider the questions in the margin. Your instructor may ask you to post your answers or discuss them in class.

1   The Hippocratic Oath binds doctors to practice ethically and, above all, to "do no harm." The doctor narrating William Carlos Williams's short story "The Use of Force" comes dangerously close to breaking that oath, yet ironically is able to justify his actions by invoking his professional image and the pretense of preserving his patient's well-being. As an account of a professional doing harm under the pretense of healing, the story uncovers how a doctor can take advantage of the intimate nature of his work and his professional status to overstep common forms of conduct, to the extent that his actions actually hurt rather than help a patient. In this way, the doctor-narrator actually performs a valuable service by warning readers, indirectly through his story, that blindly trusting members of his profession can have negative consequences.

2   In the way the story and its characters introduce us to the narrator, we see how people automatically grant a doctor status and privilege based on his profession alone, creating an odd sort of intimacy that is uncommon in ordinary social relations. At the story's beginning, the narrator identifies the family he visits as "new patients" (p. 414), and he establishes that they are virtual strangers to him — "all [he] had was the name, Olson" (p. 414). After the mother confirms that he is the doctor, however, she immediately invites him into the most intimate part of her home, the kitchen, where her husband and sick daughter are waiting (p. 414). Later, the mother reassures the child that the doctor is a "nice man" and "won't hurt you," though she can base those assertions only on what little she knows of him: his occupation (p. 415). At the same time, the narrator senses that the family is "very nervous, eyeing me up and down distrustfully" (p. 414). The parents' eagerness in offering their home and hospitality, coupled with the betrayal of their nervousness, hints at the dubious nature of the intimacy between a doctor and his patient. Although the doctor's profession gives him privilege to overstep certain boundaries, the basis of real trust is lacking, thus casting the doctor-patient relationship as something strange and artificial.

3   The narrator communicates to readers that he perceives both sides of the interaction and also admits to intentionally using the weight of his professional status against the family's natural distrust of outsiders. The young girl, who is not yet "adult" enough to follow social conventions (p. 415), might be read as representing the family's instinct for self-protection. In the face of the child's resistance, the narrator "smiled in [his] best professional manner" (p. 415), trying to invoke the special form of trust that doctors typically assume. The phrase "professional manner" shows that the narrator acknowledges he is using the power of his

Basic Features

A Clear, Arguable Thesis

A Well-Supported Argument

A Clear, Logical Organization

How do the highlighted transitions help the reader? Is this merely plot summary, or does it serve an analytical purpose?

Highlight the topic sentences of paragraphs 3–5. How well do they work?

occupation, while also admitting that his reassuring smile is only part of his professional performance. As the doctor's struggle to examine the little girl's throat becomes more heated, he repeatedly brings up his expert concern to justify his rough actions. He tells readers, "I had to do it . . . for her own protection" (p. 415). Later, he reminds readers (and himself) that "I have seen at least two children lying dead in bed of neglect in such cases, and [feel] that I must get a diagnosis now or never" (pp. 415–16). He also notes that "others must be protected" against the sick child before him (p. 416). The narrator repeatedly brings up his duty as a doctor and the privilege that comes with it to defend his use of force. Yet at other points, he admits to having "grown furious" (p. 415), to being unable to "hold [himself] down" (p. 415), and to have "got beyond reason" (p. 416). In acknowledging the loss of his capacity for reason and self-control, he essentially admits that his "professional manner" and attempts to be gentle in getting the girl to follow his commands are empty artifice (p. 415). When these attempts fail, emotion alone drives his actions. In effect, he uses the medical art as a pretense to justify otherwise unacceptable interventions.

4   Beyond admitting his personal motivations in his treatment of the girl, the narrator sketches a more disturbing and potentially incriminating image of himself in his use of militaristic diction, for it aligns his character more with harming than healing — the perfect contradiction of a doctor. Examples of militaristic diction include calling his struggle with the girl a "battle" (p. 415), the tongue depressor a "wooden blade" (p. 415), his bodily effort an "assault" (p. 416). She too is a party in this war, moving from fighting "on the defensive" to surging forward in an attack (p. 416). Such metaphors of fighting and warfare, especially those associated with the doctor and his actions, figuratively convey that his character crosses a crucial boundary. They present the argument that, despite his honorable pretentions, his actions — at least during the height of his conflict with the girl — align more with violence than with healing. The doctor's thoughts even turn more obviously (and more consciously) violent at times, such as when, in a bout of frustration, he wants "to kill" the girl's father (p. 415), or when he says, "I could have torn the child apart in my own fury and enjoyed it" (p. 416). Although these statements are arguably exaggerated or hyperbolic, they, like the metaphors of war, imply a tendency to do harm that goes directly against the narrator's duty as a doctor. While the story's opening introduces him as a person whose occupation is enough to overcome the parents' distrust, by the end of the story he leaves his readers thoroughly horrified by his forceful handling of the little girl. By investigating the calculated artifice and military metaphors, we might

How clear is Lee's analysis in par. 3? How does she support it?

How well do the quoted words illustrate Lee's analysis?

conclude that the narrator is conscious both of his deceptive rhetoric and of the harm it allows him to inflict upon his patient.

5   Curiously, the narrator readily pleads guilty on both counts, which leads one to wonder why any person would willingly paint such a damning picture of himself — one that would surely destroy his livelihood. I would argue that the doctor of this story does not take ownership of his despicable actions but uses them to blame the parents and more generally to warn against blindly trusting those in positions of authority. Looking back to the story's opening, we note that the narrator presents himself generically. He does not name or describe himself or provide any information beyond the fact that he is a doctor. The lack of specification renders him the "every doctor" and expands the possible reference points for the pronoun "I" as it is used in this story. That is to say, although the story is told in the first person, attaching the actions and events to the singular narrator, that narrator turns himself into a placeholder for every doctor by leaving out all identifying features. I would argue, furthermore, that speaking in the first person, as he must to make his story credible, the narrator offers a cautionary tale about a doctor who exploits the privileges of his profession. The warning implied in the story of a doctor's exploitation of professional privilege is for patients to protect themselves. Thus, through his cautionary tale, the doctor-as-narrator does the opposite of the doctor-as-actor in the story: he performs a doctor's duty to his readers of preventing harm.

6   For readers who distinguish between the different layers of Williams's first-person narrator, the story is ultimately both a damning and a flattering depiction of the doctor figure. The doctor-as-actor in the story becomes a despicable specimen of professionalism corrupted, someone capable of brutality and rhetorical manipulation. Above him stands another — the doctor-as-narrator — who counteracts these crimes through his art. The way he tells the story conveys a powerful story and serious message.

> Why do you think Lee poses an implied question ("leads one to wonder why")? How do her answers (beginning "I would argue" in this paragraph and the next) make her analysis deeper?

> Why do you think Lee provides so many transitions, highlighted here?

> What are the strengths of this ending? How could it be improved?

Work Cited

Williams, William Carlos. "The Use of Force." *The St. Martin's Guide to Writing,* by Rise B. Axelrod and Charles R. Cooper, 12th ed., Bedford/St. Martin's, 2016, pp. 414–16.

To learn about how Isabella Wright used the activities in the "Analyze the Story" section of the Guide to Writing (pp. 392–94), turn to A Writer at Work on pp. 404–07.

Isabella Wright | *"For Heaven's Sake!"*

USING THE WAYS IN ACTIVITIES in the Guide to Writing section "Analyze the Story" (pp. 392–94), Isabella Wright explored and wrote about how the doctor's thoughts and actions in "The Use of Force" might be justified. We have not annotated or highlighted this essay, but you may want to do so as you read and as you respond to the Analyze & Write questions in the sections that follow. As you read, notice how Wright's analysis differs from Lee's. Consider which essay you find more convincing, and why.

1   By any reasonable standards, the story of a doctor prying a little girl's mouth open as she screams in pain and fear should leave readers feeling nothing but horror and disgust at the doctor's actions. William Carlos Williams's story "The Use of Force" is surprising in that it does not completely condemn the doctor for doing just that. Instead, through his actions and words (uttered or thought), readers are able to see the freeing, transformative power of breaking with social conventions. Thus, they are also encouraged to rethink what is acceptable and unacceptable in polite society.

2   Social conventions and proper conduct are prominent themes in Williams's story, in which the mother and father of the sick little girl are fixated on acting and speaking within the boundaries of politeness. The parents demonstrate this tendency most obviously in how they go out of their way to be respectful to the doctor. Upon his arrival at their home, the mother preemptively says that "[he] must excuse [them]" for bringing him into the kitchen, where they are keeping the child warm (p. 414). There, the father makes an effort to "get up" to greet the doctor (p. 414). The parents' efforts continue and take on even greater urgency when the child is uncooperative with the doctor as he tries to examine her throat. When she succeeds in knocking his glasses to the floor, her parents "almost [turn] themselves inside out in embarrassment and apology" (p. 415). At certain moments, keeping up appearances seems to become disproportionately important, overshadowing their concern for their daughter's well-being. The mother's ultimate argument, meant to be stronger even than her threat to take the girl to the hospital, is to shame her daughter over her discourteous behavior. "Aren't you ashamed to act like that in front of the doctor?" she asks (p. 415). The ending of her statement is key because it raises the question, would the daughter's misbehavior be shameful if no one outside the family witnessed it? In other words, to what extent should concerns over appearances determine rightful and wrongful conduct?

3   In contrast to the little girl's parents, the doctor breaks social conventions in his interactions with the family and in doing so highlights the absurdity of these rules. From the beginning we see him as someone who pushes aside polite but pointless practices; for example, he "motion[s] for [the father] not to bother" standing for a greeting when it would have disturbed the child on his lap (p. 414). The doctor's disregard for social conventions applies most to his tendency to give voice to thoughts rather than to keep them to himself for fear of sounding rude or causing discomfort. When the mother scolds her daughter for knocking the glasses off the "nice man" (p. 415), the doctor's reaction borders on outright rudeness: "For heaven's sake, I broke in. Don't call me a nice man to her. I'm here to look at her throat on the chance that she might have diphtheria and possibly die of it" (p. 415).

4   But is the doctor *really* giving voice to such reactions? The absence of quotation marks in the story leaves it uncertain which lines are and are not spoken aloud, creating a thought-provoking ambiguity. For example, does the doctor actually respond with "Oh yeah?" to the mother's threat to take the girl to the hospital, or does he care enough to keep such an irreverent reaction to himself (p. 415)? In any case, readers are presented with the possibility of imagining that all the doctor's thoughts — no matter how offensive, belittling, or inappropriate — are expressed aloud. In fact, the very existence of the text and our reading of it give these thoughts expression, turning a stylistic choice into the ultimate statement on how social considerations limit our actions and expressions.

5   The doctor also breaks with social conventions by willingly engaging in a physical struggle with the little girl. This conflict might be interpreted as a process of reverse socialization or reverse civilization, a transformation that, surprisingly, the story presents as a potentially positive change. While the doctor stoops to the primitive tactics of the little girl, he does not view her in a negative light. To the contrary, from the beginning, he — and, through him, readers — sees the little girl as "unusually attractive" and "strong," with "magnificent blonde hair" (p. 414). This description of her seems almost angelic. Through the doctor's conflict with her, his admiration grows. He comes to respect, even "love," the girl for her raw spirit that allows her to "[rise] to magnificent heights" in her struggle against him (p. 415). Such worshipful language — note the repetition of the word "magnificent," for example — leads readers to understand the girl and her strength as something closer to glory and divinity than to savagery. The doctor's entering a similar state might thus be read as his reeducation into a finer, truer self.

Indeed, it is at these points in the story when he uses the most sophisticated language and the most involved metaphors. Thus, the story demonstrates, through the doctor's transformation, that the casting off of social conventions might lead not to a reduced state of humanity but to a purer, more admirable state of being.

6   In a story where politeness is made to seem absurd, the doctor's tactless words and his inappropriate use of force actually have the potential to be improvements on his character. By tossing aside social conventions, he brings himself closer to the glorious heights of the little girl, who, from the story's beginning, is magnificent and strong in her stubbornness. In the characters of the mother and father, readers come to understand also that politeness can stand in the way of accomplishing a task or communicating a clear meaning, and thus the doctor's actions are in the service of honesty and efficiency. Thus framed, the story leads readers to a point where they cannot fully condemn the doctor's outwardly abhorrent actions and instead must reconsider their own metric of what is and is not socially appropriate.

Work Cited

Williams, William Carlos. "The Use of Force." *The St. Martin's Guide to Writing,* by Rise B. Axelrod and Charles R. Cooper, 12th ed., Bedford/St. Martin's, 2016, pp. 414–16.

[ANALYZE]

Use the basic features.

Take a moment . . .
What do you think teachers mean when they talk about a writer needing to go below the surface to discover a story's deeper meaning?

A CLEAR, ARGUABLE THESIS: GETTING BENEATH THE SURFACE

Earlier, we discussed how the thesis of a literary analysis can contradict or complicate a surface reading of a work. After asserting her thesis about how "The Use of Force" helps readers see the "freeing, transformative power of breaking with social conventions," Wright supports her thesis with examples from the text and with her own analysis. Often, she returns to a key term from her thesis: "social conventions."

| ANALYZE & WRITE |

Write a paragraph or two about how well Wright gets below the surface in her reading of "The Use of Force."

1 Reread the thesis statement, and highlight the term "social conventions" whenever it appears later in the essay, paying attention to what Wright says about it in each instance.

2 Do you think Wright's thesis accurately forecasts the argument she develops in the rest of her essay? If not, what changes to the thesis might you suggest?

3 In her discussion of how the doctor breaks with social conventions, do you think Wright makes an adequate case for the "freeing, transformative power" of his thoughts and actions? Why or why not?

A WELL-SUPPORTED ARGUMENT: PAIRING TEXTUAL EVIDENCE WITH ANALYSIS

As we have noted, an essay about a short story relies primarily on textual evidence—gleaned from a close reading of the story—to support the argument. We have also discussed how simply quoting, summarizing, or paraphrasing passages from the text is not enough; instead, effective writing about a literary work must use such evidence in support of an analysis: the writer's original, thoughtful examination of the text. Earlier, we looked at Lee's analysis of militaristic diction in "The Use of Force," an analysis that drew on quotations from the story. Now let's turn to Wright's essay.

ANALYZE & WRITE

Write a paragraph or two about how well Wright uses textual evidence and analysis:

1 Focus on quotations, highlighting the one in the title as well as those in paragraphs 2–5. Consider how — and how well — these quotations support Wright's argument.

2 What improvements might you suggest to the choice of quotations? For example, in paragraph 5, Wright refers to the "most involved metaphors" of the story but does not quote any of them. Which metaphors, if any, might she have quoted? Or is summarizing these parts of the story sufficient to support her analysis?

3 What improvements might you suggest to Wright's analysis of textual evidence? For example, in paragraph 2, Wright discusses how the parents of the sick child go out of their way to be polite and respectful to the doctor. However, paragraph 3 of the story (p. 414) provides a slightly different take: Consider in what ways this part of the story might complicate Wright's analysis of the parents' behavior.

A CLEAR, LOGICAL ORGANIZATION: COORDINATING KEY WORDS AND TOPIC SENTENCES

As we have seen, writers try to help readers follow their argument by making their plan or organization clear to readers. For example, topic sentences that repeat key terms from the thesis statement help readers connect individual paragraphs to the larger argument the writer is making.

Consider . . .

Why do you think guiding readers through a writing project is especially valued in academic writing?

ANALYZE & WRITE

Write a paragraph or two about Wright's use of key words in topic sentences:

1 Underline the topic sentences of paragraphs 2, 3, and 5, and circle any key terms that are repeated in these sentences.

2 Pay special attention to the key terms, noting the way they are used in each topic sentence and built upon in the paragraph. Assess how well each topic sentence helps you follow the argument as it is developed in these paragraphs.

The Writing Assignment

Write an essay analyzing one or more aspects of a story. Aim to convince readers that your analysis is interesting and contributes to the conversation about the story. Back up your ideas with supporting quotations and examples from the story.

This Guide to Writing is designed to help you write your own analysis of a story and apply what you have learned from reading other students' essays. The Starting Points chart will help you find answers to questions you might have about analyzing a story. Use it to find the guidance you need, when you need it.

STARTING POINTS: ANALYZING STORIES

How can I find a good story to write about?

- Find a story to write about. (p. 391)
- Analyze the story. (pp. 392–94)
- Test Your Choice: Choosing a Topic (p. 396)

A Clear, Arguable Thesis

How do I decide on a main idea and develop a thesis?

- Assess the genre's basic features: A clear, arguable thesis. (pp. 379–80)
- A Clear, Arguable Thesis: Getting Beneath the Surface (pp. 388–89)
- Analyze the story. (pp. 392–94)
- Formulate a working thesis. (pp. 396–97)
- A Troubleshooting Guide: A Clear, Arguable Thesis (p. 402)

A Well-Supported Argument

How do I support my ideas?

- Assess the genre's basic features: A well-supported argument. (pp. 380–81)
- A Well-Supported Argument: Pairing Textual Evidence with Analysis (p. 389)
- Provide support for your argument. (pp. 397–98)
- To build on your support, consider doing outside research. (p. 399)
- A Troubleshooting Guide: A Well-Supported Argument (p. 403)

A Clear, Logical Organization

> How can I help my readers follow my argument?

- Assess the genre's basic features: A clear, logical organization. (pp. 381–82)
- A Clear, Logical Organization: Coordinating Key Words and Topic Sentences (p. 389)
- Create an outline that will organize your argument effectively. (pp. 399–400)
- A Troubleshooting Guide: A Clear, Logical Organization (p. 403)

Writing a Draft: Invention, Research, Planning, and Composing

The activities in this section will help you find a story to write about, analyze it thoughtfully, and develop and organize an essay that argues for the position you are taking on the story. Your writing in response to many of these activities can be used as part of your rough draft, which you will be able to improve after receiving feedback from your classmates and instructor. Do the activities in any order that makes sense to you (and your instructor), and return to them as needed as you revise.

⊞ Find a story to write about.

Your instructor may have given you a list of stories to choose from or assigned a particular story for the class to write about. If so, go on to the next section, "Analyze the Story" (pp. 392–94). If you need to find a story on your own, look for one that meets your instructor's approval and does one or more of the following:

- deals with a culturally, politically, or historically significant theme
- surprises or puzzles you with apparent contradictions
- leads you to wonder what is left out of the story—the backstory, or *context*
- raises questions about characters' motivations, relationships, or development
- uses conventional story motifs, setting, or other features in unconventional ways
- resonates emotionally, perhaps giving you insight into human frailty or moral ambiguity

To find a story on your own, browse any literature anthology or short story collection in a library or bookstore, or try one of these two online sites:

- *American Literature* short story library (americanliterature.com)
- *Classic Short Stories* (classicshorts.com)

⊞ Analyze the story.

Use the following suggestions as a way into the story. Try out more than one to discover how different aspects of the story work together and to generate ideas for a thoughtful analysis. To read the story closely and critically, *annotate* it as you work through the suggestions, highlighting key passages and noting your ideas and questions.

For more on annotating, see Chapter 12.

Take a moment . . .

Think about which, if any, of these Ways In suggestions may lead you to surprising discoveries about the story?

WAYS IN

WHAT ELEMENTS COULD I ANALYZE, AND WHY?	WHAT APPROACH MIGHT I TAKE?	WHAT SHOULD I ASK MYSELF?
Character You want to know ■ why a character acts in a particular way ■ how gender or ethnicity affects relationships ■ whether a character changes or grows ■ whether we should approve of a character's actions or accept his or her justifications	Psychological	■ Does the character change/learn anything in the course of the story? ■ How does the character relate to other characters? For instance, how does he or she deal with intimacy, commitment, and responsibility? ■ Does the character seem depressed, manic, abusive, fearful, egotistical, or paranoid? ■ Does any other character seem to represent the character's double or opposite?
	Ethical or moral	■ What are the character's virtues and/or vices? ■ What influences my judgment of the character? Something in the story (such as what the narrator or another character says)? Something I bring to the story (my views of right and wrong, based on my family upbringing or religious teachings)? Something else? ■ Do any of the other characters have different moral values that could be compared or contrasted to the character's values?
	Social or cultural	■ How does the character fit into and appear to be defined by society in terms of race, ethnicity, socioeconomic class, sexual orientation, age, or gender? ■ Who in the story exercises power over whom? What causes the difference in power? What are the effects of this difference? Does the balance of power change during the story?

Writing a Draft

Guide to Reading
GUIDE TO WRITING
A Writer at Work
Reflection

393

Setting	In relation to the mood, characters, or actions	▪ How does the setting affect the mood? For example, does it create feelings of suspense or foreboding?
You want to know		▪ Are there any cause-effect connections between the setting and what characters are doing, thinking, or feeling?
▪ how much time and place matter		
▪ what the description of the setting symbolizes	Historical or cultural	▪ How does the historical period or cultural context in which the story is set affect what happens and does not happen?
▪ how the setting affects characters		
	Metaphoric or symbolic	▪ How might the story's meaning be different if the historical time or cultural situation were changed?
		▪ Assuming that the setting is a projection of the thoughts and feelings of the narrator, what does the setting tell me about the narrator's state of mind?
		▪ Assuming that the setting symbolizes the social relations among characters in the story, what does the setting tell me about these relationships?
		▪ Assuming that the setting stands for something outside the characters control (such as nature, God, or some aspect of society), what does the setting tell me about the pressures and rules under which the characters function?
Plot Structure	As realistic (resembling real-life experience)	▪ After marking where each new stage of the story begins, how can the sequence of scenes or events be understood? In what ways do subplots mirror, undercut, or comment on the main plot?
You want to know		
▪ what the ending means		
▪ whether there is a turning point in the story	As surrealistic (having symbolic rather than literal meaning)	▪ Thinking of the story as a series of images (more like a collage or a dream than a realistic portrayal of actual events), what meanings do I find in the arrangement of these images?
▪ how a subplot relates to the main plot		

(continued)

Point of View You want to know • whether the narrator can be believed • whose values and interests are represented • how readers' sympathies are manipulated	In terms of what the narrator actually sees	• Is the narrator a character in the story or an all-knowing, disembodied voice who knows what every character thinks, feels, and does? • What important insights or ideas does the narrator have? • How do factors such as the narrator's gender, age, and ethnicity influence what he or she notices as important? • Are there things that the narrator is not able to see or that he or she distorts—for example, certain truths about himself or herself, about other characters, or about what happens in the story?
	In terms of how the narrator represents what he or she sees	• How would I characterize the narrator's tone at various points in the story? For example, is the tone satirical, celebratory, angry, bitter, or optimistic? • What about the narrator (or about the situation) might account for each tone I identify? • What special agenda or motive might have led the narrator to this particular way of describing characters and scenes or telling the story?
Literary Motif or Theme You want to know • whether the story is about a break with social conventions, the initiation into adulthood, or some other common literary motif	In terms of a traditional story motif (or an ironic reversal of the tradition)	• Could I analyze the text as an initiation (or coming-of-age or rite-of-passage) story? a quest (for love, truth, fame, fortune, or salvation of oneself or the community)? a story about a character's disillusionment or fall from innocence? a story about family or surrogate families? a story about storytelling (or some other art) or becoming a writer or an artist?

Writing a Draft

Guide to Reading
GUIDE TO WRITING
A Writer at Work
Reflection

395

■ what the story says about war, poverty, love, alienation, or some other general theme ■ how the story illuminates a historical or current issue	In terms of a common literary theme	■ Might I focus on the theme of the American Dream? the social construct of femininity or masculinity? race relations in America? alienation? the urban or suburban experience?

Generate ideas by moving from specific to general or the reverse.

In addition to generating ideas by taking one of the approaches listed above, you can consider the details and use those to generate an approach. Or you can list ideas you had while reading the story and use those to locate supporting details. The Ways In box that follows can help you generate ideas using these two approaches.

WAYS IN

HOW CAN I GENERATE IDEAS BY MOVING FROM SPECIFIC DETAILS TO GENERAL IDEAS?

1. Select two or three quotations, and write several sentences answering this question: What idea or ideas does each quotation suggest, and what in the quotation makes you think so?

2. Write a paragraph analyzing one or more patterns you found in the story. Here are a few patterns to help you get started:

 ■ imagery (for example, the militaristic images in "The Use of Force" that Lee analyzes)

 ■ characters as contrasts (for example, differences between the parents and the doctor in "The Use of Force" that Wright discusses)

 ■ events that echo or reverse one another (for example, the doctor's fury echoes that of the young girl)

HOW CAN I GENERATE IDEAS BY MOVING FROM GENERAL IDEAS TO SPECIFIC DETAILS?

1. List ideas you thought of as you analyzed the story, without worrying about how those ideas relate to one another or whether they are contradictory. For example, here are two of Isabella Wright's ideas about the doctor in "The Use of Force" (see A Writer at Work, pp. 404–7).

 He has no time for the social conventions upheld by the parents.

 His break with social conventions feels freeing—maybe even transformative.

2. Review the story to find quotations or other details you could use to illustrate your ideas.

3. Write for a few minutes on your most interesting ideas and how they connect. For example, in exploring her ideas about "The Use of Force," Wright connected ideas about breaking social conventions to develop her main claim about the transformative power of disobeying the rules of social behavior.

TEST YOUR CHOICE

Choosing a Topic

Get together with two or three other students who have read the story and share your ideas.

Presenters.   Take turns telling the other students your two or three most promising ideas, giving an example from the story to support each idea.

Listeners.   Briefly respond to each presenter's ideas, identifying what you find interesting in them, what you agree or disagree with, and how the ideas could be extended or complicated productively.

▥ Formulate a working thesis.

Remember that an arguable thesis is not a simple statement of fact or an obvious conclusion. To get a sense of how you might formulate an arguable thesis, take a look at the thesis statements from the student essays you've studied in this chapter.

> As an account of a professional doing harm under the pretense of healing, the story uncovers how a doctor can take advantage of the intimate nature of his work and his professional status to overstep common forms of conduct, to the extent that his actions actually hurt rather than help a patient. In this way, the doctor-narrator actually performs a valuable service by warning readers, indirectly through his story, that blindly trusting members of his profession can have negative consequences. (Lee, par. 1)

> Through [the doctor's] actions and words (uttered or thought), readers are able to see the freeing, transformative power of breaking with social conventions. Thus, they are also encouraged to rethink what is acceptable and unacceptable in polite society. (Wright, par. 1)

You may have already decided on the main claim you want to make in your short story analysis; if so, try drafting a working thesis statement now. The Ways In activities that follow may help. (Alternatively, if you prefer to develop your analysis before trying to formulate a thesis, skip this activity and return to it when you're ready.)

Did you know?

Research shows that suggestions like those in the Ways In activities help writers new to field research. How helpful do you find them?

WAYS IN

HOW CAN I FORMULATE AN ARGUABLE THESIS?

Write for ten minutes about your most promising ideas. After writing, read what you have written and see if you can find one main idea or claim that can serve as the thesis for your essay. Focus your exploratory writing on questions like these:

- How can readers understand a character's internal conflict or apparent change?

- How is the story's theme reflected in the way the story is told, the way the setting is described, how characters relate to one another, or some other aspect of the story?

- How does the language used to describe the setting or the characters' actions illuminate such things as the main character's internal conflict, the relationship between characters, or the theme? (For example, the doctor-patient struggle described in "The Use of Force" forms the basis of Iris Lee's argument that the story warns readers against blindly trusting doctors.)

Writing a Draft

Guide to Reading
▶ **GUIDE TO WRITING**
A Writer at Work
Reflection

397

- What does the trajectory of the story (the plot structure) say about the characters or the culture? (For example, Isabella Wright's analysis of the increasing tension between repression and expression, social conventions and human willfulness, underlies her argument about the value of breaking with these conventions.)

Reread the story with one of the following questions (or a question of your own) in mind, underlining passages or taking notes as you read:

- How do my ideas about the story form links in a chain leading to some general conclusion? For example, Wright links two ideas: (1) pressure to adhere to social conventions and (2) reasons for breaking with these conventions. She is *not* simply retelling the story; she is stating her ideas about what happens in the story.

- How can I present my ideas as a response to a question—either a question my instructor asked or one I composed myself? For example, in their essays, Lee and Wright responded to the first question we pose in the Analyze & Write section for "The Use of Force" (p. 414).

- What, if anything, does the story say about what may be universally true about people and society versus what may result from specific historical, economic, or cultural conditions? About what is usually considered normal versus what is considered abnormal? About how some groups exert power while others may be oppressed or subversive?

Now reread your notes. Do they suggest one **MAIN IDEA** or **CLAIM** that can serve as the thesis for your essay?

Use the sentence strategies that follow as a jumping-off point. You can put your thesis into your own words when you revise, or use your own words and sentence patterns now:

- ▶ Many readers of X point to .... [state feature(s) of the story], but an important aspect of the story that is often overlooked is ....

- ▶ A common/superficial reading of X [name of story or character] is that .... [common conclusion], but in fact, ... [your own conclusion].

- ▶ Through the actions of X [name of character], we are led to this surprising conclusion: ....

- ▶ Through the events unfolded in X [name of story], readers are led to this disturbing conclusion: ....

⊞ Provide support for your argument.

Look back on the ideas that you have generated so far, and ask yourself these questions:

- How can I present my ideas as reasons supporting my central claim, the essay's thesis? For example, Isabella Wright shaped the ideas she generated moving from general ideas to specific details (pp. 406–7) into reasons supporting her thesis about the value of breaking with social conventions.

- Have I remembered to include my own analysis in the support instead of just retelling the story through quotation, paraphrase, or summary? (If you are unsure, work through the Ways In activities that follow.)

Reflect on . . .

Think about what teachers mean when they advise against "just retelling the story through quotation, paraphrase, or summary." How does analysis go beyond retelling the story?

WAYS IN

HOW CAN I INTEGRATE EVIDENCE FROM THE STORY?

As noted earlier, to provide support for a short story analysis, writers may QUOTE, PARAPHRASE, or SUMMARIZE parts of the story. However, this evidence should be offered in the service of a thoughtful examination of the story and go beyond a simple repetition of description, dialogue, and so on. To effectively integrate material from a story, try these strategies:

- **Use short quotations frequently to support your ANALYSIS.** Brief quotations are not in themselves superior to sentence-length and longer quotations, but they allow you to stay focused on your own argument while bringing in key information or vivid details from the story. Look at these examples from the student essays in this chapter:

  > To the contrary, from the beginning, he—and, through him, readers—sees the little girl as "unusually attractive" and "strong," with "magnificent blonde hair" (p. 414). This description of her seems almost angelic. (Wright, par. 5)

  > Later, the mother reassures the child that the doctor is a "nice man" and "won't hurt you," though she can base those assertions only on what little she knows of him: his occupation (p. 415). (Lee, par. 2)

- **Comment directly on what you have QUOTED, PARAPHRASED, or SUMMARIZED so that readers will understand the relevance of this material to your ANALYSIS.** These comments should connect the quotation, paraphrase, or summary to the idea you are trying to support. One good strategy is to refer to quotations or paraphrases with *this, these,* or *they* statements, which Lee does in the following example:

  > The doctor's thoughts even turn more obviously (and more consciously) violent at times, such as when . . . he says, "I could have torn the child apart in my own fury and enjoyed it" (p. 416). Although these statements are arguably exaggerated or hyperbolic, they, like the metaphors of war, imply a tendency to do harm that goes directly against the narrator's duty as a doctor. (par. 4).

Another good strategy is to repeat key nouns from quotations, paraphrases, or summaries in your analysis, as Wright does in the example below:

> Social conventions and proper conduct are prominent themes in William's story, in which the mother and father of the sick little girl are fixated on acting and speaking within the boundaries of politeness. (par. 2)

> In a story where politeness is made to seem absurd, the doctor's tactless words and his inappropriate use of force actually have the potential to be improvements on his character. (par. 6)

Writing a Draft

Guide to Reading
GUIDE TO WRITING
A Writer at Work
Reflection

399

⠿ To build on your support, consider doing outside research.

Many analyses of short stories rely on a close reading of the text alone; the writer's analysis is the only tool brought to bear on the work. Some approaches to analysis, however, also consider biographical information on the author, his or her other works, or various critical responses to the short story in question. If your instructor has asked you to include such information, or if you are curious about some aspect of the text that you do not understand — or that you suspect your readers will not understand — you might want to conduct some research and include your findings in your essay. Here are a few suggestions for getting started:

- Do a *Google* search, using keywords relevant to your analysis. For example, if you want more information about the context of "The Use of Force," you could try key words such as *diphtheria epidemic*.

- To see what others have said about an author's work, conduct a search using a specialized periodical database, such as the *MLA International Bibliography,* which specializes in academic writing about languages and literature. You should have access to periodical databases through your school's library.

As you work, bookmark or keep a record of promising sites. If you download or copy information you could use in your essay, remember to record source information.

To learn more about using library databases to conduct research, see Chapter 17.

⠿ Create an outline that will organize your argument effectively.

Whether you have rough notes or a complete draft, making an outline of what you have written can help you organize your essay effectively for your audience. One way to outline a literary analysis is to lay out your argument as a series of *because* sentences. For example, here's how Iris Lee might have outlined her argument:

I. The story performs a valuable service because, through the doctor's actions, readers see that it's unwise to trust members of his profession blindly.

    A. Although he displays his "best professional manner," the doctor does so only because he knows it will encourage the family's deference to him despite his rude and rough behavior.

    B. The doctor shows his untrustworthiness because he seems more interested in harming the girl than healing her.

II. Readers who see the doctor purely as a bad person are wrong because the author presents two sides of him.

    A. The doctor-as-actor deserves our scorn because he is capable of brutality under the guise of professionalism.

    B. The doctor-as-narrator deserves our thanks because he depicts the crimes of the doctor-as-actor, warning readers about the dangers of placing too much trust in medical professionals.

Once you have a working outline, you should not hesitate to change it as necessary while drafting and revising. For instance, you might find you left out an important idea that is needed to make the chain of reasoning complete. Remember that the purpose of an outline is to help you organize your ideas logically, not to lock you into a particular structure.

Write the opening sentences.

The section "Formulate a working thesis" (pp. 396–97) and the Ways In activities there suggest several ways to present an arguable thesis. In writing your introduction, avoid creating a "funnel paragraph," which begins with a broad generalization and then becomes more and more focused and narrow, culminating in what is usually the essay's thesis. The problem with this kind of paragraph structure is that broad generalizations are not very interesting and add nothing to the essay. Look, for example, at the italicized sentences in this modified version of Isabella Wright's opening paragraph:

> *As all of us know, being the subject of a medical examination, especially if you are a child, is rarely fun. Patients can be nervous and uncooperative, and in the worst cases, doctors can act like real jerks.* William Carlos Williams's story "The Use of Force" is surprising in that it does not completely condemn the doctor for doing just that.

It is best to get rid of sentences like these and simply begin by presenting your ideas about the story.

Draft your analysis.

By this point, you have done a lot of writing to

- come up with ideas for your short story analysis;
- draft an arguable thesis;
- provide support for your argument;
- organize your ideas to present them logically to readers.

Now stitch that material together to create a draft. As you write, ask yourself questions like the following:

- Early in my essay, should I name the story and also identify the author?
- How much do I need to tell my readers about what happens in the story? Should I assume, as both Iris Lee and Isabella Wright do, that my readers have read the story?
- Should I consider placing the story in the context of the author's other writing or in its historical context?
- How can I revise my topic sentences to use the key terms introduced in my thesis? What synonyms could I use to avoid repeating my key terms too often?
- How can I use logical transitions to help readers see how one point connects to the next? For example, could I use transitions that announce contrasts, such as *but, although,* and *yet*?
- Should I consider ending with a new idea that grows out of my argument? Could I, for example, expand on the cultural or historical implications of my reading of the story?

Evaluating the Draft

Guide to Reading
▶ **GUIDE TO WRITING**
A Writer at Work
Reflection

401

Evaluating the Draft: Using Peer Review

Your instructor may arrange a peer review session in class or online, where you can exchange drafts with your classmates and give one another a thoughtful critical reading, pointing out what works well and suggesting ways to improve the draft. A good critical reading of a literary analysis does three things:

1. It lets the writer know how well the point of his or her analysis comes across to readers.

2. It praises what works best.

3. It indicates where the draft could be improved and makes suggestions on how to improve it.

One strategy for evaluating a draft is to use the basic features of a literary analysis as a guide. Also, be sure to respond to any concerns the writer has shared with you.

A PEER REVIEW GUIDE

A Clear, Arguable Thesis

> **How well does the writer present the thesis?**

Summarize: Tell the writer what you understand the essay's thesis to be and what its key terms are.

Praise: Tell the writer what seems most interesting to you about his or her main claim about the story, whether you agree with it or not.

Critique: If you cannot find the thesis statement or cannot identify the key terms, let the writer know. Evaluate the thesis statement on the basis of whether
- it makes an interesting and arguable assertion (rather than making a statement of fact or an obvious point);
- it is clear and precise (neither ambiguous nor vague);
- it is appropriately qualified (neither overgeneralized nor exaggerated).

A Well-Supported Argument

> **How well does the writer develop and support the argument?**

Summarize: Underline the thesis statement and the major support for it. (Often, the major support appears in the topic sentences of paragraphs.)

Praise: Give an example in the essay where support for a reason is presented especially effectively — for instance, note where brief quotations (words and short phrases), a longer quotation, or summaries of particular events are introduced and explained in a way that clearly illustrates a particular point that is being argued.

Critique: Tell the writer where the connection between a reason and its support seems vague, where too much plot is being relayed with no apparent point, or where a quotation is left to speak for itself without explanation. Let the writer know if any part of the argument seems to be undeveloped or does not support the thesis.

(continued)

A Clear, Logical Organization

> Has the writer clearly and logically organized the argument?

Summarize: Underline the sentence(s) in which the writer forecasts supporting reasons, and circle transitions or repeated key words and phrases.

Praise: Give an example of something that makes the essay especially easy to read — where, for example, the key terms introduced in the thesis recur throughout the essay in topic sentences and elsewhere, or where transitions are used logically.

Critique: Tell the writer where readability could be improved. For example, point to places where key terms could be added or where a topic sentence could be made clearer, indicate where the use of transitions might be improved, or note where transitions are lacking and could be added.

Improving the Draft: Revising, Editing, and Proofreading

Start improving your draft by reflecting on what you have written thus far:

- Review critical reading comments from your classmates, instructor, or writing center tutor: What problems do your readers identify?

- Consider your invention writing: What else should you consider?

- Review your draft: What can you do to present your argument more compellingly?

Revise your draft.

If your readers are having difficulty with your draft, or if you think there is room for improvement, try some of the strategies listed in the Troubleshooting Guide that follows. They can help you fine-tune your presentation of the genre's basic features.

A TROUBLESHOOTING GUIDE

A Clear, Arguable Thesis

> My thesis is unclear or overgeneralized.

- Add more explanation.
- Refer to the story specifically.
- Add qualifying words like *some* or *usually*.

> My thesis is not arguable or interesting.

- Respond to a question or a class discussion.
- Summarize an alternative argument.
- Try additional suggestions for analysis from the Ways In activities on pp. 392–94.

Improving the Draft

Guide to Reading
GUIDE TO WRITING
A Writer at Work
Reflection

403

A Well-Supported
Argument

> My argument seems superficial or thin.

- Develop your ideas by connecting them.
- Link your ideas to make a chain of reasoning.
- Connect to a literary motif or theme.
- Add textual evidence by quoting, paraphrasing, or summarizing important passages.
- Focus on the writer's choice of words, explaining how particular word choices support your ideas.
- Consider using other kinds of support, such as information about the story's historical or cultural context.

> The connection between a reason and its support seems vague.

- Explain why the support illustrates the point you are making.
- Explain what the quoted words imply — their connotative (cultural or emotional) associations as well as their denotative (literal or dictionary) meanings.
- Introduce quotations, and follow them with some analysis or explanation.
- Explain more fully and clearly how your reasons relate logically to one another as well as to your thesis.
- Fill in the gaps.
- Use contradictions or gaps to extend or complicate your argument.

A Clear, Logical
Organization

> My essay is hard to follow.

- Repeat key terms from the thesis and other introductory text.
- Provide explicit topic sentences.
- Add logical transitions.

Edit and proofread your final draft.

Editing means making changes to the text to ensure that it follows the conventions of style, grammar, spelling, and mechanics appropriate to the rhetorical situation. **Proofreading** involves checking to make sure the text follows these conventions and that no words are repeated or omitted. You have probably done some editing and proofreading while composing and improving your draft, but it is always good practice to edit and proofread a draft after you have revised it and before you submit it.

Most writers get the best results by leaving time — even just an hour or two — between the stages of revising, editing, and proofreading, so that they can return to their writing project with fresh eyes. When possible, enlist a friend or classmate to proofread the final draft of your writing projects. When that is not possible, proofread from the last line to the first, to avoid seeing what you expect to find rather than what is actually on the page (or screen).

As rhetorical situations change, so, too, do the conventions or expectations readers bring to the text. For example, whereas e-mail messages to friends are usually quite informal, filled with abbreviations, emojis, and sentence fragments, final drafts of writing projects for college classes or the workplace are expected to follow a more formal set of conventions concerning clarity, style, grammar, and punctuation.

We recommend that you make a list of the problems your instructors frequently point out in your writing, then use that list to guide your editing and proofreading. A Guide to Editing and Proofreading (at the end of this text) provides a checklist of the most common problems writers face. For issues that go beyond those on this list, consult a handbook* or search for advice online at sites like the Purdue Online Writing Lab (owl.english.purdue.edu) or Grammarly (grammarly.com). For practice identifying and correcting errors, try the activities in LearningCurve, a gamelike adaptive quizzing program available on LaunchPad for *The St. Martin's Guide to Writing*. The less well you do on activities in one topic area, the more LearningCurve focuses on it; the better you do, the more challenging the questions become.

A Note on Grammar and Spelling Checkers
Spelling checkers cannot catch misspellings that are themselves words, such as *to* for *too*, and grammar checkers miss problems, give faulty advice, and even flag correct items as wrong. Use these tools as a second line of defense after your own (and, ideally, another reader's) proofreading efforts.

A WRITER AT WORK

Isabella Wright's Invention Work

In this section, you will see some of the work that Isabella Wright did in developing her essay analyzing the story "The Use of Force." Using the Guide to Writing in this book, Wright chose the suggestions for interpreting character to guide her analysis of the story. As you will see,

- she annotated a portion of the story focusing on the doctor's first attempts to examine the young patient's throat;
- she wrote to explore her annotations on the passages;
- she listed ideas for formulating her tentative thesis statement.

You will be able to infer from her invention work how her ideas came to form the thesis she developed for her final essay.

---

* The full version of *The St. Martin's Guide to Writing* includes a handbook.

Isabella Wright's Invention Work

Guide to Reading
Guide to Writing
▶ **A WRITER AT WORK**
Reflection

405

Annotating

With the suggestions for analyzing character in mind, Wright annotated paragraphs 12–22 of "The Use of Force" as she reread them. The annotated passages are reproduced here. Notice the variety of her annotations:

- In the text itself, she underlined key words and circled words to be defined.
- In the margin, she defined words, made comments, and posed questions. She also expressed her tentative insights, reactions, and judgments.

smile really sincere? 12 Well, I said, suppose we take a look at the throat first. I <u>smiled</u> in my best professional manner and asking for the child's first name I said, come on, Mathilda, open your mouth and let's take a look at your throat.

13 Nothing doing.

14 Aw, come on, I coaxed, just open your mouth wide and let me take a look. <u>Look, I said opening both hands wide, I haven't anything in my hands. Just open up and let me see.</u>   *he's trying to come across as unthreatening*

mother's politeness continues 15 Such a <u>nice man</u>, put in the mother. Look how kind he is to you. Come on, do what he tells you to. He won't hurt you.

16 At that I ground my teeth in <u>disgust</u>. If only they wouldn't use the word "hurt" I might be able to get somewhere. But I did not allow myself to be hurried or disturbed but speaking quietly and slowly I approached the child again.   *not willing to promise he won't hurt girl*

unlike parents, child showing her true self 17 As I moved my chair a little nearer suddenly with one catlike movement both her hands clawed instinctively for my eyes and she almost reached them too. In fact she knocked my glasses flying and they fell, though unbroken, several feet away from me on the kitchen floor.

18 Both the mother and father almost turned themselves inside out in <u>embarrassment</u> and <u>apology</u>. You bad girl, said the mother, taking her and shaking her by one arm. Look what you've done. The nice man . . .   *parents very embarrassed — concerned with social conventions*

19 For heaven's sake, I broke in. Don't call me a nice man to her. I'm here to look at her throat on the chance that she might have ⊙diphtheria⊙ and possibly die of it. But that's nothing to her. Look here, I said to the child, we're going to look at your throat. You're old enough to understand what I'm saying. Will you open it now by yourself or shall we have to open it for you?   *Rude. Is he really saying this? No quotation marks*

possibly deadly infection

he's losing his patience

battle of the wills as much as a physical battle?

20   Not a move. Even her expression hadn't changed. Her breaths however were coming faster and faster. Then the <u>battle</u> began. I had to do it. I had to have a throat culture for <u>her own protection</u>. But first I told the parents that it was entirely up to them. I explained the danger but said that I would not insist on a throat examination so long as they would take the responsibility.

"her own protection"—he's trying to justify his actions

21   If you don't do what the doctor says you'll have to go to the hospital, the mother admonished her severely.

22   Oh yeah? <u>I had to smile to myself.</u> After all, I had already fallen in love with the savage brat, the parents were contemptible to me. In the ensuing struggle they grew more and more (abject,) crushed, exhausted while she surely rose to magnificent heights of insane fury of effort bred of her terror of me.

Now here's a sincere smile!

struggle has transformed him—and his view of her?

hopeless

As you can see, annotating this section of the story with the suggestions for analyzing character in mind led Wright to notice how much the doctor's direct, and sometimes rude, manner is butting up against the parents' politeness and embarrassment over their child's behavior.

Examining Patterns in the Story

Following the instructions in the section "Generate ideas by moving from specific to general or the reverse" (p. 395), Wright explored a pattern of contrast she saw between the doctor and the parents in the story. Here is what she wrote:

> From the start of this scene, it feels like the whole experience between the doctor and the family is going to go from bad to worse. The doctor's smile feels forced, almost as if he's warning the little girl that she's in for an unpleasant time. The parents' attempts to smooth things over do nothing but irritate him, and he's actually angered by being referred to as a "nice man." It's as if he has no time for the social conventions so important to the parents; these rules mean nothing to him, much less to the girl. In some ways, the doctor and the girl seem more alike than the doctor and the parents because he and the girl are showing their true selves. For that reason, maybe he even respects her more than he does the parents. The longer the two of them struggle, the more he seems to admire her. From the parents' and the girl's point of view, the experience is pretty clearly a bad one, but perhaps there's something freeing about it from the doctor's perspective.

As Wright wrote about the contrasts between the characters, she became increasingly confident that she not only had an interesting idea but also had one she could find support for in the story.

Reflecting on Reading and Writing a Literary Analysis

Guide to Reading
Guide to Writing
A Writer at Work
▶ REFLECTION

407

Listing Ideas

Wright tried out the activity on listing ideas from the Ways In activity on p. 395. In doing so, she drew on both her annotations and on the exploratory writing she did about the doctor and the family:

> The doctor comes across in a bad light: He's rude and impatient and able to justify the use of force against the girl.
>
> He has no time for the social conventions upheld by the parents.
>
> He's more annoyed than flattered by the mother's compliments and attempts to smooth things over.
>
> In this way, maybe he is more like the little girl than the parents.
>
> They both seem to be showing their true selves.
>
> In the end, it's hard to condemn the doctor.
>
> His break with social conventions feels freeing — maybe even transformative.

From these ideas about the doctor's behavior and how his views about social conventions differ from those of the parents, Wright was able to devise the thesis statement she eventually used in her essay.

REFLECTION

The benefit of reflection is proven and important: It helps consolidate what you have learned so that you can remember and apply it well beyond this class. That is why we have included questions and comments in the margins and at the end of this: to stimulate your thinking about what you have read, your rhetorical situation, and the choices you make as a writer.

Reflecting on Reading and Writing a Literary Analysis

To reflect on your experience reading literary analyses and writing one of your own, try writing a blog post, a letter to your instructor, or an e-mail message to a student who will take this course next term that draws on what you have learned. Use any of these writing prompts that seem productive:

- Explain how your purpose and audience influenced *one* of your decisions as a writer, such as how you chose the suggestions for analysis you used, the key words you used in presenting your thesis, or the quotations you chose to support your argument.

- Discuss what you learned about yourself as a writer in the process of writing this essay. For example, what part of the process did you find most challenging? Did you try anything new, like getting a critical reading of your draft or summarizing an alternative argument to improve your thesis? If so, would you do it again?

- Choose one of the readings in this chapter, and explain how it influenced your essay. Be sure to cite specific examples from your essay and the reading.

- If you got good advice from a critical reader, explain exactly how the person helped you—perhaps by questioning the way you stated your thesis or how you explained one of your reasons.

Reflecting on Your Composing Process

Thinking about your process for writing a literary analysis can be useful in helping you decide what works best for you. Using one or more of the following questions as a starting point, write a paragraph or two about your composing process:

- How did you go about choosing an aspect of the story for analysis? Did you try out a few possibilities before making a final decision?

- Explain how peer review helped you—perhaps by helping you choose the most convincing causes or effects to develop or helping you strengthen your refutation of alternative causes or effects.

- What was the hardest part of the process: coming up with an aspect of the story to analyze, deciding on your point of view, crafting an interesting arguable thesis, finding supporting evidence in the story, or something else?

- How satisfied are you with the process you used? If you could go back in time, what would you have done differently? If you could continue working on your literary analysis, what would you like to do?

AN ANTHOLOGY OF SHORT STORIES

In this section, you will find four short stories: "The Story of an Hour," by Kate Chopin; "Araby," by James Joyce; "The Use of Force," by William Carlos Williams; and "Girl" by Jamaica Kincaid. Each is followed by questions to help you get started analyzing the story. Your instructor may ask you to choose one of these stories for your essay analyzing a story.

Kate Chopin | *The Story of an Hour*

KATE CHOPIN (1851–1904) was born in St. Louis and lived in Louisiana until her husband died in 1882, leaving her with six children. Encouraged by friends, Chopin wrote her first novel, *At Fault* (1890), when she was nearly forty years old. She wrote many short stories for such popular magazines as *Century, Harper's,* and *Vogue,* in which "The Story of an Hour" first appeared in 1894. She published two collections of stories and a second novel, her best-known work, *The Awakening* (1899).

1 Knowing that Mrs. Mallard was afflicted with a heart trouble, great care was taken to break to her as gently as possible the news of her husband's death.

2 It was her sister Josephine who told her, in broken sentences; veiled hints that revealed in half concealing. Her husband's friend Richards was there, too, near her. It was he who had been in the newspaper office when intelligence of the railroad disaster was received, with Brently Mallard's name leading the list of "killed." He had only taken the time to assure himself of its truth by a second telegram, and had hastened to forestall any less careful, less tender friend in bearing the sad message.

3 She did not hear the story as many women have heard the same, with a paralyzed inability to accept its significance. She wept at once, with sudden, wild abandonment, in her sister's arms. When the storm of grief had spent itself she went away to her room alone. She would have no one follow her.

4 There stood, facing the open window, a comfortable, roomy armchair. Into this she sank, pressed down by a physical exhaustion that haunted her body and seemed to reach into her soul.

5 She could see in the open square before her house the tops of trees that were all aquiver with the new spring life. The delicious breath of rain was in the air. In the street below a peddler was crying his wares. The notes of a distant song which some one was singing reached her faintly, and countless sparrows were twittering in the eaves.

6 There were patches of blue sky showing here and there through the clouds that had met and piled one above the other in the west facing her window.

7 She sat with her head thrown back upon the cushion of the chair, quite motionless, except when a sob came up into her throat and shook her, as a child who has cried itself to sleep continues to sob in its dreams.

8 She was young, with a fair, calm face, whose lines bespoke repression and even a certain strength. But now there was a dull stare in her eyes, whose gaze was fixed away off yonder on one of those patches of blue sky. It was not a glance of reflection, but rather indicated a suspension of intelligent thought.

9 There was something coming to her and she was waiting for it, fearfully. What was it? She did not know; it was too subtle and elusive to name. But she felt it, creeping out of the sky, reaching toward her through the sounds, the scents, the color that filled the air.

10 Now her bosom rose and fell tumultuously. She was beginning to recognize this thing that was approaching to possess her, and she was striving to beat it back with her will—as powerless as her two white slender hands would have been.

11 When she abandoned herself a little whispered word escaped her slightly parted lips. She said it over and over under her breath: "free, free, free!" The vacant stare and the look of terror that had followed it went from her eyes. They stayed keen and bright. Her pulses beat fast, and the coursing blood warmed and relaxed every inch of her body.

12 She did not stop to ask if it were or were not a monstrous joy that held her. A clear and exalted perception enabled her to dismiss the suggestion as trivial.

13 She knew that she would weep again when she saw the kind, tender hands folded in death; the face that had never looked save with love upon her, fixed and gray and dead. But she saw beyond that bitter moment a long procession of years to come that would belong to her absolutely. And she opened and spread her arms out to them in welcome.

14 There would be no one to live for during those coming years; she would live for herself. There would be no powerful will bending hers in that blind persistence with

which men and women believe they have a right to impose a private will upon a fellow-creature. A kind intention or a cruel intention made the act seem no less a crime as she looked upon it in that brief moment of illumination.

15   And yet she had loved him—sometimes. Often she had not. What did it matter! What could love, the unsolved mystery, count for in face of this possession of self-assertion which she suddenly recognized as the strongest impulse of her being!

16   "Free! Body and soul free!" she kept whispering.

17   Josephine was kneeling before the closed door with her lips to the keyhole, imploring for admission. "Louise, open the door! I beg; open the door—you will make yourself ill. What are you doing, Louise? For heaven's sake open the door."

18   "Go away. I am not making myself ill." No; she was drinking in a very elixir of life through that open window.

19   Her fancy was running riot along those days ahead of her. Spring days, and summer days, and all sorts of days that would be her own. She breathed a quick prayer that life might be long. It was only yesterday she had thought with a shudder that life might be long.

20   She arose at length and opened the door to her sister's importunities. There was a feverish triumph in her eyes, and she carried herself unwittingly like a goddess of Victory. She clasped her sister's waist, and together they descended the stairs. Richards stood waiting for them at the bottom.

21   Some one was opening the front door with a latchkey. It was Brently Mallard who entered, a little travel-stained, composedly carrying his gripsack and umbrella. He had been far from the scene of accident, and did not even know there had been one. He stood amazed at Josephine's piercing cry; at Richards' quick motion to screen him from the view of his wife.

22   But Richards was too late.

23   When the doctors came they said she had died of heart disease—of joy that kills.

ANALYZE & WRITE

Use the following questions to begin analyzing "The Story of an Hour":

1 **Irony** refers to a gap or discrepancy between what is said and what is true, or between a result that is expected and what actually happens. In literature, readers often perceive irony that characters are unable to see. What is the central irony of "The Story of an Hour"? To get started, take a look at how the story is framed in the opening and closing paragraphs. What gap or discrepancy do you notice? Do the characters share your insight?

2 What do you learn from the setting and, in particular, the language Chopin uses to describe what Mrs. Mallard experiences when, beginning in paragraph 4, she sits in her armchair, looking out the window?

3 This story was originally published at the end of the nineteenth century. With this context in mind, what do you think Chopin is saying about marriage, gender, power, and sexuality in American society? To get started, you could look at how Richards tries to "screen [Mr. Mallard] from the view of his wife" (par. 21).

James Joyce | *Araby*

JAMES JOYCE (1882–1941), a native of Dublin, Ireland, is considered one of the most influential writers of the early twentieth century. "Araby," one of his most often anthologized stories, first appeared in the collection *Dubliners* in 1914. Like his novel *Portrait of the Artist as a Young Man*, published two years later, it relies on scenes from Joyce's own boyhood.

1 North Richmond Street, being blind,[1] was a quiet street except at the hour when the Christian Brothers' School set the boys free. An uninhabited house of two storeys stood at the blind end, detached from its neighbours in a square ground. The other houses of the street, conscious of decent lives within them, gazed at one another with brown imperturbable faces.

2 The former tenant of our house, a priest, had died in the back drawing-room. Air, musty from having been long enclosed, hung in all the rooms, and the waste room behind the kitchen was littered with old useless papers. Among these I found a few paper-covered books, the pages of which were curled and damp: *The Abbot*, by Walter Scott, *The Devout Communicant* and *The Memoirs of Vidocq*.[2] I liked the last best because its leaves were yellow. The wild garden behind the house contained a central apple-tree and a few straggling bushes under one of which I found the late tenant's rusty bicycle-pump. He had been a very charitable priest; in his will he had left all his money to institutions and the furniture of his house to his sister.

3 When the short days of winter came dusk fell before we had well eaten our dinners. When we met in the street the houses had grown sombre. The space of sky above us was the colour of ever-changing violet and towards it the lamps of the street lifted their feeble lanterns. The cold air stung us and we played till our bodies glowed. Our shouts echoed in the silent street. The career of our play brought us through the dark muddy lanes behind the houses where we ran the gauntlet of the rough tribes from the cottages, to the back doors of the dark dripping gardens where odours arose from the ashpits, to the dark odorous stables where a coachman smoothed and combed the horse or shook music from the buckled harness. When we returned to the street light from the kitchen windows had filled the areas. If my uncle was seen turning the corner we hid in the shadow until we had seen him safely housed. Or if Mangan's sister came out on the doorstep to call her brother in to his tea we watched her from our shadow peer up and down the street. We waited to see whether she would remain or go in and, if she remained, we left our shadow and walked up to Mangan's steps resignedly. She was waiting for us, her figure defined by the light from the half-opened door. Her brother always teased her before he obeyed and I stood by the railings looking at her. Her dress swung as she moved her body and the soft rope of her hair tossed from side to side.

4 Every morning I lay on the floor in the front parlour watching her door. The blind was pulled down to within an inch of the sash so that I could not be seen. When she came out on the doorstep my heart leaped. I ran to the hall, seized my books and followed her. I kept her brown figure always in my eye and, when we came near the point at which our ways diverged, I quickened my pace and passed her. This happened morning after morning. I had never spoken to her, except for a few casual words, and yet her name was like a summons to all my foolish blood.

5 Her image accompanied me even in places the most hostile to romance. On Saturday evenings when my aunt went marketing I had to go to carry some of the parcels. We walked through the flaring streets, jostled by drunken men and bargaining women, amid the curses of labourers, the shrill litanies of shop-boys who stood on guard by the barrels of pigs' cheeks, the nasal chanting of street-singers, who sang a *come-all-you* about O'Donovan Rossa,[3] or a ballad about the troubles in our native land. These noises converged in a single sensation of life for me: I imagined that I bore my chalice safely through a throng of foes. Her name sprang to my lips at moments in strange prayers and praises which I myself did not understand. My eyes were often full of tears (I could not tell why) and at times a flood from my heart seemed to pour itself out into my bosom. I thought little of the future. I did not know whether I would ever speak to her or not or, if I spoke to her, how I could tell her of my confused adoration. But my body was like a harp and her words and gestures were like fingers running upon the wires.

---

[1] A dead end. The young Joyce in fact lived for a time on North Richmond Street in Dublin. [Editor's note]

[2] *The Abbot* is a historical romance set in the court of Mary, Queen of Scots, a Catholic, who was beheaded for plotting to assassinate her Protestant cousin, Queen Elizabeth I. *The Devout Communicant* is a collection of religious meditations. *The Memoirs of Vidocq* is a collection of sexually suggestive stories about a French criminal turned detective. [Editor's note]

[3] A contemporary leader of an underground organization opposed to British rule of Ireland. [Editor's note]

6   One evening I went into the back drawing-room in which the priest had died. It was a dark rainy evening and there was no sound in the house. Through one of the broken panes I heard the rain impinge upon the earth, the fine incessant needles of water playing in the sodden beds. Some distant lamp or lighted window gleamed below me. I was thankful that I could see so little. All my senses seemed to desire to veil themselves and, feeling that I was about to slip from them, I pressed the palms of my hands together until they trembled, murmuring: *"O love! O love!"* many times.

7   At last she spoke to me. When she addressed the first words to me I was so confused that I did not know what to answer. She asked me was I going to Araby. I forgot whether I answered yes or no. It would be a splendid bazaar, she said she would love to go.[4]

8   "And why can't you?" I asked.

9   While she spoke she turned a silver bracelet round and round her wrist. She could not go, she said, because there would be a retreat that week in her convent. Her brother and two other boys were fighting for their caps and I was alone at the railings. She held one of the spikes, bowing her head towards me. The light from the lamp opposite our door caught the white curve of her neck, lit up her hair that rested there and, falling, lit up the hand upon the railing. It fell over one side of her dress and caught the white border of a petticoat, just visible as she stood at ease.

10   "It's well for you," she said.

11   "If I go," I said, "I will bring you something."

12   What innumerable follies laid waste my waking and sleeping thoughts after that evening! I wished to annihilate the tedious intervening days. I chafed against the work of school. At night in my bedroom and by day in the classroom her image came between me and the page I strove to read. The syllables of the word *Araby* were called to me through the silence in which my soul luxuriated and cast an Eastern enchantment over me. I asked for leave to go to the bazaar on Saturday night. My aunt was surprised and hoped it was not some Freemason affair.[5] I answered few questions in class. I watched my master's face pass from amiability to sternness; he hoped I was not beginning to idle. I could not call my wandering thoughts together. I had hardly any patience with the serious work of life which, now that it stood between me and my desire, seemed to me child's play, ugly monotonous child's play.

13   On Saturday morning I reminded my uncle that I wished to go to the bazaar in the evening. He was fussing at the hallstand, looking for the hatbrush, and answered me curtly:

14   "Yes, boy, I know."

15   As he was in the hall I could not go into the front parlour and lie at the window. I left the house in bad humour and walked slowly towards the school. The air was pitilessly raw and already my heart misgave me.

16   When I came home to dinner my uncle had not yet been home. Still it was early. I sat staring at the clock for some time and, when its ticking began to irritate me, I left the room. I mounted the staircase and gained the upper part of the house. The high cold empty gloomy rooms liberated me and I went from room to room singing. From the front window I saw my companions playing below in the street. Their cries reached me weakened and indistinct and, leaning my forehead against the cool glass, I looked over at the dark house where she lived. I may have stood there for an hour, seeing nothing but the brown-clad figure cast by my imagination, touched discreetly by the lamplight at the curved neck, at the hand upon the railings and at the border below the dress.

17   When I came downstairs again I found Mrs. Mercer sitting at the fire. She was an old garrulous woman, a pawnbroker's widow, who collected used stamps for some pious purpose. I had to endure the gossip of the tea-table. The meal was prolonged beyond an hour and still my uncle did not come. Mrs. Mercer stood up to go: she was sorry she couldn't wait any longer, but it was after eight o'clock and she did not like to be out late, as the night air was bad for her. When she had gone I began to walk up and down the room, clenching my fists. My aunt said:

---

[4] Traveling bazaars featured cafés, shopping stalls, and entertainment. Araby was the name of an English bazaar that visited Dublin when Joyce was a boy. [Editor's note]

[5] The Freemasons is a secretive fraternal order that has a long history and that has traditionally been opposed by the Catholic Church. [Editor's note]

18 "I'm afraid you may put off your bazaar for this night of Our Lord."

19 At nine o'clock I heard my uncle's latchkey in the halldoor. I heard him talking to himself and heard the hallstand rocking when it had received the weight of his overcoat. I could interpret these signs. When he was midway through his dinner I asked him to give me the money to go to the bazaar. He had forgotten.

20 "The people are in bed and after their first sleep now," he said.

21 I did not smile. My aunt said to him energetically:

22 "Can't you give him the money and let him go? You've kept him late enough as it is."

23 My uncle said he was very sorry he had forgotten. He said he believed in the old saying: "All work and no play makes Jack a dull boy." He asked me where I was going and, when I had told him a second time he asked me did I know *The Arab's Farewell to His Steed*. When I left the kitchen he was about to recite the opening lines of the piece to my aunt.

24 I held a florin tightly in my hand as I strode down Buckingham Street towards the station. The sight of the streets thronged with buyers and glaring with gas recalled to me the purpose of my journey. I took my seat in a third-class carriage of a deserted train. After an intolerable delay the train moved out of the station slowly. It crept onward among ruinous houses and over the twinkling river. At Westland Row Station a crowd of people pressed to the carriage doors; but the porters moved them back, saying that it was a special train for the bazaar. I remained alone in the bare carriage. In a few minutes the train drew up beside an improvised wooden platform. I passed out on to the road and saw by the lighted dial of a clock that it was ten minutes to ten. In front of me was a large building which displayed the magical name.

25 I could not find any sixpenny entrance and, fearing that the bazaar would be closed, I passed in quickly through a turnstile, handing a shilling to a weary-looking man. I found myself in a big hall girdled at half its height by a gallery. Nearly all the stalls were closed and the greater part of the hall was in darkness. I recognised a silence like that which pervades a church after a service. I walked into the centre of the bazaar timidly. A few people were gathered about the stalls which were still open. Before a curtain, over which the words *Café Chantant*[6] were written in coloured lamps, two men were counting money on a salver. I listened to the fall of the coins.

26 Remembering with difficulty why I had come I went over to one of the stalls and examined porcelain vases and flowered tea-sets. At the door of the stall a young lady was talking and laughing with two young gentlemen. I remarked their English accents and listened vaguely to their conversation.

27 "O, I never said such a thing!"

28 "O, but you did!"

29 "O, but I didn't!"

30 "Didn't she say that?"

31 "Yes. I heard her."

32 "O, there's a . . . fib!"

33 Observing me the young lady came over and asked me did I wish to buy anything. The tone of her voice was not encouraging; she seemed to have spoken to me out of a sense of duty. I looked humbly at the great jars that stood like eastern guards at either side of the dark entrance to the stall and murmured:

34 "No, thank you."

35 The young lady changed the position of one of the vases and went back to the two young men. They began to talk of the same subject. Once or twice the young lady glanced at me over her shoulder.

36 I lingered before her stall, though I knew my stay was useless, to make my interest in her wares seem the more real. Then I turned away slowly and walked down the middle of the bazaar. I allowed the two pennies to fall against the sixpence in my pocket. I heard a voice call from one end of the gallery that the light was out. The upper part of the hall was now completely dark.

37 Gazing up into the darkness I saw myself as a creature driven and derided by vanity; and my eyes burned with anguish and anger.

---

[6] Literally, *singing café* (French), a music hall. [Editor's note]

ANALYZE & WRITE

Use the following questions to begin analyzing "Araby":

1 "Araby" can be read as a coming-of-age story about an adolescent boy's first crush. If you read it on this level, what changes would you say the boy goes through? What, if anything, does he learn? To get started, take a look at paragraph 4.

2 The boy describes himself as carrying the "image" of Mangan's sister like a "chalice," "even in places the most hostile to romance," such as the crowded, raucous streets of early twentieth-century Dublin, Ireland (par. 5). How does the boy's experience on Saturday evening shopping trips with his aunt compare to his experience at Araby (25)? What makes the experiences so different?

3 This story is saturated with the culture of Dublin, particularly its Catholicism and its attitudes about gender and sexuality. How are these or other important cultural influences expressed in the story? To get started, take a look at paragraph 2.

William Carlos Williams | *The Use of Force*

Library of Congress

WILLIAM CARLOS WILLIAMS (1883–1963) is one of the most important poets of the twentieth century, best known for his long poem *Paterson* (1946–1958). He also wrote essays, plays, novels, and short stories. "The Use of Force" was initially published in *The Doctor Stories* (1933), a collection loosely based on Williams's experiences as a pediatrician.

1   They were new patients to me, all I had was the name, Olson. Please come down as soon as you can, my daughter is very sick.

2   When I arrived I was met by the mother, a big startled-looking woman, very clean and apologetic, who merely said, Is this the doctor? and let me in. In the back, she added. You must excuse us, doctor, we have her in the kitchen where it is warm. It is very damp here sometimes.

3   The child was fully dressed and sitting on her father's lap near the kitchen table. He tried to get up, but I motioned for him not to bother, took off my overcoat and started to look things over. I could see that they were all very nervous, eyeing me up and down distrustfully. As often, in such cases, they weren't telling me more than they had to, it was up to me to tell them; that's why they were spending three dollars on me.

4   The child was fairly eating me up with her cold, steady eyes, and no expression to her face whatever. She did not move and seemed, inwardly, quiet; an unusually attractive little thing, and as strong as a heifer in appearance. But her face was flushed, she was breathing rapidly, and I realized that she had a high fever. She had magnificent blonde hair, in profusion. One of those picture children often reproduced in advertising leaflets and the photogravure sections of the Sunday papers.

5   She's had a fever for three days, began the father, and we don't know what it comes from. My wife has given her things, you know, like people do, but it don't do no good. And there's been a lot of sickness around. So we tho't you better look her over and tell us what is the matter.

6   As doctors often do I took a trial shot at it as a point of departure. Has she had a sore throat?

7   Both parents answered me together, No . . . No, she says her throat don't hurt her.

8   Does your throat hurt you? added the mother to the child. But the little girl's expression didn't change nor did she move her eyes from my face.

9   Have you looked?

10   I tried, said the mother, but I couldn't see.

11   As it happens we had been having a number of cases of diphtheria in the school to which this child went during that month and we were all, quite apparently, thinking of that, though no one had as yet spoken of the thing.

12   Well, I said, suppose we take a look at the throat first. I smiled in my best professional manner and asking for the child's first name I said, come on, Mathilda, open your mouth and let's take a look at your throat.

13   Nothing doing.

14   Aw, come on, I coaxed, just open your mouth wide and let me take a look. Look, I said opening both hands wide, I haven't anything in my hands. Just open up and let me see.

15   Such a nice man, put in the mother. Look how kind he is to you. Come on, do what he tells you to. He won't hurt you.

16   At that I ground my teeth in disgust. If only they wouldn't use the word "hurt" I might be able to get somewhere. But I did not allow myself to be hurried or disturbed but speaking quietly and slowly I approached the child again.

17   As I moved my chair a little nearer suddenly with one catlike movement both her hands clawed instinctively for my eyes and she almost reached them too. In fact she knocked my glasses flying and they fell, though unbroken, several feet away from me on the kitchen floor.

18   Both the mother and father almost turned themselves inside out in embarrassment and apology. You bad girl, said the mother, taking her and shaking her by one arm. Look what you've done. The nice man . . .

19   For heaven's sake, I broke in. Don't call me a nice man to her. I'm here to look at her throat on the chance that she might have diphtheria and possibly die of it. But that's nothing to her. Look here, I said to the child, we're going to look at your throat. You're old enough to understand what I'm saying. Will you open it now by yourself or shall we have to open it for you?

20   Not a move. Even her expression hadn't changed. Her breaths however were coming faster and faster. Then the battle began. I had to do it. I had to have a throat culture for her own protection. But first I told the parents that it was entirely up to them. I explained the danger but said that I would not insist on a throat examination so long as they would take the responsibility.

21   If you don't do what the doctor says you'll have to go to the hospital, the mother admonished her severely.

22   Oh yeah? I had to smile to myself. After all, I had already fallen in love with the savage brat, the parents were contemptible to me. In the ensuing struggle they grew more and more abject, crushed, exhausted while she surely rose to magnificent heights of insane fury of effort bred of her terror of me.

23   The father tried his best, and he was a big man, but the fact that she was his daughter, his shame at her behavior and his dread of hurting her made him release her just at the critical times when I had almost achieved success, till I wanted to kill him. But his dread also that she might have diphtheria made him tell me to go on, go on though he himself was almost fainting, while the mother moved back and forth behind us raising and lowering her hands in an agony of apprehension.

24   Put her in front of you on your lap, I ordered, and hold both her wrists.

25   But as soon as he did the child let out a scream. Don't, you're hurting me. Let go of my hands. Let them go I tell you. Then she shrieked terrifyingly, hysterically. Stop it! Stop it! You're killing me!

26   Do you think she can stand it, doctor! said the mother.

27   You get out, said the husband to his wife. Do you want her to die of diphtheria?

28   Come on now, hold her, I said.

29   Then I grasped the child's head with my left hand and tried to get the wooden tongue depressor between her teeth. She fought, with clenched teeth, desperately! But now I also had grown furious—at a child. I tried to hold myself down but I couldn't. I know how to expose a throat for inspection. And I did my best. When finally I got the wooden spatula behind the last teeth and just the point of it into the mouth cavity, she opened up for an instant but before I could see anything she came down again and gripping the wooden blade between her molars she reduced it to splinters before I could get it out again.

30   Aren't you ashamed, the mother yelled at her. Aren't you ashamed to act like that in front of the doctor?

31   Get me a smooth-handled spoon of some sort, I told the mother. We're going through with this. The child's mouth was already bleeding. Her tongue was cut and she was screaming in wild hysterical shrieks. Perhaps I should have desisted and come back in an hour or more. No doubt it would have been better. But I have

seen at least two children lying dead in bed of neglect in such cases, and feeling that I must get a diagnosis now or never I went at it again. But the worst of it was that I too had got beyond reason. I could have torn the child apart in my own fury and enjoyed it. It was a pleasure to attack her. My face was burning with it.

32   The damned little brat must be protected against her own idiocy, one says to oneself at such times. Others must be protected against her. It is a social necessity. And all these things are true. But a blind fury, a feeling of adult shame, bred of a longing for muscular release are the operatives. One goes on to the end.

33   In a final unreasoning assault I overpowered the child's neck and jaws. I forced the heavy silver spoon back of her teeth and down her throat till she gagged. And there it was—both tonsils covered with membrane. She had fought valiantly to keep me from knowing her secret. She had been hiding that sore throat for three days at least and lying to her parents in order to escape just such an outcome as this.

34   Now truly she was furious. She had been on the defensive before but now she attacked. Tried to get off her father's lap and fly at me while tears of defeat blinded her eyes.

ANALYZE & WRITE

Use the following questions to begin analyzing "The Use of Force":

1 This story is told from the doctor's point of view. How does he justify his use of force? What are the pros and cons he weighs in using it? To get started, look at paragraph 34.

2 How do the sexual overtones of the story — for example, in the doctor's describing the girl as "an unusually attractive little thing" (par. 4) and admitting "I had already fallen in love with the savage brat" (22) — affect your understanding and judgment of the doctor's and the girl's behavior?

3 Because this story came out of the era of the Great Depression, you might expect it to say something about the impoverished material conditions in which people lived at the time and how these hardships affected them. Are these expectations borne out? What seems to be the economic status of the family and the doctor, and how does class affect what happens in the story? To get started, take a look at paragraphs 2 and 3.

Jamaica Kincaid | *Girl*

Cosima Scavolini/ZUMA
Press/Roma/rm/Italia

JAMAICA KINCAID was born Elaine Potter Richardson in 1949 in St. Johns, Antigua, in the West Indies. As Kincaid's mother had more children, the once-close relationship between mother and daughter became strained, and Kincaid began to feel increasingly restricted by life in Antigua under British rule. At seventeen, she left Antigua to work as an au pair in New York, where she attended night classes and began working as a freelance writer. At the start of her writing career, she changed her name to Jamaica Kincaid to shed the "weights" (as she put it) of her past life. Kincaid's stories have appeared in such prestigious venues as *Rolling Stone,* the *Paris Review,* and the *New Yorker,* where she became a staff writer in 1978. "Girl" was published first in the *New Yorker* and later in Kincaid's first book, *At the Bottom of the River* (1984), an anthology of short stories that won the Morton Dauwen

Zabel Award. Her next book, *Annie John* (1985), also a collection of stories, centered on a girl growing up in the West Indies. In addition to stories and novels, such as *See, Now, Then* (2013), *Mr. Potter* (2002), and *Lucy* (1990), Kincaid has published several books of nonfiction, including *My Brother* (1997), the story of her brother Devon Drew's short life; *A Small Place* (2000), an examination of her native Antigua; and *Among Flowers: A Walk in the Himalayas* (2005), a memoir of her travels in Nepal. Kincaid now makes her home in Vermont, where her husband is a composer and professor of music at Bennington College.

As you read "Girl," listen to the rhythms of the language, and consider how the almost poetic litany of instructions reflects and shapes the relationship between mother and daughter.

Wash the white clothes on Monday and put them on the stone heap; wash the color clothes on Tuesday and put them on the clothesline to dry; don't walk barehead in the hot sun; cook pumpkin fritters in very hot sweet oil; soak your little cloths right after you take them off; when buying cotton to make yourself a nice blouse, be sure that it doesn't have gum on it, because that way it won't hold up well after a wash; soak salt fish overnight before you cook it; is it true that you sing benna[1] in Sunday school?; always eat your food in such a way that it won't turn someone else's stomach; on Sundays try to walk like a lady and not like the slut you are so bent on becoming; don't sing benna in Sunday school; you mustn't speak to wharf-rat boys, not even to give directions; don't eat fruits on the street—flies will follow you; *but I don't sing benna on Sundays at all and never in Sunday school;* this is how to sew on a button; this is how to make a button-hole for the button you have just sewed on; this is how to hem a dress when you see the hem coming down and so to prevent yourself from looking like the slut I know you are so bent on becoming; this is how you iron your father's khaki shirt so that it doesn't have a crease; this is how you iron your father's khaki pants so that they don't have a crease; this is how you grow okra—far from the house, because okra tree harbors red ants; when you are growing dasheen,[2] make sure it gets plenty of water or else it makes your throat itch when you are eating it; this is how you sweep a corner; this is how you sweep a whole house; this is how you sweep a yard; this is how you smile to someone you don't like too much; this is how you smile to someone you don't like at all; this is how you smile to someone you like completely; this is how you set a table for tea; this is how you set a table for dinner; this is how you set a table for dinner with an important guest; this is how you set a table for lunch; this is how you set a table for breakfast; this is how to behave in the presence of men who don't know you very well, and this way they won't recognize immediately the slut I have warned you against becoming; be sure to wash every day, even if it is with your own spit; don't squat down to play marbles—you are not a boy, you know; don't pick people's flowers—you might catch something; don't throw stones at blackbirds, because it might not be a blackbird at all; this is how to make a bread pudding; this is how to make doukona;[3] this is how to make pepper pot;[4] this is how to make a good medicine for a cold; this is how to make a good medicine to throw away a child before it even becomes a child; this is how to catch a fish; this is how to throw back a fish you don't like, and that way something bad won't fall on you; this is how to bully a man; this is how a man bullies you; this is how to love a man; and if this doesn't work there are other ways, and if they don't work don't feel too bad about giving up; this is how to spit up in the air if you feel like it, and this is how to move quick so that it doesn't fall on you; this is how to make ends meet; always squeeze bread to make sure it's fresh; *but what if the baker won't let me feel the bread?;* you mean to say that after all you are really going to be the kind of woman who the baker won't let near the bread?

---

[1] Calypso, popular Afro-Caribbean music from the West Indies. [Editor's note]

[2] Taro, a starchy root vegetable with edible leaves that is a staple crop of the Caribbean. [Editor's note]

[3] Spicy pudding made from plantains. [Editor's note]

[4] A West Indian stew that is typically made for special occasions. [Editor's note]

ANALYZE & WRITE

Use the following questions to begin analyzing "Girl":

1 This story is told almost exclusively from the mother's point of view; with the exception of two italicized interjections from the daughter ("but I don't sing benna on Sundays at all and never in Sunday school"; "but what if the baker won't let me feel the bread?"), the words are entirely the mother's. How does the language the mother uses, and the instructions she gives, shape your understanding of the mother's character? How would you describe her relationship with her daughter based on her litany of advice?

2 If irony is the discrepancy between the truth and what is said or the gap between what is expected and what actually happens, is "Girl" ironic? Why or why not?

3 Kincaid grew up in St. John's, Antigua, in the 1950s and 1960s, and while the setting is not specified, "Girl" seems to have been set in a similar place and time. What can you infer about the society in which "Girl" is set from the advice the mother gives and the language she uses? How might the story's first readers (subscribers to the *New Yorker* in 1978) have reacted, and why? How might your reaction differ from that of the story's initial audience?

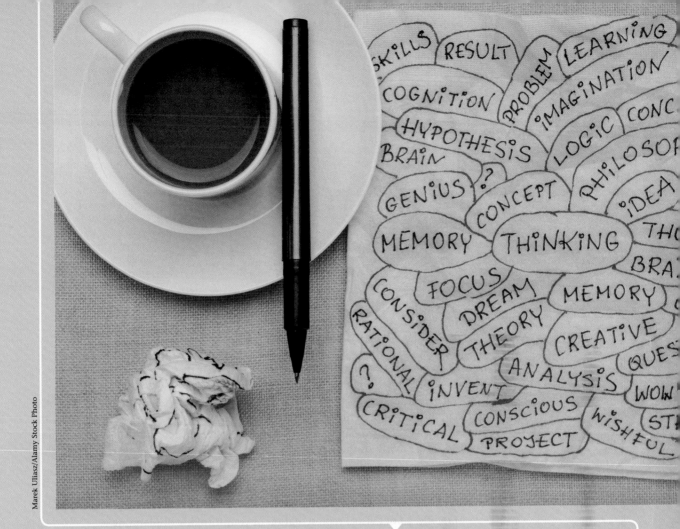

PART 2

Critical Thinking Strategies

11

A Catalog of Invention and Inquiry Strategies

Writers are like scientists: They ask questions, systematically inquiring about how things work, what they are, where they occur, and how more information can be learned about them. Writers are also like artists in that they use what they know and learn to create something new and imaginative.

The invention and inquiry strategies described in this chapter are not mysterious or magical. They represent ways that writers, engineers, scientists, composers—in fact, all of us—solve problems. Once you have mastered these strategies, you can use them to tackle many of the writing situations you will encounter in college, on the job, and in the community.

The strategies for invention and inquiry in this chapter are arranged alphabetically within two categories:

Mapping: a brief visual representation of your thinking or planning

Writing: the composition of phrases or sentences to discover information and ideas and to make connections among them

These invention and inquiry strategies will help you explore and research a topic fully before you begin drafting, and then help you creatively solve problems as you draft and revise.

Mapping

Mapping strategies, like clustering, listing, and outlining, involve making a visual record of invention and inquiry. In making maps, writers usually use key words and phrases to record material they want to remember, questions they need to answer, and new sources of information they want to check. The maps show the ideas, details, and facts as well as possible ways to connect and focus them. Mapping can be especially useful for working collaboratively, preparing presentations, and creating multimedia illustrations for written texts you will submit either on paper or electronically.

Create a cluster diagram to reveal relationships among ideas.

Clustering is a strategy for revealing possible relationships among facts and ideas. Clustering works as follows:

1. In a word or phrase, write your topic in the center of a piece of paper. Circle it.

2. Also in words or phrases, write down the main parts or ideas of your topic. Circle these, and connect them with lines to the topic in the center.

3. Next, write down facts, details, and examples related to these main parts or ideas. Circle these, and connect them with lines to the relevant main parts or ideas.

Clustering can be useful in the early stages of composing to narrow a topic, find subtopics, and organize information. You may try out and discard several clusters before finding one that is promising. Many writers also use clustering to plan brief sections of a writing project as they are drafting or revising. (A model of clustering is shown in Figure 11.1.)

Software-based diagramming tools
Software vendors have created a variety of electronic tools to help people better visualize complex projects. These flowcharts, webs, and outlines can make it easier for you to see how to proceed at any stage of your project.

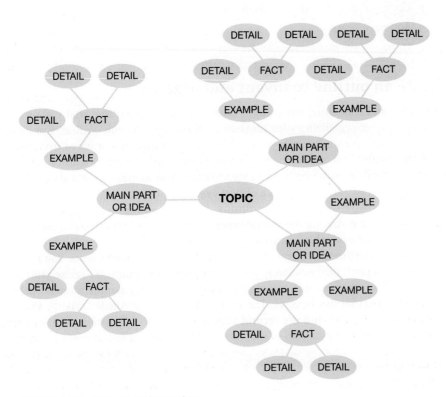

FIGURE 11.1   A Model of Clustering

Make a list to generate a plan quickly.

Listing is a familiar activity. You probably make shopping or to-do lists every day. But listing can also be a great help in planning a writing project. It enables you to recall what you already know about a topic and suggests what you may still need to find out. Listing is especially useful to those who have little time for planning—for example, reporters facing deadlines and college students taking essay exams—because it lets you order your ideas quickly. It can also serve as a first step in discovering possible writing topics.

Here is how listing works best for invention work:

1. Give your list a title that indicates your main idea or topic.

2. Write as fast as you can, relying on short phrases.

3. Include anything that seems at all useful. Try not to be judgmental at this point.

4. After you have finished or even as you write, reflect on and organize the list:

   - Put an asterisk next to the most promising items.
   - Number or reorder key items in order of importance.
   - Put items in related groups.
   - Cross out or delete items that do not seem promising.
   - Add new items.

Create an outline to invent and organize.

Like listing and clustering, **outlining** is both a means of inventing what you want to say and a way of organizing your ideas and information. As you outline, you nearly always see new possibilities in your subject, discovering new ways of dividing or grouping information and seeing where you need additional information to develop your ideas. Because outlining lets you see strengths and weaknesses at a glance, it can also help you read and revise with a critical eye.

There are two main forms of outlining: informal outlining and formal topic or sentence outlining. Among the several types of informal outlining, *scratch outlines* are perhaps the most adaptable to a variety of situations.

A **scratch outline** is little more than a list of the essay's main points. You have no doubt made scratch outlines many times—to plan essay exams, to revise your own writing, and to analyze a difficult reading passage. Here are sample scratch outlines for two different kinds of essays. The first is an outline of Annie Dillard's essay in Chapter 2 (pp. 22–24), and the second shows one way to organize a position paper (Chapter 6):

Scratch Outline: Essay about a Remembered Event

¶1. explains what she learned from playing football

¶2. identifies other sports she learned from boys in the neighborhood

¶3. sets the scene by describing the time and place of the event

¶4. describes the boys who were playing with her

¶5. describes what typically happened: a car would come down the street, they would throw snowballs, and then they would wait for another car

¶6. describes the iceball-making project she had begun while waiting

¶7. describes the Buick's approach and how they followed the routine

Scratch Outline: Essay Arguing a Position

Presentation of the issue

Concession of some aspect of an opposing position

Thesis statement

First reason with support

Second reason with support

(etc.)

Conclusion

Remember that the items in a scratch outline do not necessarily coincide with paragraphs. Sometimes two or more items may be developed in the same paragraph, or one item may be covered in two or more paragraphs.

Chunking, a type of scratch outline commonly used by professional writers in business and industry and especially well suited to collaborative and multimodal composing, consists of a set of headings describing the major points to be covered in the final document. What makes chunking distinctive is that the blocks of text—or "chunks"—under each heading are intended to be roughly the same length and scope. These headings can be discussed and passed around among several writers and editors before writing begins, and different chunks may be written by different authors, simply by typing notes into the space under each heading. The list of headings is subject to change during the writing, and new headings may be added or old ones subdivided or discarded as part of the drafting and revising processes.

The advantage of chunking in your own writing is that it breaks the large task of drafting into smaller tasks in a simple, evenly balanced way; once the headings are determined, the writing becomes a matter of filling in the specifics that go in each chunk. Organization tends to improve as you get a sense of the weight of different parts of the document while filling in the blanks. Places where the writing project needs more information or where there is a problem with pacing tend to stand out because of the chunking structure, and the headings can be either taken out of the finished project or left in as devices to help guide readers. If they are left in, they should be edited into parallel grammatical form like the items in a formal topic or sentence outline, as discussed below.

For more on parallelism, see Chapter 13, p. 468.

Topic outlines and **sentence outlines** are considered more formal than scratch outlines because they follow a conventional format of numbered and lettered headings and subheadings:

Period follows numbers and letters

First word of each item is capitalized

```
I.  Main topic
    A. Subtopic of I
    B.
        1. Subtopic of I.B
        2.
            a. Subtopic of I.B.2
            b.
                (1) Subtopic of I.B.2.b
                (2)
    C.
        1. Subtopic of I.C
        2.
```

The difference between a topic and sentence outline is obvious: Topic outlines simply name the topics and subtopics, whereas sentence outlines use complete or abbreviated sentences. To illustrate, here are two partial formal outlines of an essay arguing a position, Jessica Statsky's "Children Need to Play, Not Compete," from Chapter 6 (pp. 198–204).

Formal Topic Outline

I. Organized sports harmful to children
 A. Harmful physically
  1. Curve ball (Koppett)
  2. Concussions and "bobble head" effect
 B. Harmful psychologically
  1. Fear of being hurt
   a. Little League Online
   b. Tutko and mother
   c. Tosches
  2. Competition
   a. Rablovsky
   b. Smith et al.

Formal Sentence Outline

I. Highly organized competitive sports such as Peewee Football and Little League Baseball can be physically and psychologically harmful to children, as well as counterproductive for developing future players.
 A. Physically harmful because sports entice children into physical actions that are bad for growing bodies.
  1. Koppett claims throwing a curve ball may put abnormal strain on developing arm and shoulder muscles.
  2. Research shows youngsters suffer concussions or "the bobble head effect" caused by a lot of minor injuries.
 B. Psychologically harmful to children for a number of reasons.
  1. Fear of being hurt detracts from their enjoyment of the sport.
   a. Little League Online ranks fear of failure, lack of playing time, disapproval, and stress among top reasons children quit.
   b. Tutko argues that tackle football is too traumatic for young kids. One mother says, "Kids get so scared. . . . They'll sit on the bench and pretend their leg hurts."
   c. Tosches (A33) tells about a child who made himself vomit to get out of playing Peewee Football.
  2. Too much competition detracts from fun and eliminates children.
   a. Rablovsky reports: "The spirit of play suddenly disappears, and sport becomes job-like."
   b. Studies show that 90% children prefer playing on a losing team to warming the bench on a winning team (Smith et al. 11).
   c. Too few get to participate. Julianna W. Minor/ *Washington Post* say 70% drop out by 13 because it's no longer fun.

Every level of a formal outline except the top level (identified by the roman numeral *I*) must include at least two items. Items at the same level of indentation in a topic outline should be grammatically parallel—all beginning with the same part of speech. For example, *I.A* and *I.B* are parallel when they both begin with an adverb (*Physically harmful* and *Psychologically harmful*) or with an adjective (*Harmful physically* and *Harmful psychologically*); they would not be parallel if one began with an adverb (*Physically harmful*) and the other with an adjective (*Harmful psychologically*).

Writing

Writing strategies—including cubing, dialoguing, dramatizing, freewriting, looping, keeping a journal, and questioning—invite you to produce complete sentences, so they provide considerable generative power. Because they are complete statements, they take you further than listing or clustering, enabling you to explore ideas and define relationships, bring ideas together or show how they differ, identify causes and effects, and develop a logical chain of thought.

Use cubing to explore a topic from six perspectives.

Cubing allows you to explore a writing topic from six different perspectives (the number of sides on a cube):

Describing: What does your subject look like? What size is it? What is its color? Its shape? Its texture? Name its parts.

Comparing: What is your subject similar to? Different from?

Associating: What does your subject make you think of? What connections does it have to anything else in your experience?

Analyzing: What are the origins of your subject? What are the functions or significance of its parts? How are its parts related?

Applying: What can you do with your subject? What uses does it have?

Arguing: What arguments can you make for your subject? Against it?

These guidelines can help you use cubing productively:

1. **Select a topic, a subject, or part of a subject.** This can be a person, a scene, an event, an object, a problem, an idea, or an issue. Hold it in focus.

2. **Limit your writing to three to five minutes for each perspective.** The whole activity should take no more than half an hour.

3. **Keep going until you have written about your subject from all six perspectives.** Remember that cubing offers the special advantage of enabling you to generate multiple perspectives quickly.

4. **As you write from each perspective, begin with what you know about your subject.** However, do not limit yourself to your present knowledge. Indicate what else you would like to know about your subject, and suggest where you might find that information.

5. **Reread what you have written.** Look for bright spots, surprises. Recall the part that was easiest for you to write. Recall the part where you felt a special momentum and pleasure in writing. Look for an angle or an unexpected insight. These special parts may suggest a focus or topic within a larger subject, or they may provide specific details to include in a draft.

Construct a dialogue to explore an experience or an alternative view.

A *dialogue* is a conversation between two or more people. You can use **dialoguing** to search for topics, find a focus, explore ideas, or consider opposing viewpoints. When you write a dialogue as an invention strategy, you need to make up all parts of the conversation (unless, of course, you are writing collaboratively). Following these steps can help:

1. **Write a conversation between two speakers.** Label the participants *Speaker A* and *Speaker B,* or make up names for them.

2. **Write brief responses to keep the conversation moving fast.** Do not spend much time planning or rehearsing responses. Write what first occurs to you, just as in a real conversation, in which people take quick turns to prevent any awkward silences.

3. **If you get stuck, you might have one of the speakers ask the other a question.**

Dialogues can be especially useful in writing based on personal experience and persuasive essays because they help you remember conversations and anticipate objections.

Use dramatizing to analyze behavior.

Dramatizing is an invention activity developed by philosopher Kenneth Burke as a way of thinking about how people interact and as a way of analyzing stories and films. Thinking about human behavior in dramatic terms can be very productive for writers. Drama has action, actors, setting, motives, and methods. A five-pointed star can help you remember these five points of dramatizing (see Figure 11.2).

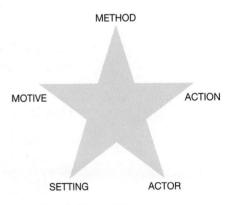

FIGURE 11.2 **Dramatizing**

Action *Action* answers the question "What?" An action is anything that happens, has happened, will happen, or could happen. Action includes events that are physical (running a marathon), mental (thinking about a book you have read), and emotional (falling in love).

Actor   The *actor* answers the question "Who?" The actor is either responsible for or affected by the action. The actor may be anything that causes an action. For example, if the action is a rise in the price of gasoline, the actor could be increased demand or short supply. Dramatizing may also include a number of actors working together or at odds.

Setting   *Setting* answers the questions "When?" and "Where?" We usually think of setting as the place and time of an event, but it may also be the historical background of an event or the childhood of a person.

Motive   *Motive* answers the question "Why?" The motive is the purpose or reason for an action—the actor's intention. Actions may have multiple, even conflicting, motives.

Method   *Method* answers the question "How?" The method explains how an action occurs, including the techniques an actor uses. It refers to whatever makes things happen.

This list answers the questions reporters typically ask. But dramatizing goes further: It enables us to consider relations among these five elements. You can also use this invention strategy to analyze the readers you want to inform or convince.

Freewrite to generate ideas freely and creatively.

Freewriting is a technique that requires you to stop judging what you write and simply let your mind wander in order to generate ideas freely and creatively. To freewrite, set a certain amount of time, say ten to fifteen minutes, and then simply write, generating as much text as you can in the allotted time. While freewriting, try not to stop; if you cannot think of anything to say, simply write "don't know what to say" over and over until an idea comes to you. If you find it difficult to avoid editing yourself, try turning down the brightness on your monitor or lowering the screen on your laptop until you can no longer see what it says.

A variation on freewriting is **focused freewriting**. In focused freewriting, you begin from a specific topic, returning to the beginning topic whenever you find yourself getting off track.

Use looping to explore aspects of a topic.

Looping is especially useful for the first stages of exploring a topic. Like focused freewriting, **looping** involves writing quickly to explore some aspect of a topic. But it differs in that the focus is on looping back to your original starting point or to a new starting point to explore another aspect. Beginning with almost any starting point, looping enables you to find a center of interest and eventually a thesis for your essay. The steps are simple:

1. **Write down your area of interest.** You may know only that you have to write about another person or a movie or a cultural trend that has caught your attention. Or you may want to search for a topic in a broad historical period or for one related to a major political event. Although you may wander from this topic as you write, you will want to keep coming back to it. Your purpose is to find a focus for writing.

2. **Write nonstop for ten minutes.** Start with the first thing that comes to mind. Write rapidly, without looking back to reread or correct anything. *Do not stop writing. Keep your pencil moving or keystrokes clacking.* Continuous writing is the key to looping. If you get stuck for a moment, rewrite the last sentence. Follow diversions and digressions, but keep returning to your topic.

3. **After ten minutes, pause to reread what you have written.** Decide what is most important—a single insight, a pattern of ideas, an emerging theme, a visual detail, anything at all that stands out. Some writers call this a "center of gravity" or a "hot spot." To complete the first loop, restate this center in a single sentence.

4. **Beginning with this sentence, write nonstop for another ten minutes.** Summarize in one sentence again to complete the second loop. Keep looping until one of your summary sentences produces a focus or thesis. You may need only two or three loops; you may need more.

Take notes in a journal.

Professional writers often use **journals** to keep notes. Starting one is easy. Buy a special notebook, or open a new file on your computer, and start writing. Here are some possibilities:

- Keep a list of new words and concepts you learn in your courses. You could also write about the progress and direction of your learning in particular courses—the experience of being in the course, your feelings about what is happening, and what you are learning.

- Respond to your reading, both assigned and personal. As you read, write about your personal associations, reflections, reactions, and evaluations. Summarize or copy memorable or especially important passages, and comment on them. (Copying and commenting have been practiced by students and writers for centuries in special journals called *commonplace books*.)

- Write to prepare for particular class meetings. Write about the main ideas you have learned from assigned readings and about the relationship of these new ideas to other ideas in the course. After class, write to summarize what you have learned. List questions you have about the ideas or information discussed in class. Journal writing of this kind involves reflecting, evaluating, interpreting, synthesizing, summarizing, and questioning.

- Write for ten or fifteen minutes every day about whatever is on your mind. Focus these meditations on your new experiences as you try to understand, interpret, and reflect on them, or write sketches of people who catch your attention, recording observations and overheard conversation.

- Organize your time. Write about your goals and priorities, or list specific things to accomplish and how you plan to do so.

- Keep a log over several days or weeks about a particular event unfolding in the news—a sensational trial, an environmental disaster, a political campaign, a campus controversy, or the fortunes of a sports team.

Ask questions to explore a subject systematically.

Asking questions about a subject is a way to learn about it and decide what to write. When you first encounter a subject, however, your questions may be scattered. Also, you are not likely to think right away of all the important questions you ought to ask. The advantage of having a basic list of questions for invention, like the ones for cubing and for dramatizing discussed earlier in this chapter, is that it provides a systematic approach to exploring a subject.

The questions that follow are based on the work of linguist Kenneth Pike. Here are the steps in using questions for invention:

1. **In a sentence or two, identify your subject.** A subject could be any event, person, problem, project, idea, or issue—in other words, anything you might write about.

2. **Start by writing a response to the first question in the lists below, then move right through the lists.** Try to answer each question at least briefly, with a word or a phrase. Some questions may invite several sentences or even a page or more of writing. You may draw a blank on a few questions. Skip them. Later, when you have more experience with questions for invention, you can start anywhere in the list.

3. **Write your responses quickly, without much planning.** Follow digressions or associations. Do not screen anything out. Be playful.

What Is Your Subject?

- What is your subject's name? What other names does it have or has it had?
- What aspects of the subject do these different names emphasize?
- Imagine a photograph or movie of your subject. What would it look like?
- What would you put into a time capsule to stand for your subject?
- What are its causes and effects?
- How would it look from different vantage points or perspectives?
- What experiences have you had with the subject? What have you learned?

What Parts or Features Does Your Subject Have, and How Are They Related?

- Name the parts or features of your subject.
- Describe each one, using the questions in the preceding subject list.
- How is each part or feature related to the others?

How Is Your Subject Similar to and Different from Other Subjects?

- What is your subject similar to? In what ways?
- What is your subject different from? In what ways?

How Much Can Your Subject Change and Still Remain the Same?

- How has your subject changed from what it once was?
- How is it changing now—moment to moment, day to day, year to year?
- How does each change alter your way of thinking about your subject?
- What are some different forms your subject takes?
- What does your subject become when it is no longer itself?

Where Does Your Subject Fit in the World?

- When and where did your subject originate?
- What would happen if at some future time your subject ceased to exist?
- When and where do you usually experience your subject?
- What is your subject a part of, and what are the other parts?
- What do other people think of your subject?

12

A Catalog of
Reading Strategies

This chapter presents strategies for reading critically, which you can apply to the selections in this book as well as to your other college reading.

- *Annotating:* recording your reactions to, interpretations of, and questions about a text as you read it
- *Taking inventory:* listing and grouping your annotations and other notes to find meaningful patterns
- *Outlining:* listing the text's main ideas to reveal how it is organized
- *Paraphrasing:* restating what you have read to clarify or refer to it
- *Summarizing:* distilling the main ideas or gist of a text
- *Synthesizing:* integrating into your own writing ideas and information gleaned from different sources
- *Contextualizing:* placing a text in its historical and cultural context
- *Exploring the significance of figurative language:* examining how metaphors, similes, and symbols are used in a text to convey meaning and evoke feelings
- *Looking for patterns of opposition:* inferring the values and assumptions embodied in the language of a text
- *Reflecting on challenges to your beliefs and values:* examining the bases of your personal responses to a text
- *Evaluating the logic of an argument:* determining whether an argument is well reasoned and adequately supported
- *Recognizing emotional manipulation:* identifying texts that unfairly and inappropriately use emotional appeals based on false or exaggerated claims
- *Judging the writer's credibility:* considering whether writers represent different points of view fairly and know what they are writing about

For more about annotating, see Chapter 5; for more about outlining, see Chapters 11 and 12; for more about paraphrasing, see Chapter 19; for more about summarizing and synthesizing, see Chapters 5 and 19; for more about logical fallacies, see Chapter 16.

Annotating

Annotations are the marks—underlines, highlights, and comments—you make directly on the page as you read. Annotating can be used to record immediate reactions and questions; outline and summarize main points; and evaluate and relate the reading to other ideas, readings, and points of view. Annotating can be done on paper with a pencil, pen, or highlighter, or on-screen by using your software's highlighting and commenting functions (or simply by typing annotations into the text using a different color or font).

Your annotations can take many forms, such as the following:

- inserting comments, questions, or definitions in the margins
- underlining or circling words, phrases, or sentences
- connecting ideas with lines or arrows
- numbering related points
- bracketing sections of the text
- noting anything that strikes you as interesting, important, or questionable

Most readers annotate in layers, adding further annotations on second and third readings. Annotations can be light or heavy, depending on your purpose and the difficulty of the material. Your purpose for reading also determines how you use your annotations.

The following selection, excerpted from Martin Luther King Jr.'s "Letter from Birmingham Jail," illustrates some of the ways you can annotate as you read. Add your own annotations, if you like.

Martin Luther King Jr. | *An Annotated Sample from "Letter from Birmingham Jail"*

MARTIN LUTHER KING JR. (1929–1968) first came to national notice in 1955, when he led a successful boycott against the policy of restricting African American passengers to rear seats on city buses in Montgomery, Alabama, where he was minister of a Baptist church. He subsequently formed the Southern Christian Leadership Conference, which brought people of all races from all over the country to the South to fight nonviolently for racial integration. In 1963, King led demonstrations in Birmingham, Alabama, that were met with violence; a bomb was detonated in a black church, killing four young girls. King was arrested for his role in organizing the protests, and while in prison, he wrote his "Letter from Birmingham Jail" to justify his strategy of civil disobedience, which he called "nonviolent direct action."

King begins his letter by discussing his disappointment with the lack of support he has received from white moderates, such as the group of clergy who published criticism of his organization in the local newspaper.

As you read, try to infer what the clergy's specific criticisms might have been, and notice the tone King uses. Would you characterize the writing as apologetic, conciliatory, accusatory, or something else?

¶1. White moderates block progress.

I must confess that over the past few years I have been gravely 1 disappointed with the white moderate. I have almost reached the regrettable conclusion that the Negro's [great stumbling block in his stride toward freedom] is not the White Citizen's Counciler or the Ku Klux Klanner, but the white moderate, who is more devoted to "order" than to justice; who prefers a negative peace which is the absence of tension to a positive peace which is the presence of justice; who constantly says: "I agree with you in the goal you seek, but I cannot agree with your methods of direct action"; who

Contrasts: order vs. justice, negative vs. positive peace, ends vs. means

(treating others like children)

paternalistically believes he can set the timetable for another man's freedom; who lives by a mythical concept of time and who constantly advises the Negro to wait for a "more convenient season." Shallow understanding from people of good will is more frustrating

more contrasts

than absolute misunderstanding from people of ill will. [Lukewarm acceptance is much more bewildering than outright rejection.]

I had hoped that the white moderate would understand that 2 law and order exist for the purpose of establishing justice and that when they fail in this purpose they become the [dangerously structured dams that block the flow of social progress.] I had hoped that the white moderate would understand that the present tension in the South is a necessary phase of the transition from an [obnoxious

¶2. What the moderates don't understand

metaphor: law and order = dams (faulty?)

repeats contrast (negative/positive)

negative peace,] in which the Negro passively accepted his unjust plight, to a [substantive and positive peace,] in which all men will respect the dignity and worth of human personality. Actually, we

Tension already exists: We help dispel it. (True?)

who engage in nonviolent direct action are not the creators of tension. We merely bring to the surface the hidden tension that is already alive. We bring it out in the open, where it can be seen and dealt with. [Like a boil that can never be cured so long as it is covered up but must be opened with all its ugliness to the natural medicines of air and light, injustice must be exposed, with all the tension its exposure creates, to the light of human conscience and the air of national opinion before it can be cured.]

In your statement you assert that our actions, even though peaceful, must be condemned because they precipitate violence. But is this a logical assertion? [Isn't this like condemning a robbed man because his possession of money precipitated the evil act of robbery? Isn't this like condemning Socrates because his unswerving commitment to truth and his philosophical inquiries precipitated the act by the misguided populace in which they made him drink hemlock? Isn't this like condemning Jesus because his unique God-consciousness and never-ceasing devotion to God's will precipitated the evil act of crucifixion?] We must come to see that, as the federal courts have consistently affirmed, it is wrong to urge an individual to cease his efforts to gain his basic constitutional rights because the question may precipitate violence. [Society must protect the robbed and punish the robber.]

I had also hoped that the white moderate would reject the myth concerning time in relation to the struggle for freedom. I have just received a letter from a white brother in Texas. He writes: "All Christians know that the colored people will receive equal rights eventually, but it is possible that you are in too great a religious hurry. It has taken Christianity almost two thousand years to accomplish what it has. The teachings of Christ take time to come to earth." Such an attitude stems from a tragic misconception of time, from the strangely irrational notion that there is something in the very flow of time that will inevitably cure all ills. Actually, time itself is neutral; it can be used either destructively or constructively. More and more I feel that the people of ill will have used time much more effectively than have the people of good will. We will have to repent in this generation not merely for the [hateful words and actions of the bad people] but for the [appalling silence of the good people.] Human progress never rolls in on [wheels of

---

Margin annotations:

simile: injustice is "like a boil"

¶3. Questions clergymen's logic: condemning his actions = condemning robbery victim, Socrates, Jesus.

repetition ("Isn't this like . . .")

(Yes!)

example of a white moderate's view

¶4. Time must be used to do right.

Silence/passivity is as bad as hateful words and actions.

*metaphor
(mechanical?)*

inevitability;] it comes through the tireless efforts of men willing to be co-workers with God, and without this hard work, time itself becomes an ally of the forces of social (stagnation.) [We must use time creatively, in the knowledge that the time is always ripe to do right.] Now is the time to make real the promise of democracy and transform our pending [national elegy] into a creative [psalm of brotherhood.] Now is the time to lift our national policy from the [quicksand of racial injustice] to the [solid rock of human dignity.]

stop developing

*metaphors (song,
natural world)*

*King accused of being
an extremist.*

You speak of our activity in Birmingham as extreme. At first I was rather disappointed that fellow clergymen would see my non-violent efforts as those of an extremist. I began thinking about the fact that I stand in the middle of two opposing forces in the Negro community. One is a [force of complacency,] made up in part of Negroes who, as a result of long years of oppression, are so drained of self-respect and a sense of "somebodiness" that they have adjusted to segregation; and in part of a few middle-class Negroes, who because of a degree of academic and economic security and because in some ways they profit by segregation, have become insensitive to the problems of the masses. The other [force is one of bitterness and hatred,] and it comes perilously close to advocating violence. It is expressed in the various black nationalist [groups that are springing up] across the nation, the largest and best-known being Elijah Muhammad's Muslim movement. Nourished by the Negro's frustration over the continued existence of racial discrimination, this movement is made up of people who have lost faith in America, who have absolutely repudiated Christianity, and who have concluded that the white man is an incorrigible "devil."

5

*¶5. Puts self in
middle of two
extremes:
complacency and
bitterness.*

Malcolm X?

*(How did nonviolence
become part of King's
movement?)*

I have tried to stand between these two forces, saying that we need emulate neither the "do-nothingism" of the complacent nor the hatred and despair of the black nationalist. For there is the more excellent way of love and nonviolent protest. I am grateful to God that, through the influence of the Negro church, the way of nonviolence became an integral part of our struggle.

6

*¶6. Offers better
choice: nonviolent
protest.*

If this philosophy had not emerged, by now many streets of the South would, I am convinced, be flowing with blood. And I am further convinced that if our white brothers dismiss as "rabble-rousers"

7

*¶7. Says movement
prevents racial
violence. (Threat?)*

and "outside agitators" those of us who employ nonviolent direct action, and if they refuse to support our nonviolent efforts, *(comfort)* millions of Negroes will, out of frustration and despair, seek solace and security in black-nationalist ideologies—a development that would inevitably lead to a frightening racial nightmare.

[Oppressed people cannot remain oppressed forever.] The 8 yearning for freedom eventually manifests itself, and that is what has happened to the American Negro. Something within has reminded him of his birthright of freedom, and something without has reminded him that it can be gained. Consciously or unconsciously, he has been caught up by the Zeitgeist, and with *(spirit of the times)* his black brothers of Africa and his brown and yellow brothers of Asia, South America and the Caribbean, the United States Negro is moving with a sense of great urgency toward the [promised land of racial justice.] If one recognizes this [vital urge that has engulfed the Negro community,] one should readily understand why public demonstrations are taking place. The Negro has many [pent-up resentments] and latent frustrations, and he must release them. So let him march; let him make prayer pilgrimages to the city hall; let him go on freedom rides—and try to understand why he must do *Not a threat but a* so. If his repressed emotions are not released in nonviolent ways, *fact—?* they will seek expression through violence; this is not a threat but a fact of history. So I have not said to my people: "Get rid of your discontent." Rather, I have tried to say that this normal and healthy *¶8. Discontent is* discontent can be [channeled into the creative outlet of nonviolent *normal, healthy,* direct action.] And now this approach is being termed extremist. *and historically*
inevitable, but it
must be channeled.

But though I was initially disappointed at being categorized as 9 an extremist, as I continued to think about the matter I gradually gained a measure of satisfaction from the label. Was not Jesus an *¶9. Redefines* extremist for love: "Love your enemies, bless them that curse you, *"extremism," embraces* do good to them that hate you, and pray for them which despite- *"extremist" label.* fully use you, and persecute you." Was not Amos an extremist for justice: "Let justice roll down like waters and righteousness like an *(Hebrew prophet)* ever-flowing stream." Was not Paul an extremist for the Christian *(Christian* gospel: "I bear in my body the marks of the Lord Jesus." Was not *apostle)* Martin Luther an extremist: "Here I stand; I cannot do otherwise, *(founder of*
Protestantism)

(English preacher)

so help me God." And John Bunyan: "I will stay in jail to the end of my days before I make a butchery of my conscience." And Abraham Lincoln: "This nation cannot survive half slave and half free." And Thomas Jefferson: "We hold these truths to be self-evident, that all men are created equal. . . ." [So the question is not whether we will be extremists, but what kind of extremists we will be.] Will we be extremists for hate or for love? Will we be extremists for the preservation of injustice or for the extension of justice? In that dramatic scene on Calvary's hill three men were crucified. We must never forget that all three were crucified for the same crime—the crime of extremism. Two were extremists for immorality, and thus fell below their environment. The other, Jesus Christ, was an extremist for love, truth and goodness, and thereby rose above his environment. Perhaps the South, the [nation and the world are in dire need of creative extremists.]

Compares self to great "extremists"—including Jesus

I had hoped that the white moderate would see this need. 10 Perhaps I was too optimistic; perhaps I expected too much. I suppose I should have realized that few members of the oppressor race can understand the deep groans and passionate yearnings of the oppressed race, and still fewer have the vision to see that [injustice must be rooted out] by strong, persistent and determined action. I am thankful, however, that some of our white brothers in the South have grasped the meaning of this social revolution and committed themselves to it. They are still all too few in quantity, but they are big in quality. Some—such as Ralph McGill, Lillian Smith, Harry Golden, James McBride Dabbs, Ann Braden and Sarah Patton Boyle—have written about our struggle in eloquent and prophetic terms. Others have marched with us down nameless streets of the South. They have languished in filthy, roach-infested jails, suffering the abuse and brutality of policemen who view them as "dirty nigger-lovers." Unlike so many of their moderate brothers and sisters, they have recognized the urgency of the moment and sensed the need for [powerful "action" antidotes] to combat the [disease of segregation.]

Disappointed in the white moderate

¶10. *Praises whites who have supported movement.*

(Who are they?)

(been left unaided)

Metaphor: segregation is a disease.

---

1 Select one of the readings in Part 1 or another text, and mark the text using annotations like these:

- Circle words to be defined in the margin.
- Underline key words and phrases.
- Bracket important sentences and passages.
- Use lines or arrows to connect ideas or words.

2 Insert marginal comments like these:

- Number and summarize each paragraph.
- Define unfamiliar words.
- Note responses and questions.
- Identify interesting writing strategies.
- Point out patterns.

3 Layer additional markings in the text and add comments in the margins as you reread for different purposes.

Taking Inventory

Taking inventory helps you analyze your annotations for different purposes. When you take inventory, you make various kinds of lists to explore patterns of meaning you find in the text. For instance, in reading the annotated passage by Martin Luther King Jr., you might have noticed that certain similes and metaphors are used or that many famous people are named. By listing the names (Socrates, Jesus, Luther, Lincoln, and so on) and then grouping them into categories (people who died for their beliefs, leaders, teachers, and religious figures), you can better understand why the writer refers to these particular people. Taking inventory of your annotations can be helpful if you plan to write about a text you are reading.

---

1 Examine the annotations you made in the preceding activity for patterns or repetitions, such as recurring images, stylistic features, repeated words and phrases, repeated examples or illustrations, and reliance on particular writing strategies.

2 List the items that make up a pattern.

3 Decide what the pattern might reveal about the reading.

Outlining

Outlining is an especially helpful reading strategy for understanding the content and structure of a reading. **Outlining**, which identifies the text's main ideas, may be part of the annotating process or may be done separately. Writing an outline in the margins of the text as you read and annotate makes it easier to find information later. Writing an outline on a separate piece of paper or online gives you more space to work with and therefore usually includes more detail.

The key to outlining is distinguishing between the main ideas and the supporting material, such as examples, quotations, comparisons, and reasons. The main ideas form the backbone that holds the various parts of the text together. Outlining the main ideas helps you uncover this structure.

For more about the conventions of formal outlines, see Chapter 11.

Making an outline, however, is not simple. The reader must exercise judgment in deciding which are the most important ideas. The words used in an outline reflect the reader's interpretation and emphasis. Readers also must decide when to use the writer's words, their own words, or a combination of the two.

You may make either a formal, multileveled outline or an informal scratch outline. You might choose to make a formal outline of a reading about which you are writing an in-depth analysis or evaluation and a scratch outline to help you identify the main idea in each paragraph of a reading assignment. For example, here is a formal outline a student wrote for an essay evaluating the logic of the King excerpt.

Formal Outline of "Letter from Birmingham Jail"

I. "[T]he Negro's great stumbling block in his stride toward freedom is . . . the white moderate. . . ." (par. 1)

  A. White moderates are more devoted to "order" than to justice; however,

    1. law and order exist only to establish justice (par. 2)

    2. law and order *without* justice actually threaten social order ("dangerously structured dams" metaphor, par. 2)

  B. White moderates prefer "negative peace" (absence of tension) to "positive peace" (justice); however,

    1. tension already exists; it is not created by movement (par. 2)

    2. tension is a necessary phase in progress to a just society (par. 2)

    3. tension must be allowed outlet if society is to be healthy ("boil" simile, par. 2)

  C. White moderates disagree with methods of movement; however,

    1. nonviolent direct action can't be condemned for violent response to it (analogies: robbed man; Socrates; Jesus, par. 3)

    2. federal courts affirm that those who seek constitutional rights can't be held responsible for violent response (par. 3)

  D. White moderates paternalistically counsel patience, saying time will bring change; however,

      1. time is "neutral" — we are obligated to use it *actively* to achieve justice (par. 4)

      2. the time for action is now (par. 4)

II. Contrary to white moderates' claims, the movement is not "extremist" in the usual sense (par. 5 ff.).

  A. It stands between extremes in the black community: passivity, seen in the oppressed and the self-interested middle-class; and violent radicalism, seen in Elijah Muhammad's followers (pars. 5–6)

  B. In its advocacy of love and nonviolent protest, the movement has forestalled bloodshed and kept more blacks from joining radicals (pars. 5–7)

  C. The movement helps blacks channel the urge for freedom, which is part of historical trend and the prevailing *Zeitgeist* (par. 8)

III. The movement can be defined as extremist if the term is redefined: "Creative extremism" is extremism in the service of love, truth, and goodness (examples of Amos, Paul, Luther, Bunyan, Lincoln, Jefferson, Jesus, par. 9)

IV. Some whites — "few in quantity, but . . . big in quality" — have recognized the truth of the arguments above and, unlike the white moderates, have committed themselves to the movement (par. 10)

     The annotations include a summary of each paragraph's topic. Here is a scratch outline that lists the topics:

For more about making a scratch outline, see Chapter 11.

Scratch Outline of "Letter from Birmingham Jail"

¶1. White moderates block progress

¶2. What the moderates don't understand

¶3. Questions clergymen's logic

¶4. Time must be used to do right

¶5. Puts self in middle of two extremes: complacency and bitterness

¶6. Offers better choice: nonviolent protest

¶7. Says movement prevents racial violence

¶8. Discontent is normal, healthy, and historically inevitable, but it must be channeled

¶9. Redefines "extremism," embraces "extremist" label

¶10. Praises whites who have supported movement

ANALYZE & WRITE

---

1 Reread each paragraph of the selection you have been working with in the previous activities in this chapter. Identify the topic and the comments made about the topic. Do not include examples, specific details, quotations, or other explanatory and supporting material.

2 List the author's main ideas in the margin, on a separate piece of paper, or in a new document.

Paraphrasing

To learn more about paraphrasing, see Chapter 19.

Paraphrasing is restating a text you have read by using mostly your own words. It can help you clarify the meaning of an obscure or ambiguous passage. It is one of the three ways of integrating other people's ideas and information into your own writing, along with **quoting** (reproducing exactly the language of the source text) and **summarizing** (distilling the main ideas or gist of the source text). You might choose to paraphrase rather than quote when the source's language is not especially arresting or memorable. You might paraphrase short passages but summarize longer ones.

Following are two passages. The first is from paragraph 2 of the excerpt from King's "Letter." The second passage is a paraphrase of the first:

Original

> I had hoped that the white moderate would understand that law and order exist for the purpose of establishing justice and that when they fail in this purpose they become the dangerously structured dams that block the flow of social progress. I had hoped that the white moderate would understand that the present tension in the South is a necessary phase of the transition from an obnoxious negative peace, in which the Negro passively accepted his unjust plight, to a substantive and positive peace, in which all men will respect the dignity and worth of human personality.

Paraphrase

> King writes that he had hoped for more understanding from white moderates — specifically that they would recognize that law and order are not ends in themselves but means to the greater end of establishing justice. When law and order do not serve this greater end, they stand in the way of progress. King expected the white moderate to recognize that the current tense situation in the South is part of a transition process that is necessary for progress. The current situation is bad because although there is peace, it is an "obnoxious" and "negative" kind of peace based on blacks passively accepting the injustice of the status quo. A better kind of peace — one that is "substantive," real and not imaginary, and "positive" — requires that all people, regardless of race, be valued.

When you compare the paraphrase to the original, you can see that the paraphrase contains all the important information and ideas of the original. Notice also that the paraphrase is somewhat longer than the original, refers to the writer by name, and encloses King's original words in quotation marks. The paraphrase tries to be *neutral,* to avoid inserting the reader's opinions or distorting the original writer's ideas.

| ANALYZE & WRITE |

1 Select an important passage from the selection you have been working with. (The passage need be only two or three sentences.) Then reread the passage, looking up unfamiliar words in a college dictionary.

2 Translate the passage into your own words and sentences, putting quotation marks around any words or phrases you quote from the original.

3 Revise to ensure coherence.

Summarizing

Summarizing is important because it not only helps you understand and remember what is most significant in a reading but also creates a condensed version of the reading's ideas and information, which you can refer to later or insert into your own writing. Along with quoting and paraphrasing, summarizing enables you to integrate other writers' ideas into your own writing.

To learn more about summarizing, see Chapter 5.

A **summary** is a relatively brief restatement, primarily in the reader's own words, of the reading's main ideas. Summaries vary in length, depending on the reader's purpose. Some summaries are very brief—a sentence or even a subordinate clause. For example, if you were referring to the excerpt from "Letter from Birmingham Jail" and simply needed to indicate how it relates to your other sources, your summary might look something like this: "There have always been advocates of extremism in politics. Martin Luther King Jr., in 'Letter from Birmingham Jail,' for instance, defends nonviolent civil disobedience as an extreme but necessary means of bringing about racial justice." If, however, you were surveying the important texts of the civil rights movement, you might write a longer, more detailed summary that not only identifies the reading's main ideas but also shows how the ideas relate to one another.

Many writers find it useful to outline the reading as a preliminary to writing a summary. A paragraph-by-paragraph scratch outline (like the one on p. 441) lists the reading's main ideas in the sequence in which they appear in the original. But summarizing requires more than merely stringing together the entries in an outline; it must fill in the logical connections between the author's ideas. Notice how, in the following summary, the reader repeats selected words and phrases and refers to the author by name, indicating, with verbs like *expresses*, *acknowledges*, and *explains*, the writer's purpose and strategy at each point in the argument.

Summary

King expresses his disappointment with white moderates who, by opposing his program of nonviolent direct action, have become a barrier to progress toward racial justice. He acknowledges that his program has raised tension in the South, but he explains that tension is necessary to bring about change. Furthermore, he argues that tension already exists, but because it has been unexpressed, it is unhealthy and potentially dangerous.

> He defends his actions against the clergy's criticisms, particularly their argument that he is in too much of a hurry. Responding to charges of extremism, King claims that he has actually prevented racial violence by channeling the natural frustrations of oppressed blacks into nonviolent protest. He asserts that extremism is precisely what is needed now — but it must be creative, rather than destructive, extremism. He concludes by again expressing disappointment with white moderates for not joining his effort as some other whites have.

A summary presents only ideas. Although it may use certain key terms from the source, it does not otherwise attempt to reflect the source's language, imagery, or tone; and it avoids even a hint of agreement or disagreement with the ideas it summarizes. Of course, a writer might summarize ideas in a source like "Letter from Birmingham Jail" to show readers that he or she has read it carefully and then proceed to use the summary to praise, question, or challenge King's argument. In doing so, the writer might quote specific language that reveals word choice, imagery, or tone. The summary itself remains impartial.

ANALYZE & WRITE

1 Make a scratch outline of the reading you have been working with, or use the outline you created in the activity on page 441.

2 Write a paragraph or more that presents the author's main ideas in your own words and sentences, omitting supporting details and examples. Use the outline as a guide, but reread parts of the original text as necessary.

3 To make the summary coherent, fill in connections between the ideas you present.

Synthesizing

For more on synthesizing information and ideas from sources, see Chapters 5 and 19.

Synthesizing involves presenting ideas and information gleaned from different sources. It can help you see how different sources relate to one another. For example, one reading might provide information that fills out the information in another reading, or a reading could present arguments that challenge arguments in another reading.

When you synthesize material from different sources, you construct a conversation among your sources, a conversation in which you also participate. Synthesizing contributes most when writers use sources not only to support their ideas but to challenge and extend them as well.

In the following example, the reader uses a variety of sources related to the King passage (pp. 433–38) and brings them together around a central idea. Notice how quotation, paraphrase, and summary are all used.

Synthesis

When King defends his campaign of nonviolent direct action against the clergymen's criticism that "our actions, even though peaceful, must be condemned because they precipitate violence" (King excerpt, par. 3), he is using what Vinit Haksar calls Mohandas Gandhi's "safety-valve argument" ("Civil Disobedience and Non-Cooperation" 117). According to Haksar, Gandhi gave a "non-threatening warning of worse things to come" if his demands were not met. King similarly makes clear that advocates of actions more extreme than those he advocates are waiting in the wings: "The other force is one of bitterness and hatred, and it comes perilously close to advocating violence" (King excerpt, par. 5). King identifies this force with Elijah Muhammad, and although he does not name him, King's contemporary readers would have known that he was referring also to his disciple Malcolm X, who, according to Herbert J. Storing, "urged that Negroes take seriously the idea of revolution" ("The Case against Civil Disobedience" 90). In fact, Malcolm X accused King of being a modern-day Uncle Tom, trying "to keep us under control, to keep us passive and peaceful and nonviolent" (*Malcolm X Speaks* 12).

ANALYZE & WRITE

1. Find and read two or three sources on the topic of the selection you have been working with, annotating the passages that give you ideas about the topic.

2. Look for patterns among your sources, possibly supporting or challenging your ideas or those of other sources.

3. Write a paragraph or more synthesizing your sources, using quotation, summary, and paraphrase to present what they say on the topic.

Contextualizing

All texts reflect historical and cultural assumptions, values, and attitudes that may differ from your own. To read thoughtfully, you need to become aware of these differences. **Contextualizing** is a critical reading strategy that enables you to make inferences about a reading's historical and cultural context and to examine the differences between its context and your own.

The excerpt from King's "Letter from Birmingham Jail" is a good example of a text that benefits from being read contextually. If you knew little about the history of slavery and segregation in the United States, it would be difficult to understand the passion expressed in this passage. To understand the historical and cultural context in which King wrote his "Letter from Birmingham Jail," you could do some library or Internet research. Comparing the situation at the time to situations with which you are familiar would help you understand some of your own attitudes toward King and the civil rights movement.

Here is what one reader wrote to contextualize King's writing:

> I have seen documentaries showing civil rights demonstrators being attacked by dogs, doused by fire hoses, beaten and dragged by helmeted police. Such images give me a sense of the violence, fear, and hatred that King was responding to. The creative tension King refers to comes across in his writing. He uses his anger and frustration to inspire his critics. He also threatens them, although he denies it. I saw a film on Malcolm X, so I could see that King was giving white people a choice between his own nonviolent way and Malcolm's more confrontational way.
>
> Things have certainly changed since the 1960s. For one: Barack Obama was elected president for two terms! When I read King's "Letter" today, I feel like I'm reading history. But then again, there have been a number of reports recently—often caught as cell-phone videos—of white supremacist rallies and police brutality. Some people have also suggested that in recent elections, there have been efforts to deprive African Americans and other minorities of the right to vote in some areas of the country.

ANALYZE & WRITE

1. Describe the historical and cultural situation as it is represented in the reading you have been working with and in other sources with which you are familiar. Your knowledge may come from other reading, television or film, school, or elsewhere. (If you know nothing about the historical and cultural context, you could do some library or Internet research.)

2. Compare the historical and cultural situation in which the text was written with your own historical and cultural situation. Consider how your understanding and judgment of the reading are affected by your own context.

Exploring the Significance of Figurative Language

Figurative language—*metaphor, simile,* and *symbolism*—enhances literal meaning by implying abstract ideas through vivid images and by evoking feelings and associations.

Metaphor implicitly compares two different things by identifying them with each other. For instance, when King calls the white moderate "the Negro's great stumbling block in his stride toward freedom" (par. 1), he does not mean that the white moderate literally trips the Negro who is attempting to walk toward freedom. The sentence makes sense only if understood figuratively: The white moderate trips up the Negro by frustrating every effort to achieve justice.

Simile, a more explicit form of comparison, uses the word *like* or *as* to signal the relationship of two seemingly unrelated things. King uses simile when he says that injustice is "like a boil that can never be cured so long as it is covered up" (par. 2). This simile makes several points of comparison between injustice and a boil. It suggests that injustice is a disease of society as a boil is a disease of the skin and that injustice, like a boil, must be exposed or it will fester and infect the entire body.

Symbolism compares two things by making one stand for the other. King uses the white moderate as a symbol for supposed liberals and would-be supporters of civil rights who are actually frustrating the cause.

How these figures of speech are used in a text reveals something of the writer's feelings about the subject. Exploring possible meanings in a text's figurative language involves (1) annotating and then listing the metaphors, similes, and symbols you find in a reading; (2) grouping and labeling the figures of speech that appear to express related feelings or attitudes; and (3) writing to explore the meaning of the patterns you have found. The following example shows the process of exploring figures of speech in the King excerpt.

Listing Figures of Speech

"stumbling block in his stride toward freedom" (par. 1)

"law and order . . . become the dangerously structured dams" (2)

"the flow of social progress" (2)

"Like a boil that can never be cured" (2)

"the light of human conscience and the air of national opinion" (2)

"the quicksand of racial injustice" (4)

Grouping and Labeling Figures of Speech

<u>Sickness</u>: "like a boil" (2); "the disease of segregation" (10)

<u>Underground</u>: "hidden tension" (2); "injustice must be exposed" (2); "injustice must be rooted out" (10)

<u>Blockage</u>: "dams," "block the flow" (2); "Human progress never rolls in on wheels of inevitability" (4); "pent-up resentments" (8); "repressed emotions" (8)

Writing to Explore Meaning

The patterns labeled <u>underground</u> and <u>blockage</u> suggest a feeling of frustration. Inertia is a problem; movement forward toward progress or upward toward the promised land is stalled. The strong need to break through the resistance may represent King's feelings about both his attempt to lead purposeful, effective demonstrations and his effort to write a convincing argument.

The simile of injustice being "like a boil" links the two patterns of underground and sickness, suggesting that something bad, a disease, is inside the people or the society. The cure is to expose or to root out the blocked hatred and injustice as well as to release the tension or emotion that has long been repressed. This implies that repression itself is the evil, not simply what is repressed. Therefore, writing and speaking out through political action may have curative power for individuals and society alike.

| ANALYZE & WRITE |

1 Annotate all the figures of speech you find in the reading you have been working with (or another selection) — metaphors, similes, and symbols — and then list them.

2 Group the figures of speech that appear to express related feelings and attitudes, and label each group.

3 Write one or two paragraphs exploring the meaning of these patterns. What do they tell you about the text?

Looking for Patterns of Opposition

All texts carry within themselves voices of opposition. These voices may echo the views and values of readers the writer anticipates or predecessors to whom the writer is responding in some way; they may even reflect the writer's own conflicting values. Careful readers look closely for such a dialogue of opposing voices within the text.

When we think of oppositions, we ordinarily think of polarities: *yes* and *no, up* and *down, black* and *white, new* and *old*. Some oppositions, however, may be more subtle. The excerpt from King's "Letter from Birmingham Jail" is rich in such oppositions: *moderate* versus *extremist, order* versus *justice, direct action* versus *passive acceptance, expression* versus *repression*. These oppositions are not accidental; they form a significant pattern that gives readers important information about the essay.

A careful reading will show that King always values one of the two terms in an opposition over the other. In the passage, for example, *extremist* is valued over *moderate* (par. 9). This preference for extremism is surprising. The reader should ask why, when white extremists like members of the Ku Klux Klan have committed so many outrages against African Americans, King would prefer extremism. If King is trying to convince his readers to accept his point of view, why would he represent himself as an extremist? Moreover, why would a clergyman advocate extremism instead of moderation?

Studying the **patterns of opposition** in the text enables you to answer these questions. You will see that King sets up this opposition to force his readers to examine their own values and realize that they are in fact misplaced. Instead of working toward justice, he says, those who support law and order maintain the unjust status quo. By getting his readers to think of white moderates as blocking rather than facilitating peaceful change, King brings readers to align themselves with him and perhaps even embrace his strategy of nonviolent resistance.

Looking for patterns of opposition involves annotating words or phrases in the reading that indicate oppositions, listing the opposing terms in pairs, deciding which term in each pair is preferred by the writer, and reflecting on the meaning of the patterns. Here is a partial list of oppositions from the King excerpt, with the preferred terms marked by an asterisk:

Listing Patterns of Opposition

moderate	*extremist
order	*justice
negative peace	*positive peace
absence of tension	*presence of justice
goals	*methods
*direct action	passive acceptance
*exposed tension	hidden tension

ANALYZE & WRITE

1 Annotate the selection you have been working with (or another selection) for words or phrases indicating oppositions.

2 List the pairs of oppositions. (You may have to paraphrase or even supply the opposite word or phrase if it is not stated directly in the text.)

3 For each pair of oppositions, put an asterisk next to the term that the writer seems to value or prefer over the other.

4 Study the patterns of opposition. How do they contribute to your understanding of the essay? What do they tell you about what the author wants you to believe?

Reflecting on Challenges to Your Beliefs and Values

To read thoughtfully, you need to scrutinize your own assumptions and attitudes as well as those expressed in the text you are reading. If you are like most readers, however, you will find that your assumptions and attitudes are so ingrained that you are not always fully aware of them. A good strategy for getting at these underlying beliefs and values is to identify and reflect on the ways the text challenges you and how it makes you feel—disturbed, threatened, ashamed, combative, pleased, exuberant, or some other way. For example, here is what one student wrote about the King passage:

Reflections

In paragraph 1, Dr. King criticizes people who are "more devoted to 'order' than to justice." This criticism upsets me because today I think I would choose order over justice. When I reflect on my feelings and try to figure out where they come from, I realize that what I feel most is fear. I am terrified by the violence in society today. I'm afraid of sociopaths who don't respect the rule of law, much less the value of human life.

> I know Dr. King was writing in a time when the law itself was unjust, when order was apparently used to keep people from protesting and changing the law. But things are different now. Today, justice seems to serve criminals more than it serves law-abiding citizens. That's why I'm for order over justice.

ANALYZE & WRITE

1 Identify challenges by marking the text you have been working with (or another text) where you feel your beliefs and values are being opposed, criticized, or unfairly characterized.

2 Write a few paragraphs reflecting on why you feel challenged. Do not defend your feelings; instead, search your memory to discover where they come from.

Evaluating the Logic of an Argument

For more on argument, including logical fallacies, see Chapter 16.

An *argument* includes a thesis backed by reasons and support. The **thesis** asserts a position on a controversial issue or a solution to a problem that the writer wants readers to accept. The **reasons** tell readers why they should accept the thesis, and the **support** (such as examples, statistics, authorities, and textual evidence) gives readers grounds for accepting it. For an argument to be considered logically acceptable, it must meet the three conditions of what we call the ABC test:

The ABC Test

A. The reasons and support must be *appropriate* to the thesis.

B. The reasons and support must be *believable*.

C. The reasons and support must be *consistent* with one another as well as *complete*.

Test for appropriateness.

To evaluate the logic of an argument, first decide whether the argument's reasons and support are appropriate. To test for appropriateness, ask these questions:

- How does each reason or piece of support relate to the thesis?
- Is the connection between reasons and support and the thesis clear and compelling?

Readers most often question the appropriateness of reasons and support when the writer argues by analogy or by invoking authority. For example, in paragraph 2, King argues that when law and order fail to establish justice, "they become the dangerously structured dams that block the flow of social progress." The analogy asserts the following logical relationship: Law and order are to progress toward justice as water is to a dam. If you do not accept this analogy, the argument fails the test of appropriateness.

For more about analogy, see Chapter 15. For more about invoking authorities, see Chapter 16.

King uses both analogy and authority in paragraph 3: "Isn't this like condemning Socrates because his unswerving commitment to truth and his philosophical inquiries precipitated the act by the misguided populace in which they made him drink hemlock?" Not only must you judge the appropriateness of the analogy comparing the

Greeks' condemnation of Socrates to the white moderates' condemnation of King, but you must also judge whether it is appropriate to accept Socrates as an authority. Since Socrates is generally respected for his teachings on justice, his words and actions are likely to be considered appropriate to King's situation in Birmingham.

Test for believability.

Believability is a measure of your willingness to accept as true the reasons and support the writer gives in defense of a thesis. To test for believability, ask the following questions:

- On what basis am I being asked to believe this reason or support is true?
- If it cannot be proved true or false, how much weight does it carry?

In judging facts, examples and anecdotes, statistics, and authorities, consider the following points:

Facts are statements that can be proved objectively to be true. The believability of facts depends on

- their *accuracy* (they should not distort or misrepresent reality);
- their *completeness* (they should not omit important details);
- the *trustworthiness* of their sources (sources should be qualified and unbiased).

King, for instance, asserts as fact that the African American will not wait much longer for racial justice (par. 8). His critics might question the factuality of this assertion by asking: Is this true of all African Americans? How does King know what African Americans will and will not do?

Examples and anecdotes are particular instances that may or may not make you believe a general statement. The believability of examples depends on

- their *representativeness* (whether they are truly typical and thus generalizable);
- their *specificity* (whether particular details make them seem true to life).

Even if a vivid example or gripping anecdote does not convince readers, it usually strengthens argumentative writing by clarifying the meaning and dramatizing the point. In paragraph 5 of the King excerpt, for example, King supports his generalization that some African American extremists are motivated by bitterness and hatred by citing the specific example of Elijah Muhammad's Black Muslim movement. Conversely, in paragraph 9, he refers to Jesus, Paul, Luther, and others as examples of extremists motivated by love and Christianity. These examples support his assertion that extremism is not in itself wrong and that any judgment of extremism must be based on its motivation and cause.

Statistics are numerical data. The believability of statistics depends on

- the *comparability* of the data (the price of apples in 1985 cannot be compared with the price of apples in 2015 unless the figures are adjusted to account for inflation);
- the *precision* of the methods employed to gather and analyze data (representative samples should be used and variables accounted for);
- the *trustworthiness* of the sources.

Authorities are people to whom the writer attributes expertise on a given subject. Not only must such authorities be appropriate, as mentioned earlier, but they must be credible as well—that is, the reader must accept them as experts on the topic at hand. King cites authorities repeatedly throughout his essay. He refers to religious leaders (Jesus and Luther) as well as to American political leaders (Lincoln and Jefferson). These figures are likely to have a high degree of credibility among King's readers.

Test for consistency and completeness.

In looking for consistency, you should be concerned that all the parts of the argument work together and that they are sufficient to convince readers to accept the thesis or at least take it seriously. To test for consistency and completeness, ask the following questions:

- Are any of the reasons and support contradictory?
- Do the reasons and support provide sufficient grounds for accepting the thesis?
- Does the writer fail to acknowledge, concede, or refute any opposing arguments or important objections?

For more on responding to objections and alternatives, see Chapter 16.

A thoughtful reader might regard as contradictory King's characterizing himself first as a moderate and later as an extremist opposed to the forces of violence. (King attempts to reconcile this apparent contradiction by explicitly redefining extremism in par. 9.) Similarly, the fact that King fails to examine and refute every legal recourse available to his cause might allow a critical reader to question the sufficiency of his argument.

| ANALYZE & WRITE |

Use the ABC test on the selection you have been working with (or another selection):

A *Test for appropriateness* by checking that the reasons and support are clearly and directly related to the thesis.

B *Test for believability* by deciding whether you can accept the reasons and support as likely to be true.

C *Test for consistency and completeness* by deciding whether the argument has any contradictions and whether any important objections or opposing views have been ignored.

Recognizing Emotional Manipulation

Writers often try to arouse emotions in readers to excite their interest, make them care, or move them to take action. There is nothing wrong with appealing to readers' emotions. What *is* wrong is manipulating readers with false or exaggerated appeals. Therefore, you should be suspicious of writing that is overly sentimental, that cites alarming statistics and frightening anecdotes, that demonizes others and identifies itself with revered authorities, or that uses potent symbols (for example, the American flag) or emotionally loaded words (such as *racist*).

King, for example, uses the emotionally loaded word *paternalistically* to refer to the white moderate's belief that "he can set the timetable for another man's freedom" (par. 1). In the same paragraph, King uses symbolism to get an emotional reaction from readers when he compares the white moderate to the "Ku Klux Klanner." To get readers to accept his ideas, he also relies on authorities whose names evoke the greatest respect, such as Jesus and Lincoln. But some readers might object that comparing his own crusade to that of Jesus is pretentious and manipulative. A critical reader might also consider King's discussion of African American extremists in paragraph 7 to be a veiled threat designed to frighten readers into agreement.

ANALYZE & WRITE

1 Annotate places in the text you have been working with (or another text) where you sense emotional appeals are being used.

2 Assess whether any of the emotional appeals are unfairly manipulative.

Judging the Writer's Credibility

Writers try to persuade readers by presenting an image of themselves in their writing that will gain their readers' confidence. This image must be created indirectly, through the arguments, language, and system of values and beliefs expressed or implied in the writing. Writers establish credibility in their writing in three ways:

- by showing their knowledge of the subject
- by building *common ground* with readers
- by responding fairly to objections and opposing arguments

Test for knowledge.

Writers demonstrate their knowledge through the facts and statistics they marshal, the sources they rely on for information, and the scope and depth of their understanding. You may not be sufficiently expert on the subject yourself to know whether the facts are accurate, the sources are reliable, and the understanding is sufficient. You may need to do some research to see what others say about the subject. You can also check credentials—the writer's educational and professional qualifications, the respectability of the publication in which the selection first appeared, and reviews of the writer's work—to determine whether the writer is a respected authority in the field. For example, King brings with him the authority that comes from being a member of the clergy and a respected leader of the Southern Christian Leadership Conference.

For more about evaluating sources, see Chapter 18.

Test for common ground.

One way writers can establish **common ground** with their readers is by basing their reasoning on shared values, beliefs, and attitudes. They use language that includes their readers (*we*) and qualify their assertions to keep them from being too extreme. Above all, they acknowledge differences of opinion. You want to notice such appeals.

King creates common ground with readers by using the inclusive pronoun *we,* suggesting shared concerns between himself and his audience. Notice, however, his use of masculine pronouns and other references ("the Negro . . . he," par. 8; "our white brothers," par. 10). Although King addressed his letter to male clergy, he intended it to be published in the local newspaper, where it would be read by an audience of both men and women. By using language that excludes women—a common practice at the time the selection was written—King may have missed an opportunity to build common ground with more than half of his readers.

Test for fairness.

Writers reveal their character by how they handle opposing arguments and objections to their argument. As a critical reader, pay particular attention to how writers treat possible differences of opinion. Be suspicious of those who ignore differences and pretend that everyone agrees with their viewpoints. When objections or opposing views are represented, consider whether they have been distorted in any way; if they are refuted, be sure that they are challenged fairly—with sound reasoning and solid support.

One way to gauge the author's credibility is to identify the tone of the argument, for it conveys the writer's attitude toward the subject and toward the reader. Is the text angry? Sarcastic? Evenhanded? Shrill? Condescending? Bullying? Do you feel as if the writer is treating the subject—and you, as a reader—with fairness? King's tone might be characterized in different passages as patient (he doesn't lose his temper), respectful (he refers to white moderates as "people of good will," par. 1) or pompous (comparing himself to Jesus and Socrates).

ANALYZE & WRITE

---

1 Using the selection you have been working with (or another selection), annotate for the writer's knowledge of the subject, how well common ground is established, and whether the writer deals fairly with objections and opposing arguments.

2 Decide what in the essay you find credible and what you question.

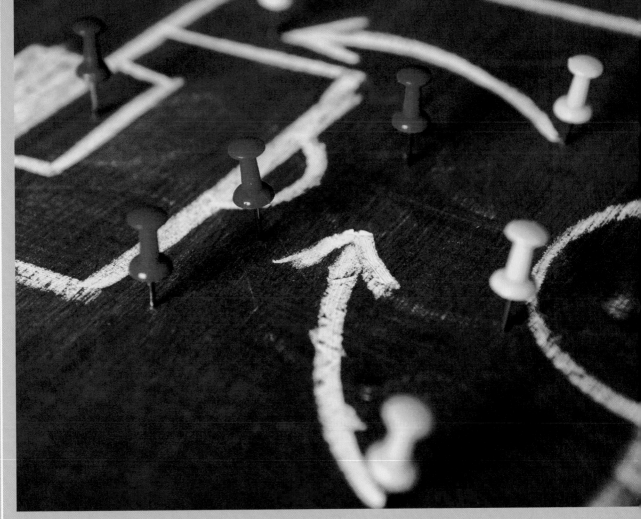

PART 3

Writing Strategies

13

Cueing the Reader

Readers need guidance. To guide readers through a piece of writing, a writer can provide five basic kinds of **cues**, or signals:

1. thesis and forecasting statements, to orient readers to ideas and organization
2. paragraphing, to group related ideas and details
3. cohesive devices, to connect ideas to one another and bring about clarity
4. transitions, to signal relationships or shifts in meaning
5. headings and subheadings, to group related paragraphs and help readers locate specific information quickly

This chapter illustrates how each of these cueing strategies works.

Orienting Statements

To help readers find their way, especially in difficult and lengthy texts, you can provide two kinds of **orienting statements**: a *thesis statement*, which declares the main point, and a *forecasting statement*, which previews subordinate points, showing the order in which they will be discussed in the essay.

Use thesis statements to announce the main idea.

To help readers understand what is being said about a subject, writers often provide a thesis statement early in the essay. The **thesis statement**, which can comprise one or more sentences, operates as a cue by letting readers know which is the most important general idea among the writer's many ideas and observations. In "Love: The Right Chemistry" in Chapter 4, Anastasia Toufexis expresses her thesis in the second paragraph:

> O.K., let's cut out all this nonsense about romantic love. Let's bring some scientific precision to the party. Let's put love under a microscope.

When rigorous people with Ph.D.s after their names do that, what they see is not some silly, senseless thing. **No, their probe reveals that love rests firmly on the foundations of evolution, biology and chemistry.**

Readers naturally look for something that will tell them the point of an essay, a focus for the many diverse details and ideas they encounter as they read. They expect to find some information early on that will give them a context for reading the essay, particularly if they are reading about a new or difficult subject. Therefore, a thesis statement placed at the beginning of an essay enables readers to anticipate the content of the essay and helps them understand the relationships among its various ideas and details.

Occasionally, however, particularly in fairly short, informal pieces, a writer may save a direct statement of the thesis until the conclusion. Ending with the thesis brings together the various strands of information or supporting details introduced over the course of the essay and makes clear the essay's main idea.

Some essays, particularly autobiographical essays, offer no direct thesis statement. Although this can make the point of the essay more difficult to determine, it can be appropriate when the essay is more expressive and personal than it is informative. In all cases, careful writers keep readers' needs and expectations in mind when deciding how—and whether—to state the thesis.

EXERCISE 13.1

In the essay by Jessica Statsky in Chapter 6, underline the thesis statement, the last sentence in paragraph 1. Notice the key terms: "overzealous parents and coaches," "impose adult standards," "children's sports," "activities . . . neither satisfying nor beneficial." Then skim the essay, stopping to read the sentence at the beginning of each paragraph. Also read the last paragraph.

Consider whether the idea in every paragraph's first sentence is anticipated by the thesis's key terms. Consider also the connection between the ideas in the last paragraph and the thesis's key terms. What can you conclude about how a thesis might assert the point of an essay, anticipate the ideas that follow, and help readers relate the ideas to one another?

Use forecasting statements to preview topics.

Some thesis statements include a **forecast**, which provides an overview of how a thesis will be developed, as in the following example:

In the three years from 1348 through 1350 the pandemic of plague known as the Black Death, or, as the Germans called it, the Great Dying, killed at least a fourth of the population of Europe. It was undoubtedly the worst disaster that has ever befallen mankind. Today we can have no real conception of the terror under which people lived in the shadow of the plague. For more than two centuries plague has not been a serious threat to mankind in the large, although it is still a grisly presence in parts of the Far East and Africa. Scholars continue to study the Great Dying, however, as a historical example of human behavior under the stress of universal catastrophe. **In these days when the threat of plague has been replaced by the threat of mass human extermination** by even more rapid means, there has been a sharp renewal of interest in the history of the fourteenth-century calamity. With new perspective, students are investigating its manifold effects: demographic, economic, psychological, moral and religious.

—WILLIAM LANGER, "The Black Death"

As a reader would expect, Langer divides his essay into explanations of the research into these five effects, addressing them in the order in which they appear in the forecasting statement.

EXERCISE 13.2

Turn to Patrick O'Malley's essay in Chapter 7, and underline the forecasting statement in paragraph 2. Then skim the essay. Notice whether O'Malley takes up every point he mentions in the forecasting statement and whether he sticks to the order he promises readers. How well does his forecasting statement help you follow his essay? What suggestions for improvement, if any, would you offer him?

Paragraphing

Paragraph cues as obvious as indentation keep readers on track. You can also arrange material in a paragraph to help readers see what is important or significant. For example, you can begin with a topic sentence, help readers see the relationship between the previous paragraph and the present one with an explicit transition, and place the most important information toward the end.

Paragraph indents signal related ideas.

One paragraph cue—the indentation that signals the beginning of a new paragraph—is a relatively modern printing convention. Old manuscripts show that paragraph divisions were not always marked. To make reading easier, scribes and printers began to use the symbol ¶ to mark paragraph breaks, and later, indenting became common practice. Indenting has been abandoned by most online and business writers, who now distinguish one paragraph from another by leaving a line of space between paragraphs.

Paragraphing helps readers by signaling when a sequence of related ideas begins and ends. Paragraphing also helps readers judge what is most important in what they are reading. Writers typically emphasize important information by placing it at the two points in the paragraph where readers are most attentive—the beginning and the end.

You can give special emphasis to information by placing it in its own paragraph.

EXERCISE 13.3

Turn again to Patrick O'Malley's essay in Chapter 7, and read paragraphs 4–7 with the following questions in mind: Does all the material in each paragraph seem to be related? Do you feel a sense of closure at the end of each paragraph? Does the last sentence offer the most significant or weighty information in the paragraph?

Topic sentences announce the paragraph's focus.

A **topic sentence** lets readers know the focus of a paragraph in simple and direct terms. It is a cueing strategy for the paragraph, much as a thesis or forecasting statement is for the whole essay. Because paragraphing usually signals a shift in focus, readers expect some kind of reorientation in the opening sentence. They need to know whether the new paragraph will introduce another aspect of the topic or develop one already introduced.

Announcing the Topic   Some topic sentences simply announce the topic. Here are some examples taken from Barry Lopez's book *Arctic Dreams:*

> A polar bear walks in a way all its own.

> What is so consistently striking about the way Eskimos used parts of an animal is the breadth of their understanding about what would work.

> The Mediterranean view of the Arctic, down to the time of the Elizabethan mariners, was shaped by two somewhat contradictory thoughts.

The following paragraph shows how one of Lopez's topic sentences (highlighted) is developed:

> **What is so consistently striking about the way Eskimos used parts of an animal is the breadth of their understanding about what would work.** Knowing that muskox horn is more flexible than caribou antler, they preferred it for making the side prongs of a fish spear. For a waterproof bag in which to carry sinews for clothing repair, they chose salmon skin. They selected the strong, translucent intestine of a bearded seal to make a window for a snowhouse—it would fold up for easy traveling and it would not frost over in cold weather. To make small snares for sea ducks, they needed a springy material that would not rot in salt water—baleen fibers. The down feather of a common eider, tethered at the end of a stick in the snow at an angle, would reveal the exhalation of a quietly surfacing seal. Polar bear bone was used anywhere a stout, sharp point was required, because it is the hardest bone.
>
> —Barry Lopez, *Arctic Dreams*

EXERCISE 13.4

Turn to Jessica Statsky's essay in Chapter 6. Underline the topic sentence (the first sentence) in paragraphs 4 and 7. Consider how these sentences help you anticipate the paragraph's topic and method of development.

Making a Transition   Not all topic sentences simply point to what will follow. Some also refer to earlier sentences. Such sentences work both as topic sentences, stating the main point of the paragraph, and as *transitions*, linking that paragraph to the previous one. Here are a few topic sentences from "Quilts and Women's Culture," by Elaine Hedges, with transitions highlighted:

Transitions tie topic sentences to a previous statement.

Within its broad traditionalism and anonymity, **however,** variations and distinctions developed.

Regionally, **too,** distinctions were introduced into quilt making through the interesting process of renaming.

Finally, out of such regional and other variations come individual, signed achievements.

Quilts, **then,** were an outlet for creative energy, a source and emblem of sisterhood and solidarity, and a graphic response to historical and political change.

Sometimes the first sentence of a paragraph serves as a transition, and a subsequent sentence states the topic, as in the following example:

No one is about to spend his or her hard-earned money on produce that has a blemish, or is in some way sub-par. For this reason, stores are pressured to supply produce that meets our unreasonably high standards. Edible food that is deemed unworthy of our dollars is sent to the dumpster.

Transition sentence
Topic sentence

The innate value of food is overlooked in the current system; monetary value seems to be all that matters. Sadly, it seems stores can't or don't try to eliminate food waste. Employees are not allowed to take food home, and expired food cannot be donated because of legal risk. Besides a separate dumpster for corrugated cardboard, there is no attempt made by stores to recycle. Some of the packaging we find even says "please recycle," "compostable," or "biodegradable," but the stores probably consider the sorting process too much of a hassle.

—Victoria C. Moré, "Dumpster Dinners: An Ethnography of Freeganism"

Occasionally, whole paragraphs serve as transitions, linking one sequence of paragraphs with those that follow, as in the following:

Transition paragraph summarizes contrasts and sets up analysis of similarities.

Yet it was not all contrast, after all. **Different as they were**—in background, in personality, in underlying aspiration—these two great soldiers **had much in common.** **Under everything else,** they were marvelous fighters. **Furthermore,** their fighting qualities were really very much alike.

—Bruce Catton, "Grant and Lee: A Study in Contrasts"

EXERCISE 13.5

Turn to Jessica Statsky's essay in Chapter 6 and underline the part of the first sentence in paragraphs 7 and 11 that refers to the previous paragraph, creating a transition from one to the next. Notice the different ways Statsky creates these transitions. Consider whether they are all equally effective.

Positioning the Topic Sentence   Although topic sentences may occur anywhere in a paragraph, stating the topic in the first sentence has the advantage of giving readers a sense of how the paragraph is likely to be developed. The beginning of the paragraph is therefore the most common position.

A topic sentence that does not open a paragraph is most likely to appear at the end. When a topic sentence concludes a paragraph, it usually summarizes or generalizes preceding information:

> "My life's an open book," people might say. "I've got nothing to hide." But now the government has large dossiers of everyone's activities, interests, reading habits, finances, and health. What if the government leaks the information to the public? What if the government mistakenly determines that based on your pattern of activities, you're likely to engage in a criminal act? What if it denies you the right to fly? What if the government thinks your financial transactions look odd—even if you've done nothing wrong—and freezes your accounts? What if the government doesn't protect your information with adequate security, and an identity thief obtains it and uses it to defraud you? **Even if you have nothing to hide, the government can cause you a lot of harm.**
>
> —Daniel Solove, "Why Privacy Matters Even if You Have 'Nothing to Hide'"

Topic sentence appears at end of paragraph.

When a topic sentence is used in a narrative, it often appears as the last sentence as a way to evaluate or reflect on events:

> A cold sun was sliding down a gray fall sky. Some older boys had been playing tackle football in the field we took charge of every weekend. In a few years, they'd be called to Southeast Asia, some of them. Their locations would be tracked with pushpins in red, white, and blue on maps on nearly every kitchen wall. But that afternoon, they were quick as young deer. They leapt and dodged, dove from each other and collided in midair. Bulletlike passes flew to connect them. Or the ball spiraled in a high arc across the frosty sky one to another. **In short, they were mindlessly agile in a way that captured as audience every little kid within running distance of the yellow goalposts.**
>
> —Mary Karr, *Cherry*

Topic sentence reflects on narrated events described earlier in paragraph.

It is possible for a single topic sentence to introduce two or more paragraphs. Subsequent paragraphs in such a sequence have no separate topic sentences of their own:

> **Anthropologists Daniel Maltz and Ruth Borker point out that boys and girls socialize differently.** Little girls tend to play in small groups or, even more common, in pairs. Their social life usually centers around a best friend, and friendships are made, maintained, and broken by talk—especially "secrets." If a little girl tells her friend's secret to another little girl, she may find herself with a new best friend. The secrets themselves may or may not be important, but the fact of telling them is all-important. It's hard for newcomers to get into these tight groups, but anyone who is admitted is treated as an equal. Girls like to play cooperatively; if they can't cooperate, the group breaks up.
>
> Little boys tend to play in larger groups, often outdoors, and they spend more time doing things than talking. It's easy for boys to get into the group, but not everyone is accepted as an equal. Once in the group, boys must jockey for their status in it. One of the most important ways they do this is through talk: verbal display such as telling stories and jokes, challenging and sidetracking the verbal

Topic sentence states topic of this paragraph and next.

displays of other boys, and withstanding other boys' challenges in order to maintain their own story—and status. Their talk is often competitive talk about who is best at what.

—DEBORAH TANNEN, *That's Not What I Meant!*

EXERCISE 13.6

Consider the variety and effectiveness of the topic sentences in your most recent writing project. Begin by underlining the topic sentence in each paragraph after the first one. The topic sentence may not be the first sentence in a paragraph, though it will often be.

Then double-underline the part of the topic sentence that provides an explicit transition from one paragraph to the next. You may find a transition that is separate from the topic sentence. You may not always find a topic sentence.

Reflect on your topic sentences, and evaluate how well they serve to orient your readers to the sequence of topics or ideas in your essay.

Cohesive Devices

Cohesive devices guide readers, helping them follow your train of thought by connecting key words and phrases throughout a passage. Among such devices are pronoun reference, word repetition, synonyms, sentence structure repetition, and collocation.

Pronouns connect phrases or sentences.

One common cohesive device is *pronoun reference*. As noun substitutes, pronouns refer to nouns that either precede or follow them and thus serve to connect phrases or sentences. The nouns that come before pronouns are called **antecedents**.

> Pronouns form a chain of connection with antecedent.

In New York from dawn to dusk to dawn, day after day, you can hear the steady rumble of tires against the concrete span of the **George Washington Bridge. The bridge** is never completely still. **It** trembles with traffic. **It** moves in the wind. **Its** great veins of steel swell when hot and contract when cold; **its** span often is ten feet closer to the Hudson River in summer than in winter.

—GAY TALESE, "New York"

This example has only one pronoun-antecedent chain, and the antecedent comes first, so all the pronouns refer back to it. When there are multiple pronoun-antecedent chains with references forward as well as back, writers have to make sure that readers will not mistake one pronoun's antecedent for another's.

Word repetition aids cohesion.

To avoid confusion, writers often use *word repetition*. The device of repeating words and phrases is especially helpful if a pronoun might confuse readers:

Some odd optical property of our highly polarized and unequal society makes **the poor** almost invisible to their economic superiors. **The poor** can see **the affluent** easily enough—on television, for example, or on the covers of magazines. But **the affluent** rarely see **the poor** or, if they do catch sight of them in some public space, rarely know what they're seeing, since—thanks to consignment stores and, yes, Wal-Mart—**the poor** are usually able to disguise themselves as members of the more comfortable classes.

—Barbara Ehrenreich, *Nickel and Dimed*

Repeated words

In the next example, several overlapping chains of word repetition prevent confusion and help the reader follow the ideas:

Natural selection is the central concept of Darwinian theory—the **fittest survive** and spread their favored traits through populations. **Natural selection** is defined by Spencer's phrase **"survival** of the **fittest,"** but what does this famous bit of jargon really mean? Who are the **fittest?** And how is **"fitness"** defined? We often read that **fitness** involves no more than "differential reproductive success"—the production of more **surviving** offspring than other competing members of the population. Whoa! cries Bethell, as many others have before him. This formulation defines **fitness** in terms of **survival** only. The crucial phrase of **natural selection** means no more than "the **survival** of those who **survive"**—a vacuous **tautology.** (A **tautology** is a phrase—like "my father is a man"—containing no information in the predicate ["a man"] not inherent in the subject ["my father"]. **Tautologies** are fine as definitions, but not as testable scientific statements—there can be nothing to test in a statement true by definition.)

—Stephen Jay Gould, *Ever Since Darwin*

Repeated words with some variation of form

Synonyms connect ideas.

In addition to word repetition, you can use **synonyms**, words with identical or very similar meanings, to connect important ideas. In the following example, the author develops a careful chain of synonyms and word repetitions:

Over time, small bits of knowledge about a **region** accumulate among local residents in the form of **stories.** These are remembered in the **community**; even what is unusual does not become lost and therefore irrelevant. These **narratives** comprise for a native an *intricate, long-term view* of a **particular** landscape. . . . Outside the **region** this *complex but easily shared "reality"* is hard to get across without reducing it to generalities, to misleading or imprecise abstraction.

—Barry Lopez, *Arctic Dreams*

Synonyms:
1. **region, community, particular landscape**
2. local residents, native
3. **stories, narratives**
4. are remembered, does not become lost
5. *intricate . . . view, complex . . . reality*

The result is a coherent paragraph that constantly reinforces the author's point.

Repetition of sentence structure emphasizes connections.

Writers occasionally use *sentence structure repetition* to emphasize the connections among their ideas, as in this example:

Repeats the if/then sentence structure

But the life forms are as much part of the structure of the Earth as any inanimate portion is. It is all an inseparable part of a whole. If any animal is isolated totally from other forms of life, **then** death by starvation will surely follow. **If** isolated from water, death by dehydration will follow even faster. **If** isolated from air, whether free or dissolved in water, death by asphyxiation will follow still faster. **If** isolated from the Sun, animals will survive for a time, but plants would die, and **if** all plants died, all animals would starve.

—Isaac Asimov, "The Case against Man"

Collocation creates networks of meaning.

Collocation—the positioning of words together in expected ways around a particular topic—occurs quite naturally to writers and usually forms recognizable networks of meaning for readers. For example, in a paragraph on a high school graduation, a reader might expect to encounter such words as *valedictorian, diploma, commencement, honors, cap and gown,* and *senior class.* The paragraph that follows uses five collocation chains:

Collocation Chains:

1. **housewife, neighbor, home**

2. **clocks, calculated, progression, precise**

3. **cooking, fire, matches, hot coals smoldering, ashes, go out, bed-warming pan**

4. **sun, clear days, cloudy ones, sundial, cast its light, angle, seasons, sun, weather**

5. *obstinacy, vagaries, problem*

The seventeenth-century **housewife** not only had to make do without thermometers, she also had to make do without clocks, which were scarce and dear throughout the sixteen hundreds. She calculated **cooking** times by the progression of the sun; her **cooking** must have been more precise on clear days than on cloudy ones. Marks were sometimes painted on the floor, providing her with a rough sundial, but she still had to make allowance for the *obstinacy* of the sun in refusing to cast its light at the same angle as the seasons changed; but she was used to allowing for the *vagaries* of sun and weather. She also had a *problem* starting her **fire** in the morning; there were no **matches**. If she had allowed the **hot coals smoldering** under the **ashes** to **go out**, she had to borrow some from a **neighbor**, carrying them **home** with care, perhaps in a **bed-warming pan**.

—Waverly Root and Richard de Rochement, *Eating in America*

EXERCISE 13.7

Now that you know more about pronoun reference, word repetition, synonyms, sentence structure repetition, and collocation, turn to Brian Cable's essay in Chapter 3 and identify the cohesive devices in paragraphs 1–5. Underline each cohesive device you can find; there will be many. You might also want to connect with lines the various pronoun, related-word, and synonym chains you find. You could also try listing the separate collocation chains. Consider how these cohesive devices help you read and make sense of the passage.

EXERCISE 13.8

Choose one of your recent writing projects, and select any three contiguous paragraphs. Underline every cohesive device you can find; there will be many. Try to connect with lines the various pronoun, related-word, and synonym chains you find. Also try listing the separate collocation chains.

You will be surprised and pleased at how extensively you rely on cohesive ties. Indeed, you could not produce readable text without cohesive ties. Consider these questions relevant to your development as a writer: Are all of your pronoun references clear? Are you straining for synonyms when repeated words would do? Do you ever repeat sentence structures to emphasize connections? Do you trust yourself to put collocation to work?

Transitions

A **transition** serves as a bridge to connect one paragraph, sentence, clause, or word with another. It also identifies the kind of connection by indicating to readers how the item preceding the transition relates to the one that follows it. Transitions help readers anticipate how the next paragraph or sentence will affect the meaning of what they have just read. There are three basic groups of transitions, based on the relationships they indicate: logical, temporal, and spatial.

Transitions emphasize logical relationships.

Transitions help readers follow the *logical relationships* within an argument. How such transitions work is illustrated in this tightly and passionately reasoned paragraph by James Baldwin:

> The black man insists, by whatever means he finds at his disposal, that the white man cease to regard him as an exotic rarity **and** recognize him as a human being. This is a very charged and difficult moment, **for** there is a great deal of will power involved in the white man's naïveté. Most people are not naturally malicious, **and** the white man prefers to keep the black man at a certain human remove **because** it is easier for him **thus** to preserve his simplicity **and** to avoid being called to account for crimes committed by his forefathers, or his neighbors. He is inescapably aware, **nevertheless,** that he is in a better position in the world than black men are, **nor** can he quite put to death the suspicion that he is hated by black men **therefore.** He does not wish to be hated, **neither** does he wish to change places, **and** at this point in his uneasiness he can scarcely avoid having recourse to those legends which white men have created about black men, the most unusual effect of which is that the white man finds himself enmeshed, so to speak, in his own language which describes hell, **as well as** the attributes which lead one to hell, **as being** black as night.
>
> —JAMES BALDWIN, "Stranger in the Village"

Transitions reinforce the logic of the argument.

Transitions Showing Logical Relationships

- *To introduce another item in a series:* first . . . , second; in the second place; for one thing . . . , for another; next; then; furthermore; moreover; in addition; finally; last; also; similarly; besides; and; as well as

- *To introduce an illustration or other specification:* in particular; specifically; for instance; for example; that is; namely

- *To introduce a result or a cause:* consequently; as a result; hence; accordingly; thus; so; therefore; then; because; since; for

- *To introduce a restatement:* that is; in other words; in simpler terms; to put it differently

- *To introduce a conclusion or a summary:* in conclusion; finally; all in all; evidently; clearly; actually; to sum up; altogether; of course

- *To introduce an opposing point:* but; however; yet; nevertheless; on the contrary; on the other hand; in contrast; still; neither; nor

- *To introduce a concession to an opposing view:* certainly; naturally; of course; it is true; to be sure; granted

- *To resume the original line of reasoning after a concession:* nonetheless; all the same; even though; still; nevertheless

Transitions can indicate a sequence in time.

In addition to showing logical connections, transitions may indicate **temporal relationships**—a sequence or progression in time—as this example illustrates:

Transitions to show
relationships of time

> **That night,** we drank tea and **then** vodka with lemon peel steeped in it. The four of us talked in Russian and English about mutual friends and American railroads and the Rolling Stones. Seryozha loves the Stones, and his face grew wistful **as we spoke** about their recent album, *Some Girls*. He played a tape of "Let It Bleed" **over and over, until** we could translate some difficult phrases for him; **after that,** he came out with the phrases **at intervals during the evening,** in a pretty decent imitation of Jagger's Cockney snarl. He was an adroit and oddly formal host, inconspicuously filling our teacups and politely urging us to eat bread and cheese and chocolate. **While he talked to us,** he teased Anya, calling her "Piglet," and she shook back her bangs and glowered at him. It was clear that theirs was a fiery relationship. **After a while,** we talked about ourselves. Anya told us about painting and printmaking and about how hard it was to buy supplies in Moscow. There had been something angry in her dark face **since the beginning of the evening;** I thought **at first** that it meant she didn't like Americans; but **now** I realized that it was a constant, barely suppressed rage at her own situation.
>
> —Andrea Lee, *Russian Journal*

Transitions Showing Temporal Relationships

- *To indicate frequency:* frequently; hourly; often; occasionally; now and then; day after day; every so often; again and again

- *To indicate duration:* during; briefly; for a long time; minute by minute; while

- *To indicate a particular time:* now; then; at that time; in those days; last Sunday; next Christmas; in 2003; at the beginning of August; at six o'clock; first thing in the morning; two months ago; when

- *To indicate the beginning:* at first; in the beginning; since; before then

- *To indicate the middle:* in the meantime; meanwhile; as it was happening; at that moment; at the same time; simultaneously; next; then

- *To indicate the end and beyond:* eventually; finally; at last; in the end; subsequently; later; afterward

Transitions can indicate relationships in space.

Transitions showing **spatial relationships** orient readers to the objects in a scene, as illustrated in these paragraphs:

> **On** Georgia 155, I crossed Troublesome Creek, then went **through** groves of pecan trees **aligned one with the next** like fenceposts. The pastures grew a green almost blue, and syrupy water the color of a dusty sunset filled the ponds. **Around** the farmhouses, **from** wires strung high **above** the ground, swayed gourds hollowed out for purple martins.
>
> The land rose **again on the other side** of the Chattahoochee River, and Highway 34 went to the ridgetops where long views **over** the hills opened **in all directions. Here** was the tail of the Appalachian backbone, its gradual descent **to** the Gulf. **Near** the Alabama stateline stood a couple of LAST CHANCE! bars.
>
> —WILLIAM LEAST HEAT-MOON, *Blue Highways*

Transitions to show
relationships in space

Transitions Showing Spatial Relationships

- *To indicate closeness:* close to; near; next to; alongside; adjacent to; facing

- *To indicate distance:* in the distance; far; beyond; away; there

- *To indicate direction:* up/down; sideways; along; across; to the right/left; in front of/behind; above/below; inside/outside; toward/away from

---

EXERCISE 13.9

Turn to William Akana's essay in Chapter 8. Relying on the lists of transitions just given, underline the transitions in paragraphs 4–6. Consider how the transitions connect the ideas from sentence to sentence. Suggest any further transitions that could be added to make the relationships even clearer.

EXERCISE 13.10

Select a recent writing project of your own. Choose at least three paragraphs, and underline the logical, temporal, and spatial transitions. Depending on the kind of writing you were doing, you may find few, if any, transitions in one category or another. For example, an essay speculating about causes may not include any spatial transitions; writing about a remembered event might not contain transitions showing logical relationships.

Consider how your transitions relate the ideas from sentence to sentence. Compare your transitions with those in the preceding lists. Do you find that you are making full use of the repertoire? Do you find gaps between any of your sentences that a well-chosen transition would close?

Headings and Subheadings

Headings and **subheadings**—brief phrases set off from the text in various ways—can provide visible cues to readers about the content and organization of a text. Headings can be distinguished from the text in numerous ways, including the selective use of capital letters, bold or italic type, or different sizes of type. To be most helpful to readers, headings should be phrased similarly and follow a predictable system.

Headings indicate sections and levels.

In this chapter, the headings in the section Paragraphing, beginning on p. 458, provide a good example of a system of headings that can readily be outlined:

Paragraphing
Paragraph indents signal related ideas.
Topic sentences announce the paragraph's focus.
Announcing the Topic
Making a Transition
Positioning the Topic Sentence

Notice that in this example, the heading system has three levels. The first-level heading sits on its own line and is set in a large red font; this heading stands out most visibly among the others. (It is one of five such headings in this chapter.) The second-level heading also sits on its own line but is set in a smaller font (and uses black type). The first of these second-level headings has no subheadings beneath it, while the second has three. These third-level headings, in black, do not sit on their own lines but run into the paragraph they introduce, as you can see if you turn back to pp. 458–60.

All of these headings follow a parallel grammatical structure: "-ing" nouns at the first level; complete sentences at the second level; and "-ing" nouns at the third level.

Headings are not common in all genres.

Headings may not be necessary in short essays: thesis statements, forecasting statements, well-positioned topic sentences, and transition sentences may be all the cues the reader needs. Headings are rare in some genres, such as essays about remembered events (Chapter 2) and essays profiling people and places (Chapter 3). Headings appear more frequently in such genres as concept explanations, opposing argument analyses, position arguments, proposals, evaluations, and cause-effect arguments (Chapters 4–9). Headings are required in résumés and lab reports (Chapter 25).

At least two headings are needed at each level.

Before dividing their essays into sections with headings and subheadings, writers need to make sure their discussion is detailed enough to support at least two headings at each level. The frequency and placement of headings depend entirely on the content and how it is divided and organized. Keep in mind that headings do not reduce the need for other cues to keep readers on track.

EXERCISE 13.11

Turn to Rosa Alexander's essay "The Meme-ing of Trigger Warnings" in Chapter 4 (pp. 111–17), and survey that essay's system of headings. If you have not read the essay, read or skim it now. Consider how the headings help readers anticipate what is coming and how the argument is organized. Decide whether the headings substitute for or complement other cues for keeping readers on track. Consider whether the headings are grammatically parallel.

EXERCISE 13.12

Select one of your writing projects that might benefit from headings. Develop a system of headings, and insert them where appropriate. Be prepared to justify your headings in light of the discussion about headings in this section.

14

Narrating and Describing

Writers use the strategies of narrating and describing to tell a vivid story, as in literacy narratives (Chapter 1), memoirs (Chapter 2), and profiles (Chapter 3), but these strategies can be used in almost any kind of writing in which a vivid anecdote or detailed information about a subject can help readers understand a topic.

Narrating

Narrating is a basic strategy for representing action and events. It can be used to report on events, present information, illustrate abstract ideas, support arguments, explain procedures, and illuminate with stories. This part of the chapter describes and illustrates five basic narrating strategies, then discusses two types of process narrative—explanatory and instructional.

Use narrating strategies to sequence and dramatize events.

Strategies such as calendar and clock time, temporal transitions, verb tense, action sequences, and dialogue give narrative its dynamic quality, the sense of events unfolding in time. They also help readers track the order in which the events occurred and understand how they relate to one another.

CALENDAR AND CLOCK TIME

One of the simplest ways of constructing a clear time sequence is to place events on a timeline, with years or precise dates and times clearly marked. Look, for example, at the excerpted portion of a timeline in Figure 14.1, which presents a series of events in the history of U.S. savings bonds. A timeline is not itself a narrative, but it shares with narrative two basic elements:

1. Events are presented in chronological order.
2. Each event is "time-stamped," so that readers can clearly understand when events occurred in relation to one another.

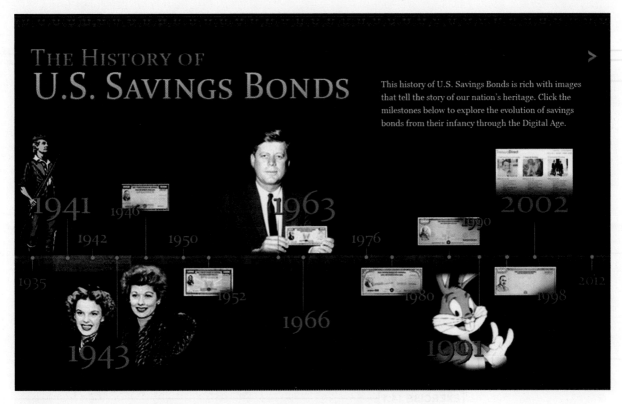

FIGURE 14.1 **Chronology of events in the history of U.S. Savings Bonds** (U.S. Department of the Treasury)

Look now at a brief but fully developed narrative reconstructing the discovery of the bacterial cause of stomach ulcers. This narrative was written by Martin J. Blaser for *Scientific American,* a journal read primarily by nonspecialists interested in science. As you read, notice the same narrating strategies you saw in the timeline in Figure 14.1: sequencing events in chronological order and specifying when each event occurred:

In 1979 J. Robin Warren, a pathologist at the Royal Perth Hospital in Australia, made a puzzling observation. As he examined tissue specimens from patients who had undergone stomach biopsies, he noticed that several samples had large numbers of curved and spiral-shaped bacteria. Ordinarily, stomach acid would destroy such organisms before they could settle in the stomach. But those Warren saw lay underneath the organ's thick mucus layer—a lining that coats the stomach's tissues and protects them from acid. Warren also noted that the bacteria were present only in tissue samples that were inflamed. Wondering whether the microbes might somehow be related to the irritation, he looked to the literature for clues and learned that German pathologists had witnessed similar organisms a century earlier. Because they could not grow the bacteria in culture, though, their findings had been ignored and then forgotten.

Blaser cites specific years, months, days, and holidays to convey passage of time and indicate when each event occurred.

Warren, aided by an enthusiastic young trainee named Barry J. Marshall, also had difficulty growing the unknown bacteria in culture. He began his efforts in 1981. By April 1982 the two men had attempted to culture samples from 30-odd patients—all without success. Then the Easter holidays arrived. The hospital laboratory staff accidentally held some of the culture plates for five days instead of the usual two. On the fifth day, colonies emerged. The workers christened them *Campylobacter pyloridis* because they resembled pathogenic bacteria of the *Campylobacter* genus found in the intestinal tract. Early in 1983 Warren and Marshall published their first report, and within months scientists around the world had isolated the bacteria.

—Martin J. Blaser, "The Bacteria Behind Ulcers"

In addition to **calendar time** (years, months, days), writers sometimes also refer to **clock time** (hours, minutes, seconds). Here is a brief narrative from an essay profiling the emergency room at Bellevue Hospital in New York City:

References to clock time establish sequence and contribute to dramatic intensity.

9:05 p.m. An ambulance backs into the receiving bay, its red and yellow lights flashing in and out of the lobby. A split second later, the glass doors burst open as a nurse and an attendant roll a mobile stretcher into the lobby. When the nurse screams, "Emergency!" the lobby explodes with activity as the way is cleared to the trauma room. Doctors appear from nowhere and transfer the bloodied body of a black man to the treatment table. Within seconds his clothes are stripped away.

— George Simpson, "The War Room at Bellevue"

EXERCISE 14.1

Skim Gabriel Thompson's "A Gringo in the Lettuce Fields" in Chapter 3, and underline the references to calendar and clock time. How do you think these time markers function in the narrative? What do they tell you about the impression Thompson wants to create about that period of his life?

Temporal Transitions

For a more extensive list of transitions showing temporal relationships, see Chapter 13.

Whereas writers tend to use calendar and clock time sparingly, they regularly use **temporal transitions**—such as *when, at that moment, before,* and *while*—to establish a clear sequence of actions.

To see how temporal transitions work, let us look at the concluding paragraphs of a remembered-event essay in which Russell Baker recounts a one-time event—what happened after his final flight test, his last chance to become a pilot. The "he" Baker refers to is the flight check pilot, T. L. (nicknamed "Total Loss") Smith:

Temporal transitions

Back at the flight line, when I'd cut the ignition, he climbed out and tramped back toward the ready room while I waited to sign the plane in. When I got there he was standing at a distance talking to my regular instructor. His talk was being illustrated with hand movements, as pilots' conversations always were, hands executing little loops and rolls in the air. After he did the falling-leaf motion with his hands, he pointed a finger at my instructor's chest, said something I couldn't hear, and trudged off. My instructor, who had flown only with the pre-hangover Baker, was slack-jawed **when** he approached me.

"Smith just said you gave him the best check flight he's ever had in his life," he said. "What the hell did you do to him up there?"

"I guess I just suddenly learned to fly," I said.

—Russell Baker, "Smooth and Easy"

Baker uses temporal transitions to show what he and Smith were doing after the flight test. Look closely at the two transitions in the first sentence. The word *when* presents actions in chronological order (first Baker stopped the plane, and then Smith got out). *While* performs a different function, showing that the next two actions occurred at the same time (Baker waited to sign in as the check pilot returned to the ready room). There is nothing complicated or unusual about this set of actions, but it would be hard to represent them in writing without temporal transitions.

Temporal transitions also enable writers to narrate recurring events. In the following narrative by Monica Sone about her daily life in an internment camp for Japanese Americans during World War II, we can see how transitions help the writer represent actions she routinely performed:

> **First** I typed on pink, green, blue and white work sheets the hours put in by the 10,000 evacuees, **then** sorted and alphabetized these sheets, and stacked them away in shoe boxes. My job was excruciatingly dull, but under no circumstances did I want to leave it. The Administration Building was the only place which had modern plumbing and running hot and cold water; **in the first few months and every morning, after** I had typed for a decent hour, I slipped into the rest room and took a complete sponge bath with scalding hot water. **During the remainder of the day,** I slipped back into the rest room **at inconspicuous intervals,** took off my head scarf and wrestled with my scorched hair. I stood upside down over the basin of hot water, soaking my hair, combing, stretching and pulling at it.
>
> — Monica Sone, "Camp Harmony"

Temporal transitions

With the time marker *first*, Sone starts describing her typical work routine. In the third sentence, she tells of her surreptitious actions in *the first few months* and *every morning*.

EXERCISE 14.2

Turn to Anastasia Toufexis's "Love: The Right Chemistry" in Chapter 4. Read paragraph 3, underlining the temporal transitions Toufexis uses to present the sequence of evolutionary changes that may have contributed to the development of romantic love. How important are these transitions in helping you follow her narrative?

Verb Tense

In addition to time markers like calendar time and temporal transitions, writers use **verb tense** to represent action in writing and to help readers understand when each action occurred in relation to other actions. Writers typically use the past tense to represent onetime events that began and ended in the past. Here is a brief passage from a remembered-person essay by Amy Wu. In addition to the temporal transitions *once* and *when* in the opening sentence, which let readers know that this particular event occurred many years earlier, the writer uses simple past-tense verbs to indicate that actions occurred in a linear sequence:

Simple past-tense verbs

> Once, when I **was** 5 or 6, I **interrupted** my mother during a dinner with her friends and **told** her that I **disliked** the meal. My mother's eyes **transformed** from serene pools of blackness into stormy balls of fire. "Quiet!" she **hissed,** "do you not know that silent waters run deep?"
>
> — Amy Wu, "A Different Kind of Mother"

In the next example, by Chang-rae Lee, we see how verb tense can be used to show more complicated relationships between past actions that occurred at different times in the past:

Simple past-tense verbs
Past-perfect verbs

> When Uncle Chul **amassed** the war chest he **needed** to open the wholesale business he <u>had hoped</u> for, he **moved** away from New York.
>
> — Chang-rae Lee, "Uncle Chul Gets Rich"

You do not have to know that *amassed* is simple past tense and *had hoped* is past perfect tense to know that the uncle's hopes came before the money was amassed. In fact, most readers of English can understand complicated combinations of tenses without knowing their names.

Let us look at another verb tense combination used frequently in narrative: the simple past and the past progressive:

Simple past-tense verbs
Past-progressive verbs

> When Dinah Washington <u>was leaving</u> with some friends, I **overheard** someone say she **was** on her way to the Savoy Ballroom where Lionel Hampton <u>was appearing</u> that night—she **was** then Hamp's vocalist.
>
> — Malcolm X, *The Autobiography of Malcolm X*

This combination of tenses plus the temporal transition *when* shows that the two actions occurred at the same time in the past. The first action ("Dinah Washington was leaving") continued during the period that the second action ("I overheard") occurred.

Occasionally, writers use the present instead of the past tense to narrate onetime events. Process narratives and profiles typically use the present tense to give the story a sense of "you are there" immediacy. In the passage that follows, Edge uses present-tense verbs to give readers a sense that they are in the room with him:

Present-tense verbs

> I . . . **stare** down at the pink juice spreading outward from a crumpled foil pouch and onto the bar.
>
> *I'm not leaving until I eat this thing,* I **tell** myself.
>
> — John T. Edge, "I'm Not Leaving Until I Eat This Thing"

Verb tense, usually combined with temporal transitions, can also help writers narrate events that occurred routinely. In the passage below, Morris uses the helping verb *would* along with temporal transitions to show recurring actions:

> <u>Many times</u>, walking home from work, I **would see** some unknowing soul venture across that intersection against the light and then freeze in horror when he saw the cars ripping out of the tunnel toward him. . . . <u>Suddenly</u>, the human reflex **would take** over, and the pedestrian **would jackknife** first one way, then another, arms flaying the empty air, and <u>often</u> the car **would literally skim** the man, brushing by him so close it would touch his coat or his tie. . . . <u>On one occasion</u>, feeling sorry for the person who had brushed against the speeding car, I hurried across the intersection after him to cheer him up a little. Catching up with him down by 32nd I said, "That was good legwork, sir. Excellent moves for a big man!" but the man looked at me with an empty expression in his eyes, and then moved away mechanically and trancelike, heading for the nearest bar.
>
> — WILLIE MORRIS, *North Toward Home*

Helping verb + main verb
Temporal transitions

Notice also that Morris shifts to the simple past tense when he moves from recurring actions to an action that occurred only once. He signals this shift with the temporal transition *on one occasion.*

EXERCISE 14.3

Turn to Jean Brandt's essay, "Calling Home," in Chapter 2. Read paragraph 3 and underline the verbs, beginning with *got, took, knew,* and *didn't want* in the first sentence. Brandt uses verb tense to reconstruct her actions and reflect on their effectiveness. Notice also how verb tense helps you follow the sequence of actions Brandt took.

Action Sequences

The narrating strategy we call **action sequences** uses active verbs and modifying phrases and clauses to present action vividly. Action sequences are especially suited to representing intense, fast-moving events, like chase scenes and sports. The following example by George Plimpton shows how well action sequences work to tell what happened during a practice scrimmage. Plimpton participated in the Detroit Lions football training camp while writing a book profiling professional football. This is what he experienced:

> Since in the two preceding plays the concentration of the play had been elsewhere, I had felt alone with the flanker. Now, the whole heave of the play was toward me, <u>flooding the zone not only with confused motion but noise</u>—the <u>quick stomp of feet, the creak of football gear, the strained grunts of effort,</u> the <u>faint *ah-ah-ah* of piston-stroke regularity,</u> and the <u>stiff calls of instruction,</u> like exhalations. "Inside, inside! Take him inside!" someone **shouted,** tearing by me, his cleats thumping in the

Modifying phrases and clauses

Active verb

grass. A call—a parrot squawk—may have erupted from me. My feet **splayed** in hopeless confusion as Barr **came** directly toward me, feinting in one direction, and then stopping suddenly, drawing me toward him for the possibility of a buttonhook pass, and as I **leaned** almost off balance toward him, he **turned** and **came on** again, downfield, moving past me at high speed, leaving me poised on one leg, reaching for him, trying to grab at him despite the illegality, anything to keep him from getting by. But he was gone, and by the time I had turned to set out after him, he **had** ten yards on me, drawing away fast with his sprinter's run, his legs pinwheeling, the row of cleats flicking up a faint wake of dust behind.

— George Plimpton, *Paper Lion*

By piling up action sequences, Plimpton reconstructs for readers the texture and excitement of his experience on the football field. He uses the two most common kinds of modifiers that writers employ to present action sequences:

> *Participial phrases: tearing by me, stopping suddenly, moving past me at high speed*

> *Absolute phrases: his cleats thumping in the grass, his legs pinwheeling, the row of cleats flicking up a faint wake of dust behind*

Combined with vivid *sensory description (the creak of football gear, the strained grunts of effort, the faint* ah-ah-ah *of piston-stroke regularity)*, these action sequences re-create the sights and sounds of people in motion.

EXERCISE 14.4

Turn to paragraph 2 of Amanda Coyne's profile essay "The Long Good-Bye: Mother's Day in Federal Prison" in Chapter 3. Underline any action sequences you find in this brief paragraph. Then reflect on how they help the reader envision the scene in the prison's visiting room.

EXERCISE 14.5

Record several brief—two- or three-minute—televised segments of a fast-moving sports competition, such as a soccer or basketball game. Then review the recording, and choose one segment to narrate, using action sequences to describe in detail what you see.

If you cannot record a televised game, narrate a live-action event (for example, people playing touch football, a dog catching a Frisbee, or a skateboarder or inline skater practicing a trick). As you watch the action, take detailed notes of what you see. Then, based on your notes, write a few sentences using action sequences to describe what you witnessed firsthand.

Dialogue

Dialogue is most often used in narratives that dramatize events. It reconstructs choice bits of conversation, rather than trying to present an accurate and complete record. In addition to showing people interacting, dialogue can give readers insight into character and relationships. Dialogue may be *quoted* to make it resemble the give-and-take of actual conversation, or it may be *summarized* to give readers the gist of what was said.

The following example from Gary Soto's *Living Up the Street* shows how a narrative can combine quoted and summarized dialogue. In this passage, Soto recalls his first experience as a migrant worker in California's San Joaquin Valley:

"Are you tired?" **she asked.**

"No, but I got a sliver from the frame," **I told her.** I showed her the web of skin between my thumb and index finger. She wrinkled her forehead but said it was nothing.

"How many trays did you do?"

I looked straight ahead, not answering at first. **I recounted** in my mind the whole morning of bend, cut, pour again and again, before answering a feeble "thirty-seven." No elaboration, no detail. Without looking at me she told me how she had done field work in Texas and Michigan as a child. But I had a difficult time listening to her stories. I played with my grape knife, stabbing it into the ground, but stopped when Mother reminded me that I had better not lose it. I left the knife sticking up like a small, leafless plant. She then talked about school, the junior high I would be going to that fall, and then about Rick and Debra, how sorry they would be that they hadn't come out to pick grapes because they'd have no new clothes for the school year. She stopped talking when she peeked at her watch, a bandless one she kept in her pocket. She got up with an "Ay, Dios," and told me that we'd work until three, leaving me cutting figures in the sand with my knife and dreading the return to work.

— GARY SOTO, "One Last Time"

> Signal phrase (noun or pronoun + verb)

Soto uses signal phrases with the first two quotations but not with the third, where it is clear who is speaking. The fourth quotation, "thirty-seven," is preceded by a narrative that tells what Soto did and thought before speaking and is followed by a summary of further conversation. Quoted dialogue is easy to recognize, of course, because of the quotation marks. Summarized dialogue can be harder to identify. In this case, however, Soto embeds *signal phrases* (*she told me* and *she then talked*) in his narrative. Summarizing leaves out information the writer decides readers do not need. In this passage about a remembered event, Soto has chosen to focus on his own feelings and thoughts rather than his mother's.

> For more on deciding when to quote, see Chapter 2 and Chapter 19.

EXERCISE 14.6

Read the essay "A Gringo in the Lettuce Fields" in Chapter 3, and consider Gabriel Thompson's use of both direct quotation and summaries for reporting speech. When does Thompson choose to quote directly, and why might he have made this decision?

EXERCISE 14.7

If you wrote a remembered-event essay in Chapter 2 or used narration in some other essay, reread your essay, looking for one example of each of the following narrating strategies: calendar and clock time, temporal transitions, verb tense, action sequences, and dialogue. Do not worry if you cannot find examples of all the strategies. Pick one strategy you did use, and comment on what it contributes to your narrative.

Use narrating strategies to explain and instruct.

Process narratives explain how something was done or instruct readers on how it could or should be done. Whether the purpose is explanatory or instructional, process narratives must clearly convey each necessary action and the exact order in which the actions occur.

Explanatory Process Narratives

Writers often use **explanatory process narratives** to relate particular experiences or elucidate processes followed by machines or organizations. Consider this excerpt from a remembered-event essay by Mary Mebane. She uses process narrative to let readers know what happened the first time she worked on an assembly line putting tobacco leaves on the conveyor belt:

Temporal transitions

> The job seemed easy enough as I picked up bundle after bundle of tobacco and put it on the belt, careful to turn the knot end toward me so that it would be placed right to go under the cutting machine. **Gradually,** as we worked up our tobacco, I had to bend more, for as we emptied the hogshead we had to stoop over to pick up the tobacco, **then** straighten up and put it on the belt just right. **Then** I discovered the hard part of the job: the belt kept moving at the same speed all the time and if the leaves were not placed on the belt at the same tempo there would be a big gap where your bundle should have been. So that meant that when you got down lower, you had to bend down, get the tobacco, straighten up fast, make sure it was placed knot end toward you, place it on the belt, and bend down again. **Soon** you were bending down, up; down, up; down, up. All along the line, heads were bobbing—down, up; down, up—**until** you finished the barrel. **Then** you could rest until the men brought you another one.
>
> —MARY MEBANE, "Summer Job"

Here, action sequences (*bend down, get the tobacco, straighten up fast*) become a series of staccato movements (*down, up; down, up; down, up*) that emphasize the speed and machinelike actions Mebane had to take to keep up with the conveyor belt.

The next example shows how a laser printer functions:

Objects performing the action

> To create a page, the **computer** sends signals to the **printer,** which shines a **laser** at a mirror system that scans across a charged **drum.** Whenever the **beam** strikes the **drum,** it removes the charge. The **drum** then rotates through a **toner** chamber filled with thermoplastic **particles.** The **toner particles** stick to the negatively charged areas of the **drum** in the pattern of characters, lines, or other elements the **computer** has transmitted and the **laser beam** mapped.
>
> Once the **drum** is coated with **toner** in the appropriate locations, a **piece of paper** is pulled across a so-called **transfer corona wire,** which imparts a positive electrical charge. The **paper** then passes across the toner-coated **drum.** The positive charge on the **paper** attracts the **toner** in the same position it occupied on the **drum.** The final phase of the process involves fusing the **toner** to the **paper** with a set of high-temperature **rollers.**
>
> —RICHARD GOLOB AND ERIC BRUS, *The Almanac of Science and Technology*

Like Mebane's process narrative, this one sequences the actions chronologically from beginning ("the computer sends signals to the printer") to end ("fusing the toner to the paper"). Temporal transitions (*then, once, final*) and present-tense verbs (*sends, shines, scans, strikes*) convey the passage of time and place the actions clearly in this chronological sequence. Because the objects performing the action change from sentence to sentence, the writers must construct a clearly marked chain, introducing the object's name in one sentence and repeating the name or using a synonym in the next.

EXERCISE 14.8

In Chapter 3, read paragraph 6 of Brian Cable's profile of a local mortuary, "The Last Stop." Here Cable narrates the process that the company follows once it has been notified of a client's death. As you read, look for and mark the narrating strategies discussed in this chapter that Cable uses. Then reflect on how well you think the narrative presents the actions and their sequence.

Instructional Process Narratives

Unlike explanatory process narratives, **instructional process narratives** must include all the information a reader needs to perform the procedure presented. Depending on the reader's experience, the writer might need to define technical terms, list tools that should be used, give background information, and account for alternatives or possible problems.

For guidelines on designing, see Chapter 22.

Figure 14.2 presents a detailed instructional process narrative from the *Home Repair Handbook,* which gives readers directions for replacing a broken plug. The graphic includes four steps that are clearly numbered, illustrated, and narrated. Each step presents several actions to be taken, and its graphic shows what the plug should look like when these actions have been completed. We can identify the actions by looking at the verbs. Step 1 in "Replacing plugs with terminal screws," for example, instructs readers to take four separate actions, each signaled by the verb (italicized here): "*Unscrew* and *remove* the new plug's insulating barrier. Using a utility knife, *split*

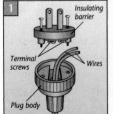 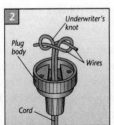 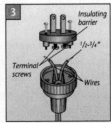 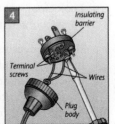

Unscrew and remove the new plug's insulating barrier. Using a utility knife, split the end of the cord to separate the wires; push the cord through the plug body.

Make two loops with the wires, pass the loose ends of the wires through the loops, and pull to form an Underwriter's knot (to prevent strain on connections).

Strip 1/2 to 3/4 inch of insulation off the wire ends, being careful not to nick the wires (page 159). Unscrew the terminal screws to allow space for the wires.

Form loops on wires and wrap them clockwise three-quarters of the way around screws. Tighten the screws, trim excess wire, and reattach the barrier to the body.

FIGURE 14.2   Replacing plugs with terminal screws

the end of the cord to separate the wires; *push* the cord through the plug body." These are active verbs, and the sentences are in the form of clear and efficient commands. The anonymous authors do not assume that readers know very much, as they label every element of each drawing, including the screws. They also instruct readers on precisely what to do. For example, in Step 4, they tell readers to "form loops on wires and wrap them clockwise three-quarters of the way around screws."

EXERCISE 14.9

Write a one- to two-page instructional process narrative that tells readers how to make a peanut butter and jelly sandwich or perform some other equally simple procedure, such as hemming a pair of pants, potting a plant, or changing a tire. Address your narrative to readers who have never done the procedure before.

Describing

Vivid **description** creates an intense, distinctive image, one that seems to bring words to life. Good description can also be evocative, calling up memories or suggesting feelings associated with the subject being described. Writers use description to give readers an impression of people and places, to illustrate abstract ideas, to make information memorable, and to support an argument. This part of the chapter presents the three basic descriptive techniques of *naming, detailing,* and *comparing;* it surveys the words writers typically use to evoke vivid sense impressions; and it examines how writers use description to create a dominant impression.

Use naming to give an overall impression.

For more on naming, see Chapter 2.

Naming calls readers' attention to observable features of the subject being described. To describe a room, for example, you might name objects you see as you look around, such as a bed, pillows, blankets, a dresser, clothes, books, and a laptop. These objects suggest what kind of room it is and begin to give readers an impression of what it is like to be in this particular room.

Look closely at the following passage describing a weasel that the writer, Annie Dillard, encountered in the woods:

> He was ten inches long, thin as a curve, a muscled ribbon, brown as fruitwood, soft-furred, alert. His **face** was fierce, small and pointed as a lizard's; he would have made a good arrowhead. There was just a dot of **chin,** maybe two brown hairs' worth, and then the pure white **fur** began that spread down his **underside.** He had two black **eyes** I didn't see, any more than you see a window.
>
> —ANNIE DILLARD, *Teaching a Stone to Talk*

With these names, readers can begin to put together a mental image of the animal Dillard is describing. She uses simple, everyday nouns, like *chin,* to identify the weasel's features, not technical words like *maxilla* or *mandible.* The piling up of simple, concrete nouns helps readers imagine what the weasel looked like to Dillard.

Although writers most commonly name what they see, sight is not the only sense that contributes to vivid descriptions:

> When the sun fell across the great white pile of the new Telephone Company building, you could smell the stucco burning as you passed; then some liquid **sweetness** that came to me from deep in the rings of the freshly cut lumber stacked in the yards, and the fresh plaster and paint on the brand-new storefronts. **Rawness,** sunshiny **rawness** down the end streets of the city, as I thought of them then—the hot ash-laden **stink** of the refuse dumps in my nostrils and the only sound at noon the resonant metal **plunk** of a tin can I kicked ahead of me as I went my way.
>
> —Alfred Kazin, *A Walker in the City*

Names smells, sounds, tastes, and tactile qualities

EXERCISE 14.10

Go to a place where you can sit for a while and observe the scene. It might be a landscape or a cityscape, indoors or outdoors, crowded or solitary. For five minutes, list everything in the scene that you can name, using nouns. (A simple way to test if a word is a noun is to see if you can put the word *the, a,* or *an* in front of it.) Remember, you can name objects you see (*dog, hydrant*) as well as impressions, such as smells or sounds, you experience at the place (*stench, hiss*).

Then write a paragraph or two that describes the scene for someone who is not there with you. Write for readers who have never been to this particular place to let them know what to expect when they get there.

EXERCISE 14.11

Turn to the excerpt from Annie Dillard's *An American Childhood* in Chapter 2. Read paragraphs 12 and 13, and underline the names that Dillard uses to describe the circuitous route she runs while the stranger is chasing her. Begin underlining with the words *house, path, tree,* and *bank* in the opening sentence. How do you think the amount of naming Dillard does contributes to the description's vividness, measured by your ability to imagine the chase scene?

Use detailing to add specifics and convey thoughts, feelings, and judgments.

Naming identifies the notable features of the subject being described; **detailing** makes the features more specific or particularized. Naming answers the questions, What is it? and What are its parts or features? Detailing answers questions like these:

For more on detailing, see Chapter 2.

- What size is it?
- How many are there?
- What is it made of?
- Where is it located?
- What is its condition?

- How is it used?
- Where does it come from?
- What is its effect?
- What is its value?

To add details to names, add modifiers—adjectives and adverbs, phrases and clauses. **Modifiers** make nouns more specific by supplying additional information. Notice how many modifying details Dillard provides in her description of the weasel:

> He was **ten inches long, thin** as a curve, a **muscled** ribbon, **brown** as fruitwood, **soft-furred, alert.** His face was **fierce, small** and **pointed** as a lizard's; he would have made a good arrowhead. There was just a dot of chin, maybe **two brown hairs'** worth, and then the **pure white** fur began that spread down his underside. He had **two black** eyes I didn't see, any more than you see a window.
>
> —ANNIE DILLARD, *Teaching a Stone to Talk*

In addition to providing details that show readers what this specific weasel looked like, Dillard conveys her thoughts and feelings during the encounter. For example, when she writes that the weasel's "face was fierce," she is making a judgment. She uses details like this to make readers see the weasel as a wild animal, not a soft and cuddly pet.

In describing people, writers often combine physical details with details characterizing aspects of the individual's personality. These characterizations or evaluations let readers know something about the writer's thoughts about the person, as the following examples illustrate:

Physical description
Evaluative details

> My father, a **fat,** funny man with beautiful eyes and a subversive wit
>
> —ALICE WALKER, "Beauty: When the Other Dancer Is the Self"

> I was afraid of her **higharched bony** nose, her eyebrows **lifted in half-circles** above her **hooded, brilliant** eyes, and of the **Kentucky** R's in her speech, and the **long** steps she took in her **hightop** shoes. I did nothing but fear her bearing-down authority.
>
> —EUDORA WELTY, "Miss Duling"

Sometimes physical details alone can be enough to symbolize a person's character or the writer's feelings toward that person, as in the following passage:

Physical details
suggesting a powerful,
threatening character

> Rick was not a friendly looking man. He wore only swim trunks, and his **short, powerful** legs rose up to meet a **bulging** torso. His **big** belly was **solid.** His shoulders, as if to offset his **front-heaviness,** were **thrown back,** creating a **deep crease of excess muscle** from his sides around the small of his back, a **crease like a huge frown. His arms were crossed, two medieval maces** placed carefully on their racks, ready to be swung at any moment. His **round** cheeks and chin were **darkened** by traces of **black** whiskers. His hair was **sparse. Huge, black, mirrored** sunglasses replaced his eyes. Below his **prominent** nose was a **thin,** sinister mustache. I couldn't believe this menacing-looking man was the legendary jovial Rick.
>
> —BRAD BENIOFF, "Rick"

EXERCISE 14.12

Return to the description you wrote in Exercise 14.10. Put brackets around the details you used to help describe the scene. Add any other details you think of now—details that indicate size, quantity, makeup, location, condition, use, source, effect, value, or any other quality that would make the description more specific and particularized for readers. Then reread your description. What do you think the detailing contributes to the description you wrote?

EXERCISE 14.13

Look again at paragraphs 12 and 13 of Annie Dillard's *An American Childhood* in Chapter 2. In Exercise 14.11, you underlined the names Dillard used. Now put brackets around the details. You might begin, for example, with the modifiers *yellow* and *backyard*. How do you think detailing contributes to Dillard's description? How do these details help you imagine Dillard's experience of the chase?

EXERCISE 14.14

Turn to paragraphs 10 and 13 of Amanda Coyne's "The Long Good-Bye: Mother's Day in Federal Prison" in Chapter 3. Read and put brackets around the words that detail the description of Stephanie and her son, Ellie. If you have not read the entire essay, read it now, and consider how Coyne uses these contrasting descriptions of the inmate and her son to emphasize her main point in the essay.

Use comparisons to make a description vivid and convey emotion.

In addition to naming and detailing, writers sometimes use **comparing** to make their description more vivid for readers. Look again at Annie Dillard's description of a weasel, paying attention this time to the comparisons:

> He was ten inches long, thin as a curve, **a muscled ribbon,** brown as fruitwood, soft-furred, alert. His face was fierce, small and pointed as a lizard's; **he would have made a good arrowhead.** There was just a dot of chin, maybe two brown hairs' worth, and then the pure white fur began that spread down his underside. He had two black **eyes I didn't see, any more than you see a window.**
>
> —ANNIE DILLARD, *Teaching a Stone to Talk*

Similes
Metaphors

Dillard uses simile and metaphor, both of which point out similarities in things that are essentially dissimilar. A **simile** expresses the similarity directly by using the words *like* or *as* to announce the comparison. A **metaphor**, by contrast, is an implicit comparison in which one thing is described as though it were the other.

Similes and metaphors can enhance the vividness of a description by giving readers additional information to help them picture the subject. For example, Dillard uses the word *thin* to detail the weasel's body shape. But *thin* is a relative term, leading readers to wonder, how thin? Dillard gives readers two images for comparison, a curve and a ribbon, to help them construct a fuller mental image of the weasel.

Comparing can also convey to readers what the writer feels about the subject. The following comparison from Brad Benioff's description of Coach Rick suggests the writer's feelings: "His arms were crossed, two medieval maces placed carefully on their racks, ready to be swung at any moment." Sometimes the similes or metaphors writers use are suggestive but hard to pin down. What do you think Dillard means, for example, by comparing the weasel's eyes to a window: "He had two black eyes I didn't see, any more than you see a window"?

EXERCISE 14.15

Return to the description you wrote in Exercise 14.10 and may have added to in Exercise 14.12. Reread it, and mark any comparing you did. Try to add one or two similes or metaphors to your description. How do you think your use of comparing may help readers imagine the subject or get a sense of what you feel about it?

Use sensory description to convey what you saw, heard, smelled, felt, and tasted.

When writers use **sensory description** to describe animals, people, or scenes, they usually rely on the sense of sight more than the other senses. In general, our vocabulary for reporting what we see is larger and more varied than our vocabulary for reporting other sense impressions. Nevertheless, writers can detail the qualities and attributes of nonvisual sensations—the loudness or tinniness or rumble of an engine, for instance. They can also use comparing to help readers imagine what something sounds, smells, feels, or tastes like.

Sight

When people describe what they see, they identify the objects in their field of vision. Here are two brief examples of visual description:

> On Christmas Eve I saw that my mother had outdone herself in creating a strange menu. She was pulling black veins out of the backs of fleshy prawns. The kitchen was littered with appalling mounds of raw food: A slimy rock cod with bulging eyes that pleaded not to be thrown into a pan of hot oil. Tofu, which looked like stacked wedges of rubbery white sponges. A bowl soaking dried fungus back to life. A plate of squid, their backs crisscrossed with knife markings so they resembled bicycle tires.
>
> —Amy Tan, "Fish Cheeks"

> She was thirty-four. She wore a white skirt and yellow sweater and a thin gold necklace, which she held in her fingers, as if holding her own reins, while waiting for

children to answer. Her hair was black with a hint of Irish red. It was cut short to the tops of her ears, and swept back like a pair of folded wings. She had a delicate cleft chin, and she was short—the children's chairs would have fit her. . . . Her hands kept very busy. They sliced the air and made karate chops to mark off boundaries. They extended straight out like a traffic cop's, halting illegal maneuvers yet to be perpetrated. When they rested momentarily on her hips, her hands looked as if they were in holsters.

—TRACY KIDDER, *Among Schoolchildren*

EXERCISE 14.16

Write a few sentences describing a teacher, friend, or family member. Do not rely on memory for this exercise; describe someone who is before you as you write so that you can describe in detail what you see. Later, when you are alone, reread what you have written, and make any changes you think will help make this visual description more vivid for your readers.

Sound

In reporting auditory impressions, writers seldom name sounds without also specifying what the sounds come from: the murmur of a voice, the rustle of the wind, the squeak of a hinge, the sputter of an engine. *Onomatopoeia* is the term for names of sounds that echo the sounds themselves: *squeak, murmur, hiss, boom, plink, tinkle, twang, jangle, rasp, chirr.* Sometimes writers make up words—like *sweesh* and *carawong*—to imitate sounds they wish to describe. Qualitative words like *powerful* and *rich* as well as relative terms like *loud* and *low* often specify sounds further. For detailing sounds, writers sometimes use a technique called *synesthesia*, taking words commonly used to describe one sense and applying them to another, such as describing sounds as *sharp* and *soft;* they sometimes also use simile or metaphor to compare one sound to another.

To write about the sounds along Manhattan's Canal Street, Ian Frazier uses many of these describing and naming techniques:

> The traffic on Canal Street never stops. It is a high-energy current jumping constantly between the poles of Brooklyn and New Jersey. It hates to have its flow pinched in the density of Manhattan, hates to stop at intersections. Along Canal Street, **it moans and screams.** Worn brake shoes of semitrucks go "Ooohhhh nooohhhh" at stoplights, and the **sound echoes in the canyons** of warehouses and Chinatown tenements. People lean on their horns from one end of Canal Street to the other. They'll honk nonstop for ten minutes at a time, **until the horns get tired and out of breath.** They'll try different combinations: shave-and-a-hair-cut, long-long-long, short-short-short-long. Some people have musical car horns; a person purchasing a musical car horn seems to be limited to a choice of four tunes—"La Cucaracha," "Theme from *The Godfather*," "Dixie," and "Hava Nagila."

—IAN FRAZIER, "Canal Street"

Metaphor

Onomatopoeia

Auditory details

EXERCISE 14.17

Find a noisy spot — a restaurant, a football game, a nursery school, a laundry room — where you can perch for about half an hour. Listen attentively to the sounds of the place, and make notes about what you hear. Then write a paragraph or two describing the place through its sounds.

Smell

The English language has a meager stock of words to express the olfactory sense. Fewer than a dozen commonly used nouns name this sensation: *odor, scent, vapor, fume, aroma, fragrance, perfume, bouquet, stench,* and *stink.* Although there are other, rarer words, like *fetor* and *effluvium,* few writers use them, probably for fear that their readers will not know them. Few verbs describe receiving or sending odors—*smell, sniff, waft*—but a fair number of detailing adjectives are available: *redolent, pungent, aromatic, perfumed, stinking, musty, rancid, putrid, rank, fetid, malodorous, foul, acrid, sweet,* and *cloying.*

Here is an example of how Amanda Coyne, in her essay in Chapter 3, uses smell in a description:

> Occasionally, a mother will pick up her present and **bring it to her nose** when one of the bearers of the single flower—her child—asks if she likes it. . . .
>
> But most of what is being **smelled** today is the children themselves. While the other adults are plunking coins into the vending machines, the mothers take deep **whiffs** from the backs of their children's necks, or kiss and **smell** the backs of their knees, or take off their shoes and tickle their feet and then **pull them close to their noses.** They hold them tight and **take in their own second scent**—the scent assuring them that these are still their children and that they still belong to them.
>
> —Amanda Coyne, "The Long Good-Bye: Mother's Day in Federal Prison"

In addition to using *smell* as a verb, Coyne describes the repeated action of bringing the object being smelled to the nose, an act that not only signifies the process of smelling but also underscores its intimacy. To further emphasize intimacy, Coyne connects smelling with other intimate acts of kissing, tickling, pulling close, and holding tight.

Because she is not describing her own experience of smell, Coyne does not try to find words to evoke the effect the odor has on her. In the next passage, however, Frank Conroy uses comparing in addition to naming and detailing to describe how the smell of flowers affected him:

Metaphor
Simile

> The perfume of the flowers rushed into my brain. A **lush aroma,** thick with sweetness, thick as blood, and **spiced** with the clear acid of tropical greenery.
>
> —Frank Conroy, *Stop-Time*

Naming the objects from which smells come can also be very suggestive:

> The odor of these houses was different, full of fragrances, sweet and nauseating. On 105th Street the smells were of **fried lard,** of **beans** and **car fumes,** of **factory**

smoke and **home-made brew** out of backyard stills. There were **chicken smells** and **goat smells** in grassless yards filled with engine parts and wire and wood planks, cracked and sprinkled with rusty nails. These were the familiar aromas: the funky earth, animal and mechanical smells which were absent from the homes my mother cleaned.

—LUIS J. RODRÍGUEZ, *Always Running: Gang Days in L.A.*

EXERCISE 14.18

Choose a place with noticeable, distinctive smells where you can stay for ten or fifteen minutes. You may choose an eating place (a cafeteria, a doughnut shop), a place where something is being manufactured (a sawmill, a bakery), or some other place that has strong, identifiable odors (a fishing dock, a garden, a locker room). While you are there, take notes on what you smell, and then write a paragraph or two describing the place primarily through its smells.

Touch

Relatively few nouns and verbs name tactile sensations besides *touch, feel, tickle, brush, scratch, sting, itch,* and *tingle*. Probably as a consequence, writers describing the sense of touch tend not to name the sensation directly or even to report the act of feeling. Nevertheless, a large stock of words describes temperature (*hot, warm, mild, tepid, cold, arctic*), moisture content (*wet, dry, sticky, oily, greasy, moist, crisp*), texture (*gritty, silky, smooth, crinkled, coarse, soft, leathery*), and weight (*heavy, light, ponderous, buoyant, feathery*). Read the following passages with an eye for descriptions of touch:

A small slab of roughly finished concrete offered a place to stand opposite a square of tar from which a splintered tee protruded.

—WILLIAM RINTOUL, "Breaking One Hundred"

The earth was moldy, a dense clay. No sun had fallen here for over two centuries. I climbed over the brick retaining wall and crawled toward the sound of the kitten. As I neared, as it sensed my presence was too large to be its mother, it went silent and scrabbled away from the reach of my hand. I brushed fur, though, and that slight warmth filled me with what must have been a mad calm because when the creature squeezed into a bearing wall of piled stones, I inched forward on my stomach.

—LOUISE ERDRICH, "Beneath My House"

Here is an example of a writer recalling a childish fantasy of aggression toward her younger sister. Notice the tactile description she uses:

She was baby-soft. I thought that I could put my thumb on her nose and push it bonelessly in, indent her face. I could poke dimples into her cheeks. I could work her face around like dough.

—MAXINE HONG KINGSTON, "The Quiet Girl"

EXERCISE 14.19

Do something with your hands, and then write a sentence or two describing the experience of touch. For example, you might pet a dog, dig a hole and put a plant into the earth, make a pizza, sculpt with clay, bathe a baby, or scrub a floor. As you write, notice the words you consider using to describe temperature, moisture content, texture, weight, or any other tactile quality.

EXERCISE 14.20

Turn to Brian Cable's "The Last Stop" in Chapter 3, and read the last paragraph. Underline the language that describes the sense of touch. What does this detail add to your understanding of the scene, and why might Cable have chosen to save it for the last paragraph of his profile?

Taste

Other than *taste, savor,* and *flavor,* few words name gustatory sensations directly. Certain words do distinguish among types of tastes—*sweet (saccharine, sugary, cloying); sour (acidic, tart); bitter (acrid, biting); salty (briny, brackish)*—and several other words describe specific tastes (*piquant, spicy, pungent, peppery, savory*).

In the following passage, M. F. K. Fisher describes the surprisingly "delicious" taste of tar:

> Tar with some dust in it was perhaps even more delicious than dirty chips from the iceman's wagon, largely because if we worked up enough body heat and had the right amount of spit we could keep it melted so that it acted almost like chewing gum, which was forbidden to us as vulgar and bad for the teeth and in general to be shunned. Tar was better than anything ever put out by Wrigley and Beechnut, anyway. It had a **high, bright** taste. It tasted the way it smelled, but better.
>
> —M. F. K. FISHER, "Prejudice, Hate, and the First World War"

Words not typically associated with taste

Fisher tries to evoke the sense of taste by comparing tar that acted like chewing gum to actual Wrigley and Beechnut chewing gum. More surprisingly, she compares the taste of tar to its smell.

Ernest Hemingway, in a more conventional passage, tries to describe taste primarily by naming the foods he consumed and giving details that indicate the intensity and quality of the tastes:

> As I ate the oysters with their **strong taste of the sea** and their **faint metallic taste** that the cold wine washed away, leaving only the **sea taste** and the **succulent texture,** and as I drank their **cold liquid** from each shell and washed it down with the **crisp taste** of the wine, I lost the empty feeling and began to be happy and to make plans.
>
> —ERNEST HEMINGWAY, *A Moveable Feast*

Combines taste and touch (the feel of the food in the mouth)

Writers often use words like *juicy, chewy,* and *chunky* to evoke both the taste and the feel of food in the mouth.

EXERCISE 14.21

In the manner of Hemingway, take notes as you eat a particular food or an entire meal. Then write a few sentences describing the tastes you experienced.

Use description to create a dominant impression.

The most effective description creates a **dominant impression**, a mood or an atmosphere that reinforces the writer's purpose. Naming, detailing, comparing, and sensory language—all the choices about what to include and what to call things—come together to create this effect, as the following passage by Mary McCarthy illustrates. Notice that McCarthy directly states the idea she is trying to convey in the last sentence of the paragraph:

> Whenever we children came to stay at my grandmother's house, we were put to sleep in the sewing room, a **bleak, shabby, utilitarian rectangle,** more office than bedroom, more attic than office, that played to the hierarchy of chambers the role of a poor relation. It was a room seldom entered by the other members of the family, seldom swept by the maid, a **room without pride;** the old sewing machine, some **cast-off chairs,** a **shadeless lamp,** rolls of wrapping paper, piles of pins, and remnants of material united with the **iron folding cots** put out for our use and the **bare floor boards** to give an impression of **intense and ruthless temporality. Thin, white spreads,** of the kind used in hospitals and charity institutions, and **naked blinds** at the windows reminded us of our orphaned condition and of the ephemeral character of our visit; there was nothing here to encourage us to consider this our home.
> —Mary McCarthy, *Memories of a Catholic Girlhood*

Like McCarthy and her brothers, the things in the room were unwanted, discarded, orphaned. Even the room itself is described in terms applicable to the children: Like them, it "played to the hierarchy of chambers the role of a poor relation."

Sometimes writers comment directly in a description, as McCarthy does. Often, however, writers want description to speak for itself, as in the following example:

> Hanging from the ceiling there was a **heavy glass chandelier** on which the **dust was so thick that it was like fur.** And covering most of one wall there was a **huge hideous piece of junk,** something between a sideboard and a hall-stand, with lots of carving and little drawers and strips of looking-glass, and there was a **once-gaudy carpet ringed by the slop-pails of years,** and **two gilt chairs with burst seats,** and one of those old-fashioned armchairs which you slide off when you try to sit on them. The room had been turned into a bedroom by **thrusting four squalid beds** in among the **wreckage.**
> —George Orwell, *The Road to Wigan Pier*

EXERCISE 14.22

Turn to "The Long Good-Bye: Mother's Day in Federal Prison" by Amanda Coyne in Chapter 3, and read paragraph 3. What seems to you to be the dominant impression of this description? What do you think contributes most to this impression?

15

Defining, Classifying, and Comparing

Writers use the strategies of defining, classifying, and comparing to create a vivid profile (Chapter 3); explain a complex concept (Chapter 4); or convince readers to accept a position, a solution, an evaluation, or a preferred cause or effect. These strategies can also be used to analyze and synthesize opposing arguments (Chapter 5) or to analyze a story (Chapter 10). In fact, they're used in just about all kinds of writing in which a writer needs to organize ideas and communicate a shared understanding.

Defining

Defining is an essential strategy for all writing. Autobiographers, for example, must occasionally define objects, conditions, events, and activities for readers likely to be unfamiliar with particular terms, as in the following example:

Term to be defined
Definition

> My father's hands are grotesque. He suffers from psoriasis, a chronic skin disease that covers his massive, thick hands with scaly, reddish patches that periodically flake off, sending tiny pieces of dead skin sailing to the ground.
>
> —JAN GRAY, "Father"

When writers share information or explain how to do something, they must often define important terms for readers who are unfamiliar with the subject, as in this example:

> Shifting baselines are the chronic, slow, hard-to-notice changes in things, from the disappearance of birds and frogs in the countryside to the increased drive time from L.A. to San Diego.
>
> —RANDY OLSON, "Shifting Baselines: Slow-Motion Disaster below the Waves"

To convince readers of a position or an evaluation or to move them to act on a proposal, a writer must often define concepts important to an argument:

> You would come across news of a study showing that the percentage of Wisconsin food-stamp families in "extreme poverty"—defined as less than 50 percent of the federal poverty line—has tripled in the last decade to more than 30 percent.
>
> —Barbara Ehrenreich, *Nickel and Dimed*

Some writing is primarily concerned with the definition of a little-understood or problematic concept or thing. Usually, however, a long piece of writing, like a term paper, textbook, or research report, will include many kinds of brief and extended definitions, all of them integrated with other writing strategies.

This part of the chapter illustrates various types of sentence definitions, the most common in writing. When writers use sentence definitions, they rely on various sentence patterns to provide concise definitions. The section also provides illustrations of multisentence extended definitions, including definition by word history, or etymology, and by stipulation.

Use sentence definitions to explain terms and concepts briefly.

Coming to a new field of study, institution, or activity for the first time, a participant is often baffled by the many unfamiliar concepts and terms. In college, introductory courses in all the academic disciplines often seem like courses in new terms. In the same way, newcomers to a sport like sailing or rock climbing often need to learn a great deal of specialized terminology. Writers of textbooks and manuals that cover such topics rely on brief **sentence definitions** to explain terms and concepts. The most obvious strategies simply announce a definition:

> A karyotype is a graphic representation of a set of chromosomes.   Term to be defined
>
>   Definition

> Then, within the first week, the cells begin to differentiate—to specialize in structure and function.

> Posthypnotic suggestions (suggestions to be carried out after the hypnosis session has ended) have helped alleviate headaches, asthma, warts, and stress-related skin disorders.

Other, less direct strategies for integrating definitions are signaled by *subordinate clauses*:

> During the oral stage, which lasts throughout the first 18 months, the infant's sensual pleasures focus on sucking, biting, and chewing.

> Hemophilia is called the bleeder's disease because the affected person's blood does not clot.

Another common defining strategy is to use an *appositive*—a brief inserted word or phrase that presents either the definition or the word to be defined:

Taxonomy, **the science of classifying groups (taxa) of organisms in formal groups,** is hierarchical.

The actual exchange of gases takes place in **small air sacs,** the alveoli, which are clustered in branches like grapes around the ends of the smallest bronchioles.

EXERCISE 15.1

Look up any three of the following words or phrases in a dictionary. Define each one in a sentence. Try to use a different sentence pattern for each of your definitions.

bull market	ecumenism	samba
carcinogen	edema	seasonal affective disorder
caricature	harangue	sonnet
clinometer	hyperhidrosis	testosterone
ectomorph	mnemonic	zero-based budgeting

EXERCISE 15.2

Turn to the essay in Chapter 8 titled "What College Rankings Really Tell Us," by Malcolm Gladwell, and analyze the sentence definition in paragraph 2. Notice the strategy Gladwell relies on. Keeping in mind that Gladwell's purpose is to persuade readers to accept his criticism of the *U.S. News* staff's college rankings, how helpful do you find this sentence definition?

Use extended definitions to convey the meaning of complex concepts.

At times a writer may need to go further than a brief sentence definition and provide readers with a fuller, **extended definition,** as in the following example:

Compares TV addiction with **drug and alcohol addiction**

People often refer to being "hooked on TV." Does this, too, fall into the light-hearted category of cookie eating and other pleasures that people pursue with unusual intensity, or is there a kind of televison viewing that falls into the more serious category of **destructive addiction?** . . .

Let us consider television viewing in the light of the conditions that define **serious addictions.**

Not unlike drugs or alcohol, the television experience allows the participant to blot out the real world and enter into a pleasurable and passive mental state. The worries and anxieties of reality are as effectively deferred by becoming absorbed in a television program as by going on a "trip" induced by drugs or alcohol. And just as alcoholics are only inchoately aware of their addiction, feeling that they control their

drinking more than they really do ("I can cut it out any time I want—I just like to have three or four drinks before dinner"), people similarly overestimate their control over television watching. Even as they put off other activities to spend hour after hour watching television, they feel they could easily resume living in a different, less passive style. But somehow or other while the television set is present in their homes, the click doesn't sound. With television pleasures available, those other experiences seem less attractive, more difficult somehow. . . .

The self-confessed <u>television addict</u> often feels he "ought" to do other things—but the fact that he doesn't read and doesn't plant his garden or sew or crochet or play games or have conversations means that those activities are no longer as desirable as television viewing. In a way a heavy viewer's life is as imbalanced by his <u>television "habit"</u> as **a drug addict's or an alcoholic's.** He is living in a holding pattern, as it were, passing up the activities that lead to growth or development or a sense of accomplishment. This is one reason people talk about their television viewing so ruefully, so apologetically. They are aware that it is an unproductive experience, that almost any other endeavor is more worthwhile by any human measure.

Finally, it is the adverse effect of television viewing on the lives of so many people that defines it as a serious addiction. The **television habit** distorts the sense of time. It renders other experiences vague and curiously unreal while taking on a greater reality for itself. It weakens relationships by reducing and sometimes eliminating normal opportunities for talking, for communicating.

And yet television does not satisfy, else why would the viewer continue to watch hour after hour, day after day? "The measure of health," writes Lawrence Kubie, "is flexibility . . . and especially the freedom to cease when sated." But the television viewer can never be sated with his television experiences—they do not provide the true nourishment that satiation requires—and thus he finds that he cannot stop watching.

—MARIE WINN, "TV Addiction"

In this example, Marie Winn offers an extended definition of television addiction that begins with a comparison. *Comparison or contrast* is often the most effective way to present an unfamiliar term or concept to readers. The key is to know your readers well enough to find a term familiar to nearly all of them to compare to the unfamiliar term.

Extended definitions may also include *negative definitions*—explanations of what the thing being defined is *not*:

It's important to be clear about the reverse definition, as well: what dinosaurs are not. **Dinosaurs are not lizards,** and vice versa. Lizards are scaly reptiles of an ancient bloodline. The oldest lizards antedate the earliest dinosaurs by a full thirty million years. A few large lizards, such as the man-eating Komodo dragon, have been called "relics of the dinosaur age," but this phrase is historically incorrect. No lizard ever evolved the birdlike characteristics peculiar to each and every dinosaur. A big lizard never resembled a small dinosaur except for a few inconsequential details of the teeth. Lizards never walked with the erect, long-striding gait that distinguishes the dinosaur like ground birds today or the birdlike dinosaurs of the Mesozoic.

—ROBERT T. BAKKER, *The Dinosaur Heresies*

> Defines by saying what dinosaurs are not

EXERCISE 15.3

Choose one term that names some concept or feature of central importance in an activity or a subject you know well. For example, if you are studying biology, you have probably encountered terms like *morphogenesis* and *ecosystem*. Choose a word with a well-established definition. Write an extended definition of several sentences for this important term. Write for readers your own age who will be encountering the term for the first time when they read your definition.

EXERCISE 15.4

In her essay in Chapter 4, "Shyness: Evolutionary Tactic?," Susan Cain presents an extended definition. After reading her essay, how would you define *shyness*? Reread the essay to see which strategies she uses to define the term.

Use historical definitions to explain how a meaning has changed over time or across cultures.

Occasionally, a writer will provide a **historical definition**, tracing the evolution of a term from its first use to its adoption into other languages to its shifting meanings over the centuries. Such a strategy can bring surprising depth and resonance to the definition of a concept. In this example, Marc Silver provides a historical definition of the term *third world*:

> More than half a century ago, the Cold War was just starting. It was Western capitalism versus Soviet socialism. But there was another group of countries. Many of them were former colonies. None of them were squarely in either the Western or the Soviet camp. Thinking of these three factions, French demographer Alfred Sauvy wrote of "Three worlds, one planet" in an article published in *L'Observateur* in 1952. The First World consisted of the U.S., Western Europe and their allies. The Second World was the so-called Communist Bloc: the Soviet Union, China, Cuba and friends. The remaining nations, which aligned with neither group, were assigned to the Third World.
>
> The Third World has always had blurred lines. "Although the phrase was widely used, it was never clear whether it was a clear category of analysis, or simply a convenient and rather vague label for an imprecise collection of states in the second half of the twentieth century and some of the common problems that they faced," writes historian B. R. Tomlinson in the essay "What Was the Third World?," published in 2003 in the *Journal of Contemporary History*. Because many countries in the Third World were impoverished, the term came to be used to refer to the poor world.
>
> This 1-2-3 classification is now out of date, insulting and confusing. Who is to say which part of the world is "first"? And how can an affluent country like Saudi Arabia, neither Western nor communist, be part of the Third World? Plus, the Soviet Union doesn't even exist anymore. And it's not like the First World is the best world in every way. It has pockets of deep urban and rural poverty, says Paul Farmer,

co-founder of the nonprofit Partners in Health and a professor at Harvard Medical School. "That's the Fourth World," Farmer says, referring to parts of the United States and other wealthy nations where health problems loom large.

—MARC SILVER, "If You Shouldn't Call It the Third World, What Should You Call It?"

This historical definition serves Silver's larger purpose in writing this blog post: to help his readers understand why the term *third world* is inaccurate and inappropriate.

EXERCISE 15.5

You can consult a historical, or etymological, dictionary — such as the *Oxford English Dictionary, A Dictionary of American English,* or *A Dictionary of Americanisms* — to trace changes in the use of a word over long periods of time or to survey different theories of a word's or phrase's origins. Online, you can search the *Phrase Finder,* search the *Urban Dictionary,* or just Google the word or phrase plus definition. Look up the historical definition of any one of the following words — or a word or phrase you're curious about — in one or more sources, and write several sentences on its roots and development.

bedrock	eye-opener	lobbying	rubberneck
bogus	filibuster	lynching	sashay
bushwhack	gerrymander	pep	23 skidoo
dugout	head over heels	podunk	two-bit

Use stipulative definitions to reach an agreement on the meaning of a term or concept.

To **stipulate** means to seek or assert agreement on something. In a stipulative definition, the writer declares a certain meaning, generally not one found in the dictionary. In the excerpt from her autobiography *An American Childhood* that appears in Chapter 2, Annie Dillard offers a stipulative definition of *football* as she understood it as a nine-year-old:

Some boys taught me to play football. This was fine sport. You thought up a new strategy for every play and whispered it to the others. You went out for a pass, fooling everyone. Best, you got to throw yourself mightily at someone's running legs. Either you brought him down or you hit the ground flat out on your chin, with your arms empty before you. It was all or nothing. If you hesitated in fear, you would miss and get hurt: you would take a hard fall while the kid got away, or you would get kicked in the face while the kid got away. But if you flung yourself wholeheartedly at the back of his knees—if you gathered and joined body and soul and pointed them diving fearlessly—then you likely wouldn't get hurt, and you'd stop the ball. Your fate, and your team's score, depended on your concentration and courage. Nothing girls did could compare with it.

—ANNIE DILLARD, *An American Childhood*

There are recognizable elements of grown-up football in Dillard's definition. Her focus is less on rules and strategy, however, than on the "concentration and courage" required to make a successful tackle and, of course, on the sheer thrill of doing so.

In the next example, the writer stipulates a definition of the term *environmentalism* to support an argument:

> A sane environmentalism, the only kind of environmentalism that will win universal public support, begins by unashamedly declaring that nature is here to serve man. A sane environmentalism is entirely anthropocentric: it enjoins man to preserve nature, but on the grounds of self-preservation.
>
> A sane environmentalism does not sentimentalize the earth. It does not ask people to sacrifice in the name of other creatures. After all, it is hard enough to ask people to sacrifice in the name of other humans. (Think of the chronic public resistance to foreign aid and welfare.) Ask hardworking voters to sacrifice in the name of the snail darter, and, if they are feeling polite, they will give you a shrug.
>
> —Charles Krauthammer, "Saving Nature, but Only for Man"

EXERCISE 15.6

Write several sentences of a stipulative definition for one of the following:

1 Define in your own way game shows, police dramas, horror movies, or some other form of entertainment. Try for a stipulative definition of what your subject is generally like. In effect, you will be saying to your readers — other students in your class who are familiar with these entertainments — "Let's define it this way for now."

2 Define in your own way some hard-to-define concept, such as "loyalty," "love," "bravery," "shyness," or "masculinity."

3 Think of a new development or phenomenon in contemporary romance, music, television, leisure, fashion, or eating habits, or in your line of work. Invent a name for it, and write a stipulative definition for it.

Classifying

Classifying is an essential writing strategy for thinking about and organizing ideas, information, and experience. The process of **classifying** involves either grouping or dividing. Writers group related items (such as *apples, oranges, bananas, strawberries, cantaloupes,* and *cherries*), then label the general class of items they grouped together (*fruit*). Or they begin classifying with a general class (*fruit*), then divide it into subclasses of particular types (*apples, oranges,* and so on). This part of the chapter shows how you can organize and illustrate a classification you have read about or constructed yourself.

Use topics and subtopics to organize classifications.

Classifying in writing serves primarily as a means of **organization** — of creating a framework for the presentation of information, whether in a few paragraphs of an essay or in an entire book. This section surveys several examples of classifying, ranging from a simple classification to a complex system.

The simplest classification divides a general topic into two subtopics, as does this one by Lindsay McGregor and Neel Doshi (writing in the *Harvard Business Review*), who analyze the types of performance critical to business success:

> Our research into over 20,000 workers of all skill levels across U.S. industries, and a review of hundreds of academic studies on the psychology of human performance, shows that most leaders and organizations tend to focus on just one type of performance. But there are two types that are important for success.
>
> The first type is known as ***tactical performance***. Tactical performance is how effectively your organization *sticks to* its strategy. It is the driver of focus and consistency. It allows organizations to increase strength by directing limited resources to the fewest targets. . . .
>
> The second type, known as ***adaptive performance***, is how effectively your organization *diverges* from its strategy. Adaptive performance manifests as creativity, problem solving, grit, innovation, and citizenship. It allows organizations to create value in a world filled with, as the U.S. military says, volatility, uncertainty, complexity, and ambiguity, where technology and strategy changes rapidly.
>
> —LINDSAY MCGREGOR AND NEEL DOSHI, "There Are Two Types of Performance—but Most Organizations Only Focus on One"

Subtopics

McGregor and Doshi argue that companies overemphasize tactical performance, which undermines creativity and the ability to solve problems. In order to persuade readers that companies neglect adaptive performance, they must first classify the components of effective performance.

The following figure offers a **diagram** of their analysis:

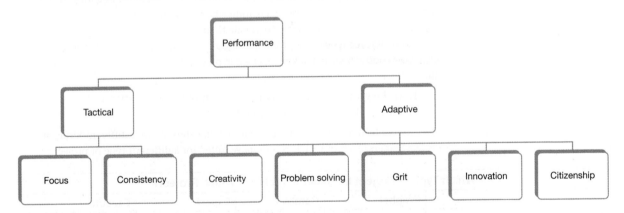

What the diagram shows at a glance is that in a classification system, some categories, such as "tactical performance" and "adaptive performance," are on the same level, or **coordinate**. In addition, some categories (in this case, "tactical performance" and "adaptive performance") are on a higher level, or **superordinate**; and some ("focus," "consistency," creativity," "problem solving," "grit," "innovation," and "citizenship") are on a lower level, or **subordinate**. The higher level represents the more general category, and the lower level the more specific. McGregor and Doshi go on to take their classification to the most specific level by offering examples of sales people, engineers, factory workers, and baristas who demonstrate both performance types.

Effective baristas, they point out, demonstrate tactical performance by making a latte the same way each time and adaptive performance by adjusting their greeting to fit each customer.

EXERCISE 15.7

Turn to Anastasia Toufexis's concept explanation in Chapter 4, "Love: The Right Chemistry," and make a diagram of the classification she offers of romantic love. What do you think is Toufexis's basis for classification? Does each item seem to be placed in an appropriate category and at the proper level?

EXERCISE 15.8

Review the essays you have written so far for this class or for another class, looking for an essay in which you used classifying. What was the purpose of your essay and your basis for classifying? Construct a diagram of your classification to see whether each item can be placed in an appropriate category and on the proper level.

Use graphics to depict a classification scheme.

Writers sometimes integrate **graphics** to make their classification easy for readers to see at a glance. Here is an example in which Carsten Lund Pedersen and Thomas Ritter (also writing in the *Harvard Business Review*) categorize project managers into four types:

> Your organization's growth opportunities fall into four different categories, and in order to develop your business in a commercially sustainable manner, you need four specific types of project manager to pursue them. . . .
>
> The **employee types** [the prophet, the gambler, the expert, and the executor] and the **growth opportunities that they are best at pursuing** can be positioned along two dimensions:
>
> 1. Is the growth opportunity in line with our existing strategy?
> 2. Can a reliable business case be made?

For more information on designing documents with graphics, see Chapter 22.

These two questions create a matrix that distinguishes the four different kinds of project leaders, each of which is optimally suited for a different type of project.

Which Type of Project Manager Is Right for Which Project?				
	Prophet	**Gambler**	**Expert**	**Executor**
Strategy should be . . .	Challenged	Followed	Challenged	Followed
The growth opportunity is . . .	A grand vision	A bet	An analysis	A sure thing
Organizational followers should . . .	Make a leap of faith	Gamble a bit and pursue rewards	Listen to the advice and act upon it	Stay within the strategy and follow the analyses
Weapon of choice	Persuasive vision	Potential reward	Well-supported arguments	Business cases and reports

—Carsten Lund Pedersen and Thomas Ritter, "The Four Types of Project Manager"

Use cues to maintain clarity and coherence in a classification.

The next example illustrates how writers can help readers follow a classification system by maintaining **clarity** and **coherence**—even when the subject is new and difficult. The passage comes from a book on physics by Gary Zukav. He uses classifying to explain the concept of mass. Simply defined, mass in physics is a measure of the matter in an object:

> **There are two kinds of mass,** which means that there are two ways of talking about it. **The first is** gravitational mass. The gravitational mass of an object, roughly speaking, is the weight of the object as measured on a balance scale. Something that weighs three times more than another object has three times more mass. Gravitational mass is the measure of how much force the gravity of the earth exerts on an object. Newton's laws describe the effects of this force, which vary with the distance of the mass from the earth. . . .
>
> **The second type** of mass **is** inertial mass. Inertial mass is the measure of the resistance of an object to acceleration (or deceleration, which is negative acceleration). For example, it takes three times more force to move three railroad cars from a standstill to twenty miles per hour (positive acceleration) than it takes to move one railroad car from a standstill to twenty miles per hour. . . . Similarly, once they are moving, it takes three times more force to stop three cars than it takes to stop the single car. This is because the inertial mass of the three railroad cars is three times more than the inertial mass of the single railroad car.
>
> —GARY ZUKAV, *The Dancing Wu Li Masters: An Overview of the New Physics*

Cues alerting readers to classification scheme

From this passage, we can see some of the cues writers use to make a classification clear and coherent. Zukav begins by *forecasting* the classification he will develop (*There are two kinds of mass*). He then introduces each category in its own paragraph, announced with a *transition* (*first* and *second*) and presented in the same sentence pattern (*The first is . . .* and *The second type of mass is . . .*). Careful *cueing* like this can help make a classification clear to readers.

EXERCISE 15.9

Look back at Anastasia Toufexis's essay "Love: The Right Chemistry" (Chapter 4), which you used to make a tree diagram in Exercise 15.7, or at the preceding example by Pedersen and Ritter to examine the strategies these authors use to make their classifications clear and coherent. Notice how each category is introduced and how transitions are used to help readers keep track of the categories. From your analysis, what conclusions can you draw about how writers maintain clarity and coherence?

EXERCISE 15.10

Look back at the classification you examined in Exercise 15.8 to see how well you were able to maintain clarity and coherence in your classification. What changes would you make, if any, to improve clarity and coherence?

General strategies for coherence are discussed in Chapter 13.

Comparing and Contrasting

Most of us compare things all the time: You might compare two people you know well, two motorcycles you are considering buying for a cross-country tour, three Stephen King novels, four tomato plants being grown under different laboratory conditions, or two theories about the relationship between inflation and wages. But as soon as you begin to compare two things, you usually begin to contrast them as well, for rarely are two things alike in all respects. The contrasts, or differences, between the two motorcycles are likely to be more enlightening than the similarities, many of which may be so obvious as to need no analysis. **Comparison**, then, brings similar things together for examination, to see how they are alike. **Contrast** is a form of comparison that emphasizes differences. According to research on learning, we acquire new concepts most readily if we can see how they are similar to or different from concepts we already know.

Chances are that you will confront many test questions and essay assignments asking you to compare and contrast—two poems, three presidents, four procedures. This strategy is popular in all academic disciplines, for it is one of the best ways to challenge students intellectually.

Use chunking or sequencing to organize comparisons and contrasts.

There are two ways to organize comparison and contrast in writing: You can present the items being compared in chunks or in sequence. In **chunking**, each object of the comparison is presented separately; in **sequencing**, the items are compared point by point. For example, a chunked comparison of two motorcycles would first detail all pertinent features of the Harley-Davidson SuperLow 1200T, and then consider all features of the Kawazuki Z1000 ABS, whereas a sequenced comparison would analyze the Harley and the Kawazuki feature by feature. In a chunked comparison, the discussion is organized around the items being compared. In a sequenced comparison, it is organized around characteristics of the items being compared.

In the following example of chunked comparison, Jane Tompkins contrasts popular nineteenth-century sentimental novels with the Western novels that provided a reaction against them:

> The female, domestic, "sentimental" religion of the best-selling women writers—Harriet Beecher Stowe, Susan Warner, Maria Cummins, and dozens of others—whose novels spoke to the deepest beliefs and highest ideals of middle-class America, is the real antagonist of the Western.
>
> You can see this simply by comparing the main features of the Western with the sentimental novel. In these books . . . a woman is always the main character, usually a young orphan girl, with several other main characters being women too. Most of the action takes place in private spaces, at home, indoors, in kitchens, parlors, and upstairs chambers. And most of it concerns the interior struggles of the heroine to live up to an ideal of Christian virtue—usually involving uncomplaining submission

Presents each point of contrast for **sentimental** and Western novels in the same order

to difficult and painful circumstances, learning to quell rebellious instincts, and dedicating her life to the service of God through serving others. In these struggles, women give one another a great deal of emotional and material support, and they have close relationships verging on what today we would identify as homosocial and homoerotic. There's a great deal of Bible reading, praying, hymn singing, and drinking of tea. Emotions other than anger are expressed very freely and openly. Often there are long, drawn-out death scenes in which a saintly woman dies a natural death at home. . . .

    The elements of the typical <u>Western plot</u> arrange themselves in stark opposition to this pattern, not just vaguely and generally but point for point. First of all, in Westerns (which are generally written by men), the main character is always a full-grown adult male, and almost all of the other characters are men. The action takes place either outdoors—on the prairie, on the main street—or in public places—the saloon, the sheriff's office, the barber shop, the livery stable. The action concerns physical struggles between the hero and a rival or rivals, and culminates in a fight to the death with guns. In the course of these struggles the hero frequently forms a bond with another man—sometimes his rival, more often a comrade—a bond that is more important than any relation he has with a woman and is frequently tinged with homoeroticism. There is very little free expression of the emotions. The hero is a man of few words who expresses himself through physical action—usually fighting. And when death occurs it is never at home in bed but always sudden death, usually murder.

           —Jane Tompkins, *West of Everything: The Inner Life of Westerns*

> Transition sentence signals shift to discussion of <u>Western novel</u>.

    Schematically, a chunked comparison looks simple enough. As the preceding example shows, it is easy to block off such a discussion in a text and then provide a clean *transition* between the various parts. And yet it can in fact be more complicated for a writer to plan than a sequenced comparison. Sequenced comparison may be closer to the way people perceive and think about similarities or differences in things. For example, you may have realized all at once that two navy jackets are different, but you would identify the specific differences—buttons, tailoring, fabric—one at a time. A sequenced comparison would point to the differences in just this way, one at a time, whereas a chunked comparison would present all the features of one jacket and then do the same for the second. A writer using the chunked strategy, then, must organize all the points of comparison before starting to write and then be sure that the points of comparison are presented in the same order in the discussion of each item being compared. With sequencing, however, the writer can take up each point of comparison as it comes to mind.

    In the next example, from a natural history of the earth, David Attenborough uses sequencing to contrast bird wings and airplane wings:

> Bird wings have a much more complex job to do than the wings of an aeroplane, for in addition to supporting the bird they must act as its engine, rowing it through the air. Even so the **wing outline** of a bird conforms to the same aerodynamic principles as those eventually discovered by man when designing his aeroplanes, and if you know how different kinds of aircraft perform, you can predict the flight capabilities of similarly shaped birds.

> **Wing shape**

Short stubby wings enable a tanager and other forest-living birds to swerve and dodge at speed through the undergrowth just as they helped the fighter planes of the Second World War to make tight turns and aerobatic manoeuvres in a dog-fight. More modern fighters achieve greater speeds by **sweeping back their wings** while in flight, just as peregrines do when they go into a 130 kph dive, stooping to a kill. Championship gliders have **long thin wings** so that, having gained height in a thermal up-current, they can soar gently down for hours and an albatross, the largest of flying birds, with a similar wing shape and a span of 3 metres, can patrol the ocean for hours in the same way without a single wing beat. Vultures and hawks circle at very slow speeds supported by a thermal and they have the **broad rectangular wings** that very slow flying aircraft have. Man has not been able to adapt wings to provide hovering flight. He has only achieved that with the whirling horizontal blades of a helicopter or the downward-pointing engines of a vertical landing jet. Hummingbirds have paralleled even this. They tilt their bodies so that they are almost upright and then beat their wings as fast as 80 times a second producing a similar down-draught of air. So the hummingbird can hover and even fly backwards.

—DAVID ATTENBOROUGH, *Life on Earth*

Attenborough finds a valid—and fascinating—basis for comparison between birds and airplanes and develops it in a way that both informs and entertains his readers. A successful comparison always has these qualities: a valid basis for comparison, a limited focus, and information that will catch a reader's attention.

EXERCISE 15.11

Identify the specific items contrasted in Tompkins's passage comparing sentimental novels and Westerns. Number in sequence each contrast, and underline both parts of the contrast. To get started, in the paragraph about sentimental novels, underline "a woman is always the main character, usually a young orphan girl," and number it "1" in the margin. In the paragraph about Westerns, underline "the main character is always a full-grown adult male," and number this "1" also, to complete your identification of both parts of the comparison. Then look for contrast 2, underline and number the contrasted items, and so on.

Look over your work, and consider the pattern of these contrasts. What, if anything, made them easy to identify? Was any contrast left incomplete? In general, how successful and informative do you find this set of contrasts?

EXERCISE 15.12

Identify the specific items compared in Attenborough's passage comparing bird wings and aircraft wings. Underline both items, and number the pair in the margin. To get started, underline "tanager" and "fighter planes" in the first sentence of the second paragraph. In the margin, number this pair "1." Then identify pair 2 and so on.

Consider the pattern and ordering of the comparisons you have identified. What, if anything, made the pairs of items easy to identify? Some comparisons begin by naming a bird, some by identifying a category of aircraft. Did this lack of predictability present problems for you? Do you see any possible justification for the writer's having given up the predictability of always beginning each comparison with either a bird or an aircraft? In general, how successful and informative did you find this comparison?

| EXERCISE 15.13 |

Write a page or so comparing or contrasting any one of the following subjects. Be careful to limit the basis for your comparison, and underline the sentence that states that basis. Use chunking or sequencing to organize the comparison.

> Two ways of achieving the same goal (for example, traveling by bus or subway, or using flattery or persuasion to get what you want)
>
> A good and bad job interview or date
>
> Your relationship with two friends or relatives
>
> Two or more forms of music, dance, film, or social networking sites
>
> Two methods of doing some task at home or on the job

| EXERCISE 15.14 |

Read paragraph 14 from "Love: The Right Chemistry" in Chapter 4 and paragraphs 2 and 3 from *"What College Rankings Really Tell Us"* in Chapter 8. How is each comparison organized? (It may or may not be neatly chunked or sequenced.) Why do you think the writer organizes the comparison in that way?

Use analogies to make comparisons clear and vivid.

An **analogy** is a special form of comparison in which one part of the comparison is used simply to explain the other, as in the following example. This passage uses two analogies—the twelve-month calendar and the "line of life" along one hand—to explain the duration of geologic time:

> In like manner, geologists will sometimes use the **calendar year** as a unit to represent the time scale, and in such terms the Precambrian runs from New Year's Day until well after Halloween. Dinosaurs appear in the middle of December and are gone the day after Christmas. The last ice sheet melts on December 31st at one minute before midnight, and the Roman Empire lasts five seconds. With your arms spread wide . . . to represent all time on earth, look at one hand with its **line of life**. The Cambrian begins in the wrist, and the Permian Extinction is at the outer end of the palm. All of the Cenozoic is in a fingerprint, and in a single stroke with a medium-grained nail file you could eradicate human history. Geologists live with the geologic scale. Individually, they may or may not be alarmed by the rate of exploitation of the

things they discover, but, like the environmentalists, they use these repetitive analogies to place the human record in perspective—to see the Age of Reflection, the last few thousand years, as a small bright sparkle at the end of time.

—JOHN MCPHEE, *Basin and Range*

Analogies are not limited to abstract, scientific concepts. Writers often use analogies to make nontechnical descriptions and explanations more vivid or to make an imaginative point of comparison that serves a larger argument. The following example suggests that the working poor in the United States are among society's "major philanthropists":

> But now that government has largely withdrawn its "handouts" [to the welfare poor], now that the overwhelming majority of the poor are out there toiling in Wal-Mart or Wendy's—well, what are we to think of them? Disapproval and condescension no longer apply, so what outlook makes sense?
>
> The **"working poor,"** as they are approvingly termed, are in fact the <u>major philanthropists</u> of our society. They neglect their own children so that the children of others will be cared for; they live in substandard housing so that other homes will be shiny and perfect; they endure privation so that inflation will be low and stock prices high. To be a member of the working poor is to be an anonymous donor, a nameless benefactor, to everyone else. As Gail, one of my restaurant coworkers put it, "you give and you give."
>
> —BARBARA EHRENREICH, *Nickel and Dimed*

Analogies are tricky. They can be useful, but they are rarely consistently accurate at all major points of comparison. For example, in the preceding analogy, the working poor can be seen as philanthropists in the sense that they have "made a great sacrifice" but not in the sense that they are selflessly sharing their wealth. Analogies can powerfully bring home a point, but skilled writers use them with caution.

Nevertheless, you will run across analogies regularly; indeed, it would be hard to find a book without at least one. For abstract information and in certain writing situations, analogy is often the writing strategy of choice.

EXERCISE 15.15

Write a one-paragraph analogy that explains a principle or process to a reader who is unfamiliar with it. Choose a principle or process that you know well. You might select a basic principle from the natural or social sciences, like dark matter or ethnocentrism; a bodily movement, like running; a physiological process, like digestion; or a process from your job, like assembling a product. Look for something very familiar to compare it with that will help the reader understand the principle or process without a technical explanation.

16

Arguing

This chapter presents the basic strategies for making *arguments* in writing. In it, we focus on asserting a thesis, backing it up with reasons and support, and anticipating readers' questions and objections.

Asserting a Thesis

Central to any argument is the **thesis**. In a sentence or two, a thesis asserts or states the main point of any argument you want to make. It can be assertive only if you make it clear and direct. The thesis statement usually appears at the beginning of an argument essay.

There are five kinds of argument essays in Part One of this book. Each of these essays requires a special kind of assertion and reasoning:

Chapters 6–10 contain essays that argue for each of these kinds of assertions, along with guidelines for constructing an argument to support such an assertion.

- *Assertion of opinion:* What is your position on a controversial issue? (Chapter 6, "Arguing a Position")

    When overzealous parents and coaches impose adult standards on children's sports, the result can be activities that are neither satisfying nor beneficial to children.

    —JESSICA STATSKY, "Children Need to Play, Not Compete"

- *Assertion of policy:* What is your understanding of a problem, and what do you think should be done to solve it? (Chapter 7, "Proposing a Solution")

    Although this last-minute anxiety about midterm and final exams is only too familiar to most college students, many professors may not realize how such major, infrequent, high-stakes exams work against the best interests of students both psychologically and cognitively. . . . If professors gave brief exams at frequent intervals, students would be spurred to learn more and worry less.

    —Patrick O'Malley, "More Testing, More Learning"

- *Assertion of evaluation:* What is your judgment of a subject? (Chapter 8, "Justifying an Evaluation")

    Although the film is especially targeted for old-school gamers, anime fans, and comic book fanatics, *Scott Pilgrim vs. the World* can be appreciated and enjoyed by all audiences because of its inventive special effects, clever dialogue, and artistic cinematography and editing.

—William Akana, "*Scott Pilgrim vs. the World*: A Hell of a Ride"

- *Assertion of cause:* What do you think made a subject the way it is? (Chapter 9, "Arguing for Causes or Effects")

    The fact *that* social networking is popular is well established. The question is *why* is it so popular? The most basic answer is that social networking is popular because it's available. . . . A better answer, though, is that social media offer people a way to satisfy their desire to connect with others and maybe also be "world-famous for fifteen minutes" (as Andy Warhol supposedly remarked).

    —Clayton Pangelinan, "#socialnetworking: Why It's *Really* So Popular"

- *Assertion of story analysis:* What does a story mean, or what is significant about it? (Chapter 10, "Analyzing Stories")

    As an account of a professional doing harm under the pretense of healing, the story uncovers how a doctor can take advantage of the intimate nature of his work and his professional status to overstep common forms of conduct, to the extent that his actions actually hurt rather than help a patient. In this way, the doctor-narrator actually performs a valuable service by warning readers, indirectly through his story, that blindly trusting members of his profession can have negative consequences.

    —Iris Lee, "Performing a Doctor's Duty"

As these different thesis statements indicate, the kind of thesis you assert depends on the occasion for which you are writing and the question you are trying to answer for your readers. Whatever the writing situation, to be effective, every thesis must satisfy the same three standards: It must be *arguable, clear,* and *appropriately qualified.*

Make arguable assertions.

Reasoned argument is called for when informed people disagree over an issue or remain divided over how best to solve a problem, as is so often the case in social and political life. Hence, the thesis statements in reasoned arguments make **arguable assertions**—possibilities or probabilities, not certainties.

Therefore, a statement of fact could not be an arguable thesis statement because facts are easy to verify—whether by checking an authoritative reference book, asking an authority, or observing the fact with your own eyes. For example, these statements assert facts:

Jem has a Ph.D. in history.

I am less than five feet tall.

Eucalyptus trees were originally imported into California from Australia.

Each of these assertions can be easily verified. To find out Jem's academic degree, you can ask him, among other things. To determine a person's height, you can use a tape measure. To discover where California got its eucalyptus trees, you can search the library or Internet. There is no point in arguing about such statements (though you might question the authority of a particular source or the accuracy of someone's measurement). If a writer asserts something broadly accepted as established fact, the resulting essay is not an argument but a *report*.

Like facts, expressions of personal feelings are not arguable assertions. Whereas facts are unarguable because they can be definitively proved true or false, feelings are unarguable because they are purely subjective.

You can declare, for example, that you detest eight o'clock classes, but you cannot offer an argument to support this assertion. All you can do is explain why you feel as you do. If, however, you were to restate the assertion as "Eight o'clock classes are counterproductive," you could then construct an argument that does not depend solely on your subjective feelings, memories, or preferences. Your argument could be based on *reasons* and *support* that apply to others as well as to yourself. For example, you might argue that students' ability to learn is at an especially low ebb immediately after breakfast and provide scientific support for this assertion—in addition, perhaps, to personal experience and reports of interviews with your friends.

Use clear and precise wording.

The way a thesis is worded is as important as its arguability. The wording of a thesis, especially its key terms, must be **clear** and **precise**.

Consider the following assertion: "Democracy is a way of life." The meaning of this claim is uncertain, partly because the word *democracy* is abstract and partly because the phrase *way of life* is inexact. Abstract ideas like democracy, freedom, and patriotism are by their very nature hard to grasp, and they become even less clear with overuse. Too often, such words take on *connotations* that may obscure the meaning you want to emphasize. *Way of life* is fuzzy: What does it mean? Does it refer to daily life, to a general philosophy or attitude toward life, or to something else?

Thus, a thesis is vague if its meaning is unclear; it is ambiguous if it has more than one possible meaning. For example, the statement "My English instructor is mad" can be understood in two ways: The teacher is either angry or insane. Obviously, these are two very different assertions. You would not want readers to think you mean one when you actually mean the other.

Whenever you write an argument, you should pay special attention to the way you phrase your thesis and take care to avoid vague and ambiguous language.

Qualify the thesis appropriately.

In addition to being arguable and clear, the thesis of an argument must make **appropriate qualifications** that suit your writing situation. If you are confident that your case is so strong that readers will accept your argument without question, state your thesis emphatically and unconditionally. If, however, you expect readers to challenge your assumptions or conclusions, you must qualify your statement. Qualifying a thesis makes it more likely that readers will take it seriously. Expressions like *probably, very likely, apparently,* and *it seems* all serve to qualify a thesis.

EXERCISE 16.1

Write an assertion of opinion that states your position on one of the following controversial issues:

- Should English be the official language of the United States and the only language used in local, state, and federal governments' oral and written communications?
- Should teenagers be required to get their parents' permission to obtain birth control information and contraceptives?
- Should high schools or colleges require students to perform community service as a condition for graduation?
- Should parents be able to demand access to the social media accounts of their children under the age of eighteen?

Constructing a persuasive argument on any of these issues would obviously require careful deliberation and research. For this exercise, however, all you need to do is construct an arguable, clear, and appropriately qualified thesis.

EXERCISE 16.2

Find the thesis in the student essays in one of the argument chapters (Chapters 6–10). Then decide whether the thesis is arguable, clear, and appropriately qualified.

EXERCISE 16.3

If you have written or are currently working on one of the argument assignments in Chapters 6–10, consider whether your thesis is arguable, clear, and appropriately qualified. If you believe it does not meet these requirements, revise it accordingly.

Giving Reasons and Support

Whether you are arguing a position, proposing a solution, justifying an evaluation, or speculating about causes, you need to give reasons and support for your thesis.

Think of **reasons** as the main points supporting your thesis. Often they answer the question *Why do you think so?* For example, if you assert among friends that you value a certain movie highly, one of your friends might ask, "Why do you like it so much?" And you might answer, "*Because* it has challenging ideas, unusual camera work, and memorable acting." Similarly, you might oppose restrictions on students' use of offensive language at your college *because* such restrictions would make students reluctant to enter into frank debates, *because* offensive speech is hard to define, and *because* restrictions violate the free-speech clause of the First Amendment. These *because* phrases are your reasons. You may have one or many reasons, depending on your subject and your writing situation.

For your argument to succeed with your readers, you must not only give reasons but also support your reasons. The main kinds of **support** writers use are examples, statistics, authorities, anecdotes, and textual evidence. Following is a discussion and illustration of each kind of support, along with standards for judging its reliability.

Use representative examples for support.

Examples may be used as support in all types of arguments. For examples to be believable and convincing, they must be representative (typical of all the relevant examples you might have chosen), consistent with the experience of your readers (familiar to them and not extreme), and adequate in number (numerous enough to be convincing and yet not likely to overwhelm readers).

The following illustration comes from a book on illiteracy in America by Jonathan Kozol, a prominent educator and writer, who uses examples to support the argument that human costs of illiteracy are high:

> Illiterates cannot read the menu in a restaurant.
>
> They cannot read the cost of items on the menu in the window of the restaurant before they enter.
>
> Illiterates cannot read the letters that their children bring home from their teachers. They cannot study school department circulars that tell them of the courses that their children must be taking if they hope to pass the SAT exams. They cannot help with homework. They cannot write a letter to the teacher. They are afraid to visit in the classroom. They do not want to humiliate their child or themselves.
>
> Illiterates cannot read instructions on a bottle of prescription medicine. They cannot find out when a medicine is past the year of safe consumption; nor can they read of allergenic risks, warnings to diabetics, or the potential sedative effect of certain kinds of nonprescription pills. They cannot observe preventive health care admonitions. They cannot read about "the seven warning signs of cancer" or the indications of blood-sugar fluctuations or the risks of eating certain foods that aggravate the likelihood of cardiac arrest.
>
> —Jonathan Kozol, *Illiterate America*

Kozol collected these examples in his many interviews with people who could neither read nor write. Though all of his readers are literate and have presumably never experienced the frustrations of adult illiteracy, Kozol assumes they will accept that the experiences are a familiar part of lives of adults who cannot read. Most readers will believe the experiences to be neither atypical nor extreme.

EXERCISE 16.4

Identify the examples in paragraphs 12 and 13 in Jessica Statsky's essay "Children Need to Play, Not Compete" and paragraphs 16–18 in Amitai Etzioni's essay "Working at McDonald's" (both in Chapter 6). If you have not read the essays, pause to skim each so that you can evaluate these examples within the context of the entire essay. How well do the examples meet the standards of representativeness, consistency with experience of readers, and adequacy in number? You will not have all the information you need to evaluate the examples — you rarely do unless you are an expert on the subject — but make a judgment based on the information available to you in the headnotes and the essays.

Use up-to-date, relevant, and accurate statistics.

In many kinds of arguments about economic, educational, or social issues, **statistics** may be essential. When you use statistics in your own arguments, you will want to ensure that they are up-to-date, relevant, and accurate. In addition, take care to select statistics from reliable sources and to cite them from the sources in which they originally appeared if at all possible. For example, you would want to get medical statistics directly from a reputable and authoritative professional periodical like the *New England Journal of Medicine* rather than secondhand from a supermarket tabloid or an unaffiliated Web site, neither of which can be relied on for accuracy. If you are uncertain about the most authoritative sources, ask a reference librarian or a professor who knows your topic.

The following selection, written by a Harvard University professor, comes from an argument speculating about the decline of civic life in the United States. It uses statistics to support the claim that Americans devote less time to civic life because they are watching more television. Civic life includes all the clubs, organizations, and communal activities in which people choose to participate:

The culprit is television.

First, the timing fits. The long civic generation was the last cohort of Americans to grow up without television, for television flashed into American society like lightning in the 1950s. In 1950 barely **10 percent** of American homes had television sets, but by 1959, **90 percent** did. . . . The reverberations from this lightning bolt continued for decades, as viewing hours grew by **17–20 percent** during the 1960s and by an additional **7–8 percent** during the 1970s. In the early years, TV watching was concentrated among the less educated sectors of the population, but during the 1970s the viewing time of the more educated sectors of the population began to converge upward. Television viewing increases with age, particularly upon retirement, but each generation since the introduction of television has begun its life cycle at a higher starting point. By 1995 viewing per TV household was more than **50 percent** higher than it had been in the 1950s.

Most studies estimate that the average American now watches roughly **four hours per day** (excluding periods in which television is merely playing in the background). Even a more conservative estimate of three hours means that television absorbs **40 percent** of the average American's free time, an increase of about one-third since 1965. Moreover, multiple sets have proliferated: By the late 1980s **three-quarters** of all U.S. homes had more than one set, and these numbers, too, are rising steadily, allowing

Statistics

ever more private viewing. . . . This massive change in the way Americans spend their days and nights occurred precisely during the years of generational civic disengagement.
— Robert D. Putnam, "The Strange Disappearance of Civic America"

These statistics come primarily from the U.S. Bureau of the Census: a nationwide count of the number of Americans and a survey, in part, of their buying habits, levels of education, and leisure activities. The Census reports are widely considered to be accurate and trustworthy. They qualify as original sources of statistics.

Chapter 18 provides help finding statistical data in the library.

EXERCISE 16.5

In Chapter 6, underline the statistics in paragraphs 7 and 8 of Jessica Statsky's essay "Children Need to Play, Not Compete." If you have not read the essay, pause to skim it so that you can evaluate the writer's use of statistics within the context of the whole essay. How well do the statistics meet the standards of up-to-dateness, relevance, accuracy, and reliance on the original source? Does the writer indicate where the statistics come from? What do the statistics contribute to the argument?

Cite reputable authorities on relevant topics.

To support an argument, writers often cite experts on the subject. **Quoting, paraphrasing,** or even just referring to a respected **authority** can add to a writer's credibility. Authorities must be selected as carefully as are facts and statistics, however. One qualification for authorities is suggested by the way we refer to them: They must be authoritative — that is, trustworthy and reputable. They must also be specially qualified to contribute to the subject you are writing about. For example, a well-known expert on the American presidency might be a perfect choice to support an argument about the achievements of a past president but a poor choice to support an argument on whether adolescents who commit serious crimes should be tried as adults. Finally, qualified authorities must have training at respected institutions or have unique real-world experiences, and they must have a record of research and publications recognized by other authorities.

The following example comes from a Vox.com article by Brian Resnick about why we resist listening to those who hold opinions that disagree with our own:

> This is the dark truth that lies at the heart of all partisan politics, and makes me pessimistic that Facebook or any other social networking site can really solve the problem of people filtering into their own content bubbles: We automatically have an easier time remembering information that fits our worldviews. We're simply quicker to recognize information that confirms what we already know, which makes us blind to facts that discount it. It's the reason why that — paradoxically — as we learn more about politics and politically charged issues, we tend to become more rigid in our thinking.
>
> "People are using their reason to be socially competent actors," **Dan Kahan, a psychologist at Yale,** told me earlier this year. Put another way: We have a lot of pressure to live up to our groups' expectations. And the smarter we are, the more we put our brain power to use for that end.
>
> — Brian Resnick, "'Motivated Ignorance' Is Ruining Our Political Discourse"

Establishes Kahan's professional qualifications by naming the university where he teaches and his area of study.

In this example, Resnick relies on **informal citation** within his article to introduce Dan Kahan, the authority he quotes, along with a reference to Kahan's professional affiliation with the renowned Yale University. Such informal citation is common in newspapers, magazines, and books intended for general audiences. In scholarly books and articles, and in other academic contexts, writers use **formal citation**, providing a list of works cited at the end of their own writing.

For examples of two formal citation styles often used in college essays, see Chapters 20 and 21.

EXERCISE 16.6

Analyze how authorities are used in paragraphs 4 and 6 of Patrick O'Malley's essay "More Testing, More Learning" in Chapter 7. Begin by underlining the authorities' contributions to these paragraphs, whether through quotation, summary, or paraphrase. On the basis of the evidence you have available, decide to what extent each source is authoritative on the subject: qualified to contribute to the subject, trained appropriately, and recognized widely. How does O'Malley establish each authority's credentials? Then decide what each authority contributes to the argument as a whole. (If you have not read the essay, take time to read or skim it.)

Use vivid, relevant anecdotes.

Anecdotes are brief stories about events or experiences. If they are relevant to the argument, well told, and true to life, they can provide convincing support. To be relevant, an anecdote must strike readers as more than an entertaining diversion; it must seem to make an irreplaceable contribution to an argument. A well-told story is easy to follow, and the people and scenes are described memorably, even vividly. A true-to-life anecdote seems believable, even if the experience is foreign to readers' experiences.

The following anecdote appeared in an argument taking a position on gun control. The writer—essayist, poet, and environmentalist Linda Hasselstrom, who is also a rancher in South Dakota—always carries a pistol and believes that other people should have the right to do so:

> One day, while driving to the highway mailbox, I saw a vehicle parked about halfway to the house. Several men were standing in the ditch, relieving themselves. I have no objection to emergency urination; we always need moisture. But I noticed they'd also dumped several dozen beer cans, which can blow into pastures and slash a cow's legs or stomach.
>
> As I drove slowly closer, the men zipped their trousers ostentatiously while walking toward me, and one of them demanded what the hell I wanted.
>
> "This is private land. I'd like you to pick up the beer cans."
>
> "What beer cans?" said the belligerent one, putting both hands on the car door and leaning in my window. His face was inches from mine, and the beer fumes were strong. The others laughed. One tried the passenger door, locked; another put his foot on the hood and rocked the car. They circled, lightly thumping the roof, discussing my good fortune in meeting them and the benefits they were likely to bestow upon me. I felt small and trapped; they knew it.

"The ones you just threw out," I said politely.

"I don't see no beer cans. Why don't you get out here and show them to me, honey?" said the belligerent one, reaching for the handle inside my door.

"Right over there," I said, still being polite, "—there and over there." I pointed with the pistol, which had been under my thigh. Within one minute the cans and the men were back in the car and headed down the road.

I believe this incident illustrates several important principles. The men were trespassing and knew it; their judgment may have been impaired by alcohol. Their response to the polite request of a woman alone was to use their size and numbers to inspire fear. The pistol was a response in the same language. Politeness didn't work; I couldn't intimidate them. Out of the car, I'd have been more vulnerable. The pistol just changed the balance of power.

> See Chapters 2 and 14 for more information about narrating anecdotes.

—LINDA M. HASSELSTROM, "Why One Peaceful Woman Carries a Pistol"

Most readers would readily agree that this anecdote is well told: It has many concrete, memorable details; there is action, suspense, climax, resolution, and even dialogue. It is about a believable, possible experience. Finally, the anecdote is clearly relevant to the author's argument about gun control.

EXERCISE 16.7

Evaluate the way an anecdote is used in paragraph 16 of Amitai Etzioni's essay "Working at McDonald's" in Chapter 6. Consider whether the story is well told and true to life. Decide whether it seems to be relevant to the whole argument. Does the writer make the relevance clear? Does the anecdote support Etzioni's argument?

Use relevant textual evidence.

When you argue claims of value (Chapter 8) and offer an analysis (Chapter 10), **textual evidence** will be very important. In your college courses, if you are asked to evaluate a controversial article, you must quote, paraphrase, or summarize passages so that readers can understand why you think the author's argument is or is not credible. If you are analyzing a novel, you must include numerous excerpts to show just how you arrived at your conclusion.

> See Chapter 5 for more about summarizing; see Chapters 12 and 19 for more about paraphrasing; see Chapter 19 for more about when to quote, paraphrase, and summarize, and how to integrate material from sources into your own writing.

For textual evidence to be considered effective support for an argument, it must be carefully selected to be relevant. You must help readers see the connection between each piece of evidence and the reason it supports. Textual evidence must also be highly selective—that is, chosen from among all the available evidence to provide the support needed without overwhelming the reader or weakening the argument with marginally relevant evidence. Textual evidence usually has more impact if it is balanced between quotation and paraphrase, and quotations must be smoothly *integrated* into the sentences of the argument.

You can read "'For Heaven's Sake!'" in Chapter 10.

The following example comes from Isabella Wright's essay "'For Heaven's Sake!'" on William Carlos Williams's story "The Use of Force" (Chapter 10). In this essay, the student writer argues that the doctor's rudeness is actually a form of exaltation that liberates him from social niceties endangering the health of the sick child he is tending:

> In contrast to the little girl's parents, the doctor breaks social conventions in his interactions with the family and in doing so highlights the absurdity of these rules. From the beginning we see him as someone who pushes aside polite but pointless practices; for example, he "motion[s] for [the father] not to bother" standing for a greeting when it would have disturbed the child on his lap (p. 414). The doctor's disregard for social conventions applies most to his tendency to give voice to thoughts rather than to keep them to himself for fear of sounding rude or causing discomfort. When the mother scolds her daughter for knocking the glasses off the "nice man" (p. 415), the doctor's reaction borders on outright rudeness: "For heaven's sake, I broke in. Don't call me a nice man to her. I'm here to look at her throat on the chance that she might have diphtheria and possibly die of it" (p. 415).

Writer's interpretation
Evidence from text

Notice how Wright quotes selected words and sentences to support her claim that politeness is actually an impediment. Notice, too, that she does not assume that the evidence speaks for itself; rather, she interprets the quotations she uses to support her point.

EXERCISE 16.8

Analyze the use of evidence in paragraphs 2 and 3 of Iris Lee's essay "Performing a Doctor's Duty" in Chapter 10. If you have not read this essay, read it now. Identify the quotes and paraphrases Lee uses, and then try to identify the phrases or sentences that comment on or explain this evidence. Consider whether Lee's evidence in these two paragraphs seems relevant to her thesis and reasons, appropriately selective, well balanced between quotes and paraphrases, integrated smoothly into the sentences she creates, and explained helpfully.

Responding to Objections and Alternatives

For more about conceding and refuting, see Chapters 6–9.

Asserting a thesis and backing it with reasons and support are essential to a successful argument. Thoughtful writers go further, however, by anticipating and responding to their readers' objections or their alternative position or solutions to a problem.

To **respond** to objections and alternatives, writers rely on three basic strategies: acknowledging, conceding, and refuting. Writers show that they are aware of readers' objections and questions (*acknowledge*), modify their position to accept those concerns they think are legitimate (*concede*), or explicitly argue that readers' objections may be invalid or that their concerns may be irrelevant (*refute*). Writers may use one or more of these three strategies in the same essay. Readers find arguments more convincing when writers have anticipated their concerns in these ways.

Acknowledge readers' concerns.

When you **acknowledge** readers' questions or objections, you show that you are aware of their point of view and take it seriously even if you do not agree with it, as in the following example:

> The homeless, it seems, can be roughly divided into two groups: those who have had marginality and homelessness forced upon them and want nothing more than to escape them, and a smaller number who have at least in part chosen marginality, and now accept, or, in a few cases, embrace it.
>
> I understand how dangerous it can be to introduce the idea of choice into a discussion of homelessness. It can all too easily be used for all the wrong reasons by all the wrong people to justify indifference or brutality toward the homeless, or to argue that they are getting only what they deserve.
>
> And I understand, too, how complicated the notion can become: Many of the veterans on the street, or battered women, or abused and runaway children, have chosen this life only as the lesser of evils, and because, in this society, there is often no place else to go.
>
> And finally, I understand how much that happens on the street can combine to create an apparent acceptance of homelessness that is nothing more than the absolute absence of hope.
>
> Nonetheless we must learn to accept that there may indeed be people on the street who have seen so much of our world, or have seen it so clearly, that to live in it becomes impossible.
>
> —PETER MARIN, "Go Ask Alice"

Acknowledges doubts readers may have

You might think that acknowledging readers' objections in this way—addressing readers directly, listing their possible objections, and discussing each one—would weaken your argument. It might even seem reckless to suggest objections that not all readers would think of. On the contrary, however, most readers respond positively to this strategy because it makes you seem thoughtful and reasonable. By researching your subject and your readers, you will be able to use this strategy confidently in your own argumentative essays. And you will learn to look for it in arguments you read and use it to make judgments about the writer's credibility.

EXERCISE 16.9

Jessica Statsky acknowledges readers' concerns in paragraphs 9 and 14 of her essay "Children Need to Play, Not Compete" in Chapter 6. How, specifically, does Statsky attempt to acknowledge her readers' concerns? What do you find most and least successful in her acknowledgments? How do the acknowledgments affect your judgment of her credibility?

Concede readers' concerns.

To argue effectively, you must often take special care to acknowledge readers' objections; questions; and alternative positions, causes, or solutions. Occasionally, however, you may have to go even further. Instead of merely acknowledging your readers' concerns, you may decide to accept some of them and incorporate them into your argument. This strategy, called **concession**, can be very disarming to readers, for it recognizes that opposing views have merit. The following example comes from an essay enthusiastically endorsing e-mail:

Concedes that e-mail poses certain problems

> **To be sure, egalitarianism has its limits.** The ease and economy of sending email, especially to multiple recipients, makes us all vulnerable to any bore, loony, or commercial or political salesman who can get our email address. It's still a lot less intrusive than the telephone, since you can read and answer or ignore email at your own convenience. . . .
>
> Another supposed disadvantage of email is that it discourages face-to-face communication. **At Microsoft, where people routinely send email back and forth all day to the person in the next office, this is certainly true.** Some people believe this tendency has more to do with the underdeveloped social skills of computer geeks than with Microsoft's role in developing the technology email relies on. I wouldn't presume to comment on that. Whether you think email replacing live conversation is a good or bad thing depends, I guess, on how much of a misanthrope you are. I like it.
>
> —MICHAEL KINSLEY, "Email Culture"

Notice that Kinsley's accommodation or concession is not grudging. He readily concedes that e-mail brings users a lot of unwanted messages and may discourage conversation in the workplace.

EXERCISE 16.10

How does Patrick O'Malley respond to readers' objections and alternatives in paragraphs 9 and 10 of his essay "More Testing, More Learning" in Chapter 7, which argues for more frequent exams? What seems successful or unsuccessful in his argument? How do his efforts to acknowledge readers' concerns or make concessions affect his argument and his credibility?

Refute readers' objections.

Your readers' possible objections and views cannot always be conceded. Sometimes they must be refuted. When you **refute** readers' objections, you assert that they are wrong and argue against them. Refutation does not have to be delivered arrogantly or dismissively, however. Because differences are inevitable, reasoned argument provides a peaceful and constructive way for informed, well-intentioned people who disagree strongly to air their differences. In the following example, Laura Beth Nielsen—a sociology professor and director of the legal studies program at Northwestern University—first acknowledges and then refutes the argument that First Amendment rights to free speech need to be protected no matter what:

> Instead of characterizing racist and sexist hate speech as "just speech," courts and legislatures need to . . . allow the restriction of hate speech as do all of the other economically advanced democracies in the world.

Many readers will find this line of thinking repellent. They will insist that protecting hate speech is consistent with and even central to our founding principles. They will argue that regulating hate speech would amount to a serious break from our tradition. They will trivialize the harms that social science research undeniably associates with being the target of hate speech, and call people seeking recognition of these affronts "snowflakes."

> Acknowledges possible objection

But these free-speech absolutists must at least acknowledge two facts. First, the right to speak already is far from absolute. Second, they are asking disadvantaged members of our society to shoulder a heavy burden with serious consequences. Because we are "free" to be hateful, members of traditionally marginalized groups suffer.

> Refutes the objection

—Laura Beth Nielsen, "The Case for Restricting Hate Speech"

Nielsen doesn't simply dismiss readers' possible concerns. Rather, she states several potential objections and then refutes them by pointing out key issues that reasonable readers would at least have to consider. Effective refutation requires a restrained tone and careful argument, and Nielsen has offered supporting evidence for her claims earlier in her argument. (The argument appears in full in Chapter 6, pp. 205–6.) Although you may not accept her refutations, you can agree that they are reasonable. Readers need not feel attacked personally just because the writer disagrees with them.

EXERCISE 16.11

Evaluate Kelly D. Brownell and Thomas R. Frieden's use of refutation in paragraphs 5 and 6 of "Ounces of Prevention: The Public Policy Case for Taxes on Sugared Beverages" (Chapter 7). How do Brownell and Frieden signal or announce the refutation? How do they support the refutation? What is the tone of the refutation, and how effective do you think the tone would be in convincing readers to take the writers' argument seriously?

Identifying Logical Fallacies

Fallacies are errors or flaws in reasoning. Although essentially unsound, fallacious arguments seem superficially plausible and often have great persuasive power. Fallacies are not necessarily deliberate efforts to deceive readers. Writers may accidentally introduce a fallacy by not examining their own reasons or underlying assumptions, by failing to establish solid support, or by using unclear or ambiguous words. Here is a summary of the most common logical fallacies (listed alphabetically):

- *Begging the question:* arguing that a claim is true by repeating the claim in different words (also called *circular reasoning*) (More and more often, writers are using *begging the question* to mean *raising the question*, but this is incorrect. Asking questions is a legitimate strategy in reasoned argument.)

- *Confusing chronology with causality:* assuming that because one thing preceded another, the former caused the latter (also called *post hoc, ergo propter hoc*—Latin for "after this, therefore because of this")

- *Either-or reasoning:* assuming that there are only two sides to a question and representing yours as the only correct one

- *Equivocating:* misleading or hedging with ambiguous word choices
- *False analogy:* assuming that because one thing resembles another, conclusions drawn from one also apply to the other
- *Hasty generalization:* offering only weak or limited evidence to support a conclusion
- *Overreliance on authority:* assuming that something is true simply because an expert says so and ignoring evidence to the contrary
- *Oversimplifying:* giving easy answers to complicated questions, often by appealing to emotions rather than logic
- *Personal attack:* demeaning the proponents of a claim instead of refuting their argument (also called *ad hominem*—Latin for "against the man"—*attack*)
- *Red herring:* attempting to misdirect the discussion by raising an essentially unrelated point
- *Slanting:* selecting or emphasizing the evidence that supports your claim and suppressing or playing down other evidence
- *Slippery slope:* pretending that one thing inevitably leads to another
- *Sob story:* manipulating readers' emotions to lead them to draw unjustified conclusions
- *Straw man:* directing the argument against a claim that nobody actually makes or that everyone agrees is very weak

Bernard Van Berg/EyeEm/Getty Images

PART 4
Research Strategies

17

Planning and Conducting Research

To research a topic effectively at the college level requires a plan. Having a clear sense of your rhetorical situation, as well as the practical needs of your research task (such as the due date and the level of detail required), will help you as you complete the following steps:

1. Choose a topic, and get an overview of it by consulting subject guides and general or subject-specific reference sources.

2. Develop an appropriate focused topic, and draft research questions to guide your research.

3. Establish a research log, listing the keywords you are using to conduct your search, and create a working bibliography.

4. Identify source types your readers will recognize as varied and appropriate.

5. Take notes on the sources that seem appropriate for your project, and create an annotated bibliography.

Analyzing Your Rhetorical Situation and Setting a Schedule

Making your research project manageable begins with defining its scope and goals. Begin by analyzing your *rhetorical situation*:

- What is your *purpose*? Is it to explain a concept, report on or argue for a position, or analyze the causes of an event or a behavior?

- Who is your *audience*, and what will your readers' interests, attitudes, and expectations for the project be? How many and what kinds of resources does your audience expect you to consult? (For college research projects, your audience will likely be your instructor.)

- What *genre* (or *type*) is the research project, and how will that affect the kinds of sources you use? An observational report in the social sciences may demand mainly *primary research,* whereas an argument essay for a history course may require a variety of *secondary* and primary sources.

- What medium will you use to present your research project? A research project presented in print will allow you to incorporate visuals and use parenthetical citations and a works-cited or references list to acknowledge your sources; a project presented using PowerPoint or Prezi slides may allow you to incorporate video and sound but require you to name your sources during the presentation.

To learn more about primary and secondary research, see pp. 525–31 and Chapters 18 and 19.

Also be sure to consider the following practical issues before you begin your research project:

- How long should the research project be?
- When is it due?
- Are any interim assignments required (such as an outline or an annotated bibliography)?

If you're not sure of the answers to these questions, ask your instructor to clarify the assignment or to define any confusing terms so that you can work most efficiently.

Finally, set a schedule. Be sure to take into consideration the projects you have due for other classes as well as other responsibilities (to work or family, for example) or activities. Some library Web sites may offer an online scheduler to help you with this process. Look for a link on your library's Web site, or try out an assignment calculator, such as one of those listed on the Guides page of the Web site for the University of Missouri Libraries: library.missouri.edu/guides/assigncalc/.

Choosing a Topic and Getting an Overview

Often students will be assigned a topic for a research project. If you are free to choose your own topic, consult course materials, such as textbooks and handouts, to get ideas, and consult your instructor to make sure your topic is appropriate. Sometimes conducting an Internet search may give you an idea for a topic. Once you've chosen an appropriate topic, an overview can help you determine the kinds of issues you should consider.

Wikipedia offers a wealth of information, and it is often the first stop for students who are accustomed to consulting the Internet first for information. Be aware, though, that *Wikipedia* is user generated rather than traditionally published, and thus the quality of information found there can be inconsistent. Many instructors do not consider *Wikipedia* a reliable source, so you should ask your teacher for advice on consulting it at this stage.

Your library will likely subscribe to databases, such as *Gale Virtual Reference Library* or *Oxford Reference Online*, that you can search to find information from general encyclopedias and dictionaries as well as from specialized, or subject-specific, encyclopedias and dictionaries.

General encyclopedias, like *Britannica Online*, provide basic information about many topics. **Specialized encyclopedias**, like *Encyclopedia of Addictions* or *Grove Art Online*, provide a comprehensive introduction to your topic, including the key terms you will need in order to find relevant material in catalogs and databases, and they present subtopics, enabling you to see many possibilities for focusing your research.

Frequently, libraries prepare **research guides**—lists of reliable sources on popular topics. A guide can suggest very useful resources for research, so check your library to find out if such a guide is available. You may also find resources that provide good overviews of topics, such as *CQ Researcher*. A reference librarian can help point you in the right direction.

Focusing Your Topic and Drafting Research Questions

The invention strategies in Chapter 11 can help you focus in on one aspect of your topic.

After you have gotten a sense of the kinds of sources available on your topic, you may be ready to narrow it. Focus on a topic that you can explore thoroughly in the number of pages assigned and the length of time available. Finding your own take on a subject can help you narrow it as well.

To learn more about crafting an effective thesis statement, see Chapter 13 and the Guides to Writing in any of the appropriate Part One chapters.

You may also want to write questions about your topic and then focus in on one or two that can be answered through research. These will become the research questions that will guide your search for information. You may need to add or revise questions as you conduct your search. The answers you come up with can form the basis of your thesis statement.

Establishing a Research Log

One of the best ways to keep track of your research is to keep all your notes in one place, in a **research log**. Your log may be digital (a folder on your computer with files for notes, lists of keywords, and your working bibliography) or analog (a notebook with pockets for copies of sources works well).

Develop a list of search terms.

Finding useful sources depends on determining the right **keywords**—words or phrases that describe your topic—to use while searching catalogs, databases, and the Internet. Start your list of keywords by noting the main words from your research questions or thesis statement. Look for useful terms in your search results, and use these to expand your list. Then add synonyms (or words with a similar meaning) to expand your list. Keep in mind that different disciplines use different terminology, and terms that work well for one subject might not be successful in another.

For example, databases covering education and psychology might index sources on some of the same subjects, but they might not use the same keywords.

For example, student Cristina Dinh, whose research project appears at the end of Chapter 20, might have started with a term like *home schooling.* She might have added *home education* or *home study.* After reading an article in an encyclopedia about her subject, she might have added *student-paced education* or *autonomous learning* to expand her scope. After consulting the thesaurus in ERIC, a database focusing on education, she might have added *parents as teachers;* after consulting the thesaurus in the database PsycARTICLES, she might have added *nontraditional education.*

Create a working bibliography.

A **working bibliography** is an ongoing record of the sources you discover as you research your subject. In your final project, you will probably not cite every source that you have listed in your working bibliography, but recording the information you will need to cite a source—*as you identify it*—will save you time later. (Just be sure to double-check that your entries are accurate!) Your working bibliography should include the same information as in the entry in your list of works cited. (You may also want to note the call number for any library books, so you can retrieve them again later.)

Online citation managers, such as RefWorks, Zotero, or EndNote, can help you create bibliographic citations in the specific style (such as MLA or APA) required by your discipline or your instructor. (Check with your instructor to confirm the documentation style you should use.) These software programs are not perfect, however; you will still need to double-check your citations against models in the style manual you are using or in Chapters 20 or 21 of this text.

See Chapter 20 for MLA-style citation models and Chapter 21 for APA-style citation models.

Annotating Your Working Bibliography

An **annotated bibliography** provides an overview of sources that you have considered for your research project. Researchers frequently create annotated bibliographies to keep a record of sources and their thoughts about them. Most entries answer these questions:

- What kind of source is this?
- What is the main point of the source?
- How might I use the source?
- How might my sources be related?
- What information will I need to cite the source?

Here's an example of an entry in an annotated bibliography written by Maya Gomez for her analysis of opposing arguments on compensating kidney donors: Maya Gomez's analysis appears in Chapter 5, pp. 165–67.

Becker, Gary S., and Julio J. Elías. "Cash for Kidneys: The Case for a Market for Organs." *The Wall Street Journal,* 18 Jan. 2014, www.wsj.com/articles/ SB10001424052702304149404579322560004817176. Op-ed.

In an op-ed published in *The Wall Street Journal,* economists Gary Becker and Julio Elías argue for a straightforward but controversial proposal to solve the kidney shortage by paying people to donate their extra kidney for transplantation. To demonstrate the serious need for kidneys to transplant, they cite statistics, illustrated by a graph showing the difference between the number of people on the waiting list and the low, flat rate of transplant surgeries. They use their own research to refute the alternative solution that changing from informed to implied consent of deceased donors would reduce the shortage and also to refute objections to paying donors.

I could either use this argument to pair with the argument made in the National Kidney Foundation's policy statement, "Financial Incentives for Organ Donation," or use the data in this proposal to provide background on the controversy.

Some annotated bibliographies also include an introduction that explains its purpose and scope and may describe how and why the researcher selected the sources. Maya Gomez's annotated bibliography, written for her composition instructor, might have included an introduction like this:

My annotated bibliography is intended to provide me with the sources I need to provide background on the kidney crisis. It includes sources that offer background on evolving government policy and data on the scope of the problem (such as the number of people on waiting lists and the number of kidneys available each year). This information will help me establish the seriousness of the problem, so readers will understand why I chose to analyze conflicting voices on compensating kidney donors.

Taking Notes on Your Sources

For more on synthesizing, see Chapters 12 and 19.

The notes that you include in an annotated bibliography or on a printed or digital copy of a source are useful reminders, but you should also make notes that analyze the text, that synthesize what you are learning with your own ideas or with ideas you have gleaned elsewhere, and that evaluate the quality of the source. You will mine these notes for language to use in your draft, so be careful to

- summarize accurately, using your own words and sentence structures;
- paraphrase without borrowing the language or sentence structure of the source;
- quote accurately and place all language from the source in quotation marks.

For more on annotating, sources, see Chapter 12; for more on avoiding plagiarism, see Chapter 19.

Whenever possible, download, print, photocopy, or scan useful sources, so that you can not only read and make notes at your leisure but also double-check your summaries, paraphrases, and quotations of sources against the original. These strategies, along with those discussed in Chapter 19, "Using Sources to Support Your Ideas," will keep you from plagiarizing inadvertently.

Finding Sources

Students are surrounded by a wealth of information—in print, online, in videos and podcasts, even face-to-face. Although much of this information is excellent, some is of dubious quality. This can make finding supporting evidence exciting, but it also means that sources must be sifted through carefully. Be sure to consider the rhetorical situation: What you are writing about, who will read your writing project, and what type, or genre, you are composing (a story for your college newspaper, a proposal for your employer, a research project for your U.S. history course). Consider, too, whether your writing project requires you to depend mainly on **secondary sources**—like books and articles that analyze and summarize a subject—or to develop **primary sources**, such as interviews with experts, surveys, or observational studies you conduct yourself, and laboratory reports, historical documents, diaries, letters, or works of literature written by others. Whatever sources you decide will best help you support your claims, the following sections will help you find or develop the resources you need.

To learn how to evaluate sources, see Chapter 18.

Search library catalogs and databases.

For most college research projects, finding appropriate sources begins with your library's home page, where you can

- find (and sometimes access) books, reference sources (such as general and subject-specific encyclopedias and dictionaries), reports, documents, multimedia resources (such as films and audio recordings), and much more;

- use your library's databases to find (and sometimes access) articles in newspapers, magazines, and scholarly journals, as well as in reference sources;

- find research guides, or lists of reliable sources on topics frequently studied by students.

Many libraries offer **unified search**, which allows patrons to search for books and articles in magazines, newspapers, and scholarly journals simultaneously, from the home page. If you aren't sure whether you will need to search for books and articles using separate catalogs and databases, consult a librarian.

Your library's home page is also the place to find information about the brick-and-mortar library—its floor plan, its hours of operation, and the journals it has available in print. You might even be able to find links to what you need in other libraries (often called "interlibrary loan") or get online help from a librarian.

Using Appropriate Search Terms

Just as with a search engine like *Google,* you can search a library catalog or database by typing your search terms—an author's name, the title of a work, a subject term or keyword, even a call number—into the search box. To search successfully, put yourself in the position of the people writing about your topic to figure out what words they might have used. If your topic is ecology, for example, you might find information under the keywords *ecosystem, environment, pollution,* and *endangered species,* as well as under a number of related keywords, depending on the focus of your research and your area of study.

Broadening or Narrowing Your Results

When conducting a search, you might get too few hits and have to broaden your topic. To broaden your search, try the following:

Replace a specific term with a more general term	Replace *sister* or *brother* with *sibling*
Substitute a synonym for one of your keywords	Replace *home study* with *home schooling* or *student-paced education*
Combine terms with *or* to get results with either or both terms	Search *home study or home schooling* to get results that include both *home study* and *home schooling*
Add a wildcard character, usually an asterisk (*) or a question mark (?)	Search *home school** or *home school?* to retrieve results for *home school, home schooling,* and *home schooled*

(Check the search tips to find the wildcard character in use.)

Most often, you'll get too many hits and need to narrow your search. To narrow a search, try the following:

Add a specific term	Instead of searching just *home schooling,* search *home schooling statistics*
Use *and* or quotation marks ("/") to combine search terms	Search *home schooling and California* or *"California home schooling"*

In many cases, using phrases will limit your results to items that include *all* the words you have specified, but check the search tips for the database, catalog, or search engine you are using.

Find books (and other sources).

Books housed in academic library collections offer two distinct advantages to the student researcher:

1. They provide in-depth coverage of topics.
2. They are likely to be published by reputable presses that strive for accuracy and reliability.

You can generally search for books and other library resources, like reference works and multimedia resources, by author name, title, keyword, or subject heading, and narrow your search by using advanced search options. (See Figure 17.1.)

Some libraries also allow you to search by call number, which makes it easy to find items on the same or a similar topic. (You might think of a call-number search as the electronic equivalent of looking at books shelved nearby.) For example, typing

FIGURE 17.1   A book's record from a college library catalog
An item's catalog record provides a lot more information than just the author, title, and call number. You can also find the subject headings by which it was catalogued and perhaps also the item's location and whether it has been checked out. Some libraries may allow you to place a hold on a book or find similar items, and some, such as the one whose catalog record is depicted here, even allow you to capture the book's record with your smartphone or have the information texted or e-mailed to you.

LC40 (the first part of the call number) into the search box calls up the records of other items on the subject of home schooling:

Title	Call number
Well-Trained Mind: A Guide to Classical Education at Home	LC40.B39 2004
Love in a Time of Homeschooling: A Mother and Daughter's Uncommon Year	LC40.B76 2010
Homeschool: An American History	LC40.G34 2008
Family Matters: Why Homeschooling Makes Sense	LC40.G88 1992
Home Schooling: Parents as Educators	LC40.H65 1995
How Children Learn at Home	LC40.T48 2007

If your search for books in your college library turns up little that is useful to you, do not give up. You may be able to request an item from another library via your library's interlibrary loan service. Inquire at your library for services available to you that can connect you to resources in other libraries.

Find articles in periodicals.

Much of the information you will use to write your research project will come from articles in **periodicals**, publications such as newspapers, magazines, or scholarly journals that are published at regular intervals. To locate relevant articles on your topic, start your search with your library's unified search bar or one of your library's databases. Why not just start with a *Google* search? There are three very good reasons:

1. *Google* will pull up articles from any publication it indexes, from personal Web sites to scholarly journals. Results rise to the top of the list based on a number of factors but not necessarily the reliability of the source. (*Google Scholar* may help you locate more reliable sources than those you might find through a typical *Google* search.)

2. Sources you find through *Google* may ask you to pay for access to articles or may require a subscription. Your library may already subscribe to these sources on your behalf.

3. Adding databases to your search strategy will diversify your search and provide you with access to resources not available through a search engine such as *Google*.

Most college libraries subscribe to **general databases** and **subject-specific databases** as well as databases that index newspapers. General databases (such as *Academic OneFile*, *Academic Search Premier* or *Elite* or *Complete*,[1] and *ProQuest Central*)

---

[1] The names of databases change over time and vary from library to library, so ask your instructor or a reference librarian if you need help.

index articles from both scholarly journals and popular magazines. Subject-specific databases (such as *ERIC, MLA International Bibliography, PsycINFO,* and *General Science Full Text*) index articles only in their discipline. Newspaper databases (such as *Alt-Press Watch, LexisNexis Academic, National Newspaper Index,* and *ProQuest Newspapers*) index newspaper articles. For college-level research projects, you may use all three types of databases to find appropriate articles. (Note that many libraries also offer ways to search multiple databases at once.) For the research project on home schooling that appears in Chapter 20, "Citing and Documenting Sources in MLA Style," Cristina Dinh might have consulted both a general database and a sub-ject-specific database like *ERIC*.

If your search returns too many unhelpful results, use the database's advanced search options to refine your search. Many databases allow users to restrict results to articles published in academic journals, for example, or to articles that were published only after a certain date (see Figure 17.2).

Increasingly, databases provide access to full-text articles, in either HTML or PDF format. When you have the option, choose the PDF format, as this will provide you with photographs, graphs, and charts in context, and you will be able to include the

FIGURE 17.2 Database search results
Database search results may allow you to access an article directly or provide the information you need to locate (and cite) it, including the title, author(s), and publication information. The database may also provide options for narrowing a search by publication date, source type (academic journal, for example), and so on.

page numbers in your citation. If you find a citation to an article that is not accessible through a database, however, do not ignore it. Check with a librarian to find out how you can get a copy of the article.

Find government documents and statistical information.

Federal, state, and local governments make many of their documents available directly through the Web. For example, you can access statistical data about the United States through the U.S. Census Bureau's Web site, and you can learn a great deal about other countries through the Web sites of the U.S. State Department and the CIA.

The Library of Congress provides a useful portal for finding government documents (federal, state, local, and international) through its Web site (www.loc.gov), and the U.S. Government Printing Office provides free electronic access to documents produced by the federal government through its Web page (www.gpo.gov/fdsys).

To learn more about the domains of Web sites, see Chapter 18.

Some libraries have collections of government publications and provide access to government documents through databases or catalogs. Your library may also offer statistical resources and data sets. See if your library has a guide to these resources, or ask a librarian for advice. You can also find government documents online using an advanced *Google* search and specifying *.gov* as the type of site, or *domain*.

Find Web sites and interactive sources.

Undoubtedly, you are quite familiar with searching the Web. This section introduces you to some tools and strategies for using it more efficiently. But first, a few cautions:

- *Your research project will be only as credible as the sources you use.* Because search engines index Web sources without evaluating them, not all the results a search engine like *Google* generates will be reliable and relevant for your purposes.

- *Web sources may not be stable.* A Web site that existed last week may not be available today, or its content may have changed. Be sure to record the information you need to cite a source when you first find it.

For guidelines on how to cite Web sources, see Chapter 20, "Citing and Documenting Sources in MLA Style," or Chapter 21, "Citing and Documenting Sources in APA Style"; for more about evaluating sources, especially Web sources, see Chapter 18.

- *Web sources must be documented.* No matter what your source—a library book, a scholarly article, or a Web site or Web page—you will need to cite and document your source in your list of works cited or references. If you are publishing your report online, check to determine whether you will need permission to reproduce an image or any other elements.

Using *Google Scholar* and *Google Book Search*

Although you may use search engines like *Google* with great rapidity and out of habit, as a college researcher you are likely to find it worthwhile to familiarize yourself with other parts of the *Google* search site. Of particular interest to the academic writer are *Google Scholar* and *Google Book Search*. *Google Scholar* retrieves articles from a number of scholarly databases and a wide range of general-interest and scholarly books. *Google Book Search* searches both popular and scholarly books. Both *Google Scholar* and *Google Book Search* offer overviews and, in some cases, the full text of a source.

Note: Whatever search engine you use, always click on the link called Help, Hints, or Tips on the search tool's home page to find out more about the commands and advanced-search techniques it offers. Most search engines allow searches using the techniques discussed earlier in this chapter (pp. 525–30). Many also provide advanced-search options that allow you to limit results to those created between specific dates, in specific languages, and so on.

Using Interactive Sources

Interactive sources—including blogs, wikis, social networking sites (like *Facebook* and *Twitter*), and discussion lists—can also be useful sources of information, especially if your research project focuses on a current event or late-breaking news.

- **Blogs** are Web sites that are updated regularly, often many times a day. They are usually organized chronologically, with the newest posts at the top, and though they may contain links to news stories, they generally focus on the opinions of the blog host and visitors. Blogs by experts in the field are likely to be more informative than blogs by amateurs or fans.

- **Wikis**—of which *Wikipedia* is the best known example—offer content contributed and modified collaboratively by a community of users. Wikis can be very useful for gleaning background information, but because (in most cases) anyone can write or revise wiki entries, many instructors will not accept them as reliable sources for college-level research projects. Use wikis cautiously.

- **Social networking sites**, like *Facebook* and *Twitter,* allow users to create groups or pages on topics of interest or to follow the thoughts and activities of newsmakers.

- **Discussion lists** are electronic mailing lists that allow members to post comments and get feedback from others interested in the same topic. The most reliable discussion lists are moderated and attract experts on the topic. Many online communities provide some kind of indexing or search mechanism so that you can look for "threads" (conversations) related to your topic.

Although you need to evaluate the information you find in all sources carefully, you must be especially careful with information from social networking sites and discussion lists. However, such sources can provide up-to-the-minute information. Also be aware that whereas most online communities welcome guests and newcomers, others may perceive your questions as intrusive or naive. It may be useful to "lurk" (that is, just read posts) before making a contribution.

Conducting Field Research

In universities, government agencies, and the business world, field research can be as important as library research. In some majors, like education or sociology, as well as in service-learning courses, primary research projects are common. Even in the writing projects covered in Part One, observations, interviews, and surveys may be useful or even necessary. As you consider how you might use field research in your writing projects, ask your instructor whether your institution requires you to obtain approval, and check Chapter 20, "Citing and Documenting Sources in MLA Style," or 21, "Citing and Documenting Sources in APA Style," for information about citing interviews you conduct yourself.

Conduct observational studies.

Observational studies, such as those you would conduct when profiling a place (see Chapter 3), are common in college. To conduct an observational study effectively, follow these guidelines:

- **Arrange access if necessary.** Visits to a private location (such as a school or business) require special permission, so be sure to arrange your visit in advance, and have a fallback plan in case your request is refused or the business or institution places constraints on you that hamper your research.

- **Develop a hypothesis.** In advance, write down a tentative assumption about what you expect to learn from your study—your **hypothesis**. This will guide your observations and notes, while allowing you to adjust your expectations in response to what you observe, if necessary. Consider, too, how your presence might affect those whom you are observing, so you can minimize your impact and take the effect of your presence into consideration.

- **Take notes when making observations, using description, narration, analysis, and classification.** Describe in detail the setting and the people you are observing. Record as many details as possible, draw diagrams or sketches if helpful, and take photographs or videos if allowed (and if those you are observing do not object). Try to be an innocent observer: Pretend that you have never seen anything like this activity or place before, and explain what you are seeing step-by-step, even if what you are writing seems obvious. Break the scene down into its component parts, identify common threads, and organize the details into categories. Take careful notes during your visit if you can do so unobtrusively or immediately afterward if you can't. You can use a notebook and pencil, a laptop or tablet, or even a smartphone to record your notes. Choose whatever note-taking tools will be least disruptive to those around you.

- **Write up your observations.** After your visit, fill in any gaps in your notes, then review them to look for meaningful patterns. Ask yourself questions like these: How did what I observed fit or undermine any of my own or my readers' likely preconceptions of the place or activity? What most interested me (or would most interest my readers) about the activity or place? What are my readers likely to find interesting about it? What did I learn?

Your purpose in writing about your visit is to share your insights into the meaning and significance of your observations. Assume that your readers have never been to the place, and provide enough detail for it to come alive for them. Decide on the perspective you want to convey, and choose the details necessary to convey your insights.

Conduct interviews.

A successful interview involves careful planning before the interview, but it also requires keen listening skills and the ability to ask appropriate follow-up questions while conducting the interview. Courtesy and consideration for your subject are crucial at all stages of the process. Follow these guidelines when planning and conducting interviews:

- **Choose an interview subject, and arrange the interview.** Prepare a list of interview candidates, as busy people might turn you down. Keep in mind that the person you want to interview will be donating valuable time to you, so call ahead to arrange the interview, allow your subject to specify the amount of time she or he can spare, and come prepared.

- **Consider your objectives.** Do you want details or a general orientation (the "big picture")? Do you want mainly facts or opinions? Do you need to clarify something you have observed or read?

- **Do some background reading beforehand.** Find out as much as you can about the organization or company (size, location, purpose, etc.), as well as the key people.

- **Write some questions in advance.** You will likely want to ask a few **closed questions** ("How do you do _____ ?" "What does _____ mean?") and a number of **open questions** ("What do you think about _____ ?" "Tell me about a time you were _____ ."). The best questions encourage the subject to talk freely but stick to the point. If you are unsure about a subject's answer, follow up by rephrasing the answer, prefacing it by saying something like "Let me see if I have this right." Avoid *forced-choice questions* ("Which do you think is the better approach: _____ or _____ ?") and *leading questions* ("How well do you think _____ is doing?").

- **Be flexible.** Ask the questions you have prepared, but also be ready to shift gears to take full advantage of what your subject can offer.

- **Take notes but also listen carefully.** Take notes during the interview, even if you are recording your discussion. Remember that how something is said is as important as what is said. Look for material that will give texture to your writing—gesture, verbal inflection, facial expression, body language, physical appearance (dress, hair), or anything that makes the person an individual. Avoid interrupting your subject or talking about yourself; rather, listen carefully and guide the discussion by asking follow-up questions and probing politely for more information.

- **Be considerate.** Do not stay longer than the time you were allotted unless your subject agrees to continue the discussion; show your appreciation for the time you have been given by thanking your subject and offering to give her or him a copy of your finished project. After the interview, reflect on what you've learned, and review and amplify your notes. Make a list of any questions that arise. You may want to follow up with your subject for more information, but limit yourself to one e-mail or phone call to avoid becoming a bother.

Conduct surveys.

Surveys let you gauge the opinions and knowledge of large numbers of people. You might conduct a survey to gauge opinion in a political science course or to assess familiarity with a television show for a media studies course. Use the following guidelines to design an effective survey, administer the survey, and report on your results:

- **Conduct background research, focus your study, and identify the population you are trying to reach.** Before starting out, decide what you expect to learn (your *hypothesis*). Make sure to limit your focus to only one or two important issues so that you can craft a questionnaire that respondents can complete quickly and easily, as well as organize and report on your results more easily. If necessary, conduct background research to draft your hypothesis or narrow your focus. Even for an informal study, you should try to get a reasonably representative group. Determine the demographic makeup of your school, and arrange to reach out to a representative sample.

- **Write questions.** Plan to use a number of *closed questions* (questions that request specific information), such as yes/no questions, multiple-choice questions, ranking-scale questions, and checklist questions. You will also likely want to include a few *open questions* (questions that give respondents the opportunity to write their answers in their own words). Whatever questions you develop, be sure that they are clear and unambiguous.

- **Design and test the questionnaire.** Begin your questionnaire with a brief introduction, clearly stating the purpose of your survey and explaining how you intend to use the results. Give advice on answering the questions, estimate the amount of time needed to complete the questionnaire, and give a due date. Organize your questions logically (such as by topic or from least to most complicated), and format your questionnaire so that it is easy to read. Once you have a draft you are happy with, ask at least three readers to complete your questionnaire before you distribute it. Time them as they respond, and discuss with them any confusion or problems they experienced. Then revise your questionnaire accordingly.

- **Administer the survey.** You can conduct the survey in person, use an online service such as *SurveyMonkey* (surveymonkey.com) or *Zoomerang* (zoomerang .com), or use a social media site such as *Facebook*. Though fewer than half the surveys you solicit using survey software are likely to be completed, online software will tabulate survey responses automatically.

- **Write the report.** When writing your report, include a summary of the results, as well as an interpretation of what they mean. Research reports in the social sciences use a standard format, with headings introducing the following categories of information: *Abstract* (a brief summary), *Introduction* (context, background, and limitations of the research program), *Methods* (a copy of the questionnaire and a description of administration methods), *Results* (survey data with limited interpretation), and *Discussion* (interpretation of results and conclusions drawn).

18

Selecting and Evaluating Sources

As soon as you start your search for sources, you should begin evaluating what you find, not only to decide whether they are *relevant* to your research project but also to determine how *credible,* or reliable, they are.

Selecting Relevant Sources

Sources are **relevant** when they help you achieve your aims with your readers. Relevant sources may

- explain terms or concepts;
- provide background information;
- provide evidence in support of your claims;
- provide alternative viewpoints or interpretations;
- lend authority to your point of view.

A search for sources may reveal more books and articles than any researcher could ever actually consult. A search on the term *home schooling* in one database, for example, got 1,172 hits. Obviously, a glance at all the hits to determine which are most relevant would take far too much time. To speed up the process, resources such as library catalogs, databases, and search engines provide tools to narrow the results. For example, in one popular all-purpose database, you can limit results by publication date, language, and publication or source type (such as articles from newspapers or scholarly journals), among other options. (Check the Help screen to learn how to use these tools.) In this particular database, limiting the *home schooling* results to articles published in scholarly journals in English over the last ten years reduced the number of hits to fifty-six, a far more reasonable number to review.

For more on focusing search results and selecting search terms, see Chapter 17.

Once you've reduced your search results to a manageable number, click on the remaining titles to look closely at each record. The analysis of an article's detailed record in Figure 18.1 shows what to look for.

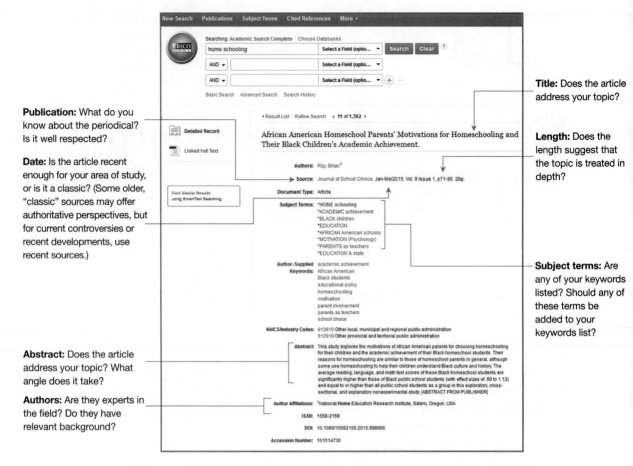

Title: Does the article address your topic?

Length: Does the length suggest that the topic is treated in depth?

Subject terms: Are any of your keywords listed? Should any of these terms be added to your keywords list?

Publication: What do you know about the periodical? Is it well respected?

Date: Is the article recent enough for your area of study, or is it a classic? (Some older, "classic" sources may offer authoritative perspectives, but for current controversies or recent developments, use recent sources.)

Abstract: Does the article address your topic? What angle does it take?

Authors: Are they experts in the field? Do they have relevant background?

FIGURE 18.1   Analyzing the detailed record of an article from a periodicals database
Analyze the detailed record of an article to determine whether the article itself is worth reading by asking yourself the following questions: Does the title suggest that the article addresses your topic? Are the authors experts in the field? Was the article published in a periodical that is likely to be reliable, was it published recently, and is it lengthy enough to indicate that the topic is treated in depth? Does the abstract (or summary) suggest that the article addresses your topic? If so, what angle does it take?

After you have identified a reasonable number of relevant sources, examine the sources themselves:

- Read the preface, introduction, or conclusion of books, or the first or last few paragraphs of articles, to determine which aspect of the topic is addressed or which approach to the topic is taken. To obtain a clear picture of a topic, researchers need to consider sources that address different aspects of the topic or take different approaches.

- Look at the headings or references in articles, or the table of contents and index in books, to see how much of the content relates specifically to your topic.

- Consider the way the source is written: Sources written for general readers may be accessible but may not analyze the subject in depth. Extremely specialized works may be too technical. Poorly written sources may be unreliable. (See the next section, Evaluating Sources, for more on scholarly versus popular sources and for a discussion of why researchers should avoid sources that are poorly written or riddled with errors.)

If close scrutiny leaves you with too few sources—or too many sources from too few perspectives—conduct a search using additional or alternative keywords, or explore links to related articles, look up references from a particularly useful article, or look for other sources by an author whose work you find useful.

Evaluating Sources

Choosing relevant sources is crucial to assembling a useful working bibliography. Determining which of those relevant sources is also likely to be *reliable* is even more important. To determine reliability, ask yourself the following questions.

Who wrote it?

Consider, first, whether the author is an *expert* in the field. The fact that someone has a PhD in astrophysics is no indication that he or she will be an expert in military history, for example, so be careful that the area of expertise is directly relevant to the topic.

To determine the author's area of expertise, look for the author's professional affiliation (where he or she works or teaches). This may be indicated at the bottom of the first page of an article (often labeled "Author Affiliations") or in an "About the Author" section in a book or on a Web site. Frequently, Googling the author will also reveal the author's affiliation, but double-check to make sure that the affiliation is current and that you have located the right person. You may also consult a biographical reference source available through a reference database at your library. Looking to see what other works the author has published, and with whom, can also help you ascertain his or her areas of expertise.

Contributors to blogs, wikis, and online discussion forums may or may not be experts in the field. Determine whether the site screens contributors, and double-check any information taken from sites for which you cannot determine the credentials of contributors.

Also consider the author's *perspective*. Most writing is not neutral or objective and does not claim to be. Knowledge of the author's perspective enables you to assess *bias* and determine whether the author's perspective affects the presentation of his or her argument. To determine the author's perspective, look for the main point and ask yourself questions like these:

- What evidence does the author provide to support this point? Is it from authoritative sources? Is it persuasive?
- Does the author make concessions to or refute opposing arguments?
- Does the author avoid fallacies, confrontational phrasing, and loaded words?

For more details on these argumentative strategies, see Chapter 16.

How recently was it published?

For help locating a source's publication date, see the documentation maps in Chapter 20.

In general, especially when you are writing about science or technology, current events, or emerging trends, you should consult the most up-to-date sources available on your subject. You may also need to consult older, "classic" sources, which establish the principles, theories, and data on which later work is based; classics may also provide a useful perspective for evaluating other works. To determine which sources are classics, note the ones that are cited most often in encyclopedia articles, lists of works cited or references, and recent works on the subject. You may also want to consult your instructor or a librarian to help you determine which works are classics in your field.

Is the source scholarly, popular, or for a trade group?

Scholarly sources (whether books or articles) are written by and for experts in a field of study, frequently professors or academic researchers. They can be challenging to read and understand because they use the language of the field, which may be unfamiliar to those outside the discipline, but they are considered reliable because the contents are written by specialists and peer-reviewed (reviewed by specialists) before publication. Scholarly sources also tend to delve deeply into a subject, often a narrowly defined subject. Scholarly sources may be published by a university press, a scholarly organization, or a commercial publisher (such as Kluwer Academic or Blackwell). Though scholarly sources may provide an overview of the subject and a survey of information from *secondary* sources, they generally focus on a specific issue or argument and contain a great deal of original, or *primary*, research.

In contrast, **popular sources** are written to entertain and educate the general public. For the most part, they are written by journalists who have conducted research and interviewed experts. They may include primary research, especially on current events or emerging trends. Mainly, though, they report on and summarize primary research and are written for interested, nonspecialist readers.

Of course, popular sources range widely along the reliability spectrum. Highly respected newspapers and magazines, such as the *New York Times,* the *Guardian,* the *Economist,* and *Harper's Magazine,* publish original research on news and culture. These newspapers and magazines check facts carefully and are often considered appropriate sources for research projects in entry-level courses (although you should check with your instructor to find out her or his expectations). Magazines that focus on celebrity gossip, such as *People* and *Us Weekly,* are unlikely to be considered appropriate sources for a college-level research project.

Trade publications—periodicals that report on news and technical advances in a specific industry—are written for those employed in the industry and include such titles as *Advertising Age, World Cement,* and *American Machinist.* Some trade publications may be appropriate for college research projects, especially in the sciences, but keep in mind that these publications are intended for a specialized audience and may focus on marketing products to professionals in the field. Table 18.1 summarizes some of the important differences between scholarly journals, popular magazines, and trade publications. (These sources may be tricky to distinguish online.)

Who published it?

Determining who published or sponsored a source you are considering can help you gauge its reliability and ascertain the publication's slant (or point of view). Look to see whether the source was published by a commercial publisher (such as St. Martin's or Random House); a university press (such as the University of Nebraska Press);

TABLE 18.1   Scholarly journals versus popular magazines and trade publications

Scholarly Journals	*Popular Magazines*	*Trade Publications*
Journals are usually published 4 to 6 times per year.	Magazines are usually published weekly or monthly.	Trade publications may be published daily, weekly, monthly, or quarterly, depending on the industry covered.
Articles are usually written by scholars (with *PhD* or academic affiliations after their names).	Authors of articles are journalists but may quote experts.	Articles may be written by professionals or by journalists with quotes from experts.
Many articles have more than one author.	Most articles have a single author.	Authors of articles may or may not be named.
In print journals, the title page often appears on the cover, and the covers frequently lack photographs.	Photographs, usually in color, appear on the covers of most print magazines and on their Web sites.	Photographs, usually in color, appear on the covers of most print trade publications and on their Web sites.
Articles may include charts, tables, figures, and quotations from other scholarly sources.	Articles frequently include color pictures and sidebars.	Articles frequently include color pictures and sidebars.
An abstract (summary) of the article may appear on the first page.	A headline or an engaging description may precede the article or appear as a teaser on the Web site.	Headlines often include names or terms familiar only to industry insiders.
Most articles are fairly long—5 to 20 pages.	Most articles are fairly short—1 to 5 pages.	Most articles are fairly short—1 to 5 pages.
Articles cite sources and provide a works-cited or reference list.	Articles rarely include a list of works cited or references but may include links.	Articles rarely include a list of works cited or references but may include links.

a corporation, an organization, or an interest group (such as the RAND Corporation, the World Wildlife Fund, or the National Restaurant Association); a government agency (such as the Internal Revenue Service or the U.S. Census Bureau); or the author on his or her own. Determining the publisher or sponsor is particularly important for material published on the Web.

If your source is a Web page, look at the URL (uniform resource locator) to find its top-level domain, which is indicated by a suffix. Some of the most useful ones are listed here:

.gov	U.S. federal government and some state or local government institutions
.org	nonprofit organizations
.edu	educational institutions
.com	businesses and commercial enterprises
.net	usually businesses or organizations associated with online networks
.mil	the U.S. military

For the most part, *.gov* and *.edu* are the most likely to offer reliable sources of information for a college research project. However, sources with any of these domains may vary in reliability. For example, a file with a *.com* suffix may offer a highly reliable history of a corporation and be an appropriate source for someone writing a history of corporate America, whereas a file with a *.edu* suffix may have been posted by a student or by a faculty member outside his or her area of expertise.

It is essential to look at Web sites carefully. Determine who sponsors the site: Is it a business, a professional group, a private organization, an educational institution, a government agency, or an individual? Look for a link, usually at the top or the bottom of the home page, called something like "Who We Are" or "About Us." If you cannot determine who sponsors a site, carefully double-check any information you find there.

Consider, too, checking how often the Web site has been linked to and the types of links provided by the Web site. That a site has been linked to repeatedly does not guarantee reliability, but that information may be helpful in conjunction with other recommendations in this chapter. To determine the number of times a Web page has been linked to, type *link:* plus the URL into a *Google* search box. To check the links provided, click on them and apply the criteria in this chapter.

If the source was published by a commercial publisher, check out the publisher's Web site, and ask yourself questions like these:

- Does the publisher offer works from a single perspective or from multiple perspectives?
- Do the works it publishes cover a wide variety of topics or focus on a particular array?
- Does the publisher's Web site host links to a particular type of site?

The Web sites of book publishers may offer a link to a catalog. If so, look at the works the catalog lists. Does the publisher seem to focus on a particular topic or take a particular point of view? Does the publisher generally offer popular, academic, or professional works?

If your source is a periodical (a magazine, newspaper, newsletter, or scholarly journal), consider whether it focuses on a particular topic or offers a single point of view. In addition to looking at the article you are considering and back issues of the periodical, visit the publisher's Web site, which may help you determine topic and point of view.

How is the source written?

Most works that are published professionally (including popular newspapers and magazines, as well as scholarly journals and trade magazines) will have been edited carefully. These sources generally avoid errors of grammar, punctuation, and spelling, and have been fact-checked carefully. Web sites sponsored by professional organizations, too, generally avoid these kinds of errors. Personal Web sites, however, are unlikely to have been professionally edited and fact-checked. If a Web site is riddled with errors, be very careful to double-check any information you take from that site.

What does the source say?

Finally, and perhaps most important, consider the source itself. Answering the following questions can help you determine whether the source is worth consideration:

- What is the intended audience of the source? Does the source address an audience of experts or a general audience?

- What is the purpose of the source? Does it review a number of different positions, or does it argue for a position of its own? Is the argument presented logically?

- What is the tone of the source? Is the tone reasonable? Does the source respond to alternative viewpoints, and are those responses logical and reasonable?

- What evidence is offered to support the argument? Is the evidence relevant and reliable? What kinds of citations or links does the source supply?

To learn more about analyzing an argument, see Chapter 16.

19

Using Sources to Support Your Ideas

Writing a college research project requires you to

- analyze sources to understand the arguments those sources are making, the information they are using to support their claims, and the ways those arguments and the supporting evidence they use relate to your topic;
- synthesize information from sources to support, extend, and challenge your own ideas;
- integrate information from sources with your own ideas to contribute something new to the "conversation" on your topic.

Synthesizing Sources

Synthesizing means making connections among information and ideas from texts and from your own experience. Once you have analyzed a number of sources on your topic, consider questions like the following to help you synthesize ideas and information:

- Do any of the sources you read use similar approaches or come to similar conclusions? What common themes do they explore? Do any of them use similar evidence (facts, statistics, research studies, examples) to support different conclusions?
- What differentiates their various points of view, such as different values, beliefs, priorities, interests, or concerns? Does one writer seem to be responding to or challenging one or more of the others?
- Do you agree with some sources and disagree with others? What makes one source more convincing than the others? Do any of the sources you have read offer support for your claims? Do any of them challenge your conclusions? If so, can you *refute* the challenge, or do you need to *concede* a point?

Sentence strategies like the following can help you clarify where you differ from or agree with the sources you have read:

▶ A study by X supports my position by demonstrating that ....

▶ X and Y think this issue is about .... But what is really at stake here is ....

▶ X claims that .... But I agree with Y, who argues that ....

▶ On this issue, X and Y say .... Although I understand and to some degree sympathize with their point of view, I agree with Z that this is ultimately a question of ....

The analysis of opposing positions by Max King (pp. 160–64) and the synthesis chart he created (p. 187) show how ideas and information from sources can be synthesized.

To learn more about synthesis, see Chapters 5 and 12.

Acknowledging Sources and Avoiding Plagiarism

In your college writing, you will be expected to use and acknowledge **secondary sources**—books, articles, published or recorded interviews, Web sites, lectures, and other print and nonprint materials—in addition to your own ideas, insights, and field research. The following information will help you decide what does and does not need to be acknowledged and will enable you to avoid *plagiarizing* inadvertently.

What does and does not need to be acknowledged?

For the most part, any ideas, information, or language you borrow from a source—whether the source is in print or online—must be acknowledged by including an in-text citation and an entry in your list of works cited (MLA style) or references (APA style). The only types of information that do not require acknowledgment are common knowledge (for example, John F. Kennedy was assassinated in Dallas), facts widely available in many sources (U.S. presidents used to be inaugurated on March 4 rather than January 20), well-known quotations ("To be or not to be / That is the question"), and material you created or gathered yourself (photographs you took or data from surveys you conducted).

For more on citing sources in MLA and APA style, see Chapters 20 and 21.

Remember that you need to acknowledge the source of any visual (photograph, table, chart, graph, diagram, drawing, map, screenshot) that you did not create yourself as well as the source of any information that you used to create your own visual. (You should also request permission from the source of a visual if your essay is going to be posted online without password protection.) When in doubt about whether you need to acknowledge a source, do so.

The documentation guidelines in the next two chapters present two styles for citing sources: MLA and APA. Whichever style you use, the most important thing is that your readers be able to tell where words or ideas that are not your own begin and end. You can accomplish this most readily by placing parenthetical source citations correctly and by separating your words from those of the source with **signal phrases** such as "According to Smith," "Peters claims," and "As Olmos asserts." (When you cite a source for the first time in a signal phrase, use the author's full name; after that, use just the last name.)

Avoid plagiarism by acknowledging sources and quoting, paraphrasing, and summarizing carefully.

When you use material from another source, you need to acknowledge the source, usually by citing the author and page or publication date in your text and including a list of works cited or references at the end of your essay. Failure to acknowledge sources—even by accident—constitutes plagiarism, a serious transgression. By citing sources correctly, you give appropriate credit to the originator of the words and ideas you are using, offer your readers the information they need to consult those sources directly, and build your own credibility.

Writers—students and professionals alike—occasionally fail to acknowledge sources properly. Students sometimes mistakenly assume that plagiarizing occurs only when another writer's exact words are used without acknowledgment. In fact, plagiarism can also apply to paraphrases as well as to such diverse forms of expression as musical compositions, visual images, ideas, and statistics. Therefore, keep in mind that you must indicate the source of any borrowed information, idea, language, or visual or audio material you use in your essay, whether you have *paraphrased, summarized,* or *quoted* directly from the source or have reproduced it or referred to it in some other way.

Remember especially the need to document electronic sources fully and accurately. Perhaps because it is so easy to access and distribute text and visuals online and to copy material from one electronic document and paste it into another, some students do not realize, or may forget, that information, ideas, and images from electronic sources require acknowledgment just as those from print sources do. At the same time, the improper (unacknowledged) use of online sources is often very easy for readers to detect.

Some people plagiarize simply because they do not know the conventions for using and acknowledging sources. Others plagiarize because they keep sloppy notes and thus fail to distinguish between their own and their sources' ideas. If you keep a working bibliography and careful notes, you will not make this serious mistake. If you are unfamiliar with the conventions for documentation, this and the next two chapters will clarify how you can incorporate sources into your writing and properly acknowledge your use of those sources.

Another reason some people plagiarize is that they feel intimidated by the writing task or the deadline. If you experience this anxiety about your work, speak to your instructor. Do not run the risk of failing a course or being expelled from your college because of plagiarism.

If you are confused about what is and what is not plagiarism, be sure to ask your instructor, or consult your school's plagiarism policy.

Using Information from Sources to Support Your Claims

When writing a research project, remember that the goal is to use the ideas and information you find in sources *to support your ideas*. Make sure that each of your supporting paragraphs does three things:

1. States a claim that supports your thesis
2. Provides evidence that supports your claim
3. Explains to readers how the evidence supports your claim

Consider this paragraph from Patrick O'Malley's proposal in Chapter 7, "More Testing, More Learning" (pp. 246–52):

> The main reason professors should give frequent exams is that when they do and when they provide feedback to students on how well they are doing, students learn more in the course and perform better on major exams, projects, and papers. It makes sense that in a challenging course containing a great deal of material, students will learn more of it and put it to better use if they have to apply or "practice" it frequently on exams, which also helps them find out how much they are learning and what they need to go over again.
> A 2006 study reported in the journal *Psychological Science* concluded that "taking repeated tests on material leads to better long-term retention than repeated studying," according to the study's coauthors, Henry L. Roediger and Jeffrey Karpicke (ScienceWatch.com, 2008). When asked what the impact of this breakthrough research would be, they responded: "We hope that this research may be picked up in educational circles as a way to improve educational practices, both for students in the classroom and as a study strategy outside of class." The new field of mind, brain, and education research advocates the use of "retrieval testing." For example, research by Karpicke and Blunt (2011) published in *Science* found that testing was more effective than other, more traditional methods of studying both for comprehension and for analysis. Why retrieval testing works is not known. UCLA psychologist Robert Bjork speculates that it may be effective because "when we use our memories by retrieving things, we change our access" to that information. "What we recall," therefore, "becomes more recallable in the future" (qtd. in Belluck, 2011).

Claim

Explanation of how evidence supports claim

Evidence

O'Malley connects this body paragraph to his thesis by beginning with the transition *The main reason* and by repeating the phrase *perform better* from his forecasting statement. He synthesizes information from a variety of sources, and doesn't merely stitch quotations and summary together; rather, he explains how the evidence supports his claim by stating that it "makes sense" that students "apply or 'practice'" what they learn on frequent exams, for example.

Decide whether to quote, paraphrase, or summarize.

As illustrated in O'Malley's paragraph (p. 545), writers integrate supporting evidence by quoting, paraphrasing, or summarizing information or ideas from sources. This section provides guidelines for deciding when to use each of these three methods and how to quote, paraphrase, and summarize effectively. Note that, with the exception of O'Malley's paragraph (which uses APA style), all examples in this section follow MLA style for in-text citations, which is explained in detail in Chapter 20.

As a rule, quote only in these situations:

- When the wording of the source is particularly memorable or vivid or expresses a technical point you can't rephrase clearly
- When a respected authority's words would lend support to your position
- When you wish to cite an author whose opinions challenge or vary greatly from those of other experts
- When you are going to discuss the source's choice of words

Paraphrase passages whose details you wish to use but whose language is not particularly striking. Summarize any long passages whose main points you wish to record as support for a point you are making.

Copy quotations exactly, or use italics, ellipses, and brackets to indicate changes.

Quotations should duplicate the source exactly, even if they contain spelling errors. Add the notation "(sic)" immediately after any such error to indicate that it is not your error but your source's. As long as you signal them appropriately, you may make changes to

- emphasize particular words;
- omit irrelevant information;
- insert information necessary for clarity;
- make the quotation conform grammatically to your sentence.

Using Italics for Emphasis   You may italicize any words in the quotation that you want to emphasize. When you do so, add a semicolon and the words *emphasis added* (in regular type, not italicized or underlined) to the parenthetical citation:

> In her 2001 exposé of the struggles of the working class, Ehrenreich writes, "The wages Winn-Dixie is offering — *$6 and a couple of dimes to start with* — are not enough,
> I decide, to compensate for this indignity" (14; emphasis added).

Using Ellipsis Marks for Omissions   You may decide to omit words from a quotation because they are not relevant to the point you are making. When you omit words from within a quotation, use **ellipsis marks**—three spaced periods (. . .)—in place of the missing words. When the omission occurs within a sentence, include a space before the first ellipsis mark and after the last mark:

> Hermione Roddice is described in Lawrence's *Women in Love* as a "woman of the new school, full of intellectuality and . . . nerve-worn with consciousness" (17).

When the omission falls at the end of a sentence, place a period *directly after* the final word of the sentence, followed by a space and three spaced ellipsis marks:

> But Grimaldi's commentary contends that for Aristotle rhetoric, like dialectic, had "no limited and unique subject matter upon which it must be exercised. . . . Instead, rhetoric as an art transcends all specific disciplines and may be brought into play in them" (6).

A period plus ellipsis marks can indicate the omission not just of the rest of a sentence but also of whole sentences, paragraphs, or even pages.

When a parenthetical reference follows ellipsis marks at the end of a sentence, place the three spaced periods after the quotation, and place the sentence period after the final parenthesis:

> But Grimaldi's commentary contends that for Aristotle rhetoric, like dialectic, had "no limited and unique subject matter upon which it must be exercised. . . . Instead, rhetoric as an art transcends all specific disciplines . . ." (6).

When you quote only single words or phrases, you do not need to use ellipsis marks because it will be obvious that you have left out some of the original:

> More specifically, Wharton's imagery of suffusing brightness transforms Undine before her glass into "some fabled creature whose home was in a beam of light" (21).

For the same reason, you need not use ellipsis marks if you omit the beginning of a quoted sentence unless the rest of the sentence begins with a capitalized word and appears to be a complete sentence.

Using Brackets for Insertions or Changes   Use brackets around an insertion or a change needed to make a quotation conform grammatically to your sentence, such as a change in the form of a verb or pronoun or in the capitalization of the first word of the quotation. In this example from an essay on James Joyce's short story "Araby," the writer adapts Joyce's phrases "we played till our bodies glowed" and "shook music from the buckled harness" to fit the grammar of her sentences:

> In the dark, cold streets during the "short days of winter," the boys must generate their own heat by "play[ing] till [their] bodies glowed." Music is "[shaken] from the buckled harness" as if it were unnatural, and the singers in the market chant nasally of "the troubles in our native land" (30).

You may also use brackets to insert or substitute explanatory material in a quotation:

> Guterson notes that among Native Americans in Florida, "education was in the home; learning by doing was reinforced by the myths and legends which repeated the basic value system of their [the Seminoles'] way of life" (159).

Some changes that make a quotation conform grammatically to another sentence may be made without any signal to readers:

- A period at the end of a quotation may be changed to a comma if you are using the quotation within your own sentence.
- Double quotation marks enclosing a quotation may be changed to single quotation marks when the quotation is enclosed within a longer quotation.

Adjusting the Punctuation within Quotations   Although punctuation within a quotation should reproduce the original, some adaptations may be necessary. Use single quotation marks for quotations within the quotation:

> Guterson claims that E. D. Hirsch "also recognizes the connection between family and learning, suggesting in his discussion of family background and academic achievement 'that the significant part of our children's education has been going on outside rather than inside the schools'" (16-17).

If the quotation ends with a question mark or an exclamation point, retain the original punctuation:

> "Did you think I loved you?" Edith later asks Dombey (566).

If a quotation ending with a question mark or an exclamation point concludes your sentence, retain the question mark or exclamation point, and put the parenthetical reference and sentence period outside the quotation mark:

> Edith later asks Dombey, "Did you think I loved you?" (566).

Avoiding Grammatical Tangles   When you incorporate quotations into your writing, and especially when you omit words from quotations, you run the risk of creating ungrammatical sentences. Avoid these three common errors:

- verb incompatibility
- ungrammatical omissions
- sentence fragments

Verb incompatibility occurs when the verb form in the introductory statement is grammatically incompatible with the verb form in the quotation. When your quotation has a verb form that does not fit in with your text, it is usually possible to use just part of the quotation, thus avoiding verb incompatibility:

> *he describes seeing himself "*
> ▶ The narrator suggests his bitter disappointment when "I saw myself as a creature
>   ^
> driven and derided by vanity" (35).

As this sentence illustrates, use the present tense when you refer to events in a literary work.

Ungrammatical omissions may occur when you delete text from a quotation. To avoid this problem, try adapting the quotation (with brackets) so that its parts fit together grammatically, or use only one part of the quotation:

▶ From the moment of the boy's arrival in Araby, the bazaar is presented as a

commercial enterprise: "I could not find any sixpenny entrance and . . .

hand[ed]
~~handing~~ a shilling to a weary-looking man" (34).

▶ From the moment of the boy's arrival in Araby, the bazaar is presented as a

He "
commercial enterprise: "~~I~~ could not find any sixpenny entrance *and*

so he had to pay a shilling to get in
. . . ~~handing a shilling to a weary-looking man~~" (34).

Sentence fragments sometimes result when writers forget to include a verb in the sentence introducing a quotation, especially when the quotation itself is a complete sentence. Make sure you introduce a quotation with a complete sentence:

leads
▶ The girl's interest in the bazaar ~~leading~~ the narrator to make what amounts to a sacred

oath: "If I go . . . I will bring you something" (32).

Use in-text or block quotations.

Depending on its length, you may incorporate a quotation into your text by enclosing it in quotation marks or by setting it off from your text in a block without quotation marks. In either case, be sure to integrate the quotation into your essay using the strategies described here:

In-Text Quotations Incorporate brief quotations into your text. (In MLA style, "brief" means four lines or fewer of prose and three lines or fewer of poetry; in APA style, "brief" means less than forty words.) You may place a quotation virtually anywhere in your sentence:

At the Beginning

"To live a life is not to cross a field," Sutherland, quoting Pasternak, writes at the beginning of her narrative (11).

In the Middle

Woolf begins and ends by speaking of the need of the woman writer to have "money and a room of her own" (4) — an idea that certainly spoke to Plath's condition.

At the End

In *The Second Sex*, Simone de Beauvoir describes such an experience as one in which the girl "becomes an object, and she sees herself as object" (378).

Divided by Your Own Words

"Science usually prefers the literal to the nonliteral term," Kinneavy writes, "—that is, figures of speech are often out of place in science" (177).

When you quote poetry within your text, use a slash (/) with spaces before and after to signal the end of each line of verse:

Alluding to St. Augustine's distinction between the City of God and the Earthly City, Lowell writes that "much against my will / I left the City of God where [faith] belongs" (4-5).

Block Quotations   In MLA style, use the block form for prose quotations of five or more typed lines; in APA style, use the block form for quotations of forty words or more. Indent the quotation half an inch from the left margin:

In "A Literary Legacy from Dunbar to Baraka," Margaret Walker says of Paul Lawrence Dunbar's dialect poems:

> He realized that the white world in the United States tolerated his literary genius only because of his "jingles in a broken tongue," and they found the old "darky" tales and speech amusing and within the vein of folklore into which they wished to classify all Negro life. This troubled Dunbar because he realized that white America was denigrating him as a writer and as a man. (70)

Note that in MLA style, the parenthetical page reference follows the period in block quotations.

In a block quotation, double-space between lines, just as you'll do in your main text. *Do not* enclose the passage within quotation marks. Use a colon to introduce a block quotation unless the context calls for another punctuation mark or none at all. When quoting a single paragraph or part of one in MLA style, do not indent the first line of the quotation more than the rest. In quoting two or more paragraphs, indent the first line of each paragraph an extra quarter inch.

Use punctuation to integrate quotations into your writing.

Statements that introduce in-text quotations take a range of punctuation marks and lead-in words. Here are some examples of the ways writers typically introduce quotations.

Introducing a Quotation Using a Colon   A colon usually follows an independent clause placed before the quotation:

As George Williams notes, protection of white privilege is critical to patterns of discrimination: "Whenever a number of persons within a society have enjoyed for a considerable period of time certain opportunities for getting wealth, for exercising power and authority, and for successfully claiming prestige and social deference, there is a strong tendency for these people to feel that these benefits are theirs 'by right'" (727).

Introducing a Quotation Using a Comma   A comma usually follows an introduction that incorporates the quotation into its sentence structure:

> Similarly, Duncan Turner asserts, "As matters now stand, it is unwise to talk about communication without some understanding of Burke" (259).

Introducing a Quotation Using *That*   No punctuation is generally needed with *that*, and no capital letter is used to begin the quotation:

> Noting this failure, Alice Miller asserts that "the reason for her despair was not her suffering but the impossibility of communicating her suffering to another person" (255).

Paraphrase sources carefully.

In a **paraphrase**, the writer restates in his or her own words all the relevant information from a passage, without any additional comments or any suggestion of agreement or disagreement with the source's ideas. A paraphrase is useful for recording details of a passage when the source's wording is not important. Because all the details of the passage are included, a paraphrase is often about the same length as the original passage. It is better to paraphrase than to quote ordinary material in which the author's way of expressing things is not worth special attention.

Here is a passage from a book on home schooling and an example of an acceptable paraphrase:

Original Source

Bruner and the discovery theorists have also illuminated conditions that apparently pave the way for learning. It is significant that these conditions are unique to each learner, so unique, in fact, that in many cases classrooms can't provide them. Bruner also contends that the more one discovers information in a great variety of circumstances, the more likely one is to develop the inner categories required to organize that information. Yet life at school, which is for the most part generic and predictable, daily keeps many children from the great variety of circumstances they need to learn well.

—David Guterson, *Family Matters: Why Homeschooling Makes Sense*, p. 172

Acceptable Paraphrase

According to Guterson, the "discovery theorists," particularly Bruner, have found that there seem to be certain conditions that help learning take place. Because individuals require different conditions, many children are not able to learn in the classroom. According to Bruner, when people can explore information in many different situations, they learn to classify and order what they discover. The general routine of the school day, however, does not provide children with the diverse activities and situations that would allow them to learn these skills (172).

The highlighting shows that some words in the paraphrase were taken from the source. Indeed, it would be nearly impossible for paraphrasers to avoid using any key terms from the source, and it would be counterproductive to try to do so, because the original and the paraphrase necessarily share the same information and concepts. Notice, though, that of the eighty-four words in the paraphrase, the paraphraser uses only a name (*Bruner*) and a few other key nouns and verbs for which it would be awkward to substitute other words or phrases. If the paraphraser had wanted to use other, more distinctive language from the source—for example, the description of life at school as "generic and predictable"—these adjectives would need to be enclosed in quotation marks. In fact, the paraphraser puts quotation marks around only one of the terms from the source: "discovery theorists"—a technical term likely to be unfamiliar to readers.

Paraphrasers must, however, avoid borrowing too many words and repeating the sentence structures from a source. Here is an unacceptable paraphrase of the first sentence in the Guterson passage:

Unacceptable Paraphrase: Too Many Borrowed Words and Phrases

Apparently, some conditions, which have been illuminated by Bruner and other discovery theorists, pave the way for people to learn.

Here, the paraphrase borrows almost all of its key language from the source sentence, including the entire phrase *pave the way for*. Even if you cite the source, this heavy borrowing would be considered plagiarism.

Here is another unacceptable paraphrase of the same sentence:

Unacceptable Paraphrase: Sentence Structure Repeated Too Closely

Bruner and other *researchers* have also *identified circumstances* that *seem to ease the path* to learning.

If you compare the source's first sentence and this paraphrase of it, you will see that the paraphraser has borrowed the phrases and clauses of the source and arranged them in an almost identical sequence, simply substituting synonyms for most of the key terms. This paraphrase could also be considered plagiarism.

Write summaries that present the source's main ideas in a balanced and readable way.

Unlike a paraphrase, a **summary** presents only the main ideas of a source, leaving out examples and details. Here is one student's summary of five pages from Guterson's book *Family Matters*. You can see at a glance how drastically summaries can condense information, in this case from five pages to five sentences. Depending on the summarizer's purpose, the five pages could be summarized in one sentence, the five sentences here, or two or three dozen sentences.

In looking at different theories of learning that discuss individual-based programs (such as home schooling) versus the public school system, Guterson describes the disagreements among "cognitivist" theorists. One group, the "discovery theorists," believes that

---

Margin notes:

Repeated words

Repeated phrase

Repeated words

Synonyms

Repeated sentence structure

For more about summarizing, see Chapter 12.

individual children learn by creating their own ways of sorting the information they take in from their experiences. Schools should help students develop better ways of organizing new material, not just present them with material that is already categorized, as traditional schools do. "Assimilationist theorists," by contrast, believe that children learn by linking what they don't know to information they already know. These theorists claim that traditional schools help students learn when they present information in ways that allow children to fit the new material into categories they have already developed (171–75).

Summaries like this one are more than a dry list of main ideas from a source. Rather, they are a coherent, readable new text composed of the source's main ideas. Summaries provide balanced coverage of a source, following the same sequence of ideas and avoiding any hint of agreement or disagreement with them.

20

Citing and Documenting Sources in MLA Style

When using the MLA system of documentation, include both an in-text citation and a list of works cited. **In-text citations** tell your readers where the ideas or words you have borrowed come from, and the entries in the **works-cited list** allow readers to locate your sources so that they can read more about your topic.

Citing Sources in the Text

In most cases, include the author's last name and the page number on which the borrowed material appears in the text of your research project. You can incorporate this information in two ways:

SIGNAL PHRASE   By naming the author in the text of your research project with a signal phrase (*Simon described*) and including the page reference (in parentheses) at the end of the borrowed passage:

Author's last name   *Appropriate verb*

Simon, a well-known figure in New York literary society, described the impression Dr. James made on her as a child in the Bronx: He was a "not-too-skeletal Ichabod Crane" (68).

Page number

PARENTHETICAL CITATION   By including the author's name and the page number together in parentheses at the end of the borrowed passage:

Author's last name + page number

Dr. James is described as a "not-too-skeletal Ichabod Crane" (Simon 68).

WORKS-CITED ENTRY   Simon, Kate. "Birthing." *Bronx Primitive: Portraits in a Childhood*. Viking Books, 1982, pp. 68-77.

In most cases, you will want to use a *signal phrase* because doing so lets you put your source in context. The signal-phrase-plus-page-reference combination also allows you to make crystal clear where the source information begins and ends.

Use a parenthetical citation alone when you have already identified the author or when you are citing the source of an uncontroversial fact.

The in-text citation should include as much information as is needed to lead readers to the source in your list of works cited and allow them to find the passage you are citing in that source. In most cases, that means the author's last name and the page number on which the borrowed material appears. In some cases, you may need to include other information in your in-text citation (such as a brief version of the title if the author is unnamed or if you cite more than one work by this author). In a few cases, you may not be able to include a page reference, as when you cite a Web site or film. In such cases, you may include other identifying information, such as a paragraph number, section heading, or time stamp (if provided by the source).

The most common types of in-text citations follow. For other, less common citation types, consult the *MLA Handbook,* Eighth Edition, and the Modern Language Association's Web site (www.mla.org). If the MLA does not provide a model citation, use the information here to create a citation that will lead your readers to the source. (Citation managers like *EndNote* and *RefWorks* will format your citations in MLA style, but check them carefully, as the software sometimes makes errors and may not be up to date.)

Directory to In-Text-Citation Models

One author   When citing most works with a single author, include the author's name (usually the last name is enough)* and the page number on which the cited material appears.

Author's last name + appropriate verb   *Page number*

SIGNAL PHRASE   Simon describes Dr. James as a "not-too-skeletal Ichabod Crane" (68).

                                                      Author's last name + page number

PARENTHETICAL CITATION   Dr. James is described as a "not-too-skeletal Ichabod Crane" (Simon 68).

---

* But see entries for "Two or more works by the same author," "Two or more authors with the same last name," and "Work without page numbers or a one-page work" on pp. 556 and 558.

Author's name

BLOCK QUOTATION   In Kate Simon's story "Birthing," the description of Dr. James captures both his physical appearance and his role in the community:

> He looked so much like a story character — the gentled Scrooge of a *St. Nicholas Magazine* Christmas issue, a not-too-skeletal Ichabod Crane. . . . Dr. James was, even when I knew him as a child, quite an old man, retired from a prestigious and lucrative practice in Boston. . . . His was a prosperous intellectual family, the famous New England Jameses that produced William and Henry, but to the older Bronx doctors, *the* James was the magnificent old driven scarecrow. (68)

Page number

(A works-cited entry for "Birthing" appears on p. 554.)

More than one author   To cite a source by two authors, include both authors' last names. To cite a source with three or more authors, provide just the first author's last name followed by *et al.* ("and others" in Latin, not italicized).

SIGNAL PHRASE   Bernays and Painter maintain that a writer can begin a story without knowing how it will end (7).

Dyal et al. identify several types of students, including the "Authority-Rebel" (4).

PARENTHETICAL CITATION   A writer should "resist the temptation to give the reader too lengthy an explanation" (Bernays and Painter 7).

The Authority-Rebel "tends to see himself as superior to other students in the class" (Dyal et al. 4).

Unknown author   If the author's name is unknown, use a shortened version of the title, beginning with the word by which the title is alphabetized in the works-cited list. Use the first noun and any modifiers. (In this example, the full title is "Plastic Is Found in the Sargasso Sea; Pieces of Apparent Refuse Cover Wide Atlantic Region.")

An international pollution treaty still to be ratified would prohibit ships from dumping plastic at sea ("Plastic" 68).

Two or more works by the same author   If you cite more than one work by the same author, include a shortened version of the title.

When old paint becomes transparent, it sometimes shows the artist's original plans: "a tree will show through a woman's dress" (Hellman, *Pentimento* 1).

Two or more authors with the same last name   When citing works by authors with the same last name, include each author's first name in the signal phrase or first initial in the parenthetical citation.

Chaplin's *Modern Times* uses montage to make an editorial statement (E. Roberts 246).

Corporation, organization, or government agency as author   In a signal phrase, use the full name of the corporation, organization, or government agency. In a parenthetical citation, use the full name if it is brief or a shortened version if it is long.

SIGNAL PHRASE	The Washington State Board for Community and Technical Colleges will raise tuition to offset budget deficits from Initiative 601 (4).
PARENTHETICAL CITATION	A tuition increase has been proposed for community and technical colleges to offset budget deficits from Initiative 601 (Washington State Board 4).

Literary work (novel, play, poem)   Provide information that will help readers find the passage you are citing no matter what edition of the novel, play, or poem they are using. In a signal phrase, spell out titles; in a parenthetical citation, abbreviate famous works. For a novel or other prose work, provide the part or chapter number as well as the page numbers from the edition you used.

NOVEL OR OTHER PROSE WORK	In *Hard Times,* Tom reveals his utter narcissism by blaming Louisa for his own failure: "'You have regularly given me up. You never cared for me'" (Dickens 262; bk. 3, ch. 9).

For a play in verse, use act, scene, and line numbers instead of page numbers.

PLAY (IN VERSE)	At the beginning, Regan's fawning rhetoric hides her true attitude toward Lear: "I profess / myself an enemy to all other joys . . . / And find that I am alone felicitate / In your dear highness' love" (*Lr.* 1.1.74-75, 77-78).

For a poem, indicate the line numbers and stanzas or sections (if they are numbered) instead of page numbers.

POEM	In "Song of Myself," Whitman finds poetic details in busy urban settings, as when he describes "the blab of the pave, tires of carts . . . the driver with his interrogating thumb" (8.153-54).

If the source gives only line numbers, use the term *lines* in your first citation and use only the numbers in subsequent citations.

> In "Before you thought of spring," Dickinson at first identifies the spirit of spring with a bird, possibly a robin — "A fellow in the skies / Inspiriting habiliments / Of indigo and brown" (lines 4, 7-8) — but by the end of the poem, she has linked it with poetry and perhaps even the poet herself, as the bird, like Dickinson, "shouts for joy to nobody / But his seraphic self!" (15-16).

Work in an anthology   Use the name of the author of the work, not the editor of the anthology, in your in-text citation.

SIGNAL PHRASE	In "Six Days: Some Rememberings," Grace Paley recalls that when she was in jail for protesting the Vietnam War, her pen and paper were taken away and she felt "a terrible pain in the area of [her] heart — a nausea" (191).
PARENTHETICAL CITATION	Writers may have a visceral reaction — "a nausea" (Paley 191) — to being deprived of access to writing implements.

Religious work   In your first citation, include the element that begins your entry in the works-cited list, such as the edition name of the religious work you are citing (see p. 564), and include the book or section name (using standard abbreviations in parenthetical citations) and any chapter or verse numbers.

> She ignored the admonition "Pride goes before destruction, and a haughty spirit before a fall" (*New Oxford Annotated Bible,* Prov. 16.18).

Multivolume work (one volume, more than one volume)   If you cite only one volume of a multivolume work, treat the in-text citation as you would any other work, but include the volume number in the works-cited entry (see below).

ONE VOLUME   Forster argued that modernist writers valued experimentation and gradually sought to blur the line between poetry and prose (150).

When you use two or more volumes of a multivolume work, include the volume number and the page number(s) in your in-text citation.

MORE THAN ONE   Modernist writers valued experimentation and gradually sought to blur
VOLUME   the line between poetry and prose (Forster 3: 150).

Indirect citation (quotation from a secondary source)   If possible, locate the original source and cite that. If not possible, name the original source but also include the secondary source in which you found the material you are citing, plus the abbreviation *qtd. in.* Include the secondary source in your list of works cited.

> E. M. Forster says, "The collapse of all civilization, so realistic for us, sounded in Matthew Arnold's ears like a distant and harmonious cataract" (qtd. in Trilling 11).

Entire work   Include the reference in the text without any page numbers or parentheses.

> In *The Structure of Scientific Revolutions,* Thomas Kuhn discusses how scientists change their thinking.

Work without page numbers or a one-page work (with/without other section numbers)
If a work (such as a Web page) has no page numbers or is only one page long, omit the page number. If it uses screen numbers or paragraph numbers, insert a comma after the author's name, an identifying term (such as *screen*) or abbreviation *(par.* or *pars.*), and the number.

WITHOUT PAGE OR   The average speed on Montana's interstate highways, for example, has
OTHER NUMBERS   risen by only 2 miles per hour since the repeal of the federal speed limit, with most drivers topping out at 75 (Schmid).

WITH OTHER   Whitman considered African American speech "a source of a native grand
SECTION NUMBERS   opera" (Ellison, par. 13).

Work in a time-based medium   To cite a specific portion of a video or an audio recording, include a time or range of times, as provided by your media player. Cite hours, minutes, and seconds, placing colons between them.

> President Obama joked that he and Dick Cheney agreed on one thing — *Hamilton* is phenomenal ("*Hamilton* Cast" 00:02:34-38).

Two or more works cited in the same parentheses If you cite two or more sources for a piece of information, include them in the same parentheses, separated by semicolons.

> A few studies have considered differences between oral and written discourse production (Gould; Scardamalia et al.).

Creating a List of Works Cited

In your MLA-style research project, every source you cite must have a corresponding entry in the list of works cited, regardless of its medium of publication (printed book, online newspaper, Tweet, text message, and so on), and every entry in your list of works cited must correspond to at least one citation in your research project.

The MLA Handbook, Eighth Edition, offers these general principles for citing sources:

- **Author or author(s).** Start with the author's name (or authors' names). Only the first author is listed last name first: *Smith, Jane. Follow the author's name with a period.*

- **Title of source.** Include the title of the source. Italicize the title if the work is self-contained (book, television series, and Web site titles fall into this category); put the title in quotation marks if the work is contained within a larger work (titles of magazines, newspapers, journal articles, and episodes of television series fall into this category). *Follow the title of the source with a period.*

- **Title of "container," or larger work in which the source appears, if any.** A newspaper, magazine, or journal contains the articles that appear in it; a Web site contains the Web pages that compose it; and a blog contains the blog posts and comments that appear in it. Container titles are typically italicized; the information that relates to the container is not. (Common types of container-related information appear in the following list.) *Follow the container title and every item that relates to the container with a comma—except for the last, which should be followed by a period.* If a source appears nested within multiple containers, add information about other containers following the first. For example, if an article appears in a journal, and you access the article through a database, then information about the journal follows the source title, and information about the database follows information about the journal.

See the citation for an article from a scholarly journal on page 567.

  - **Other contributors.** Translators, editors, producers, narrators, and illustrators are examples of other contributors.

  - **Version.** Edition names or numbers (*revised edition, eighth edition*) and *director's cut* are examples of versions.

  - **Number.** The volume number of a multivolume work, the volume and issue number of a journal, and the disk number of a set of DVDs fall into this category.

  - **Publication information.** The name of the publisher, government and agency, and site sponsor fall into this category.

  - **Publication date.** The date might be a day, month, and year for weekly magazines, daily or weekly television episodes, and daily newspapers; a month and year for journals and monthly magazines; or just a year for books and movies.

- **Source locator.** The source locator might be the page number(s) of the section you used from a printed text, the DOI (digital object identifier, a permanent code) or URL of an online source, or the time stamp of a Tweet or video.

- **Additional information.** Include additional information if your readers are likely to need it to identify your source. For an undated online source, you might include the date on which you accessed the source. A source might require a label if the type of source you are citing (such as an editorial or a lecture) is unclear from the citation. *Follow any additional information you provide with a period.*

To cite a source without a model, use a similar model, or devise your own using the general principles.

Nowadays, many print sources are also available in an electronic format, either online or through a database your school's library subscribes to. For most online versions of a source, follow the form of the corresponding print version. Then add the information about the online source.

For example, if you are citing an article from a journal that appears in print but that you accessed through a database, start with the citation for the print journal. Then add the information about the online source (a second container).

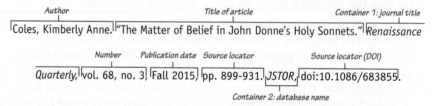

For sources accessed through a database, include the following:

- Title of the database (in italics), *followed by a comma*

- Location where you accessed the source, *followed by a period*; ideally this is a DOI, or digital object identifier (a permanent code), but when one is not available, provide a URL (if available, use a permalink)

For other online sources, include the following:

- Title of the Web site (in italics), *followed by a comma*

- Version or edition used (if any), *followed by a comma*

- Publisher of the site, but only if distinct from the title of the publication, *followed by a comma*

- Date of publication or last update, *followed by a comma*; if no date of publication or update is available, provide the date you last accessed the source at the end of the entry

- DOI, if one is available; if not, a URL (ideally a permalink), *followed by a period*

You may not always find the exact model you need to cite your sources, but MLA style is flexible. Using these general principles, you can adapt another model or devise your own.

Format your list of works cited.

Follow these rules when formatting your list of works cited in MLA style:

- On a new page, type "Works Cited" (centered), and double-space the whole works-cited list, from the heading on.

- Alphabetize entries by the first word in the citation, usually the first author's last name or the title if the author is unknown (ignore *A, An,* or *The*).

- Use a hanging indent for all entries: Do not indent the first line, but indent second and subsequent lines of the entry by half an inch. (Your word processor can be set to create a hanging indent automatically.)

- Abbreviate the names of university presses, shortening the words *University* and *Press* to *U* and *P*. Spell out other publishers' names in full, including words like *Press* or *Books*. Omit only initial articles like *The* and corporate-sounding words or abbreviations (*Limited, Co.*). If a work has more than one publisher, separate them with a slash: *University of Texas / International Digital Media Arts*.

Directory to Works-Cited-List Models

(Continued)

Author Listings

One author   List the author last name first (followed by a comma), and insert a period at the end of the name.

> Isaacson, Walter.

Two authors   List the first author last name first (followed by a comma). List the second author in the usual first-name/last-name order. Insert the word *and* before the second author's name, and follow it with a period.

> Bernays, Anne, and Pamela Painter.

Three or more authors   List the first author last name first (followed by a comma). Then insert *et al.* (which means *and others* in Latin) in regular type (not italics).

> Hunt, Lynn, et al.

Unknown author   Begin the entry with the title.

> *Primary Colors: A Novel of Politics.*
>
> "Out of Sight."

Corporation, organization, or government agency as author   Use the name of the corporation, organization, or government agency as the author. (But see the entry on government documents, p. 566, for what to do when author and publisher are the same.)

> RAND Corporation.
>
> United States, National Commission on Terrorist Attacks.

Two or more works by the same author   Replace the author's name in subsequent entries with three hyphens, and alphabetize the works by the first important word in the title:

> Eugenides, Jeffrey. *The Marriage Plot.*
>
> —. *Middlesex.*
>
> —. *"Walkabout."*

Books (Print, Electronic, Database)

Basic format

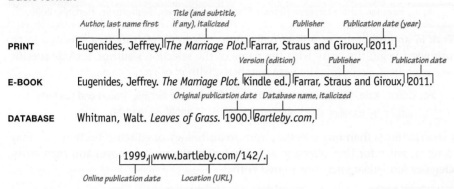

PRINT

Author, last name first
Title (and subtitle, if any), italicized
Publisher
Publication date (year)

Eugenides, Jeffrey. *The Marriage Plot.* Farrar, Straus and Giroux, 2011.

E-BOOK

Version (edition)
Publisher
Publication date

Eugenides, Jeffrey. *The Marriage Plot.* Kindle ed. Farrar, Straus and Giroux, 2011.

DATABASE

Original publication date   Database name, italicized

Whitman, Walt. *Leaves of Grass.* 1900. *Bartleby.com,*

1999, www.bartleby.com/142/.

Online publication date   Location (URL)

Figure 20.1 shows you where to find the source information you will need to create a works-cited entry for a book.

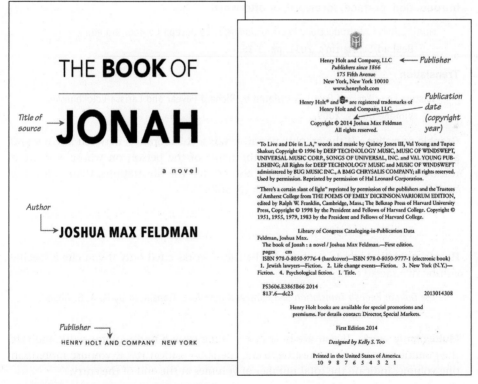

FIGURE 20.1   Documentation Map for a Book
Look for the author, title, and publisher on the title page (at the front of the book) and the year of publication (or copyright date) on the copyright page (usually on the back of the title page in print books). The title page and copyright page may appear in a different location or look a little different in an e-book or a book accessed through a database.

Anthology or edited collection   If you are referring to the anthology as a whole, put the editor's name first.

> Masri, Heather, editor. *Science Fiction: Stories and Contexts.* Bedford/St. Martin's, 2009.

Work in an anthology or edited collection   If you're referring to a selection in an anthology, begin the entry with the name of the selection's author. Include specific page references, preceding the page number(s) with *p.* or *pp.*

> Hopkinson, Nalo. "Something to Hitch Meat To." *Science Fiction: Stories and Contexts,* edited by Heather Masri, Bedford/St. Martin's, 2009, pp. 838-50.

If you cite more than one selection from an anthology or edited collection, you may create an entry for the collection as a whole (see the model above) and then cross-reference individual selections to that entry.

Selection author	Selection title	Anthology editor

Hopkinson, Nalo. "Something to Hitch Meat To." Masri, pp. 838-50.

Selection pages in anthology

Introduction, preface, foreword, or afterword

> Murfin, Ross C. Introduction. *Heart of Darkness*, by Joseph Conrad, 3rd ed., Bedford/St. Martin's, 2011, pp. 3-16.

Translation

> Tolstoy, Leo. *War and Peace*. Translated by Richard Pevear and Larissa Volokhonsky, Vintage Books, 2009.

Graphic narrative   If the graphic narrative was a collaboration between a writer and an illustrator, begin your entry with the name of the person on whose work your research project focuses. If the author also created the illustrations, then follow the basic model for a book with one author (p. 562).

> Pekar, Harvey, and Joyce Brabner. *Our Cancer Year*. Illustrated by Frank Stack, Four Walls Eight Windows, 1994.

Religious work   Include an entry in the list of works cited only if you cite a specific edition of a sacred text.

> *The Qu'ran: English Translation and Parallel Arabic Text*. Translated by M. A. S. Abdel Haleem, Oxford UP, 2010.

Multivolume work   If you use only one volume from a multivolume work, indicate the volume number after the title, using the abbreviation *vol.* If you use more than one volume, indicate the total number of volumes at the end of the entry.

One volume cited

Sandburg, Carl. *Abraham Lincoln.* Vol. 2, Charles Scribner's Sons, 1939.

More than one volume cited

Sandburg, Carl. *Abraham Lincoln*. Charles Scribner's Sons, 1939. 6 vols.

Later edition of a book   Include the edition name (such as *Revised*) or number following the title.

> Rottenberg, Annette T., and Donna Haisty Winchell. *The Structure of Argument*. 6th ed.,
>   Bedford/St. Martin's, 2009.

Republished book   Provide the original year of publication (plus a period) after the title of the book, followed by publication information for the edition you are using.

Original publication date

> Alcott, Louisa May. *An Old-Fashioned Girl*. 1870. Puffin Books, 1995.

Republication information

More than one publisher named   If the book was published by two or more publishers, separate the publishers with a slash, and include a space before and after the slash.

> Hornby, Nick. *About a Boy*. Riverhead / Penguin Putnam, 1998.

Title within a title   When a title that is normally italicized appears within a book title, do not italicize it. If the title within the title would normally be enclosed in quotation marks, include the quotation marks and also set the title in italics.

> Hertenstein, Mike. *The Double Vision of* Star Trek: *Half-Humans, Evil Twins, and Science
>   Fiction*. Cornerstone Press, 1998.

> Miller, Edwin Haviland. *Walt Whitman's "Song of Myself": A Mosaic of Interpretation*. U of
>   Iowa P, 1989.

Book in a series   Include the series title (without italics) and number (if any) at the end of the entry, after a period (never a comma). (This information will appear on the title page or on the page facing the title page.)

> Zigova, Tanya, et al. *Neural Stem Cells: Methods and Protocols*. Humana Press, 2002.
>   Methods in Molecular Biology 198.

Dictionary entry or article in another reference book   If no author is listed, begin with the entry's title. (But check for initials following the entry or article and a list of authors in the front of the book.) For familiar reference works, the publication information is probably not necessary.

PRINT   "Homeopathy." *Webster's New World College Dictionary*, 4th ed., 1999.

PRINT   Trenear-Harvey, Glenmore S. "Farm Hall." *Historical Dictionary of Atomic Espionage*,
        Scarecrow Press, 2011.

Web site (same name as publisher)   Most recent update

ONLINE   "Homeopathy." *Merriam-Webster*, 2011, www.merriam-webster.com/dictionary/
        homeopathy.

DATABASE   Powell, Jason L. "Power Elite." *Blackwell Encyclopedia of Sociology*,
        edited by George Ritzer, Wiley, 2007. *Blackwell Reference Online*,
        doi:10.1111/b.9781405124331.2007.x.   *Database (italics)*

Location (DOI)

Government document   If no author is named, begin with the government and agency that issued the document. If the work does have an author, begin with this information and place the government information after the source's title. In the United States, the publication information for most official government documents is *Government Printing Office,* both in print and online.

Authors

PRINT   Newes-Adeyi, Gabriella, et al. *Trends in Underage Drinking in the United States,*

Issuing government   *Issuing department*

 1991-2007. United States, Department of Health and Human Services, Government Printing Office, 2009.

ONLINE   United States, Department of Health and Human Services, Centers for Disease Control. "Youth Risk Behavior Surveillance — United States, 2009." *Morbidity and Mortality Weekly Report,* vol. 59, no. SS5, 4 June 2010, www.cdc.gov/mmwr/pdf/ss/ss5905.pdf.

Publication date

Published proceedings of a conference   If the name of the conference is part of the title of the publication, it need not be repeated. If it isn't part of the title, insert the name of the conference following the title. Use the format for a work in an anthology (p. 564) to cite an individual presentation. Include the location (city) where the conference took place after its date. Separate conference information from publication information with a period.

Conference name included in title

 Duffett, John, editor. *Against the Crime of Silence: Proceedings of the* International War Crimes Tribunal. Nov. 1967, Stockholm. Simon and Schuster, 1970.

Pamphlet or brochure

 Hypothermia and Cold Water Survival. U.S. Foundation for Boating Safety and Clean Water, 2001.

Doctoral dissertation   Cite a published dissertation as you would a book, but add pertinent dissertation information before the publication data. Enclose the title of an unpublished dissertation in quotation marks.

Title in italics

PUBLISHED   Jones, Anna Maria. *Problem Novels/Perverse Readers: Late-Victorian Fiction and the Perilous Pleasures of Identification.* Dissertation, U of Notre Dame, 2001.

Dissertation information

Title in quotation marks

UNPUBLISHED   Bullock, Barbara. "Basic Needs Fulfillment among Less Developed Countries: Social Progress over Two Decades of Growth." Dissertation, Vanderbilt U, 1986.

Dissertation information

Articles (Print, Online, Database)

Articles appear in periodicals—works that are issued at regular intervals, such as scholarly journals, newspapers, and magazines. Most periodicals today are available both in print and in electronic form (online or through an electronic database); some are available only in electronic format. If you are using the online version of an article, use the models provided here. If no model matches your source exactly, choose the closest match, and add any other information your reader will need to track down the source.

From a scholarly journal   Scholarly journals are typically identified using their volume and issue numbers, and date of publication. If a journal does not use volume numbers, provide the issue number only. Online journals may not include page numbers; if paragraph or other section numbers are provided, use them instead. If an article in a printed journal is not on a continuous sequence of pages, give the first page number followed by a plus sign. (See entry for a print version of a newspaper for an example.)

For help distinguishing between scholarly journals and magazines, see Chapter 18.

Figure 20.2 (p. 568) shows where to find the source information you will need to create works-cited entries for articles in print, online, and in a database.

Author, last name first   Article in quotation marks

PRINT   Haas, Heather A. "The Wisdom of Wizards — and Muggles and Squibs: Proverb
Use in the World of *Harry Potter*." *Journal of American Folklore*, vol. 124,
no. 492, Spring 2011, pp. 29-54.

Date of publication Page numbers

Garas-York, Keli. "Overlapping Student Environments: An Examination of the
Homeschool Connection and Its Impact on Achievement." *The Journal of
College Admission*, vol. 42, no. 4, May 2010, pp. 430-39.

ONLINE   Markel, J. D. "Religious Allegory and Cultural Discomfort in Mike Leigh's
Happy-Go-Lucky: And Why *Larry Crowne* Is One of the Best Films of 2011."
Bright Lights Film Journal, no. 74, 2011, brightlightsfilm.com/religious
-allegory-and-cultural-discomfort-in-mike-leighs-happy-go-luckyand-why
-larry-crowne-is-one-of-the-best-films-of-2011/.

URL

Saho, Bala S. K. "The Appropriation of Islam in a Gambian Village: Life and
Times of Shaykh Mass Kay, 1827-1936." *African Studies Quarterly*,
vol. 12, no. 4, 2011, asq.africa.ufl.edu/files/Saho-Vol12Is4.pdf.

DATABASE Coles, Kimberly Anne. "The Matter of Belief in John Donne's Holy Sonnets."
Renaissance Quarterly, vol. 68, no. 3, Fall 2015, pp. 899-931.
JSTOR, doi:10.1086/683855.

Database (italics)   DOI

From a newspaper   Newspapers are identified by date, not by volume and issue numbers, with the names of months longer than four letters abbreviated. If articles are not on a continuous series of pages, give only the first page number followed by a plus sign. If an article is unsigned, start with the title (in quotation marks); ignore articles (*A, An, The*) when alphabetizing. (See *Editorial or letter to the editor*, p. 569, for an example.)

Article from Printed Journal

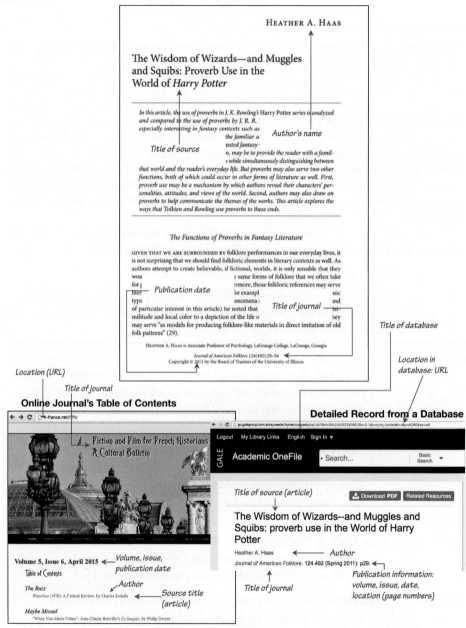

Heather A. Haas

The Wisdom of Wizards—and Muggles and Squibs: Proverb Use in the World of *Harry Potter*

Author's name

In this article, the use of proverbs in J. K. Rowling's Harry Potter series is analyzed and compared to the use of proverbs by J. R. R.

Title of source

especially interesting in fantasy contexts such as the familiar a eated fantasy n, may be to provide the reader with a famil- while simultaneously distinguishing between that world and the reader's everyday life. But proverbs may also serve two other functions, both of which could occur in other forms of literature as well. First, proverb use may be a mechanism by which authors reveal their characters' personalities, attitudes, and views of the world. Second, authors may also draw on proverbs to help communicate the themes of the works. This article explores the ways that Tolkien and Rowling use proverbs to these ends.

The Functions of Proverbs in Fantasy Literature

GIVEN THAT WE ARE SURROUNDED BY folklore performances in our everyday lives, it is not surprising that we should find folkloric elements in literary contexts as well. As authors attempt to create believable, if fictional, worlds, it is only sensible that they wou .... e same forms of folklore that we often take

Publication date

for .... rmore, those folkloric references may serve liter .... 'or exampl .... isic type .... enomena .... ind of particular interest in this article) he noted that .... isi-militude and local color to a depiction of the life o .... hey may serve "as models for producing folklore-like materials in direct imitation of old folk patterns" (29).

Title of journal

Title of database

HEATHER A. HAAS is Associate Professor of Psychology, LaGrange College, LaGrange, Georgia

Journal of American Folklore 124(492):29–54
Copyright © 2011 by the Board of Trustees of the University of Illinois

Location in database: URL

Location (URL)

Title of journal

Online Journal's Table of Contents

Detailed Record from a Database

Fiction and Film for French Historians
A Cultural Bulletin

Volume 5, Issue 6, April 2015 — *Volume, issue, publication date*

Table of Contents

The Buzz

Waterloo (1970): A Critical Review, by Charles Esdaile — *Author* — *Source title (article)*

Maybe Missed

"When Vice Meets Crime": Jean-Claude Brisville's *Le Souper*, by Philip Dwyer

GALE Academic OneFile — Search... — Basic Search

Title of source (article) — Download PDF | Related Resources

The Wisdom of Wizards--and Muggles and Squibs: proverb use in the World of Harry Potter

Heather A. Haas ← *Author*

Journal of American Folklore. 124.492 (Spring 2011): p29. ←

Title of journal

Publication information: volume, issue, date, location (page numbers)

FIGURE 20.2 Documentation Map for a Journal Article For a print journal, look for the title of the journal on the front cover or in the table of contents. The author and article title will also be listed there; they will, of course, appear on the first page of the article (shown here) as well. The information you will need to cite an article you access through a database will appear in the list of results, the detailed record of the article, and the PDF (or HTML) version of the article itself. For an article published in an electronic journal, look for the information you need to create the works-cited entry on the journal's home page, the table of contents, or the page on which the article appears. Sometimes the URL that appears in your browser's address bar is not the best way to cite your source. Some databases provide shorter, more stable permalinks for journal articles, often as part of a sharing feature or detailed record. If your source has a DOI, use this instead of the URL. DOIs may be listed near the beginning of an article, on the top or bottom of all pages in a PDF, or in the detailed record for the source in a database. You can look up the DOI for any source that has one at www.crossref.org.

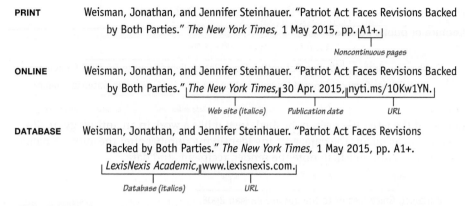

PRINT   Weisman, Jonathan, and Jennifer Steinhauer. "Patriot Act Faces Revisions Backed
by Both Parties." *The New York Times,* 1 May 2015, pp. A1+.

Noncontinuous pages

ONLINE   Weisman, Jonathan, and Jennifer Steinhauer. "Patriot Act Faces Revisions Backed
by Both Parties." *The New York Times,* 30 Apr. 2015, nyti.ms/1OKw1YN.

Web site (italics)   *Publication date*   *URL*

DATABASE   Weisman, Jonathan, and Jennifer Steinhauer. "Patriot Act Faces Revisions
Backed by Both Parties." *The New York Times,* 1 May 2015, pp. A1+.
LexisNexis Academic, www.lexisnexis.com.

Database (italics)   *URL*

From a magazine Magazines (like newspapers) are identified by date, with the names
of months longer than four letters abbreviated. For magazines published weekly or
biweekly, include the day, month, and year; for magazines published monthly or
bimonthly, include the month and year. If the article is unsigned, alphabetize entries
by the first important word in the title (ignoring *A, An,* and *The*).

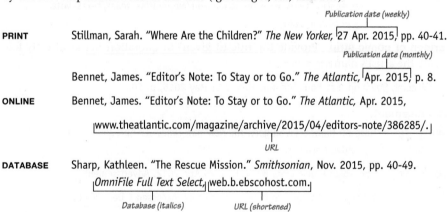

Publication date (weekly)

PRINT   Stillman, Sarah. "Where Are the Children?" *The New Yorker,* 27 Apr. 2015, pp. 40-41.

Publication date (monthly)

Bennet, James. "Editor's Note: To Stay or to Go." *The Atlantic,* Apr. 2015, p. 8.

ONLINE   Bennet, James. "Editor's Note: To Stay or to Go." *The Atlantic,* Apr. 2015,
www.theatlantic.com/magazine/archive/2015/04/editors-note/386285/.

URL

DATABASE   Sharp, Kathleen. "The Rescue Mission." *Smithsonian,* Nov. 2015, pp. 40-49.
OmniFile Full Text Select, web.b.ebscohost.com.

Database (italics)   *URL (shortened)*

Editorial or letter to the editor

"City's Blight Fight Making Difference." *The Columbus Dispatch,* 17 Nov. 2015, www.dispatch
.com/content/stories/editorials/2015/11/17/1-citys-blight-fight-making-difference
.html. Editorial.

Fahey, John A. "Recalling the Cuban Missile Crisis." *The Washington Post,* 28 Oct. 2012,
p. A16. Letter. *LexisNexis Library Express,* www.lexisnexis.com.

Review If the review does not include an author's name, start the entry with the title of
the review; then add *Review of* and the title of the work being reviewed. If the review is
untitled, include the *Review of* description immediately after the author's name. For a
review in an online newspaper or magazine, add the URL, ideally a permalink. For a
review accessed through a database, add the database title (in italics) and the DOI or URL.

Deparle, Jason. "Assimilation Nation." Review of *Exodus: How Migration Is Changing Our
World,* by Paul Collier. *The Atlantic,* Nov. 2013, pp. 44-46.

Multimedia Sources (Live, Print, Electronic, Database)

Lecture or public address

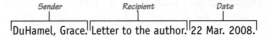

Title of lecture

Stephenson, Brittany. "'Wading Out of Web Stew: Reader-Centric Course Design.'" Conference on College Composition and Communication, 20 Mar. 2015, Marriott Waterside, Tampa.

Date of lecture   *Location of conference*

Letter If the letter has been published, treat it like a work in an anthology (p. 564), but add the recipient, the date, and any identifying number after the author's name. If the letter is unpublished, note the sender, recipient, and date.

Sender   *Recipient*   *Date*

DuHamel, Grace. Letter to the author. 22 Mar. 2008.

Map or chart

PRINT *Map of Afghanistan and Surrounding Territory*. GiziMap, 2001.

ONLINE "Vote on Secession, 1861." *Perry-Castañeda Library Map Collection*, U of Texas at Austin, 1976, www.lib.utexas.edu/maps/atlas_texas/texas_vote _secession_1861.jpg.

Cartoon or comic strip Provide the title (if given) in quotation marks directly following the artist's name.

Wheeler, Shannon. Cartoon. *The New Yorker,* 11 May 2015, p. 50.

Advertisement

PRINT Hospital for Special Surgery. *The New York Times,* 13 Apr. 2009, p. A7. Advertisement.

BROADCAST Norwegian Cruise Line. *WNET,* PBS, 29 Apr. 2012. Advertisement.

ONLINE Volkswagen Passat. *Slate,* www.slate.com/. Accessed 1 Dec. 2011. Advertisement.

Access date (no pub date available)

Work of art Include the year the work was created, and provide the museum or collection and its location. If you accessed the work online, include the Web site name and the URL.

Location

MUSEUM Palmer Payne, Elsie. *Sheep Dipping Time*. c. 1930s, Nevada Museum of Art, Reno.

PRINT Chihuly, Dale. *Carmine and White Flower Set*. 1987, Tacoma Art Museum. *Dale Chihuly: A Celebration,* Abrams Press, 2011, p. 109.

Print publication information   *Web site*

ONLINE Sekaer, Peter. *A Sign Business Shop, New York*. 1935, *International Center of Photography,* www.icp.org/exhibitions/signs-of-life-photographs-by-peter -sekaer.

Location (URL)

Musical composition

> Beethoven, Ludwig van. Violin Concerto in D Major, op. 61. 1809. IMSLP Music Library,
>
>   imslp.org/wiki/Violin_Concerto_in_D_major,_Op.61_(Beethoven,_Ludwig_van).
>
> Gershwin, George. *Porgy and Bess*. 1935. Alfred A. Knopf, 1999.

Performance

> *The Draft*. Directed by Diego Arciniegas, 10 Sept. 2015, Hibernian Hall, Boston.
>
> Beethoven, Ludwig van. Piano Concerto no. 3. Conducted by Andris Nelsons, performances
>
>   by Paul Lewis and Boston Symphony Orchestra, 9 Oct. 2015, Symphony Hall, Boston.

Television show, radio program, or podcast Include the network and broadcast date. If you streamed the program, treat the streaming service like a second "container" (see p. 559): At the end of your entry, include information about the streaming service (its name and a URL). Separate program information from database information with a period. If you streamed or downloaded the program through an app, like an iPhone's *Podcasts*, list the app as you would a streaming service or database. Treat a podcast that you listened to or watched online as you would a streamed television or radio program.

	Episode / Program / Key contributors
BROADCAST	"Being Mortal." *Frontline*, written by Atul Gawande and Tom Jennings, directed by Tom Jennings and Nisha Pahuja, PBS, 22 Nov. 2011.

Network Broadcast date

STREAMED	"The Choice." *The Borgias*, directed by Kari Skogland, season 2, episode 5, Showtime, 6 May 2012. *Netflix*, www.netflix.com/watch/70261634.
DOWNLOADED (OR VIA APP)	"Patient Zero." *Radio Lab*, hosted by Jad Abumrad and Robert Krulwich, season 10, episode 4, National Public Radio, 14 Nov. 2011. *Podcasts*, iTunes.

Film

THEATER	*Space Station*. Produced and directed by Toni Myers, narrated by Tom Cruise, IMAX, 2002.
DVD	*Casablanca*. Directed by Michael Curtiz, performances by Humphrey Bogart, Ingrid Bergman, and Paul Henreid, 1942. Warner Home Video, 2003.

Online video

> Film School. "Sunny Day." *YouTube*, 12 June 2010, www.youtube.com/watch?v=8oTJFUCbsfI.

Music recording

> Beethoven, Ludwig van. Violin Concerto in D Major, op. 61. Performances by David Oistrakh
>
>   and the U.S.S.R. State Orchestra, conducted by Alexander Gauk, Allegro Music, 1980.
>
> Maroon 5. "Moves Like Jagger." *Hands All Over*, A&M Octone Records, 2011.

Interview

PRINT   Ashrawi, Hanan. "Tanks vs. Olive Branches." Interview by Rose Marie Berger.
            Sojourners, Feb. 2005, pp. 22-26.

BROADCAST   Dobbs, Bill. "Occupy Wall Street." Interview by Brooke Gladstone. *On the
            Media,* National Public Radio, 7 Oct. 2011, www.wnyc.org/story/163283
            -occupy-wall-street/.

PERSONAL   Ellis, Trey. Personal interview, 3 Sept. 2015.

Other Electronic Sources

Online sources have proliferated in the last ten years. With that proliferation has come
access to more information than ever before. But not all of that information is of equal
value. Before including a source found on *Google* in your research project, be sure that
it is appropriate for a college-level writing project, and evaluate its reliability carefully.

  If you are using the online version of a source for which there is no model shown
here, choose the model that best matches your source and add any other information
that readers will need to find the source themselves. If an online source does not
include a publication date or information about its latest update, provide the date
you accessed it at the end of your entry. Separate access information from source
information with a period.

For help evaluating online
sources, see Chapter 18.

Web page or other document on a Web site

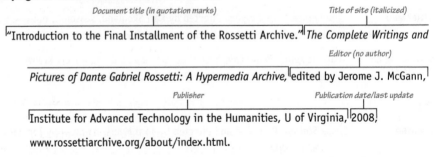

Figure 20.3 shows where to find the source information you will need to create a
works-cited entry for the Web page cited here.

Entire Web site or online scholarly project   If the author's name is not given, begin
the citation with the title.

Gardner, James Alan. *A Seminar on Writing Prose.* 2001, www.thinkage.ca/~jim/prose/
    prose.htm.

McGann, Jerome J., editor. *The Complete Writings and Pictures of Dante Gabriel Rossetti:
    A Hypermedia Archive.* Institute for Advanced Technology in the Humanities, U of
    Virginia, 2008, www.rossettiarchive.org/index.html.

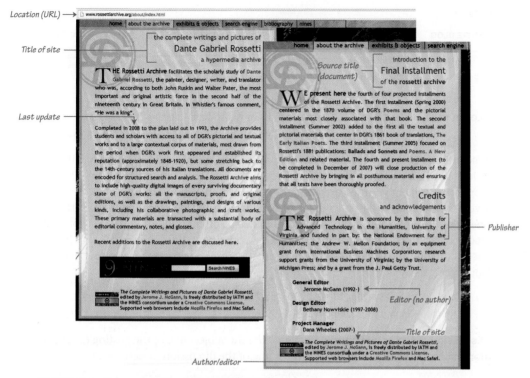

Location (URL) — www.rossettiarchive.org/about/index.html

Title of site

Last update

Source title (document)

Publisher

Editor (no author)

Title of site

Author/editor

FIGURE 20.3   Documentation Map for a Web Page

Look for the author or editor and title of the Web page on the Web page itself. The title of the Web site may appear on the Web page, on the site's home page, or both. The publisher (sponsor) may be listed at the bottom of the Web page, on the home page, or somewhere else. (Look for an "About Us," "Who We Are," or "Contact Us" page.) If no publication or copyright date or "last update" appears on the Web page, the home page, or elsewhere on the site, include a date of access at the end of your works-cited entry. Otherwise, conclude with a permalink or the URL provided in your browser's address bar.

Book or a short work in an online scholarly project   Treat a book or a short work in an online scholarly project as you would a Web page or another document on a Web site, but set the title in italics if the work is a book and in quotation marks if it is an article, an essay, a poem, or some other short work, and include the print publication information (if relevant to your particular use) following the title.

> Heims, Marjorie. "The Strange Case of Sarah Jones." *The Free Expression Policy Project*, 2 Nov. 2011, www.fepproject.org/commentaries/sarahjones.html.

Original publication date

> Corelli, Marie. *The Treasure of Heaven.* 1906. *Victorian Women Writers Project,* edited by Percy Willett, Indiana U, 10 July 1999, webapp1.dlib.indiana.edu/vwwp/ view?docId=VAB7176.

Blog   Cite an entire blog as you would an entire Web site (see p. 572). If the author of the blog or blog post uses a pseudonym (or *handle*), use it in place of the author's real name. If you know the author's real name, include it in parentheses following the pseudonym.

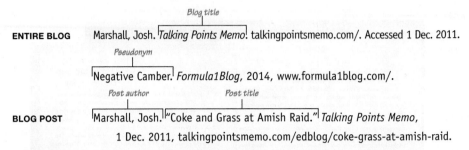

ENTIRE BLOG   Marshall, Josh. *Talking Points Memo*. talkingpointsmemo.com/. Accessed 1 Dec. 2011.

Negative Camber. *Formula1Blog*, 2014, www.formula1blog.com/.

BLOG POST   Marshall, Josh. "Coke and Grass at Amish Raid." *Talking Points Memo*,
1 Dec. 2011, talkingpointsmemo.com/edblog/coke-grass-at-amish-raid.

Wiki article   Since wikis are written and edited collectively, start your entry with the title of the article you are citing. But check with your instructor before using information from a wiki in your research project; because content is written and edited collectively, it is difficult to assess its reliability and impossible to determine the expertise of the contributors. Some wikis, such as *Wikipedia*, offer unique permalinks for each updated version of every article (click on "Permanent link" under "Tools" in the menu). If you cannot locate a unique permalink for the version you're citing, include your access date.

"John Lydon." *Wikipedia*, 19 Mar. 2016, 3:17 a.m., en.wikipedia.org/w/index.php ?title=John_Lydon&oldid=710801155.

Discussion group or newsgroup posting   Use the subject line of the posting (in quotation marks) as the title, and include the name of the discussion or newsgroup.

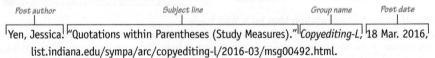

Yen, Jessica. "Quotations within Parentheses (Study Measures)." *Copyediting-L*, 18 Mar. 2016, list.indiana.edu/sympa/arc/copyediting-l/2016-03/msg00492.html.

E-mail message

Olson, Kate. "Update on State Legislative Grants." Received by Alissa Brown, 5 Nov. 2015.

Tweet

@grammarphobia (Patricia T. O'Conner and Steward Kellerman). "Is 'if you will,' like, a verbal tic? http://goo.gl/oYrTYP #English #language #grammar #etymology #usage #linguistics #WOTD." Twitter, 14 Mar. 2016, 9:12 a.m., twitter.com/grammarphobia.

Student Research Project in MLA Style

Student Cristina Dinh uses MLA documentation style in her research project on home schooling, which follows. As you work on college writing projects in the humanities, use the formatting instructions in this paper as a guide, but be sure to check with your instructor before preparing a final draft. Some instructors may prefer that you use APA or another style.

1"

1/2"

1"

Dinh 1

1"

Cristina Dinh

Professor Cooper

English 100

15 May 2015

Educating Kids at Home

Every morning, Mary Jane, who is nine, doesn't have to worry about gulping down her cereal so she can be on time for school. School for Mary Jane is literally right at her doorstep.

In this era of serious concern about the quality of public education, increasing numbers of parents across the United States are choosing to educate their children at home. These parents believe they can do a better job teaching their children than their local schools can. *Home schooling,* as this practice is known, has become a national trend over the past thirty years, and according to education specialist Brian D. Ray, the home-schooled population is growing at a rate between 5% and 12% per year. A 2008 report by the U.S. Department of Education's Institute of Education Sciences estimated that, nationwide, the number of home-schooled children rose from 850,000 in 1999 to approximately 1.5 million in 2007 (*Issue Brief* 1). Some home-schooling advocates believe that even these numbers may be low because not all states require formal notification when parents decide to teach their children at home.

What is home schooling, and who are the parents choosing to be home-schoolers? David Guterson, a pioneer in the home-schooling movement, defines home schooling as "the attempt to gain an education outside of institutions" (5). Home-schooled children spend the majority of the conventional school day learning in or near their homes rather than in traditional schools; parents or guardians are the prime educators. Former teacher and home-schooler Rebecca Rupp notes that home-schooling parents vary considerably in what they teach and how they teach, ranging from those who follow a highly traditional curriculum within a structure that parallels the typical classroom to those who essentially

1"

Double-spaced

Double-spaced

Title centered; no underlining, quotes, or italics

Paragraphs indented one-half inch

Author named in text; no parenthetical page reference because source is not paginated

Author named in text; parenthetical page reference falls at end of sentence

Dinh 2

allow their children to pursue whatever interests them at their own pace (3). Home-schoolers commonly combine formal instruction with life skills instruction, learning fractions, for example, in terms of monetary units or cooking measurements (Saba and Gattis 89). According to the U.S. Department of Education's 2008 report, while home-schoolers are also a diverse group politically and philosophically — libertarians, conservatives, Christian fundamentalists — most say they home school for one of three reasons: they are concerned about the quality of academic instruction, the general school environment, or the lack of religious or moral instruction (Stevens 2).

The first group generally believes that children need individual attention and the opportunity to learn at their own pace to learn well. This group says that one teacher in a classroom of twenty to thirty children (the size of typical public-school classes) cannot give this kind of attention. These parents believe they can give their children greater enrichment and more specialized instruction than public schools can provide. At home, parents can work one-on-one with each child and be flexible about time, allowing their children to pursue their interests at earlier ages. Many of these parents, like home-schooler Peter Bergson, believe that

> home schooling provides more of an opportunity to continue the natural learning process that's in evidence in all children.
>
> [In school,] you change the learning process from self-directed to other-directed, from the child asking questions to the teacher asking questions. You shut down areas of potential interest. (qtd. in Kohn 22)

This trend can be traced back to the 1960s, when many people began criticizing traditional schools. Various types of "alternative" schools were created, and some parents began teaching their children at home (Friedlander 150). Parents like this mention several reasons for their disappointment with public schools and for their decision to home school. A lack of funding, for example, leaves children without new textbooks. In a

Annotations (left margin):

Work by two authors cited

Quotation of more than four lines typed as a block and indented a half inch

Brackets indicate alteration of quotation

Parenthetical citation of secondary source falls after period when quotation is indented as a block

Dinh 3

2002 survey, 31% of teachers said that their students are using textbooks that are more than ten years old, and 29% said that they do not have enough textbooks for all of their students (National Education Association). Many schools also cannot afford to buy laboratory equipment and other teaching materials. At my own high school, the chemistry teacher told me that most of the lab equipment we used came from a research firm he worked for. In a 2006 Gallup poll, lack of proper financial support ranked first on the list of the problems in public schools (Rose and Gallup 45).

> Corporate author's name cited

Parents also cite overcrowding as a reason for taking their kids out of school. The more students in a classroom, the less learning that goes on, as Cafi Cohen discovered before choosing to home school; after spending several days observing what went on in her child's classroom, she found that administrative duties, including disciplining, took up to 80% of a teacher's time, with only 20% of the day devoted to learning (6). Moreover, faced with a large group of children, a teacher ends up gearing lessons to the students in the middle level, so children at both ends miss out. Gifted children and those with learning disabilities particularly suffer in this situa-tion. At home, parents of these children say they can tailor the material and the pace for each child. Studies show that home-schooling methods seem to work well in preparing children academically. Lawrence Rudner, director of the ERIC Clearinghouse on Assessment and Evaluation at the University of Maryland and a researcher on home schooling, found that testing of home-schooled students showed them to be between one and three years ahead of public school students their age (xi). Home-schooled children have also made particularly strong showings in academic competitions; since the late 1990s, 10% of National Spelling Bee participants have been home schooled, as have two National Spelling Bee and two National Geographic Bee winners (Lyman). More and more selective colleges are admitting, and even recruit-ing, home-schooled applicants (Basham et al. 15).

> Work by three or more authors cited

Parents in the second group — those concerned with the general school environment — claim that their children are more well-rounded

Dinh 4

than those in school. Because they don't have to sit in classrooms all day, home-schooled kids can pursue their own projects, often combining crafts or technical skills with academic subjects. Home-schoolers participate in outside activities, such as 4-H competitions, field trips with peers in home-school support groups, science fairs, musical and dramatic productions, church activities, and Boy Scouts or Girl Scouts (Saba and Gattis 59-62). In fact, they may even be able to participate to some extent in actual school activities. A 1999 survey conducted by the United States Department of Education's Institute of Education Sciences found that 28% of public schools allowed home-schooled students to participate in extracurricular activities alongside enrolled students, and 20% allowed home-schooled students to attend some classes (Princiotta and Bielick 12).

Many home-schooling parents believe that these activities provide the social opportunities kids need without exposing their children to the peer pressure they would have to deal with as regular school students. For example, many kids think that drinking and using drugs are cool. When I was in high school, my friends would tell me a few drinks wouldn't hurt or affect driving. If I had listened to them, perhaps I wouldn't be alive today. Four of my friends were killed under the influence of alcohol. Between 1992 and 2008, the number of high school seniors surveyed who had used any illicit drug in the last year climbed from 27.1% to 36.6% (Johnston et al. 59).

Work by three or more authors cited

Another reason many parents decide to home school their kids is that they are concerned for their children's safety. Samuel L. Blumenfeld notes that "physical risk" is an important reason many parents remove their children from public schools as "[m]ore and more children are assaulted, robbed, and murdered in school" and a "culture of violence, abetted by rap music, drug trafficking, . . . and racial tension, has engulfed teenagers" (4). Beginning in the mid-1990s, a string of school shootings — including the 1999 massacres in Littleton, Colorado, and Conyers, Georgia, and the 2001 massacre in Santee, California — has led to increasing fears that young people are simply not safe at school.

Dinh 5

While all of the reasons mentioned so far are important, perhaps the single most significant cause of the growing home-schooling trend is Christian fundamentalist dissatisfaction with "godless" public schools. Sociologist Mitchell L. Stevens, author of one of the first comprehensive studies of home schooling, cites a mailing sent out by Basic Christian Education, a company that markets home-schooling materials, titled "What Really Happens in Public Schools." This publication sums up the fears of fundamentalist home-schoolers about public schools: that they encourage high levels of teenage sexual activity and pregnancies "out of wedlock"; expose children to "violence, crime, lack of discipline, and, of course, drugs of every kind"; present positive portrayals of communism and socialism and negative portrayals of capitalism; and undermine children's Christian beliefs by promoting "New Age philosophies, Yoga, Tran-scendental Meditation, witchcraft demonstrations, and Eastern religions" (51).

As early as 1988, Luanne Shackelford and Susan White, two Christian home-schooling mothers, were claiming that because schools expose chil-dren to "[p]eer pressure, perverts, secular textbooks, values clarification, TV, pornography, rock music, bad movies[,] . . . [h]ome schooling seems to be the best plan to achieve our goal [to raise good Christians]" (160). As another mother more recently put it:

> I don't like the way schools are going. . . . What's wrong with
> Christianity all of a sudden? You know? This country was founded
> on Christian, on religious principles. [People] came over here for
> religious freedom, and now all of a sudden all religious references
> seem to be stricken out of the public school, and I don't like that
> at all. (qtd. in Stevens 67)

Although many nonfundamentalist home-schoolers make some of these same criticisms, those who cite the lack of "Christian values" in public schools have particular concerns of their own. For example, home-schooling leader Raymond Moore talks of parents who are "'sick and tired of the teaching of evolution in the schools as a cut-and-dried fact,' along with other evidence of so-called secular humanism" (Kohn 21),

Dinh 6

such as textbooks that contain material contradicting Christian beliefs. Moreover, parents worry that schools undermine their children's moral values. In particular, some Christian fundamentalist parents object to sex education in schools, saying that it encourages children to become sexually active early, challenging values taught at home. They see the family as the core and believe that the best place to instill family values is within the family. These Christian home-schooling parents want to provide their children not only with academic knowledge but also with a moral grounding consistent with their religious beliefs.

Still other home-schooling parents object to a perceived government-mandated value system that they believe attempts to override the values, not necessarily religious in nature, of individual families. For these parents, home schooling is a way of resisting what they see as unwarranted intrusion by the federal government into personal concerns ("Is").

Armed with their convictions, parents such as those who belong to the Christian Home School Legal Defense Association have fought in court and lobbied for legislation that allows them the option of home schooling. In the 1970s, most states had compulsory attendance laws that made it difficult, if not illegal, to keep school-age children home from school. Today, home schooling is permitted in every state, with strict regulation required by only a few ("State Action Map"). As a result, Mary Jane is one of hundreds of thousands of American children who can start their school day without leaving the house.

Internet source cited by a shortened form of the title; author name and page numbers unavailable

Source cited by title

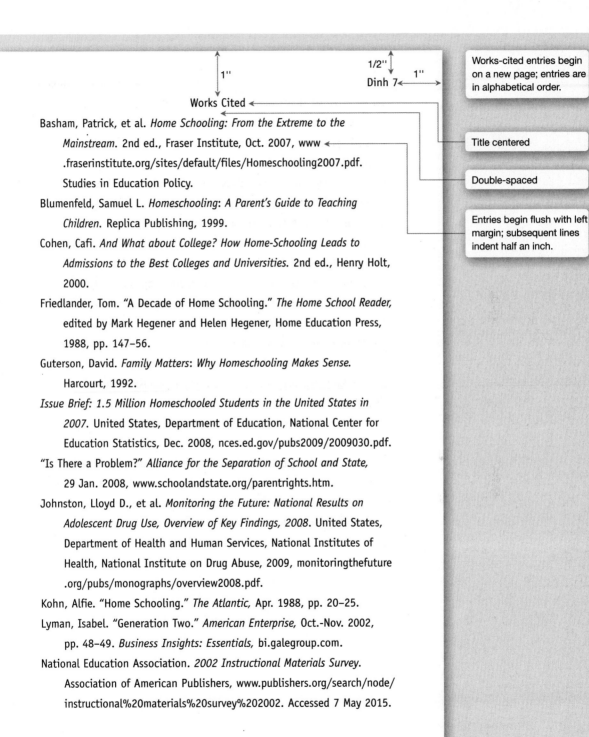

1/2" 1"
Dinh 7

Works Cited

Basham, Patrick, et al. *Home Schooling: From the Extreme to the Mainstream.* 2nd ed., Fraser Institute, Oct. 2007, www.fraserinstitute.org/sites/default/files/Homeschooling2007.pdf. Studies in Education Policy.

Blumenfeld, Samuel L. *Homeschooling: A Parent's Guide to Teaching Children.* Replica Publishing, 1999.

Cohen, Cafi. *And What about College? How Home-Schooling Leads to Admissions to the Best Colleges and Universities.* 2nd ed., Henry Holt, 2000.

Friedlander, Tom. "A Decade of Home Schooling." *The Home School Reader,* edited by Mark Hegener and Helen Hegener, Home Education Press, 1988, pp. 147–56.

Guterson, David. *Family Matters: Why Homeschooling Makes Sense.* Harcourt, 1992.

Issue Brief: 1.5 Million Homeschooled Students in the United States in 2007. United States, Department of Education, National Center for Education Statistics, Dec. 2008, nces.ed.gov/pubs2009/2009030.pdf.

"Is There a Problem?" *Alliance for the Separation of School and State,* 29 Jan. 2008, www.schoolandstate.org/parentrights.htm.

Johnston, Lloyd D., et al. *Monitoring the Future: National Results on Adolescent Drug Use, Overview of Key Findings, 2008.* United States, Department of Health and Human Services, National Institutes of Health, National Institute on Drug Abuse, 2009, monitoringthefuture.org/pubs/monographs/overview2008.pdf.

Kohn, Alfie. "Home Schooling." *The Atlantic,* Apr. 1988, pp. 20–25.

Lyman, Isabel. "Generation Two." *American Enterprise,* Oct.-Nov. 2002, pp. 48–49. *Business Insights: Essentials,* bi.galegroup.com.

National Education Association. *2002 Instructional Materials Survey.* Association of American Publishers, www.publishers.org/search/node/instructional%20materials%20survey%202002. Accessed 7 May 2015.

Dinh 8

Princiotta, Daniel, and Stacey Bielick. *Homeschooling in the United States:
2003.* United States, Department of Education, Institute of Education
Sciences, National Center for Education Statistics, 2006, nces.ed.gov/
pubs2006/2006042.pdf.

Ray, Brian D. "Research Facts on Home Schooling." *National Home
Education Research Institute,* 23 Mar. 2015, www.nheri.org/research/
research-facts-on-homeschooling.html.

Rose, Lowell C., and Alec M. Gallup. "The 38th Annual Phi Delta Kappa/
Gallup Poll of the Public's Attitudes toward the Public Schools."
Phi Delta Kappan, vol. 88, no. 1, Sept. 2006, pp. 41–56. *Larry Cuban
on School Reform and Classroom Practice,* larrycuban.files.wordpress
.com/2012/10/k0609pol.pdf.

Rudner, Lawrence. Foreword. *The McGraw-Hill Home-Schooling Companion,*
by Laura Saba and Julie Gattis, McGraw-Hill, 2002, pp. xi–xiii.

Rupp, Rebecca. *The Complete Home Learning Source Book.* Three Rivers
Press, 1998.

Saba, Laura, and Julie Gattis. *The McGraw-Hill Home-Schooling Companion.*
McGraw-Hill, 2002.

Shackelford, Luanne, and Susan White. *A Survivor's Guide to Home Schooling.*
Crossway, 1988.

"State Action Map." *Home School Legal Defense Association,* 2011, www
.hslda.org/hs/state/.

Stevens, Mitchell L. *Kingdom of Children: Culture and Controversy in the
Homeschooling Movement.* Princeton UP, 2001.

Untitled section labeled

21

Citing and Documenting Sources in APA Style

When using the APA system of documentation, include both an in-text citation and a list of references at the end of the research project. **In-text citations** tell your readers where the ideas or words you have borrowed come from, and the entries in the **list of references** provide readers with the information they need to locate your sources so that they can read more about your topic.

The most common types of in-text citations and reference-list models follow. For other, less common citation types, consult the *Publication Manual of the American Psychological Association,* Sixth Edition. Most libraries will own a copy.

Citing Sources in the Text

When citing ideas, information, or words borrowed from a source, include the author's last name and the date of publication in the text of your research project. In most cases, you will want to use a *signal phrase* to introduce the works you are citing, since doing so gives you the opportunity to put the work and its author in context. A signal phrase includes the author's last name, the date of publication, and a verb that describes the author's attitude or stance:

Smith (2015) complained that . . .

Jones (2015) defended her position by . . .

Use a parenthetical citation — *(Jones, 2015)* — when you have already introduced the author or the work or when citing the source of an uncontroversial fact. When quoting from a source, also include the page number: *Smith (2015) complained that he "never got a break" (p. 123).* When you are paraphrasing or summarizing, you may omit the page reference, although including it is not wrong.

Directory to In-Text-Citation Models

One author

SIGNAL PHRASE   Upton Sinclair (2005), a crusading journalist, wrote that workers sometimes "fell into the vats; and when they were fished out, there was never enough of them left to be worth exhibiting" (p. 134).

PARENTHETICAL CITATION   *The Jungle,* a naturalistic novel inspired by the French writer Zola, described in lurid detail the working conditions of the time, including what became of unlucky workers who fell into the vats while making sausage (Sinclair, 2005, p. 134).

Author's last name + Date + Page

REFERENCE-LIST ENTRY   Sinclair, U. (2005). *The jungle.* New York, NY: Oxford University Press.
   (Original work published 1906)

More than one author   In a signal phrase, use the word *and* between the authors' names; in a parenthetical citation, use an ampersand (&). When citing a work by three to five authors, list all the authors in your first reference; in subsequent references, just cite the first and use *et al.* (Latin for *and others*).

SIGNAL PHRASE   As Jamison and Tyree (2001) have found, racial bias does not diminish merely through exposure to individuals of other races.

PARENTHETICAL CITATION   Racial bias does not diminish through exposure (Jamison & Tyree, 2001).

FIRST CITATION   Rosenzweig, Breedlove, and Watson (2005) wrote that biological psychology is an interdisciplinary field that includes scientists from "quite different backgrounds" (p. 3).

LATER CITATIONS   Biological psychology is "the field that relates behavior to bodily processes, especially the workings of the brain" (Rosenzweig et al., 2005, p. 3).

For works with more than five authors, cite the first author and use *et al.* for the first and subsequent references.

Unknown author   To cite a work when the author is unknown, the APA suggests using a shortened version of the title. (The full title of the article cited below is "Plastic Is Found in the Sargasso Sea; Pieces of Apparent Refuse Cover Wide Atlantic Region.")

> An international pollution treaty still to be ratified would prohibit all plastic garbage from being dumped at sea ("Plastic Is Found," 1972).

Two or more works by the same author in the same year   When your list of references includes two works by the same author, the year of publication is usually enough to distinguish them. Occasionally, though, you may have two works by the same author in the same year. If this happens, alphabetize the works by title in your list of references, and add a lowercase letter after the date (2005a, 2005b).

> Middle-class unemployed are better off than their lower-class counterparts, because they "are likely to have some assets to invest in their job search" (Ehrenreich, 2005b, p. 16).

Two or more authors with the same last name   Include the author's initials.

> F. Johnson (2010) conducted an intriguing study on teen smoking.

Corporation, organization, or government agency as author   Spell out the name of the organization the first time you use it, but abbreviate it in subsequent citations if readers will know what the abbreviation refers to.

> (National Institutes of Health, 2015)
> (NIH, 2015)

Indirect citation (quotation from a secondary source)   To quote material taken not from the original source but from a secondary source that quotes the original, give the secondary source in the reference list, and acknowledge the original but cite the secondary source in your essay.

> E. M. Forster said "the collapse of all civilization, so realistic for us, sounded in Matthew Arnold's ears like a distant and harmonious cataract" (as cited in Trilling, 1955, p. 11).

Two or more works cited in the same parentheses   List sources in alphabetical order, separated by semicolons.

> (Johnson, 2014; NIH, 2015)

Creating a List of References

Directory to Reference-List Models

Author Listings

When the list of references includes several works by the same author, the APA provides the following rules for arranging these entries in the list:

- Same-name single-author entries precede multiple-author entries:

    Zettelmeyer, F. (2000).

    Zettelmeyer, F., Morton, F. S., & Silva-Risso, J. (2006).

- Entries with the same first author and a different second author are alphabetized under the first author according to the second author's last name:

    Dhar, R., & Nowlis, S. M. (2004).

    Dhar, R., & Simonson, I. (2003).

- Entries by the same authors are arranged by year of publication, in chronological order:

    Golder, P. N., & Tellis, G. J. (2003).

    Golder, P. N., & Tellis, G. J. (2004).

- Entries by the same authors with the same publication year should be arranged alphabetically by title (according to the first word after *A, An,* or *The*), and lower-case letters (*a, b, c,* and so on) should be appended to the year in parentheses:

Aaron, P. (1990a). Basic . . .

Aaron, P. (1990b). Elements . . .

One author

Schneier, B. (2015). *Data and Goliath: The hidden battles to collect your data and control your world*. New York, NY: Norton.

More than one author

Robinson, K., & Aronica, L. (2015). *Creative schools: The grassroots revolution that's transforming education*. New York, NY: Viking.

Hunt, L., Po-Chia Hsia, R., Martin, T. R., Rosenwein, B. H., Rosenwein, H., & Smith, B. G. (2001). *The making of the West: Peoples and cultures*. Boston, MA: Bedford.

If there are more than seven authors, list only the first six, insert ellipsis marks (. . .), and add the last author's name.

Unknown author   Begin the entry with the title.

Communities blowing whistle on street basketball. (2003, June 2). *USA Today*, p. 20A.

If an author is designated as "Anonymous," include the word *Anonymous* in place of the author, and alphabetize it as "Anonymous" in the reference list.

Anonymous. (2006). *Primary colors*. New York, NY: Random House.

Corporation, organization, or government agency as author

American Medical Association. (2004). *Family medical guide*. Hoboken, NJ: Wiley.

Two or more works by the same author

When you cite two or more works by the same author, arrange them in chronological (time) order.

Pinker, S. (2005). So how does the mind work? *Mind and Language, 20*(1), 1–24. doi:10.1111/j.0268-1064.2005.00274.x

Pinker, S. (2011). *The better angels of our nature: Why violence has declined*. New York, NY: Viking.

When you cite two works by the same author in the same year, alphabetize entries by title and then add a lowercase letter following each year.

Pinker, S. (2005a). *Hotheads*. New York, NY: Pocket Penguins.

Pinker, S. (2005b). So how does the mind work? *Mind and Language, 20*(1), 1–24. doi:10.1111/j.0268-1064.2005.00274.x

Books (Print, Electronic)

When citing a book, capitalize only the first word of the title and subtitle and any proper nouns (*Dallas, Darwin*). Book titles are italicized.

Basic format for a book

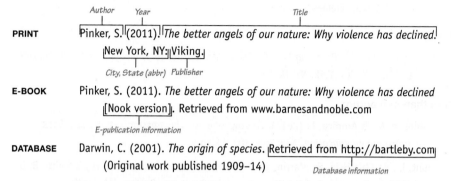

PRINT

Pinker, S. (2011). *The better angels of our nature: Why violence has declined.* New York, NY: Viking.

E-BOOK

Pinker, S. (2011). *The better angels of our nature: Why violence has declined* [Nook version]. Retrieved from www.barnesandnoble.com

DATABASE

Darwin, C. (2001). *The origin of species.* Retrieved from http://bartleby.com (Original work published 1909–14)

If an e-book has been assigned a **digital object identifier** (or *doi*)—a combination of numbers and letters assigned by the publisher to identify the work—add that information at the end of the citation.

Author and editor

Arnold, M. (1994). *Culture and anarchy.* (S. Lipman, Ed.). New Haven, CT: Yale University Press. (Original work published 1869)

Edited collection

Waldman, D., & Walker, J. (Eds.). (1999). *Feminism and documentary.* Minneapolis: University of Minnesota Press.

Work in an anthology or edited collection

Fairbairn-Dunlop, P. (1993). Women and agriculture in western Samoa. In J. H. Momsen & V. Kinnaird (Eds.), *Different places, different voices* (pp. 211–226). London, England: Routledge.

Translation

Tolstoy, L. (2002). *War and peace* (C. Garnett, Trans.). New York, NY: Modern Library. (Original work published 1869)

Dictionary entry or article in another reference book

Rowland, R. P. (2001). Myasthenia gravis. In M. Shally-Jensen (Ed.), *Encyclopedia Americana* (Vol. 19, p. 683). Danbury, CT: Grolier.

Introduction, preface, foreword, or afterword

Graff, G., & Phelan, J. (2004). Preface. In M. Twain, *Adventures of Huckleberry Finn* (pp. iii–vii). Boston, MA: Bedford.

Later edition of a book

Axelrod, R., & Cooper, C. (2019). *The St. Martin's guide to writing* (12th ed.). Boston, MA: Bedford.

Government document

U.S. Department of Health and Human Services. (2009). *Trends in underage drinking in the United States, 1991–2007*. Washington, DC: Government Printing Office.

Note: When the author and publisher are the same, use the word *Author* (not italicized) as the name of the publisher.

Unpublished doctoral dissertation

Bullock, B. (1986). *Basic needs fulfillment among less developed countries: Social progress over two decades of growth* (Unpublished doctoral dissertation). Vanderbilt University, Nashville, TN.

Articles (Print, Electronic)

For articles, capitalize only the first word of the title, proper nouns (*Barclay, Berlin*), and the first word following a colon (if any). Omit quotation marks around the titles of articles, but capitalize all the important words of journal, newspaper, and magazine titles, and set them in italics. If you are accessing an article through a database, follow the model for a comparable source.

From a scholarly journal

Author   *Year*   *Article title*

PRINT   Kardefelt-Winther, D. (2015). A critical account of DSM-5 criteria for Internet gaming disorder. *Addiction Research and Theory, 23*(2), 93–98.

Journal title   *Volume (issue) Pages*

Goodboy, A. K., & Martin, M. M. (2015). The personality profile of a cyberbully: Examining the dark triad. *Computers in Human Behavior, 49,* 1–4.

Volume only Pages

Include the digital object identifier (or *doi*) when available. When a doi has not been assigned, include the journal's URL.

ELECTRONIC   Goodboy, A. K., & Martin, M. M. (2015). The personality profile of a cyberbully: Examining the dark triad. *Computers in Human Behavior, 49,* 1–4. doi:10.1016/j.chb.2015.02.052

DOI

Houston, R. G., & Toma, F. (2003). Home schooling: An alternative school choice. *Southern Economic Journal, 69*(4), 920–936. Retrieved from http://www.southerneconomic.org

URL

From a newspaper

Year Month Day

PRINT   Peterson, A. (2003, May 20). Finding a cure for old age. *The Wall Street Journal*, pp. D1, D5.

ELECTRONIC   Zimmer, C. (2015, May 6). Under the sea, a missing link in the evolution of complex cells. *The New York Times*. Retrieved from http://www.nytimes.com

From a magazine

If a magazine is published weekly or biweekly (every other week), include the full date following the author's name. If it is published monthly or bimonthly, include just the year and month (or months).

Weekly or biweekly

PRINT   Gladwell, M. (2013, September 9). Man and superman. *The New Yorker, 89*(27), 76–80.

Monthly or bimonthly

Freeland, C. (2015, May). Globalization bites back. *The Atlantic, 315*(4), 82–86.

ELECTRONIC   Freeland, C. (2015, May). Globalization bites back. *The Atlantic, 315*(4). Retrieved from http://theatlantic.com

Editorial or letter to the editor

Kosinski, T. (2012, May 15). Who cares what she thinks? [Letter to the editor]. *The Chicago Sun-Times*. Retrieved from http://www.suntimes.com/opinions/letters/12522890-474/who-cares-what-she-thinks.html

Review

"Review of" + item type + title of item reviewed

Deparle, J. (2013, November). Assimilation Nation [Review of the book *Exodus: How Migration Is Changing Our World*, by P. Collier]. *The Atlantic, 312*(4), 44–46.

If the review is untitled, use the bracketed information as the title, retaining the brackets.

Multimedia Sources (Print, Electronic)

Television program

Label

O'Connell, C. (Writer and director). (2015, Jan. 6). Ripley: Believe it or not [Television series episode]. In H. Hampton & S. Fitzmeyer (Creators), *American experience*. Boston, MA: WGBH.

Film, video, or DVD

Label

Nolan, C. (Writer and director). (2010). *Inception* [Motion picture]. Los Angeles, CA:
Warner Bros.

Sound recording

PODCAST   Dubner, S. (2012, May 17). Retirement kills [Audio podcast]. *Freakonomics*
radio. Retrieved from http://www.freakonomics.com

Label

RECORDING   Maroon 5. (2010). Moves like Jagger. On *Hands all over* [CD]. New York, NY:
A&M/Octone Records.

Interview   Do not list personal interviews in your reference list. Instead, cite the interviewee in your text (last name and initials), and in parentheses give the notation *personal communication* (in regular type, not italicized) followed by a comma and the date
of the interview. For published interviews, use the appropriate format for an article.

Other Electronic Sources

A rule of thumb for citing electronic sources not covered in one of the preceding
sections is to include enough information to allow readers to access and retrieve the
source. For most online sources, provide as much of the following as you can:

- Name of author
- Date of publication or most recent update (in parentheses; if unavailable, use the
  abbreviation *n.d.*)
- Title of document (such as a Web page)
- Title of Web site
- Any special retrieval information, such as a URL; include the date you last
  accessed the source only when the content is likely to change or be updated
  (as on a wiki, for example)

Web site   The APA does not require an entry in the list of references for entire Web
sites. Instead, give the name of the site in your text with its Web address in
parentheses.

Web page or document on a Web site

American Cancer Society. (2011, Oct. 10). *Child and teen tobacco use*. Retrieved
from http://www.cancer.org/Cancer/CancerCauses/TobaccoCancer/
ChildandTeenTobaccoUse/child-and-teen-tobacco-use-what-to-do

Heins, M. (2014, September 4). Untangling the Steven Salaita case. In *The free expression
policy project*. Retrieved from http://www.fepproject.org/commentaries/Salaita.html

Discussion list and newsgroup postings   Include online postings in your list of references only if you can provide data that would allow others to retrieve the source.

Label

Paikeday, T. (2005, October 10). "Esquivalience" is out [Electronic mailing list message].
   Retrieved from http://listserv.linguistlist.org/cgi-bin/wa?A1=ind0510b&L=ads-1#1

Label

Ditmire, S. (2005, February 10). NJ tea party [Newsgroup message]. Retrieved from
   http://groups.google.com/group/TeaParty

Blog post

Label

Mestel, R. (2012, May 17). Fructose makes rats dumber [Web log post]. Retrieved from
   http://www.latimes.com/health/boostershots/la-fructose-makes-rats-stupid
   -brain-20120517,0,2305241.story?track=rss

Wiki entry   Start with the article title and include the post date (or *n.d.,* if there is no date), since wikis may be updated frequently, as well as the retrieval date.

Sleep. (2011, November 26). Retrieved February 23, 2018, from Wiki of Science: http://
   wikiofscience.wikidot.com/science:sleep

E-mail message   Personal correspondence, including e-mail, should not be included in your reference list. Instead, cite the person's name in your text, and in parentheses give the notation *personal communication* (in regular type, not italicized) and the date.

Computer software   If an individual has proprietary rights to the software, cite that person's name as you would for a print text. Otherwise, cite as you would for an anonymous print text.

For more information
on finding sources, see
Chapter 18.

Label

How Computers Work [Computer software]. (1998). Retrieved from Que: http://www
   .howcomputerswork.net/

A Sample Reference List in APA Style

To see the complete text of this student research project in APA style, see Patrick O'Malley's proposal, "More Testing, More Learning" in Chapter 7, pp. 246–52.

1"
1"

References

1"

Beilock, S. (2010, September 3). Stressing about a high-stakes exam

1/2"
carries consequences beyond the test [Web log post]. Retrieved from

http://www.psychologytoday.com/blog/choke/201009/stressing

-about-high-stakes-exam-carries-consequences-beyond-the-test

Belluck, P. (2011, January 20). To really learn, quit studying and take

a test. *The New York Times*. Retrieved from http://www.nytimes

.com/2011/01/21/science/21memory.html

Dendato, K. M., & Diener, D. (1986). Effectiveness of cognitive/relaxation

therapy and study skills training in reducing self-reported anxiety and

improving the academic performance of test-anxious students. *Journal

of Counseling Psychology, 33,* 131–135.

Frederiksen, N. (1984). The real test bias: Influences of testing on

teaching and learning. *American Psychologist, 39,* 193–202.

Karpicke, J. D., & Blunt, J. R. (2011, February 11). Retrieval practice

produces more learning than elaborative studying with concept

mapping. *Science, 331*(6018), 772–775. doi:10.1126/science.1199327

Light, R. J. (1990). *Explorations with students and faculty about teaching,

learning, and student life*. Cambridge, MA: Harvard University Graduate

School of Education and Kennedy School of Government.

Rothblum, E. D., Solomon, L., & Murakami, J. (1986). Affective, cognitive,

and behavioral differences between high and low procrastinators.

Journal of Counseling Psychology, 33, 387–394.

ScienceWatch.com (2008, February). Henry L. Roediger and Jeff Karpicke

talk with ScienceWatch.com and answer a few questions about

this month's fast breaking paper in the field of psychiatry/

psychology [Interview]. Retrieved from http://sciencewatch.com/dr/

fbp/2008/08febfbp/08febfbpRoedigerETAL

Nicolas Ayer/EyeEm/Getty Images

PART 5

Composing Strategies for College and Beyond

22

Analyzing and Composing Multimodal Texts

As readers, we are often confronted by multimodal texts—such as advertisements, videos, or podcasts—that involve more than just words on a page. Whether their purpose is to sell us an idea or a car, spur us to action, or inspire us to dream, these texts require careful analysis of both their key components and their *rhetorical context*. As we "read" a multimodal text, we should ask ourselves a series of questions: Who created it? Where was it published? What *audience* is it addressing? What is it trying to get this audience to think and feel about the subject? How does it attempt to achieve this *purpose*?

As writers, too, we must consider not only what we want to say but also how best we can deliver that message. This means determining who will consume the message (your audience); what you are trying to get your audience to think, feel, or do about the subject; and how you can best achieve your purpose, given the goals, preferences, experiences, and knowledge of your readers. Often we can achieve our purpose with text presented in sentences and organized into paragraphs. But sometimes words alone cannot convey the exact meaning that we have in mind.

Understanding Multimodality

Increasingly, we consume, create, and convey texts in different media (print, digital, or face-to-face) using multiple modes of communication:

- linguistic (words, written or spoken)
- visual (photos, drawings, videos)
- aural (speech, music)
- spatial (layout, white space, paragraph indents)
- gestural (movements of hands, bodies, or text)

Forms of communication that once used only the written word (thank-you notes, books, term papers) or the spoken word (telephone conversations, lectures) are today **multimodal**: They are enhanced with visual or audio components (such as calls on FaceTime or Skype) or even gestural elements (think of the various ways information enters or leaves the screen in Prezi or PowerPoint presentations) for greater impact.

In a sense, all texts are multimodal. Even an essay written in words and printed on paper uses more than just the linguistic mode and the print medium. The fact that a printed text has margins, paragraph indents, headings, or a title centered on the page means that it also uses the spatial mode. If that essay were also illustrated or used color, it would include the visual mode. However, we typically talk about texts as being multimodal when they are composed in a mode that is not primarily linguistic or printed on paper, such as video or images.

Analyzing Multimodal Texts

The primary purpose of this chapter is to help you analyze multimodal texts and give you strategies for composing your own multimodal projects. In your college courses, you may be asked to write entire papers analyzing one or more multimodal texts (paintings or films, for example). You may also find yourself writing papers in which analysis of one or more multimodal texts is included within the context of the larger paper (for example, when analyzing the brochures, television ads, and social media posts authorized by a political candidate in an argument about his or her campaign).

FIGURE 22.1   "Wedding," from the WWF's Beautiful Day U.S. Series

The chart Criteria for Analyzing Multimodal Texts (pp. 598–99) outlines key criteria for analyzing multimodal texts, including questions that will help you think critically about them.

With the Criteria for Analyzing Multimodal Texts in mind, consider the World Wildlife Fund public service announcement (PSA) shown in Figure 22.1. This PSA is primarily visual; its central image is a photo of attractive, smiling young newlyweds. The photo-mounting corners make the image seem as if it is a photo from a wedding album, rather than an ad agency's creation (which would be easier to ignore). The couple's body language (angled toward each other), posture, and facial expressions (gestural mode), as well as their position in the center of the frame (spatial mode), reveal a seemingly conventional photo. But something is wrong: A hurricane rages in the background, and the gale blows the couple's hair forcefully to one side (gestural mode), showers the bride's white gown with mud, and threatens to rip the bouquet from her hand.

CRITERIA FOR ANALYZING MULTIMODAL TEXTS

OVERALL COMPOSITION

- What modes are used in the text: linguistic, visual, aural, spatial, or gestural? What modes are emphasized? Why were these modes chosen over others? What might be lost if other modes were emphasized?

- What tone or mood does the text convey? Is it lighthearted, somber, frightening, shocking, joyful?

- What elements in the text (color, sound, composition, words, people, setting) convey this tone or contribute to the mood?

Linguistic Mode

- What do the words say? Are they recognizable—a well-known slogan, a famous quotation, song lyrics?

- What role do the words play: explanation, identification, or something else?

- Is the tone of the language used humorous? Elegiac? Ironic?

- How are the words incorporated into the text? Are they written or spoken? Are they spoken by someone on- or off-screen or page? How do they relate to the rest of the text?

Visual Mode

- If the text is primarily visual, what is depicted? What is the focal point—that is, the place your eyes are drawn to?

- From what perspective do you view the focal point? Are you looking straight ahead at it, down at it, or up at it? If the text is a photograph, video, or panel from a comic or graphic work, what is the viewer's angle on the work?

- What colors are used? Do these colors have cultural significance? How do they function with other colors (contrast for emphasis, soothing tones for mood, or something else)?

- Are there obvious special effects employed? Are there additional graphic elements? If so, what

do these elements contribute to your reading of the text?

- Who or what is represented? If people are depicted, how would you describe their age, gender, subculture, ethnicity, profession, level of attractiveness, and socioeconomic class? How do these factors relate to other elements in the text and to the intended audience?

- Who is looking at whom? Do the people represented seem conscious of the viewer's gaze?

- What is its setting? Is it recognizable? What is in the background and the foreground?

Aural Mode

- How might the voices heard, songs played, or sound effects used affect the listener's reception of the audio and other elements of the text?

- How does the sound (timbre, cadence, volume, pitch) of the speaker's voice contribute to his or her credibility (authority, trustworthiness, or expertise)?

- If there are multiple voices (such as in interviews or podcast roundtables), what is their relationship?

- Are sound clips recognizable (a popular song, famous speech, sound effect)? What cultural significance do these sound bites have, and how does that affect the message or achieve the author's purpose?

(Continued)

- What tone or mood does the audio create?
- If the audio is a piece of music, does it belong to a recognizable genre (pop, hip-hop, classical)? What is the significance of the genre?

Spatial Mode

- What is the layout of the text? How are the elements arranged on the page or screen?
- How is information grouped (paragraphs, a montage, layers)? How does the organization help the audience read through the text?
- How close do elements appear? Is there a lot of white space, and how does the white space affect the way the audience reads the text?

Gestural Mode

- What do the facial expressions and body language tell you about the attitudes (self-confident, vulnerable, anxious, subservient, angry, aggressive, sad) of and relationships among the people featured (equal, subordinate, in charge)?
- Do the facial expressions and body language complement or contradict the spoken or written language? Is this intentional? What does the relationship reveal?
- How does the text control the way in which you interpret it? If the text is a presentation, are there arrows or special effects that guide your attention? If it is an infographic, a comic strip, or a film, what elements inform you of the order in which you're supposed to read?

RHETORICAL SITUATION

- What is the text's main purpose? Are we being asked to buy a product? Form an opinion or judgment about something? Support a political party's candidate? Take some other kind of action?
- Who is the text's target audience? Is it the instructor? Children? Men? Women? Some sub- or super-set of these groups (African American men, tweens, seniors)?
- Who is the author? Who sponsored its publication? What background/associations do the author and the sponsoring publication have? What other works have they produced?
- How do the words and media elements relate to each other? Do they convey the same message, or are they at odds in any way? Are the media elements essential or merely decorative?
- Where and in what form was the text published? Does it appear online? On television? In print? In a commercial publication (a sales brochure, billboard, ad) or an informational one (newspaper, magazine)?
- What is the immediate social and cultural context within which the text is operating? What other social/cultural/historical knowledge does the text assume its audience already has? How do references to prior knowledge relate to the text's audience and purpose?
- How does the text connect, relate to, or contrast with any other significant texts (in any mode) that you are aware of? How do such considerations inform your ideas about this particular text?

The text below the image (linguistic mode) is needed to make sense of the disruption of the conventional wedding photo. It reads: "Ignoring global warming won't make it go away." The disjunction between the couple's blissful expression and the storm raging around them turns out to be the point of the PSA: Like the young couple in the image, we are blithely ignoring the impending disaster that global warming represents. The reputable nonprofit's logo and URL, which constitute its "signature," are meant to be an assurance that this threat is real—not just the idea of a profit-seeking ad agency dreamed up to manipulate us. (It is also a hint as to where we can send our contributions.)

Not everyone will be convinced by the PSA to support the work of the WWF, and some viewers may feel manipulated by the visual image. Nevertheless, most people would agree that with a single cleverly constructed image, a single line of text, and a logo, the PSA delivers its message clearly and forcefully. Scientific papers on global warming and the dire effects it will have on our planet abound, and while such papers are an effective means of communicating with an audience of scientists, this PSA is intended to speak to a general audience and to elicit contributions; thus, it uses multiple modes—visual, linguistic, gestural, and spatial—to communicate its message.

| **EXERCISE 22.1** |

For more about crafting a thesis, see Chapter 13, as well as the writing assignment chapters in Part 1.

Analyze one of the ads that follow, or another ad that you can study online or on television, by using the Criteria for Analyzing Multimodal Texts on pp. 598–599. Be sure to consider the role that writing plays in the ad's overall meaning. Write an essay with a thesis that discusses the ad's central meaning and significance.

Coca-Cola TV ad

MINI Cooper magazine ad

EXERCISE 22.2

Find a video ad or public service announcement on television or online, or a short documentary with a strong persuasive purpose aimed at spurring the audience to action. Analyze your chosen multimodal text by using the Criteria for Analyzing Multimodal Texts on pp. 598–99. Be sure to consider the role that the modes (linguistic, visual, aural, spatial, and gestural) play in the text and how each contributes to the text's overall meaning and purpose. Write an essay with a thesis that discusses the text's central meaning and significance.

Composing Multimodal Texts

When composing a project for a college course, your instructor may define many of the characteristics of the project in the assignment itself. Traditional assignments, such as a research project or an essay, are primarily linguistic. For an art history course, you may choose to include a photograph of the visual you are analyzing, but the focus of the composition will be a verbal analysis of the image. In many college classrooms, however, what constitutes an acceptable essay or project is in transition. Many instructors now allow—and in some cases require—the creation of multimodal and multimedia projects in place of traditional essays. These projects may include blogs, collages, timelines, videos, Prezi or PowerPoint presentations, and even playlists.

When the mode(s) and medium (print, oral, digital) are not specified, how do you decide which will be most effective? Start by analyzing the **rhetorical situation**. Recall that a rhetorical situation is essentially any situation in which you create or consume a text of any kind (essay, photograph, advertisement, Web site, blog post, podcast, film, and so on). You analyze the rhetorical situation by considering the text's *purpose, audience, context, genre* (or type), and *medium*.

To learn more about the rhetorical situation, see Chapter 1.

Reimagine your writing in a new genre or medium.

Sometimes a change in one or more aspects of the rhetorical situation requires writers to adapt their message to a new genre or medium. Consider, for example, study results published by a team of research scientists in a scholarly journal. The scientists format the article in the journal's style, using text and simple charts to report their findings and using language appropriate for members of the scientific community, who will read their report (the audience). Now imagine if the audience and context change, and the results of the study are being published online for a general audience. This happens often with online magazines and newspapers, when a reporter translates the findings of an article and embeds hyperlinks to cite the original study, or when a designer creates an infographic to depict the data.

Your instructor may ask you to reimagine one of your essays in a new genre or medium. This type of assignment is often called a *remix*. A remix challenges you to rethink your earlier decisions about purpose, audience, context, genre, and medium to deepen your understanding of the rhetorical situation. For example, Brian Cable revised his profile of the Goodbody Mortuary in Chapter 3 (pp. 59–65) as a treatment for a documentary (see Figure 22.2). He was hoping to raise enough money to produce a documentary about the business. Viewers would be intrigued, he thought, by a documentary that takes them behind the scenes of the "death business," a view most people never get.

Student Maya Gomez remixed information as a timeline that she had gathered while conducting research on the shortage of kidneys for donation in Chapter 5 (pp. 165–67). With the timeline, interested readers could get an overview of the history of kidney transplantation at a glance (Figure 22.3, p. 604).

Design a multimodal text.

In our increasingly multimodal world, design plays a prominent role in gaining readers' interest and in communicating the ideas of a text clearly. By designing a text, you are making rhetorical choices about how to use different modes. At a minimum, the design should make texts easy for the audience to navigate and understand. But design can also have a more profound effect. Consider this familiar phrase, rendered in four different ways:

The words in each rendering are the same, but the different uses of fonts, colors, and white space encourage us to read them very differently. The first message is vaguely unsettling (Is that a ransom note? A message from a stalker?); the second seems conventionally sweet; the third carries no emotional or context clues, but the spacing makes it irritatingly difficult to read; and the fourth offers no tone or context clues whatsoever (though this in itself might strike us as odd, given the meaning of

---

Treatment for *"Come In. We're Always Open.": The Goodbody Mortuary*

Overview

From the cost of a top-of-the-line coffin to the process of embalming and preparing the corpse for viewing, this short (15-minute) documentary will bring viewers behind the scenes at the Goodbody Mortuary, where they will get an insider's view of the death business.

Film Outline

- **Introduction:** A detached observer (or spectator) point of view will convey a "you are there" feeling, as viewers first observe the outside of the funeral home and then walk inside. The mood is wary as will be suggested by the music. The music will fade out as Howard Deaver, the funeral director, greets us.

- **Body:** Deaver will guide us past rose-pink sofas and quasi-religious visitation rooms to his office, with its bone-clean desk, where he will list the services the Goodbody Mortuary provides, from removing the body to preparing the body for viewing, embalming the corpse, placing it in the casket, and moving the casket to a visitation room. Before moving off, the camera will linger on the "Visa and MasterCard Welcome Here" sign on Deaver's desk.

  Deaver will then escort us to the sample room, where a number of casket options are on display. The camera will pan over the array, lingering over the most expensive model—the Promethean—as Deaver describes the costs and luxury features.

  Deaver will lead us downstairs to the preparation area, a white-tiled basement that looks like an operating room, where we will meet Tim, Goodbody's mortician. Tim will tell us about his work, the chemicals used in embalming, and the cosmetic work he does to achieve a resting expression. A body will appear in the background, but we will blur the features of the corpse, so that the privacy of the deceased's family members will be protected.

- **Resolution:** The film will end with an escape to the sunny day outside the gloomy funeral home. An upbeat tune will play and the viewer will get the sense of escape from a dark, confining, slightly oppressive space.

FIGURE 22.2   Brian Cable's treatment for a documentary about the Goodbody Mortuary

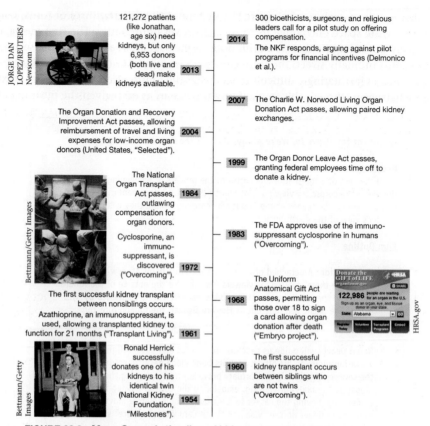

FIGURE 22.3   Maya Gomez's timeline of kidney transplantation

the words). Thus, design does far more than add visual interest: It actually directs how we read and, to a certain extent, determines the meaning we derive.

The freedom you have in terms of using design elements in the college projects you compose will vary quite a bit, depending on your instructor's preference, the nature of the assignment, and the media you choose. For instance, if you are designing a poster representing your research, your text will likely contain more text and fewer images than a flyer advertising a campus music festival. If you are creating a video, your design choices must take into account the abilities or limits of the software tools at your disposal.

If you are writing an essay for a college course, you can expect that your instructor will read it carefully. Your design decisions should therefore make sustained reading as easy as possible; fonts that are too small to read easily or margins that are too narrow to comment in will make the reader's job unnecessarily difficult. In most college courses, guidelines on design have traditionally followed a "less is more" rule, with written assignments printed on white $8^1/_2$" × 11" paper, and the use of extravagant fonts, decorative visuals, and the like discouraged. The growing number of multimodal assignments has obviously required some adjustments to traditional notions of acceptable design for college writing. In principle, however, "less is more" still applies. Good design gives priority to clarity.

Frequently, too, your design decisions will be determined by the genre (or type) of text you are preparing. Business letters and e-mails, for example, follow specific formats; movie trailers and TED talks have a familiar pacing and appearance. Because your readers will bring certain expectations to these kinds of texts, altering an established format can cause confusion and should therefore be considered carefully.

For more about business writing, see Chapter 25.

It is impossible to cover effective design in all modes and media. Since the majority of your college writing will primarily be in the linguistic mode, it is important to consider how to design written texts. A few key design elements are central:

- Use readable fonts.
- Select legible colors with adequate contrast.
- Use white space to chunk content and make it easy to read.

Choosing a Font

Typography is a design term for the letters and symbols that make up the print on a page or a screen. You are already using important aspects of typography when you use capital letters, italics, boldface, or different sizes of type to signal a new sentence, identify the title of a book or presentation, or distinguish a heading from body text. Perhaps the most important advice for working with typography is to choose fonts that are easy to read. Lengthy passages in italics, a decorative font, or too small a font, for example, can detract from readability.

Considering the audience and purpose of the text will help you decide what style of font is most appropriate for a specific writing situation. For most academic and business writing, you will probably want to choose a traditional font style that is easy to read, such as Arial or Times New Roman. Texts that will be read on paper may be easier to read if composed in a serif font, such as Georgia, Times Roman, or Century. (A serif is the little line projecting from the ends of a letter.) Texts that will be read on-screen may be easier to read if composed in a sans serif font, like Univers, Helvetica, or Verdana. Sentences and paragraphs printed in fonts that imitate calligraphy (typically called *script fonts*) or those that mimic *handwriting* are not only difficult to read but also too informal for most academic and business purposes.

To ensure that your text can be easily read, you also need to choose an appropriate font size (traditionally measured in units called *points*). For most types of academic writing, a 12-point font is standard for the main (body) text. For Web pages, however, you should consider using a slightly larger font to compensate for the difficulty of reading from a computer monitor. For presentations, you should use an even larger font size (such as 32-point, and typically no smaller than 18-point) to ensure that the text can be read from a distance.

Although technology now makes hundreds of font styles and sizes available to writers, avoid confusing readers with too many fonts in one composition. Limit the number of fonts to one or two that complement each other well. A common practice, for instance, is to choose one font for all titles and headings (such as 14-point Arial boldface for printed texts) and another for the body text (such as 12-point Times New Roman for printed texts). For texts delivered and read online, you might reverse the fonts, using 12-point Arial for the body text and 14-point Times New Roman boldface for headings.

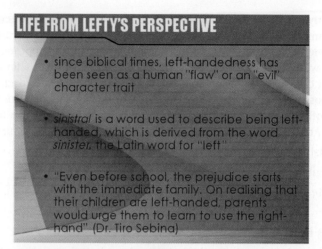

FIGURE 22.4   Document with Too Little Color Contrast

Using Colors

Color printers, photocopiers, and online technology facilitate the use of color, but color does not necessarily make text easier to read. In most academic documents, the only color you should use is black. Though color is typically used more freely in academic writing delivered on Web pages or in multimodal presentations, it should still be used in moderation and always with the aim of increasing readers' understanding of what you have to say. Always consider, too, whether your readers might have low vision or be color-blind and whether they will have access to a full-color version of the document.

Although the slide design in Figure 22.4 is visually interesting and the heading is readable, the bulleted text is very hard to read because there is too little contrast between the text color and the background color.

Also consider the meanings associated with different colors. For example, in the United States and other Western cultures, white is typically associated with goodness and purity; in China, however, white represents grief and mourning. Although your use of color in a report, blog, or multimodal presentation might not carry such deep meaning, bear in mind that most people have emotional or psychological responses to colors and color combinations. Without considering who is likely to read a text and what social or cultural factors are associated with that group, you may invite unintended interpretations, which can affect the specific meaning that a reader develops from a text.

Most people with color blindness have difficulty distinguishing between reds and greens of the same density. If designing in color, make sure that you do not convey important information in confusing colors or that you include a secondary means of distinguishing, such as by including a label or an explanation in the text.

Using White Space

Another basic element of design is white space, the open (or blank) space on a page. White space is typically used between a heading and the text that follows it and in the area surrounding visuals to emphasize an image or to create a clean, modern look.

In documents, you also use white space when you set the margins on a page and when you indent or leave a space between paragraphs. In all these cases, the white space makes your text easier to read. When used generously, white space facilitates reading by helping the eye find and follow the words or images.

Chunking, the breaking up of text or visuals into smaller units, also facilitates reading. In comics, individual frames or panels group images and text into a scene or moment. In documents, paragraphing is a form of chunking that divides text into units of closely related information. In most academic essays and reports, text is double-spaced, and paragraphs are distinguished by indenting the first line one-half inch. In single-spaced text or text that will be read on-screen, adding extra space between paragraphs serves to chunk the content. This format, referred to as block style, is often used in business letters, e-mails, and other electronic documents. When creating electronic documents—especially Web pages—you might consider chunking your material into separate pages or screens, with links connecting the chunks.

For more about creating effective Web pages or writing for business, see Chapter 25.

Embed visuals and media in texts.

Tables, graphs, charts, diagrams, photographs, maps, and screenshots, as well as embedded video and audio files, add interest and are often more effective in conveying information than prose alone. When integrating a visual or media file into your text, introduce and discuss it before revealing it. In an academic composition, include a figure number both in your text and in the caption accompanying the visual or media file, and make clear in your text the kind of information it contains and the point it makes or supports.

For an example of an academic essay with images used as support, see "Scott Pilgrim vs. the World: A Hell of a Ride" in Chapter 8; for a model student essay showing layout conventions, see "Educating Kids at Home" in Chapter 20.

If your composition is going to be posted online on a site that is not password-protected and you borrow a visual or media file from a copyrighted source, you may need to request written permission from the copyright holder (such as the photographer, publisher, or site sponsor).

Caution: Though media can enhance your writing, visuals, videos, and sound clips may distract readers and work against the goals of the text. Keep the following advice in mind when including visuals:

- **Make the decisions that your computer cannot make for you.** A computer can automatically turn spreadsheet data into a chart or graph, but only you can decide which visual—or what use of color, if any—is appropriate given your rhetorical situation.

- **Avoid "chart junk."** Many computer programs provide an array of special effects that can be used to alter visuals, including three-dimensional renderings, textured backgrounds, and shadowed text. Such special effects often detract from the intended message of the visual by calling attention to themselves instead. Use these effects sparingly, and only when they emphasize key information.

- **Use visual or audio files purposefully.** Consider your audience, context, and genre when incorporating visuals or other inserts. Academic audiences typically want visuals included only if they serve a specific purpose. Including items for merely decorative purposes is frowned on.

The following chart, Criteria for Analyzing Document Design, includes questions that will help you think about how to design your multimodal compositions.

CRITERIA FOR ANALYZING DOCUMENT DESIGN

- Does the design follow the conventions of the genre, or type of text, you are creating?

- Does the design enhance the content of the text or distract from the message in any way?

VISUAL MODE

- What do the colors in the design signify? Is there effective contrast between elements? Is the typography (font type, size, and treatment) appropriate?

- How do images, charts, graphs, or graphics convey information? What is their relationship to the words in the text? What is their relationship to other visuals?

SPATIAL MODE

- What is placed where, and why? What elements come first in the text? Next? Last?

- How are words and other elements grouped in the text? Do these "chunks" effectively divide related information for the audience?

- How is white space used throughout the text? What does it help to emphasize? Minimize?

Creating a Multimodal Presentation

This chapter has discussed at length the characteristics of a multimodal text. Now let's apply these considerations to one of the most common types of multimodal texts—the presentation.

Presentations make use of multiple modes and sometimes multiple media: Speakers use linguistic and gestural modes as they speak, move about, and advance the presentation for the audience. Presentation slides demonstrate the spatial mode in their bulleted and numbered lists and other textual elements; they demonstrate the gestural mode in the way that they enter and leave the screen. If speakers incorporate images, videos, or sound files in their presentation slides, then they expand to use all five modes of communication.

Assess your rhetorical situation.

As with any text, to make an effective presentation you must assess your rhetorical situation. Even for an impromptu presentation, take a few moments to think about why, to whom, and where you are speaking.

Define your purpose by completing the following statement:

▶ In this presentation, I want to _____ .

For instance, you may want to speculate on the causes of companies' hiring part-time rather than full-time workers, or you may want to argue your position on the ethics of this new hiring policy.

To assess your audience, ask questions like these: Why are the members of my audience here? What do they already know about my subject? How do they feel about my topic? What objections might they have to my argument? What media will help me convey my points most effectively, given my audience and what kind of media (including presentation slides, like PowerPoint or Prezi) they will expect?

Consider the context within which you will be presenting and how that will affect your content and delivery. The amount and type of media you use will differ depending on whether you are speaking at the front of your classroom, in a large auditorium, or online via Skype or Google Hangouts.

Determine how much information you can present in the allotted time.

Your presentation should be exactly as long as the time allotted. Using substantially less time will make your presentation seem incomplete or superficial; using substantially more time may alienate your audience. Plan your presentation to allocate sufficient time for an introduction, concluding remarks, and follow-up questions (if a question-and-answer session is to be part of the presentation). If you are giving a scripted presentation, each double-spaced page of text will probably take two minutes to deliver. To get a realistic sense of how long your presentation will take, rehearse several times, using any multimedia aids you plan to use. Then time yourself.

Use cues to orient audience members.

Listening is one of the most difficult ways to comprehend information, in part because listeners cannot look back at previous information or scan forward, as readers can. To help your audience follow your presentation, use the same kinds of cues that you would use for readers, but use them more frequently and overtly. Here are four basic cues that are especially helpful for listeners:

- **Thesis and forecasting statements.** Begin by announcing to the audience what you intend to communicate (your thesis) and the order in which you will present your materials (your forecast).

- **Transitions.** Provide transitions when you move from point to point. For example, when you finish discussing your first reason, state explicitly that you are now turning to your second reason.

- **Summaries.** End your presentation with a summary of your main points, and look for opportunities to include summaries at the end of each section. A brief summary that indicates the point you are making and its relation to your overall thesis can help listeners understand how the parts of your argument fit together to support your thesis.

- **Presentation slides.** An outline of your presentation, including your thesis and main topics (in a bulleted or numbered list), can be shown on an introductory slide. Slides indicating each main point and key supporting evidence can be displayed as you arrive at each point.

To learn more about creating thesis statements and forecasts and about using effective cohesive devices, including transitions, see Chapter 13. To learn more about summarizing, see Chapter 19.

Design your presentation effectively.

As mentioned previously, presentation software, such as PowerPoint or Prezi, allows you to list the major points of your presentation, which helps your listeners understand and remember what you say. Presentation slides also allow you to incorporate photographs and pie charts, videos and audio files that can be used to illustrate your points and provide supporting evidence. Simple presentation slides can be created and displayed with relative ease.

Presentation software has the advantage of allowing the use of animation, video, and audio. Online sites and apps such as Prezi allow you to create more visual and gestural presentations that zoom in and out, engaging your audience and freeing your narrative from the linear movement of slides. After writing his essay proposing a solution to the problem of "high-stakes exams," student writer Patrick O'Malley thought his target audience (professors) would be more likely to replace a few high-stakes exams with a greater number of lower-stakes quizzes and tests if he remixed his essay as a presentation that laid out the evidence clearly. (A snapshot of his Prezi presentation appears in Figure 22.5.)

Patrick O'Malley's essay "More Testing, More Learning" appears in Chapter 7.

Color scheme and typography emphasize information appropriately

Title is large, contrasts with supporting text

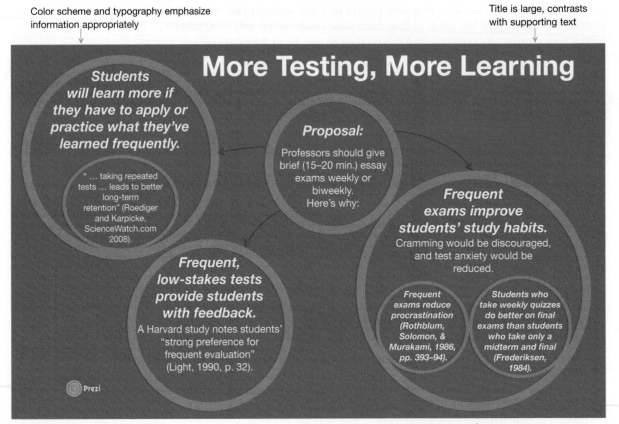

FIGURE 22.5   Sample Prezi

Text chunking, spatial arrangement, and arrows show relationships between information and provide visual interest; dynamic presentation and zoom function make all text clearly legible

As you prepare your presentation:

- Use a large, easy-to-read font; allow generous amounts of space around text; and maintain sharp contrast. Make sure fonts are large enough that your slides can be read by audience members at the back of the room.

- The text you include should be concise, easy to read, and uncluttered. Remember that audience members will have only a few moments to examine each slide, so avoid filling them with text.

- If using sound or video files, make sure the volume is consistent and clearly audible but not deafening.

- If using software or apps with more capabilities in animation, video, or sound, make sure the bells and whistles don't drown you out or distract your audience from your message.

Finally, keep in mind that the point of a presentation is to convey information to the audience, not present lengthy presentation slides. Slides should support your presentation, not dominate it.

23

Taking Essay Examinations

To learn more about comparison and contrast, see Chapter 15; for more about analysis and synthesis, see Chapters 5, 12, and 19; for more on argument, see Chapter 16 as well as Chapters 6–9.

Many instructors believe that essay exams are the best way to find out what you have learned and, more important, help you consolidate and reinforce your learning. Essay exams demonstrate that you can sort through the large body of information covered in a course, identify what is significant, and explain your decision. They show whether you understand basic concepts and can use those concepts to interpret specific materials, make connections, draw comparisons and find contrasts, and synthesize information in support of an original assertion. They may even show that you can justify your own evaluations and argue for your opinions with convincing reasons and supporting evidence. All instructors want students to think critically and analytically about a subject; many feel that essay exams provide the best demonstration that you can do so.

As a college student, then, you will face a variety of essay exams, from short-answer identifications to take-home exams. The writing activities and strategies discussed in Parts One and Three of this book—particularly narrating, describing, defining, classifying, comparing and contrasting, and arguing—as well as the critical thinking strategies in Part Two will help you do well on these exams. This chapter provides specific guidelines for you to follow in preparing for and taking essay exams, and analyzes a group of typical exam questions and answers to help you determine which strategies will be most useful.

Preparing for an Exam

The best way to ensure that you will do well on essay exams is to keep up with readings and assignments from the very start of the course: Do the reading, go to lectures, take careful notes, participate in discussion sessions, and organize study groups with classmates to explore and review course material throughout the term. Trying to cram weeks of information into a single night of study will never allow you to do your best.

As you study, avoid simply memorizing information aimlessly. Instead, clarify the important issues of the course, and use these issues to focus your understanding of specific facts and particular readings. Try to see relations among topics; concentrate on the central concerns of each study unit, and see what connections you can discover; and place all you have learned into a meaningful context.

As an exam approaches, find out what you can about the form it will take. No question is more irritating to instructors than "Do we need to know this for the exam?" but it is generally legitimate to ask whether the questions will require short or long answers, how many questions there will be, whether you may choose which questions to answer, and what kinds of thinking and writing will be required of you.

Some instructors may hand out study guides for exams or even lists of potential questions. If yours does not, make up questions you think the instructor might ask and then plan answers to them with classmates. Returning to your notes and to assigned readings with specific questions in mind can help enormously in your process of understanding. The important thing to remember is that an essay exam tests more than your memory of specific information; it requires you to use this information to demonstrate a comprehensive grasp of the material covered in the course.

Taking the Exam

Doing well on an essay exam begins with a plan of attack. Once you analyze the questions to determine what is being asked, apportion your time.

Read the exam carefully.

Before you answer a question, read the entire exam so that you can apportion your time realistically. Pay particular attention to how many points you may earn on different parts of the test; notice any directions that suggest how long an answer should be or how much space it should take up. As you are doing so, you may wish to make tentative choices about which of the questions you will answer and decide on the order in which you will answer them. If you have ideas about how you would organize any of your answers, you might also jot down some scratch outlines. But before you start to complete any answers, write down the actual clock time you expect to be working on each question or set of questions. Careful time management is crucial to your success on essay exams; devoting some time to each question is always better than using up your time on only a few.

To learn more about creating a scratch outline, see Chapters 11 and 12.

Before beginning to write your first answer, analyze the question carefully so that you can focus your attention on the information that will be pertinent to your answer. Consider this question from a sociology final:

> Drawing from lectures and discussions on the contradictory aspects of American values, the "bureaucratic personality," and the behaviors associated with social mobility, discuss the problems of attaining economic success in a relatively "open," complex, post-industrial society such as the United States.

Though the question looks confusing at first, once you sort it out, you will find that it contains the key terms for the answer's thesis, as well as the main points of development. Look first at the words that give you directions: *draw from* and *discuss*. The term *discuss* invites you to list and explain the problems of attaining economic success. The categories of these problems are already identified in the opening phrases: "contradictory . . . values," "bureaucratic personality," and "behaviors associated

To learn more about crafting a thesis, see Chapter 13 and each of the chapters in Part 1.

with social mobility." Therefore, you would begin with a thesis that includes the key words in the final clause ("attaining economic success in a relatively open, complex, post-industrial society") and then take up each category of problem—and perhaps other problems you can think of—in separate paragraphs.

Review typical essay exam questions.

The next section presents questions (on the left) in nine common categories, with an explanation of how students should respond to each question (on the right). All the examples are drawn from short quizzes, midterms, and final exams for a variety of first- and second-year courses. These questions demonstrate the range of writing you may be expected to do on exams. Pay particular attention to how the directions and key words in each case help you define the writing task.

Notice that each question indicates the amount of time students should devote to their answer. In reality, students are often expected to determine how much time to spend, depending on the number of points allocated to the question—for example, students should spend half the exam period answering a question that could earn half the exam's points. In general, instructors expect students to need the entire exam period to produce an effective essay exam. If you find that you have finished the exam in half the time, review your answers: Most likely you have not included all the information your instructor was looking for.

See Chapter 15 for more about defining.

Define or Identify   Questions that require you to write a few sentences defining or identifying material from readings or lectures may ask for a brief overview of a large topic, or a more detailed definition or identification of a more narrowly defined topic. In composing a *definition* or identification, always ask yourself why this item is important enough to be on the exam.

Question 23.1 (15/100 points; 15 minutes)

What are the three stages of African literature?

This question asks for a brief overview of a large topic. Answering this question would involve naming the periods in historical order and then describing each period in a sentence or two.

Question 23.2 (20/100 points; 20 minutes)

Define and state some important facts concerning each of the following:
a. demographics
b. Instrumental model
c. RCA
d. telephone booth of the air
e. penny press

With no more than three or four minutes for each part, students answering Question 23.2 would offer a concise definition for each item (probably in a sentence) and add facts relevant to the main topics in the course.

Recall Details of a Specific Source   Sometimes instructors will ask for a straightforward *summary* or *paraphrase* of a specific source (often, an assigned reading). To answer such questions, the student must recount details directly from the source, without interpretation or evaluation. In the following example from a sociology exam, students were allowed about fifteen minutes to complete the answer on one lined page provided with the exam.

For more about paraphrasing and summarizing, see Chapters 12 and 19.

Question 23.3 (10/100 points; 15 minutes)

In his article "Is There a Culture of Poverty?" Oscar Lewis addresses a popular question in the social sciences: What is the "culture of poverty"? How is it able to come into being, according to Lewis? That is, under what conditions does it exist? When does he say a person is no longer a part of the culture of poverty? What does Lewis say is the future of the culture of poverty?

The phrasing in Question 23.3 invites a fairly clear-cut structure: Each of the questions can be turned into an assertion and supported with examples from Lewis's article. For example, the first question could become an assertion: "Lewis defines the culture of poverty as _____," and "According to Lewis, the culture of poverty comes into being through _____." The important thing in this case is to summarize accurately what the writer said and not waste time evaluating or criticizing his ideas.

Explain the Importance or Significance   Another kind of essay exam question asks students to explain the importance of something covered in the course. Such questions require specific examples as the basis for a more general discussion of what has been studied. This type of question is often used when instructors want students to interpret a text or visual work by concentrating on a particular aspect of it.

Question 23.4 (10/100 points; 15 minutes)

In the last scene of *Paths of Glory,* the owner of a café brings a young German woman onto a small stage in his café to sing for the French troops, while Colonel Dax looks on from outside the café. Briefly explain the significance of this scene in relation to the movie as a whole.

In answering this question, a student's first task would be to reconsider the whole movie, looking for ways in which this one brief scene illuminates or explains larger issues or themes. Then, in a paragraph or two, the student would summarize these themes and point out how each element of the scene fits into the overall context.

Question 23.5 (10/100 points; 20 minutes)

Chukovsky gives many examples of cute expressions and statements uttered by small children. Give an example of two of the kinds of statements that he finds interesting. Then state their implications for understanding the nature of language in particular and communication more generally.

For Question 23.5 (on a communications exam), students would start by choosing examples of children's utterances from Chukovsky's book. These examples would then provide the basis for demonstrating the student's grasp of the larger subject. Questions like these require students to decide for themselves the significance of the information and to organize the answer so that the general ideas are clearly developed.

See Chapter 4 for more on explaining a concept.

Apply Concepts   Very often, courses in the humanities and the social sciences emphasize significant themes, ideologies, or concepts. A common type of essay exam question asks students to apply the concepts to works studied in the course.

Question 23.6 (45/130 points; 40 minutes)

Several works studied in this course depict scapegoat figures. Select two written works and two films, and discuss how their authors or directors present and analyze the social conflicts that lead to the creation of scapegoats.

In answering Question 23.6, a student would provide an introductory paragraph defining the concept "scapegoat" and referring to the works to be discussed. Then the student would devote a paragraph or two to the works, pointing out specific examples to illustrate the concept. A concluding paragraph would probably attempt to bring the concept into clearer focus.

Comment on a Quotation   On essay exams, an instructor will often ask students to comment on a quotation they are seeing for the first time. Usually, such quotations will express some surprising or controversial opinion that complements or challenges basic principles or ideas in the course. Sometimes the writer being quoted is identified, sometimes not. In fact, it is not unusual for instructors to write the quotation themselves.

Question 23.7 (75/100 points; 90 minutes)

"Some historians believe that economic hardship and oppression breed social revolt, but the experience of the United States and Mexico between 1900 and 1920 suggests that people may rebel also during times of prosperity."

Question 23.7, from a midterm exam in a history course, asks students to "comment," but the three questions make clear that a successful answer would require an *argument:* a clear *thesis* stating a position on the views

See Chapter 16 for more about these components of an argument.

Comment on this statement. Why did large numbers of Americans and Mexicans wish to change conditions in their countries during the years from 1900 to 1920? How successful were their efforts? Who benefited from the changes that took place?

expressed in the quotation, specific *reasons* for that thesis, and *support* for the thesis from readings and lectures. In general, such questions do not have a "correct" answer: Whether students agree or disagree with the quotation is not as important as whether they can argue their case reasonably and convincingly, demonstrating a firm grasp of the subject matter.

Compare and Contrast   Instructors are particularly fond of essay exam questions that require a *comparison and contrast* of two or three principles, ideas, works, activities, or phenomena. To answer this kind of question, you need to explore fully the relations between the things to be compared, analyze each one separately, and then search out specific points of likeness or difference. Students must thus show a thorough knowledge of the things being compared, as well as a clear understanding of the basic issues on which comparisons and contrasts can be made. Whether the point of comparison is stated in the question or left for you to define for yourself, your answer needs to be limited to the aspects of similarity or difference that are most relevant to the general concepts or themes covered in the course.

See Chapter 15 for more about comparing and contrasting.

Question 23.8 (50/100 points; 1 hour)

Compare and analyze the views of colonialism presented in Memmi's *Colonizer and the Colonized* and Pontecorvo's *Battle of Algiers*. What are the significant differences between these two views?

Often, as in Question 23.8, the basis of comparison will be limited to a particular focus; here, for example, students are asked to compare two works in terms of their views of colonialism.

Question 23.9 (50/100 points; 1 hour)

What was the role of the United States in Cuban affairs from 1898 until 1959? How did its role there compare with its role in the rest of Spanish America during the same period?

Sometimes instructors will simply identify what is to be compared, as in Question 23.8. In this question from a Latin American history exam, students are left the task of choosing the basis of the comparison.

Synthesize Information from Various Sources   In a course with several assigned readings, an instructor may ask students to pull together, or *synthesize*, information from several or even all the readings.

For more about synthesizing, see Chapters 5, 12, and 19.

Question 23.10 (25/100 points; 30 minutes)

On the basis of the articles read on El Salvador, Nicaragua, Peru, Chile, Argentina, and Mexico, what would you say are the major problems confronting Latin America today? Discuss the major types of problems, with references to particular countries as examples.

Question 23.10, from the final in a Latin American studies course, asks students to decide which major problems to discuss, which countries to include in each discussion, and how to use material from many readings to develop their answers, all in half an hour. To compose a coherent essay, a student will need a carefully developed *forecasting statement.*

For more about forecasting statements, see Chapter 13.

See Chapter 9 for more about analyzing causes.

Analyze Causes   In humanities and social science courses, much of what students study concerns the causes of trends, actions, and events. Hence, it is not surprising to find questions about causes on essay exams. In such cases, the instructor expects students to *analyze* causes of various phenomena discussed in readings and lectures.

Question 23.11 (25/100 points; 30 minutes)

Given that we occupy several positions in the course of our lives and given that each position has a specific role attached to it, what kinds of problems or dilemmas arise from those multiple roles, and how are they handled?

Question 23.11 comes from a midterm exam in sociology. The question requires students to develop a list of causes in their answer. The causes would be organized under a thesis statement, and each cause would be argued and supported by referring to lectures or readings.

See Chapter 8 for more about evaluation.

Criticize or Evaluate   Occasionally, instructors will include essay exam questions that invite students to *evaluate* a concept or a work. They want more than opinion: They expect a reasoned, documented evaluation based on appropriate standards of judgment. Such questions test students' ability to recall and synthesize pertinent information and to understand and apply criteria taught in the course.

Question 23.12 (10/85 points; 20 minutes)

Eisenstein and Mukerji both argue that movable print was important to the rise of Protestantism. Cole extends this argument to say that print set off a chain of events that was important to the history of the United States. Summarize this argument, and evaluate any part of it you choose.

Question 23.12 appeared on a communications course midterm that asked students to answer "in two paragraphs." The question asks students to summarize and evaluate an argument that appears in several course readings. The students would probably use the writing strategies of comparison and contrast to analyze and evaluate the authors' views.

Write your answer.

Your strategy for writing depends on the length of your answer. For short identifications and definitions, start with a general identifying statement and then move on to describe specific applications or explanations. Two complete sentences will almost always suffice.

For longer answers, begin with a clear and explicit thesis statement. Use key terms from the question in your thesis, and use the same key terms throughout your essay. If the question does not supply any key terms, provide your own. Outlining your answer will enable you to forecast your points in your opening sentences. Use transitions such as *first, second, moreover, however,* and *thus* to signal clear relations among paragraphs.

See Chapter 13 for more about forecasting and transitions.

As you write, you will certainly think of new ideas or facts to include. If you find that you want to add a sentence or two to sections you have already completed, write them in the margin or at the top of the page, with a neat arrow pointing to where they fit in your answer. Strike out words or even sentences you want to change by drawing through them neatly with a single line. If you run out of time when you are writing an answer, jot down the remaining ideas, just to show that you know the material and with more time could have continued your answer.

Model Answers

Here we analyze several successful answers and give you an opportunity to analyze one for yourself. These analyses, along with the information we have provided elsewhere in this chapter, should greatly improve your chances of writing successful exam answers.

Short Answers   A literature midterm opened with ten items to identify, each worth 3 points. Students had about two minutes for each item. Here are three of Brenda Gossett's answers, each one earning her the full 3 points:

> Rauffenstein: He was the German general who was in charge of the castle where Boeldieu, Maréchal, and Rosenthal were finally sent in *The Grand Illusion*. He, along with Boeldieu, represented the aristocracy, which was slowly fading out at that time.

> Iges Peninsula: This peninsula is created by the Meuse River in France. It is there that the Camp of Hell was created in *The Debacle*. The Camp of Hell is where the French army was interned after the Germans defeated them in the Franco-Prussian War.

> Pache: He was the "religious peasant" in the novel *The Debacle*. It was he who inevitably became a scapegoat when he was murdered by Loubet, Lapoulle, and Chouteau because he wouldn't share his bread with them.

The instructor said only "identify the following" but clearly wanted students both to identify the item and to indicate its significance to the work in which it appeared. Gossett does both and gets full credit. She mentions particular works, characters, and events. Although she is rushed, she answers in complete sentences. She does not misspell any words or leave out any commas or periods. Her answers are complete and correct.

Paragraph-Length Answers   The following question is from a weekly literature quiz. With only a few minutes to respond, students were instructed to "answer in a few sentences." Here is the question and Camille Prestera's answer:

> In *Things Fall Apart,* how did Okonkwo's relationship with his father affect his attitude toward his son? (20/100 points)

> Okonkwo despised his father, who was lazy, cowardly, and in debt. Okonkwo tried to be everything his father wasn't. He was hardworking, wealthy, and a great warrior and wrestler. Okonkwo treated his son harshly because he was afraid he saw the same weakness in Nwoye that he despised in his father. The result of this harsh treatment was that Nwoye left home.

Prestera begins by describing Okonkwo and his father, contrasting the two sharply. Then she explains Okonkwo's relationship with his son Nwoye. Her answer is coherent and straightforward.

Long Answers   Many final exams include at least one question requiring an essay-length answer. John Pixley had an hour to plan and write this essay for a final exam in a literature course in response to the following question applying a concept:

> Many American writers have portrayed their characters or their poetic speaker as being engaged in a quest. The quest may be explicit or implicit, it may be external or psychological, and it may end in failure or success. Analyze the quest motif in the work of four of the following writers: Edwards, Franklin, Hawthorne, Thoreau, Douglass, Whitman, Dickinson, James, Twain.

Key term, *quest,* mentioned in introduction and thesis

1   Americans pride themselves on being ambitious and on being able to strive for goals and to tap their potential. Some say that this is what the "American Dream" is all about. It is important for one to do and be all that one is capable of. This entails a quest or search for identity, experience, and happiness. Hence, the idea of the quest is a vital one in the United States, and it can be seen as a theme throughout American literature.

First writer identified immediately

2   In eighteenth-century colonial America, Jonathan Edwards dealt with this theme in his autobiographical and personal writings. Unlike his fiery and hard-nosed sermons, these autobiographical writings present a sensitive, vulnerable man trying to find himself and his proper, satisfying place in the world. He is concerned with his spiritual growth, in being free to find and explore religious experience and happiness. For

Edwards's work and the details of his quest presented

example, in *Personal Narrative,* he very carefully traces the stages of religious beliefs. He tells about periods of abandoned ecstasy, doubts, and rational revelations. He also notes that his best insights and growth came at times when he was alone in the wilderness, in nature. Edwards's efforts to find himself in relation to the world can also be seen in his "Observations of the Natural World," in which he relates various meticulously observed and described natural phenomena to religious precepts and occurrences. Here, he is trying to give the world and life, of which he is a part, some sense of meaning and purpose.

3   Although he was a contemporary of Edwards, Benjamin Franklin, who was very involved in the founding of the United States as a nation, had a different conception of the quest. He sees the quest as being one of practical accomplishment, success, and wealth. In his *Autobiography*, he stresses that happiness involves working hard to accomplish things, getting along with others, and establishing a good reputation. Unlike Edwards's, his quest is external and bound up with society. He is concerned with his morals and behavior, but as seen in part 2 of the *Autobiography*, he deals with them in an objective, pragmatic, even statistical way, rather than in sensitive pondering. It is also evident in this work that Franklin, unlike Edwards, believes so much in himself and his quest that he is able to laugh at himself. His concern with society can be seen in *Poor Richard's Almanac*, in which he gives practical advice on how to find success and happiness in the world, how to "be healthy, wealthy, and wise."

4   Still another version of the quest can be seen in the mid-nineteenth-century poetry of Walt Whitman. The quest that he portrays blends elements of those of Edwards and Franklin. In "Song of Myself," which is clearly autobiographical, the speaker emphasizes the importance of finding, knowing, and enjoying oneself as part of nature and the human community. He says that one should come to realize that one is lovable, just as are all other people and all of nature and life. This is a quest for sensitivity and awareness, as Edwards advocates, and for great self-confidence, as Franklin advocates. Along with Edwards, Whitman sees that peaceful isolation in nature is important; but he also sees the importance of interacting with people, as Franklin does. Being optimistic and feeling good — in both the literal and the figurative sense — are the objects of this quest. Unfortunately, personal disappointment and national crisis (i.e., the Civil War) shattered Whitman's sense of confidence, and he lost the impetus of this quest in his own life.

5   This theme of the quest can be seen in prose fiction as well as in poetry and autobiography. One interesting example is "The Beast in the Jungle," a short story written by Henry James around 1903. It is interesting in that not only does the principal character, John Marcher, fail in his lifelong quest, but his failure comes about in a most subtle and frustrating way. Marcher believes that something momentous is going to happen in his future. He talks about his belief to only one person, a woman named May. May decides to befriend him for life and watch with him for the momentous occurrence to come about, for "the beast in the jungle" to "pounce." As time passes, May seems to know what this occurrence is and eventually even says that it has happened; but John is still in the dark. It is only long after May's death that the beast pounces on him in his recognition that the "beast" was his failure to truly love May, the one woman of his life, even though she gave him all the encouragement that she possibly, decently could. Marcher never defined the terms of his quest until it was too late. By just waiting and watching, he failed to find feeling and passion. This tragic realization, as someone like Whitman would view it, brings about John Marcher's ruin.

Second writer identified in transition sentence; key term (*quest*) repeated

Contrast with Edwards added for coherence

Another key term from question, *external*, used

Franklin's particular kind of quest described

Third writer identified in transition sentence; key term repeated

Coherence sustained by comparison of Whitman to Edwards and Franklin

Whitman's quest defined

Transition: Key term repeated; fourth writer identified

Quest of James character described

Key term repeated in
conclusion

6   As seen in these few examples, the theme of the quest is a significant one in American literature. Also obvious is the fact that there are a variety of approaches to, methods used in, and outcomes of the quest. This is an appropriate theme for American literature, seeing how much Americans cherish the right of "the pursuit of happiness."

Pixley's answer is strong for two reasons: He has the information he needs, and he has organized it carefully and presented it coherently.

EXERCISE 23.1

The following essay was written by Dan Hepler. He answered the same essay exam question as his classmate John Pixley. Analyze Hepler's essay to discover whether it meets the criteria of a good essay exam answer. Review the criteria mentioned earlier in this chapter (in the section "Write Your Answer," pp. 619–22) and in the annotated commentary of John Pixley's answer. Try to identify the features of Hepler's essay that contribute to or work against its success.

Dan Hepler's Answer

The quest motif is certainly important in American literature. By considering Franklin, Thoreau, Douglass, and Twain, we can see that the quest may be explicit or implicit, external or psychological, a failure or a success. Tracing the quest motif through these four authors seems to show a developing concern in American literature with transcending materialism to address deeper issues. It also reveals a drift toward ambiguity and pessimism.   1

Benjamin Franklin's quest, as revealed by his *Autobiography*, is for material comfort and outward success. His quest may be considered an explicit one because he announces clearly what he is trying to do: perfect a systematic approach for living long and happily. The whole *Autobiography* is a road map intended for other people to use as a guide; Franklin apparently meant rather literally for people to imitate his methods. He wrote with the assumption that his success was reproducible. He is possibly the most optimistic author in American literature because he enjoys life, knows exactly *why* he enjoys life, and believes that anyone else willing to follow his formula may enjoy life as well.   2

By Franklin's standards, his quest is clearly a success. But his *Autobiography* portrays only an external, not a psychological, success. This is not to suggest that Franklin was a psychological failure. Indeed, we have every reason to believe the contrary. But the fact remains that Franklin *wrote* only about external success; he never indicated how he really felt emotionally. Possibly it was part of Franklin's overriding optimism to assume that material comfort leads naturally to emotional fulfillment.   3

Henry David Thoreau presents a more multifaceted quest. His *Walden* is, on the simplest level, the chronicle of Thoreau's physical journey out of town and into the woods. But the moving itself is not the focus of *Walden*. It is really more of a metaphor for some kind of   4 spiritual quest going on within Thoreau's mind. Most of the action in *Walden* is mental, as Thoreau contemplates and philosophizes, always using the lake, the woods, and his own daily actions as symbols of higher, more eternal truths. This spiritual quest is a success in that Thoreau is able to appreciate the beauty of nature and to see through much of the sham and false assumptions of town life and blind materialism.

Thoreau does not leave us with nearly as explicit a "blueprint" for success as Franklin does. Even Franklin's plan is limited to people of high intelligence, personal discipline, and sound character; Franklin sometimes seems to forget that many human beings are in fact weak and evil and so would stand little chance of success similar to his own. But at least Franklin's quest could be duplicated by another Franklin. Thoreau's quest is more problematic, for even as great a mystic and naturalist as Thoreau himself could not remain in the woods indefinitely. This points toward the idea that the real quest is all internal and psychological; Thoreau seems to have gone to the woods to develop a spiritual strength that he could keep and take elsewhere on subsequent dealings with the "real world."   5

The quest of Frederick Douglass was explicit in that he needed physically to get north and escape slavery, but it was also implicit because he sought to discover and redefine himself through his quest, as Thoreau did. Douglass's motives were more sharply focused than either Franklin's or Thoreau's; his very humanness was at stake, as well as his physical well-being and possibly even his life. But Douglass also makes it clear that the most horrible part of slavery was the mental anguish of having no hope of freedom. His learning to read, and his maintenance of this skill, seems to have been as important as the maintenance of his material comforts, of which he had very few. In a sense, Douglass's quest is the most psychological and abstract so far because it is for the very essence of freedom and humanity, both of which were mostly taken for granted by Franklin and Thoreau. Also, Douglass's quest is the most pessimistic of the three; Douglass concludes that physical violence is the only way out, as he finds with the Covey incident.   6

Finally, Mark Twain's *Huckleberry Finn* is an example of the full range of meaning that the quest motif may assume. Geographically, Huck's quest is very large. But again, there is a quest defined implicitly as well as one defined explicitly, as Huck (without consciously realizing it) searches for morality, truth, and freedom. Twain's use of the quest is ambiguous, even more so than the previous writers', because while he suggests success superficially (i.e., the "happily ever after" scene in the last chapter), he really hints at some sort of ultimate hopelessness inherent in society. Not even Douglass questions the good or evil of American society as deeply as Twain does; for Douglass, everything will be fine when slavery is abolished; but for Twain, the only solution is to "light out for the territories" altogether—and when Twain wrote, he knew that the territories were no more.   7

Twain's implicit sense of spiritual failure stands in marked contrast to Franklin's buoyant confidence in material success. The guiding image of the quest, however, is central to American values and, consequently, a theme that these writers and others have adapted to suit their own vision.   8

| EXERCISE 23.2 |

Analyze the following essay exam questions to decide what kind of writing task they present. What is being asked of the student as a participant in the course and as a writer? Given the time constraints of the exam, what plan would you propose for writing the answer? Following each question is the number of points it is worth and the amount of time allotted to answer it.

1 Cortázar is a producer of fantastic literature. Discuss first what fantastic literature is. Then choose any four stories by Cortázar as examples, and discuss the fantastic elements in these stories. Refer to the structure, techniques, and narrative styles that he uses in these four stories. If you like, you may refer to more than four, of course. (Points: 30 of 100. Time: 40 of 150 minutes.)

2 During the course of the twentieth century, the United States experienced three significant periods of social reform — the progressive era, the age of the Great Depression, and the decade of the 1960s. What were the sources of reform in each period? What were the most significant reform achievements of each period as well as the largest failings? (Points: 35 of 100. Time: 75 of 180 minutes.)

3 Since literature is both an artistic and an ideological product, writers comment on their material context through their writing.

   a. What is Rulfo's perspective of his Mexican reality, and how is it portrayed through his stories?

   b. What particular themes does he deal with, especially in these stories: "The Burning Plain," "Luvina," "They Gave Us the Land," "Paso del Norte," and "Tell Them Not to Kill Me!"?

   c. What literary techniques and structures does he use to convey his perspective? Refer to a specific story as an example.

   (Points: 30 of 100. Time: 20 of 50 minutes.)

4 Why is there a special reason to be concerned about the influence of television watching on kids? In your answer, include a statement of the following:

   a. Your own understanding of the *general communication principles* involved for any television watcher.

   b. What is special about television and kids.

   c. How advertisers and producers use this information. (You should draw from the relevant readings as well as lectures.)

   (Points: 20 of 90. Time: 25 of 90 minutes.)

5 Analyze the autobiographical tradition in American literature, focusing on differences and similarities among authors and, if appropriate, changes over time. Discuss four authors in all. In addition to the conscious autobiographers — Edwards, Franklin, Thoreau, and Douglass — you may choose one or two figures from among the following fictional or poetic quasi-autobiographers: Hawthorne, Whitman, Dickinson, and Twain. (Points: 50 of 120. Time: 60 of 180 minutes.)

6 How does the system of (media) sponsorship work, and what, if any, ideological control do sponsors exert? Be specific and illustrative. (Points: 33 of 100. Time: 60 of 180 minutes.)

7 Several of the works studied in this course analyze the tension between myth and reality. Select two written works and two films, and analyze how their authors or directors present the conflict between myth and reality and how they resolve it, if they resolve it. (Points: 45 of 130. Time: 60 of 180 minutes.)

8 *Man's Hope* is a novel about the Spanish Civil War written while the war was still going on. *La Guerre Est Finie* is a film about Spanish revolutionaries depicting their activities nearly thirty years after the civil war. Discuss how the temporal relationship of each of these works to the civil war is reflected in the character of the works themselves and in the differences between them. (Points: 58 of 100. Time: 30 of 50 minutes.)

9 Write an essay on one of these topics: The role of the narrator in *Tom Jones* and *Pride and Prejudice* or the characters of Uncle Toby and Miss Bates. (Points: 33 of 100. Time: 60 of 180 minutes.)

24

Creating a Portfolio

A **portfolio** displays your work. Portfolios for college composition courses usually include a selection of your writing for the course and an essay reflecting on your writing and on what you learned in the course. The contents of a portfolio will, of course, vary from writer to writer and from instructor to instructor. This chapter provides some advice for assembling a writing portfolio using the resources in *The St. Martin's Guide to Writing*.

Purposes of a Writing Portfolio

Portfolios are generally used to display an individual's accomplishments. Artists present portfolios of their best work to gallery owners. Designers and architects present portfolios of their most successful work to potential clients. Writing students may be asked to submit a portfolio of their work for evaluation. No matter what the occasion, a portfolio presents a rich opportunity to show what you can do.

Creating a portfolio for a composition course enables you to present your best, most representative, or most extensively revised writing. Your instructor will assign the final grade, but how you select the materials included in your portfolio and describe them in your introductory essay may have some influence on your instructor's judgment. Most important, selecting your work and composing an introductory reflective essay give you an opportunity to review, reinforce, and therefore better remember and apply what you have learned. Reviewing your work can increase your satisfaction with the course, give you insights into your intellectual development, and help you recognize your strengths and weaknesses.

Assembling a Portfolio for Your Composition Course

Some instructors give students free rein in deciding what to include in their portfolio, but most specify what the portfolio should include. Instructors usually ask students to select a certain number of essays, and they may specify that certain types of essays be included, such as one based on personal experience or observation and another based on research, along with other materials, like in-class writing or responses to readings. Many instructors also ask students to include materials that reflect their writing process (such as invention work, drafts, and critical responses). In addition to a selection of course materials, instructors usually require a reflective essay or a letter that introduces the portfolio and evaluates the writer's own work.

Instructors who require portfolios often do not assign grades to individual drafts or revisions but wait until the end of the term to grade the entire portfolio. In such cases, instructors may ask students to submit a midterm portfolio for an in-progress course evaluation. A midterm portfolio usually includes plans for revising one or more of the essays included.

There are many ways to assemble portfolios, and you will need to determine exactly what your instructor expects your portfolio to include. Here are some of the variables to consider:

- How many essays should be included in the portfolio?
- Will there be an opportunity to revise essays further for the portfolio?
- What other material should be included (such as invention or research notes, exercises, notes from collaborative activities, analyses of readings, or downloaded Web pages)?
- May material from other courses, workplace projects, or service-learning projects be included?

For more about service learning, see Chapter 26.

- Should the portfolio be introduced by a reflective essay or a letter? If so, how long should it be? Are there any special requirements for it?
- How should the portfolio be organized?

The following sections review specific resources in the *Guide* that can help you compose your portfolio.

Select your work.

Even if your instructor specifies what to include in your portfolio, you have some important decisions to make. Here are some suggestions to help you:

- If you are asked to select only your best essays, begin by rereading them to see how well each one develops the basic features of its genre. Also review any feedback you received from your instructor, classmates, writing center tutors, or other readers.
- If you are asked to make further revisions to one or more of your essays, reread the essay, using the Peer Review Guide for that genre, or get a response to it from your instructor, a classmate, or a writing center tutor. It may also help to review any responses you received on earlier drafts as well as the Troubleshooting Guide for that genre to see what else you could do to improve the essay. Be sure to edit and proofread your essays carefully.
- If you are asked to select an essay based on personal experience, you might choose the literacy narrative you wrote for Chapter 1 or the remembered event essay you wrote for Chapter 2. If you are asked for essays based on firsthand

observation and analysis, look at what you wrote for the profile (Chapter 3), the concept explanation (Chapter 4), the comparative analysis (Chapter 5), or the short story analysis (Chapter 10). If you are asked to include argument essays, review the writing you did for Chapters 6–9.

- If you are asked to select essays incorporating research, look at the essays you wrote for Chapters 4–9.

- If you are asked to select essays with a range of different purposes and audiences, you might begin by reviewing the Determine the Writer's Purpose and Audience sections of the Part One chapters you used. Then reread your invention notes, defining the particular purpose and audience for each essay you wrote.

- If you are asked to include examples of your writing process work, look for your most thoughtful invention work; a first draft from the Writing a Draft section in any of the Guides to Writing in Chapters 2–10; one or more revisions showing significant rethinking or reorganization; your critical reading response to another student's draft showing perceptive criticism and helpful suggestions; or a draft you edited heavily.

- If you are asked to include a complete process for one essay, you should choose process materials that show the quality as well as the quantity of work you have done. Look for examples of thoughtful invention and substantive revision you can point out in your reflective essay.

- If you are asked to select essays that show the progress you have made in the course, you may want to choose those that underwent radical change during the term.

Reflect on your work and what you have learned.

Many instructors require a written statement in the form of an essay or a letter introducing the portfolio. Some may ask for a simple description of the work presented in your portfolio; others may prefer an evaluation of your work; still others may want you to connect your learning in this course to other courses and to work you hope to do in the future. Keeping the following considerations in mind will help you write a thoughtful, well-organized statement to your instructor about what you have learned:

- ***Introduce and describe your work.*** Because you will need to refer to several works or parts of a work, name each item in your portfolio in a consistent way. In describing an essay, give its title, genre (using the title of the chapter in *The St. Martin's Guide*), purpose, audience, and topic.

If you need help writing an evaluation, review Chapter 8.

- ***Justify your choices.*** When you justify what you see as your "best" work, you think critically about the standards you are using to evaluate good writing in each genre. The *Guide* sets forth clear criteria for each kind of writing in the Use the Basic Features and Peer Review Guide sections in Chapters 2–10. Review these sections as you judge the success of your essay, and refer to them as you explain your analysis.

- ***Illustrate your growth as a writer with specific examples.*** You may have selected work to show how you have grown as a writer, but you should not assume your readers will read the portfolio as you do without some guidance. You need to show them where they can find evidence that supports your analysis by citing relevant examples from the work included in your portfolio. Summarize or quote your examples, and be sure to tell readers what you think the examples illustrate. Also refer to them in a way that will help readers locate them with ease—perhaps by page and paragraph number (see the next section for some suggestions for organizing your portfolio).

- *Use the Guide to help you reflect on your learning.* Your instructor may ask you to consider what you learned in writing and revising a particular essay or what you learned about the process of writing that essay. In either case, doing so will help you anchor your reflections in the specific work you have done using this book. Consider what you have learned analyzing and discussing the readings, drafting and researching, participating in groups, getting and giving critical comments, and revising and editing. Look again at the Reflection sections in Chapters 2–10. There you will find questions that will help you reflect on how you solved problems when revising an essay and how your writing can be situated and understood in a larger social context. You may well be able to use your responses to these questions in your portfolio's reflective essay.

Organize your portfolio.

Some instructors prescribe the portfolio's design and organization, while others allow students to be creative. Follow your instructor's specific guidelines. If your instructor doesn't supply guidelines, here are some possibilities for organizing your portfolio:

- *Include a table of contents.* Portfolios need a table of contents so that readers can see at a glance what is included and where it is located. Be sure to identify all the parts and specify the page on which each part begins. For online portfolios, link each item in your table of contents to your work.

- *Label each item.* If your instructor does not specify how you should label your work, develop a clear system on your own. You may need to explain your system briefly in a note on the table of contents or in your introductory reflective essay, where you refer to particular items in your portfolio. For example, you could use the *Guide* chapter number to identify each essay assignment. To indicate process materials, consider using the chapter number and title and the relevant heading from that chapter's Guide to Writing section (such as Chapter 2, Writing a Draft). To identify different drafts, you could write on the top left margin of every page the chapter number, essay title, and draft number. For drafts that received a critical reading, you might want to add the notation "Read by *S.*" You should also date all your work.

- *Sequence the material.* If your instructor does not indicate how you should order the work included in your portfolio, you will have to decide yourself. If your instructor asks you to present two or more examples of your best work, you may want to begin with the essay you consider your very best. If your instructor asks you to show the progress you have made in the course, you could begin with your weakest essay and either show how you improved it or present later essays that were stronger. If your instructor asks you to demonstrate growth, you might organize your work by the particular areas that improved. For example, you could show that you learned to rework your writing substantially by presenting multiple drafts. Or to show that you learned to edit effectively or to avoid certain sentence errors, you could give examples of a particular error you made one or two times early on but avoided in later drafts.

25

Writing in Business and Scientific Genres

Genres are simply categories or types of texts. Movies, for example, may be categorized into genres such as action adventure, romantic comedy, or film noir. Audiences for each of these genres of film have likely seen romantic comedies or noir films in the past, so they bring certain expectations based on that experience to the next romantic comedy or film noir they see. The same is true for genres that you are likely to read or create: Many of your decisions—from what to write about to the organizational structure, length, formatting, and design—are affected by the audience's genre expectations. While writers usually try to satisfy readers' expectations, genre conventions also provide opportunities for creativity. Depending on the *rhetorical situation* and the audience's openness to innovation, writers may play with genre conventions. But anticipating when your audience will respond to a genre surprise with delight rather than rejection is crucial.

Each of the genres you will encounter in this chapter—from business documents such as résumés and business letters to laboratory reports—are highly conventional genres in which surprises are unlikely to be met with delight. Readers of each of these genres expect writers to get directly to the point in clear, unadorned prose and to follow the format prescribed for the genre. As you examine the documents in this chapter, analyze the way language and design (*typography, color, white space,* and *visuals*) are used to inform and guide readers. What language choices and design features make the documents easy to read? What choices and features make finding specific information within the documents easy? What choices and features make the documents easy to use?

For more about design, see Chapter 22.

Business Letters

The **business letter** (such as the one shown in Figure 25.1) is the document most often used for correspondence between representatives of one organization and another, though e-mail messages are increasingly being used in place of business

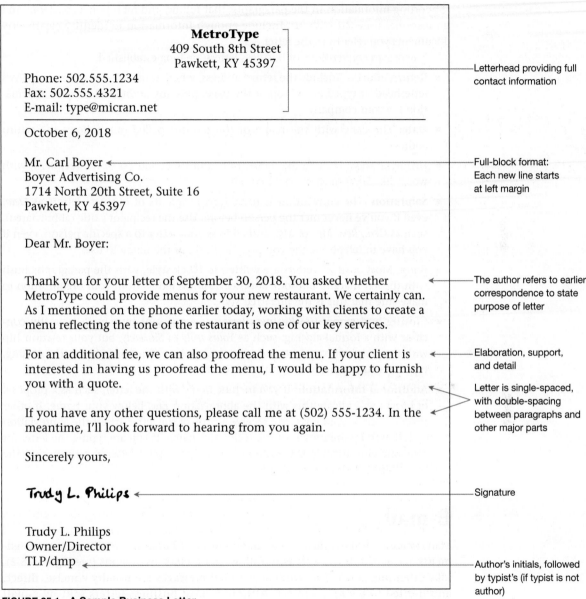

FIGURE 25.1   A Sample Business Letter

letters. Business letters are written to obtain information about a company's products, to register or respond to a complaint, to introduce other documents (such as a proposal) that accompany the letter, or to apply for a job.

Whether a letter is delivered electronically or in print, the expectations are the same: The writer should state the purpose of the letter in the first few lines, provide supporting information in the paragraphs that follow, and maintain a courteous and professional tone throughout. Include enough information to identify clearly any documents you refer to in the letter.

The design conventions of business letters are long established:

- **Return address:** Include the return address, whether included in your company's letterhead or typed at the top of the page, plus any additional contact information for your company.

- **Date:** The date, with the name of the month spelled out, follows the return address.

- **Inside address:** Include the name, title, and street address of the recipient, with words like *Street* or *Avenue* spelled out.

- **Salutation:** The convention is to address recipients of business letters as *Dear,* even if you've never met the person before. Use the recipient's title (abbreviated), such as *Gen., Rev., Mr.,* or *Ms.,* and address your letter to a specific person, even if you have to telephone the company to find out the name to use.

- **Body:** Most business letters are written in block style, with the paragraphs flush with the left margin. But look at other business letters from your organization to make sure that this is the preferred style.

- **Closing and signature:** Business letters, even if sent by e-mail, typically conclude with a formal closing, such as *Yours truly* or *Sincerely,* but your relationship with the recipient may influence your choice here. Four lines below the closing, type your full name, and sign the letter above it.

- **Additional information:** If you include items with the letter, such as a proposal or brochure, indicate this with the abbreviation *Enc.* below your name. If other people, such as your boss, will receive a copy of the letter, insert the abbreviation *cc:* followed by the initials of the recipient's name. If you are typing the letter for someone else, include the author's initials (in capital letters), a slash, and the typist's initials (in lowercase letters).

E-mail

Many students and instructors rely on **e-mail** to exchange information about assignments and schedules as well as to follow up on class discussions (see Figure 25.2). Like other business correspondence, e-mail messages are usually concise, direct, and limited to a single subject. Although most business letters sent by e-mail should be fairly formal, other e-mail messages may be polite but informal. Because of the deluge of e-mails, e-mail messages should always include a clear, accurate subject line.

If you are part of a large or complex organization, you may want to repeat your name and add such information as your job title, division, and telephone extension in a "signature" at the end of the document.

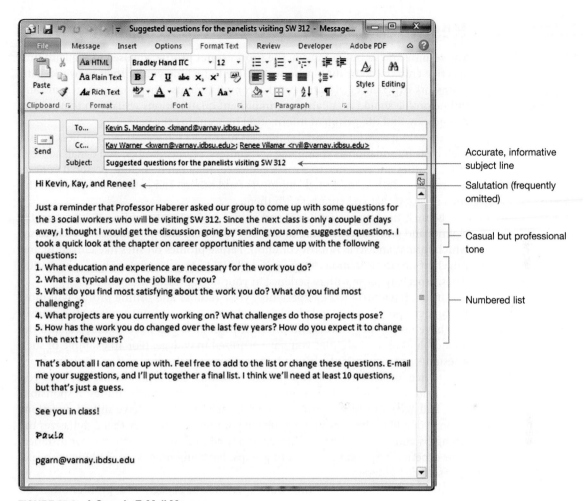

Accurate, informative subject line

Salutation (frequently omitted)

Casual but professional tone

Numbered list

FIGURE 25.2   A Sample E-Mail Message

E-mail is a broader medium of communication than the business letter. Nevertheless, in anything other than quick e-mails to friends, you should maintain a professional tone. Avoid sarcasm and humor, which may not come across as you intend, and be sure to proofread and spell-check your message before sending it. Also, because e-mail messages are accessible to many people besides the intended recipient, always be careful about what you write in an e-mail message.

Though e-mail messages themselves are among the simplest forms of electronic documents, software programs allow you to attach files, insert hypertext links, and insert pictures and graphics into your e-mail documents. If you have promised to insert an attachment to an e-mail message, always pause before sending to make sure the promised attachment is included.

Résumés and Online Professional Profiles

The **résumé** and its online cousin, the **professional profile**, are used to acquaint prospective employers (or those who would like to include you in their network) with your work experience, education, and accomplishments. Therefore, your résumé and online profile should highlight your important qualifications visually so that readers can quickly find the pertinent information by scanning the page.

To make it easy for potential employers to contact job seekers, all résumés contain such basic information as your name and address, phone number, and e-mail address. Since profiles are available to a mass audience, they rarely include personal contact information; rather, interested employers (and others) can contact you through the site or request that you connect with them.

Because the format of résumés and online professional profiles varies among disciplines and professions, be sure to research your field and potential employers to see which format and style is most common. Peruse profiles on sites like Linked In and AngelList (for those in or hoping to join tech fields) to get a sense of how other candidates, especially those with experience in your field, present themselves.

If you have little work experience, your résumé and online profile will most likely focus on your academic background—your grade point average, the courses you have taken, the projects and internships (if any) you have completed, and the applicable skills and abilities you have acquired in college. (For an example of such a résumé, see Figure 25.3.) If you have extensive, relevant, and continuous work experience, create a reverse-chronological résumé or profile, listing the jobs you have held (beginning with the most recent) and describing the duties, responsibilities, and accomplishments associated with each one. If you have shifted directions during your adult life, consider organizing your résumé in a way that emphasizes the strengths and skills you have acquired and used in different settings—for instance, your experience speaking in front of groups, handling money, or working with specific software programs.

In addition to summarizing your experience or background, profiles offer you an opportunity to reinforce your personal brand or career goals, so use the space to impress readers and inspire them to connect with you. Résumés, too, may start with a personal statement that emphasizes the writer's goals and achievements.

Résumés typically do not include photographs or personal information about age, height, or weight. Profiles frequently do include a photograph, but check to see whether others in your field have included one, and make sure that the photograph you include reinforces a professional image.

Résumés and professional profiles offer a potential employer a first impression of you. If you hope to have an opportunity to make a second impression, review your résumé and profile carefully, and proofread your documents multiple times before you post them. Is all the information accurate? Do your résumé and profile present you in the best possible light without exaggerating or misleading readers? Are they error-free? Although you can update and revise online profiles, anything you include could potentially be archived and thus could follow you throughout your career.

Kim Hua
Current Address: MS 1789, Union College, Union, PA 55342
Permanent Address: 702 Good Street, Borah, ID 83702
Phone: (412) 555-1234 E-mail: khua@mailer.union.edu — Contact information

EDUCATION

| Union College | Bachelor of Arts, | Anticipated May 2019 |
| Union, PA | Child Development | GPA: 3.7 |

Relevant Courses: Lifespan Human Development, Infancy and Early Childhood, Parent-Child Relations, Fundamentals of Nutrition, Education of the Preschool Child

Relevant Projects: Coordinator, collaborative research project analyzing educational goals for local Head Start program. Lead writer, report on parent-child relations, delivered to the Borah, Idaho, School Board.

CHILD DEVELOPMENT WORK EXPERIENCE

- *Summer 2017, Union College Child-Care Center, Union College, Union, PA* ← Work experience begins with most current employment

  Child Care Provider: Provided educational experiences and daily care for three 2-year-olds and four 3-year-olds. Prepared daily activity agendas.

- *Summer 2016, St. Alphonsus Day Care Center, St. Alphonsus Hospital, Union, PA*

  Child Care Provider: Provided educational experiences and daily care for a group of nine children ages six through ten.

- *Fall 2015, Governor's Commission for the Prevention of Child Abuse, Union, PA* — Relevant volunteer work

  Intern: Located online resources relevant to the prevention of child abuse. Recommended which resources to include in the Web site of the Governor's Commission.

OTHER WORK EXPERIENCE

2016 to present, Union Falls Bed & Breakfast, Union, PA
Payroll Manager: Maintain daily payroll records for all employees, ← Other experience showing compile daily and weekly reports of payroll costs for the manager, and dependability and ensure compliance with all applicable state and federal laws governing responsibility payroll matters.

PROFESSIONAL AFFILIATIONS

Past President, Union College Child and Family Studies Club; Student Member, American Society of Child Care Professionals; Member, National Child Care Providers

FIGURE 25.3 A Sample Résumé

Job-Application Letters

A **job-application letter** (sometimes called a **cover letter**) is sent with a résumé when you apply for a job. The primary purpose of the job-application letter is to persuade your reader that you are a qualified candidate for employment and to introduce your résumé. For college students and recent graduates, most job-application letters (such as the one shown in Figure 25.4) consist of four paragraphs:

1. **Paragraph 1:** Identify the position you are applying for and how you became aware of its availability. If you are not applying for a specific position, the first paragraph should express your desire to work for the particular organization.

2. **Paragraph 2:** Briefly describe your education, focusing on specific achievements, projects, and relevant coursework.

3. **Paragraph 3:** Briefly describe your work experience, focusing on relevant responsibilities and accomplishments.

   Note that paragraphs 2 and 3 should not merely restate what is in your résumé; rather, they should help persuade your reader that you are qualified for the job.

4. **Paragraph 4:** Express your willingness to provide additional information and to be interviewed at the employer's convenience.

Job-application letters follow the format for a business letter (see pp. 630–32). If sending the application packet electronically, you will be required to copy and paste the letter into a text box. If possible, send the letter as a PDF to avoid the possibility of formatting or other errors creeping in. If you are applying for a job via e-mail, follow the advice in the section on pp. 632–33.

Web Sites

Although Web sites offer the potential for expanded use of color, visuals (including animation and video), and audio files, the general principles of design used for paper documents can be applied to them. Start by considering your rhetorical situation: What is your purpose—to entertain, inform, or persuade? Who are your readers—your family and friends or a broader group? What is the occasion prompting the creation of your site—are you chronicling a gap year or persuading other students of the benefits of taking a year off between high school and college? In what context will your Web site be accessed—from a computer screen or on a mobile device? All these factors will affect the decisions you make as you compose, design, and post your Web pages.

Most nonprofessionals use WYSIWYG (what you see is what you get) platforms like WordPress to create Web sites. Such platforms make creating a Web page easy: You simply need to choose a design, then add text and photos to create effective Web pages.

308 Fairmont Street ← ——————— Modified block format:
Warren, CA 07812   Address, date, and signature
June 6, 2018   block begins five spaces to
                                             the right of center

Ms. Ronda Green
Software Engineer
Santa Clara Technology
P.O. Box 679
Santa Clara, CA 09145

Dear Ms. Green:

I am responding to your June 5 posting on Monster.com (reference ← ———— Purpose of the letter
#91921) announcing that Santa Clara Technology is accepting résumés
for an entry-level engineer position in the Quality Assurance Department.
I think that my experience as an intern in quality assurance and my educational background qualify me for this position.

As my résumé states, I graduated this past May from the University of Southern ← ——— Education paragraph
California (USC) with a bachelor of science degree in Interdisciplinary Studies.
The Interdisciplinary Studies program at USC allows students to develop
a degree plan spanning at least two disciplines. My degree plan included
courses in computer science, marketing, and technical communication. In
addition to university courses, I have completed courses in team dynamics;
project management; and C, C++, and C# programming offered by the
training department at PrintCom, a manufacturer of high-end laser printers.

Throughout last summer, I worked as an intern in the quality-assurance ← ——— Work-experience paragraph
department of PrintCom. I assisted quality-assurance engineers in testing
printer drivers, installers, and utilities. In addition, I maintained a database
containing the results of these tests and summarized the results in weekly
reports. This experience gave me valuable knowledge of the principles of
quality assurance and of the techniques used in testing software.

I would appreciate the opportunity to discuss further the education, skills, ← ——— Concluding paragraph
and abilities I could bring to Santa Clara Technology. You can reach me any
workday after 3 p.m. (PDT) at (907) 555-1234 or by e-mail at sstur17@axl.com.

Sincerely yours,

Shelley Sturman

Shelley Sturman

Enc.: résumé

FIGURE 25.4   A Sample Job-Application Letter

When choosing a template or theme from the preexisting designs, consider your audience and purpose. A Web page created to share a chronicle of your gap year with friends and family is likely to have a very different look from one created to showcase your portfolio for potential employers.

To post your site, you will need to obtain a domain name and choose a hosting service. When devising a domain name, choose one that is

- unique—if your preferred name is chosen, you can add a noun to the end of the string;
- short and easy to type and remember;
- an accurate reflection of your site's content.

There are many Web hosting services to choose from. Do some research to make sure the host is appropriate, and choose a plan that is in keeping with your needs. If you're planning to write a blog for friends or to chronicle your college experience, there's no need to go for the most expensive plan.

Consider the following guidelines when designing a Web site:

To learn more about creating a cluster diagram, see Chapter 11.

- ***Design the navigation of your site***. Sketch out the Web pages you want to include in your Web site, and think about how users will navigate from page to page. Even creating a simple cluster diagram can help. Put the home page in the center of your diagram, and make sure that all the pages of your Web site include a link back to your home page, so that readers can access it easily. Because Web pages include links to other Web pages, as well as to video, animation, or sound files, readers are likely to navigate your text in a nonlinear fashion, starting almost anywhere they like and branching off whenever a link piques their curiosity. To help readers find their way around, provide a site map or "index" page. You can also make your text easier to read by judiciously limiting the number of links you embed in it. Once your site is complete, check your links to make sure they all lead where they are supposed to.

- ***Make your Web site accessible***. For the visually impaired, add features for screen readers, such as alt tags (words that can be read by a screen reader when a mouse hovers over an image) to describe images accurately; transcripts for videos; links that explain the content they connect to ("check out my profile of University of Maryland lacrosse coach John Tillman" rather than just "click here"); and periods between the letters of abbreviations (*F.B.I.*), so that screen readers can pronounce them. Also choose colors that color-blind users can differentiate. For the hearing impaired, include subtitles for all audio files.

To learn more about design, see Chapter 22.

- ***Use the elements of document design***. Most principles of good design apply to Web page design as well. Also keep in mind elements of design that make it easier to read online: Keep the background of a Web page light in tone so that your text can be read with ease. Because colored type can also be difficult to read, avoid vibrant colors for long blocks of text. Bear in mind that most readers are used to reading dark (typically black) text on a light (typically white) background.

This simplicity will also make it easier for the elderly and visually impaired to access your site.

- *Chunk information carefully, and keep your Web pages short*. Because many people have difficulty reading long documents on a computer screen, be sure to chunk your information into concise paragraphs. Also, readers often find it difficult to read a Web page that requires extensive scrolling down the screen. Break up long text blocks into separate Web pages that require no more than one or two screens of scrolling. Use links to connect the text blocks and to help readers navigate across the pages.

- *Include the date posted or updated*. To help readers who will want to know whether your Web site has been updated recently and who may need to cite your Web site in their list of works cited or references, always include the date you post or update your Web page.

- *Include an "About the Author" page*. Provide relevant information about yourself to enhance your *ethos*, or credibility. If you are interested in hearing from readers, you may want to include your e-mail address, but avoid providing a link. Instead, write out your e-mail address—johnsmithatgmaildotcom, not johnsmith@gmail.com—to avoid getting robot-generated messages.

Lab Reports

A **lab report** is written to summarize the results of an experiment or test and to provide a road map for others who wish to repeat the experiment; it generally consists of the following five sections:

1. **Introduction:** provides background information: the hypothesis of the experiment, the question to be answered, how the question arose

2. **Methods:** describes how the research was conducted or the experiment performed

3. **Results:** describes what happened as a result of your research or experiment

4. **Discussion:** explains your results

5. **References:** cites the sources used in conducting the research, performing the experiment, or writing the report

The content, style, and format of a lab report may vary from discipline to discipline or from course to course. Before writing a lab report, be certain that you understand your instructor's requirements, and look at sample lab reports in your field. The sample in Figure 25.5 shows excerpts from a lab report written by two students in a soils science course. It uses the documentation format advocated by the Council of Science Editors (CSE).

Title, authors, course number, and date (centered) on title page

Bulk Density and Total Pore Space

Joe Aquino and Sheila Norris

Soils 101, Lab Section 1

October 6, 2018

Background information that the reader will need to understand the experiment

Introduction

Soil is an arrangement of solids and voids. The voids, called pore spaces, are important for root growth, water movement, water storage, and gas exchange between the soil and the atmosphere. A medium-textured soil good for plant growth will have a pore-space content of about 0.50 (half solids, half pore space). The total pore space is the space between sand, silt, and clay particles (micropore space) plus the space between soil aggregates (macropore space).[1]

Detailed explanation of the methods used

Methods

To determine the bulk density[2] and total pore space of two soil samples, we hammered cans into the wall of a soil pit (Hagerstown silt loam). We collected samples from the Ap horizon and a Bt horizon. We then placed a block of wood over the cans so that the hammer did not smash them. After hammering the cans into the soil, we dug the cans, now full of soil, out of the horizons; we trimmed off any excess soil. The samples were dried in an oven at 105°C for two days and weighed. We then determined the volume of the cans by measuring the height and radius, as follows:

volume = $1/4\ r^2h$

We used the formulas noted in the Introduction to determine bulk density and porosity of the samples. Particle density was assumed to be 2.65 g/cm^3. The textural class of each horizon was determined by feel; that is, we squeezed and kneaded each sample and assigned it to a particular textural class.

FIGURE 25.5   A Sample Lab Report

Results

We found both soils to have relatively light bulk densities and large porosities, but the Bt horizon had greater porosity than the Ap. Furthermore, we determined that the Ap horizon was a silt loam, whereas the Bt was a clay (see Table 1).

Table 1

Textural class, bulk density, and porosity of two Hagerstown soil horizons

Textural Class	Ap Silt Loam	Bt Clay
Bulk density (g/cm^3)	1.20	1.08
Porosity	0.55	0.59

Presents the results of the experiment, with a table showing quantitative data

Discussion

Both soils had bulk densities and porosities in the range we would have expected from the discussions in the lab manual and textbook. The Ap horizon is a medium-textured soil and is considered a good topsoil for plant growth, so a porosity around 0.5 is consistent with those facts. The Bt horizon is a fine-textured horizon (containing a large amount of clay), and the bulk density is in the predicted range.

Explains what was significant about the results of the research

References

1. Brady NC, Weil RR. The nature and properties of soils. 11th ed. New York (NY): Prentice-Hall; 1996. 291 p.
2. Blake GR, Hartge KH. Bulk density. In: Klute A, editor. Methods of soil analysis. Part 1. 2nd ed. Madison (WI): American Society of Agronomy/Soil Science Society of America; 1986. pp. 363–376. (Agronomy; vol. 9).

The references are in the format recommended by the Council of Science Editors (CSE). They begin on a new page.

26

Writing for and about Your Community

Service learning combines classroom education with life experience. In service-learning programs, students are most often placed in off-campus positions with government bureaus, such as local parks and recreation departments, or nonprofit organizations that offer community support services, such as tutoring or computer skills. In these positions, students have an opportunity to apply what they are studying in class. Here are a few examples:

- Nursing students teach expectant mothers about prenatal and infant care.
- Chemistry students tour local elementary schools demonstrating science "magic."
- Botany students teach fourth graders about plants native to their region.
- Zoology students help researchers gather samples for a study of local amphibian populations.
- Political science students work with the local government to increase voter turnout.
- English-speaking students tutor grade school children who are having trouble learning to read and write English.

Though you will probably find much to write about in your community service experience, you may also find writing to a wider audience to be part of your service.

Writing *about* Your Service Experience

Service learning may put you in a position to write for a nonacademic audience. For example, you might write an editorial for your campus or local newspaper in which you argue for increased support for your service organization or project. You might craft a letter to local government officials or even representatives to the state or national legislature suggesting a solution to a specific problem.

For many of the writing assignments in Part One, you might also draw on your service experience for source material. Here are some ideas for using the writing activities discussed in Part One of this textbook:

Chapter 2: Remembering an Event

- Write about your first day of service. What happened? How did you feel? What did you learn? How did it differ from what you expected to learn?

- Write about a particularly difficult day. Why was it difficult? How did you handle the situation? What would you do differently? What did you learn from the experience?

Chapter 3: Writing Profiles

- Write about the place where you are doing your service. What does it look like? How does it make you feel? How does the location reflect or affect what goes on there? What *does* go on there?

- Write about one of the people you have met doing your service. What is he or she like? How is he or she typical (or atypical) of other people in the same position? What makes this person special or different?

Chapter 4: Explaining a Concept

- Write about a concept with which you were unfamiliar before you did your service. What does the concept mean? How is it important in the context of your service experience? How does what you learned about this concept make you think differently now?

- Write about a concept that you knew but now understand differently because of your service. How has your understanding of the concept changed? What caused that change? How might you explain that change to someone who does not share your experience?

Chapter 5: Analyzing and Synthesizing Opposing Arguments

- Write about a debate that is relevant to the type of service you are doing, and analyze each position in the debate. (Note that there may be more than two.) Who are the major proponents of each position? What are the main reasons and evidence given to support each position? What are factors motivating the adherents of each position?

Chapter 6: Arguing a Position

- Write an argument in support of the service organization you are working with. Why should people support it? How can they support it? Why is it a worthwhile endeavor?

- Write an argument about the value of service learning. What have you gained from this experience? Who should participate? What are the advantages of service learning to individuals and the community?

Chapter 7: Proposing a Solution

- Write about a process or procedure within or affecting the organization you are working with that you think needs to be improved. Why does it need to be improved? How might it be improved?

- Write about a policy, law, or practice that you think should be eliminated or revised because it negatively affects the organization you are working with. What would be the benefit of eliminating or revising it? What steps would need to be taken in order to change the policy, law, or practice?

Chapter 8: Justifying an Evaluation

- Write about how effectively the organization you are working with satisfies its objectives. How do you measure its effectiveness?

- Write about your school's service-learning program. In what ways is it most successful? In what ways could it be improved?

Chapter 9: Arguing for Causes or Effects

- Write about the underlying causes of a problem or situation that you have encountered through your service-learning experience. What brought the problem about? What circumstances perpetuate it?

- Write about why service-learning programs have become common. What function do they serve that traditional education models do not? What demands do they meet?

Find a topic.

One of the many advantages of service learning is that it can present numerous topics that might be fruitfully explored through your writing. To generate a substantial list of ideas, you need only ask yourself some simple questions:

- Who is most affected by the situation, and how are these people affected?
- How long has this situation existed?
- What forces shape the situation? Can anything be done to alter them?
- How have other organizations handled this issue? How might the situation be improved?
- What common perceptions do people hold about this situation? What are my own perceptions?
- How might an audience's perceptions be changed?

Gather sources.

A service-learning environment can provide field research sources that would otherwise be difficult to tap. The most significant of these potential sources are the people who run the organization in which you are doing your service. If you have focused your writing on the kinds of issues that are relevant to your service, these people can provide expertise. Many of the people you work with will have years of experience and specialized training and will probably have researched the subject themselves. Take advantage of your opportunity to tap their knowledge. When approached courteously, people are often more than willing to share what they know.

Depending on the situation, your service site might also be a good place to circulate a questionnaire or conduct a survey to help you gather information about your subject. Of course, your own observations and experiences as you perform your service will be valuable as well. You might consider keeping a daily journal in which you record these experiences and observations. When you are ready to begin writing, you will have already done some early invention work.

The service organization itself might also be a good source of information. Such organizations often collect and produce literature that is relevant to their mission. Your organization might even maintain its own small library of resource materials. Frequently, such organizations are also part of a network of similar groups that share their expertise through newsletters, trade journals, Web sites, or online discussion groups. Explore these unique resources.

Keep in mind the ethical considerations that are involved. Many service-learning environments, such as those that involve counseling, tutoring, or teaching, can give you access to information that should be kept confidential, especially if you are working with minors. Be sure that you are open about your information gathering and that everyone whom you might use as a source knows your intentions. Any questionnaires should state what you intend to do with the information gathered. Any information gained from interviews should be properly attributed, but obtain your subjects' explicit permission before using their names. Err on the side of caution and consideration, and ask your instructor for guidance if you have any questions about how to treat sensitive material.

For suggestions on making observations, conducting interviews, and creating questionnaires, see Chapter 17. See also Chapter 3.

Writing *for* Your Service Organization

Some service-learning situations will put you in a position not just to write *about* your service experience but also to write *for* your service experience. You might be asked to create flyers, brochures, press releases, or Web pages for a community organization. You might help craft presentations or reports. Though these may not be academic writing activities, the strategies presented in this text still apply. You might be asked, for example, to write a brochure that explains the purpose and function of the organization. In effect, you would be writing an explanation, and you would need to keep in mind the basic features of this genre.

For more about explaining, see Chapter 4.

In such writing situations, it is important to consider your rhetorical situation: What is your purpose? Who is your audience? How do you want readers to think of you or the organization you represent? In what medium will you be communicating? Whereas in class you might be asked to select a topic and write an essay in which you argue for a position or a solution, in your service experience you might be asked to create a presentation that explains the importance of a no-kill animal shelter to potential donors or a brochure that urges commuters to carpool to reduce pollution and ease traffic congestion. Identifying your rhetorical situation will help you communicate your goals more effectively.

For more about arguing for a position, see Chapter 6; for more about arguing for a solution, see Chapter 7; for more about creating an effective presentation, see Chapter 22.

For suggestions on how to make such a collaboration run smoothly and successfully, see Chapter 27.

Writing in organizations is frequently a collaborative process. Everyone involved in the process is expected to do his or her part. When your written document will be used to represent your organization in any way, respect the expertise of the staff, especially when their assessment of the audience differs from your own. In some situations, your service writing may be heavily edited—or not used at all. Make sure your instructor and service-learning program administrators are aware of any instances in which you and members of the organization are having difficulty reaching a consensus.

For more about design, see Chapter 22.

Finally, remember that nonacademic writing often requires greater attention to presentation than most kinds of academic writing. One-inch margins and double-spaced text are simply not enough when you are trying to create eye-catching documents such as brochures and press releases. Document design can not only make a piece of writing more visually attractive and thereby stimulate readers' interest but also help readers with different needs identify which parts of the document are most relevant. Therefore, carefully consider the layout and configuration of your document, and take advantage of the flexibility that even a simple word processing program can give you.

27

Writing Collaboratively

Writers often seek advice and feedback from friends, colleagues, or mentors on individual writing projects. For instance, they may consult a librarian for advice on research, try out an argument on a coworker or fellow student, or ask a trusted friend to check for grammar errors. On some occasions, writers also work in small groups to research, plan, and compose joint writing projects.

Working with others is often referred to as *collaboration*. Collaborating with others on individual projects and especially on joint writing projects can be challenging but also rewarding. The following advice will help you anticipate the difficulties so that you can get the most out of the collaboration.

Working with Others on Your Individual Writing Projects

This book assumes that you will collaborate with others, at least with your instructor and classmates, to write your essays. Class discussion of the readings will help you understand more about the genres you will be writing, and responses to your invention work and to drafts of your essays will give you ideas for writing more effectively.

Collaboration is also built directly into the activities in the writing assignment chapters. In every assignment chapter, four activities ask you to collaborate with other students in a purposeful way. Chapter 6, "Arguing a Position," for example, has these activities:

> *Practicing the Genre: Debating a Position.* This activity asks you to get together with a small group of your classmates to develop reasons for and against a position. Afterward, your group is encouraged to discuss the process, reflecting on what parts presented the biggest challenges, and why.

> *Make connections.* This activity, following each of the professional readings, invites you to examine some of the important ideas and underlying assumptions of the reading. In small-group discussion—face-to-face or online—you can explore your responses and develop your understanding.

Test Your Choice. As you choose an issue and decide how best to frame it for your audience, you can get feedback to determine whether your choice will be effective with readers.

Peer Review Guide. Once you have a draft of your essay, anyone using the Peer Review Guide can give you a comprehensive evaluation of your work, and you can do likewise for others. Because the Chapter 6 Peer Review Guide reflects the particular requirements of an essay arguing a position, anyone using it to evaluate your draft will be able to give you focused, relevant advice.

In these four activities, you collaborate with others to develop your individual writing by discovering what you may know about a project before you get very far into it, assessing your progress after a period of initial work, and evaluating your first attempts to draft a complete essay. There are many other occasions for fruitful collaboration in the assignment chapters. For instance, in Chapter 6 you might work with other students to complete the Analyze & Write activities that follow the readings. You and another student might exchange revisions of your essays to help each other with final editing and proofreading. Working collaboratively on these activities may not only be easier and more enjoyable but also be more productive, as you'll likely come up with many more ideas than you would on your own.

Following are guidelines for successful collaboration on individual writing projects:

- Whenever you read someone else's writing, have the writer tell you about his or her purpose and readers. Collaboration is always more effective when writers focus on helping other writers achieve their purposes for their particular readers. If a writer is explaining a concept to readers who know nothing about it, as might be the case in Chapter 4, "Explaining a Concept," your comments are likely to be unhelpful if you assume the essay is addressed to those who share your understanding of the concept.

- Know the genre the writer is working in. If a writer is proposing a solution to a problem and you are evaluating the writing as though it were an essay arguing a position, your advice is likely to be off the mark.

- When you evaluate another writer's work, be sure you know the stage of its development. Is it a set of tentative notes for a first draft? A partial draft? A complete draft? A revision? If it is a draft, you want to focus on helping the writer develop and organize ideas; if it is a revision, you might focus exclusively on cueing and coherence or editing and proofreading.

- When you evaluate someone's writing, be helpful and supportive but also frank and specific. You do a writing partner no favor if you shrink from criticizing and giving advice. If your criticism seems grounded in the purpose, audience, and genre, it will probably not seem arbitrary or personal to your partner.

- Bring as much writing as possible to a scheduled meeting with other writers. The further along your writing is, the more you can learn from the collaboration.

- Try to be receptive to criticism. Later, you can decide whether to change your essay, and how.

Collaborating on Joint Writing Projects

In addition to collaborating with others on your individual writing projects, you may have the opportunity to collaborate to produce a single essay. For instance, in Chapter 6, "Arguing a Position," you could collaborate to construct a persuasive argument for a position you share with two or three other students. In Chapter 4, "Explaining a Concept," you could work with a few other students to research and explain a concept, perhaps using graphics or hands-on activities to help others grasp the concept and its implications. In Chapter 7, "Proposing a Solution," you have an opportunity to practice researching and writing proposals, by far the most common type of joint writing project in college, the workplace, and the community.

When people collaborate on joint projects, they often share responsibility for the final product but divide up tasks for the preparation of the final draft. For example, each team member might take on responsibilities related to his or her area of expertise. Someone who knows the problem firsthand might work on developing ways to explain the problem to those who have not experienced it directly. People who have experience making forecasts and planning budgets might be assigned to research and draft those aspects of the proposal. Or you might divide the work in sections, with one person conducting the research, another doing the initial drafting, and a third taking responsibility for revising.

Everyone in the group might suggest ways of improving the draft, and individuals might be assigned parts to strengthen and clarify. When a final draft seems near, one person might be assigned the job of improving cueing and coherence, another might be in charge of editing and proofreading, and a third might work on document design. Because the team shares responsibility for the final document, most teams collectively review the final draft so that errors do not slip through the cracks.

Consider the following workplace writing example. A pharmaceuticals company decided to invest time and money in finding a solution to a problem the company saw as damaging to its business as well as to the community. The company assigned a team of seven division managers and a technical writer, gave them a budget to pay for outside consultants, and asked them to present a written proposal to the state legislature and local school board in six months' time. The pharmaceuticals team divided the project into a series of research and writing tasks like those outlined in the Guide to Writing in Chapter 7. The team members scheduled due dates for each task and progress reports to identify problems as they arose. They assigned responsibility for each task and identified which tasks might need consultation with outside experts.

Writing collaboratively on a joint project certainly has benefits. Collaboration not only draws on the expertise and energy of different people but also creates an outcome that is greater than the sum of its parts. One difficulty of collaborative writing projects, however, is that learning how to work effectively with others takes time and effort. Writers working on a joint project need to spend a lot of time communicating with one another, anticipate conflicts and resolve them constructively, be realistic in scheduling and complete their assigned tasks responsibly, be flexible in their writing process, and be open to different points of view.

To help group members work together constructively on joint writing projects, here are some ground rules you will want to discuss and implement:

- Begin by establishing clear and easy means of communicating with one another. Will you e-mail, text, or call? Exchange e-mail addresses, but also exchange phone numbers as a backup.

- Think about the technology that will enable you to work together most easily. For example, you may decide that creating documents on a sharing site like *Google Drive* will make it easiest for all members of the group to access the documents. Or you may decide to e-mail versions to group members as the work progresses to make sure all group members can work independently until it is time to share.

- Expect to spend a lot of time planning the project together and discussing who will do what and when. Discuss how the group should divide responsibilities. Remember, however, to remain flexible, and keep the lines of communication open to deal with problems as they arise.

- Set a schedule of regular meetings, and agree on how to run the meetings. For example, should someone lead each discussion? Should the role of discussion leader fall to one person or rotate among group members? Should each meeting have an agenda? If so, how and when should it be set?

- Make sure each team member has a say in major decisions, such as choosing a topic and devising a thesis statement. This isn't always easy: Some team members might be inclined to agree with whatever the team seems to want, even if they privately have concerns. However, you can get frank input from every person on the team if you periodically collect comments or votes anonymously.

- Treat one another with respect and consideration, but do not be surprised by disagreements and personality conflicts. Arguing can stimulate thinking—inspiring creativity as well as encouraging each person to explain ideas clearly and systematically—but arguing can also encourage aggressiveness in some people and withdrawal in others. If there is a problem in the way the group interacts, address it immediately, perhaps by calling a special meeting to work out a solution. Try to avoid placing blame. Consider, for example, whether taking turns would ensure that everyone contributes to the discussion and no one dominates. Urge everyone to refrain from characterizing other people and instead to speak only about what they themselves think and feel by making "I" rather than "you" statements.

- Keep track of everyone's progress. Consider creating a chart so that all members can see at a glance what they need to do and when. Schedule regular progress reports so that any problems can be identified immediately.

For more on multimodal presentations, see Chapter 22.

- If the group will make a presentation of the final proposal, plan it carefully, giving each person a role. Rehearse the presentation as a group to make sure it satisfies the time limit and other requirements of the assignment.

Handbook

Contents

How to Use This Handbook

You may use the Handbook on your own when you edit your essays, or your instructor may refer you to specific sections to correct errors in your writing. If using the Handbook on your own, check the Handbook Contents on the previous page, or look in the index for the kind of error you are concerned about.

Your instructor may use the Handbook's letter-and-number system to lead you directly to information about a specific topic—for example, if your instructor noted "P1-b" in the margin of your essay, it would mean you had omitted a necessary comma following an introductory word, phrase, or clause. The Handbook Contents connects codes to page numbers (in this case, H-51) in the Handbook. As an alternative, you can find P1-b by looking through the tabs at the tops of the pages. Each tab indicates the section code for that page and an abbreviation or symbol for the topic covered. If your instructor indicates errors with correction symbols such as *frag* or *ww,* you can find the section where the error is covered by checking the list of correction symbols in the back of this book.

When you locate the section that will help you correct an error or make a sentence more concise or graceful, you will find a brief explanation and examples of correct usage, along with one or more hand-corrected sentences that demonstrate how to edit a sentence. Terms are defined in the margin. If your instructor has assigned this book with LaunchPad (an online course space and e-book), use your activation code to practice these skills in LearningCurve, an adaptive, gamelike quizzing program that quickly learns what you already know and helps you practice what you don't yet understand. LearningCurve activities appear in the Handbook and other relevant sections of the e-book.

While developing this Handbook, ten college writing instructors and four professional editors worked together to identify the twenty-five most common errors* in more than five hundred student essays written in first-year composition courses. These errors are listed below in order of descending frequency. The codes in bold following each error indicate the section number in this Handbook where you can find help with understanding and correcting each error in your own writing.

Top 25 Errors in Student Papers

1. Wordiness **W1-a–W1-c**
2. Misused word **W2-a, W2-e**
3. Incorrect or ambiguous pronoun reference **G1**
4. Verb tense errors **G5-a, G5-b**
5. Missing comma between independent clauses **P1-a**
6. Problems with hyphens between compound adjectives **M1-a**
7. Missing comma after introductory elements **P1-b**
8. Capitalization of proper or common nouns **M2-a**
9. Unnecessary comma between compound elements **P2-a**

---

* Spelling errors were not included.

10. Incorrect spacing **M3**

11. Missing words **E1-a–E1-d**

12. Missing comma with nonrestrictive word groups **P1-c**

13. Comma splice or fused sentence **S1, S2**

14. Problems in using quotation marks with other punctuation **P6-b**

15. Missing or unnecessary hyphens in compound nouns **M1-b**

16. Missing comma with transitional and parenthetical expressions, absolute phrases, and contrasted elements **P1-d**

17. Problems of pronoun-antecedent agreement **G2**

18. Incorrect preposition **W2-b, T3**

19. Misuse of *who, which,* or *that* **G3**

20. Unnecessarily complex sentence structure **W1-b**

21. Spelling out or using figures for numbers incorrectly **M4**

22. Problems with apostrophes in possessive nouns **P7-a**

23. Sentence fragment **S3**

24. Missing comma in items in a series **P1-e**

25. Unnecessary comma with restrictive word groups **P2-b**

This list of the top twenty-five errors can be categorized into the following five major patterns of errors. You may find it useful to keep these patterns in mind as you edit your work.

1. Missing or unnecessary commas **(P1-a–P1-d, P2-a–P2-g)**

2. Errors in word choice **(W1-a–W1-d, W2-a–W2-d)**

3. Errors in pronoun reference, agreement, or use **(G1, G2, G3)**

4. Verb tense errors **(G5-a, G5-b)**

5. Errors in recognizing and punctuating sentences—comma splices, fused sentences, and fragments **(S1, S2, S3)**

Keeping a Record of Your Errors

In addition to checking your work for the errors college students usually make, you will find it useful to keep a record of the errors that *you* usually make. You can then work toward avoiding them.

To use the Record of Errors form on the next page, note the name and section number of each error you make in the left-hand column. (See the Handbook Contents on p. H-1 or the list of correction symbols at the back of the book for the names of errors.) For example, if in your first essay your instructor or another student marks a vague use of the pronoun *this* at the beginning of two of your sentences, locate the section that provides help in correcting this error (G1), and enter the error name in the left column along with the section number. Then under *Essay 1* and next to the name of the error, enter the number *2* to indicate how many times you made this error. As you edit subsequent essays, you can easily review this section in the Handbook to make sure you have avoided this pronoun problem.

By your second or third essay, you should begin to see patterns in the errors you make and to understand how to recognize and correct them.

RECORD OF ERRORS

Name of Error and Section Number in the Handbook	Essay 1	Essay 2	Essay 3	Essay 4	Essay 5	Essay 6	Essay 7

S Sentence Boundaries

S1 Comma Splices

In a comma splice, two **independent clauses** are improperly joined by a comma.

COMMA SPLICE

┌─independent clause─┐ ┌──────── independent clause ────────┐
I know what to do, I just don't know how to do it.
          comma

Because a comma splice can be edited in many ways, first consider how the ideas in the two independent clauses relate. For example, are they equally important, or does one depend on or explain the other? Then select the strategy from the following that will best clarify this relationship for a reader.

Add a subordinating conjunction to one clause, rewording as necessary.

> *After*
> ▶ I started to exercise, my health began to improve.
>   ^

> *Though*
> ▶ I know what to do, I just don't know how to do it.
>   ^

By beginning a clause with a subordinating conjunction, you indicate that the clause is subordinate to—and dependent on—the main clause. Usually, the **dependent clause** explains or qualifies the independent clause. Select the subordinating conjunction carefully, so that it tells the reader how the ideas in the clauses relate to each other.

Separate the independent clauses with a comma and a coordinating conjunction.

> ▶ On *Muppets: The Green Album,* a wide variety of musicians and bands covered songs
>
>   *and*
> made famous by the beloved puppets, the result inspired cross-generational nostalgia
>   ^
> and extra buzz for 2011's new Muppets movie.

>   *but*
> ▶ In 2015, the average fuel consumption by a Japanese car was 40 mpg, the average
>   ^
> American car was still getting only 22 mpg.

The coordinating conjunction tells the reader that the ideas in the two clauses are closely related and equally important.

independent clause A word group with a subject and a predicate that can stand alone as a separate sentence.

subordinating conjunction A word or phrase (such as *although* or *because*) that introduces a dependent clause and relates it to an independent clause.

dependent clause A word group that has a subject and a predicate but cannot stand by itself as a sentence; it must be connected to an independent clause.

coordinating conjunction A word that joins comparable and equally important sentence elements: *for, and, or, but, nor, yet,* or *so.*

Separate the independent clauses with a semicolon.

▶ The tattoo needle looked like an extension of his arm/ the needle was his

brush, and the human body, his canvas.

▶ Nate was very lucky/ he lived to see his hundredth birthday.

The semicolon tells the reader that the ideas in the two clauses are closely connected, but it *implies* the connection rather than stating it. Occasionally, a colon may be used to introduce a second independent clause. See P4-a.

Separate the independent clauses with a semicolon or a period, and add a conjunctive adverb.

conjunctive adverb A word or phrase (such as *finally*, *however*, or *therefore*) that tells how the ideas in two sentences or independent clauses are connected.

▶ He doesn't need the map right now, he is following the direction Kiem pointed

out to him and checking it with the compass.

; instead

▶ He doesn't need the map right now, he is following the direction Kiem pointed out to

him and checking it with the compass.

. Instead

The period shows a stronger break. Conjunctive adverbs are used more frequently in formal than in informal writing.

Turn the independent clauses into separate sentences.

▶ At high noon we were off, paddling down the Potomac River, we were two

to a canoe, with space in the middle for our gear.

. We

The period at the end of the first independent clause tells the reader that one complete sentence is ending and another is beginning.

Turn one independent clause into a phrase that modifies the other.

▶ At high noon we were off, paddling down the Potomac River, ~~we were~~ two to a

canoe, with space in the middle for our gear.

modifying phrase A word group that serves as an adjective or adverb.

Eliminating the subject and verb in the second clause turns it into a **modifying phrase**, reducing the number of words and closely connecting the ideas.

S2 Fused Sentences

A fused or run-on sentence consists of two **independent clauses** run together with no punctuation.

┌── independent clause ──┐┌──────────── independent clause ────────────┐

FUSED <u>Her mood was good I took</u> the opportunity to ask if she had a few minutes

SENTENCE to answer some questions.

Because a fused sentence can be edited in many ways, first consider how the ideas in the two independent clauses are related, and then select the most appropriate strategy from among the following.

Make one of the clauses subordinate to the other by adding a subordinating conjunction and rewording as necessary.

            so   that

▶ Her mood was good I took the opportunity to ask if she had a few minutes to answer

  some questions.

    Although childhood

▶ ~~Childhood~~ is often remembered as delightful, kids can be extremely cruel to one another.

By beginning a clause with a subordinating conjunction, you indicate that the clause is subordinate to—and dependent on—the main clause. Usually, the **dependent clause** explains or qualifies the independent clause. Choose the subordinating conjunction carefully, so that it tells the reader how the dependent clause relates to the independent clause. For example, the writer might emphasize the causal relationship between two clauses by using the word *because*.

    Because her

▶ Her mood was good I took the opportunity to ask if she had a few minutes

  to answer some questions.

Add a comma and a coordinating conjunction to separate the independent clauses.

             , and

▶ The beast was upon me I could feel his paws pressing down on my chest.

The coordinating conjunction tells the reader that the ideas in the two clauses are equally important.

independent clause A word group with a subject and a predicate that can stand alone as a separate sentence.

subordinating conjunction A word or phrase (such as *although* or *because*) that introduces a dependent clause and relates it to an independent clause.

dependent clause A word group that has a subject and a predicate but cannot stand by itself as a sentence; it must be connected to an independent clause.

coordinating conjunction A word that joins comparable and equally important sentence elements: *for, and, or, but, nor, yet,* or *so.*

Separate the independent clauses with a semicolon.

▶ I looked around at the different displays⌃ most were large plasma screens, many

of which were connected to the central unit.

The semicolon tells the reader that the ideas in the two clauses are closely connected, but it *implies* the connection rather than stating it. Occasionally, a colon may be used to introduce a second independent clause. See P4-a.

Separate the independent clauses with a semicolon or a period, and add a conjunctive adverb or a transitional phrase, such as *for example* or *in other words*.

▶ Most students do not do their homework during the day they do it in the evening.
      ⌃*instead*⌃

▶ Most students do not do their homework during the day they do it in the evening.
      ⌀ *Instead*⌃

The period indicates a stronger break.

Turn the independent clauses into separate sentences.

▶ He was only eight⌀ ~~his~~ life hadn't even started.
      His

▶ I couldn't believe it⌀ I had fallen into the campus fountain.

The period at the end of the first independent clause tells the reader that one complete sentence is ending and another is beginning.

Turn one independent clause into a phrase that modifies the other.

▶ I almost dropped my phone⌃ ~~I could feel~~ my hand slipping as I tried to text and use

the self-checkout lane at the same time.

Eliminating the subject and verb in the second clause turns it into a **modifying phrase**, reducing the number of words and closely linking the ideas.

S3   Sentence Fragments

A fragment is either an incomplete sentence, lacking a complete **subject** or **predicate**, or a **dependent clause** punctuated incorrectly as a sentence.

FRAGMENT   Tonight it's my turn. *A ride-along with Sergeant Rob Nether of the Green Valley Police Department.*

---

conjunctive adverb A word or phrase (such as *finally, however,* or *therefore*) that tells how the ideas in two sentences or independent clauses are connected.

modifying phrase A word group that serves as an adjective or adverb.

subject The part of a clause that identifies who or what is being discussed.

predicate The part of a clause that includes a complete verb and describes the action or state of the subject.

dependent clause A word group that has a subject and a predicate but cannot stand by itself as a sentence; it must be connected to an independent clause.

Because a fragment can often be edited in several ways, begin by considering what the fragment lacks and how its ideas relate to those in the sentences before and after it. Then use one of the following strategies to change the fragment into a complete sentence.

Connect the fragment to a complete sentence.

To edit the fragment in the opening example, the writer might connect it to the preceding sentence.

▶ Tonight it's my turn*,* ~~A~~ *for a* ride-along with Sergeant Rob Nether of the Green Valley

Police Department.

▶ A unique design has the advantage of becoming associated with its

role*,* ~~For~~ *for* example, the highly successful Coke bottle shape, which is now

associated with soft drinks.

Eliminate the subordinating word(s) that make a clause dependent.

▶ The world that I was born into demanded continuous work. ~~Where nobody~~ *Nobody* got

ahead, and everyone came home tired.

Add or complete the verb or subject to change a fragment into a complete sentence.

▶ The crowd in the lounge is basically young. Teenagers and twentysomethings*,* *gather there.*

▶ Children are brought up in different ways. Some*,* *grow up* around violence.

Exception: Use fragments intentionally for emphasis or special effect.

▶ The bare utility of the clock echoes the simplicity of the office. No sign of a large hardwood desk, a pillowy leather chair, or even a wall of imposing law books.

Use intentional fragments cautiously. Especially in academic writing, readers may perceive them as errors, regardless of your intentions. In the preceding example, the same impact might also be achieved by using a colon or a dash.

▶ The bare utility of the clock echoes the simplicity of the office*;* No sign of a large

hardwood desk, a pillowy leather chair, or even a wall of imposing law books.

G Grammatical Sentences

G1 Pronoun Reference

Make sure that each **pronoun** clearly refers to one specific **antecedent**.

pronoun A word that replaces a specific noun (such as *it, his, them, yours, myself,* or *which*), points out a specific noun (such as *this, these,* or *that*), or refers to an unspecified person or object (such as *everybody* or *each*).

▶ ┌── antecedent ──┐   pronoun
  The elderly and children are victims when no one bothers to check on *them*.

Eliminate vague uses of *they, it,* or *you*.

antecedent The word or words that a pronoun replaces and to which it refers.

▶ Lani explained that everything is completely supported by individual

                The organization receives
  contributions. ~~They receive~~ no tax support.
        ^

▶ Often, a guest such as Neil deGrasse Tyson or Al Franken appears

               having the same guest return
  more than once. Although it may seem repetitious, it is not when the
                 ^

  guest discusses different topics each time.

▶ Parents argue that beginning the program in the sixth grade is too early.

  They say that   *encourages*
  ~~By~~ exposing teens to sex education early, ~~you encourage~~ them to go out and
  ^   ^

  have sex.

Add a noun, change the pronoun to a noun, or eliminate vague uses of *this, that,* or *which*.

▶ Researchers have found that men interrupt women more than women

            finding
  interrupt men. This may explain why women sometimes find it difficult to start
             ^

  and sustain conversations with men.

                     getting good grades
▶ I was an *A* student, and I thought ~~that~~ should have been enough for any teacher.
                                    ^

Add a missing antecedent, or eliminate a pronoun with no clear antecedent.

▶ In addition to the cars your tenants actually drive, five or six vehicles are

your tenants
always on and around the property. As a result, not only do ~~they~~ park ~~some of~~
^

~~them~~ in front of their neighbors' homes, but their questionable visitors park up

and down the street as well.

Adding an antecedent (specifying *your tenants* instead of *they*) and eliminating a pronoun (reducing *park some of them* to *park*) simplify and clarify the sentence.

Identify a specific antecedent if a pronoun refers vaguely to a clause or a whole sentence.

▶ After the long ride, we reached the place for our expedition at Pine Heaven

the trip
Forest in western Virginia. At my age, ~~it~~ seemed to take forever.
^

Clarify an ambiguous reference to two possible antecedents.

if
▶ Students may now sue their schools ~~if they~~ are underperforming.
^

underperforming
▶ Students may now sue their schools⊙ ~~if they are underperforming.~~
^

Specify an implied reference.

In this   ↝the singer
▶ ~~This~~ song tells about being carefree and going through life without any worries.
^   ^

Years later, though, he starts to remember his past, and things do not seem so

problem-free anymore.

In this example, adding *the singer* specifies an antecedent for *he*.

Note: Sometimes the implied noun may be present in another form, perhaps as a possessive (*Mary's* for *Mary*) or as part of another word (*child* in *childhood*).

▶ Radaker~~'s arguments~~ irritated everyone at the lecture because he failed to

his arguments
support ~~them~~ with examples or evidence.
^

G2 Pronoun Agreement

Make sure that a **pronoun** and its **antecedent** agree in **number**, in **person**, and in **gender**. In the following examples, the arrows connect the pronouns to their antecedents.

▶ The *scientists* did not know what *they* were creating.

▶ *I* thought about Punita's offer while watching the movie. *My* curiosity won.

▶ After we went back to the lab, *Punita* started concentrating on *her* work.

The form of the antecedent and the form of the pronoun must correspond so that a reader is not troubled by inconsistencies or confused about how many, who, or which gender you mean.

G2-a Use pronouns and antecedents that agree in number.

If the antecedent of a pronoun is singular, the pronoun must be singular so that both agree in number. Likewise, if the antecedent is plural, the pronoun must be plural.

▶ The *shelter* gets most of *its* cats and dogs from *owners* who cannot keep *their* pets.

When the pronoun and its antecedent do not agree, change one so that both are singular or plural, or rewrite the sentence to eliminate the inconsistency. (See also E2-b.)

Change either the pronoun or its antecedent so that both are singular or plural.

▶ The patient is fully aware of the decision that ~~they are~~ making.
   he or she is

▶ ~~The patient is~~ fully aware of the decisions that they are making.
   Patients are

Note: As an alternative, you may be able to eliminate the pronoun.

▶ The patient is fully aware of ~~the~~ decision ~~that they are making.~~
   each

Revise the sentence to eliminate the inconsistency.

▶ Roommates get agitated at always being told to clean, and the roommate
   doing the telling gets tired of ~~hearing their own voice complain.~~
   complaining.

Use a singular pronoun to refer to a singular indefinite pronoun, or reword the sentence.

▶ Whether student, teacher, faculty member, graduate, or parent, each wants
   ~~their~~ school to be the one that remains open.
   his or her

---

pronoun A word that replaces a specific noun (such as *it, his, them, yours, myself,* or *which*), points out a specific noun (such as *this, these,* or *that*), or refers to an unspecified person or object (such as *everybody* or *each*).

antecedent The word or words that a pronoun replaces and to which it refers.

number The form of a word that shows whether it refers to one thing (singular: *parent*) or more than one thing (plural: *parents*).

person The form of a word that shows whether it refers to *I* or *we* (first person), to *you* (second person), or to *he, she, it,* or *they* (third person).

gender The form of a word that shows whether it refers to a male (*he*) or a female (*she*).

indefinite pronoun A pronoun that does not refer to a particular person or object. Examples: **Singular**—*anybody, anyone, each, everyone, everything, somebody, something, neither, none,* and *nobody;* **Plural**—*few, many,* and *several;* **Singular or plural**—*all, most,* and *some.*

> *All students, teachers, faculty members, graduates, and parents want*
> ▶ ~~Whether student, teacher, faculty member, graduate, or parent, each wants~~

their school to be the one that remains open.

> *students*
> ▶ This event would be a good chance for ~~everyone~~ to come out, socialize, and

enjoy themselves.

Consider the level of formality of your writing. Friends in a casual conversation may not mind if an indefinite pronoun and its antecedent do not agree, but such errors are not acceptable in formal writing.

Use a singular pronoun if the antecedent is a collective noun.

> *its*
> ▶ The Santa Barbara School District has a serious problem on ~~their~~ agenda.

Exception: A collective noun may sometimes be considered plural if it refers to the group members as individuals: The *couple* decided it was time to consolidate *their* bank accounts. (See also G6-b.)

collective noun A noun (such as *class* or *family*) that refers to a group as a unit and is usually considered singular.

G2-b **Use masculine, feminine, or gender-free forms to match a pronoun with its antecedent.**

Match a masculine pronoun with a masculine antecedent and a feminine pronoun with a feminine antecedent so that the pronoun and its antecedent agree in gender.

> ▶ I first met *Mark* the day *he* was hired.

If an antecedent might be either masculine or feminine, avoid using a pronoun that stereotypes by gender. (See also W3-c.)

Match a plural antecedent with a plural pronoun to include both sexes.

> *children are*
> ▶ Many people believe that ~~a boy or girl is~~ better off with a family that is able to

provide for all their needs than with a poverty-stricken parent.

Use a phrase that includes both masculine and feminine singular pronouns (such as *his or her*) to refer to both sexes.

> ▶ Many people believe that a child is better off with a family that is able to
>
> *his or her*
> provide for all ~~their~~ needs than with a poverty-stricken parent.

Note: If repeating a phrase such as *his or her* seems cumbersome or repetitious, try using plural forms or eliminating the pronouns altogether, as the following strategy suggests.

Eliminate unneeded or awkward pairs of masculine and feminine pronouns.

▶ This solution, of course, assumes that the bus ~~driver~~ *drivers* will be where ~~he/she is~~ *they are*

   supposed to be; boredom sometimes inspires ~~a driver~~ *drivers* to make up new and exciting

   variations on ~~his or her~~ *their* designated routes.

Note: Avoid using *he/she* in all but the most informal writing situations.

G3   Relative Pronouns

relative pronoun A pronoun that introduces an adjective clause.

Use personal **relative pronouns** to refer to people: *who, whom, whoever, whomever,* and *whose.*

▶ This reaction is unlike the response of the boys, *who* had trouble focusing on a

   subject.

Use nonpersonal relative pronouns to refer to things—*which, whichever, whatever,* and *whose.* **Note:** *Whose* can be used as a nonpersonal relative pronoun as well as a personal one.

▶ These interruptions, 75 percent of *which* come solely from males, disrupt

   conversations.

Use *that* for general references to things and groups.

▶ Sensory modalities are governed by the side of the brain *that* is not damaged.

(See also G6-e.)

nonrestrictive clause A clause, set off by commas, that provides extra or nonessential information and could be eliminated without changing the meaning of the noun or pronoun it modifies.

restrictive clause A clause, not set off by commas, that provides information essential to defining or identifying the noun or pronoun it modifies.

G3-a   Select who for references to people, *which* for nonrestrictive references to things, and *that* for restrictive references to groups and things.

▶ My attention focused on a little dark-haired boy *who* was crying.

▶ The tournament, *which* we had worked for all year, was the most prestigious event

   of the season.

▶ Save Our Sharks tried to promote a bill *that* would forbid the killing of certain sharks.

Change *that* to *who* to refer to a person.

▶ Illness phobics have countless examinations despite the reassurance of each

physician ~~that~~ examines them.
             ^who

Note: Rewriting a sentence to simplify its structure sometimes eliminates a problem with pronouns.

▶ ~~It was his~~ parents ~~that~~ made him run for student council, play the piano, and
  ^His

go out for sports.

(See also G3-b for information on *who* and *whom*.)

Change *that* to *which* when a nonrestrictive clause supplies extra, nondefining information.

▶ Caroline had the prettiest jet-black hair, ~~that~~ went down to the middle of her back.
                                             ^which

See P1-c on using commas with nonrestrictive word groups.

Change *which* to *that* when a restrictive clause supplies essential information defining a thing or a group.

▶ From the moment we are born, we come into a society ~~which~~ assimilates us into
                                                      ^that

its culture.

Introduce a restrictive clause with *that,* not *which.*

▶ In addition to the equipment and technology ~~which~~ fill the trauma room,
                                               ^that

a team of experts assembles before the patient arrives.

See P2-b on unnecessary commas with restrictive word groups.

G3-b **Use *who* as a subject and *whom* as an object.**

Two strategies can help you figure out whether to use *who* or *whom.*

1. Arrange the phrase's or clause's words in subject-verb-object order or **preposition-object** order. In this standard order, a subject (*who*) is followed by a verb, but an object (*whom*) follows a subject and verb or a preposition.

object The part of a clause that receives the action of the verb, or the part of a phrase that follows a preposition.

preposition A word (such as *between, in,* or *of*) that indicates the relation between a word in a sentence and its object.

2. Look for the subject of the clause. If the verb in the clause has another subject, use *whom;* if the verb in the clause has no other subject, use *who.* If it is the object of a preposition, use *whom.*

SUBJECT	We remember [*who* tips well] and [*who* doesn't].
OBJECT OF VERB	*I will always admire Mr. Stewart.* Mr. Stewart is someone [*whom* I will always admire].
OBJECT OF PREPOSITION	The university employs a large number of international teaching assistants [for *whom* English is a second language].

Change *who* to *whom* when the pronoun is an object within another clause that has a subject and a verb.

> ► He has the ability to attract guests ~~who~~ *whom* people want to hear.

Change *who* to *whom* when the pronoun is the object of a preposition.

> ► He also met his wife, ~~who~~ he was married *to whom* for fifty-two years.

Change *whom* to *who* when the pronoun is the subject of a clause and is followed by a verb.

> ► The libraries are staffed by professionals ~~whom~~ *who* have instituted methods to keep
>
> students informed of new materials.

G4   Pronoun Case

A pronoun can take different forms or cases, depending on its role in a sentence.

subject complement A word or word group that follows a linking verb and describes or restates the subject.

■ Subject or **subject complement**: *I, we, you, he, she, it, they* (subjective form)

> ► "*You*'d better be careful," *she* said.

> ► It is *we* you owe the money to.

preposition A word (such as *between, in,* or *of*) that indicates the relation between a word in a sentence and its object.

■ Object of a verb or a **preposition**: *me, us, you, him, her, it, them* (objective form)

> ► This realization spurred *me* to hasten the search.

> ► Her dog, Peter the Great, went with *her* on the excavation in southern Siberia.

■ Possession or ownership: *mine, ours, yours, his, hers, theirs, my, our, your, her, its, their* (possessive form)

▶ I trusted *his* driving.

▶ I finished putting *my* gear on and rolled over backward into the ocean.

See R2-a for more on pronouns.

Replace a reflexive pronoun that does not refer to another noun or pronoun in the clause.

▶ Kyle and ~~myself~~ I went upstairs to see how she was doing.

A reflexive pronoun does not belong in this sentence because *myself* does not refer to a preceding *I*.

reflexive pronoun A pronoun such as *myself* or *ourselves* that refers to a noun or a personal pronoun in the same clause.

Change a pronoun to the subjective form if it is part of a compound subject.

▶ Even though Annie and ~~me~~ I went through the motions, we did not understand the customs of our host.

compound subject Two or more words acting as a subject, linked by *and*.

Change a pronoun to the objective form if it is an object (or part of a compound object) of a preposition or a verb.

▶ There was an invisible wall between ~~she~~ her and ~~I~~ me.

compound object Two or more words acting as an object, linked by *and*.

Change a pronoun to the possessive form when it modifies a gerund.

▶ One of the main reasons for ~~me~~ my wanting to stay home with my children until they enter grade school is that otherwise I would miss so much.

gerund A verb form that is used as a noun and ends in *-ing: arguing, throwing*.

Change the form of a pronoun to fit the implied or understood wording of a comparison using *than* or *as*.

▶ I was still faster than ~~her~~ she.

Test whether a pronoun form fits by filling in the implied wording.

INCORRECT PRONOUN   I was still faster than *her* [was fast].

CORRECT PRONOUN   I was still faster than *she* [was fast].

Use *we* to precede a subject, or *us* to precede an object.

We is the subjective form, and *us* is the objective form. Select the form that matches the role of the noun in the sentence.

>   *we*
> ▶ Whenever ~~us~~ neighborhood kids would go out to play, I would always be goalie.
>   ^

Test your choice of pronoun by reading the sentence with the noun left out.

INCORRECT PRONOUN   Whenever *us* would go out to play, I would always be goalie.

CORRECT PRONOUN   Whenever *we* would go out to play, I would always be goalie.

G5   Verbs

Use standard verb forms in the appropriate **tense**, **mood**, and **voice**.

G5-a   **Select the appropriate verb tense to place events in past, present, and future time.**

When selecting the correct verb tense for a sentence, pay special attention to conventional usage or to the relationships among different verbs within the context of your essay. See R2-a for a review of the basic verb tenses.

FOR MULTILINGUAL WRITERS

See T2 for advice on how to use the correct tense in conditional clauses, two-word verbs, and helping (auxiliary) verbs and whether to use a gerund or an infinitive form after a verb.

Change verbs from the past tense to the present when discussing events in a literary work or film, general truths, ongoing principles, and facts.

Readers expect the use of the present tense in a literary analysis, as if the action in a work were ongoing.

>   *knows*   *is*
> ▶ In "The Monkey Garden," the girl ~~knew~~ it ~~was~~ time to grow up but still
>   ^   ^
>
>   *wants*
> ~~wanted~~ to play with the other kids in her make-believe world.
>   ^

>   *is*
> ▶ In the show *The Good Wife,* Alicia (Julianna Margulies) ~~was~~ an attorney
>   ^
>
>   *returns*
> who ~~returned~~ to work after her husband is imprisoned.
>   ^

tense The form of a verb that shows the time of the action or state of being.

mood The form of a verb that shows the writer's attitude toward a statement.

voice The form of a verb that either emphasizes the performer of an action (active) or de-emphasizes it (passive).

Readers also expect general truths, facts, and ongoing principles to be stated in the present tense. (See also E2-a.)

GENERAL TRUTH   The family *is* the foundation for a child's education.

FACT   The earth *is tilted* at an angle of 23 degrees.

ONGOING PRINCIPLE   Attaining self-sufficiency *is* one of the most important priorities of our energy policy.

Note: Some style guides make different recommendations about verb tense, depending on the field and its conventions. The style guide of the American Psychological Association (APA), for example, recommends using the past tense for past studies but using the present tense for research implications and conclusions.

APA STYLE   Davidson *stated* that father absence *is* more than twice as common now as in our parents' generation.

Change the verb from the past tense to the past perfect (using *had*) to show that one past action took place before another.

▶ The student's roommate also claimed that she ^*had*^ called the dorm office two days

before the suicide attempt.

The past action identified by the verb *had called* occurred before the past action identified by the verb *claimed*.

FOR MULTILINGUAL WRITERS

Certain verbs—ones that indicate existence, states of mind, and the senses of sight, smell, touch, and so on—are rarely used in the **progressive tense**. Such verbs include *appear, be, belong, contain, feel, forget, have, hear, know, mean, prefer, remember, see, smell, taste, think, understand,* and *want*.

▶ I am ~~belonging~~ ^*belong*^ to the campus group for foreign students.

> **progressive tense** A tense that shows ongoing action, consisting of a form of *be* plus the *-ing* form of the main verb: I *am waiting*.

G5-b   Use the correct verb endings and verb forms.

The five basic forms of regular verbs (such as *talk*) follow the same pattern, adding *-s, -ed,* and *-ing,* as shown here. The forms of irregular verbs (such as *speak*) do not consistently follow this pattern in forming the past and the past participle (see R2-a).

- Infinitive or base: *talk* or *speak*

  ▶   Every day I *talk* on the phone and *speak* to my friends.

- Third-person singular present (*-s* form): *talks* or *speaks*

  ▶   He *talks* softly, and she *speaks* slowly.

- Past: *talked* or *spoke*

  ▶ I *talked* to my parents last week, and I *spoke* to Jed on Tuesday.

- Present participle (*-ing* form): *talking* or *speaking*

  ▶ She is *talking* on the phone now, and he is *speaking* to a friend.

- Past participle (*-ed* form): *talked* or *spoken*

  ▶ I have *talked* to her many times, but she has not *spoken* to him yet.

Add an *-s* or *-es* ending to a verb when the subject is in the third-person singular (*he, she, it,* or a singular noun).

▶ The national drug control policy ~~treat~~ *treats* drug abuse as a law enforcement problem.

▶ This group ~~account~~ *accounts* for more than 10 percent of the total U.S. population.

FOR MULTILINGUAL WRITERS

Choosing the correct verb form is sometimes complicated by English expressions. For example, *used to* followed by the base form of the verb does not mean the same as *get used to* followed by a gerund.

▶ In the United States, most people *used to live* in rural areas. [This situation existed in the past but has changed.]

▶ My daughter *is getting used to going* to school every day. [She is getting in the habit of attending school.]

For more on choosing correct word forms, see W2.

Delete an *-s* or *-es* ending from a verb when the subject is in the first person (*I, we*), second person (*you*), or third-person plural (*they*).

▶ Because I think you'll really like it, I ~~suggests~~ *suggest* that you go see the movie *Boyhood*.

Add a *-d* or an *-ed* ending to a regular verb to form the past tense or the past participle.

▶ This movie was filmed in New Orleans because it resembles the city where the story is ~~suppose~~ *supposed* to take place.

▶ As we walked through the library, she ~~explain~~ *explained* the meaning of the yellow signs.

Check to be sure you have used the correct form of an irregular verb.

If you are uncertain about a verb form, refer to the list of irregular verbs in R2-a, or check your dictionary.

▶ The hostess greeted us and ~~lead~~ ^led^ us to our seats.

▶ We could tell our food had just ~~came~~ ^come^ off the grill because it still sizzled.

Note: Some verbs with different meanings are confusing because they have similar forms. For example, the verb *lie* (*lie, lay, lain, lying*) means "recline," but the verb *lay* (*lay, laid, laid, laying*) means "put or place." Consult the Glossary of Frequently Misused Words on pp. H-111–H-114 or a dictionary to make sure that you are using the correct form of the word you intend.

▶ I thought everyone was going to see my car ~~laying~~ ^lying^ on its side.

G5-c Choose the correct form of a verb to show the indicative, imperative, or subjunctive mood.

INDICATIVE	There *is* Homer, the father, who *serves* as sole provider for the family.
	Where *are* the Simpsons today?
IMPERATIVE	*Take* me to the mall.
SUBJUNCTIVE	If it *were* to rain on the day of the picnic, we would simply bring everything indoors.

indicative mood The verb form ordinarily used for statements and questions.

imperative mood The verb form used for commands or directions.

subjunctive mood The verb form used for wishes, suggestions, and conditions that are hypothetical, impossible, or unlikely.

The subjunctive is often used in clauses with *if* or *that*. Always use the **base form** of the verb for the present subjunctive. (See G5-b.) For the past tense of the verb *be*, the subjunctive form is *were*, not *was*.

base form The uninflected form of a verb: I *eat;* to *play.*

▶ Even if this claim ~~was~~ ^were^ true, it would raise a very controversial issue.

G5-d Use verbs primarily in the active voice.

The **active voice** calls attention to the actor performing an action. By contrast, the **passive voice** emphasizes the recipient of the action or the action itself over the actor.

ACTIVE	The monkey *lived* in the garden.
PASSIVE	The story *is told* by the girl as she reflects on her childhood.

active voice The verb form that shows the subject in action.

passive voice The verb form that shows something happening to the subject.

Change passive verbs to active in most writing situations.

Straightforward and direct, the active voice creates graceful, clear writing that emphasizes actors.

▶ The ~~story is told by the~~ girl *girl tells the story* as she reflects on her childhood.

▶ ~~Physicians are attracted by the~~ *The* monetary rewards of high-tech research, *attract physicians.*

Eliminate awkward, unnecessary passive verbs.

▶ The guests cluster like grapes ~~as similar interests are sought.~~ *seeking others with similar interests.*

Note: The passive voice is sometimes useful if you want to shift information to the end of a sentence. It is also frequently used in impersonal writing that focuses on an action rather than an actor, as in a scientific research report.

▶ When the generator *is turned on,* water *is forced* down the tunnel, and the animals swim against the current. Their metabolism *is measured.* They have participated in this experiment before, and the results from that run and this new one *will be compared.*

G6   Subject-Verb Agreement

Use **subjects** and **verbs** that agree in **person** and **number**. Agreement problems often occur when a sentence has a complicated subject or verb, especially when the subject and verb are separated by other words.

▶ The large amounts of money that are associated with sports is not the problem.
[subject]   [verb] *are*

The plural subject, *amounts,* requires a plural verb, *are.* (See also R2-a to check the correct forms of *be* and other irregular verbs.)

G6-a   Make sure the subject and verb agree even if they are separated by other words.

▶ The *relationship* between artists and politicians *has become* a controversial issue.
[subject]   [verb]

First identify the subject and the verb; then change one to agree with the other.

▶ The pattern of echoes from these sound waves ~~are~~ *is* converted by computer into a visual image.

▶ The ~~pattern of~~ echoes from these sound waves are converted by computer into a visual image.

---

subject The part of a clause that identifies who or what is being discussed.

verb A word or phrase that expresses action or being and, along with a subject, is a basic component of a sentence.

person The form of a word that shows whether it refers to *I* or *we* (first person), to *you* (second person), or to *he, she, it,* or *they* (third person).

number The form of a word that shows whether it refers to one thing (singular) or more than one thing (plural): *parent, parents; child, children.*

G6-b **Use a singular verb with a subject that is a collective noun.**

> The *association distributes* information on showing bison, selling bison, and

marketing bison meat.

(collective noun ─ Singular verb)

Change the verb to a singular form if the subject is a collective noun.

> *fights*
> If a military team fight without spirit and will, it will probably lose.

Note: A collective noun is generally considered singular because it treats a group as a single unit. If it refers to the members of the group as individuals, however, it may be considered plural.

SINGULAR **(GROUP AS A UNIT)**	The *staff is* amiable.
PLURAL **(INDIVIDUAL MEMBERS)**	The *staff exchange* greetings and small talk as *they begin* putting on *their* surgical garb.

G6-c **Use a verb that agrees with a subject placed after it.**

In most sentences, the subject precedes the verb, but some sentences are inverted. For example, sentences beginning with *there is* and *there are* put the subject after the verb.

> ┌verb┐┌──────subject──────────┐
> There are no busy lines and brushstrokes in the paintings.

> ┌verb┐┌──subject──┐
> There is interaction between central and peripheral visual fields.

In inverted sentences, change the verb so that it agrees with the subject that follows it, or rewrite the sentence to put the subject (which still must agree with the verb) first.

> *were*
> The next morning, there was Mike and Cindy, acting as if nothing had happened.

> *were*
> The next morning, there was Mike and Cindy, acting as if nothing had happened.

G6-d **Use a plural verb with a compound subject.**

> ┌──────subject──────┐┌verb┐
> She and her husband have a partnership with her in-laws.

Two subjects joined by *and* require a plural verb.

> *accumulate;*
> Dust and dirt accumulates, bathrooms get mildewy, and kitchens get greasy.

collective noun A noun (such as *class* or *family*) that refers to a group as a unit and is usually considered singular.

compound subject Two or more words acting as a subject, linked by *and*.

Note: If two subjects are joined by *or* or *nor*, the verb should agree with the subject that is closer to it.

▶ Most nights, my daughter or my sons *start* dinner.

---

antecedent The word or words that a pronoun replaces and to which it refers.

G6-e Use a verb that agrees with the **antecedent** of the pronouns *who*, *which*, or *that*.

▶ Its staff consists of nineteen people who drive to work in any kind of weather to make sure the station comes through for its listeners.

To check agreement, identify the antecedent of the pronoun.

▶ Within the ordered chaos of the trauma room are diagnostic tools, surgical devices, and X-ray equipment, which *are* ~~is~~ required for Sharp to be designated a trauma center.

▶ Some students choose topics that enable them to establish dominance over classmates in the group, while others tell personally moving stories that *encourage* ~~encourages~~ partners to show their feelings.

Note: With the phrase *one of the* followed by a plural noun, use a verb that agrees with that noun.

▶ One of the *features* that *make* the player different is that it doubles as a streaming device.

---

indefinite pronoun A pronoun that does not refer to a particular person or object. Examples: **Singular**—*anybody, anyone, each, everyone, everything, somebody, something, neither, none*, and *nobody*; **Plural**—*few, many*, and *several*; **Singular or plural**—*all, most*, and *some*.

G6-f Use a singular verb with an **indefinite pronoun**.

▶ Everything on the playground is child friendly.

In formal writing, an indefinite pronoun usually refers to a single person or object and agrees with a singular verb.

▶ There are two alternatives to this solution, and neither *seems* ~~seem~~ feasible.

If an indefinite pronoun such as *all, none*, or *some* refers to a plural noun, use a plural form of the verb. If it refers to a singular noun, use a singular form.

▶ *Some manage* to find jobs that fit their schedule, the surf schedule.

▶ *Most are* respectable people.

G6-g **Use a verb that agrees with the subject rather than the subject complement.**

subject complement A word or word group that follows a linking verb and describes or restates the subject.

subject
[and verb]────── subject complement ──────
▶ The shark's favorite diet is elephant seals and sea lions.

When either the subject or the subject complement names a group or category, the choice between a singular or plural verb can be confusing. Make sure that the verb agrees with the actual subject.

are
▶ Big blocks of color in a simple flat shape ~~is~~ his artistic trademark.
                                            ^

He favors big
▶ ~~Big blocks of color in a simple flat shape~~ ~~is his artistic trademark.~~
  ^

G7 Adjectives and Adverbs

Distinguish **adjectives** from **adverbs** so that you select the correct forms of these **modifiers**. (See also R2-a.)

adjective A word that modifies a noun or a pronoun, adding information about it.

adverb A word that modifies a verb, an adjective, or another adverb.

modifier A word, phrase, or clause functioning as an adjective or adverb that adds information about another word.

ADJECTIVES   Because *angry* drivers are *dangerous* drivers, it is *imperative* that the county implement *a* solution.

ADVERB   Installing traffic lights would *quickly* alleviate three important aspects of the problem.

G7-a **Select an adverb, not an adjective, to modify an adjective, another adverb, or a verb.**

Often ending in *-ly,* adverbs tell how, when, where, why, and how often.

▶ Despite a *very* busy work schedule, Caesar finds time in the afternoon to

come *directly* to the high school and work as a volunteer track coach.

Change an adjective that modifies another adjective, an adverb, or a verb to an adverb form.

loudly
▶ The man yelled at me so ~~loud~~ that I began to cry.
                          ^

Adjective forms that are common in informal, spoken conversation should be changed to adverb forms in more formal writing.

SPOKEN   The day was going *slow,* and I repeatedly caught my lure on the riverbed or a tree limb.

WRITTEN   The day was going *slowly,* and I repeatedly caught my lure on the riverbed or a tree limb.

G7-b Select an adjective, not an adverb, to modify a noun or a pronoun.

▶ I am enamored of the *cool* motor, the *massive* boulder in the middle of the lake, and the sound of the *splashing* wake against the side of the two-seater.

Change an adverb that modifies a noun or a pronoun to an adjective.

▶ Working within a ~~traditionally~~ *traditional* chronological plot, Joyce develops the

protagonist's emotional conflict.

An adjective generally appears immediately before or after the word it modifies. When an adjective acts as a **subject complement**, however, it is separated from the word it modifies by a **linking verb**.

▶ My grandfather is *amazing*.

subject complement
A word or word group that follows a linking verb and describes or restates the subject.

linking verb *Be, seem, appear, become, taste,* or another verb that connects a subject with a subject complement that describes or modifies it: The chips *taste* salty.

Note: Some verbs (such as *looked*) act as linking verbs only in certain contexts. When one of these verbs connects a subject and its complement, use an adjective form: She looked *ill*. However, when the verb expresses an action and is modified by the word that follows it, use an adverb: She looked *quickly*.

FOR MULTILINGUAL WRITERS

Multilingual writers sometimes have trouble choosing between past and present participles (*looked, looking*) used as adjectives. See T6 for help in selecting the correct form.

G7-c Select the correct forms of adjectives and adverbs to show comparisons.

Add *-er* or *-est* to short words (one or two syllables), and use *more, most, less,* and *least* with longer words and all *-ly* adverbs.

▶ The southern peninsula's *smallest* kingdom was invaded continually by its two *more powerful* neighbors.

Use *-er, more,* or *less* (the comparative form) to compare two things.

▶ I had always been a little bit *faster* than she was.

Use *-est, most,* or *least* (the superlative form) to compare three or more things.

▶ The team's undefeated status soon gained it the respect of even its *bitterest* rivals.

Change the forms of adjectives and adverbs to show comparison precisely.

▶ She has clearly been the ~~least~~ *less* favored candidate in the sense that she is not as well known or as experienced as her opponent.

E Effective Sentences

E1 Missing Words

To write effective prose, you need to supply all words necessary for clarity, completeness, and logic. Proofread your essays carefully, even out loud, to catch any omitted words.

FOR MULTILINGUAL WRITERS

If English is not your native language, you may have trouble with omitted words. See also T4.

E1-a Supply prepositions, conjunctions, infinitive parts, and articles when needed for clarity.

In many instances, when you forget to include these small words, the reader may be puzzled or have to pause to figure out what you mean.

Insert missing prepositions.

> ▶ The car began to skid *in* the other direction.
>   ^

> ▶ He graduated *from* high school at the top of his class.
>   ^

> ▶ A child his age shouldn't be playing outside *at* that time of night.
>   ^

FOR MULTILINGUAL WRITERS

If you are not a native speaker of American English, prepositions may be challenging because native speakers of English use prepositions in ways that do not translate directly. The best way to understand when prepositions are needed is to read widely and study the work of other writers. See also T3.

Insert missing conjunctions.

> ▶ Most families and patients will accept the pain, inconvenience, financial *and*
>   ^
>
>   emotional strain as long as the patient can achieve a certain quality of life.

preposition A word (such as *between, in,* or *of*) that indicates the relation between a word in a sentence and its object.

conjunction A word that relates sentence parts by coordinating, subordinating, or pairing elements, such as *and, because,* or *either . . . or.*

> ▶ The heads of these golf clubs can be made of metal, wood, graphite and often
> *or* ^
>
> have special inserts in the part of the club that hits the ball.

A conjunction is generally needed to connect the final item in a series, such as *financial and emotional strain* in the first example and *graphite* in the second.

infinitive A verb form consisting of the word *to* plus the base form of the verb: *to run*.

Restore the *to* omitted from an infinitive if needed for clarity.

> ▶ They decided start the following Monday morning.
> *to* ^

> ▶ I noticed how he used his uncanny talent for acting make a dreary subject
> *to* ^
>
> come alive.

article An adjective that precedes a noun and identifies a definite reference to something specific (*the*) or an indefinite reference to something less specific (*a* or *an*).

Insert missing articles.

> ▶ This incident ruined the party, but it was only beginning of the trouble.
> *the* ^

> ▶ But such condition could be resolved by other means.
> *a* ^

FOR MULTILINGUAL WRITERS

Nonnative speakers of English may be unsure when and when not to use the articles *a, an,* and *the.* For more advice on the use of articles, see T1.

Insert other words that help clarify or complete a sentence.

> ▶ Malaria was once a widespread disease and become so again.
> *it may* ^ ^

> ▶ In these scenes, women are often with long, luxurious hair.
> *shown* ^

> ▶ Finally, and I'm embarrassed to admit, I pushed Bella.
> *it* ^ ^

E1-b **Insert the word *that* if needed to prevent confusion or misreading.**

CONFUSING   I would like to point out golf is not just a game for rich old men in ugly pants.

CLEARER   I would like to point out *that* golf is not just a game for rich old men in ugly pants.

Without *that,* the reader may think at first that the writer is pointing out *golf* and have to double back to understand the sentence. In the revised sentence, *that* tells the reader exactly where the **dependent clause** begins.

dependent clause A word group that has a subject and a predicate but cannot stand by itself as a sentence; it must be connected to an independent clause.

▶ Dryer says/ *that* as people grow older, they may find themselves waking up early,

   usually at dawn.

▶ One problem parents will notice is *that* the child leaves out certain words.

Note: If the meaning of a sentence is clear without *that,* it may be left out.

E1-c **Add words to a comparison to make it logical, clear, and complete.**

Because a comparison connects two or more things for the reader, you should name both things and state the comparison fully. In addition, the items compared should be of the same kind. For example, compare a person with another person, not with an activity or a situation. This sentence compares two stores:

▶ The old student center has a *general store* that carries *as many books or supplies as*

   the *Saver Center.*

(See also E7-c.)

Reword a comparison to specify comparable items of the same kind.

▶ Five-foot-five-inch Maria finds climbing to be more challenging *for her than it is for* than her six-

   foot-five-inch companions, who can reach the handholds more easily.

The original version of this sentence says that climbing is more challenging than companions (illogically comparing an activity to people). The edited sentence says that climbing is more challenging for Maria than it is for her companions (logically comparing one person to other people).

Reword a comparison to identify clearly and completely all items being compared.

▶ Danziger's article is definitely more entertaining/ *than Solomon's article.*

In some comparative sentences, formal academic English requires the coordinated use of *as.*

▶ Millie is *as* graceful *as,* if not more graceful than, Margot.

▶ Students opting for field experience credits would learn as much/ or more/ than/
  as

students who take only classes.

compound structure
A sentence element, such as a subject or a verb, that consists of two or more items linked by *and* or another conjunction.

E1-d **Supply all words needed to clarify the parts of a compound structure.**

Although words may be left out of compound structures to avoid unnecessary repetition, omitted words must fit grammatically in each part of the compound.

▶ Women tend to express feelings *in the form of* requests, whereas men tend to

express them *in* [*the form of*] commands.

When the same structure would not fit in each part, you need to supply the missing words—even if they are simply different forms of the same word.

▶ Water buffalo meat has been gaining popularity in America and being sold to
  is

the public.

▶ Observable behaviors that relate to classroom assault can be dealt with prior/
  to

during, and after an attack.

E2 Shifts

Follow the same pattern throughout a sentence or passage to avoid a shift in tense, person, number, mood, voice, or type of discourse.

tense The form of a verb that shows the time of the action or state of being.

E2-a **Use one verb tense consistently in a passage unless a tense change is needed to show a time change.**

▶ The nurse tried to comfort me by telling jokes and explaining that the needle
                                                          pierced
  wouldn't hurt. With a slight push, the long, sharp needle pierces my skin
         found
  and finds its way to the vein.

If you tend to mix verb tenses as you draft, perform a special edit of your entire essay, concentrating on this one issue.

Change the tense of any verbs that do not follow the established tense in a passage unless they show logical time changes.

▶ I noticed much activity around the base. Sailors and chiefs ~~are~~ walking all over *were*

the place. At 8:00 a.m., all traffic, foot and vehicle, halted. Toward the piers,

the flag ~~is rising~~ up its pole. After the national anthem ~~ends,~~ salutes ~~are~~ *rose* *ended* *were*

completed, and people ~~go~~ on with what they ~~are~~ doing. *went* *had been*

Change verbs to the present tense to discuss events in literature, general truths, facts, and other ongoing principles.

▶ In 2003, the Supreme Court ruled that antisodomy laws are unconstitutional

because such laws ~~went~~ against "our tradition [that] the state is not *go*

omnipresent in our homes."

▶ In the story, when the boy ~~died,~~ Kathy ~~realized~~ that it ~~was~~ also time for her *dies* *realizes* *is*

childhood to die, and so she ~~returned~~ to her South African home as an adult. *returns*

Discussing such events may require tense shifts in a sentence or text. (See also G5-a.)

PRESENT TENSE
WITH LOGICAL
SHIFT TO FUTURE   Each cell *has* forty-six chromosomes, which *carry* the
genetic traits the individual *will have* when he or she *is* born.

E2-b **Change the nouns and pronouns in a passage to a consistent person and number.**

▶ Lynn informs all the members about helpful programs for ~~you and your pet.~~ *them and their pets.*

▶ Lynn informs ~~all the members~~ about helpful programs for you and your pet. *you*

In casual conversation, people often shift between singular and plural or between the third person and the second. In writing, however, such shifts may be confusing.

Note: Also consider how your choice of person suits the tone or approach of your essay. The first or second person, for example, will usually strike a reader as less formal than the third person.

person The form of a word that shows whether it refers to *I* or *we* (first person), to *you* (second person), or to *he, she, it,* or *they* (third person).

number The form of a word that shows whether it refers to one thing (singular: *parent*) or more than one thing (plural: *parents*).

mood The form of a verb that shows the writer's attitude toward a statement.

voice The form of a verb that either emphasizes the performer of an action (active) or de-emphasizes it (passive).

E2-c   Establish a consistent mood and voice in a passage.

▶ Each time I entered his house, I ~~could~~ always ~~know~~ *knew* when he was home.

The original sentence shifts from the indicative mood (*I entered*), used for statements and questions, to the subjunctive mood (*I could know*), used to indicate hypothetical, impossible, or unlikely conditions.

▶ I stepped out of the car with my training permit, a necessary document ~~for the~~ *for taking the test.*

~~test to be taken.~~

Although mood and voice may need to change to fit the context of a sentence, unneeded shifts may seem inconsistent. (See also G5-c on mood, G5-d on voice, and T2-a on conditional clauses.)

Change the verbs in a conditional clause or passage to a consistent mood.

▶ If the mother should change her mind and keep the child, the couple ~~will~~ *would* be

reimbursed for their expenses.

▶ If the mother ~~should change~~ *changes* her mind and ~~keep~~ *keeps* the child, the couple will be

reimbursed for their expenses.

Make the verbs in a passage consistent, preferably using the active voice.

▶ I will judge the song according to the following criteria: the depth with which

the lyrics treat each issue, and the clarity with which ~~each idea is presented in~~ *the music presents each idea.*

~~the music.~~

(See also G5-d.)

E2-d   Use either direct or indirect quotation, without mixing the two.

Writers use direct quotation to present statements or questions in a speaker's or another writer's own words; they use indirect quotation to present the person's words without quoting directly.

▶ "Do whatever ~~they wanted to her,~~ *you want to me,*" she cried, "but don't harm Reza."

▶ ~~Do~~ *They could do* whatever they wanted to her, she cried, but ~~don't~~ *they shouldn't* harm Reza.

To avoid shifts between direct and indirect quotation, make sure that your pronouns are consistent in **person** (see G2) and that your verbs are consistent in mood (see G5-c).

person The form of a word that shows whether it refers to *I* or *we* (first person), to *you* (second person), or to *he, she, it,* or *they* (third person).

E3 Noun Agreement

In most instances, use nouns that agree in **number** when they refer to the same topic, person, or object.

number The form of a word that shows whether it refers to one thing (singular: *parent*) or more than one thing (plural: *parents*).

- ▶ The treatment consists of *injections* of minimal *doses* of the *allergens*, given at regular *intervals*.

Sometimes, however, the context calls for both singular and plural nouns.

- ▶ *Students* who want to make the most of *their* college years should pursue *a major course of study* while choosing *electives* or *a few minor courses of study* from the liberal arts.

E3-a Select corresponding singular or plural forms for related references to a noun.

When several nouns are used to develop a topic, they may describe and expand the characteristics of a key noun, act as synonyms for one another, or develop related points in the discussion. A sentence or passage that includes such nouns will generally be clearer and more effective if the nouns agree in number.

- ▶ Many people tend to "take their jobs to bed" with them and lie awake, thinking about what needs to be done the next day. They also worry about ~~a~~ *promotions,* ~~promotion, layoffs, or a shift~~ *layoffs, or shifts* in responsibilities.

E3-b Decide whether a noun should be singular or plural.

A noun may need to agree with another word in the sentence or may need to be singular or plural to fit the context or idiomatic usage. Be sure to consider the meaning of the sentence as a whole.

- ▶ *Minnows* are basically inedible because *they* have very little meat on *their bodies*.

In this sentence, the writer consistently uses plural forms (*they, their,* and *bodies*) to refer to the minnows but also uses *meat,* which takes a singular form in this context.

Note: Nouns such as *kind* are singular, although they have plural forms (*kinds*). Use *this* and *that* instead of *these* and *those* to modify the singular forms of *kind* and similar words. Expressions with *kind of* or *sort of* are usually singular.

> ▶ To comprehend ~~these~~ *this* type of ~~articles,~~ *article,* it helps to have a strong background in statistics.

> ▶ RAs are allowed to choose what kind of ~~programs~~ *program* they want to have.

Change a noun to singular or plural to agree with a preceding indefinite adjective.

indefinite adjective A word that modifies a noun or another adjective and indicates an unspecific quantity, such as *each, few, many,* or *some.*

> ▶ Under some ~~circumstance,~~ *circumstances,* parents aren't there to supervise their kids.

Consider changing a noun to singular or plural to reflect its context.

Sometimes it is customary to treat an abstract quality (such as *justice* or *power*) as a singular noun. In other cases, a noun should be singular or plural to fit with the grammar or logic of the rest of the sentence.

> ▶ As soon as immigrants get to the United States, they realize that to get ~~a better~~ *better jobs*
>
> ~~job~~ and better living conditions, they need to learn English.

Some common idiomatic expressions mix singular and plural forms.

IDIOMATIC WORDING   The penalties set for offenders might be enough to help them see *the error of their ways* and eventually reform their social habits.

E4 Modifiers

modifier A word, phrase, or clause functioning as an adjective or adverb that adds information about another word.

A **modifier**'s position in a sentence generally tells the reader what word the modifier qualifies.

E4-a Place a word, phrase, or clause next to or close to the word it modifies.

> ▶ My *frozen* smile faltered as my chin quivered.

> ▶ The flurry *of fins, masks, weights, and wet suits* continued.

> ▶ Beyond the chairs loomed the object *that I feared most*—
>
> *a beautiful, black Steinway grand* piano *that gleamed under the bright stage lights.*

If a modifier is too far away from the word it modifies, a reader may assume that it modifies another word closer to it. As a result, a *misplaced modifier* can create confusion, ambiguity, or even unintended humor.

Move a modifier closer to the word it modifies.

▶ The ~~attempted~~ number of *attempted* suicides this semester was four.

▶ The women have to do all the hard work*/ needed to maintain the family*, especially in subsistence cultures*/* ~~needed to maintain the family~~.

▶ He and the others start to look for any sign of a boat, an island, or an oil *as hard as they can* platform, ~~as hard as they can~~.

Rewrite to clarify the sentence.

▶ ~~Community~~ *When organizing meetings open to all neighbors,* community leaders should *select* ~~organize meetings open to all neighbors at~~ convenient times and locations.

▶ We were friends until I *turned eighteen and* became too popular and obnoxious for anyone to stand, ~~when I turned eighteen~~.

E4-b **Place a modifier so that it qualifies the meaning of a particular word in the sentence instead of dangling.**

A phrase that does not modify a specific word is called a *dangling modifier*. A dangling modifier usually occurs at the beginning of a sentence and is likely to be a **participial phrase** or a **prepositional phrase**.

▶ Rather than receiving several painful shots in the mouth before a cavity is *a patient may find that* filled, hypnosis can work just as effectively.

▶ After surveying the floor on which I live, *I concluded that* the residents of my dorm don't care much for floor programs.

Place a word or phrase being modified immediately after the modifying phrase.

▶ By far the best song on the album, ~~the~~ *"Rolling in the Deep" has a* vocal performance and musical arrangement of ~~"Rolling in the Deep"~~ *that* create a perfect harmony.

participial phrase A group of words that begins with a present participle (*dancing, freezing*) or a past participle (*danced, frozen*) and modifies a noun or a pronoun: We boarded the bus, *expecting to leave immediately*.

prepositional phrase A group of words that begins with a preposition and indicates the relation between a word in a sentence and the object following the preposition: Her sunglasses slid *under the seat*.

dependent clause A word group that has a subject and a predicate but cannot stand by itself as a sentence; it must be connected to an independent clause.

subject The part of a clause that identifies who or what is being discussed.

predicate The part of a clause that includes a complete verb and describes the action or state of the subject.

Change the modifying phrase into a **dependent clause**.

Unlike a phrase, a clause includes both a **subject** and a **predicate**. By changing a phrase to a clause, you can correct a dangling modifier by supplying the information or connection that is missing. Be sure to revise so that both the subject and the predicate are clearly stated and the clause fits the rest of the sentence.

▶ *If the school board decides to close*
~~By closing~~ Dos Pueblos, the remaining high schools ~~would~~ *will* have larger student

bodies and increased budgets.

▶ *I concluded*
After ~~concluding~~ my monologue on the hazards of partying, she smiled broadly

and said, "Okay, Mom, I'll be more careful next time."

limiting modifier A modifier such as *almost, just,* or *only* that should directly precede the word or word group it limits.

E4-c Place a limiting modifier **just before the word it modifies.**

A limiting modifier can create confusion or ambiguity when it is misplaced because it could modify several words in the same sentence.

▶ Landfills in Illinois are going to be filled to capacity by 2020, and some

even
experts ~~even~~ say sooner.

When *even* precedes *say* in the example above, the sentence suggests that the experts are "even saying," not that the date will be even sooner.

infinitive A verb form consisting of the word *to* plus the base form of the verb: *to run.*

E4-d Keep the two parts of an infinitive **together.**

When other words follow the *to*, they "split" the infinitive, separating *to* from the base form of the verb. These other words can usually be moved elsewhere in the sentence. Be especially alert to limiting modifiers that split infinitives. (See also E4-c.)

always
▶ His stomach seemed to ~~always~~ hang over his pants.

Note: Occasionally, moving intervening words creates a sentence more awkward than the version with the split infinitive. In such cases, leaving the split infinitive may be the better choice.

E5 Mixed Constructions

The beginning and ending of a sentence must match, and its parts should fit together. If a sentence changes course in the middle or its parts are mixed up, a reader will have to guess at the pattern or connection you intend.

E5-a   Begin and end a sentence with the same structural pattern.

A sentence is mixed if it combines several grammatical patterns. You usually need to rewrite a mixed construction so that its parts fit together.

▶ ~~The~~ *If we save* more oil ~~that we save~~ now ~~means~~ *we will have* much more in the future.

Choose one of the grammatical patterns in a mixed sentence, and use it consistently throughout the sentence.

▶ School is another ~~resource for~~ *place where* children who don't have anyone to talk to ~~so they~~ can get educated about the problem of teen pregnancy.

▶ School is another resource for children who don't have anyone to talk to~~so they~~ can *provide information* ~~get educated~~ about the problem of teen pregnancy.

Rewrite a mixed sentence if neither part supplies a workable pattern for the whole.

▶ ~~This is something the~~ *The* shelter prides itself on ~~and is~~ always looking for new volunteers and ideas~~for the shelter.~~

▶ The ~~next part of the essay was where~~ *next detailed* the results of the study ~~were detailed~~ and ~~finally included~~ *concluded with* a commentary section~~concluding the article.~~

E5-b   Match the subject and the predicate in a sentence so that they are compatible.

You can solve the problem of a logically mismatched subject and predicate—called *faulty predication*—by rewriting either the subject or the predicate so that the two fit together.

▶ ~~Schools~~ *Students attending schools* that prohibited corporal punishment behaved as well as *students at* schools that permitted it.

To test a sentence for faulty predication, ask yourself whether the subject can do what the predicate says: For example, do schools behave? If not, revise the sentence.

Revise the subject so that it can perform the action described in the predicate.

▶ Bean's service is top-notch *the staff* and is continually striving to meet student needs.

Revise the predicate so that it fits logically with the subject.

▶ Ironically, the main character's memory of Mangan's sister on the porch step

always includes
~~cannot recall the image without~~ the lamplight.
^

E5-c Order words logically so that the meaning of the sentence will be clear.

Entering traffic
▶ ~~Traffic entering~~ will be dispersed into a perimeter pattern of flow.
^

E5-d Eliminate the phrase *is where*, *is when*, or *the reason is because*, and then rewrite the sentence so that it is clear and logical.

Often you can replace an *is where* or *is when* phrase with a noun specifying a category or type.

part makes   *seem*
▶ This ~~is where~~ the irony ~~seems to be~~ most evident.
^   ^

a stance taken by someone who
▶ An absolutist position is ~~when someone~~ strongly opposes any restrictions on speech.
^

To eliminate *the reason is because,* rewrite the sentence, or use either *the reason is that* or *because* instead.

In addition^
▶ ~~Another reason~~ radio stations should not play songs with sexually explicit lyrics
^

is because children like to sing along.

▶ Another reason radio stations should not play songs with sexually explicit lyrics

that
is ~~because~~ children like to sing along.
^

E6 Integrated Quotations, Questions, and Thoughts

When you use sources or write dialogue, merge your quotations, questions, and thoughts smoothly into your text so that the reader can tell who is speaking, thinking, or providing information.

▶ The expense of being a teenager has caused many young people to join the workforce just because "they were offered a job" (Natriello 60).

▶ "Hello," I replied, using one of the few words I knew in her language.

▶ I told myself, *Don't move.*

Use introductory phrases to link ideas and provide necessary background and context. Refer to the source or the speaker in the sentence. (See also P6.)

E6-a Integrate direct quotations into sentences responsibly and correctly.

direct quotation A speaker's or writer's exact words, which are enclosed in quotation marks.

Writers often introduce quotations by mentioning the name of the person being quoted. Although *says* and *states* are acceptable, consider using more precise verbs and phrases that establish logical connections and provide variety. Examples include *agrees, asserts, charges, claims, confirms, discusses, emphasizes,* and *suggests.*

▶ As American Motors President M. Paul Tippitt asserts, "The cardinal rule of the new ballgame is change" (Sobel 259).

Readers expect quotations and text to fit gracefully so that the writer's ideas and the material from supporting sources are both distinct and coherent. (See also E2-d.)

Cite a source smoothly, guiding readers from text to quotation.

Identifying the author of your source in the main part of your sentence often supplies the context and transition a reader needs.

For more on integrating source information in an academic essay, see Chapter 19; for more on citing and documenting sources, see Chapters 20 (MLA) and 21 (APA).

▶ Most people are not even aware of the extent to which television plays a role
    As Mitroff and Bennis point out,
  in their lives. "Television defines our problems and shapes our actions; in
                                              (xi).
  short, [it is] how we define our world" ~~(Mitroff and Bennis xi).~~

  Mitroff and Bennis assert that most
▶ ~~Most~~ people are not even aware of the extent to which ~~television plays a role~~
          television
  ~~in their lives.~~ "~~Television~~ defines our problems and shapes our actions; in   (xi).

  short, ~~how we define our world" (Mitroff and Bennis xi).~~

Carefully select the text that introduces or integrates the quotation, as well as the exact words you are quoting.

▶ The average American child is exposed to "violence from every medium
    and
  ~~. . . in addition listens to~~ music that advocates drug use" (Hollis 624).

E6-b Integrate a question so that its source is clear.

indirect quotation A restatement of a speaker's or writer's ideas without quoting directly or using quotation marks.

Enclose a direct quotation in quotation marks, identifying the speaker and using his or her exact words. Do not use quotation marks for an **indirect quotation** or a question that you address to the reader.

DIRECT QUOTATION	"Can you get my fins?" he asked.
INDIRECT QUOTATION	Without much hesitation, I explained my mission to her and asked whether she would help me out.
QUESTION ADDRESSED TO READER	Should sex education be a required class in public schools?

Begin a new paragraph to show each change of speaker.

▶ "The refrigeration system is frozen solid. Come back later/ ~~Once~~ again   *he said, once*

turning his back to me. ~~I asked~~

I asked,
   "When would it be best for me to come back?"

E6-c   Integrate thoughts so that they are clearly identified and consistently punctuated.

If you supply the exact words that you or someone else thinks, follow the guidelines for direct quotations. Quotation marks (or sometimes italics, for emphasis) are optional, but be consistent throughout an essay.

▶ Go north eighty miles, she reminded herself.

▶ /Wife and kids?/ I thought.

▶ "/Wife and kids?/ I thought.

E7   Parallelism

Use parallel form to present items as a pair or in a series.

PAIR	Imagine that you and your daughter are *walking* in the mall or *eating* in a popular restaurant.
SERIES	By implementing this proposal, administrators could enhance the reputation of the university with quality *publications, plays, concerts,* and *sports teams.*
SERIES OF PHRASES	An interruption has the potential *to disrupt turns at talk, to disorganize the topic of conversation,* and *to violate the current speaker's right to talk.*

The grammatical similarity of the items in the pair or series strongly signals to the reader that they are equally important, similar in meaning, and related in the same way to the rest of the sentence.

E7-a **Each item in a series must follow the same grammatical pattern as the other items.**

Items in a series are usually linked by *and* or *or*. Each item should be parallel to the others, presented as a **noun**, an **infinitive**, a **gerund**, or another grammatical form.

▶ The children must deal with an overprotective parent, sibling rivalry, and ~~living~~ *life*

in a single-parent home.

▶ Drivers destined for Coronado can choose to turn left, *turn* right, or ~~proceeding~~ *proceed*

straight into the city.

> **noun** A word that names a specific or general thing, person, place, concept, characteristic, or other idea.
>
> **infinitive** A verb form consisting of the word *to* plus the base form of the verb: *to run.*
>
> **gerund** A verb form that is used as a noun and ends in *-ing: arguing, throwing.*

E7-b **Both items in a pair must follow the same grammatical pattern.**

Items in a pair are usually linked by *and* or *or*.

▶ While Maddox is growing up, he is told of things he should do and things *he should* not ~~to~~ do.

E7-c **In a comparison using *than* or *as*, the items must use the same grammatical form.**

▶ They feel that using force is more comprehensible to the children than *threatening* abstract

consequences.

In this example, "using force" was not parallel with "abstract consequences," so the latter has been changed to "threatening abstract consequences."

E7-d **Use parallel form for items joined by correlative conjunctions.**

▶ At that time, the person is surprised not only about where he is but also

about
~~unable to account for~~ what has happened.

Also position the conjunctions so that each introduces a comparable point.

> **correlative conjunctions** Word pairs that link sentence elements; the first word anticipates the second: *both . . . and, either . . . or, neither . . . nor, not only . . . but also.*

E8 Coordination and Subordination

Use coordination and subordination to indicate the relationships among sentence elements.

E8-a **Use coordination to join sentence elements that are equally important.**

▶ The sheriff's department lacks both the *officers* and the *equipment* to patrol every road in the county.

▶ The evil queen's magic mirror declares that this Disney girl, with her *skin as white as snow, lips as red as blood,* and *hair as black as ebony,* is "the fairest one of all."

Writers use coordination to bring together in one sentence two or more elements of equal importance to the meaning. These elements can be words, phrases, or clauses, including **independent clauses** within the same sentence.

> **independent clause** A word group with a subject and a predicate that can stand alone as a separate sentence.

▶ ⎡————— independent clause 1 —————⎤ ⎡— independent clause 2 —————⎤
The sport of windsurfing dates back only to 1969, but it has already achieved full

⎡——————————⎤
status as an Olympic event.

▶ ⎡————————— independent clause 1 —————————⎤ ⎡—⎤
Children like to sing along with songs their parents listen to; consequently, radio

⎡————————————— independent clause 2 —————————————⎤
stations should not play songs with language that demeans women.

E8-b **Use subordination to indicate that one sentence element is more important than other elements.**

▶ *After Dave finished his mutinous speech,* the corners of Dan's mouth slowly formed a nearly expressionless grin.

▶ Political liberals, *who trace their American roots to the Declaration of Independence,* insist that the federal government should attempt to reduce inequalities of income and wealth.

> **phrase** A group of words that does *not* contain both a subject and a verb and is always part of an independent clause.
>
> **dependent clause** A word group that has a subject and a predicate but cannot stand by itself as a sentence; it must be connected to an independent clause.

Writers frequently subordinate information within a single sentence. The most important information appears in an independent clause, and the less important (or subordinate) information appears in words, **phrases,** or **dependent clauses** attached to the independent clause or integrated into it.

W Word Choice

Effective language is concise and appropriate for the context.

W1 Concise Sentences

Sentences with redundant phrasing, wordy expressions, and unnecessary intensifiers are tiresome to read and may be difficult to understand. Concentrate on choosing words well, simplifying sentence stucture, and avoiding words that are unnecessary or evasive.

▶ *This* ~~In many cases, this~~ situation may ~~be due to the fact that~~ *occur because* these women ~~were~~ *have had no*

~~not given the~~ opportunity to work.

Note: Even though you may need to add details or examples to clarify your ideas, cutting out useless words will make your writing more focused.

W1-a   Eliminate redundancies and repetition.

Redundant phrasing adds unnecessary words to a sentence. Repetitive wording says the same thing twice.

Eliminate or rewrite redundant expressions.

The phrase *blue in color* is redundant because it repeats obvious information. Expressions such as *past memories, advance planning,* and *mix together* include modifiers that repeat information already provided in the word being modified. Expressions such as *the fact is true* and *in my opinion, I believe* are redundant because they contain obvious implications.

▶ Many machines in the drilling area need to be *modernized.* ~~updated to better and more~~

~~modern equipment.~~

▶ All these recommendations are interconnected. ~~to one another.~~

▶ *California colleges* ~~The colleges in the state of California~~ rely too much on the annual income of a

student's parents and not enough on the parents' true financial situation.

Delete extra words from a redundant or repetitive sentence.

▶ In addition, there is a customer service center. *convenient* ~~for the convenience of the~~

~~customers.~~

▶ Student volunteers will no longer be *exhausted* ~~overworked, overburdened, and~~

~~overexhausted~~ from working ~~continuously at the jobs~~ without any breaks

because of the shortage. *labor* ~~of labor.~~

W1-b Eliminate words that do not add to a sentence's meaning.

Rewrite a wordy sentence to reduce the number of clauses and phrases.

Concentrate on turning clauses into phrases or replacing phrases, especially strings of **prepositional phrases**, with individual words. Sometimes you can even consolidate a series of sentences into one.

prepositional phrase A group of words that begins with a preposition and indicates the relation between a word in a sentence and the object following the preposition: Her sunglasses slid *under the seat.*

> ▸ *One of the best examples* of an athlete, being completely
>
> *Michael Phelps is an excellent example   overexposed*
>
> overexposed is that of Michael Phelps.

> ▸ There are many other possible alternative solutions to teen pregnancy. One
>
> *No single alternative will solve the problem of teen pregnancy, and all the possible*
>
> solution is not going to work alone to solve the problem. But there are
>
> *solutions have disadvantages.*
>
> disadvantages that come along with them.

Eliminate wordy expressions.

Extra, empty words can creep into a sentence in many ways.

> ▸ Demanding Eldridge's resignation at this point in time will not solve the problem.
>
> *now*

> ▸ However, in most neighborhoods, the same group of people who write the
>
> newsletters are the ones who organize and participate in the activities.
>
> *also*

Here are examples of common wordy phrases and more concise alternatives.

Wordy Phrases	*More Concise Alternatives*
due to the fact that	
in view of the fact that	
the reason for	
for the reason that	for, because, why, since
this is why	
in light of the fact that	
on the grounds that	
despite the fact that	
regardless of the fact that	although, though

as regards in reference to concerning the matter of where . . . is concerned	concerning, about, regarding
it is necessary that there is a need for it is important that	should, must
has the ability to is able to is in a position to	can
in order to for the purpose of	to
at this point in time	now
on the subject of	on, about
as a matter of fact	actually
be aware of the fact that	know [that]
to the effect that	that
the way in which	how
in the event that	if, when

Rewrite a wordy sentence to simplify its structure.

Often you can express your ideas more directly and forcefully by editing to eliminate *there is* or *there are* from the beginning of a sentence, or by changing from the passive to the active **voice**. (See also G5–d.)

> ~~There are always~~ Five or six spots open at the ends of the rows.

                        Five   *are always*

> ~~The topic is initiated by a~~ member who has nothing to gain by the discussion ~~of~~

                        A   *initiates*

the topic.

voice The form of a verb that either emphasizes the performer of an action (active) or de-emphasizes it (passive).

Note: Whenever possible, replace *am, are, is, was,* and other forms of *be* with a stronger verb that clearly defines an action.

W1-c Eliminate unnecessary intensifiers or hedges.

Delete unnecessary intensifiers.

Although intensifiers such as *very, really, clearly, quite,* and *of course* can strengthen statements, eliminating them or substituting more forceful words is often more effective.

▶ The plot of this movie is ~~really great.~~ *thrilling.*

Some intensifiers are unnecessary because the words they modify are already as strong as possible, such as *unique.*

▶ The arrangement of the plain blocks ~~is so unique that it~~ *unique* makes the sculpture

   seem textured.

Eliminate unnecessary hedges.

Writers use hedges such as *apparently, seem, perhaps, possibly, to a certain extent, tend,* and *somewhat* to avoid making claims that they cannot substantiate. Hedges add subtlety to prose and acknowledge the possibility of important exceptions. Too many hedges, however, make writing too tentative.

▶ ~~In most cases, realistic~~ *Realistic* characteristics ~~tend to~~ *often* undermine comedy's primary

   function of making us laugh at exaggerated character traits.

W1-d Eliminate unnecessary prepositions.

preposition A word (such as *between, in,* or *of*) that indicates the relation between a word in a sentence and its object.

If the word following a preposition is the object of a verb, the preposition may be unnecessary.

▶ Nothing happened, and my doctor ordered ~~for~~ them to stop inducing labor.

Another alternative is to change the verb.

▶ Consequently, student volunteers will not be inclined to leave and ~~look for~~ *seek*

   smaller hospitals with less intense shifts.

┤ **FOR MULTILINGUAL WRITERS** ├────────────────────

Prepositions also combine with verbs to form two- or three-word (or phrasal) verbs whose meaning cannot be understood literally (*handed in, longed for*). When a preposition is part of a two- or three-word verb, it is called a *particle*. See T2-b.

W2 Exact Words

Effective writers choose words carefully, paying attention to meaning, form, idiomatic phrasing, and freshness.

W2-a Replace incorrect words with intended words.

Check a dictionary when you are uncertain of meaning. Watch for incorrect words and for words similar in meaning or sound. (See also the Glossary of Frequently Misused Words.)

> ▸ Louis kicked him into a river ~~invested~~ *infested* with crocodiles.

> ▸ How do we stop offshore oil drilling and yet offer an alternative to ~~appease~~ *alleviate* the energy crisis?

W2-b Use correct prepositions.

Short as they generally are, prepositions define crucial relationships for the reader.

> ▸ A building's beauty must be determined *by* the harmony *of* its design.

If prepositions are a problem in your writing, note how other writers use them.

> ▸ Unlike many of the other pieces of art ~~about~~ *on* campus, the statues seem to fit well.

FOR MULTILINGUAL WRITERS

If you find prepositions difficult, pay special attention to them as you read. For a review of the meanings of some common prepositions, see T3.

W2-c Use standard idioms.

Read and listen carefully to get a sense of standard idioms, especially the ones that consist of small words, such as prepositions, and verb forms.

> ▸ The most serious problems of many developing countries stem ~~to~~ *from* lack of educational and economic opportunities.

idiom An expression whose meaning cannot be determined from its parts but must be learned (*call off* for "cancel").

FOR MULTILINGUAL WRITERS

Idiomatic two- and three-word verbs (*put down, set up*) and combinations of verbs or adjectives and prepositions (*look for, afraid of*) can be especially troublesome for writers whose first language is not English. See T2-b.

---

cliché An overused expression that has lost its original freshness, such as *hard as a rock*.

W2-d Eliminate clichés or overused expressions.

Readers prefer lively, original expressions to worn phrases.

▶ The audience ~~is on pins and needles,~~ *erupts in gasps and nervous giggles*⌃ wondering whose plan will falter first.

W2-e Select the correct form of the word that you intend.

If you are learning to use an unfamiliar word or are struggling to find a word whose meaning fits, you may end up using the wrong form. A good dictionary can help you determine which form of a word fits your context.

▶ The phrase "you know" ~~is an introductory to~~ *introduces*⌃ someone's opinion.

figures of speech Images such as similes and metaphors that suggest a comparison between objects that are generally unlike each other.

simile A direct comparison that uses *like* or *as*.

metaphor An indirect comparison that refers to or describes one thing as if it were the other.

W2-f Use appropriate figures of speech.

Figures of speech, such as **similes** and **metaphors**, can express comparisons, make a complex idea easier to understand, or bring a scene or character to life for your readers.

SIMILE To Sam, high school was like a nursing home.

METAPHOR Tupac was the Beethoven of his age.

Make sure that any figure of speech that you use is clear, appropriate, and consistent.

INACCURATE METAPHOR The children would jump from car to car, *as if they were mushrooms*. [Mushrooms cannot jump.]

mixed metaphor An inconsistent metaphor, one that mixes several images rather than completing one.

Also avoid **mixed metaphors**, as in the following example, in which the soul is compared to both a criminal defendant and a plant.

MIXED METAPHOR Karma is an inorganic process of development in which the soul not only *pays the price* for its misdeeds but also *bears the fruit* of the *seeds sown* in former lives.

W3 Appropriate Words

Choose words carefully to give your writing the appropriate level of formality, without slang, bias, or pretentious language. The following sentences illustrate how appropriate words can convey a sense of environment.

▶ At 6:50 p.m., the hospital's paging system comes alive.

▶ Lying on the stretcher, the unidentified victim can only groan and move his left leg.

W3-a   Use the level of formality expected in your writing situation.

Many problems with inappropriate language occur when writers use informal language in a more formal writing situation.

INFORMAL   Treating old people badly gets everyone upset because that's your family, and no one wants to get judged for putting their mom in a home.

MORE FORMAL   Mistreatment of the elderly is an unusually sensitive problem because it involves such value-laden ideas as *home* and *family*.

Taking your essay assignment into account, reword as necessary to avoid shifts in the level of formality.

▶ What makes an excellent church, auditorium, or theater makes a ~~lousy~~ *poor* library.

W3-b   Limit the use of slang in formal writing situations.

slang Informal language that tends to change rapidly.

Although slang may be appropriate in dialogue used to define a character or a situation in a narrative, it should not be used in formal academic writing. Replace inappropriate slang expressions with more formal words.

▶ The ~~guy~~ *investor* is ~~for real~~ *completely serious*⊙

▶ The cast of the movie was ~~awesome~~ *impressive*⊙

W3-c   Use nonsexist language.

Avoid using gender-based pronouns (such as *he* or *his*) to refer to people who might be either men or women. (See also G2-b.)

Revise a sentence that uses masculine pronouns to represent people in general.

Use plural forms, eliminate the pronouns, or use both masculine and feminine pronouns.

▶ ~~A student's~~ *Students'* eligibility for alternative loans is based on whether or not ~~his~~ *their* school decides ~~he is~~ *they are* entitled to financial aid.

▶ Abstract expressionism is art that is based on the artist's spontaneous feelings at the moment when he is *or she* creating ~~his~~ *a* work.

Substitute more inclusive words to represent people in general.

▶ Oligarchies have existed throughout ~~the history of man.~~ *human history.*

Rewrite language that implies or reinforces stereotypes or discrimination.

▶ Oligarchies were left to ~~barbaric~~ *tribes* ~~tribesmen~~ and herders ~~who were beyond the~~ *outside the empire.*

~~reach of civilization.~~

▶ Doctors who did not keep up with *their* colleagues would be forced to update

their procedures.

W3-d   Replace pretentious language **with simpler, more direct wording.**

pretentious language Fancy or wordy language used primarily to impress.

Use words that best express your idea, and balance or replace distractingly unusual words with simpler, more familiar choices.

▶ Perhaps ~~apprehension toward instigating~~ *fear of making* these changes stems from financial

concern.

▶ Expanded oil exploration may seem relatively innocuous, but this proposal is a

deplorable suggestion to all but the most ~~pernicious, specious entities.~~ *deceptive destructive groups.*

P   Punctuation

P1   Commas

Use a comma to set off and separate sentence elements.

P1-a   Add a comma between independent clauses **joined by a coordinating conjunction.**

independent clause A word group with a subject and a predicate that can stand alone as a separate sentence.

coordinating conjunction A word that joins comparable and equally important sentence elements: *for, and, or, but, nor, yet,* or *so.*

When independent clauses are joined by a coordinating conjunction, a comma is required to tell the reader that another independent clause follows the first one.

━━━ independent clause ━━━   ━━━ independent clause ━━━

▶ Perhaps my father had the same dream and perhaps my grandfather did as well.
                                          ^
                                          ,

If the independent clauses are brief and unambiguous, a comma is not required, though it is never wrong to include it.

▶ The rescue attempt fails and the climber must let go.

P1-b Place a comma after an introductory word, phrase, or clause.

Sentences often begin with words, phrases, or clauses that precede the independent clause and modify an element within it. The comma following each introductory element lets the reader know where the modifying word or phrase ends and the main clause begins.

▶ *Naturally,* this result didn't help him any.

▶ *With a jerk,* I lofted the lure in a desperate attempt to catch a fish and please my dad.

▶ *When we entered the honeymoon suite,* the room smelled of burnt plastic and was the color of Pepto-Bismol.

If an introductory phrase or clause is brief—four words or fewer—the comma may be omitted unless it is needed to prevent misreading.

▶ Without hesitation I dived into the lake.

P1-c Use commas to set off a nonrestrictive word group.

To test whether a word group is *nonrestrictive* (supplemental, nondefining, and thus nonessential) or *restrictive* (defining and thus essential), read the sentence with and without the word group. If the sentence is essentially unchanged in meaning without it, the word group is nonrestrictive. Use commas to set it off.

NONRESTRICTIVE The oldest fishermen, *grizzly sea salts wrapped in an aura of experience,* led the way.

Conversely, if omitting the word group changes the meaning of the sentence, it is restrictive. In this case, do not use commas.

RESTRICTIVE Body-mapping technologies can give video games a sense of realism *that was not previously available.*

Use a comma to set off a nonrestrictive word group at the end of a sentence.

▶ We all stood anxious and prepared for what he was about to say.

Use a pair of commas to set off a nonrestrictive word group in the middle of a sentence.

▶ The most common moods are happiness when the music is in a major key or

sadness, when the music is in a minor key.

(See also P2-b.)

P1-d Use commas to set off a transitional, parenthetical, or contrasting expression or an absolute phrase.

Transitional expressions help the reader follow a writer's movement from point to point. *Parenthetical comments* interrupt a sentence with a brief aside. *Contrasting expressions* are introduced by *not, no,* or *nothing. Absolute phrases* modify the whole clause and often include a past or present **participle** as well as modifiers. By using commas to set off such expressions, you signal that they are additions, supplementing or commenting on the information in the rest of the sentence.

> **participle** A verb form showing present tense (*dancing, freezing*) or past tense (*danced, frozen*) that can also act as an adjective.

TRANSITIONAL	*Besides* it is summer.
PARENTHETICAL	These are all indications *I think* of Jan's drive for power and control.
CONTRASTING	Nick is the perfect example of a young, hungry manager trying to climb to the top *not bothered by the feelings of others.*
ABSOLUTE	"Did I ever tell you about the time I danced with the Rockettes at Radio City Music Hall?" she asked *her eyes focusing dreamily into the distance.*

P1-e Use commas to separate three or more items in a series, placing the final comma before the conjunction.

The commas in a series separate the items for the reader.

▶ He always tells me about the loyalty, honor and pride he feels as a Marine.

▶ Our communities would get relief from the fear and despair that come from having

unremitting violence, addiction and open-air drug markets in their midst.

Note: Newspapers, magazines, and British publications often omit the comma before the conjunction. In your academic writing, however, include it for clarity.

P1-f Use a comma before a trailing nonrestrictive participial phrase.

Participial phrases are generally **nonrestrictive word groups**. When they follow the **independent clause** in a sentence, they should be set off with commas. See P1-c.

PARTICIPIAL
PHRASE
The plane taxied as he turned on his phone, *expecting to find a mushy text* from his girlfriend.

The comma before the phrase signals the end of the main clause and sets off the modifying phrase.

▶ Every so often, a pelican agilely arcs high over the water͜twisting downward gracefully

to catch an unsuspecting mackerel.

Note: If the participial phrase is restrictive, providing essential information, do not use a comma. See P1-c and P2-b.

P1-g Place a comma between a complete direct quotation and the text identifying the speaker.

The comma, along with the quotation marks, helps the reader determine where the quotation begins and ends. (See also P6.)

▶ "It will be okay͜," Coach reassured me, as he motioned for the emergency

medical technicians to bring a board.

P1-h Add a comma (or pair of commas in the middle of a sentence) to set off expressions commonly included in dialogue.

Use commas to set off from the main part of the sentence names or words used in **direct address**, words such as *yes* and *no,* and mild **interjections**. Also use a comma to set off questions added to the end of sentences.

▶ "Well͜son, what are you doing?"

▶ "No͜sir."

▶ "Boy͜did we underestimate her."

---

participial phrase A group of words that begins with a present participle (*dancing, freezing*) or a past participle (*danced, frozen*) and modifies a noun or a pronoun.

nonrestrictive word group A group of words, set off by commas, that provides non-essential information and could be eliminated without changing the meaning of the noun or pronoun it modifies.

independent clause A word group with a subject and a predicate that can stand alone as a separate sentence.

direct quotation A speaker's or writer's exact words, which are enclosed in quotation marks.

direct address Words that are spoken directly to someone else who is named.

interjection An exclamatory word that indicates strong feeling or attempts to command attention: *Shhh! Oh! Ouch!*

▶ "That's not very efficient, is it?"

▶ "Besides, it'll be good for me."

P1-i Use a comma between coordinate adjectives.

coordinate adjectives Two or more adjectives that modify a noun equally and independently: the *smooth, shiny* tabletop.

If you can change the order of a series of adjectives or add *and* between them without changing the meaning, they are coordinate and should be separated with a comma.

▶ There are reasons for her *erratic, irrational* behavior.

The comma signals that the adjectives are equal, related in the same way to the word modified.

If the adjectives closest to the noun cannot be logically rearranged or linked by *and,* they are **cumulative adjectives** and should not be separated by commas.

cumulative adjectives Two or more adjectives that do not modify a noun equally. Instead, one or two of the adjectives closest to the noun form a noun phrase that the remaining adjectives modify: *colorful hot-air* balloons.

▶ I pictured myself as a *professional race car* driver.

P1-j Add commas where needed to set off dates, numbers, and addresses.

When you include a full date (month, day, and year), use a pair of commas to set off the year.

▶ In the May 11, 2015 issue of the *New Yorker,* Emily Nussbaum describes "Inside Amy

Schumer" as a "destablizing mixture of daffy and caustic" (68).

If you present a date in reverse order (day, month, and year) or if the date is partial, do not add commas.

In large numbers (except four-digit years), separate groups of three digits (thousands, millions, and so forth) with commas.

▶ As of 2015, there were about 905 000 speakers of Russian in the United States.

When you write out an address, add commas between the street address, the city, and the state.

▶ Mrs. Wilson relocated to Bowie Maryland after years of telecommuting from

Delaware.

P2 Unnecessary Commas

Because commas are warranted in so many instances, it is easy to use them unnecessarily or incorrectly.

P2-a Omit the comma when items in a pair are joined by a coordinating conjunction.

Many word pairs can be joined by *and* or another coordinating conjunction, including **compound predicates**, **compound objects**, and **compound subjects**. None of these pairs should be interrupted by a comma.

▶ I grabbed my lunchbox⸝and headed out to the tree.
   [compound predicate]

▶ As for me, I wore a pink short set with ruffles⸝and a pair of sneakers.
   [compound object]

▶ My father⸝and brother wore big hiking boots.
   [compound subject]

Note: This rule does not apply when the items in a pair are both independent clauses.

P2-b Omit any comma that sets off a restrictive word group.

A *restrictive word group* distinguishes the noun it modifies from similar nouns or precisely defines its distinguishing characteristics. See P1-c for a review of nonrestrictive word groups that need commas.

   If a comma incorrectly sets off a restrictive word group, it undermines the meaning, suggesting to the reader that essential information is not important.

▶ Although divorce is obviously a cause of the psychological problems⸝ a child

   will face, the parents need to support their child through the anxiety and turmoil.

P2-c Omit any commas that unnecessarily separate a subject and verb or a verb and its object.

A comma that separates two of a sentence's core elements—**subject**, **verb**, and **object**—confuses matters by suggesting that some other material has been added.

▶ *Bilateral*⸝means that both the left and the right sides of the brain are involved
   [subject] [verb]

   in processing a stimulus.

▶ Many singers try without success to incorporate in their works⸝music from different
   [verb] [object]

   cultures.

---

coordinating conjunction A word that joins comparable and equally important sentence elements: *for, and, or, but, nor, yet,* or *so.*

compound predicate Two or more verbs or verb phrases linked by *and.*

compound object Two or more words acting as an object and linked by *and.*

compound subject Two or more words acting as a subject and linked by *and.*

subject The part of a clause that identifies who or what is being discussed.

verb A word or phrase that expresses action or being and, along with a subject, is a basic component of a sentence.

object The part of a clause that receives the action of the verb, or the part of a phrase that follows a preposition: At the checkpoint, we unloaded *the canoes.*

no ⌃
P2

adverbial clause A clause that nearly always modifies a verb, indicating time, place, condition, reason, cause, purpose, result, or another logical relationship.

P2-d **Omit a comma that separates the main part of the sentence from a trailing adverbial clause.**

When an adverbial clause appears at the end of a sentence, a comma is ordinarily not needed.

▸ I found the tables turned,/when he interviewed me about the reasons for my tattoo.

cumulative adjectives Two or more adjectives that do not modify a noun equally. Instead, one or two of the adjectives closest to the noun form a noun phrase that the remaining adjectives modify: *colorful hot-air balloons.*

P2-e **Leave out commas that separate cumulative adjectives.**

           —— coordinate adjectives ——

▸ Wearing a pair of jeans, *cutoff, bleached,* and *torn,* with an embroidered blouse

    cumulative adjectives

and *soft leather* sandals, she looked older and more foreign than Julie.

Leather modifies *sandals,* and *soft* modifies *leather sandals* as a unit. Thus the meaning is cumulative, and a comma would interrupt the connection between the adjectives and the noun. (See P1-i to review the use of commas with coordinate adjectives.)

P2-f **Omit any comma that appears before or after a series of items.**

Although commas should be used to separate the items in a list, they should not be used before the first item or after the final one.

▸ Race, sex, religion, financial situation, or any other circumstance beyond the control of the applicant,/should not be considered.

(See also P1-e.)

P2-g **Omit or correct any other unnecessary or incorrect commas.**

Check your essays carefully to correct typical comma problems.

Omit commas that follow coordinating conjunctions.

coordinating conjunction A word that joins comparable and equally important sentence elements: *for, and, or, but, nor, yet,* or *so.*

▸ But,/since sharks are not yet classified as endangered species, the members of

Congress were not very sympathetic, and the bill was not passed.

Omit commas that follow coordinating conjunctions joining two independent clauses.

▸ The ominous vision of the piano wavered before my eyes and,/before I knew it,

I was at the base of the steps to the stage, steps that led to potential public

humiliation.

▶ I had finally felt the music deep in my soul, and/when I sang, I had a great

feeling of relief knowing that everything was going to be all right.

Omit commas following subordinating conjunctions, such as *who, that, although*, or *since*.

Watch for *who, which, that, whom, whose, where, when, although, because, since, though*, and other subordinating conjunctions.

▶ The drinking age should be raised because/drunk driving has become the leading

cause of death among young people between the ages of fifteen and twenty-five.

subordinating conjunction A word or phrase (such as *although* or *because*) that introduces a dependent clause and relates it to an independent clause.

Omit commas preceding *that* when it introduces an indirect quotation.

Unlike a direct quotation, an indirect quotation is not set off by a comma or quotation marks.

▶ After looking at my tests, the doctor said/that I had calcification.

indirect quotation A restatement of a speaker's or writer's ideas without quoting directly or using quotation marks.

Omit commas immediately following a preposition.

▶ Despite/multiple recruitment and retention problems, the number of public

school teachers remained about the same between 2000 and 2014.

preposition A word (such as *between, in*, or *of*) that indicates the relation between a word in a sentence and its object: The water splashed *into* the canoe.

Omit commas setting off a prepositional phrase in the middle or at the end of a sentence.

When a prepositional phrase appears in the middle or at the end of a sentence, it is usually not set off by commas.

▶ The children's trauma team gathered in the Resuscitation Room/at the same time

that John Doe was being treated.

prepositional phrase A group of words that begins with a preposition and indicates the relation between a word in a sentence and the object following the preposition: Her sunglasses slid *under the seat*.

Rewrite a sentence that is full of phrases and commas to simplify both the sentence structure and the punctuation.

▶ ~~The researchers could monitor,~~ ^{By} looking through a porthole window, how ^{the researchers could monitor}

much time ^{Noah spent} ~~was spent, by Noah,~~ in the dome.

P3   Semicolons

Use semicolons to join closely related independent clauses and to make long sentences with commas easier to read.

independent clause A word group with a subject and a predicate that can stand alone as a separate sentence.

P3-a **Use a semicolon to join independent clauses if the second clause restates or sets up a contrast to the first.**

Although two independent clauses could be separated by a period, the semicolon tells the reader that they are closely related, emphasizing the restatement or sharpening the contrast.

▶ Davie was not an angel/ he was always getting into trouble with the teachers.

Note: When the independent clauses are linked by *and, but,* or another coordinating conjunction, use a comma rather than a semicolon (see P1-a) unless the independent clauses include internal punctuation (see P3-c).

P3-b **Use semicolons to separate items in a series when they include internal commas.**

Because the reader expects items in a series to be separated by commas, other commas within items can be confusing. The solution is to leave the internal commas as they are but to use a stronger mark, the semicolon, to signal the divisions between items.

▶ Appliances that use freon include air conditioners, small models as well as

central systems/ refrigerators/ and freezers, both home and industrial types.

P3-c **Use a semicolon to join a series of independent clauses when they include other punctuation.**

When independent clauses include elements set off by internal punctuation, use semicolons between them if other punctuation may confuse the reader or make the sentence parts difficult to identify.

▶ He was the guide/ and he was driving us in this old Ford sedan, just the two of

us and him/ and I had noticed early on that the car didn't have a gas cap.

conjunctive adverb A word or phrase (such as *finally, however,* or *therefore*) that tells how the ideas in two sentences or independent clauses are connected.

transitional expression A word or group of words that expresses the relationship between one sentence and the next.

P3-d **Use a semicolon to join two independent clauses when the second clause contains a conjunctive adverb or a transitional expression.**

Because a semicolon shows a strong relationship between independent clauses, writers often use it to reinforce the connection expressed by the adverb or transition.

▶ Ninety-five percent of Americans recognize the components of a healthy diet/,

however, they fail to apply their nutritional IQ when selecting foods.

P3-e **Omit a semicolon used incorrectly to replace a comma or another punctuation mark.**

Take care not to use semicolons in place of other punctuation.

Replace a semicolon with a colon, dash, or comma to link an independent clause to a phrase or to set off an appositive.

> ▶ The threat of a potentially devastating malpractice suit promotes the practice of
>
> defensive medicine, doctors ordering excessive and expensive tests to confirm a
>
> diagnosis.

appositive A word or word group that identifies or gives more information about a noun or pronoun that precedes it.

Replace a semicolon with a comma to join two independent clauses linked by a coordinating conjunction.

> ▶ We can relocate the ashtrays to that area, and it could then become
>
> an outdoor smoking lounge.
>
> (See also P1-a.)

coordinating conjunction A word that joins comparable and equally important sentence elements: *for, and, or, but, nor, yet,* or *so.*

Replace a semicolon with a colon to introduce a list.

> ▶ Our county ditches fill up with old items that are hard to get rid of:
>
> refrigerators, mattresses, couches, and chairs, just to name a few.

Note: For introducing an in-text list, as in this example, a dash (see P5-b) is a less formal and more dramatic alternative to the colon (see P4-a).

P4 Colons

Besides introducing specific sentence elements, colons conventionally appear in works cited or bibliography entries, introduce subtitles, express ratios and times, and follow salutations in formal letters.

P4-a **Use a colon to introduce a list, an appositive, a quotation, a question, or a statement.**

Usually, a colon follows an independent clause that makes a general statement; after the colon, the rest of the sentence often supplies specifics—a definition, a quotation or question, or a list.

Use the colon selectively to alert readers to closely connected ideas, a significant point, a crucial definition, or a dramatic revelation.

independent clause A word group with a subject and a predicate that can stand alone as a separate sentence.

Note: Because a colon follows but does not interrupt an **independent clause**, do not use a colon after words such as *is, are, consists of, including, such as, for instance,* and *for example* to introduce a list (see P4-b).

Consider using a colon to introduce a list.

You can use a colon to introduce a list if the list is preceded by an independent clause. Be careful not to interrupt the clause in the middle (see P4-b).

▶ Most young law school graduates become trial lawyers in one of three ways⫶ by

going to work for a government prosecutor's office, by working for a private law

firm, or by opening private offices of their own.

appositive A word or word group that identifies or gives more information about a noun or pronoun that precedes it.

Consider using a colon to emphasize an appositive.

Although you can always use commas to set off an appositive, try using a colon occasionally when you need special emphasis.

▶ The oldest fishermen are followed by the younger generation of middle-aged

fathers, excited by the chance to show their sons what their fathers once taught

them. Last to arrive are the novices⫶ the thrill seekers.

Consider using a colon to introduce a formal quotation, a question, a statement, or another independent clause.

▶ We learn that the narrator is a troublemaker in paragraph twelve⫶ "I got thrown

out of the center for playing pool when I should've been sewing."

▶ I ran around the office in constant fear of his questions⫶ What do you have

planned for the day? How many demonstrations are scheduled for this week?

How many contacts have you made?

▶ Both authors are clearly of the same opinion⫶ Recycling scrap tires is no longer

an option.

▶ I guess the saying is true⫶ Absence does make the heart grow fonder.

Do not capitalize the word following a colon if it introduces an incomplete sentence. However, when the word group following a colon is a complete sentence, you can either capitalize the first word or not, depending on your preference. Whichever choice you prefer, be consistent. When you introduce a quotation with a colon, always capitalize the word that begins the quotation. (See also M2-c.)

P4-b Correct unnecessary or incorrect colons.

Omit a colon that interrupts an independent clause, especially after words such as *is, are, include, composed of, consists of, including, such as, for instance,* and *for example.*

▶ The tenets include: courtesy, integrity, perseverance, self-control, indomitable

  spirit, and modesty.

Replace an inappropriate colon with the correct punctuation mark.

▶ As I was touring the different areas of the shop, I ran into one of the owners:

  "Hi, Kim," she said, with a smile on her face.

P5 Dashes

A dash breaks the rhythm or interrupts the meaning of a sentence, setting off information with greater emphasis than another punctuation mark could supply. Writers often use dashes to substitute for other punctuation in quick notes and letters to friends. In many kinds of published writing, dashes are used sparingly—but often to good effect.

P5-a Type, space, and position a dash correctly.

Type a dash (—) as two hyphens (--) in a row, with no spaces before or after. (Your word processing program likely provides the option of converting two hyphens into a dash.) Use one dash before a word or words set off at the end of the sentence. Use two dashes—one at the beginning and one at the end—if the word or words are in the middle of the sentence.

▶ The rigid structure and asymmetrical arrangements of the sculpture blend well with
  three different surroundings—the trees, the library building, and the parking lots.

Use a pair of dashes, not just one, to mark the beginning and end of a word group that needs emphasis.

▶ I could tell that the people in the room work in uncomfortable conditions —

they all wear white lab coats, caps, and gloves/ but they joke or laugh while

building the guns.

P5-b Consider using a dash to set off material from the rest of the sentence.

Because the dash marks a strong break, it alerts the reader to the importance of the material that follows it.

Use a dash or a pair of dashes to emphasize a definition, a dramatic statement, a personal comment, or an explanation.

▶ Binge eating/ larger than normal consumption of high-calorie foods/ starts with

emotional distress and depression.

▶ But unlike the boys, the girls often turn to something other than violence/

motherhood.

Consider inserting a dash or a pair of dashes to emphasize a list.
If the list appears in the middle of the sentence, use one dash at the beginning and another at the end to signal exactly where the list begins and ends.

▶ Another problem is that certain toy figures The Hulk, Spider-Man, and the

X-Men, to name just a few/ are characters from movies that portray violence.

P5-c Rewrite a sentence that uses the dash inappropriately or excessively.

Use dashes purposefully; avoid relying on them instead of using other punctuation marks or developing clear sentences and transitions.

▶ Finally the TV people were finished with their interviewing ~~— now~~ *and* they wanted

to do a shot of the entrance to the restaurant.

If you are not sure whether you have used a dash or a pair of dashes appropriately, try removing the material that is set off. If the sentence does not make logical and grammatical sense, one or both of the dashes are misused or misplaced.

▶ That's a tall order — and a reason to start ~~a~~ amassing some serious capital soon.

P6 Quotation Marks

Use double quotation marks, always in pairs, to indicate direct quotations and to mark some types of titles.

P6-a Set off direct quotations with quotation marks.

A direct quotation is set off by a pair of quotation marks and by an initial capital letter. **Indirect quotations**, however, do not use quotation marks or capital letters.

DIRECT QUOTATION	Ms. Goldman told her colleagues: "It's time to face the real issues!"
INDIRECT QUOTATION	Ms. Goldman told her colleagues that it was time to face the real issues.

When a phrase such as *she said* interrupts the quotation, do not capitalize the first word after the phrase unless the word actually begins a new quoted sentence. (See also M2-c.)

▶ "The only way to get rid of a temptation," says Lord Henry in Oscar Wilde's *The Picture of Dorian Gray*, "~~I~~is to yield to it" (29; ch. 2).

Note: In a research paper, indent a long quotation as a block, double-spaced, and omit quotation marks.

P6-b Follow convention in using punctuation at the end of a quotation, after a signal phrase or speaker tag (*she said*), and with other punctuation.

Place a comma or a period inside the closing quotation mark.

▶ Fishman also discusses utterances such as "umm,"/ "oh,"/ and "yeah."

▶ Grandpa then said, "I guess you haven't heard what happened."/

---

direct quotation A speaker's or writer's exact words, which are enclosed in quotation marks.

indirect quotation A restatement of a speaker's or writer's ideas without quoting directly or using quotation marks.

For more on using block quotations in MLA and APA style, see Chapter 19.

In a research paper following either MLA style or APA style, the closing quotation mark should follow the last quoted word, but the period at the end of the sentence should follow the parentheses enclosing the citation.

▶ Senator Gabriel Ambrosio added that "an override would send a terrible

message, particularly to the young people" (Schwaneberg 60).

Note: Place a colon or semicolon outside the closing quotation mark.

▶ The doctor who tells the story says that the girl is "furious"; she shrieks

"terrifyingly, hysterically" as he approaches her.

Follow an introductory phrase with either a comma or the word *that*.

▶ I looked down and said, "I was trying on your dress blues."

When you introduce a formal quotation with an independent clause, you can instead follow the introduction with a colon. (See P4-a.)

Place a question mark or an exclamation point inside the closing quotation mark if it is part of the quotation, or outside if it is part of your own sentence.

PART OF QUOTATION   My father replied, "What have I ever done to you?"

PART OF SENTENCE   How is it possible that he could have kept repeating to our class,

"You are too dumb to learn anything?"?

You do not need to add a period if a question mark or an exclamation point concludes a quotation at the end of the sentence.

▶ Miriam produced a highlighter from her bookbag with an enthusiastic "Voilà!"

Supply a closing quotation mark at the end of a paragraph to show that a new quotation begins in the next paragraph.

▶ "Come on, James," Toby said. "Let's climb over the fence." [new ¶] "I don't think it's a

good idea!" I replied.

Omit the closing quotation mark if a quotation continues in the next paragraph.

▶ "I enjoy waiting on these people because they also ask about my life, instead

of treating me like a servant.ʰ

"However, some customers can be rude and very impatient."

P6-c   Enclose titles of short works in quotation marks.

Short works include articles, chapters, essays, short stories, short poems, episodes in a television program, and songs. Place the quotation marks around the exact title of the work mentioned. Titles of longer works, such as books, magazines, and newspapers, are italicized; see M5-a.

"The Use of Force,"

▶ The short story ~~The Use of Force,~~ by William Carlos Williams, is an account of
                              ^

a doctor's unpleasant experience with his patient.

Note: Do not enclose the title of your own essay in quotation marks.

P6-d   Use single quotation marks inside double quotation marks to show a quotation within a quotation.

▶ Flanagan and McMenamin say, "Housing values across the United States have

acted more like a fluctuating stock market than the ʹsureʹ investment they

once were."

P6-e   Omit or correct quotation marks used excessively or incorrectly.

Omit unneeded quotation marks used for emphasis, irony, or distance.
Avoid using quotation marks just to emphasize certain words, to show irony, or to distance yourself from **slang**, **clichés**, or trite expressions.

▶ Environmental groups can wage war in the hallways of Washington and

Sacramento and drive oil companies away from our ⱽsacred shores.ⱽ

slang Informal language that tends to change rapidly.

cliché An overused expression that has lost its original freshness, such as *hard as a rock*.

indirect quotation
A restatement of a speaker's or writer's ideas without quoting directly or using quotation marks.

Omit quotation marks from indirect quotations.

> ► He said that ~~"~~when he was eighteen years old and living in Liberty, Texas, a vision
>
> inspired him to move to Houston.~~"~~

P7 Apostrophes

Use an apostrophe to mark the **possessive form** of nouns and some pronouns, the omission of letters or figures, and (in some cases) the plural of letters or figures.

possessive form The form that shows that a thing belongs to someone or to something.

P7-a Use an apostrophe to show the possessive form of a noun.

The form of a possessive noun depends on whether it is singular (one item) or plural (two or more items).

Add -'s to a singular noun to show possession.

> a student's parents   the rabbit's eye   Ward's essay

Be sure to include the apostrophe and to place it before the -s so that the reader does not mistakenly think that the noun is plural.

> ► The apartment*'s* design is spare to the point of dullness.

Indicate shared or joint possession by adding -'s to the final noun in a list; indicate individual possession by adding -'s to each noun.

> ► father and mother's room (joint or shared possession)
>
> ► father's and mother's patterns of conversation (individual possession)

Indicate possession by adding -'s to the last word in a compound.

> ► mother-in-law's

Even if a singular noun ends in s, add an apostrophe and -s.

> ► Louis's life
>
> ► Williams's narrator
>
> ► Cisneros's story

If the second s makes the word hard to pronounce, it is acceptable to add only an apostrophe.

> ► Sophocles' plays

To make plural nouns possessive, add -'s if the noun does not already end in s, and add only an apostrophe if it does.

▶ The guard was horrified by the children's behavior in the museum.

▶ Males tend to interrupt ~~females~~ *females'* conversations.

Note: Form the plural of a family name by adding *-s* without an apostrophe (the Harrisons); add the apostrophe only to show possession (the Harrisons' house).

P7-b **Add an apostrophe to show where letters or figures are omitted from a contraction.**

▶ "~~Lets~~ *Let's* go back inside and see if you can do it my way now."

▶ Many people had cosmetic surgery in the ~~90s~~ *'90s.*

P7-c **Check your style guide to determine whether to include an apostrophe to form the plural of a number, a letter, or an abbreviation.**

Some style guides encourage writers to form the plural of a number, a letter, or an abbreviation by adding *-'s*.

▶ The participants were shown a series of ~~3s~~ *3's* that configured into a large 5.

However, the *MLA Handbook* (the most commonly used style guide in courses in English literature and composition) does not. So check with your instructor to be sure what is appropriate.

P7-d **Add *-'s* to form the possessive of an indefinite pronoun but not a personal pronoun.**

INDEFINITE PRONOUN   Everyone knows that good service can make or break ~~ones~~ *one's* dining experience.

The possessive forms of **personal pronouns**, however, do not have apostrophes: *my, mine, your, yours, her, hers, his, its, our, ours, their, theirs.*

PERSONAL PRONOUN   That company does not use animals to develop ~~it's~~ *its* products.

P7-e **Omit unnecessary or incorrect apostrophes.**

Watch for an apostrophe incorrectly added to a plural noun ending in *s* when the noun is not a possessive.

▶ Autistic ~~patient's~~ *patients* can be high, middle, or low functioning.

indefinite pronoun A pronoun that does not refer to a particular person or object, such as *all, anybody, anywhere, each, enough, every, everyone, everything, one, somebody, something, either, more, most, neither, none,* and *nobody.*

personal pronoun A pronoun that refers to a specific person or object and changes form depending on its function in a sentence, such as *I, me, my, we, us,* and *our.*

( )
P8

P8 Parentheses

Parentheses are useful for enclosing material—a word, a phrase, or even a complete sentence—that interrupts a sentence.

P8-a Add parentheses to enclose additions to a sentence.

Parentheses are useful for enclosing citations of research sources (following the format required by your style guide); for enclosing an **acronym** or abbreviation at first mention; for adding dates, definitions, illustrations, or other elaborations; and for numbering or lettering a list (always using a pair of marks).

acronym A word formed from the first letters of the phrase that it abbreviates, such as *BART* for *Bay Area Rapid Transit*.

▶ Americans are not applying their knowledge, and as a result, their children are

not benefiting (*American Dietetic Association* 582)

▶ People for the Ethical Treatment of Animals (PETA) is a radical animal liberation group.

▶ The bill ~~called~~ (S-2232) was introduced to protect people who smoke off the job

against employment discrimination.

▶ Signals would (1) prevent life-threatening collisions, (2) provide more efficient and

speedy movement of traffic, and (3) decrease frustration and loss of driver judgment.

Note: Use commas to separate the items in a numbered list. If the items include internal commas, use semicolons. (See P3-b.)

P8-b Correct the punctuation used with parentheses, and omit unnecessary parentheses.

When you add information in parentheses, the sentence should remain logical and complete, and the punctuation should be the same. Delete any comma *before* a parenthesis mark.

▶ As I stood at the salad bar, a young lady asked if the kitchen had any cream

cheese (normally served only at breakfast).

Parentheses are unnecessary if they enclose information that could simply be integrated into the sentence.

▶ He didn't exhibit the uncontrollable temper and the high-velocity swearing

(typical of many high school coaches).

P9 Brackets

Use brackets to insert editorial notes into a quotation and to enclose parenthetical material within text that is already in parentheses. In a quotation, the brackets tell the reader that the added material is yours, not the original author's. (See also P10.)

For more about brackets, see Chapter 19.

▶ " 'The gang is your family,' he [Hagan] explains."

If the original quotation includes a mistake, add (sic), the Latin word for "so," in brackets to tell the reader that the error occurs in the source. Often you can reword your sentence to omit the error.

Replace inappropriate brackets with parentheses.

▶ The American Medical Society has linked "virtual" violence (violence in the media) to real-life acts of violence (Hollis 623).

P10 Ellipsis Marks

Use ellipsis marks to indicate a deliberate omission within a quotation or to mark a dramatic pause in a sentence. Type ellipsis marks as three spaced periods (. . .), with a space before the first period and following the last period.

▶ Aries also noticed this reaction in her research: "The mixed group setting seems to benefit men more than women . . . allowing men more variation in the ways they participate in discussions" (32).

If you omit the end of a quoted sentence or if you omit a sentence or more from the middle of a quoted passage, add a sentence period and a space before the first ellipsis mark.

Do not use opening or closing ellipsis marks if the quotation is clearly only part of a sentence.

▶ According to the environmental group Earthgreen, U.S. oil reserves ". . . will be economically depleted by 2018 at the current consumption rate . . ."

(Miller 476).

For more about ellipsis marks, see Chapter 19.

P11 Slashes

Use a slash to separate quoted lines of poetry and to separate word pairs that present options or opposites.

▶ In "A Poison Tree," William Blake gives the same advice: "I was angry with my friend: / I told my wrath, my wrath did end."

Note: When you use a slash to show the lines in poetry, leave a space before and after the mark. If you quote four lines or more, omit the quotation marks and slashes and present the poetry line for line as a block quotation.

P12   Periods

declarative sentence A sentence that makes a statement rather than asks a question or exclaims.

indirect question A restatement of a question asked without directly asking the question.

Use a period to mark the end of a **declarative sentence**, an **indirect question**, or an abbreviation.

▶ Another significant use for clinical hypnosis would be to replace anesthesia.

▶ She asked her professor why he was not as tough on her as he was on the male

students?.

▶ Mrs. Drabin was probably one of the smartest people I knew.

Note: Some abbreviations do not include periods (see M6); always check your dictionary to be sure. In addition, many specialized professional and academic fields have their own systems for handling abbreviations.

P13   Question Marks

Add a question mark after a direct question.

▶ Did they even read my information sheet/?

Avoid using question marks to express irony or sarcasm. Use them sparingly to question the accuracy of a preceding word or figure.

P14   Exclamation Points

Use an exclamation point to show strong emotion or emphasis.

▶ He fell on one knee and exclaimed, "Marry me, my beautiful princess!"

Use exclamation points sparingly. Replace inappropriate or excessive exclamation points with periods.

▶ If parents know which disciplinary methods to use, they can effectively protect

their children!.

M   Mechanics

M1   Hyphens

Hyphens are used to form select **compound words** and to break words at the end of a line.

M1-a   Use a hyphen to join compound adjectives that *precede* nouns.

Before Noun	After Noun
after-school activities	activities after school
well-known athlete	athlete who is well known

When a compound adjective precedes a noun, the hyphen clarifies that the compound functions as a unit.

▶ People usually think of locusts as hideous‸looking creatures that everyone dislikes

  and wants to squash.

▶ I was a nineteen‸year old second‸semester sophomore.

▶ People are becoming increasingly health‸conscious.

When two different prefixes or initial words go with the same second word, use a hyphen and a space at the end of the first prefix or word.

▶ An army of green- and blue-hooded medical personnel crowded the small trauma room.

Note: Some compound adjectives are nearly always hyphenated, before or after a noun, including those beginning with *all-* or *self-*. Check a dictionary if you are not sure whether a hyphen is needed.

▶ The use of ethanol will be a self‸perpetuating trend.

A compound with an *-ly* **adverb** preceding an **adjective** or a **participle** is always left as two words.

▶ brilliantly clever scheme

▶ rapidly growing business

compound word A word formed from two or more words that function together as a unit.

compound adjective An adjective formed from two or more words that function as a unit.

adverb A word that modifies a verb, an adjective, or another adverb.

adjective A word that modifies a noun or a pronoun, adding information about it.

participle A verb form showing present tense (*dancing, freezing*) or past tense (*danced, frozen*) that can also act as an adjective.

M1-b **Present a compound noun as one word, as separate words, or as a hyphenated compound.**

Close up the parts of a compound noun spelled as one word.

▶ Another road in our county now looks like an appliance grave yard.

Omit hyphens in a compound noun spelled as separate words.

▶ First, make the community aware of the problem by writing a letter to the editor.

Hyphenate fractions, compound numbers (up to ninety-nine), and other nouns that are hyphenated in your dictionary.

▶ Almost two thirds of couples married before age eighteen end up divorced,

twice the number of couples married at twenty one or older.

Note: If using compound words that have more than one acceptable spelling (*work-force* and *work force,* for example), choose one spelling and use it consistently. If you are unsure about whether to use a hyphen, check your dictionary, or follow the common usage of professional publications in the field in which you are writing.

M1-c **Spell words formed with most prefixes as one word with no hyphen.**

| antismoking | coauthor | multicultural | nonviolent |
| postwar | repossess | submarine | unskilled |

▶ This possibility is so rare as to be non existent.

Insert a hyphen in a compound noun beginning with *ex-, great-,* or *self-* (unless it is followed by a suffix, as in *selfhood*) or ending in *-elect* or *-in-law.*

| ex-husband | self-esteem | secretary-elect |

▶ Self sufficiency is not the only motivation.

proper noun The capitalized name of a specific person, group, place, or thing.

Use a hyphen in a word that includes a prefix and a **proper noun**.

| un-American | anti-American | pro-American |

M1-d **Use a hyphen when necessary to avoid ambiguity.**

Sometimes a hyphen is necessary to prevent a reader from confusing a word with a prefix (*re-cover, re-creation*) with another word (*recover, recreation*) or from stumbling over a word in which two or three of the same letters fall together (*anti-inflammatory, troll-like*).

▶ The police officers asked for the *recreation* facility's log to help them *re-create* the circumstances surrounding the crime.

M1-e   **Insert a hyphen between syllables to divide a word at the end of a line.**

If you must divide a word, look for a logical division, such as between syllables, between parts of a compound word, or between the root and a prefix or suffix. If you are uncertain about where to divide a word, check your dictionary.

go-ing	height-en	mus-cu-la-ture	back-stage
dis-sat-is-fied	com-mit-ment	hon-or-able	phi-los-o-phy

Although many published works divide words, writing is easier to read without numerous broken words.

M2   Capitalization

Capitalize proper nouns, the first word in a sentence or a quotation that is a sentence, and the main words in a title.

M2-a   **Capitalize proper nouns.**

Capitalize specific names of people, groups, places, streets, events, historical periods, monuments, holidays, days, months, and directions that refer to specific geographic areas.

World War II	the Great Depression	Lincoln Memorial
Independence Day	Passover	Ramadan
Monday	January	Colorado College
the Northeast	Native Americans	Magnolia Avenue

▶ It is difficult for ͢A͢mericans to comprehend the true meaning of freedom.

Capitalize adjectives derived from proper nouns.

Mexican   Dickensian

▶ The ͢S͢ocratic method is a teaching style based on questioning.

When a reference is general, use a **common noun** (uncapitalized) rather than a proper one (capitalized). Do not capitalize general names of institutions, seasons, compass directions, or words that you simply want to emphasize.

summer vacation	last winter	university requirements
church service	southern exposure	western life

▶ I work in a ͢l͢aw ͢o͢ffice that specializes in settling accident cases.

common noun The general name of a person, place, or thing.

Note: Common nouns such as *street* and *river* are capitalized only when they are part of a proper noun: *Main Street, the Mississippi River.*

**cap
M2**

M2-b **Capitalize the word that begins a sentence.**

> *T*
> ‸the garden was their world.

If a complete sentence appears within parentheses and is not part of a larger sentence, capitalize the first word.

See P4-a for information on capitalizing **independent clauses** following colons.

independent clause A word group with a subject and a predicate that can stand alone as a separate sentence.

M2-c **Capitalize the first word in a quotation unless it is integrated into your own wording or continues an interrupted quotation.**

> Lucy Danziger says, "Forget about the glass ceiling" (81).

> Lucy Danziger argues that we should "forget about the glass ceiling."

> Marilyn describes the adult bison as having an "ugly, shaggy, brown coat."

Writers often incorporate short quotations and quotations introduced by *that* into their sentences; neither needs an initial capital letter. When a phrase such as *she said* interrupts a quotation, capitalize the first word in the quotation but not the first word after the phrase unless it begins a new sentence. (See also P6-a.)

> *T*
> Toby said, "‸trust me — we won't get caught."

> *R*
> "‸renting," she insists, "deprives you of big tax breaks."

Note: If you quote from a poem, capitalize words exactly as the poet does.

article An adjective that precedes a noun and identifies a definite reference to something specific (*the*) or an indefinite reference to something less specific (*a* or *an*).

coordinating conjunction A word that joins comparable and equally important sentence elements: *for, and, or, but, nor, yet,* or *so.*

preposition A word (such as *between, in,* or *of*) that indicates the relation between a word in a sentence and its object.

M2-d **Capitalize titles and subtitles of longer works, such as books, magazines, and newspapers.**

Capitalize the first and last words in a title and subtitle plus all other words except for **articles**, **coordinating conjunctions**, and **prepositions**.

War and Peace	*The Grand Canyon Suite*
Tragedy: Vision and Form	"On First Looking into Chapman's Homer"

(See also P6-c and M5-a.)

> *i   t*
> In her article "The Gun ‸In ‸The Closet," Straight tells of booming Riverside,
>
> California, a city east of Los Angeles.

M2-e   **Capitalize a title that precedes a person's name.**

Capitalize titles only when they precede a name, not when they follow a name or appear without a name.

> Professor John Ganim   Aunt Alice
>
> John Ganim, my professor   Alice Jordan, my favorite aunt

▶ At the state level, Reverend Green is ˚President of the State Congress of Christian

   Education and ͫModerator of the Old Landmark Association.

M2-f   **Avoid overusing capitalization for emphasis.**

Although in some writing situations a word that appears entirely in capital letters can create a desired effect, you should limit this use of capital letters to rare occasions.

▶ The powerful SMACK of the ball on the rival's thigh brings an abrupt, anticlimactic end to the rising tension.

   In most cases, follow the conventions for capitalizing described in this section.

▶ The principles are called the *tenets of tae kwon do.* ~~TENETS OF TAE KWON DO.~~

M3   Spacing

Allow standard spacing between words and punctuation marks. Most style guides recommend leaving one space after a sentence and supply specific directions about spacing source citations.

M3-a   **Supply any missing space before or after a punctuation mark.**

Although spell-checkers can help identify some misspelled words, they do not indicate spacing errors unless the error links two words or splits a word. Always proofread carefully for spacing errors around punctuation marks.

▶ My curiosity got the best of me,‸so I flipped through the pages to see what would happen.

▶ "I found to my horror, "‸Nadine later wept, "that I was too late!"

▶ "I would die without bread!" Roberto declared.‸"In my village, they made fresh bread every morning."

▶ Pet adoption fees include the cost of spaying or neutering all dogs and cats four

months old or older(if needed).

M3-b   **Close up any unnecessary space between words and punctuation marks.**

▶ Karl did not know why this war was considered justifiable⌢.

▶ The larger florist shops require previous experience⌢, but the smaller⌢, portable

wagons require only a general knowledge of flowers.

▶ Do you remember the song "⌢The Wayward Wind"⌢?

M4   Numbers

Conventions for the treatment of numbers vary widely. In the humanities, writers tend to spell out numbers (*one out of ten*), but in the sciences and social sciences, writers are far more likely to use numerals (*1 out of 10*).

M4-a   **Spell out select types of numbers in most nonscientific college writing.**

Spell out whole numbers *one* through *ninety-nine*.

▶ A hefty $7,000 per week is paid to Wells Fargo Security for ⌄4 guards who patrol the *four*

grounds ⌄24 hours a day. *twenty-four*

▶ Only ⌄~~15~~ years ago, it was difficult to find any public figures who were openly gay. *fifteen*

Note: Depending on the type of writing that you do and the conventions of your field, you may decide to spell out only numerals up to ten. Choose a rule and follow it consistently.

If two numbers occur in succession, use a combination of spelled-out words and numerals for clarity.

eight 45-cent stamps   ten 3-year-olds

Spell out a number that begins a sentence, or rewrite so that the number is no longer the first word.

▶ ⌄~~41,000~~ women die from breast cancer each year. *Forty-one thousand*

▶ ⌄41,000 women die from breast cancer~~each year~~. *Each year,*

Spell out very large round numbers, or use a combination of numerals and words.

$3.5 million   nearly 14 million

five thousand   a billion

M4-b **Use numerals for numbers over a hundred, in fractions and percentages, with abbreviations and symbols, in dates and addresses, and for page numbers and sections of books.**

289 cards	1/2	18.5	99%
73 percent	5 a.m.	10:30 p.m.	3 cm
185 lb	$200	May 6, 2022	175 Fifth Avenue
page 44	part 5	chapter 2	volume 8

▶ A woman with the same skills as her coworkers may earn an additional ~~eight~~ 8 to ~~twenty~~ 20 percent just by being well groomed.

Note: Depending on the style guide you are using, either the word *percent* or the % symbol will be required. Whichever you choose, use it consistently throughout a paper.

M5 Italics

M5-a **Italicize titles of long or self-contained works.**

Titles of books, newspapers, magazines, scholarly journals, pamphlets, long poems, movies, television and radio programs, long musical compositions, plays, comic strips, and works of art are italicized.

the *Georgia Review*	*Beowulf*	*Citizen Kane*
the *Washington Post*	*60 Minutes*	*Pride and Prejudice*

▶ I found that the article in the *Journal of the American Medical Association* had more information and stronger scientific proof than the article in *American Health*.

Note: The Bible and its divisions are not italicized.

▶ ~~"The Hunger Games"~~ *The Hunger Games* film was based on the novel by Suzanne Collins.

Titles of short works or works contained in other works are not italicized but are placed in quotation marks. (See also P6-c.)

▶ The original ~~"Star Trek"~~ *Star Trek* episode "The Trouble with Tribbles" was hugely popular.

M5-b **Italicize words used as words and letters and numbers used as themselves.**

the word *committed*   three 7s   a *q* or a *g*

▶ *Rank order* is a term that Aries uses to explain the way that some individuals take the role as the leader and the others fall in behind.

M5-c **Italicize names of planes, ships, and other vehicles; foreign words not commonly used in English; and, on occasion, words that need special emphasis.**

Lindbergh's *Spirit of St. Louis*   Amtrak's *Silver Star*

Resist the temptation to emphasize words by putting them in bold type. In most writing situations, italics provides enough emphasis.

                                                                    amore
▶ On every table is a vase adorned with a red carnation, symbolizing **amore**.

                                                          reverse
▶ This situation could exist because it is just that, **reverse** socialization.

M5-d **Italicize when appropriate, but not in place of or in addition to other conventional uses of punctuation and mechanics.**

Eliminate any unusual uses of italics.

UNUSUAL   Former NFL commissioner Paul Tagliabue said, *"I do not believe playing [football] in Arizona is in the best interests of the NFL."*

APPROPRIATE   Former NFL commissioner Paul Tagliabue said, "I do not believe playing [football] in Arizona is in the best interests of the NFL."

M6 Abbreviations

Although abbreviations are more common in technical and business writing than in academic writing, you may sometimes want to use them to avoid repetition. Use the full word in your first reference, followed by the abbreviation in parentheses. Then use the abbreviation in subsequent references.

▶ She was a member of the San Diego Humane Society (SDHS).

Abbreviations composed of all capital letters are generally written without periods or spaces between letters. When capital letters are separated by periods, do not include a space after the period except for the initials of a person's name, which should be spaced.

USA   CNN   UPI   B.A.   Ph.D.   T. S. Eliot

M6-a **Use abbreviations that your readers will recognize for names of agencies, organizations, countries, and common technical terms.**

FBI   IRS   CBS   NATO   NOW   DNA   GNP   CPM

▸ NOW is an independently run nonprofit organization.

Note: Do not abbreviate geographic names in formal writing unless the areas are commonly known by their abbreviations (*Washington, D.C.*).

M6-b **Use a.m., p.m., no., and $ only with specific numerals or dates.**

7:15 a.m.   10:30 p.m.

$172.18 or $38   No. 18 or no. 18 [item or issue number of a source]

M6-c **Use commonly accepted abbreviations for titles, degrees, and Latin terms.**

Use an accepted abbreviation for titles and degrees.

Rev. Jesse Jackson   Mr. Roger Smith   Ring Lardner Jr.

Diana Lee, M.D.   Dr. Diana Lee   James Boyer, D.V.M.

Avoid duplication by using a title before a person's name or a degree after the name but not both.

▸ According to Dr. Ira Chasnoff, M.D., cocaine produces a dramatic fluctuation in blood pressure.

Use Latin terms, such as those listed here, primarily for source citations or comments in parentheses rather than in the text of your essay.

c. (*or* ca.)   "circa" or about (used with dates)

cf.   compare

e.g.   for example

et al.   and others (used with people)

etc.   and so forth

i.e.   that is

M6-d **Use abbreviations when appropriate, but do not use them to replace words in most writing.**

In formal writing, avoid abbreviating units of measurement or technical terms (unless your essay is technical), names of time periods, titles of courses or names of departments, names of states or countries (unless the abbreviation is the more common form), names of companies, and parts of books.

▶ The Pets for People program gives older people the companionship they need, ~~esp.~~ *especially* if they live alone.

▶ I called the closest site on Hancock ~~St.~~ *Street* to ask for a tour.

▶ The walkout followed an incident on ~~Sept.~~ *September* 27.

M7   Spelling

Spell-checkers can be helpful, but they will not catch all errors. To be sure that your spelling is correct, you must proofread your final draft yourself. The following suggestions for catching and correcting spelling errors will help:

- Proofread your writing carefully to catch transposed letters (*becuase* for *because*), omitted letters (*becaus*), and other careless errors (*then* for *than*). When you proofread for spelling, read the text backward, beginning with the last word. This strategy keeps you from reading for content and lets you focus on each word.

- Check a good dictionary for any words you are uncertain about. When you are writing and doubt the spelling of a word, put a question mark by the word but wait to check it until you have finished drafting.

- Keep a list of words you often misspell so that you can try to pinpoint your personal patterns. Although misspellings nearly always follow a pattern, you are not likely to misspell every word of a particular type, or you may spell the same word two different ways in the same essay.

prefix A word part, such as *pre-*, *anti-*, or *bi-*, that is attached to the beginning of a word to form another word: *preconceived, unbelievable.*

suffix A word part, such as *-ly*, *-ment*, or *-ed*, that is added to the end of a word to change the word's form (*bright, brightly*) or tense (*call, called*) or to form another word (*govern, government*).

M7-a   Study the spelling rules for adding **prefixes** and **suffixes** to words.

Although English has a large number of words with unusual spellings, many follow the patterns that spelling rules describe.

Add a prefix to a root without doubling or dropping letters.

dis<u>trust</u>	mis<u>behave</u>	un<u>able</u>
dis<u>satisfy</u>	mis<u>spell</u>	un<u>natural</u>

Add a suffix beginning with a vowel (such as *-ing*) in accord with the form of the root word.

Double the final consonant if the word has a single syllable that ends in a single consonant preceded by a single vowel.

be<u>gg</u>ing	hi<u>dd</u>en	fi<u>tt</u>ing

Do the same if the word has a final stressed syllable that ends in a single consonant preceded by a single vowel.

beginn<u>ing</u>   occurr<u>ence</u>

The final consonant does not double if the word ends in two consonants or a
consonant preceded by two vowels.

act<u>ing</u>   part<u>ed</u>   seem<u>ing</u>   stoop<u>ed</u>

In some cases, the stress shifts to the first syllable when a suffix is added. When it
does, do not double the final consonant.

pref<u>é</u>r: pref<u>é</u>rring,   pref<u>é</u>rred

                    <u>p</u>réference,   <u>p</u>réferable

Add a suffix that begins with *y* or a vowel by dropping a final silent *e*.

achieving   icy   location

grievance   lovable   continual

Keep the final silent *e* to retain a soft *c* or *g* sound, to prevent mispronunciation, or to
prevent confusion with other words.

changeable   courageous   noticeable

eyeing   mileage   canoeist

dyeing   singeing

Add a suffix that begins with a consonant by keeping a final silent *e*.

achievement   discouragement   sincerely

Exceptions: acknowledgment, argument, awful, judgment, truly, wholly

Form the plural of a singular noun in accord with its form.

If a singular noun ends in a consonant followed by *y,* change *y* to *i* and add -*es.*

▶ baby, babies   ▶ cry, cries

Note: Simply add -*s* to names: her cousin *Mary,* both *Marys.*

If a singular noun ends in a vowel followed by *y,* add -*s.*

▶ trolley, trolleys   ▶ day, days

If a singular noun ends in a consonant and *o,* add -*es.*

▶ potato, potatoes   ▶ echo, echoes   ▶ veto, vetoes

Exceptions: autos, dynamos, pianos, sopranos

If a singular noun ends in a vowel and *o,* add -*s.*

▶ video, videos   ▶ rodeo, rodeos   ▶ radio, radios

If a singular noun ends in *s, ss, sh, ch, x,* or *z,* add *-es.*

- ▶ Jones, Joneses
- ▶ hiss, hisses
- ▶ bush, bushes
- ▶ match, matches
- ▶ suffix, suffixes
- ▶ buzz, buzzes

Note: The plural of *thesis* is *theses.*

Check the dictionary for the plural of a word that originates in another language.

criterion, criteria   datum, data

medium, mediums *or* media

hors d'oeuvre, hors d'oeuvres *or* hors d'oeuvre

M7-b   **Study the spelling rules (and the exceptions) that apply to words you routinely misspell.**

Add *i* before *e* except after *c*.

Most people remember this rule because of the jingle "Write *i* before *e* / Except after *c* / Or when sounded like *ay* / As in *neighbor* and *weigh*." *Exceptions:* either, foreign, forfeit, height, leisure, neither, seize, weird

Spell most words ending in the sound "seed" as *-cede*.

precede   recede   secede   intercede

Exceptions: proceed, succeed, supersede

FOR MULTILINGUAL WRITERS

If you have learned Canadian or British English, you may have noticed some differences in the way that words are spelled in U.S. English.

U.S. English	Canadian or British English
color	colour
realize	realise (*or* realize in Canadian English)
center	centre
defense	defence

M7-c   **Watch for words that are often spelled incorrectly because they sound like other words.**

In English, many words are not spelled as they sound. The endings of some words may be dropped in speech but need to be included in writing. For example, speakers often pronounce *and* as *an'* or drop the *-ed* ending on verbs. Other common words sound the same but have entirely different meanings. Watch carefully for words such as the following:

> *already* ("by now": He is *already* in class.)
>
> *all ready* ("fully prepared": I'm *all ready* for the test.)
>
> *an* (article: Everyone read *an* essay last night.)
>
> *and* (conjunction: The class discussed the problem *and* the solution.)
>
> *its* (possessive pronoun: The car lost *its* shine.)
>
> *it's* ("it is": *It's* too cold to go for a walk.)
>
> *maybe* ("perhaps": *Maybe* we should have tacos for dinner.)
>
> *may be* (verb showing possibility: They *may be* arriving tonight.)
>
> *than* (conjunction showing comparison: The house was taller *than* the tree.)
>
> *then* (adverb showing time sequence: First she knocked and *then* she opened the door.)
>
> *their* (possessive pronoun: They decided to sell *their* old car.)
>
> *there* (adverb showing location: The car dealer is located *there* on the corner.)
>
> *they're* ("they are": *They're* going to pick up the new car tonight.)
>
> *your* (possessive pronoun: I can see *your* apartment.)
>
> *you're* ("you are": Call me when *you're* home.)

For distinctions between other words, such as *affect/effect, principal/principle,* and *to/too,* see the Glossary of Frequently Misused Words.

Watch for and correct misspelled words that sound the same as other words.

▶ I started packing my gear, still ~~vary~~ *very* excited about the trip.

▶ I just ~~new~~ *knew* it was a bear, and I was going to be its dinner.

▶ Students need to pay ~~there~~ *their* fees, as part of this money goes toward purchasing new books and materials.

M7-d   Watch for words that are often misspelled.

Check your essays for the following words, which are often spelled incorrectly. Look up any other questionable words in a dictionary, and keep a personal list of words that you tend to misspell.

absence	choose	friend	preferred
accidentally	chose	government	prejudice
accommodate	coming	harass	preparation
accomplish	commitment	height	privilege
achievement	committed	heroes	probably
acknowledge	competitive	immediately	proceed
acquaintance	conscience	incredible	professor
acquire	conscious	indefinitely	quiet
against	convenient	interesting	quite
aggravate	criticize	irrelevant	receive
all right	definitely	knowledge	recommend
a lot	dependent	loose	reference
although	desperate	lose	referred
analyze	develops	maintenance	roommate
apparently	disappear	maneuver	schedule
appearance	eighth	mischievous	separate
appropriate	eligible	necessary	similar
argument	embarrass	noticeable	studying
arrangement	emphasize	occasion	succeed
attendance	environment	occur	success
basically	especially	occurred	successful
before	every day	occurrences	therefore
beginning	exaggerated	particularly	thorough
believe	exercise	performance	truly
benefited	exercising	phenomena	unnecessarily
business	experience	phenomenon	until
businesses	explanation	physically	usually
calendar	finally	playwright	whether
cannot	foreign	practically	without
categories	forty	precede	woman
changeable	fourth	preference	women

T Troublespots for Multilingual Writers

This section provides advice about problems of grammar and standard usage that are particularly challenging for writers whose first language is not English.

T1 Articles

The rules for using articles (*a, an,* and *the*) are complicated. Your choice depends on whether the article appears before a **count, noncount,** or **proper noun.** An *article* is used before a common noun to indicate whether the noun refers to something specific (*the* moon) or whether it refers to something that is one among many or has not yet been specified (*a* planet, *an* asteroid). In addition, for some nouns, the absence of an article indicates that the reference is not specific.

count noun A noun that names people and things that can be counted: one *teacher,* two *teachers;* one *movie,* several *movies.*

noncount noun A noun that names things or ideas that are not or cannot be counted: thunder, money, happiness.

proper noun The capitalized name of a specific person, group, place, or thing.

T1-a Select the correct article to use with a count noun.

- Use *a* or *an* with nonspecific singular count nouns.
- Use no article with nonspecific plural count nouns.
- Use *the* with specific singular and plural count nouns.

Note: The article *a* is used before a consonant and *an* before a vowel; exceptions include words beginning with a long *u* sound, such as *unit.*

Use *a* or *an* before a singular count noun when it refers to one thing among many or something that has not been specifically identified.

> ▸ We, as ‸a society, have to educate our youth about avoiding teen pregnancy.

> ▸ *A darkroom*
> ‸D̶a̶r̶k̶r̶o̶o̶m̶ is a room with no light where photographs are developed.

Use *the* before a singular or plural count noun when it refers to one or more specific things.

After you have used *a* or *an* with a count noun, subsequent references to the noun become specific and are marked by *the.*

> ▸ When I walked into the office, *a* woman in her midforties was waiting to be called. As I sat down, I looked at *the* woman.

Exceptions include a second reference to one among many.

> ▸ I was guided to *a* classroom. It was *a* bright room, filled with warm rays of Hawaiian sunlight.

In most situations, use *the* with a count noun modified by a superlative adjective.

the most frightening moment   the smallest person

Nouns such as *sun* generally refer to unique things. Nouns such as *house* and *yard* often refer to things that people own. In most situations, both types of nouns can be preceded by the definite article *the*.

▶ Don't look directly at *the sun*. [Only one sun could be meant.]

▶ I spent Saturday cleaning *the house*. [The reader will infer that the writer is referring to his or her own house.]

You can also introduce count nouns referring to specific entities with possessive nouns or pronouns (*Maya's* friends) or demonstrative pronouns (*these* friends). Indefinite count and noncount nouns can also be introduced by words that indicate amount (*few* friends, *some* sand).

COUNT NOUN   She starred in a reality show with *her* eight children.

NONCOUNT NOUN   Her family wanted *some* happiness.

Delete any article before a nonspecific plural count noun.

▶ ~~The people~~ like Dee cannot forget their heritage.
   ^People^

T1-b   Select the correct article to use with a noncount noun.

The many kinds of noncount nouns include the following:

Natural phenomena: *thunder, steam, electricity*

Natural elements: *gold, air, sunlight*

Manufacturing materials: *steel, wood, cement*

Fibers: *wool, cotton, rayon*

General categories made up of a variety of specific items: *money, music, furniture*

Abstract ideas: *happiness, loyalty, adolescence, wealth*

Liquids: *milk, gasoline, water*

Some nouns naming foodstuffs are always noncount (*pork, rice, broccoli*); others are noncount when they refer to food as it is eaten (*We ate barbecued chicken and fruit*) but count when they refer to individual items or varieties (*We bought a plump chicken and various fruits*).

Delete any article before a general noncount noun.

▶ What is needed is ~~a~~ reasonable and measured legislation.

▶ The destruction caused by the war drew artists away from ~~the~~ reality, which is painful

   and cruel, and toward ~~the~~ abstract art, which avoids a sense of despair.

Use *the* before a noncount noun when it refers to something specific or when it is specified by a **prepositional phrase** or an **adjective clause**.

▶ *The* coffee is probably cold by now.

▶ *The* water on the boat has to be rationed.

▶ *The* water that we have left has to be rationed.

You can also introduce noncount nouns referring to specific things with possessive nouns or pronouns (*her* money) or with demonstrative pronouns (*that* money). Indefinite noncount nouns can also be introduced by words that indicate amount (*some* money).

T1-c **Select the correct article to use with a proper noun.**

Most plural proper nouns require *the*: *the* United States, *the* Philippines, *the* Black Hills, *the* Clintons, *the* Los Angeles Dodgers. Exceptions include business names (Hillshire Farms, Miller Auto Sales).

Delete any article before most singular proper nouns.

In general, singular proper nouns are not preceded by an article: Dr. Livingston, New York City, Hawaii, Disneyland, Mount St. Helens, Wrigley Field.

▶ ~~The~~ Campus Security is a powerful deterrent against parties because if you are written up twice, you can lose your housing contract.

The is used before proper noun phrases that include *of* (*the* Rock of Gibraltar, *the* Gang of Four). *The* is also required before proper nouns that name the following things:

1. Bodies of water, except when the generic part of the name precedes the specific name: *the* Atlantic Ocean, *the* Red River, but Lake Erie

2. Geographic regions: *the* West Coast, *the* Sahara, *the* Grand Canyon

3. Vehicles for transportation: *the* Concorde

4. Named buildings and bridges: *the* Empire State Building, *the* Golden Gate Bridge

5. National or international churches: *the* Russian Orthodox Church

6. Governing bodies preceded by a proper adjective: *the* British Parliament

7. Titles of religious and political leaders: *the* Dalai Lama

8. Religious and historical documents: *the* Bible, *the* Magna Carta

9. Historical periods and events: *the* Gilded Age, *the* Civil War

T2 Verbs

Section R2-a reviews the basic English verb forms and includes a list of common irregular verbs. As you edit your writing, pay particular attention to conditional clauses, two-word verbs, helping (auxiliary) verbs, and gerund or infinitive forms after verbs.

---

prepositional phrase A group of words that begins with a preposition and indicates the relation between a word in a sentence and the object following the preposition: Her sunglasses slid *under the seat.*

adjective clause A clause that modifies a noun or pronoun and is generally introduced by a relative pronoun (such as *that* or *which*).

proper noun The capitalized name of a specific person, group, place, or thing.

vb
T2

main (independent) clause
A word group with a subject and a predicate that can stand alone as a separate sentence.

T2-a **Select verb tenses carefully in main clauses and conditional clauses.**

Conditional clauses beginning with *if* or *unless* generally indicate that one thing causes another (a factual relationship); predict future outcomes or possibilities; or speculate about the past, present, or future, or impossible events or circumstances.

─────── conditional clause ───────┬─────── main clause ───────
If we *use* media outlets responsibly, they *can give* us information and entertainment.

─────── conditional clause ───────┬─────── main clause ───────
If we *use* the media carelessly, it *will control* our families and our society.

Change both verbs to the same tense to express general or specific truths or actions that happen together habitually.

► When we moved to America, my family ~~has~~ ^had^ good communication.

Change the verb in the main clause to the future and the verb in the conditional clause to the present to express future possibilities or predictions.

► If you ask about the servers in any of her restaurants, the manager ~~could~~ ^will^ tell you

about their quirks.

base form The uninflected form of a verb: I *eat*; to *play*.

To speculate about events or conditions that are unreal, improbable, or contrary to fact, change the verb in the main clause to *would, could,* or *might* plus the **base form**, and change the verb in the *if* conditional clause to the past tense.
Use *were* rather than *was* in an *if* clause.

► Some people believe that if the Health Department ~~gives~~ ^were to give^ out clean needles, the

number of people using drugs would increase.

participle A verb form showing present tense (*dancing, freezing*) or past tense (*danced, frozen*) that can also act as an adjective.

To speculate about past actions that did not in fact occur, change the verb in the main clause to *would have, might have, could have,* or *should have* plus the past **participle**, and change the verb in the *if* clause to the past perfect.

► If the lab ~~added~~ ^had^ more hours during finals week, students would not have had

to wait to use a computer.

Note: Do not add *would have* to the *if* clause.

T2-b **Learn the meanings of idiomatic two- and three-word verbs used in English.**

Idiomatic two- or three-word (or phrasal) verbs usually combine a verb with a word that appears to be a preposition or an adverb (called a *particle*). The combined meaning cannot be understood literally, and similar expressions often have very different meanings.

hand in means "submit"

hand out means "distribute"

look into means "investigate"

look out for means "watch carefully"

run away means "leave without warning"

run into means "meet by chance"

walk out on means "abandon"

want out means "desire to be free of responsibility"

Native speakers of English will notice misuses of these idiomatic verbs even though they use the verbs without thinking about their literal meanings. When you are unsure of the meaning or usage of such verbs, consult a dictionary or ask a native speaker.

T2-c **Use the correct verb forms after helping verbs.**

After the helping (auxiliary) verbs *do, does,* and *did,* always use the **base form** of the main verb. After the helping verbs *have, has,* and *had,* always use the **past participle** form of the main verb. (See R2-a and G5.)

> ► They do not ~~cooperated~~ ^cooperate^ with the police.

> ► They have ~~doing~~ ^done^ these things for a long time.

base form The uninflected form of a verb: I *eat; to play.*

A **modal** such as *will* sometimes precedes *have, has,* or *had.*

> ► By Friday I *will have finished* this project.

Following the helping verbs *be, am, is, are, was, were,* and *been* (forms of *be*), use the present participle to show ongoing action (progressive tense).

> ► The president is ~~given~~ ^giving^ a speech on all major networks.

Use one of the modal verbs with *be.* Use *have, has,* or *had* with *been.*

> ► Terence *could be making* some calls while I am out.

> ► I *have been working* hard.

modals The helping verbs *can, could, may, might, must, shall, should, will,* and *would,* which must be used in conjunction with another (main) verb: I *may go* to the bank.

passive voice The verb form that shows something happening to the subject.

After the helping verbs *am, is, are, was,* and *were* (forms of *be*), use the past participle to form the **passive voice**.

▶ Regular programming is ~~cancel~~ *canceled* for tonight.

To form the passive, *be, being,* and *been* need a helping verb in addition to the past participle.

▶ Tonya *will be challenged* in graduate school this fall.

After a modal, use the base form.

▶ The Senate *might* vote on this bill next week.

gerund A verb form that is used as a noun and ends with *-ing: arguing, throwing.*

infinitive A verb form consisting of the word *to* plus the base form of the verb: *to run.*

T2-d   Follow verbs with gerunds or infinitives.

1. Some verbs can be followed by either a gerund or an infinitive with no change in meaning:

begin	continue	like	prefer
can't stand	hate	love	start

▶ The roof *began leaking.*

▶ The roof *began to leak.*

2. Some verbs change their meaning, depending on whether a gerund or an infinitive follows:

forget	remember	stop	try

▶ Salam *remembered going* to the park on Saturday. [Salam recalled a weekend visit to the park.]

▶ Salam *remembered to go* to the park on Saturday. [Salam remembered that he had to go to the park on Saturday.]

3. Some verbs can be followed by a gerund but not an infinitive:

admit	deny	keep	recall
appreciate	discuss	miss	resist
avoid	dislike	postpone	risk
can't help	enjoy	practice	suggest
consider	finish	put off	tolerate
delay	imagine	quit	

▶ I recall ~~to see~~ *seeing* Michel there.

Not or *never* can separate the verb and the gerund.

▶ We discussed *not* having a party this year.

4. Some verbs can be followed by an infinitive but not a gerund:

agree	expect	need	refuse
ask	fail	offer	venture
beg	have	plan	wait
choose	hope	pretend	want
claim	manage	promise	wish
decide	mean		

▶ Children often only pretend ~~eating~~ *to eat* food they dislike.

In a sentence with a verb followed by an infinitive, the meaning changes depending on the placement of a negative word such as *not* or *never*.

▶ I *never* promised to eat liver. [I did not make the promise.]

▶ I promised *never* to eat candy. [I promised not to do it.]

5. Some verbs must be followed by a noun or pronoun and an infinitive:

advise	encourage	order	teach
allow	force	persuade	tell
cause	instruct	remind	urge
command	invite	require	warn
convince	need		

▶ Magda taught *her parrot to say* a few words.

Use an infinitive, not *that,* following a verb such as *want* or *need.*

▶ José wants ~~that~~ his new car ~~stays~~ *to stay* in good condition.

6. The verbs *let, make* ("force"), and *have* ("cause") must be followed by a noun or pronoun and the base form of the verb (not the infinitive):

▶ He *let me borrow* the car.

▶ The drill sergeant *makes the recruits stand* at attention.

▶ I *had the children draw* in their notebooks.

T3 **Prepositions**

Use the **prepositions** *in, on,* and *at* to indicate location and time.

preposition A word (such as *between, in,* or *of*) that indicates the relation between a word in a sentence and its object.

Location

- *In* usually means within a geographic place or an enclosed area (*in* Mexico, *in* a small town, *in* the park, *in* my bedroom, *in* a car).

- *On* means *on top of* (*on* the shelf, *on* a hill, *on* a bicycle); it is also used with modes of mass transportation (*on* a train, *on* the subway), streets (*on* Broadway), pages (*on* page 5), floors of buildings (*on* the tenth floor), and tracts of private land (*on* a farm, *on* the lawn).

- *At* refers to specific addresses and named locations (*at* 1153 Grand Street, *at* Nana's house, *at* Macy's), to general locations (*at* work, *at* home, *at* the beach), and to locations that involve a specific activity (*at* the mall, *at* the gym, *at* a party, *at* a restaurant).

Time

- *In* is used with months (*in* May), years (*in* 1999), and seasons (*in* the fall), as well as with *morning, afternoon,* and *evening* (*in* the morning).

- *On* is used with days of the week (*on* Wednesday) and dates (*on* June 2, 2006).

- *At* is used with specific times (*at* 7:30, *at* noon, *at* midnight) and with *night* (*at* night).

Change any incorrect prepositions so that *in, on,* and *at* convey location and time correctly.

> on
> ▶ People are driving at 55 or 60 miles per hour in the highway.
>   ^

Change any incorrect prepositions to idiomatic usage.

>   in
> ▶ Is life worse in the refugee camps or in Vietnam? You would find answers from
>   ^
>
>   his article.

>   into
> ▶ Williams gives readers insight to the doctor's insecurity.
>   ^

subject The part of a clause that identifies who or what is being discussed.

verb A word or phrase that expresses action or being and, along with a subject, is a basic component of a sentence.

T4 **Omitted or Repeated Words**

In English, every sentence, with rare exceptions, should have both a **subject** and a **verb**.

> ┌─ subject ─┐ ┌─ verb ─┐
> ▶ My brother has been very successful in his job.

If your native language allows you to omit either subject or verb, check your drafts carefully to be sure that you include both in your writing. Supply both a subject and a verb in each sentence, but do not repeat the subject or other words that duplicate grammatical functions.

Add a missing subject.

the compliments
▶ On the contrary, increase his irritability.
                   ^

Add a missing verb.

is
▶ Mr. Yang a man who owns a butcher shop.
           ^

Supply a missing expletive (*there* or *it*) if the subject follows the verb.

There are
▶ ~~Are~~ many ways to help the unemployed get jobs.
  ^

Delete a repeated subject.

▶ The elderly woman ~~she~~ must have an eye infection.

Delete other words that repeat grammatical functions.

▶ People say that the cost of insurance ~~has~~ never goes down anymore.

▶ Only a few people ~~that~~ are rich.

T5 Adjective Order

Adjectives generally appear in the following order in English sentences.

1. Article, pronoun, or other determiner: *a, an, the, that, his, their, Janine's*

2. Evaluation or judgment: *beautiful, ugly, elegant, magnificent, impressive*

3. Size or dimension: *short, tall, long, large, small, big, little*

4. Shape: *round, rectangular, square, baggy, circular, octagonal*

5. Age: *new, young, old, aged, antique*

6. Color: *pink, turquoise, gray, orange*

7. History or origin (country and religion): *Asian, Norwegian, Thai, American, Protestant, Mongolian, Buddhist, Muslim, Catholic, Jewish*

8. Material: *copper, cotton, plastic, oak, linen*

9. Noun used as a descriptive adjective: *kitchen* (sink), *bedroom* (lamp)

When you use several adjectives to modify a noun, arrange them in the order expected in English.

 1 2   4   6   1   3   5

▶ a beautiful, round, turquoise stone   ▶ her skinny, young cousin

T6 Participles

participle A verb form showing present tense (*dancing, freezing*) or past tense (*danced, frozen*) that can also act as an adjective.

Use the present form of the **participle** (-*ing*) if it describes someone or something *causing* or *producing* a mental state. Use the past form (-*ed*) if it describes someone or something *experiencing* the mental state. Problem participles include the following pairs:

annoying/annoyed	exhausting/exhausted
boring/bored	pleasing/pleased
confusing/confused	surprising/surprised
disappointing/disappointed	terrifying/terrified
exciting/excited	tiring/tired

▶ The class was *confused* by the *confusing* directions.

▶ The teacher was *surprised* by the *surprising* number of questions.

Change a participle to its present form (-*ing*) if it describes someone or something causing or producing a situation.

　　　　　　　　　　　frightening
▶ Parents must not accept the ~~frightened~~ behavior that their children learn in gangs.
　　　　　　　　　　　^

Change a participle to its past form (-*ed*) if it describes someone or something experiencing a situation.

　　　　　pleased
▶ I was not ~~pleasing~~ with the information about religion in this article.
　　　　　^

R Review of Sentence Structure

As you write, your primary concern will be with the ideas you want to convey to your audience, not parts of speech or sentence structure. Still, writing clear and correct sentences is an important part of communicating effectively with your audience. This and the other sections in the Handbook will help you achieve that goal.*

R1 Basic Sentence Structure

This review of basic sentence structure will look first at the elements that make up simple sentences and then at how simple sentences produce compound and complex sentences.

R1-a Words, Phrases, and Clauses

The basic building blocks of sentences are, of course, words, which can be combined into discrete groupings or *phrases*.

Words and phrases are further combined to create *clauses,* groups of at least two words that both name a topic and make some point about that topic; every clause can be divided into a subject and a predicate. The *subject* identifies the topic or theme of the sentence—what is being discussed—and the *predicate* says something about the subject and is the focus of information in the clause.

R1-b Sentence Units

A *simple sentence* includes a single independent clause made up of a subject and a predicate. The subject and the predicate may each be a single word or a group of words. In addition to its verb, the predicate may include **objects**, **complements**, and **adverbial modifiers**.

> ┌──── subject ────┐ ┌──────────────── predicate ────────────────┐
> ▶ Native Americans introduced baked beans to the New England settlers.

Simple sentences, then, are composed of some combination of these basic units:

Subject (S)   The simplest subject can be a single noun or pronoun, but a subject may also consist of a noun phrase (including adjectives and other sentence elements) or even a noun clause. Subjects may also be *compound* when two or more nouns or

object The part of a clause that receives the action of the verb, or the part of a phrase that follows a preposition.

complement A word or word group that describes or restates a subject or an object.

adverbial modifier A word or word group that modifies a verb, an adjective, or another adverb.

---

* This brief review is based on an extraordinary book: *A Grammar of Contemporary English* (New York: Harcourt, 1972). If you need more information than is provided here, consult a stand-alone handbook, such as Diana Hacker and Nancy Sommers's *The Bedford Handbook* or Andrea Lunsford's *The St. Martin's Handbook.*

pronouns are linked by a conjunction. (See R2 for definitions and examples of these various elements.)

Verb (V)   These can be classified as *transitive*, when they occur with an object, or *intransitive*, when they occur without an object. Intransitive verbs that occur with complements are often called *linking verbs*. Like subjects, verbs may be compound.

Objects (DO, IO)   These include *direct objects* (DO) and *indirect objects* (IO), which, like subjects, can be nouns, noun phrases, noun clauses, or pronouns. Objects usually follow the subject and verb.

Complements (SC, OC)   These are either subject complements or object complements: *Subject complements* (SC) refer to the subject, *object complements* (OC) to an object. Like subjects and objects, complements can be nouns or pronouns, noun phrases, or noun clauses (sometimes referred to as *predicate nominatives*). Complements can also be adjectives or adjective phrases (sometimes called *predicate adjectives*). Like objects, complements usually follow the subject and verb. They also follow any objects.

Adverbial (A)   These are modifiers that refer to the verb in the sentence. They can be adverbs, adverb phrases, or adverb clauses.

Of these seven units, two—subject and verb—are required in every sentence.

R1-c   Types of Simple Sentences

The basic sentence elements listed in R1-b can be put together in various ways to produce seven general types of simple sentences.

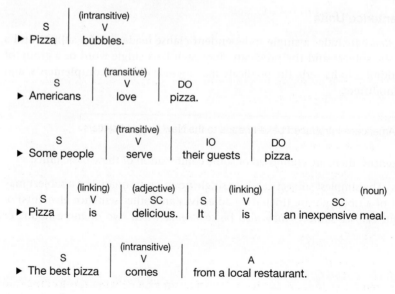

S	(transitive) V	DO	OC
▶ Vegetarians	consider	pepperoni pizza	appalling.

S	(transitive) V	DO	A
▶ They	prefer	cheese pizza	any day.

R1-d Combinations and Transformations

The simple sentence patterns shown in R1-c can be combined and transformed to produce all the sentences writers of English need.

Two or more clauses may be combined with a coordinating conjunction (such as *and* or *but*) or a pair of correlative conjunctions (such as *either . . . or*) to create a **compound sentence**:

COMPOUND   Pizza is delicious, and it is an inexpensive meal.

Either Americans love pizza, or they consider it junk food.

Writers create **complex sentences** by combining independent clauses with a subordinating conjunction (such as *although* or *because*) or by linking two clauses with a relative pronoun (such as *which* or *who*):

COMPLEX   Vegetarians consider pepperoni pizza appalling

┌──── dependent clause ────┐
because pepperoni is red meat.

Clauses that contain subordinating conjunctions or relative pronouns are *dependent clauses* and cannot stand on their own as simple sentences.

Clauses can also be combined to produce **compound-complex sentences**, compound sentences that contain dependent clauses:

┌──────── dependent clause ────────┐
COMPOUND-   Even though pepperoni pizza is unhealthy, it is a delicious meal,
COMPLEX   and Americans love it.

(Conjunctions and dependent clauses are discussed in more detail in R2.) Simple sentences can take the form of *questions, commands,* and *exclamations*:

QUESTION   Why is pizza popular?

COMMAND   Bake the pizza in a brick oven.

EXCLAMATION   This pizza is delicious!

(In addition, sentences that are in the *active voice* can generally be transformed into the *passive voice* if they have transitive verbs and objects.)

PASSIVE   Pepperoni pizza is considered unhealthy.

R2   Basic Sentence Elements

This section reviews the parts of speech and the types of clauses and phrases.

R2-a   Parts of Speech

There are ten parts of speech: nouns, pronouns, adjectives, adverbs, verbs, prepositions, conjunctions, articles, demonstratives, and interjections.

subject The part of a clause that identifies who or what is being discussed.

object The part of a clause that receives the action of the verb or the part of a phrase that follows a preposition.

subject complement A word or word group that follows a linking verb and describes or restates the subject.

appositive A word or word group that identifies or gives more information about a noun or pronoun that precedes it.

Nouns   Nouns function in sentences or clauses as **subjects**, **objects**, and **subject complements**. They also serve as objects of various kinds of phrases and as **appositives**. They can be proper (*Burger King, Bartlett pear, Rachael Ray, Trader Joe's*) or common (*tomato, food, lunch, café, waffle, gluttony*). Common nouns can be abstract (*hunger, satiation, indulgence, appetite*) or concrete (*spareribs, soup, radish, champagne, gravy*). Nouns can be singular (*biscuit*) or plural (*biscuits*); they may also be collective (*food*). They can be marked to show possession (*gourmet's choice, lambs' kidneys*). Nouns take determiners (*that lobster, those clams*), quantifiers (*many hotcakes, several sausages*), and articles (*a milk shake, the eggnog*). They can be modified by adjectives (*fried chicken*), adjective phrases (*chicken in a basket*), and adjective clauses (*chicken that is finger-licking good*). (See also E3.)

Pronouns   Pronouns come in many forms and have a variety of functions in clauses and phrases.

    Personal pronouns function as replacements for nouns and come in three case forms:

1. Subjective, for use as subjects or subject complements: *I, we, you, he, she, it, they.*

2. Objective, for use as objects of verbs and prepositions: *me, us, you, him, her, it, them.*

3. Possessive: *mine, ours, yours, his, hers, theirs.* Possessive pronouns also have a determiner form for use before nouns: *my, our, your, his, her, its, their.*

                                                    subjective

▶ Calvin Trillin says the best restaurants in the world are in Kansas City, but *he* was born there.

▶ If *you* ever have the spareribs and french-fried potatoes at Arthur Bryant's, *you* will

                  objective
never forget *them.*

  possessive   possessive
▶ *Your* memory of that lunch at Bryant's is clearer than *mine.*

    Personal pronouns also come in three persons (first person: *I, me, we, us*; second person: *you*; third person: *he, him, she, her, it, they, them*), three genders (masculine: *he, him*; feminine: *she, her*; neuter: *it*), and two numbers (singular: *I, me, you, he, him, she, her, it*; plural: *we, us, you, they, them*).

Reflexive pronouns, like personal pronouns, function as replacements for nouns, nearly always replacing nouns or personal pronouns in the same clause. Reflexive pronouns include *myself, ourselves, yourself, yourselves, himself, herself, oneself, itself,* and *themselves*.

▶ Aunt Odessa prided *herself* on her chocolate sponge cake.

Reflexive pronouns may also be used for emphasis.

▶ Barry baked the fudge cake *himself*.

Indefinite pronouns do not refer to a specific person or object: *each, all, everyone, everybody, everything, everywhere, both, some, someone, somebody, something, somewhere, any, anyone, anybody, anything, anywhere, either, neither, none, nobody, many, few, much, most, several, enough*.

▶ Not *everybody* was enthusiastic about William Laird's 1698 improvement on apple cider—Jersey lightning applejack.

▶ In the Colonies, *most* preferred rum.

▶ Taverns usually served *both*.

Relative pronouns introduce **adjective (or relative) clauses**. They come in three forms: personal, to refer to people (*who, whom, whose, whoever, whomever*), nonpersonal (*which, whose, whichever, whatever*), and general (*that*).

▶ In 1846, Nancy Johnson invented a small hand-operated machine, *which* was the forerunner of today's portable ice-cream freezer.

▶ It was Jacob Fussell of Baltimore *who* established the first wholesale ice-cream business in 1851.

▶ The fact *that* we had to wait until 1896 for someone to invent the ice-cream cone is surprising.

Interrogative pronouns have the same forms as relative pronouns but have different functions. They serve to introduce questions.

▶ *Who* invented the ice-cream sundae?

▶ Of chocolate and vanilla ice cream, *which* do you prefer?

▶ The waiter asked, "*Whose* chocolate walnut sundae is this?"

Demonstrative pronouns are pronouns used to point out particular persons or things: *this, that, these, those*.

▶ *This* dish is what Mandy likes best for brunch: pecan waffles with blueberry syrup.

▶ Of everything on the menu, *these* must be the most fattening.

(See also G1–G4.)

adjective (or relative) clause A clause that modifies a noun or pronoun and is generally introduced by a relative pronoun (such as *that* or *which*).

Adjectives   Adjectives modify nouns and pronouns, and they usually appear immediately before or after the noun they modify. As subject complements (sometimes called predicate adjectives), they may be separated from the noun or pronoun they modify by the verb.

▶ *Creole* cooking can be found in *many* diners along the Gulf of Mexico.

▶ Gumbo is a *spicy* soup.

▶ Jambalaya tastes *delicious*, and it is *cheap*.
　　　　　　　　　　subject complements

Some adjectives change form in comparisons.

　　　　　　　comparative
▶ Gumbo is *spicier* than crawfish pie.

　　　　　　　superlative
▶ Gumbo is the *spiciest* Creole soup.

Some words can be used as both pronouns and adjectives; nouns are also sometimes used as adjectives.

　　adj.　　　　　　adj.　　　　　pron.
▶ *Many* people love *crawfish* pie, and *many* prefer gumbo.

(See also G7-b.)

Adverbs   Adverbs modify verbs (*eat well*), adjectives (*very big appetite*), and other adverbs (*extremely well done*). They often tell when, how, where, why, and how often.

▶ Walter started the charcoal fires *early*. [when]

▶ He basted the sizzling ribs *liberally* with marinade. [how]

▶ Pots of beans simmered *nearby*. [where]

Like adjectives, adverbs can change form for comparison.

▶ He ate the buttermilk biscuits *fast*. [*faster* than Bucky ate his biscuits, *fastest* of all the hungry diners]

A number of adverbs are formed by adding *-ly* to an adjective (*hearty* appetite, eat *heartily*). With adverbs that end in *-ly*, the words *more* and *most* are used when making comparisons.

▶ Junior drank the first cold lemonade *quickly*. [*more quickly* than Billy Joe, *most quickly* of all those at the table]

The *conjunctive adverb* is a special kind of adverb, used to connect the ideas in two sentences or independent clauses. Familiar connectives include *consequently, however, therefore, similarly, besides,* and *nevertheless.*

▶ The inspiration for Tex-Mex food came from Mexico. *Nevertheless*, it is considered a native American cuisine.

Finally, adverbs may evaluate or qualify the information in a sentence.

▶ *Barbecue* comes from *barbacoa*, a word the Spaniards *probably* picked up from the Arawak Indians.

(See also G7-a.)

Verbs   Verbs tell what is happening in a sentence by expressing action (*cook, stir*) or a state of being (*be, stay*). Depending on the structure of the sentence, a verb can be **transitive** (*Jerry bakes cookies*) or **intransitive** (*Jerry bakes for a living*); an intransitive verb that is followed by a subject complement (*Jerry is a fine baker, and his cookies always taste heavenly*) is often called a **linking verb**.

Nearly all verbs have several forms (or principal parts), many of which may be irregular rather than follow a standard pattern. In addition, verbs have various forms to indicate *tense* (time of action or state of being), *voice* (performer of action), and *mood* (statement, command, or possibility). Studies have shown that because verbs can take so many forms, the most common errors in writing involve verbs. (See also G5.)

Verb phrases.   Verbs divide into two primary groups: (1) *main* (*lexical*) *verbs* and (2) *auxiliary* (*helping*) *verbs* that combine with main verbs to create verb phrases. The three primary auxiliary verbs are *do, be,* and *have*, in all their forms.

> *do:* does, did, doing, done
> *be:* am, is, are, was, were, being, been
> *have:* has, had, having

These primary auxiliary verbs can also act as main verbs in sentences. Other common auxiliary verbs (*can, could, may, might, shall, should, will, would, must, ought to, used to*), however, cannot be the main verb in a sentence but are used in combination with main verbs in verb phrases. The auxiliary verb works with the main verb to indicate tense, mood, and voice.

▶ When the cheese curd forms, it *must be* separated from the whey.

▶ After cheddar cheese is shaped into a block, it *should be* aged for at least several months.

▶ By the year 2061, Americans *will have been* eating cheese for 450 years.

Principal parts of verbs.   All main verbs (as well as the primary auxiliary verbs *do, be,* and *have*) have five forms. The forms of a large number of verbs are regular, but many verbs have irregular forms.

---

transitive verb A verb that needs an object — something that receives the action of the verb — to make its meaning complete.

intransitive verb A verb that does not need an object to make its meaning complete.

linking verb *be, seem, appear, become, taste,* or another verb that connects a subject with a subject complement that describes or modifies it: The chips *taste* salty.

Form	Regular	Irregular
Infinitive or base	sip	drink
Third-person singular present (-s form)	sips	drinks
Past	sipped	drank
Present participle (-ing form)	sipping	drinking
Past participle (-ed form)	sipped	drunk

The past and past participle for most verbs in English are formed by simply adding *-d* or *-ed* (*posed, walked, pretended, unveiled*). However, a number of verbs have irregular forms, most of which are different for the past and the past participle.

For regular verbs, the past and past participle forms are the same: *sipped*. All new verbs coming into English have regular forms: *format, formats, formatted, formatting*.

Irregular verbs have unpredictable forms. Their *-s* and *-ing* forms are generally predictable, just like those of regular verbs, but their past and past participle forms are not. In particular, be careful to use the correct past participle form of irregular verbs.

Listed here are the principal parts of fifty-three commonly troublesome irregular verbs. Check your dictionary for a more complete listing.

Base	Past Tense	Past Participle
be: am, is, are	was, were	been
beat	beat	beaten
begin	began	begun
bite	bit	bitten
blow	blew	blown
break	broke	broken
bring	brought	brought
burst	burst	burst
choose	chose	chosen
come	came	come
cut	cut	cut
deal	dealt	dealt
do	did	done
draw	drew	drawn
drink	drank	drunk
drive	drove	driven
eat	ate	eaten
fall	fell	fallen
fly	flew	flown
freeze	froze	frozen

Base	Past Tense	Past Participle
get	got	got (gotten)
give	gave	given
go	went	gone
grow	grew	grown
have	had	had
know	knew	known
lay	laid	laid
lead	led	led
lie	lay	lain
lose	lost	lost
ride	rode	ridden
ring	rang	rung
rise	rose	risen
run	ran	run
say	said	said
see	saw	seen
set	set	set
shake	shook	shaken
sink	sank	sunk
sit	sat	sat
speak	spoke	spoken
spring	sprang (sprung)	sprung
steal	stole	stolen
stink	stank	stunk
swear	swore	sworn
swim	swam	swum
take	took	taken
teach	taught	taught
tear	tore	torn
throw	threw	thrown
wear	wore	worn
win	won	won
write	wrote	written

Tense.   As writers, even native speakers may find it difficult to put together sentences that express time clearly through verbs: Time has to be expressed consistently from sentence to sentence, and shifts in time perspective must be managed smoothly. In addition, certain conventions permit time to be expressed in unusual ways: History can be written in present time to dramatize events, and characters in novels can be presented as though their actions are in present time. The following examples of verb **tense** provide only a partial demonstration of the complex system indicating time in English.

tense The form of a verb that shows the time of the action or state of being.

Present. There are three basic types of present time: timeless, limited, and instantaneous. Timeless present-tense verbs express habitual action.

▶ Some Americans *grow* their own fruits and vegetables.

Limited present-tense verbs express an action in process and of limited duration.

▶ The neighbors *are preparing* watermelon rind preserves this week.

Instantaneous present-tense verbs express action being completed at the moment.

▶ Laura *is eating* the last ripe strawberry.

Present-tense verbs can also be emphatic.

▶ I certainly *do enjoy* homemade strawberry preserves in the middle of winter.

Past. There are several kinds of past time. Some actions must be identified as having taken place at a particular time in the past.

▶ While he *was waiting*, Jake *ordered* a ham sandwich on whole wheat bread.

In the *present perfect tense,* actions may be expressed as having taken place at no definite time in the past or as occurring in the past and continuing into the present.

▶ Jake *has eaten* more ham sandwiches than he can count.

▶ The Downtown Deli *has sold* delicious ham sandwiches on homemade bread for as long as he can remember.

Action can even be expressed as having been completed in the past prior to some other past action or event (the *past perfect tense*).

▶ Before he *had taken* a bite, Jake dropped his sandwich on the floor.

Future. The English verb system offers writers several ways of expressing future time. Future action can be indicated with the modal auxiliary *will.*

▶ Fast-food restaurants *will grow* in popularity.

A completed future action can even be viewed from some time further in the future (the *future perfect tense*).

▶ Within a decade or two, Americans *will have given up* cooking their own meals.

Continuing future actions can be expressed with *will be* and the *-ing* form of the verb.

▶ Americans soon *will be eating* every second meal away from home.

The right combination of verbs with *about* can express an action in the near future.

▶ Jeremiah *is about to eat* his third hamburger.

Future arrangements, commands, or possibilities can be expressed.

▶ Junior and Mary Jo *are to be married* at McDonald's.

▶ You *have to be* there by noon to get a good table.

▶ If Fred *is to lose* weight, he must give up french fries.

Voice. A verb is in the *active* voice when it expresses an action taken by the subject. A verb is said to be in the *passive* voice when it expresses something that happens to the subject.

   In sentences with active verbs, it is apparent who is performing the action expressed in the verb.

▶ The chef *disguised* the tasteless broccoli with a rich cheese sauce.

In sentences with passive verbs, it may not be clear who is performing the action.

▶ The tasteless broccoli *was disguised* with a rich cheese sauce.

The writer could reveal the performer by adding a phrase (*by the chef*), but the revision would also create a clumsy sentence. Graceful, clear writing relies on active, rather than passive, verbs. Passive forms do fulfill certain purposes, however, such as expressing the state of something.

▶ The broccoli *is disguised*.

▶ The restaurant *was closed*.

Passives can give prominence to certain information by shifting it to the end of the sentence.

▶ *Who* closed this restaurant? It was closed by *the Board of Health*.

Writers also use passives to make sentences more readable by shifting long **noun clauses** to the end.

ACTIVE	*That the chef disguised the tasteless broccoli* with cheese sauce disgusted Elvira.
PASSIVE	Elvira was disgusted *that the chef disguised the tasteless broccoli* with cheese sauce.

noun clauses Word groups that can function like nouns, acting as subjects, objects, or complements in independent clauses.

Mood. Mood refers to the writer's attitude toward a statement. There are three moods: indicative, imperative, and subjunctive. Most statements or questions are in the *indicative mood*.

▶ The chuck wagon *fed* cowboys on the trail.

▶ *Did* cowboys ever *tire* of steak and beans?

Commands or directions are given in the *imperative mood*.

▶ *Eat* those beans!

The *subjunctive mood* is used mainly to indicate hypothetical, impossible, or unlikely conditions.

▶ If I *were* you, I'd compliment the cook.

▶ *Had* they *been* here yesterday, they would have had hot camp bread.

phrase A group of words that does *not* contain both a subject and a verb and is always part of an independent clause.

object The part of a clause that receives the action of the verb or the part of a phrase that follows a preposition.

Prepositions   Prepositions occur in **phrases**, followed by **objects**. (The uses of prepositional phrases are explained in R2-c.) Most prepositions are single words (*at, on, by, with, of, for, in, under, over, by*), but some consist of two or three words (*away from, on account of, in front of, because of, in comparison with, by means of*). They are used to indicate relations—usually of place, time, cause, purpose, or means—between their objects and some other word in the sentence.

▶ I'll meet you *at* El Ranchero *for* lunch.

▶ The enchiladas are stuffed *with* cheese.

▶ You can split an order *with* [Georgette and me].

objective case The form a pronoun takes when it is an object (receiving the action of the verb).

Objects of prepositions can be single or compound nouns or pronouns in the **objective case** (as in the preceding examples), or phrases or clauses acting as nouns.

▶ Herman began making nachos *by* [grating the cheese].

▶ His guests were happy *with* [what he served].

Conjunctions   Like prepositions, conjunctions show relations between sentence elements. There are coordinating, subordinating, and correlative conjunctions.

Coordinating conjunctions (*and, but, for, nor, or, so,* or *yet*) join logically comparable sentence elements.

▶ Guacamole is made with avocados, tomatoes, onions, *and* chiles.

▶ You may add a little lemon or lime juice, *but* be careful not to add too much.

Subordinating conjunctions (*although, because, since, though, as though, as soon as, rather than*) introduce **dependent clauses**.

dependent clause A word group that has a subject and a predicate but cannot stand by itself as a sentence; it must be connected to an independent clause.

▶ *As soon as* the waitress came, Susanna ordered an iced tea.

▶ She dived into the salsa and chips *because* she was too hungry to wait for her combination plate.

Correlative conjunctions come in pairs, with the first element anticipating the second (*both . . . and, either . . . or, neither . . . nor, not only . . . but also*).

▸ Charley wanted to order *both* the chiles rellenos *and* the enchiladas verdes.

Articles   There are only three articles in English: *the, a,* and *an. The* is used for definite reference to something specific; *a* and *an* are used for indefinite reference to something less specific. *The Mexican restaurant in Westbury* is different from *a Mexican restaurant in Westbury.* (See T1.)

Demonstratives   *This, that, these,* and *those* are demonstratives. Sometimes called demonstrative adjectives, they are used to point to something specific.

▸ Put one of *these* maraschino cherries at each end of the banana split.

▸ The accident left pineapple milk shake all over the front seat of *that* pickup truck.

Interjections   Interjections indicate strong feeling or an attempt to command attention: *phew, shhh, damn, oh, yay, yikes, ouch, boo.*

R2-b   Dependent Clauses

Like independent clauses, all dependent clauses have a **subject** and a **predicate**. Unlike independent clauses, however, dependent clauses cannot stand by themselves as complete sentences; they always occur with independent clauses as part of either the subject or the predicate.

INDEPENDENT	Ribbon-shaped pasta is popular in northern Italy.
DEPENDENT	. . . , while tubular-shaped pasta is popular in southern Italy.
	. . . , which is generally made by hand, . . .
	Although it originally comes from China, . . .

There are three types of dependent clauses: adjective, adverb, and noun.

Adjective clauses   Also known as *relative clauses,* adjective clauses modify nouns and pronouns in independent clauses. They are introduced by relative pronouns (*who, whom, which, that, whose*) or adverbs (*where, when*), and most often they immediately follow the noun or pronoun they modify. Adjective clauses can be either *restrictive* (essential to defining the noun or pronoun they modify) or *nonrestrictive* (not essential to understanding the noun or pronoun); nonrestrictive clauses are set off by commas, and restrictive clauses are not (see P1-c and P2-b).

▸ Vincent bought a package of agnolotti, *which is a pasta used in soup.*

▸ We went back to the restaurant *where they serve that delicious veal.*

▸ Everyone *who likes Italian cooking* knows Romano cheese well.

subject The part of a clause that identifies who or what is being discussed.

predicate The part of a clause that includes a complete verb and describes the action or state of the subject.

Adverb clauses   Introduced by subordinating conjunctions (such as *although, because,* and *since*), adverb clauses nearly always modify verbs in independent clauses, although they may occasionally modify other elements (except nouns). Adverb clauses are used to indicate a great variety of logical relations with their independent clauses: time, place, condition, concession, reason, cause, circumstance, purpose, result, and so on. They are generally set off by commas.

▶ *Although the finest olive oil in Italy comes from Lucca*, good-quality olive oil is produced in other regions of the country. [concession]

▶ *When the tomato sauce comes to a boil*, reduce the heat and simmer. [time]

▶ *If you know mushrooms*, you probably prefer them fresh. [condition]

▶ Ken carefully watches the spaghetti *because he does not like it to be overcooked.* [reason]

Noun clauses   Like nouns, noun clauses can function as subjects, objects, or complements (or predicate nominatives) in independent clauses. They are thus essential to the structure of the **independent clause** in which they occur and so, like restrictive adjective clauses, are not set off by commas. A noun clause usually begins with a relative pronoun, but the introductory word may sometimes be omitted.

▶ *That we preferred the sausage* surprised us. [subject]

▶ Harold did not know for sure *whether baloney came from Bologna.* [object]

▶ He assumed *that it did*. [subject/complement]

▶ Hillary claims *no one eats pizza in Italy.* [relative pronoun *that* dropped] [direct object]

▶ Gnocchi may be flavored with *whatever fresh herbs are available.* [prep./object of preposition]

independent clause A word group with a subject and a predicate that can stand alone as a separate sentence.

R2-c   Phrases

Like **dependent clauses**, phrases can function as nouns, adjectives, or adverbs in sentences. However, unlike clauses, phrases do not contain both a subject and a verb. (A phrase, of course, cannot stand on its own but occurs as part of an **independent clause**.) The six most common types of grammatical phrases are *prepositional, appositive, participial, gerund, infinitive,* and *absolute.*

Prepositional phrases   Prepositional phrases always begin with a **preposition** and function as either an adjective or an adverb.

▶ Food *in Hunan* is noticeably different from that *in Sichuan.*
adjective phrase   adjective phrase

dependent clause A word group that has a subject and a predicate but cannot stand by itself as a sentence; it must be connected to an independent clause.

preposition A word (such as *between, in,* or *of*) that indicates the relation between a word in a sentence and its object.

▶ The perfect egg roll is crisp on the outside and crunchy on the inside.
    adjective phrase   adjective phrase

Appositive phrases Appositive phrases identify or give more information about a noun or pronoun just preceding. They take several forms. A single noun may also serve as an appositive.

▶ The baguette, *the most popular bread in France,* is a loaf about two feet long.

▶ The king of the breakfast rolls, *the croissant,* is shaped like a crescent.

▶ The baker *Marguerite* makes superb croissants.

Participial phrases Participles are verb forms used to indicate certain tenses (present: *sipping;* past: *sipped*). They can also be used as verbals—words derived from verbs—and function as adjectives.

▶ At breakfast, we were first served *steaming* coffee and a simple *buttered* roll.

A participial phrase is an adjective phrase made up of a participle and any complements or modifiers it might have. Like participles, participial phrases modify nouns and pronouns in sentences.

▶ Two-thirds of the breakfasts *consumed in the diner* included sausage and eggs.

▶ *Prepared in the chef's personal style,* the vegetable omelets are served with a cheese sauce *flavored with garlic and herbs.*

▶ *Mopping up the cheese sauce with the last of his roll,* Mickey thought to himself, I could get used to this.

Gerund phrases Like a participle, a gerund is a verbal. Ending in *-ing,* it even looks like a present participle, but it functions as a noun, filling any noun slot in a clause. Gerund phrases include **complements** and any modifiers of the gerund.

complement A word or word group that describes or restates a subject or an object.

┌─ subject ─┐
▶ Roasting is the quickest way to cook a turkey.

┌──────── subject ────────┐
▶ Preparing a stuffed turkey takes several hours.

▶ You begin by mixing the dressing.
           object of preposition

Infinitive phrases Like participles and gerunds, infinitives are verbals. The infinitive is the base form of the verb, preceded by *to: to simmer, to broil, to fry.* Infinitives and infinitive phrases function as nouns, adjectives, or adverbs.

▶ Tamales can be complicated *to prepare.*
                  adverb

▶ *To assemble the tamales,* begin by cutting the kernels off the corncobs.
    adverb

▶ Remembering *to save the corn husks* is important.

noun (bracket over "to save the corn husks")

object of gerund phrase

▶ Anyone's first tamale dinner is a meal *to remember for a long time.*

adjective

Absolute phrases

The absolute phrase does not modify or replace any particular part of a clause; it modifies the whole clause. An absolute phrase includes a noun or pronoun and often includes a past or present participle as well as modifiers. Nearly all modern prose writers rely on absolute phrases. Some style historians consider them a hallmark of modern prose.

▶ *Her eyes glistening,* Lucy checked out the cases of doughnuts at Krispy Kreme Doughnuts.

▶ She stood patiently in line, *her arms folded to control her hunger, her backpack hanging off one shoulder.*

GL Glossary of Frequently Misused Words

Sometimes writers choose a word that is incorrect, imprecise in meaning, pronounced the same as the correct word (a homophone), or used widely but unacceptable in formal writing situations. In addition, problems can arise with idiomatic phrases, common everyday expressions that may or may not fit, or words whose denotations or connotations do not precisely suit the context of a particular sentence. This list will help you avoid imprecise popular usages in formal writing.

accept/except *Accept* is a verb ("receive with favor"). *Except* may be a verb ("leave out") but is more commonly used as a preposition ("excluding"). Other forms: *acceptance, acceptable; exception.*

- ▶ None of the composition instructors will *accept* late papers *except* Mr. Siu.

- ▶ Her *acceptance* of the bribe *excepts* her from consideration for the position.

adapt/adopt *Adapt* means "adjust to make more suitable." *Adopt* means "take as one's own." Other forms: *adaptable, adaptation; adoption.*

- ▶ To *adopt* an older child, parents must be willing to *adapt* themselves to the child's needs.

advice/advise *Advice* is a noun; *advise* is a verb. Other forms: *advisable, adviser.*

- ▶ Everyone *advised* him to heed the expert's *advice.*

affect/effect *Affect* is commonly used as a verb, most often meaning "influence"; in psychology, the noun *affect* is a technical term for an emotional state. *Effect* is generally a noun ("result or consequences"); it is only occasionally used as a verb ("bring about"), although the adjective form (*effective*) is common.

- ▶ Researchers are studying the *effect* of stress.

- ▶ How does stress *affect* the human body?

all right *All right* is the preferred spelling, rather than *alright,* which many people regard as unacceptable.

a lot A common expression meaning "a large number," *a lot* is always written as two words. Because it is vague and informal, avoid it in college writing.

among/between Use *among* when you are referring to more than two objects; limit *between* to references to only two objects.

- ▶ It is hard to choose one winner *among* so many highly qualified candidates for the scholarship.

- ▶ *Between* the two extreme positions lies a vast middle ground.

amount/number *Amount* refers to the quantity of a unit ("amount of water," "amount of discussion"), whereas *number* refers to the quantity of individual items ("number of papers," "number of times"). In general, use *amount* only with a singular noun.

anxious/eager *Anxious* means "nervous" or "worried"; *eager* means "looking forward [impatiently]." Avoid using *anxious* to mean *eager.*

- ▶ The students were *eager* to learn their grades.

- ▶ They were *anxious* they wouldn't pass.

between/among See **among/between.**

capital/capitol *Capital* is the more common word and has a variety of meanings, among them the principal city in a state or country; *capitol* refers to the government building in which a legislature meets.

cite/sight/site *Cite* as a verb means "refer to as proof" or "summon to appear in court." *Sight* may be a verb or a noun and always refers to seeing or what is seen ("a sight for sore eyes"). *Site* is a noun meaning "place or location."

▶ Can you *cite* your sources for these figures?

▶ When she *sighted* the speeding car, the officer *cited* the driver for recklessness.

▶ A new dormitory will be built at this *site*.

complement/compliment *Complement* refers to completion, the making of a satisfactory whole, whereas *compliment* indicates admiration or praise; both can be used as either nouns or verbs. *Complementary* means "serving to complete" or "contrasting in color"; *complimentary* means "given free."

▶ The dean *complimented* the school's recruiters on the full *complement* of students registered for the fall.

▶ The designer received many *compliments* on the way the elements of the room *complemented* one another.

▶ Buy a new refrigerator and receive a *complimentary* ice maker in a *complementary* color.

could of/should of/would of In standard speech, "could have," "should have," and "would have" sound very much like "could of," "should of," and "would of"; however, substituting *of* for *have* in this construction is too casual for written work. The same holds true for "might of," "must of," and "will of."

council/counsel *Council* is a noun ("an assembly of people who deliberate or govern"). *Counsel* is a verb meaning "advise" or a noun meaning "advice." Other forms: *councilor* ("member of a council"); *counselor* ("one who gives advice").

▶ The *council* on drug abuse has issued guidelines for *counseling* troubled students.

▶ Before voting on the important fiscal issue, City *Councilor* Lopez sought the *counsel* of her constituents.

desert/dessert As a noun or an adjective, *desert* (dez´ ert) means "a dry, uncultivated region"; as a verb, *desert* (di zurt´) means "abandon." A *dessert* is a sweet dish served at the end of a meal.

▶ The hunters were alone in the arid *desert*, *deserted* by their guides.

▶ After a heavy meal, sherbet is the perfect *dessert*.

eager/anxious See **anxious/eager**.

effect/affect See **affect/effect**.

emigrant/immigrant An *emigrant* moves out of a country; an *immigrant* moves into a country. Other forms: *emigrate, emigration, émigré; immigrate, immigration.*

▶ Congress passed a bill to deal with *immigrants* living in the United States illegally.

▶ Members of her family *emigrated* from Cuba to Miami and Madrid.

etc. An abbreviation of the Latin words *et cetera* ("and other things"), *etc.* should never be preceded by *and* in English. Also be careful to spell the abbreviation correctly (*not* "ect."). In general, use *etc.* sparingly, if at all, in college writing.

except See **accept/except**.

fewer/less Use *fewer* when referring to **count nouns** (nouns that name people or things that can be counted: one *teacher*, several *teachers*); reserve *less* for amounts you cannot count.

▶ The new cookies have *fewer* calories than the other brand because they contain *less* sugar.

fortuitous/fortunate Often used incorrectly, the adjective *fortuitous* means "by chance" or "unplanned" and should not be confused with *fortunate* ("lucky").

▶ Because the two candidates wished to avoid each other, their *fortuitous* meeting in the parking lot was not a *fortunate* event for either party.

hisself/theirselves In nonstandard speech, "hisself" is sometimes used for *himself* and "theirselves" for *themselves,* but such usage is not acceptable in written work.

hopefully In conversation, *hopefully* is often used as a convenient shorthand to suggest that some outcome is generally to be hoped for ("Hopefully, our nominee will win the election"); this usage, however, is not acceptable in most written work. Better substitutes include *I hope, let's hope, everyone hopes,* and *it is to be hoped,* depending on your meaning. The adverb *hopefully* ("full of hope") should always modify a specific verb or adverb.

- I *hope* my brother wins the election.

- We should all *hope* his brother wins the election.

- Her sister is *hopeful* that she will win the election.

- The candidate inquired *hopefully* about the results.

immigrant See **emigrant/immigrant**.

its/it's *Its* is a possessive pronoun; *it's* is the contraction of *it is*.

- This job has *its* advantages.

- When *it's* well grilled, there's nothing like a steak.

lay/lie The verb *lay*, meaning "put, place," is transitive (forms of *lay* are *lay, laid, laid*): It needs an object—something that receives the action of the verb—to make its meaning complete. The verb *lie*, meaning "recline," is intransitive (forms of *lie* are *lie, lay, lain*): It does not need an object to make its meaning complete. Writers may incorrectly use *laid* as the past tense of *lie*, or *lay* as the present tense of *lie*. Other forms: *laying, lying*.

- The lion *lies* in wait for the approach of its prey.

- Joseph *laid* down his shovel, took a shower, and *lay* down for a nap.

less/fewer See **fewer/less**.

literally *Literally* means "exactly as stated, actually" and is often used to suggest that a cliché has in fact come true. However, to say, "The movie made my hair literally stand on end" is to misuse the word (although a person who suffered a fatal heart attack brought on by a fearful shock might correctly be said to have *literally* died of fright).

lose/loose *Lose* is a verb ("mislay, fail to maintain"); *loose* is most often used as an adjective ("not fastened tightly").

- A *loose* board may make someone *lose* his or her balance.

number/amount See **amount/number**.

persecute/prosecute *Persecute* means "mistreat or oppress"; *prosecute* most often means "bring a legal suit or action against."

- A biased majority can easily *persecute* minority groups.

- The law may *prosecute* only those who are indicted.

prejudice/prejudiced *Prejudice* is a noun or a verb. When used adjectivally, it should take the form of the past tense of the verb: *prejudiced*.

- We should fight *prejudice* wherever we find it.

- He was *prejudiced* against the candidate because she spoke with an accent.

principal/principle *Principal* implies "first in rank, chief," whether it is used as an adjective ("the principal cities of the Midwest") or a noun ("the principal of a midwestern high school"). *Principle* is generally a noun meaning "a basic law or truth."

- The *principle* of free speech will be the *principal* topic of discussion.

- In *principle*, you are correct.

prosecute/persecute See **persecute/prosecute**.

sensual/sensuous Both *sensual* and *sensuous* suggest the enjoyment of physical pleasure through the senses. However, *sensual* generally implies self-indulgence, particularly in terms of sexual activity; *sensuous* has a more positive meaning and suggests the ability to appreciate intellectually what is received through the senses. Other forms: *sensuality; sensuousness*.

- When drunk, the emperor gave himself up to brutal *sensuality*.

- Anyone can enjoy a *sensuous* spring night.

set/sit The difference between the verbs *sit* and *set* is similar to that between *lie* and *lay: Sit* is generally intransitive ("rest on one's buttocks"), and *set* is transitive ("put [something] in a certain place"). *Set* also has a number of uses as a noun. The past tense and past **participle** forms of *sit* are both *sat;* these forms for *set* are both *set*. (Remember that a participle is a verb form showing present tense [*dancing, freezing*] or past tense [*danced, frozen*] that can also act as an adjective.)

▶ He *set* his suitcase on the ground and then *sat* on it.

▶ He would rather *sit* than stand and would rather lie than *sit*.

should of See **could of/should of/would of.**

sight/site See **cite/sight/site.**

stationary/stationery *Stationary* is an adjective meaning "fixed, remaining in one place" ("Concrete will make the pole stationary"). *Stationery* refers to writing paper. One way to keep the distinction in mind is to associate the *er* in *paper* with that in *stationery*.

that/which When used as a subordinating conjunction (a word or phrase [such as *although, because, since,* or *as soon as*] that introduces a dependent clause and relates it to an independent clause), *that* always introduces a restrictive word group (a group of words, not set off by commas, that provides information essential to defining or identifying the noun or pronoun it modifies). The word *which* is generally used for nonrestrictive word groups (groups of words, set off by commas, that provide extra or nonessential information). (See the discussion of restrictive and nonrestrictive word groups in P1-c and P2-b, and the review of sentence structure and sentence elements in R1 and R2.)

▶ Her first bid for the Senate was the only election *that* she ever lost.

▶ Her first bid for the Senate, *which* was unsuccessful, brought her to prominence.

▶ The Senate election *that* resulted in her defeat took place in 1968.

their/there/they're *Their* is a possessive pronoun, *there* specifies a place or functions as an expletive, and *they're* is a contraction of *they are.*

▶ The coauthors say *there* are no copies of *their* script in *their* office, but *they're* not telling the truth.

theirselves See **hisself/theirselves.**

to/too/two *To* is a preposition, *too* is an adverb, and *two* is generally an adjective. The most common error here is the substitution of *to* for *too.*

▶ It is *too* early *to* predict either of the *two* scores.

unique To be precise, *unique* means "one of a kind, like no other." Careful writers do not use it loosely to mean simply "unusual or rare." Nor can it correctly take a comparative form ("most unique"), although advertisers sometimes use it this way.

▶ Her generosity is not *unique*, although today it is increasingly rare.

▶ This example of Mayan sculpture is apparently *unique*; none other like it has so far been discovered.

used to In colloquial speech, *used to* often sounds like "use to." However, *used to* is the correct form for written work.

▶ My grandfather *used to* be a Dodgers fan, until the team moved to Los Angeles.

weather/whether *Weather* is a noun ("atmospheric conditions"); *whether* is a conjunction.

▶ The *weather* forecast indicates *whether* there will be sun or rain.

which See **that/which.**

who's/whose *Who's* is the contraction of *who is* or *who has; whose* is a possessive pronoun.

▶ *Who's* up next?

▶ She's the only student *who's* done her work correctly.

▶ *Whose* work is this?

▶ The man *whose* job I took has retired.

would of See **could of/should of/would of.**

Acknowledgments

David J. Smith, "Getting to 'E Pluribus Unum,'" *Inside Higher Ed,* January 5, 2017. Copyright © 2017. Reprinted by permission.

Daniel J. Solove, "Why Privacy Matters Even if You Have 'Nothing to Hide,'" excerpt as published in the *Chronicle of Higher Education,* May 15, 2011, adapted from *Nothing to Hide: The False Tradeoff between Privacy and Security.* Copyright © 2011 by Daniel J. Solove. Reprinted by permission of the publisher, Yale University Press.

Gabriel Thompson, "A Gringo in the Lettuce Fields," *The Week,* January 29, 2010; excerpted from the book *Working in the Shadows: A Year of Doing the Jobs That (Most) Americans Won't Do* by Gabriel Thompson. Copyright © 2010 by Gabriel Thompson. Republished with permission from Hachette Books Group; permission conveyed through the Copyright Clearance Center.

Anastasia Toufexis, "Love: The Right Chemistry," *TIME,* June 24, 2001, first published February 15, 1993. © 2001 Time Inc. All rights reserved. Reprinted from *TIME* and published with permission of Time Inc. Reproduction in any manner in any language in whole or in part without written permission is prohibited.

Jean M. Twenge, "Have Smartphones Destroyed a Generation?," *Atlantic Magazine,* September 2017. From *iGen* by Jean M. Twenge, PhD. Copyright © 2017 by Jean M. Twenge, PhD. Reprinted with the permission of Atria Books, a division of Simon & Schuster, Inc. All rights reserved.

Shankar Vedantam, "The Telescope Effect," from Shankar Vedantam, *The Hidden Brain: How Our Unconscious Minds Elect Presidents, Control Markets, Wage Wars, and Save Our Lives.* Copyright © 2010 by Shankar Vedantam. Used by permission of Spiegel & Grau, an imprint of Random House, a division of Penguin Random House LLC. All rights reserved. Any third-party use of this material, outside of this publication, is prohibited. Interested parties must apply directly to Penguin Random House LLC for permission.

William Carlos Williams, "The Use of Force," from *The Collected Stories of William Carlos Williams.* Copyright © 1938 by William Carlos Williams. Reprinted by permission of New Directions Publishing Corp.

Index

Index for Multilingual Writers

A Guide to Editing and Proofreading

Error	Identification of the Error	Quick Fix
Sentence Fragment	A word group that looks like a sentence but lacks a **subject**, a **verb**, or both; or a **dependent clause** that looks like a sentence	Determine what is missing—a **subject**, a **verb**, or both—and add the missing part. ▸ ~~Worrying~~ about rain. We watched the sky. *(We were worried)* Connect the fragment to a complete sentence. ▸ Worrying about rain~~.~~ We watched the sky. *(, we)* If the fragment is a **dependent clause**, either connect it to an independent clause or remove the **subordinating conjunction**. ▸ We traveled to Oregon~~.~~ ~~Because~~ we wanted to see the eclipse. *(because)* ▸ ~~Because~~ we wanted to see the eclipse. *(We)*
Fused (Run-On) Sentence	Two **independent clauses** that are joined with no punctuation or **conjunctions**	Turn one clause into a dependent **clause** by adding a **subordinating conjunction**. ▸ ~~We~~ waited for the eclipse clouds moved in. *(As we)* *(,)* Turn one clause into a phrase. ▸ We waited for the eclipse ~~clouds moved~~ in. *(with clouds moving)* Separate the clauses with a comma and add a **coordinating conjunction**. ▸ We waited for the eclipse clouds moved in. *(, but)* Separate the clauses with a semicolon. ▸ We waited for the eclipse clouds moved in. *(;)* Create two separate sentences. ▸ We waited for the eclipse ~~clouds~~ moved in. *(. Clouds)*
Comma Splice	Two **independent clauses** that are joined with only a comma	Turn one clause into a **dependent clause** by adding a **subordinating conjunction**. ▸ ~~We~~ waited for the eclipse, clouds moved in. *(As we)* Turn one clause into a phrase. ▸ We waited for the eclipse, ~~clouds moved~~ in. *(with clouds moving)* Add a **coordinating conjunction** after the comma. ▸ We waited for the eclipse, clouds moved in. *(but)*

Error	Identification of the Error	Quick Fix
Comma Splice	Two **independent clauses** that are joined with only a comma	Change the comma to a semicolon. ▶ We waited for the eclipse, ⌃;⌃ clouds moved in. Create two separate sentences. . Clouds ▶ We waited for the eclipse, ~~clouds~~ moved in.
Pronoun Reference Error	A **pronoun** that does not refer clearly to one specific **antecedent** (Note: Gender-neutral pronouns, like *they* and *their,* are less cumbersome than *he or she* or *he/she.*)	Replace a vague **pronoun** with a clear **noun** or **noun phrase**. ▶ People need special glasses to view an eclipse. *Experts* ~~They~~ say not to look directly at the sun. ▶ An eclipse viewer can easily be made from a cardboard box. *Constructing a box viewer* ~~This~~ is economical and fun. Add a missing **antecedent**. *birds* ▶ During an eclipse, bird behavior changes, so they may return to their nests. Clarify an ambiguous **antecedent**. antecedent ,"You ▶ Melissa told Beth ~~she~~ should have seen the eclipse."
Pronoun Agreement Error	A **pronoun** that does not agree with its **antecedent** in **number, person,** or **gender**	Change either the **pronoun** or the **antecedent** to ensure that the pronoun and antecedent agree in **person, number,** and **gender**. antecedent — pronoun *Students* ▶ A ~~student~~ can plan their schedule online. pronoun *their* antecedent ▶ Students can plan ~~your~~ schedule online. Revise the sentence to eliminate the **pronoun**. *the* ▶ Either Sheena or Tom will complete ~~his~~ work first.
Subject-Verb Agreement Error	A **subject** and **verb** that do not agree in **person, number,** or both	When the **subject** and **verb** are separated by other words, identify the subject and make the verb agree with it. subject — verb *were* ▶ Stars normally hidden by the sun ~~was~~ visible during the eclipse. Make the **verb** agree with a **subject** that follows it. verb — subject *come* ▶ Onto the field ~~comes~~ the players, ready for action.

Error	Identification of the Error	Quick Fix
Subject-Verb Agreement Error	A **subject** and **verb** that do not agree in **person**, **number**, or both	Use a **singular verb** when the **subject** is a **collective noun**. ┌ verb ┐ ┌subject┐ *travels* ▶ The team often ~~travel~~ to out-of-town games on weekends. ^ Make the verb agree with a **compound subject**. verb compound *are* subject ▶ Donuts and coffee ~~is~~ always available in the break room. ^ Make the **verb** agree with the **antecedent** of a **relative pronoun**. relative pronoun antecedent verb *run* ▶ The office is staffed by two people who ~~runs~~ it calmly and efficiently. ^ Make the **verb** agree with an **indefinite pronoun subject**. indefinite pronoun subject ▶ Two people know how to operate the alarm system, and neither verb *is* ~~are~~ here right now. ^ Make the **verb** agree with the **subject**, not a **subject complement**. ┌verb┐ subject ┌subject┐*was* complement ▶ Our special dinner ~~were~~ burgers and fries. ^
Misplaced or Dangling Modifier	A **modifier** that is too far from the word it modifies (misplaced) or that does not modify any word or phrase in the sentence (dangling)	Move a misplaced **modifier** closer to the word it modifies. ┌──── modifier ────┐ *Spewing clouds of dust and dog hair, the* ▶ ~~The~~ broken vacuum cleaner infuriated my ^ father~~, spewing clouds of dust and dog hair~~. If the **modifier** dangles, rewrite the sentence to include the words being modified. ┌ words being modified ┐ *With the vacuum cleaner spewing* ▶ ~~Spewing~~ clouds of dust and dog hair, we failed to get the carpet clean. ^
Wordiness	Words or phrases that do not add meaning to the writing	Eliminate repetitive or unnecessary words and phrases. ▶ The treasurer returned ~~back~~ to the account books. Replace wordy phrases with brief, clear language. *now.* ▶ The committee will adjourn ~~at this point in time~~. ^ Rewrite to simplify sentence structure. *The* *should* ▶ ~~There is a need for the~~ organization ~~to~~ recruit new members. ^ ^